Lesbian, Gay, and Bisexual Identities Over the Lifespan

Lesbian, Gay, and Bisexual Identities Over the Lifespan

Psychological Perspectives

Edited by

Anthony R. D'Augelli
The Pennsylvania State University

Charlotte J. Patterson
University of Virginia

OXFORD UNIVERSITY PRESS
New York   Oxford

Oxford University Press

Oxford   New York
Athens   Auckland   Bangkok   Bogota   Bombay
Buenos Aires   Calcutta   Cape Town   Dar es Salaam
Delhi   Florence   Hong Kong   Istanbul   Karachi
Kuala Lumpur   Madras   Madrid   Melbourne
Mexico City   Nairobi   Paris   Singapore
Taipei   Tokyo   Toronto

and associated companies in
Berlin   Ibadan

Copyright © 1995 by Oxford University Press, Inc.

First published in 1995 by Oxford University Press, Inc.
198 Madison Avenue, New York, New York 10016

First issued as an Oxford University Press paperback, 1996

Oxford is a registered trademark of Oxford University Press

Library of Congress Cataloging-in-Publication Data
Lesbian, gay, and bisexual identities over the lifespan : psychological
perspectives, edited by Anthony R. D'Augelli and Charlotte J. Patterson.
ISBN 0-19-508231-1; ISBN 0-19-510899-X (pbk.)
1. Homosexuality—United States.
2. Bisexuality—United States.
3. Gender identity—United States.
I. Patterson, Charlotte
HQ76.25.L49   1994   155.3'4—dc20
94-14398

2 4 6 8 9 7 5 3 1

Printed in the United States of America
on acid-free paper

Preface

Though often hidden in the past, lesbians, gay men, and bisexual women and men are a substantial and increasingly visible minority of the population. With the growing cultural openness about lesbian and gay identities in recent years, issues relating to sexual orientation have become more and more prominent in public discourse. In the 1980s and 1990s, psychological research and theory on gay, lesbian, and bisexual issues have mushroomed. At the same time, however, few authoritative books presenting this new scholarship have appeared.

This book reviews recent psychological research and theory on lesbian, gay, and bisexual identities and identifies promising directions for future work. Our perspective is influenced by the need to recognize individual differences across the lifespan, variations in family and close relationship patterns, and the impact of context on lesbian, gay, and bisexual identities. We are also committed to encouraging the explication of ways in which sexual identities are influenced by variations in lesbian, gay, and bisexual lives attributable to gender, cultural, ethnic, racial, and social class differences. An ecological perspective which conceptualizes the individual as embedded in family, community, and cultural contexts is central to our approach. To provide definitive reviews of the literature in each area, we have solicited new analyses by leading scholars who are active in advancing psychological knowledge. We believe that, taken together, the chapters present an up-to-date overview of psychological research and theory on lesbian, gay, and bisexual identities across the lifespan. In addition, these reviews provide much valuable direction for future developments in theory, research, and policy.

The first part of the book explores concepts of sexual identity. The first chapter, "Lesbian Identities: Concepts and Issues" by Laura S. Brown, explicates critical issues in sexual identity formation and change among lesbian and bisexual women. The second, "Gay Male Identities: Concepts and Issues" by John C. Gonsiorek, describes the processes involved in the articulation by men of gay identities, formulating some of the issues in terms of contemporary self psychology. Ronald C. Fox, in the third chapter, describes the development of research and theory on bisexual identities, reporting on the results of a major survey of bisexual individuals in the United States. Using the example of Chinese Americans, Connie S. Chan then discusses the challenges faced by ethnic minorities who are also lesbian, gay, or bisexual. In the next chapter, J. Michael Bailey provides an overview of research and theory on biological contributions to sexual orientation, including some of his own research on genetic factors. In the final chapter in this part, Celia Kitzinger describes the metatheoretical challenge of social constructionism for theory and research on sexual identities.

The second part focuses on personal development during different periods of the lifespan. Ritch C. Savin-Williams reviews his own extensive research, as well as that of others, to describe the developmental challenges faced by "Lesbian, Gay Male, and Bisexual Adolescents." Douglas C. Kimmel and Barbara E. Sang have integrated the often disparate literatures on lesbian and gay midlife issues into their chapter on "Lesbians and Gay Men in Midlife." In his chapter "Development in Later Life: Older Lesbian and Gay Lives," James D. Reid presents the new and growing literature on older adults who are lesbian, gay, and bisexual, linking these advances to current themes in gerontology.

Relationships and families, the interpersonal contexts of development, are the focus of the third part of the book. In the chapter on "Lesbian and Gay Couples," Lawrence A. Kurdek presents the increasingly sophisticated research on close relationships among lesbians and gay men. The second chapter in this part, authored by Charlotte J. Patterson, concerns "Lesbian Mothers, Gay Fathers, and Their Children"; it describes the historical context of research as well as the history and contemporary status of psychological research and theory in this area.

Consistent with our ecological approach, community and contextual issues are the focus of the fourth and final part. The first chapter in this part, "Lesbian, Gay, and Bisexual Communities," written by Anthony R. D'Augelli and Linda D. Garnets, focuses on the ways in which individuals and social groups are embedded in, influenced by, and in turn influence their larger communities. One core challenge facing lesbian, gay, and bisexual people in contemporary society is antigay and antilesbian bias. In his chapter, Gregory M. Herek reviews "Psychological Heterosexism in the United States." "The Impact of the HIV Epidemic on U.S. Gay Male Communities" is the topic of the next chapter, coauthored by Jay P. Paul, Robert B. Hays, and Thomas J. Coates. Finally, Kristin A. Hancock provides a definitive review of critical issues related to "Psychotherapy with Lesbians and Gay Men."

We hope that the reviews contained in this book will be helpful in identifying directions for the future psychological study of issues related to sexual orientation. We hope the book will also contribute to the training of the next generation of psychological researchers. It is intended for an audience of advanced undergraduate students, graduate students, and faculty in the fields of developmental, social, clinical, community, and counseling psychology. Psychologists in professional practice will also, we hope, find these chapters useful. In addition, the book should be of interest to those in related disciplines such as social work, sociology, anthropology, education, gay and lesbian studies, family studies, and women's studies, and to professionals in various fields such as law, nursing, psychiatry, and education who seek current knowledge of lifespan human development from a lesbian or gay perspective.

For her enthusiasm about this project and her cooperation throughout, we thank our editor, Joan Bossert, at Oxford University Press. We also thank the friends, relatives, and colleagues who helped in various ways in the preparation of this book. In particular, we thank Charlene Depner and Barbara Rogoff for their timely advice and Ellen Stern, under whose roof much of the editing of these chapters was completed. Our greatest vote of thanks goes to our partners, George Dempsie and Deborah Cohn, whose support has meant and continues to mean so much.

January 1994   A.R.D.
                                                                                                          C.J.P.

Contents

I

Concepts of
Sexual Identity

1

Lesbian Identities: Concepts and Issues

Laura S. Brown

The concept of a lesbian *identity*, a sense of oneself as lesbian, which gives meaning to behavior across dimensions of time and place, as distinct from simply being an unidentified participant in certain kinds of sexual behavior between two women, is a relatively new one. Until the work of such late nineteenth- and early twentieth-century sexologists as Ellis (1922) and Hirschfield (1936) came to the intellectual foreground, lesbian relationships, when they were identifiable to the outside world, tended to be perceived as perverse relationships between women who were essentially heterosexual. This view prevailed largely because there was no framework for understanding the concept that a person might be fundamentally homosexual. We know little about how such women perceived themselves, aside from knowing that many of them identified themselves as loving and bonded to one another. More commonly, close affectional ties between women were not seen by the larger culture as possessing a sexual cast; as Faderman (1982) and other historians of lesbian heritage have noted, intimate and romantic (although not necessarily sexual) relationships between women have been normative in many cultures over time without a lesbian identity attaching to the behavior. Following the arrival of psychoanalytic concepts on the Western intellectual scene, such relationships were construed as containing an inevitable sexual component.

In addition, the notion of lesbian identity is culture bound as well as time bound. Outside of Western, Eurocentric cultures, definitions of sexuality differ widely from those currently subscribed to by European

and North American behavioral scientists and in popular culture. Although women behave as lesbians cross-culturally—that is, having sexual and affectionate relationships with one another—"lesbian identity"
as such may be absent in contexts which do not define persons as having particular sexual orientations or which are not directly influenced
by Western cultural concepts of sexuality (Weinrich & Williams, 1991;
Williams, 1986).

The definition of lesbian identity that I work with in this chapter is
one I have found useful in organizing my thinking on this matter. I
define lesbian identity as primarily a self-ascribed definition held by
a woman over time and across situations as having primary sexual,
affectional, and relational ties to other women. This identity may or
may not be congruent with overt behavior at any point during the lifespan, and the variables making up this definition may come and go
from the foreground of a woman's definition as life circumstances
change. A lesbian identity may also be ascribed to a woman by others,
even if she does not accept this definition, and the development of
such a woman's sexual identity must also be considered in any discussions of lesbian identity development. One of the issues to be examined in this chapter is the question of how to define and describe the
process of sexual identity development for women to whom lesbian
identity is ascribed by others, who behave in ways that both dominant
and lesbian cultures would describe as lesbian, and who intentionally
define themselves as nonlesbian. Because such women fall within what
Rich (1980) has described as a "lesbian continuum," the development
of their identity falls within my discussion even though they may reject
the terminology of the self-defined lesbian.

This very broad, flexible, and somewhat ambiguous definition defines the contours of the concepts under discussion in this chapter.
They include these three questions: Who decides what makes a woman
a lesbian? By what paths do women arrive at a definition of themselves
as lesbian? And, related to the second, are there paths by which a
woman who has so identified herself then departs from that definition?
In those cultural contexts where there is no separate lesbian social
identity or role, what are the processes of sexual identity development;
how do cultural differences in understanding the nature of attraction
and intimate pair-bonding in humans transform the meaning of being
or behaving in a lesbian fashion?

Who Are the Lesbians?

The arguments over who and what makes a lesbian can be found
throughout both modern and postmodern literature, psychology, and
philosophy, not to mention in the pages of popular magazines pub-

lished for this sexual minority. It is useful to review these questions here to demonstrate the complexities inherent in defining the parameters of empirical study of lesbian identity development. The singer Holly Near personifies some of the issues in the current debate; a woman who has been sexually and romantically involved with women, who currently, as well as prior to her brief period of same-sex relationships, is sexually and romantically involved with men, and who yet proudly describes herself as a lesbian in writing and in performance. Is she, or isn't she? Then there is another public figure, Patricia Ireland, the president, as of this writing, of the National Organization for Women. She has recently revealed that she lives with a female companion, although she also maintains her marriage to a man. Is she bisexual? lesbian? Or, as she stated, does it matter what her behavior is named? She has chosen to have an ambiguous public sexual identity. And what of the women in a Boston marriage; that is, two women who live together as a couple, are tied by bonds of affection and emotional intimacy, but who have never or rarely been sexual with one another (Rothblum & Brehony, 1993). This pair will probably be perceived as lesbian by others, although they may or may not identify themselves as such.

Some women describe themselves as having known of their attraction to their own gender from a very young, even prepubescent age. Others may feel heterosexually attracted in adolescence, then gradually find their interest becoming more directed to other women as they grow older. Still other women may be securely ensconced in heterosexual adult relationships, even marriage, then find themselves strongly drawn to another woman or women. This may occur as late as the sixth or seventh decade of life, judging by some first-person accounts (Adleman, 1986). A woman who is strongly politically feminist may make a conscious choice, regardless of feeling, to relate sexually and emotionally to other women because of strong belief in the importance of women bonding with one another or in protest against the dominance hierarchies in which most heterosexual relationships are embedded. In this case her socially defined sexual orientation and lesbian identity exist to some degree detached from her actual experiences of arousal and sexual attraction. Some of these women identify themselves as lesbians; some, including those who have had life-long exclusive sexual and affectional attraction to women, do not, or do so only with difficulty. Who among these women is the "real" lesbian, whose identity development we are attempting to comprehend?

This question of who are "genuine" lesbians betrays several interesting underlying concerns both from the dominant culture and from the perspective of lesbians. The dominant culture has wished to know who lesbians were at times because special, negative treatment is reserved for lesbians that is not considered appropriate for women who merely "appear" to be lesbian but are not. In addition, women who are lesbian, but who actively deny or hide their status, are treated similarly to women who are not lesbian, "forgiven," as it were, their sexual orientation as long is it is hidden from public view; intentional and public commitment to a lesbian identity carries meaning within a dominant cultural context above and beyond an individual woman's self-perceptions.

Well-defined boundaries around the concept of lesbian are important in dominant North American culture for purposes of discrimination, for the same reasons it is important in this culture to know whether a person has any African ancestry so that she or he may be classified as "African–American." The need for a strict definition of lesbian reflects the tendency toward dichotomous thinking that typifies much white, Eurocentric cultural philosophies, a dichotomy which for the most part assumes separate and mutually exclusive categories of sexual orientation. At the same time, the dominant culture has tried to define certain women as "not lesbian" because the value accorded a particular woman was at odds with the devaluation of lesbians. The extended public debate over the nature of Eleanor Roosevelt's relationship with the journalist Lorena Hickok, which judging by their letters was at least emotionally intimate, sensuous, and passionate, is an example of this phenomenon. Various biographers, depending on their degree of discomfort with lesbianism, have argued for or against the notion that Roosevelt, seen as a paragon of public virtue, might have had a lesbian relationship or identity (Cook, 1992).

For lesbians ourselves, the question has different meanings that have to do with safety, affiliation, and the possibilities of sexual and intimate relations, as well as the importance of having roles and lesbian women models of superlative function available in both historical and contemporary context. As lesbian author and theorist Julia Penelope has pointed out (1992), the question of who is a lesbian can become extremely important for women who wish to define a space as "lesbian-only." It may also enter, for individual women, into questions of to whom one will disclose one's own lesbian identity, or with whom one will contemplate the possibility of an intimate sexual relationship. It is not uncommon for women newly coming into a lesbian identity after a history of heterosexual experience to find themselves rebuffed by other women for not being "sufficiently" lesbian, somehow tainted in their "purity" by having related to men. How then, is lesbian to be defined by lesbians, and which lesbians possess the authority to define? Is one lesbian's definition of herself adequate to the needs of another lesbian's quest to create boundaries defining to whom and in what circumstances she will reveal herself most intimately?

One recent controversy in white U.S. lesbian cultural feminist circles, which reveals the dimensions of the definitional question, centers on whether a male-to-female transsexual who is now partnered with a woman can be considered a lesbian for purpose of inclusion in such lesbian-only spaces, and whether the woman in a relationship with this newly created female person is herself in a lesbian relationship (Letters, *Lesbian Connection*, Spring 1992). Arguments strongly for and against each position have appeared (Raymond, 1982), with nothing resembling consensus emerging in the public discourse (although consensus is not really to be expected). The question raised in these debates of whether a person must be born and raised female to be socially constructed and accepted as a woman, and thus lesbian, highlights all aspects of the discourse over the parameters of lesbian identity.

As Golden (1987) has pointed out, these definitional debates also raise questions regarding the degree to which a lesbian identity (as differentiated from an erotic orientation to which no particular identity may be attached) is fixed, invariant, and stable, in contrast to flexible and changeable over time. This is not a trivial concern for either the student of lesbianism or lesbians ourselves. For theorists and researchers of lesbian identity development, the tendency to see sexual identity in one or another manner leads to models which are descriptive and predictive of those outcomes. A model which encompasses the ambiguous definition described by Golden and others may in turn lead to more ambiguous outcomes, although perhaps more interesting questions regarding the overall construction, both socially and phenomenologically, of women's sexual identity development in general. For lesbians, the fixedness of a lesbian identity speaks more strongly to issues of trust and predictability. If a woman has always and only related sexually and affectionally to other women, she may be perceived as "safer" to invest in for relationships than a woman who has past experiences of heterosexual relationships. Golden suggests that as this definitional question is played out, in some lesbian communities whether a woman has ever been sexual with men is more important than whether she has been sexual with women. In this analysis, a formerly celibate woman has no apparent loyalties to heterosexual relationships, while a women who has behaved heterosexually may be perceived as at risk for returning to men.

A model such as Golden has proposed implies that a lesbian identity may, at some point, be a possible outcome for any woman's sexual identity development, whereas biological models such as those currently popular among some students of gay male identity restrict lesbian identity to those women who diverge biologically from a heterosexual "norm," or those with an erotic orientation entirely consistent with their sexual identity. Questions of fixed versus fluid also inform debates over whether conversion therapies aimed at "reorienting" women to heterosexuality are ethical or efficacious (Haldeman, 1991), as well as public policy questions regarding civil rights protections for sexual minority persons.

A history of lesbian relationships does not appear to be a necessary predictor of ongoing lesbianism, however, as the first-person accounts of several women who now identify themselves as bisexual illustrate quite clearly (Wiese, 1992). Such narratives illustrate the degree to which sexual orientation and sexual identity are not always congruent. These women describe their distress at discovering in midlife that they wish to take up an intimate relationship with a man, perhaps for the first time in their lives. Not only is the individual identity of such a woman challenged; her identity within a social context and community will also undergo transformation. The transformation to bisexuality in later adulthood from a prior life history of lesbian identity raises questions about the fixed nature of sexual orientation and identity. The "bisexual lesbian" perceives herself as having a lesbian identity, independent of her sexual orientation or her current sexual behavior. Ironically, the woman who describes herself in this manner may have a stronger attachment to a lesbian identity in the public context than might a woman who has always related sexually and affectionally only with women, but for reasons of culture or homophobia has an asexual or heterosexual public identity. While the frequency with which such transitions occur is currently unknown, given the very closeted nature of many women in this position, evidence exists that lesbian identity development is a process with not only several different initial stages, but variations in later stages as well.

Motherhood and the possibility of motherhood in the past decade and a half through donor insemination have also raised questions in some lesbian cultures about what constitutes a "genuine" lesbian self-definition. Some separatist lesbians (Penelope, 1992; Ruston, Jo, & Strega, 1986) have argued that lesbian motherhood, which requires contact with sperm, constitutes an oxymoron in which lesbian "energy" is diverted from its proper place among lesbians to a task which is paradigmatic of women's enslavement in patriarchal cultures. For these authors, contact with sperm, however divorced from sexual experience, renders a woman no longer lesbian. In addition, for many lesbians in age cohorts preceding the baby boom generation, motherhood was thought to be excluded by lesbian identity, except for those women who had borne children out of prior heterosexual connections. Lesbian mothers, in addition, have written about their sense of being "invisible" to other lesbians in their parental role; in effect, these women describe feeling stripped of their lesbian identity by the more visible identity of motherhood, which is strongly tied to heterosexuality in the dominant discourse.

This discourse reflects the struggle over who is to control the definition of lesbian identity, and what other features of women's identity in general are included in or excluded from the boundaries of lesbian identity. Dominant cultural definitions tend to contain direct or indirect inferences of deficit and deviance, while lesbian cultural definitions tend to use lesbian experience as normative and orthogonal to questions of abnormality. Psychology as a discipline has wavered from one stance to another, depending on the politics and identities of the psychologists writing about lesbian issues. However, even within these categories disagreement exists over a number of factors which leave definitions uncertain. Within each setting, distinguished simplistically here for purposes of outlining the conceptual problems, the discourse is not unitary.

In understanding the concept of lesbian identity development, in developing research or theory, one is first faced with this complex definitional question. Which answer a scholar chooses reflects a willingness to align primarily with certain explanatory models, which in turn define the parameters of ensuing theory or research. For example, if one adopts a model of lesbian definition that rests solely on overtly expressed sexual behavior, then questions of how and when arousal to same-sex stimuli and sexual contact in same-sex contexts first occurred will be important because they represent data about important defining variables. If one adopts the writer Adrienne Rich's model of a "lesbian continuum" (1980), in which overt sexual expression is simply one of several forms of lesbian relating to be examined, then questions of affection, bonding, and valuing of women as aspects of lesbian identity development become paramount. If one uses a political model of lesbians as resisters to culturally imposed norms of femininity, this might lead to attempts to study and understand gender nonconformity. Attention to multicultural issues raises questions regarding the degree to which the external dominant context informs the process of identifying oneself as lesbian, and the degree to which cultural perceptions regarding gender role nonconformity enter into consideration for individuals defining themselves as not-heterosexual. Because our current state of knowledge does not lend stronger support to one or another definition, scholars of lesbian identity development will continue to need to clarify what paradigm of lesbianism they are adopting and embedding in their work. In addition, the ethical scholar needs to attend to whether, how, and to what degree the model adopted attributes deviance or pathology to lesbians. The definitional questions are foundational to our understanding and critiques of models currently advanced for describing the development of lesbian identity.

To organize a discussion of the diverse models of how lesbian identity develops, I define a lesbian as a woman whose primary sexual and affectional attractions are to other women and who has a sexual minority identity, that is, recognizes through the use of language or symbolic expressions that her sexual orientation places her apart from a sexual mainstream, even though she may not use the term "lesbian" per se. (For example, she may call herself "gay," purposely eschewing the term lesbian, reflecting class and cultural origins where the latter term is more stigmatized than the former. Or she may call herself "queer," a more inclusive term arising from postmodern constructions of sexual identity popular in some groups of younger women, in which gender politics has lost the significance it held in an earlier generation of lesbian-feminists.) This definition does not speak to questions of gender-role stereotypy and leaves open the question of how the term "woman" is socially constructed. Overt sexual expression of lesbian identity is not required, only that any such expression if it occurs be primarily invested in women. In addition, women who have related to men, and some who continue to relate to men sexually and affectionally, are not necessarily excluded from this definition, depending on the position in which such heterosexual behavior in placed. What is core to this definitional model is that the lesbian sees her relationships and connections to women as *primary*, whether acted upon or not, and identifies herself as outside the sexual mainstream.

Models of Identity Development

Following on the diversity of paradigms arising from definitional questions is the variability of models of identity development themselves. I categorize lesbian identity development into biological models, traditional psychodynamic models, feminist psychodynamic models, and cognitively mediated "stage" models. Each model reflects different definitional assumptions and inferences regarding the nature of lesbianism, and each is problematic in its own way. Many such models have been derived from paradigms of gay male identity development, or are subsumed under such paradigms, reflecting what this writer believes to be an erroneous and sexist assumption regarding the isomorphism of homosexuality in women and men, as well as the historical neglect of lesbians in the research and theoretical literatures. One important factor informing my own critique of models of lesbian identity is whether and to what degree they make the experiences of lesbians as women, with distinct forms of socialization experiences, primary in their understanding of the development of erotic and affectional same-gender connections for women. Lesbians and gay men often have only sexual minority status in common. As the following review of the literature notes, women's experience of our sexual selves, an important component of lesbian identity, appears to be sufficiently different from the parallel process in men as to render suspect any model that purports to explain both gay men and lesbians equally well.

In addition, some of these models explored here arise within a context of more general models of women's psychosexual development. It is my bias that lesbian identity is an aspect of female identity which cannot be completely understood apart from a general understanding of women's development within a particular cultural context. This placement of lesbian identity development within a framework of women's development conceives of lesbianism as a common and normal, if minority, outcome of the development of sexual and affectional relating and overall self-development in women. In fact, my own tendency is to wonder, given some recently proposed models of women's identity development, why more women are not lesbian, since such models tend to highlight women's attachments and affectional connections to other women as central to the development of identity and self. I believe this question to be important, and address it at length in discussions of feminist models of lesbian identity.

In evaluating the various paradigms for lesbian identity development, it is useful to ask whether and to what degree such models posit a set of necessary and sufficient conditions for the development of a lesbian self. I believe that the utility of any model which fails to do so will be truncated, and the model will be unable to stand alone as a paradigm for understanding lesbian identity development. In addition, any model that will be useful to current scholars and clinicians must encompass the range of lesbian phenomenological experiences, accounting for the variability of realities exposed in the rich autobiographical literature by lesbians. The inherent assumptive frameworks of a variety of models of "coming out"—that is, coming to identify oneself as lesbian or gay—are that something unspecified is a precursor to the awareness of same-sex affection and attraction. Thus, an ideal model will be able to describe that precursor state. While the ethical implications of pursuing such a line of questioning are challenging, since risk is inherent in the exploration of questions of the origins of lesbian identity, the ethics of neglecting to ask such important questions about the nature of sexual orientation override concerns about how findings will be used.

Biological Models

Biological models have been proposed since Ellis to explain the presence of homosexuality in both women and men. Early models arise from a construction of homosexuality as a disease, deficit, or error. These paradigms include, most famously, Hirschfield's description of homosexuals as a "third sex," as well as many folk stereotypes of lesbians as "mannish" women. As a result of this underlying assumptive stance, such models tend to contain several prominent and consistent metamessages. First, there is usually an assumption of pathology: too much or too little or a particular hormone, pre- or-postnatally, "wrong" sizes of genital organs, malfunction of reproductive capacity. This image of the lesbian as a biological "invert" or "third sex" was especially popular in the late nineteenth and early twentieth centuries. These views were often used to support calls for tolerance and understanding of behavior that, since biologically fixed, could not be changed. Second, there is a message of inevitability and fixedness of sexual orientation. That is, such models either state or infer that a woman's lesbianism is innately present for her to discover, and will be present in such a woman regardless of external experience.

Difficulties with such models are both empirical and conceptual. Despite many attempts to uncover meaningful, nonoverlapping biological differences between lesbian and heterosexual women, the weight of the evidence does not support this position (Kirsch & Weinrich, 1991). Lesbians tend to demonstrate the same within-group variability on such factors as level of sex hormones, size of clitoris, and reproductive capacity as do heterosexual women. There also appears to be no evidence of difference in size or development of central nervous system structures of the sort recently reported to differentiate gay and heterosexual men. The only current piece of empirical research suggesting some biological component to lesbianism is a recent study that found greatly increased numbers of lesbian or bisexual sisters of a group of lesbians compared to a matched sample of heterosexual women (Bailey & Benishay, 1993). The concept of the biological "invert" first promulgated by Ellis and Hirschfield and popularized by Hall's lesbian classic *The Well of Loneliness,* in which lesbians and gay men represent a biological third sex, betrays the confusion between gender role and anatomical sex that permeates biological models in which lesbians are masculinized, "butch" women only.

Conceptually, such models are problematic because of their assumption of a fixed, nonchanging sexual self for lesbians and, by implication, for all women. Arguably, such a model may be important in understanding gay men, who subjectively report a more unchanging experience of sexual identity; but lesbian sexuality, like other aspects of female sexuality, does not appear to be well-described by any model assuming fixed sexual orientation. If, as proposed earlier, lesbian identity development is placed within a context of the overall development of female sexual identity, the biological models appear to be even less useful. In addition, such biological models do not account well, if at all, for the nonsexual, affectional aspects of lesbian identity. They are reductionistic, paring lesbianism down to *only* sexual acts and arousal, rather than placing lesbianism in the broader frame of affiliation, affection, and sense of community which are the subjective experiences of many lesbians.

Such models are seductive, however, because of their potential value in the political arena. Lesbian and gay rights activists have argued that if homosexuality is fixed and primarily biologically determined, then lesbians and gays should not be discriminated against. Such an argument plays into a dominant paradigm, but this position should be adopted only with extreme caution by both scholars and activists, since it implies that the dominant culture may freely punish those who have any choice in their deviance from a dominant norm and accord fair treatment only to those who are "victims," so to speak, of their biology. The degree to which biological models fail to reflect lesbian phenomenology in many cases makes them problematic and suspect.

Traditional Psychodynamic Models

As is the case for biological models, traditional psychodynamic formulations of lesbian identity development carry the message of psychopathology. These models address questions of etiology as linked to the genesis of lesbian identity. Despite his focus on female sexuality, Freud himself addressed the question of lesbian identity only briefly, in one of his famous "Three Essays" on sexuality in which he hypothesized it mirrored in some ways the development of male homosexuality, representing a perverse as distinguished from neurotic adaptation to internal conflict. In addition he published one case study of a lesbian patient (Freud, 1920). The proposed mechanisms leading to lesbian identity were unclear. Freud suggested that homosexuality in women represented a failure to resolve issues at the oedipal stage of development, leading to an identification with the father and a desire to possess the mother sexually, while simultaneously rejecting the mother because of her deficient lack of penis. Freud's followers have embellished considerably upon this formulation, increasing the degree of pathology ascribed to lesbianism, and describing it as an important aspect of failure to accept normal femininity (Deutsch, 1933; Jones, 1927; Socarides, 1968). One school of psychodynamic thought on lesbianism proposes that such an identity develops out of a wish to return to and merge with the mother (Eisenbud, 1981).

Attempting to provide empirical support for the notion that pathological processes are at the foundation of lesbian identity, Kaye et al. (1967) queried the psychoanalytic therapists of a small number of lesbian patients and purported to find a disturbance of gender role arrangements in the families of these women. More recent psychoanalytic thinking on lesbianism (Siegel, 1988) has placed it within the framework of characterological personality disturbance; interestingly, none of the women described in the dozen or so case studies in Siegel's volume were self-defined as lesbian; most had strong heterosexual self-definitions and patterns of sexual behavior interspersed with some same-sex fantasy or incidental same-sex contact.

Traditional psychodynamic formulations appear extremely problematic on the surface because of their pathologizing bent and the tendency to infer patterns of identity development from the case histories of women in distress. These models are also quite monocultural, assuming Eurocentric paradigms of family structure and process, which severely limits their usefulness in describing identity development for lesbians from non-Western cultures or non-nuclear family structures. Largely because of these limitations, such classic psychoanalytic formulations have understandably been avoided by most modern scholars of lesbian identity (Golden, 1987; Kitzinger, 1987).

However, these models contain a paradigm of sexual identity development as fluid and changeable over time and in response to certain types of interpersonal and social/contextual experiences. As a consequence, such psychodynamic models potentially provide useful conceptual and heuristic steppingstones, once their normative assumptions have been critiqued and stripped away. If we abandon (as I suggest) the heterosexist notion of one normal stream of sexual identity development, in which outcomes other than heterosexual identity and behavior are constructed as deviant and pathological, and instead adopt a paradigm of multiple, diversely normal streams of sexual identity development with many possible successful outcomes, then the questions traditional psychodynamic models raise are very intriguing; they ask us to consider how the complex experiences of girls within their familial and social contexts can lead to identification with a certain sense of self and attention to certain aspects of erotic and affectional arousal.

Politically, such questions are dangerous. Because these identity development models also contain assumptions about the origins of lesbianism within potentially fluid, modifiable interactive experience, there is always a risk that dominant cultural institutions might attempt to use such information to prevent the emergence of lesbianism. This is not a paranoid concern, since there is ample evidence of such attempts based on folk "wisdom" about the origins of lesbian identity (e.g., the campaigns of Anita Bryant, framed as a "saving of children" from homosexuals, or recent ballot measures in Colorado and Oregon aimed at stopping homosexuality by declaring it illegal and perverse). Consequently, many students of lesbian identity development have been understandably wary about the use of such a conceptual framework, preferring to ignore causal questions and simply assume that the required (if unspecified) seeds upon which to construct a lesbian identity are present in personality.

Feminist Psychodynamic Models

Feminist psychodynamic models of the development of sexual self in women avoid some, if not all, of the problematic normative assumptions of traditional psychodynamic formulations and biological models. These models tend to address lesbian identity development within a broader framework of women's sexual identity processes, thus framing a lesbian outcome as one of several normative possibilities for women (Galenson, 1986; Golden, 1987). Although, as Palladino and Stephenson (1990) have noted, these models are flawed by their monocultural nature, with assumptions about family structure, child-rearing patterns, and gender role norms that almost exclusively reflect white, northern European paradigms, they tend to be more encompassing of women's phenomenology than are other models of lesbian identity development. Feminist psychodynamic models use the object relations formulations popularized by Nancy Chodorow (1979), which posit that the core of female personality development rests in the mother–infant daughter relationship. This pairing enables the daughter to develop a sense of self through interaction and projective identification. One prominent feminist model of female personality development, the self-in-relation paradigm (Jordan, Kaplan, Miller, Stiver, & Surrey, 1992; Surrey, 1985), expands upon the possibilities Chodorow proposed to posit that women's adult development, which includes the development of a sexual self, occurs in a relational matrix characterized by increasing competence in relationality and for which the sense of self is constructed as self-in-relation to others. Empathy and the capacity for mutuality in relations are defined as successful outcomes of this developmental process.

Curiously, few of these theorists (aside from Carla Golden, cited earlier) have commented directly on the development of lesbian identity. In fact, much of the theoretical literature in the feminist psychodynamic field can be described as heterosexist, since it assumes heterosexuality of women implicitly even while explicitly endorsing a diverse-outcome norm for women's sexual development. As Palladino and Stephenson (1990) note, the feminist psychodynamicists fail to explicate how a girl whose passionate relational attachments are to a woman (the mother) is transformed into a woman whose relational self is directed to men, while similarly failing to address what might occur in the developmental process of those girls who, to some degree, continue to direct their passion, arousal, and relationality toward women throughout the lifespan. They note how Eichenbaum and Orbach (1987), another prominent pair of feminist psychodynamic theorists, describe their own erotic charge for one another without ever examining the erotic implications of their friendship, thus falsely separating questions of lesbian identity development from those of women's over-all relational process. These problems and critiques aside, feminist psychodynamic formulations are potentially powerful paradigms for the study of lesbian identity development.

Golden's (1987) work exemplifies how feminist psychodynamic formulations can be extrapolated to understand certain patterns of lesbian identity development in some groups of women. In her examples, feminist psychodynamic formulations provide important elements for understanding lesbian identity as a normal aspect of female sexuality. In addition, Golden's work reflects other useful assumptions of the feminist psychodynamic literature. These elements include a foundation in women's embodied experiences rather than a view of women as "other," an (at least theoretical) embrace of a normative stance in which lesbianism is one of many equally valued outcomes of female adult development, and a broader, less genitally focused model of passionate relating than is found in male-dominant paradigms. Such conceptual threads could be woven together so as to allow a more complex and rich response than would otherwise be possible to some of the definitional questions addressed earlier in this chapter.

Such models, with their emphasis on the quality of relationships, place lesbian identity within the broader question about how women come to love and bond with other women, and ask the more subversive question as to why some women *fail* to develop primary sexual and affectional bonds to women, rather than seeing the development of such bonds as representing a separate, relatively infrequently taken, and possibly deviant developmental pathway. However, it is incumbent upon researcher or theoretician using these paradigms to address the very real limits of phenomenology, to borrow a phrase from Lerman (1992) in response to questions of cultural diversity as they affect the development of sexual self in women. Because the phenomenologically based models proposed by feminist psychodynamicists have been so seductive to white women, their reduced applicability and usefulness for women of color in North America and women in non-Euro-American cultures is often not noticed. As Espin (1987) has noted, one cannot simply "add women of color and stir" to make an intrapsychic model generalizable beyond its culture of origin, even when that model is feminist.

"Stage" Models

The period since 1970 has seen a flurry of proposed models to explicate the "coming out" process in lesbians and gay men (for a complete review see Gonsiorek & Rudolph, 1991). These models derive from Atkinson, Morten, and Sue's (1979) model of minority identity development, and attempt to identify stages by which the individual lesbian learns, within the social context, to identify to self and others as lesbian. Stages usually consist of such elements as noticing same-gender attractions, working through ambivalent feelings about these attractions, ascribing meaning and names to those feelings, and then attaching the feelings to a minority group identity.

In stage models, identity development is construed as a process of learning to name one's sexual self, and then place oneself within various social contexts at increasing degrees of social distance from the person. Many of the models developed to date have taken the experience of gay men as their norm, extrapolating this to assumptions about lesbians. Each of these models proposes that becoming lesbian requires a process of identifying oneself as such, giving meaning to that self-identification, and then communicating that identity to other lesbians, gay men, and members of the general community. The sine qua non of identity development is hypothesized as the ability to be more open about one's sexual orientation in more settings.

Like traditional psychodynamic formulations, these stage models lack explanations for the roots of lesbian feelings. Same-sex attraction is simply assumed to exist. This can be read as either a taking for granted the normative nature of such feelings (i.e., they are simply there, like the color of one's hair) or a strategy for avoiding politically dangerous etiological considerations. Depending on the other intellectual traditions influencing the individual who is generating these paradigms, one can detect assumptions regarding the possible biological and/or psychological roots of sexual identity development. For example, Malyon's (1982) model of identity development in gay men demonstrates clearly the author's grounding in psychodynamic theory, whereas DeMonteflores and Schultz's (1978) proposal reflects a social constructivist perspective. All of the models reviewed by Gonsiorek and Rudolph also have a hint of the biological in their explanatory fictions.

Such models are also limited by the inherent assumption that the process of sexual identity development have one outcome. That is, such models do not account for the fluidity and changing nature of sexual identities, or for nonlinear processes of coming to terms intellectually with one's felt and embodied experiences. Such models explain the woman who comes to a lesbian identity later in her adult life by defining the period of heterosexual behavior and/or identity as one of denial or repression of awareness of same-sex attraction. These models reflect their genesis in a period when the notion of bisexuality did not receive serious consideration, however, and fail to make sense of the woman who identifies initially as lesbian, based on her behaviors and the meanings ascribed to them in the social discourse, then relates heterosexually either again or for the first time, and finally arrives at a bisexual or heterosexual identity. The models manifest the influence of the dichotomous model of sexual orientation, in which one is either lesbian or heterosexual for life, but not both at various points in the life cycle.

The strength of the stage models is their power to explain and describe how the development of sexual self in lesbians is one of constant interaction and interchange between internal reality and external cultural context. They demonstrate how social discourse influences the process of naming oneself lesbian as well as the meaning ascribed to that name. They offer the scholar or researcher frames within which to raise questions about what might happen in lesbian identity development in a lesbian-defined, lesbian-affirmative social context rather than the heterosexist and antilesbian social discourse which informs the developmental process of almost every lesbian.

Empirical research derived from these models has also underscored the importance of examining lesbian identity development separate from that of gay men; a number of researchers note that the awareness of same-sex attraction for women begins as a primarily affectional rather than sexual phenomenon (Gramick, 1984; Schippers, 1990; Sears, 1989). While such an awareness is essential for taking the next step of naming such feelings as lesbian, our knowledge that these feelings are not narrowly sexually defined in women can lead to further questions regarding what happens to those women who feel affection for member of their own gender but do not name themselves lesbian. This might fruitfully enlarge the discourse regarding the definitions of lesbianism, and will probably point the way toward situating questions of lesbian identity development within the broader framework of the development of female sexuality.

Conclusion

As I have noted elsewhere (Brown, 1989), the psychological study of lesbian and gay issues has been severely hampered by our tendency, until recently, to engage in such study from the models and constructs of dominant, heterosexist paradigms in which assumptions about the non-normative, if not deviant, nature of lesbianism and the dichotomous nature of sexual orientation were embedded. These problems are reflected in the conceptual issues discussed in this chapter. That is, our definitional questions and theoretical models have arisen to one degree or another from outside lived lesbian experience. This limits them in various ways.

A problem common to all extant models is that they have been overly Eurocentric; no well-developed models of lesbian identity development speak to the meaning of same-sex relationships for women in cultures where no clearly demarcated lesbian identity exists. Similarly, only partial explorations are available in the behavioral science literature of how race, culture, and class interact with the process of lesbian identity development in the North American and European cultural matrices from which most of the current models spring, although several authors have begun to address this question regarding African–American (Greene, 1986, 1994), Latina (Espin, 1987), and Asian–American (Chan, 1989) lesbian groups. The autobiographical literature is repleat with such material from personal and phenomenological perspectives, offering rich conceptual possibilities for the psychological theoretician and researcher.

A related problem of extant models is the failure of any one model to account for the diversity of lesbian definitions and experiences in the development of lesbian identity. Partly because the discussion of this topic in a nonpathologizing manner is relatively recent, the thinking reflected in many paradigms has been overly simplistic, attempting to narrow the scope of discussion prematurely to impose some order on the creative chaos of the material at hand. What is needed in the future is models that use a biopsychosocial framework to understand the interaction of humans with both physical and emotional environmental contexts. Such models must eschew the concept of sexual orientations as dichotomous and mutually exclusive and embrace a paradigm of human sexuality as a collection of complex and fluid phenomena.

In this chapter I have chosen not to address questions of gender role as they relate to lesbian identity. This is partially to narrow the focus of my discussion. It also reflects my difficulties with what I believe to be a conflation of gender role and sexual orientation in many definitions of lesbian identity, and my view that much of this confusion represents certain limited points in temporal and cultural discourses on female sexuality. The discussion of such matters as butch and femme roles in certain North American lesbian communities, while fascinating aspects of the public invention of lesbian erotic selves, falls beyond the scope of the present chapter. However, future studies of lesbian identity development will need to inquire about the relationship of these phenomena in the more general framework of human development. That is, where and when are the seeds of erotic and affectional orientation sown as children gain a sense of themselves as members of a gender, then move toward gendered schemata of their own and others' behavior? One cannot, after all, have a gender orientation until gender becomes an important emotional category of analysis.

We also need to ask ourselves how we can apply a lesbian voice and vision to our understanding of lesbian identity development. That is, how can we assume a lesbian stance to be central rather than marginal; and what questions and frameworks can we expect to arise from such a different view of lesbian realities? As Kitzinger (1987) has noted, the social constructions of lesbianism by the general public and by theoreticians and researchers have tended to distort our views of lesbian realities and to depoliticize the discussion by ignoring the subversive nature of lesbian existence in heterosexist and misogynist dominant cultures.

This transformational dilemma continues to be a demanding task for theoreticians and researchers because our professional socialization in heterosexist dominant cultures is a powerful limiting factor on our imaginations. Models derived from qualitative studies of lesbian communities and lesbian families have promise, because they will begin to offer us the experiences of women for who being lesbian has always been a viable and valuable possibility rather than a hidden, feared, or stigmatized one. As we approach the second decade of lesbian liberation, the social cradle for the age cohort of these women, the possible models for understanding lesbian identity will be changed by the differences between these women's realities and those of their foresisters. As it is difficult to separate our understanding of gendered phenomena from those that are simply the result of power and dominance hierarchies (Unger, 1989), so it is extremely difficult to differentiate theoretically or empirically those aspects of lesbian identity development that are primarily or solely about the management of stigma or marginality from those that are simply about being lesbian.

Concretely, all of these suggestions may require scholars of lesbian identity development to reinvent our methodologies in light of the currently available data. The questions that have informed research on lesbian issues until the present have largely reflected earlier knowledge bases. Our knowledge, much of which is experiential, has expanded exponentially in the past two decades. Ironically, our best hopes for better understanding lesbian identity may lie in the development of a lesbian-informed study of women's overall sexual development, including the development of heterosexuality in women. Those models, arising from feminist psychodynamic formulations, seem to best describe embodied lesbian experience and assume the primacy of women's passionate relationships to other women. It may be possible to better understand how lesbians hold on to and eroticize these attachments if we comprehend how such passions are lost or distorted for women who are not lesbian. In other words, we may be asking the wrong questions. We may need to ask not only why are some women lesbians and how do they come to that identity, but also why do some women lose their lesbianism as they develop?

Scholarship in this field is arriving at a new level of maturity after two decades of increasingly public and affirmative discourse by lesbians and our allies regarding the processes by which we come to name and know ourselves as lesbian. The challenge for the future is to move beyond the limitations imposed by dominant cultural norms and to develop definitions and paradigms based in the diversity and variability of embodied lesbian experiences across time and culture.

References

Adleman, J. (1986). Falling and rising in love. In M. Adelman (Ed.), *Long time passing: Lives of older lesbians* (pp. 35–50). Boston: Alyson Publications.

Atkinson, D. R., Morten, G, & Sue, D. W. (1979). *Counseling American minorities*. Dubuque, IA: Brown.

Bailey, J. M., & Benishay, D. S. (1993). Familial aggregation of female sexual orientation. *American Journal of Psychiatry, 150,* 272–277.

Brown, L. S. (1989). New voices, new visions: Toward a lesbian/gay paradigm for psychology. *Psychology of Women Quarterly, 13,* 445–458.

Chan, C. S. (1989). Issues of identity development among Asian–American lesbians and gay men. *Journal of Counseling and Development, 68,* 16–20.

Chodorow, N. (1979). *The reproduction of mothering.* Berkeley, CA: University of California Press.

Cook, B. W. (1992). *Eleanor Roosevelt, Volume One, 1884–1933.* New York: Viking.

DeMonteflores, C., & Schultz, S. (1978). Coming out: Similarities and differences for lesbians and gay men. *Journal of Social Issues, 34,* 59–72.

Deutsch, H. (1933). Female sexuality (homosexuality in women). *International Journal of Psychoanalysis, 14,* 34–56.

Eichenbaum, L., & Orbach, S. (1987). *Between women: Love, envy and competition in women's friendships.* New York: Viking.

Eisenbud, R. J. (1981). Early and late determinants of lesbian choice. *Psychoanalytic Review, 69,* 85–109.

Ellis, H. (1922). *Studies in the psychology of sex: Vol. 2* (3rd ed.) Philadelphia: F. A. Davis.

Espin, O. M. (1987). Issues of identity in the psychology of Latina lesbians. In Boston Lesbian Psychologies Collective (Eds.), *Lesbian psychologies: Explorations and challenges* (pp. 35–55). Urbana, IL: University of Illinois Press.

Faderman, L. (1982). *Surpassing the love of men: Romantic friendship and love between women from the Renaissance to the present.* New York: William Morrow.

Freud, S. (1953). Three essays on the theory of sexuality. In *Standard Edition, 7* (pp. 125–243). London: Hogarth Press.

Freud, S. (1920). Psychogenesis of a case of homosexuality in a woman. In *Standard Edition, 18.* (pp. 143–175). London: Hogarth Press.

Galenson, E. (1986). Early pathways to female sexuality in advantaged and disadvantaged girls. In T. Bernay & D. W. Cantor (Eds.), *The psychology of today's woman: New psychoanalytic visions* (pp. 37–50). Hillsdale, NJ: The Analytic Press.

Golden, C. (1987). Diversity and variability in women's sexual identities. In Boston Lesbian Psychologies Collective (Eds.), *Lesbian psychologies: Ex-*

plorations and challenges (pp. 18–34). Urbana, IL: University of Illinois Press.

Gonsiorek, J., & Rudolph, J. (1991). Homosexual identity: Coming out and other developmental events. In J. Gonsiorek & J. Weinrich (Eds.), *Homosexuality: Research implications for public policy* (pp. 161–176). Newbury Park, CA: Sage.

Gramick, J. (1984). Developing a lesbian identity. In T. Darty & S. Potter (Eds.), *Women-identified women* (pp. 31–44). Palo Alto, CA: Mayfield.

Greene, B. (1986). When the therapist is white and the patient is Black: Considerations for psychotherapy in the feminist heterosexual and lesbian communities. *Women and Therapy, 5,* 41–66.

Greene, B. (1994). Mental health concerns of lesbians of color. In L. Comas-Diaz & B. Greene (Eds.), *Women of color and mental health.* New York: Guilford.

Haldeman, D. (1991). Sexual orientation conversion therapy for gay men and lesbians: A scientific examination. In J. Gonsiorek & J. Weinrich (Eds.), *Homosexuality: Research implications for public policy* (pp. 149–160). Newbury Park, CA: Sage.

Hirschfield, M. (1936). The homosexual as an intersex. In V. Robinson (Ed.), *Encyclopaedia sexualis.* New York: Dingwall-Rock.

Jones, E. (1927). Early development of female homosexuality. *International Journal of Psychoanalysis, 8,* 459–472.

Jordan, J., Kaplan, A. G., Miller, J. B., Stiver, I., & Surrey, J. (1992). *Women's growth in connection: Writings from the Stone Center.* New York: Guilford.

Kaye, H. S., et al. (1967). Homosexuality in women. *Archives of General Psychiatry, 17,* 626–634.

Kirsch, J. A. W., & Weinrich, J. (1991). Homosexuality, nature, and biology: Is homosexuality natural? Does it matter? In J. Gonsiorek & J. Weinrich (Eds.), *Homosexuality: Research implications for public policy* (pp. 13–31). Newbury Park, CA: Sage.

Kitzinger, C. (1987). *The social construction of lesbianism.* London: Sage.

Lerman, H. (1992). The limits of phenomenology: A feminist critique of the humanistic personality theories. In L. S. Brown & M. Ballou (Eds.), *Personality and psychopathology: Feminist reappraisals* (pp. 8–19). New York: Guilford.

Letters Column (1992, Spring). *Lesbian Connection.* Lansing, MI: Elsie Publishing.

Malyon, A. (1982). Biphasic aspects of homosexual identity formation. *Psychotherapy: Theory, Research, and Practice, 19,* 335–340.

Palladino, D., & Stephenson, Y. (1990). Perceptions of the sexual self: Their impact on relationships between lesbian and heterosexual women. In L. S. Brown & M. P. P. Root (Eds.), *Diversity and complexity in feminist therapy* (pp. 231–254). New York: Haworth.

Penelope, J. (1992). *Call me lesbian: Lesbian lives, lesbian theory.* Freedom, CA: The Crossing Press.

Raymond, J. (1982). *The transsexual empire: The making of a she-male.* Boston: Beacon.

Rich, A. (1980). Compulsory heterosexuality and lesbian existence. *Signs: Journal of Women in Culture and Society, 5,* 631–660.

Rothblum, E. D. & Brehony, K. A. (Eds.) (1993). *Boston marriages: Romantic, but asexual relationships among contemporary lesbians.* Amherst: University of Massachusetts Press.

Ruston, Jo, B., & Strega, L. (1986). Heterosexism causes lesbophobia causes butch-phobia: Part II of the big sellout: Lesbian femininity. *Lesbian Ethics, 2,* 22–41.

Sears, J. T. (1989). The impact of gender and race on growing up lesbian and gay in the South. *National Women's Studies Association Journal, 1,* 422–457.

Schippers, J. (1990, August). "Gay affirmative counseling and psychotherapy in the Netherlands." Paper presented at the Convention of the American Psychological Association, Boston MA.

Siegel, E. V. (1988). *Female homosexuality: Choice without volition.* Hillsdale, NJ: The Analytic Press.

Socarides, C. W. (1968). *The overt homosexual.* New York: Grune and Stratton.

Surrey, J. (1985). The "self-in-relation": A theory of women's development. *Work in progress.* Wellesley, MA: Stone Center Working Papers Series.

Unger, R. K. (1989). Explorations in feminist ideology: Surprising consistencies and unexamined conflicts. In R. K. Unger (Ed.), *Representations: Social constructions of gender* (pp. 203–211). Amityville, NY: Baywood Publishing.

Weinrich, J., & Williams, W. (1991). Strange customs, familiar lives: Homosexualities in other cultures. In J. Gonsiorek & J. Weinrich (Eds.), *Homosexuality: Research implications for public policy* (pp. 44–59). Newbury Park, CA: Sage.

Wiese, R. B. (Ed.) (1992). *Closer to home: Bisexuality and feminism.* Seattle: Seal Press.

Williams, W. L. (1986). *The spirit and the flesh: Sexual diversity in American Indian culture.* Boston: Beacon.

2

Gay Male Identities: Concepts and Issues

John C. Gonsiorek

Beginning with Evelyn Hooker's study in 1957, which provided the first empirical evidence that homosexuality was not indicative of psychological disturbance, we witnessed for the next two decades a line of research addressing this issue. As reviewed by Gonsiorek (1991), the data overwhelmingly indicate that homosexuality is not indicative of mental illness. This data base is sufficiently compelling that one can argue that theories which continue to purport an illness model of homosexuality represent egregious distortions of scientific information about homosexuality in the service of hatred and bigotry.

In the mid-1970s, following the depathologizing of homosexuality, a new wave of lesbian and gay affirmative research attempted to elucidate the psychological processes involved as lesbian and gay individuals navigate the development of a viable identity in a typically hostile society (see Gonsiorek & Rudolph, 1991, for review of this literature). This chapter reviews these new lesbian and gay affirmative concepts with emphasis on gay men, critiques certain features and limitations, and suggests future directions.

Unique Developmental Events in the Lives of Gay and Lesbian Individuals

Research, however, suggests a subset of homosexual individuals who, particularly in adolescence and young adulthood, have a greater than average likelihood of psychological problems, particularly attempted suicide and perhaps chemical abuse (see Gonsiorek, 1991, for review of this literature). The most parsimonious explanation of these data is that although homosexuality per se is not related to psychopathology, stresses in the lives of some gay and lesbian individuals may result, particularly in adolescence and young adulthood, in higher rates of certain kinds of symptomatology.

It is important to note that the demise of the illness model of homosexuality created a theoretical and clinical vacuum for understanding sexual orientation as well as responding to lesbian and gay clients who seek psychological services. Furthermore, the paradox of the lack of empirical support for the illness model of homosexuality versus suggestions of a subgroup of homosexual individuals who experience certain kinds of psychiatric symptomatology in adolescence or young adulthood required an explanation. More important, central tasks that have emerged are to develop truly psychological understandings of the lives of lesbian, gay, and bisexual individuals, including what might be unique versus shared with heterosexual persons, and of how these understandings can operate across varying contexts of gender, race, ethnicity, age, class, and others.

The material reviewed in this chapter contains such an explanatory framework. Homosexuality and bisexuality are viewed as nonpathological variations in human behavior, and perhaps identity, which can elicit certain predictable stresses which gay, lesbian, and bisexual individuals negotiate, acquiring an affirmative sense of self in a hostile and disparaging society generally, and specifically within their families and communities. As a result, there may be some consistencies in these developmental experiences and psychological processes, perhaps even particular identities.

These consistencies in experience and psychological process are not the same as gay, lesbian, or bisexual personalities. The same data that showed no evidence for intrinsic psychopathology also showed no consistency in personality variables among gay and lesbian populations. Rather, gay and lesbian individuals are conceptualized as a diverse group who experience some similarity in the external pressures they face. As a result, some consistency in psychological processes exists. These events, however, are filtered through diverse early personality structures and personal and family histories; race, gender, ethnicity, class, and other contexts; and development over time and life experience. This way of understanding may have considerable significance for any group of individuals who cope with a disparaging or oppressive society, although it is likely the experiences of any specific group are likely to be particular enough that application from one group to another is inexact. Gay, lesbian, and bisexual affirmative theorizing during the 1980s focused on the development and explication of such concepts. This information is now reviewed with an emphasis on gay men.

Some Particular Features of Maleness and Sexual Orientation

While it is commonplace to assume that sexual orientations mean roughly the same thing across gender, this may not be a wise assumption. For example, Golden (1990) describes how some women perceive choice as an important element in their sexual orientations. Gay men, on the other hand, typically perceive that their sexual orientation is a given, a central aspect of themselves, and choice has little to do with it. Lesbians appear to perceive affectional orientation and political perspectives as central to self-definition, while gay men appear to view sexual behavior and sexual fantasy as central. It may even be that the nature of sexual orientation is different for men and women. Certainly, perceptions about the nature of sexual orientation differ between men and women.

There are also suggestions that identity development differs between lesbians and gay men in a number of ways. They are especially prominent during adolescence and the coming out process. Gonsiorek (1988) has described that the coming out process for males appears to be more abrupt and is likely to be associated with psychiatric symptoms, whereas the process for women appears to be characterized by greater fluidity and ambiguity. Differences in the tempo of identity development may be influenced by patterns of sexual socialization. Because women are allowed a broader range of behavioral and emotional interactions with other women, some lesbians may experience their emerging sexual and emotional intimacy as friendship. Because men are confined to narrower patterns, longing for emotional and physical contact with other males is apt to be perceived as clearly homosexual. Consistent with traditional sex role socialization, men are more prone to sexual activity during the coming out process and women are more likely to respond with reflection and self-absorption. These generalizations are more or less true of each individual, depending on the flexibility of his or her sex role and other aspects of personality structure. Accumation of research about gay and lesbian individuals currently in their teens and early twenties will also be informative. Some of these observations may be generational cohort effects, intermingling with sex role socialization.

Stereotypic sex role behaviors may persist as the homosexual individual begins intimate relationships. Men are apt to sexualize their relationships to be competitive or autonomous and independent rather than intimate. Women, on the other hand, are socialized to develop and express intimacy but may be less skilled in maintaining autonomy and individuality in the context of a relationship. Based on these stereotypes, problems in gay male relationships can be expected early on, as the two men struggle to develop a sense of being a couple and to contain their tendency toward competition and independence. Sexual aspects of the relationship may predominate and disagreement about sexual expression may be perceived as a threat to self-esteem. If the men can develop a greater capacity for intimacy and mutual cooperation, however, problems with autonomy and competitiveness tend to diminish with time.

A different pattern of strengths and weaknesses is anticipated for lesbian relationships. A sense of being coupled often emerges quickly and with considerable vigor. At later stages in the relationship, problems may develop if autonomy and individuality do not counterbalance the forces toward merger and dependency.

The constraints of sex role socialization are not unique to gay and lesbian relationships. However, they may be intense and quickly apparent because both partners in the relationship share the same gender. Another way of saying this is that the problems challenging gay male couples are very much male problems and the problems challenging lesbian couples are very much female problems.

Gender and sexual orientation can interact in other ways. For gay men, particularly those who are English-speaking and educated, their future before they come out is that of a member of the most enfranchised class of society. Bigotry against homosexuality probably remains the most virulent prejudice in our society, and the status of homosexuality rarely enjoys legal protection. Gay men, particularly white, English-speaking, well-educated gay men, face a comparatively great loss of status during the coming out process. Women and nonwhite men have already experienced status loss through sexism and racism. English-speaking, white, middle-class or above gay men have often had little experience with overt bigotry. This may be part of the reason, in addition to sex role socialization, why the coming out process has a sharp edge for some men.

On a more intrapsychic level, if the perception that the self-esteem of many men is strongly tied to sexuality is accurate, this loss of status may become an ongoing process. It is possible then that the effects of societal disparagement (or narcissistic injury, in the self psychology perspective) may be more acute and dramatic for men than for women, although this is speculative. Certainly, many indications suggest that sexual orientation and coming to terms with it operate in contexts heavily influenced by gender, socioeconomic status, and racial/ethnic variables. Given how powerful an effect gender plays in many other aspects of human behavior, there is every reason to suspect that as identity development is further researched among gay men and lesbians, these two groups are likely to be more different than similar.

Finally, as sex roles and definitions evolve over time, the influences just described will likely warrant revision. If, as some have suggested, we are in a period when different cohorts experience significantly different socialization regarding sex roles, there may be no fixed relationship between sexual orientation and maleness or femaleness; rather, a variety of interplay of forces with different outcomes, may be the "norm."

The Beginnings of a Developmental Perspective

Much theory about personality structure assumes that characteristics are laid down relatively early in life, and that events in later childhood, adolescence, and adulthood represent an unfolding of these characteristics over time. Such approaches, however, tend to be static. They have difficulty incorporating ongoing development, such as Erikson's (1980) theory of personality development throughout adulthood. They also have trouble accommodating events that occur later in life but powerfully influence psychological functioning, such as posttraumatic stress disorder, coping with physical illness, aging, and so on. While recent decades have seen greater emphasis on development over the lifespan, it is probably fair to say that the "tyranny of early development" remains.

More important, most personality theories operate at a "micro" level, that is, the family is the most important influence. They do not easily incorporate such "macro" effects as larger sociopolitical forces of poverty, racism, sexism, homophobia, and similar kinds of oppression, especially as these forces may have their impact over the lifespan, not just in early childhood. Finally, most theories have difficulty conceptualizing interaction between micro and macro levels. Theories that accommodate important influences and change over the lifespan, incorporate the effects of macro forces on the individual, and can explain interaction between levels I label *developmental*, to signify an ongoing identity development process instead of a relatively static identity structure that merely manifests over time.

Perhaps the first individual to apply a developmental perspective to the experience of oppressed groups was Allport (1954), who examined the nature and effects of stereotyping and prejudice. Allport theorized about the personality characteristics that develop in individuals who are targets of prejudice. He described these characteristics as coping mechanisms, which may be developed in response to prejudice but eventually can become relatively stable personality traits. These *traits due to victimization* he believed were common in most persecuted groups. They include: excessive concern and preoccupation with minority or deviant group membership, feelings of insecurity, denial of membership in the group, withdrawal and passivity, self-derision, strong in-group ties coupled with prejudice against out groups, slyness and cunning, self-hate, aggression against one's own group, militancy, enhanced striving, neuroticism, and acting out self-fulfulling prophecies about one's own inferiority.

Allport developed his ideas by observing the effects of prejudice against Blacks and Jews. His analysis did not include homosexuals, yet the personality traits and coping mechanisms he describes closely parallel descriptions of personality characteristics certain psychoanalytic writers (Bergler, 1956; Bieber et al., 1962; Hatterer, 1970; Socarides, 1968) describe as inherent and pathological features of homosexuals and "evidence" that homosexuality per se is a neurotic illness. This is a clear example of the same phenomena being viewed as intrinsic and structural by one school of thought and as reactive to an external situation by another. Allport's work is different from the theories on stereotyping described by Herek (1991) in that Allport places greater emphasis on how social situations shape and alter *personality characteristics* of stereotyped individuals. The material described by Herek emphasizes how the processes of stereotyping affect target individual's *behavior* in given situations.

Examining factors that facilitate general adjustment to homosexuality, Weinberg and Williams (1974) found that individuals who were well adjusted as homosexuals had rejected the idea that homosexuality was an illness, had close and supportive associations with other homosexuals, and were not interested in changing their homosexuality. It is noteworthy that writers who advocate an illness model of homosexuality and attempt to "cure" homosexuals agree on many points. These theorists (Bergler, 1956; Bieber, et al., 1962; Caprio, 1954; Hatterer, 1970; Nicolosi, 1991; Socarides, 1968, 1978) agree that in order to "cure" a homosexual, he or she must be convinced that such behavior is disturbed, be motivated to change, avoid homosexual relationships, and avoid social contacts with other homosexuals. These are precisely the attitudes that Weinberg and Williams (1974) found related to poor psychological adjustment in homosexuals. The question arises whether theorists who advocate curing homosexuals are creating or exacerbating maladjustment in their homosexual patients, or as Silverstein (1991) notes, psychiatry teaches patients to suffer.

Later research supports and amplifies the findings of Weinberg and Williams. Hammersmith and Weinberg (1973) found that positive commitment to homosexuality was related to psychological adjustment and the existence of significant others who support that identity. Farrell and Morrione (1974) found that membership in a homosexual group had positive psychological effects in a lower socioeconomic status subject group. Jacobs and Tedford (1980) found that membership in a homosexual group was positively related to self-esteem. Schmitt and Kurdek (1987) found that gay men living with a partner had a more positive self-concept, and that gay men involved in long-term relationships had less depression and anxiety, and a greater internal locus of control.

These discussions share the idea that a gay or lesbian person's response to the external oppression he or she faces has significant effects on psychological functioning. They set the stage for the idea that some of the problems gay and lesbian people experience can be best understood from a *developmental* perspective; that is, from an understanding that events which occur psychologically "late" can nonetheless be powerful and are filtered through the myriad influences of what has occurred before.

The Coming Out Process

As noted earlier, there are suggestions that in adolescence and young adulthood some gay and lesbian individuals experience a great deal of psychological turmoil. In the 1970s clinicians working with gay men and lesbians began to notice patterning to these struggles and to describe a developmental process of coming to terms with homosexuality, labeled the "coming out" process.

These theorists and observers, who include Cass (1979), Coleman (1982), Dank (1971), Grace (1979), Hencken and O'Dowd (1977), Lee (1977), Plummer (1975), and Troiden (1979), suggested that gay individuals progress through a series of stages typically occurring in adolescence or young adulthood. While varying in the number and description of the stages, they generally run as follows. There is an initial stage when individuals block recognition of same-sex feelings through a variety of defensive strategies, which may exact a high psychological price for their maintenance. Some individuals maintain these defensive strategies indefinitely and constrict their same-sex feelings. In the process they usually consume much psychological energy and incur constriction in general functioning style and damage to self-esteem. For many individuals, however, a gradual recognition of same-sex interests emerges. The individual gradually begins to tolerate that significant same-sex feelings are present.

This is usually followed by a period of emotional and behavioral experimentation with homosexuality, and often an increasing sense of normality about same-sex feelings. Some models postulate a second crisis after the dissolution of a first relationship when negative feelings about being gay or lesbian reemerge. As the individual again begins to accept his or her same-sex feelings, a sense of identity as gay or lesbian is successfully integrated and accepted as a positive aspect of the self. The models vary somewhat on the particulars of these later stages. While most writers describe this process in discrete stages, they often note that it is generally unpredictable, with stops, starts, and back-tracking. In particular, denial of same-sex feelings may weave in and out, periodically halting development.

This coming out process represents a shift in the person's core sexual identity and may be accompanied by dramatic emotional distress. In general, the best predictor of an individual's long-term adjustment during this phase is his or her level of functioning prior to this process rather than the presenting symptomatology. Most gay and lesbian individuals weather these crises and emerge with minimal or no symptomatology and improved functioning. A more detailed description of these events, particularly for adolescents, is presented by Gonsiorek (1988).

There appear to be differences between gay men and lesbians during this process. As noted earlier, this process appears to be more abrupt for men, and more likely to be associated with psychiatric symptoms; for women the process appears to be characterized by greater fluidity and ambiguity. It may well be that differences in the pacing of identity development are influenced by sex role socialization. Because women are allowed a broader range of behavioral and emotional interactions with other women, they may experience emerging sexual and emotional intimacy as "mere friendship." Because men are confined to narrower patterns of expression, longing for emotional and physical contact with other men is apt to be perceived as clearly "homosexual." Consistent with traditional sex role socialization, males are more prone to sexualizing distress during the coming out process and women are more likely to respond with reflection and self-absorption.

Sears (1989) noted in his research that "important differences among males and females in the meanings constructed around these sexual feelings and experiences were evident. Lesbian participants, more often than gay men, attached emotional–romantic meaning to same-sex relationships prior to engaging in homosexual behavior, defined the term *homosexual* in an emotional romantic context, and denied the legitimacy of their own sexual feelings. . . . Some scholars have concluded that lesbians have more in common with heterosexual women than they do with gay men" (p. 437). Schippers (1990) summarizes this idea in the following way: "The psychological discourse on lesbian sexuality differs from the one about gay male sexuality . . . it is of a more exploratory nature . . ." (p. 14). These generalizations are more or less true of any individual, depending on the flexibility of his or her sex role and other aspects of personality structure and personal history.

The coming out models are an important theoretical development. They essentially describe *additional* developmental processes unique to the lives of lesbians and gay men. These processes occur in addition to, *not* instead of, standard psychological processes and other aspects of identity development of adolescence and adulthood. In other words, these additional developmental processes are filtered through other aspects of the personality structure and personal and family history. The coming out models themselves vary in how sensitive they are to this variation. For example, Cass' model contains a well-developed explication of the psychological processes involved, whereas others, such as Coleman's, are relatively unelaborated and nonpsychological.

Though these coming out theories are useful as observations about certain developmental events, however, as a group they suffer serious limitations. It is currently unknown if they are generalizable beyond the generational cohort which entered adolescence in the 1960s and 1970s. Anecdotal observations suggest that some adolescents of the 1990s may experiences these events in a more truncated or rapid manner, perhaps because some "come out" earlier. Perhaps these differences are sufficiently qualitative that the processes described earlier are simply not a faithful rendering. The models are relatively silent about the psychological processes occurring in lesbian and gay individuals before the discrete and dramatic processes termed "coming out." This limitation began to be remedied with the work of Alan Malyon.

Internalized Homophobia

Malyon (1981, 1982a, 1982b) theorized that gay and lesbian persons, like heterosexuals, are raised with culturally sanctioned antihomosexual biases. Such biases mobilize other psychological processes that extend beyond the development of prejudice. Children who will eventually be bisexual or homosexual often develop an awareness of being different at an early age. They may not understand the sexual nature or precise meaning of their differentness, but they soon learn it is negatively regarded. As these individuals develop and mature, they reach a fuller understanding of the nature of this difference and the considerable negative societal reaction to it. These negative feelings may be incorporated into their self-image, resulting in varying degrees of *internalized homophobia*. Negative feelings about one's sexual orientation may be overgeneralized to encompass the entire self. Effects of this may range from a mild tendency toward self-doubt in the face of prejudice to overt self-hatred and self-destructive behavior.

Another important concept is that the manifestations of internalized homophobia can be expressed in a variety of ways. Overt manifestations include individuals consciously viewing themselves as evil, second class or inferior on account of their homosexuality. Such individuals may engage in substance abuse or other self-destructive or abusive behaviors. However, because overt internalized homophobia is so psychologically painful and destabilizing, it is less prevalent than covert forms. Few persons who have not been seriously damaged by earlier childhood events can tolerate such conscious self-deprecation.

Covert forms of internalized homophobia are the most common. Such individuals may appear to accept themselves and their same-sex orientation but sabotage their own lives in a variety of subtle ways. For example, they may abandon career or educational goals with the excuse that external bigotry will keep them from their objectives. Internalized homophobia also takes the form of excessively tolerating discriminatory or abusive behavior from others. When gay and lesbian persons are met with bigotry and oppression, as they invariably are, they are forced to make a choice. Neutrality is not among the options. To say no, either behaviorally or symbolically is self-affirming; to tolerate second-class status is in effect to affirm a view of oneself as inferior.

The coming out processes are additional, superimposed on whatever psychological and developmental processes are particular to the individual. In adulthood, other processes occur in later periods which are relatively unique to gay and lesbian persons. Chief among these is the management of disclosure. As I describe later, the management of disclosure has special significance for gay, lesbian, and bisexual individuals because they are the only minority group whose disclosure of their minority status is optional and not thrust upon them. Management of a full range of options concerning disclosure is therefore required, which often demands considerable psychological sophistication and well-tuned reality testing. In other words, gay and lesbian persons must develop the skills to perform a complex "cost-benefit analysis" when faced with external bigotry and oppression. They can err by not standing up for themselves and thereby undermining their sense of self-worth; or they can err by allowing themselves to be provoked into rash, ill-advised disclosure, also with negative consequences.

Similarly, the degree of self-disclosure determines the extent and depth of one's support system as a gay or lesbian individual. Insufficient disclosure constricts one's potential social support system. Disclosing too much exposes the individual to greater harshness and hostility from the external disparaging world. As one can easily imagine, individuals who have a significant degree of internalized homophobia have a difficult time with this process. Overtly, such individuals may view themselves as inferior and not deserving of an adequate support system. More subtly, they may set themselves up for rejection with poorly planned and impulsive disclosure in an environment that is likely to produce a harsh response.

Others have theorized about different psychological processes. Grace (1977) theorized that gay and lesbian adolescents generally do not partake of typical adolescent social and romantic experimentation. This creates a sense of loss, which predisposes some individuals to depression, despair, and self-esteem problems in adulthood. Gonsiorek (1982) described how certain developmental routes can result in an overlay of other symptomatology, which with time becomes a more pronounced part of the personality structure. For example, he described how married or closeted individuals who covertly engage in anonymous sexual behavior with the same sex can develop an overlay of highly maladaptive coping mechanisms. Daher (1981) explicated how the sense of differentness in gay male adolescents can lead to development of feelings of inferiority.

This is one of the most productive areas in terms of theory development about gay men and lesbians. These models, however, derive heavily from middle-class, white, non-Hispanic samples from the English-speaking world. One would expect developmental events such as these to be highly sensitive to cultural, class, socioeconomic, racial, and ethnic variation. Therefore, the developmental sequence described in these models should not be assumed to hold true for other populations. The application of this identity/developmental perspective to more diverse populations is one of the most important and illuminating of current research efforts.

Diversity Enriches the Model

Icard (1985–86, 1986) has applied similar ideas to U.S. black men; Loiacano (1989) to black lesbians and gay men; Greene (1986) to U.S. black lesbians; Chan (1989) to Asian–American lesbians and gay men; Gock (1985) to Asian Pacific gay men; Allen (1984) to Native American lesbians; Wooden, Kawasaki, and Mayeda (1983) to Japanese–American men; Hidalgo (1984) and Hidalgo and Christensen (1976–77) to Puerto Rican lesbians in the United States; and Espin to Latina lesbians (1987). Morales (1983) attempted a model that would be general to Third World gay men and lesbians.

Comparable work in a variety of populations is currently in progress. While the specifics of this identity/developmental perspective change between populations, the general perspective appears to be broadly useful. Since this perspective stresses the relationship between the individual, social forces, and sense of self, these differing cultural perspectives are not variations on a theme epitomized by the white, middle-class, North American, English-speaking world. Rather, the entire developmental process and outcomes in the sense of self can vary greatly as the social forces that shape them vary. In other words, as the experiences of diverse groups are observed and described, the model begins to shift qualitatively, rather than merely quantitatively. Or, to use an analogy from statistics, the relationships between the different factors are more akin to path analysis, in which both the variables and their weights can change, than to multiple regression, in which only the weights of the variables change.

For example, both the nature of homophobia and concepts of "maleness" and "femaleness" can differ significantly in African–American communities; the relationship between individual and family is less clearly drawn in the more cohesive multigenerational Hispanic communities than in the relatively atomized, one-generational Anglo family; and pressures on gay and lesbian members of Asian families to prevent dishonor and loss of face for the family are especially high. The model described here could accommodate cultural and other sources of variation and predict differing effects on identity development and sense of self.

These writers generally agree that there is commonality in the psychological processes experienced by lesbian and gay members of racial and ethnic minorities. Many writers speak of double (in the case of lesbians, triple) minority statuses. For example, Gock (1985) described the perceived choice of having to identify with the homosexual community (and so address expression of intimacy) versus the ethnic minority community (and so retain cultural groundedness). Morales (1983) terms this a "conflict of allegiance," and offers a four-stage model on how ethnic lesbians and gay men resolve such conflicts of multiple identities.

Icard (Icard, 1985–86, 1986) describes how gay black men are subject to an unusually harsh triple prejudice, coming not only from the white heterosexual majority, but also from the white gay male and black heterosexual minorities. The strong pressures for social sex role conformity in black communities further exacerbate these stresses. Sears (1989), in his study of growing up lesbian in the U.S. South, describes "fragmentation of identity in the attempt to integrate multiple identities." He also notes that ethnic identity acquisition occurs first, and therefore the later lesbian identity can create a sense of betrayal to one's ethnic group.

Espin (1987) applied the minority identity development model (Atkinson, Morten, & Sue, 1979) to understand identity development among Latina lesbians. This model shares many features with the lesbian/gay developmental models described earlier. Espin suggests that the psychological processes may be similar in the integration of various disparaged identities. The task at hand, however, is somewhat different for ethnic/racial minority lesbians and gay men; namely, the integration of all minority identities in a context in which all are disparaged and in which one minority group typically disparages the others. The picture is more complicated yet: one researcher found sex differences in the relative strength of which minority status is most disparaged. In her study on Asian–American lesbians and gay men, Chan (1989) found that lesbians experienced more discrimination because of being Asian, while gay men experienced more discrimination because of being homosexual. The final outcomes are complex: "The development of homosexual identity is shaped by the racial and gendered contexts in which the person is situated" (Sears, 1989: 447).

Sex differences between gay men and lesbians in this process have been explicated by DeMonteflores and Schultz (1978), Gonsiorek (1988), Henderson (1984), and Lewis (1984). Cass (1984) measured aspects of the different stages and compared similarities and differences between men and women. Kimmel (1978) noted that the existing information on lesbian and gay identity formation is cross-sectional (different people, at different stages, at one point in time), and that longitudinal studies (the same people followed across time) are needed to fully understand identity development.

Wasserman and Storms (1984) critiqued various theories about coming out and identity formation. MacDonald (1982) researched various milestone events during the coming out process, finding evidence for many of the events described in the models. Troiden and Goode (1980) also found support for gay identity development occurring over time, and related to distinct behavioral events. In Holland, the work of Deenen (Deenen, 1986; Deenen & Naerssen, 1988) also provides empirical support for aspects of these theories.

This identity/developmental perspective has reached sufficient maturity that one commentator (Schippers, 1990) has reviewed the meaning of the concept and proposed renaming it the "acceptance and appreciation process." Schippers makes the legitimate point that this term is more accurate psychologically. The term "coming out" "really is a political term" (p. 8). There are other problems with the term coming out. It can be seen as trivializing in that it connotes a single point in time and a deliberate choice. Further, the term is most specific to a particular juncture of social and political events in the mid- and late twentieth-century Western world. Coming out may also be subtly sexist in that it implies a linear "male" process, which is reasonably descriptive for some men but ignores the fluidity described by many women (see Golden, 1990).

These developments in theory and research have been important. Many of the ideas about the coming out process, identity development, and internalized homophobia, however, stand apart as theoretical conceptions not tied into other developmental psychological theories. In particular, explication of how these ideas interact with general and earlier psychological development is lacking. This constricts the further development of these ideas and also risks their underutilization by clinicians.

The next section attempts to unify ideas pertaining to internalized homophobia, gay and lesbian identity formation, and the coming out process with an emerging theory about personality development, Kohut's self psychology. This theory focuses on the effects on the sense of self caused by traumatizing, disappointing, or disparaging events. Thus, we believe it can serve as a bridge between theories of identity development based on the experience of disparaged minorities and theories of personality development which emphasize general and earlier development. It is also an *example*—but in no sense the final word—of how the emerging ideas of gay and lesbian affirmative theory can incorporate select portions of other "depth" psychological theory. But first, some background is needed to effect this bridge. Self psychology terminology is retained to bring the models together.

A Self Psychology Perspective

A self psychology perspective on the coming out process and gay/lesbian identity development is explicated by Gonsiorek and Rudolph (1991). Most simply put, a narcissistic injury is a profound blow to one's self-esteem. For the majority of gay and lesbian youth, the point of awareness of their differentness, and eventually, homosexuality (and for some time thereafter) is an experience in narcissistic injury. As Moses and Hawkins (1982) observed, those who encounter few problems in accepting their homosexuality, or having it accepted, are "probably fairly rare" (p. 84).

Becoming aware of one's homosexuality is a wounding both by commission and ommission. The gay or lesbian youth, upon discovering that his or her sexuality is devalued and rejected by society generally and more personally by parents, peers, and teachers, suffers a clear and explicit narcissistic injury. Equally powerfully wounding, if less obviously, is having one's sexuality—a fundamental aspect of the self (defined as "the core of personality"; Greene, 1984: 40)—left unresponded to and unadmired by parents and others (see Kohut, (1977, p. 26, about the importance of responding to the "whole child"). That is, the heterosexual child's heterosexuality is anticipated, embraced, and cultivated; the homosexual child's homosexuality is not. Woodman and Lenna (1982) remarked that "[a coming out crisis] occurs when the person encounters inner conflict between what he or she feels about

self and what has been learned about acceptable social and sexual behavior. Fear and anxiety arise not only from internal stress but also
from perceptions that external support systems are either absent or
hostile" (p. 25).

The result of this neglect and devaluation of a basic part of the personality of the gay or lesbian youth is a loss, in many cases a drastic
loss, of self-esteem, initiative, and legitimate entitlement. The self is
prone to fragmentation, enfeeblement, and disharmony. The coming
out process can serve to heal this narcissistic injury and restore integrity and functioning to the damaged self.

Provided the gay or lesbian youth arrives at the coming out stage
not otherwise psychologically crippled or severely traumatized (e.g.,
from prolonged involvement with pathological parents or other toxic
childhood experiences), the narcissistic injury is temporary albeit non-
trivial, a developmental challenge to be mastered. Since this wounding
occurs relatively later in childhood than other critical developmental
events, its effects are likely to be less damaging. The gay or lesbian
youth who has been *chronically* narcissistically injured throughout
childhood by events prior to and separate from those described here,
however, reaches the coming out stage in a different, and highly vulnerable state. To them, the narcissistic injury of disparaged sexuality is
not met as a developmental challenge to be surmounted, but rather as
another danger that threatens to shatter an already tenuous psychological constitution.

It is suggested that these fragile gay and lesbian youth comprise a
majority of the casualities of the coming out period, those for whom a
resilient homosexual identity is beyond their personal resources to
achieve and for whom the narcissistic injury of their homosexuality is
a coup de grace that leaves them emotionally debilitated. These individuals are theorized to constitute the bulk of those with histories of
suicide attempts, alcohol and drug abuse, and increased use of mental
health services, as noted earlier.

Self Psychology and the Coming Out Process

Heinz Kohut wrote extensively on narcissistic injury and developed an
analytical psychotherapy for the healing of narcissistic injuries, or self-
deficits (e.g., 1971, 1977, 1984). Although he wrote of the narcissistic
injuries in children as a function of unresponsive, unempathic, and
unavailable parents, his theoretical model can be applied, heuristically,
to the narcissistic injuries of gay and lesbian youth as a function of
their disparaged sexuality.

The process of healing the narcissistic injury of disparaged sexuality
in otherwise healthy gay or lesbian youth is analogous to the process

involved in healing the narcissistic injuries of early childhood (i.e., a process analogous to psychotherapy). The gay or lesbian youth who successfully works through his or her internalized homophobia and adopts an affirmative homosexual identity frequently does so in the context of a positive, ongoing gay/lesbian social support network. This support network, through its individual members and collectively as a group, serves the gay or lesbian youth as a selfobject, paralleling the role of the psychotherapist as selfobject to a client narcissistically injured in early childhood, or, more radically, serves as the good or wholesome parent by accepting and admiring, stabilizing and inspiring, and being a companion to the coming out youth. That is, the support network helps to heal the narcissistically injured gay or lesbian youth in all three sectors of the self. The research data on the positive relationships between self-esteem, involvement in community, and acceptance of self in lesbians and gay men, cited earlier in this chapter, are in line with this self-psychology perspective. Simply stated, a positive affirming community heals the wounds of external oppression.

Kohut (1977) argues that, although we become "independent centers of initiative" (p. 99) through the acquisition of a naturally healthy or reconstituted self, we never "out grow" our need for selfobjects; rather we replace archaic with maturely chosen selfobjects, as in "a strong self enables us to experience love and desire more intensely" (Kohut, 1984: 53). We still need to be admired, uplifted, and shared to feel good about ourselves. Thus, after the narcissistic injury of disparaged homosexuality heals over, the gay or lesbian youth chooses more developmentally mature selfobjects, those with whom he or she can experience relationships of deeper empathic resonance. Examples of behavior indicating a healing, or healed over, narcissistic injury include a young gay man who is able without self-derision to walk away from, or object to, the telling of a homophobic joke; a young lesbian who is able to compose herself following the negative reaction of a long-time acquaintance to the disclosure of her homosexuality; or a young gay or lesbian youth who is able, despite parental disapproval, to volunteer in the campaign of a self-identified homosexual candidate or is able for the first time to go to a same-sex social club and ask someone attractive to dance. Through a multitude of such experiences during the coming out period (optimal frustrations followed by transmuting internalization), the selves of gay and lesbian youth, narcissistically injured by the disparagement of their sexuality by society and significant others, are restored to wholeness, vigor, and harmony.

The preceding discussion simplifies Kohut's theory of self psychology, and its application to the narcissistic injuries and coming out period of gay and lesbian youth is inexact. In particular, we apply his concepts to a later developmental period than the one on which he developed his theory. Nonetheless, we believe these ideas can help create a better understanding of the dynamics of homosexual youth mediating between a self which is "different" and a society which disparages that differentness. These ideas also have clear implications for clinical practice, consistent with available research, suggesting that affirmation of a gay or lesbian identity, involvement in community, and services for gay and lesbian adolescents are likely to be important in the primary prevention and remediation of mental health problems.

Comparisons have been made throughout this chapter between lesbian and gay individuals as a minority group and other minority groups, particularly racial and ethnic minorities. It is important to note that minority status of lesbian and gay individuals differs in some important ways from other minority statuses.

The Unique Minority Status of Gay and Lesbian Individuals

The minority status of gay and lesbian individuals has unique features. Unlike racial and ethnic minorities, disclosure of sexual orientation status is optional, except perhaps in the most gender-atypical individuals, who are a minority of gay and lesbian individuals. Even in this group, management of gender-atypical behavior is a skill that one can usually acquire. Racial and ethnic minorities typically have little choice in disclosure: it is made for them by appearance.

While this reduction in options can initially expose racial and ethnic minority individuals to the full force of bigotry and ostracism, later consequences may be ameliorating. The predictability of prejudice can create cohesive bonds among racial and ethnic individuals whose inherent diversity might otherwise impair cohesion. Psychologically, the range of options is simplified. For racial and ethnic minority individuals, the prejudice is there, and it will be directed toward them: the main options revolve around how best to respond.

With gay and lesbian individuals, disclosure of minority status is usually optional; the choices are more complex. One need not necessarily disclose: the psychological task involves not only considering a range of responses should disclosure occur, but weighing the pros and cons of nondisclosure. Further, cohesion and unification are more elusive, as one's minority status peers may choose not to disclose and may not be available as support.

A second crucial feature is that the economic oppression which is often the core of bigotry toward racial and ethnic minorities, is considerably less predictable with gay and lesbian individuals. While some gay and lesbian individuals are economically devastated by prejudice, many are not. Lesbian women face consistent economic oppression primarily because they are women, not lesbians. Within gay and lesbian communities then, male–female differences around economic issues can be noteworthy. Gay white men whose minority status is not known enjoy the most enfranchised status in the economic hierarchy, whereas lesbians are discriminated against as women, thus dividing gay men and lesbians on an economic basis. Nonwhite lesbians and gay men face economic and other discrimination based on color, creating further divisions within gay and lesbian communities. Predictable economic discrimination can be a powerful unifying force, one lacking in the economically divided (along gender and color lines) gay and lesbian communities where optional disclosure, with its variable overt discrimination, further weakens cohesion.

The final and perhaps most crucial difference is that gay and lesbian individuals are the only minority status organized horizontally, not vertically. In other words, it is not intergenerational. Racial and ethnic minority individuals are born into racial and ethnic minority families. Religious minorities are often born into religious minority families or if they convert, it is often into a community where family and social supports are highly valued and well developed. Gay and lesbian individuals are usually born into heterosexual families and are raised with heterosexual norms. Therefore, the ameliorating influence that parents, grandparents, and other relatives and peer community can have in training the individual to handle the strains of minority status, inculcate group norms, and provide support are not only absent but frequently replaced by lack of understanding, confusion, and at times outright rejection by one's family and original community. Within lesbian and gay communities, the lack of intergenerational bonds may exacerbate general tendencies to "generation gaps" and magnify cohort differences, as each generation "reinvents the wheel," more or less in isolation.

The net effect of these unique features of gay and lesbian minority status is that gay and lesbian individuals may appear to have a "better deal" than other minority groups. They can "choose" to disclose or not to disclose, which may seem like a luxury to other minorities. Overt economic oppression is either highly inconsistent, in the case of gay males; along gender lines, in the case of lesbian women, who thereby have some solidarity and comradeship with women in general; or along racial/ethnic lines.

Underneath these apparent "advantages" are some distinct disadvantages. Intergenerational support and transmission of community wisdom in handling one's minority status is lacking. The option of disclosure not only produces a lack of cohesion, but introduces levels of complexity to the psychological decision-making process that can balance or even outweigh the "luxury."

The intent of this discussion is not to suggest that individuals of different minority statuses have a better or worse deal then others. Rather, different minorities experience different combinations of assets and liabilities in dealing with the oppressive forces arrayed against them. Gay and lesbian individuals are faced with a variety of factors in their minority status that are easily overlooked because they are atypical. Finally, it is important to recognize that, with any minority group member regardless of the nature of the status, the particular acuity of oppression varies from individual to individual and across time for the same individual. Minority status, or minority statuses for those who have multiple statuses, is a moving target as the nature and severity of a disparaging environment change over time and one's life experience in handling this disparagement changes one over time.

The unique features of gay and lesbian minority statuses can have a number of effects. First, gay and lesbian individuals can avoid their minority status because of its potential for invisibility. This allows individuals who have some awareness ranging from dim to fully conscious of their same-sex orientation to avoid coming to terms with it or to deny its existence altogether. This creates a "shadowy" psychological process of coming to terms with this identity. Further, homosexual identity is often something that an individual develops in late adolescence or adulthood.

In most situations, gay and lesbian individuals begin the process of understanding and integrating their minority status entirely alone, quite different from most other minority statuses. Ignorance, misinformation, isolation, and fear can color the process more heavily. This minority status is initially forged in isolation; minority status peers are not immediately available in the early stages.

Because sexual orientation cuts across virtually all demographic variables, gay and lesbian communities are as heterogeneous as larger society. The inconsistency of the economic oppression relating to sexual orientation and the considerable diversity inherent in lesbian and gay communities often creates lesbian and gay identities which wax and wane in strength, depending on the sharpness of external oppression. Gay and lesbian individuals are challenged to integrate sexual-orientation identity among a host of other identities relating to ethnicity, gender, class, education level, profession or occupation, and others. Depending on external circumstances and one's consciousness, the relevance of sexual-orientation identity varies from trivial to profound in relation to these other aspects of identity.

One of the challenges facing this area of study is to explicate how changing external forces alter intrapsychic outcomes. The features of minority status often change over time, and in so doing, can profoundly alter the kinds of intrapsychic processes described in the self psychology section earlier.

Summary

Recent theoretical developments supported by a small but growing amount of research suggest that gay men and lesbians experience unique and particular stresses and developmental variations in identity formation. It is clear that a supportive environment, self-acceptance, and positive role models facilitate mental health. Gay men and lesbians experience additional developmental events as they negotiate the emergence of positive identity in a context of external oppression, which are in addition to, not instead of, other aspects of child, adolescent, and adult development.

These events are not only an additional developmental process, but the culmination of a series of psychological processes extending much earlier than the discreet events of coming out. The concept of internalized homophobia, particularly applied through a lens of self psychology or other elaborated theories of intrapsychic structure, begins to flesh out an understanding of the psychological experience of gay men and lesbians and also explains why some individuals are overwhelmed by the challenges involved and become temporarily or permanently psychiatrically troubled. Particular and unique features are involved in gay and lesbian minority status, which can make it a particularly elusive minority status with which to come to terms. All indications suggest that gender differences in understanding sexual orientation and in the processes by which individuals come to understand, accept, and affirm it are likely to be profound.

The ideas outlined here can be useful in a number of ways. They can serve as a framework for articulating the psychological experience and identity formation of any group of individuals who are oppressed by the majority culture and suggest ways that the wounds of oppression can be healed. They help explicate differences and similarities within gay and lesbian people and offer an explanation for why some consistencies exist against a backdrop of considerable psychological variation. The concept of internalized homophobia and analogous forms developed for other minority groups may be useful in explaining the distinct tendency of minority groups to discharge their frustration primarily against each other instead of the majority culture. These ideas help form the basis of future psychological theory development and research pertaining to gay men and lesbians.

Finally, the external influences on the individual evolve over time and, in our time, appear to be evolving both rapidly and in different ways for different groups of people. The self psychology perspective offered here should not be construed as a "truth," but rather as a method of understanding how larger forces can exert profound psychological influences on the individual. Above all, it should be applied flexibly, and with sensitivity to the changing character of these forces.

References

Allen, P. G. (1984). Beloved women: The lesbian in American Indian culture. In T. Darty & S. Potter (Eds.), *Women-identified women* (pp. 83–96). Palo Alto, CA: Mayfield.

Allport, G. W. (1954). *The nature of prejudice*. Reading, MA: Addison-Wesley.

Atkinson, D. R., Morten, G., & Sue, D. W. (1979). *Counseling American minorities*. Dubuque, IA: Brown.

Bergler, E. (1956). *Homosexuality: Disease or way of life?* New York: Collier.

Bieber, I., Dain, H. J., Dince, P. R., Drellich, M. G., Grand, H. G., Gundlach, R. H., Kremer, M. W., Rifkin, A. H., Wilbur, C. B., & Bieber, T. B. (1962). *Homosexuality: A psychoanalytic study*. New York: Basic Books.

Caprio, F. S. (1954). *Female homosexuality: A modern study of lesbianism*. New York: Grove Press.

Cass, V. C. (1979). Homosexual identity formation: A theoretical model. *Journal of Homosexuality, 4*, 219–236.

Cass, V. C. (1984). Homosexual identity formation: Testing a theoretical model. *Journal of Sex Research, 20*, 143–167.

Chan, C. S. (1989). Issues of identity development among Asian–American lesbians and gay men. *Journal of Counseling and Development, 68*, 16–20.

Coleman, E. (1982). Developmental stages of the coming out process. In J. C. Gonsiorek (Ed.), *Homosexuality and psychotherapy* (pp. 31–44). New York: Haworth.

Daher, D. (1981). The loss and search for the puer: A consideration of inferiority feelings in certain male adolescents. *Adolescence, 16*, 145–158.

Dank, B. M. (1971). Coming out in the gay world. *Psychiatry, 34*, 180–197.

Deenen, A. (1986). "Homoseksuele identiteit in ontwikkeling" [The developing homosexual identity]. unpublished doctoral dissertation, Catholic University of Nijmegen, The Netherlands.

Deenen, A., & Naerssen, A. X. van (1988). *Een onderzoek naar enkele aspecten van de homoseksuele identiteitsontwikkeling* [An investigation into some aspects of the development of homosexual identity]. *Tijdschrift voor Seksuologie, 12*, 105–116.

DeMonteflores, C., & Schultz, S. (1978). Coming out: Similarities and differences for lesbians and gay men. *Journal of Social Issues, 34*, 59–72.

Erikson, E. H. (1980). *Identity and the life cycle*. New York: Norton.

Espin, O. M. (1987). Issues of identity in the psychology of Latina lesbians. In Boston Lesbian Psychologies Collective (Eds.), *Lesbian psychologies: Explorations and challenges* (pp. 35–51). Urbana: University of Illinois Press.

Farrell, R. A., & Morrione, T. J. (1974). Social interation and stereotypic responses to homosexuals. *Archives of Sexual Behavior, 3*, 425–442.

Gock, T. S. (1985, August). Psychotherapy with Asian/Pacific gay men: Psychological issues, treatment approach and therapeutic guidelines. Paper presented at Asian-Amaerican Psychological Association, Los Angeles, CA.

Golden, C. (1990, August). *Our politics and our choices: The feminist movement and sexual orientation.* Paper presented at American Psychological Association, Boston.

Gonsiorek, J. C. (1982). The use of diagnostic concepts in working with gay and lesbian populations. In J. Gonsiorek (Ed.), *Homosexuality and psychotherapy: A practitioner's handbook of affirmative models* (pp. 9–20). New York: Haworth.

Gonsiorek, J. C. (1988). Mental health issues of gay and lesbian adolescents. *Journal of Adolescent Health Care, 9,* 114–122.

Gonsiorek, J. C. (1991). The empirical basis for the demise of the illness model of homosexuality. In J. C. Gonsiorek & J. D. Weinrich (Eds.), *Homosexuality: Research implications for public policy* (pp. 115–136). Newbury Park, CA: Sage Publications.

Gonsiorek, J. C., & Rudolph, J. R. (1991). Homosexual identity: Coming out and other developmental events. In J. C. Gonsiorek & J. D. Weinrich (Eds.), *Homosexuality: Research implications for public policy* (pp. 161–176). Newbury Park, CA: Sage Publications.

Gonsiorek, J. C., & Weinrich, J. D. (1991). The definition and scope of sexual orientation. In J. C. Gonsiorek & J. D. Weinrich (Eds.), *Homosexuality: Research implications for public policy* (pp. 1–12). Newbury Park, CA: Sage Publications.

Grace, J. (1977, November). Gay despair and the loss of adolescence. Paper presented at Fifth Biennial Professional Symposium of the National Association of Social Workers, San Diego, CA.

Grace, J. (1979, November). Coming out alive. Paper presented at Sixth Biennial Professional Symposium of the National Association of Social Workers, San Antonio, TX.

Greene, A. G. (1984). The self psychology of Heinz Kohut: A synopsis and critique. *The Bulletin of the Menninger Clinic, 48*(11), 37–53.

Greene, B. A. (1986). When the therapist is white and the patient is black: Considerations for psychotherapy in feminist heterosexual and lesbian communities. *Women and Therapy, 5,* 41–65.

Hammersmith, S. K., & Weinberg, M. S. (1973). Homosexual identity: Commitment, adjustment, and significant others. *Sociometry, 36,* 56–79.

Hatterer, L. (1970). *Changing homosexuality in the male.* New York: McGraw-Hill.

Hencken, J. D., & O'Dowd, W. T. (1977). Coming out as an aspect of identity formation. *Gay Academic Union Journal: Gai Saber, 1,* 18–22.

Henderson, A. I. (1984). Homosexuality in college years: Developmental differences between men and women. *Journal of American College Health, 32,* 216–219.

Herek, G. M. (1991). Stigma, prejudice and violence against lesbians and gay men. In J. C. Gonsiorek & J. D. Weinrich (Eds.), *Homosexuality: Research implications for public policy* (pp. 60–80). Newbury Park, CA: Sage Publications.

Hidalgo, H. A. (1984). The Puerto Rican lesbian in the United States. In T. Darty & S. Potter (Eds.), *Women-identified women* (pp. 105–115). Palo Alto, CA: Mayfield.

Hidalgo, H. A., & Christensen, E. H. (1976–77). The Puerto Rican lesbian and the Puerto Rican community. *Journal of Homosexuality, 2,* 109–121.

Hooker, E. A. (1957). The adjustment of the male overt homosexual. *Journal of Projective Techniques, 21,* 17–31.

Icard, L. (1985–86). Black gay men and conflicting social identities: Sexual orientation versus racial identity. *Journal of Social Work and Human Sexuality,* 4(1–2), 83–93.

Icard, L. (1986). Black gay men and conflicting social identities: Sexual orientation vs. racial identity. In J. Gripton & M. Valentich (Eds.), *Social work practice in sexual problems* (pp. 83–93). New York: Haworth.

Jacobs, J. A. & Tedford, W. H. (1980). Factors affecting self-esteem of the homosexual individual. *Journal of Homosexuality, 5,* 373–382.

Kimmel, D. (1978). Adult development and aging: A gay perspective. *Journal of Social Issues, 43,* 113–130.

Kohut, H. (1971). *The analysis of the self.* New York: International Universities Press.

Kohut, H. (1977). *The restoration of the self.* New York: International Universities Press.

Kohut, H. (1984). *How does analysis cure?* Chicago: The University of Chicago Press.

Lee, J. A. (1977). Going public: A study into the sociology of homosexual liberation. *Journal of Homosexuality,* 3(1), 49–78.

Lewis, L. A. (1984). The coming out process for lesbians: Integrating a stable identity. *Social Work,* 29(5), 464–469.

Loiacano, D. K. (1989). Gay identity issues among black Americans: Racism, homophobia and the need for validation. *Journal of Counseling and Development, 68,* 21–25.

MacDonald, G. J. (1982). Individual differences in the coming-out process for gay men: Implications for theoretical models. *Journal of Homosexuality,* 8(1), 47–60.

Malyon, A. K. (1981). The homosexual adolescent: Developmental issues and social bias. *Child Welfare, 60,* 321–330.

Malyon, A. K. (1982a). Biphasic aspects of homosexual identity formation. *Psychotherapy: Theory, Research & Practice, 19,* 335–340.

Malyon, A. K. (1982b). Psychotherapeutic implications of internalized homophobia in gay men. In J. C. Gonsiorek (Ed.), *Homosexuality and psychotherapy: A practitioner's handbook of affirmative models* (pp. 59–69). New York: Haworth.

Morales, E. (1983, August). Third world gays and lesbians: A process of multiple identities. Paper presented at American Psychological Association, Anaheim, CA.

Moses, A. E., & Hawkins, R. D., Jr. (1982). *Counseling lesbian women and gay men.* St. Louis: C. V. Mosby.

Nicolosi, J. (1991). *Reparative therapy of male homosexuality.* Northvale, NJ: Jason Aronson.

Plummer, K. (1975). *Sexual stigma.* London: Routledge & Kegan Paul.

Schippers, J. (1990, August). Gay affirmative counseling and psychotherapy in the Netherlands. Paper presented at meeting of the American Psychological Association, Boston, MA.

Schmitt, K. P., & Kurdek, L. H. (1987). Personality correlates of positive identity and relationship involvement in gay men. *Journal of Homosexuality, 13*(4), 101–109.

Sears, J. T. (1989). The impact of gender and race on growing up lesbian and gay in the South. *National Women's Studies Association Journal, 1,* 422–457.

Silverstein, C. (1991). Psychological and medical treatments of homosexuality. In J. C. Gonsiorek & J. D. Weinrich (Eds.), *Homosexuality: Research implications for public policy.* (pp. 101–114). Newbury Park, CA: Sage.

Socarides, C. W. (1968). *The overt homosexual.* New York: Grune & Stratton.

Socarides, C. (1978). *Homosexuality.* New York: Jason Aronson.

Troiden, R. R. (1979). Becoming homosexual: A model of gay identity acquisition. *Psychiatry, 42,* 362–373.

Troiden, R. R., & Goode, E. (1980). Variables related to the acquisition of a gay identity. *Journal of Homosexuality, 5*(4), 383–392.

Wasserman, E. B., & Storms, M. D. (1984). Factors influencing erotic orientation development in females and males. *Women and Therapy, 3*(2), 51–60.

Weinberg, M. S., & Williams, C. J. (1974). *Male homosexuals: Their problems and adaptations.* New York: Oxford University Press.

Wooden, W. S., Kawasaki, H., & Mayeda, R. (1983). Lifestyles and identity maintenance among Japanese-American gay males. *Alternative Lifestyles, 5,* 236–243.

Woodman, N. J., & Lenna, H. R. (1982). *Counseling with gay men and women.* San Francisco: Jossey-Bass.

3

Bisexual Identities

Ronald C. Fox

Scholarly and scientific understanding of sexual orientation has been hindered by two assumptions: that homosexuality is an indication of psychopathology and that sexual orientation is dichotomous. The movement toward a descriptive, multidimensional approach has greatly facilitated understanding of the complexity of sexual orientation and sexual identity and brought theory and research on both homosexuality and bisexuality into focus.

The theoretical and research literature on the development of lesbian and gay identities emerged following the American Psychiatric Association's 1973 decision to remove homosexuality as a clinical diagnostic category. The literature on bisexual identities, however, is more recent. This is due to the historical polarization of sexual orientation into heterosexuality and homosexuality, as well as the variety of ways in which the term "bisexuality" has been used and defined in theory, clinical practice, and research.

In fact, bisexuality has existed as a concept and descriptive term in the literature since the process of psychosexual development was first conceptualized by Freud and his contemporaries. For example, bisexuality has been used as a theoretical construct to explain aspects of evolutionary theory, psychosexual development, psychopathology, masculinity and femininity, and homosexuality. The designation *bisexual* has been used as a descriptive term to refer to individuals with heterosexual and homosexual attractions or relationships, just as the designations *gay* and *lesbian* have referred to individuals with homosexual attractions or relationships. Finally, individuals themselves have used the self-designations *homosexual, lesbian, gay,* and *bisexual* to describe their sexual orientations. This chapter examines how bisexuality has appeared in the literature as a concept, a descriptive term, a sexual orientation category, and a sexual identity and compares theory and research on bisexual, gay, and lesbian identities.

Bisexuality in Psychoanalytic Theory

The view that homosexuality is a mental illness has been part of medical and psychological writing since the late nineteenth century. Early theorists found the concept of bisexuality useful in understanding homosexuality from the perspective of evolutionary theory (Ellis, 1905/1942; Krafft-Ebing, 1886/1965; Moll, 1897/1933; Weininger, 1903/1908). They believed that the human species evolved from a primitive hermaphroditic state to today's gender-differentiated physical form and that the physiological and psychological development of the individual parallels this evolutionary process.

Freud, who was familiar with evolutionary theory, incorporated the concept of bisexuality as a basic element of his theory of psychosexual development (Freud, 1905/1962, Ritvo, 1990; Sulloway, 1979). Like his contemporaries, he used the concept of bisexuality to account for homosexuality, which he saw as an indication of arrested psychosexual development (Freud, 1925/1963). At the same time, he emphasized that all individuals have some homosexual feelings: "The most important of these perversions, homosexuality . . . can be traced back to the constitutional bisexuality of all human beings. . . . Psychoanalysis enables us to point to some trace or other of a homosexual object-choice in everyone" (pp. 71–72). Other psychoanalysts, in particular Stekel (1922/1946a), expressed the view that bisexuality is normative during childhood and adult sexual orientation results from repression that occurs during the developmental process:

> All persons originally are bisexual in their predisposition. There is no exception to this rule. Normal persons show a distinct bisexual period up to the age of puberty. The heterosexual then represses his homosexuality. . . . If the heterosexuality is repressed, homosexuality comes to the forefront. (p. 39)

Freud and his contemporaries used *invert* and *homosexual* as generic clinical and descriptive terms to refer to persons with any same-gender sexual attractions or behavior. At the same time, Freud (1905/1962) differentiated three types of homosexuals, including persons with both same- and opposite-gender sexual attractions or behavior:

(a) They may be absolute inverts. In that case their sexual objects are exclusively of their own sex. . . . (b) They may be amphigenic inverts, that is psychosexual hermaphrodites. In that case their sexual objects may equally well be of their own or of the opposite sex. . . . (c) They may be contingent inverts. In that case, under certain external conditions . . . they are capable of taking as their sexual object someone of their own sex and of deriving satisfaction from sexual intercourse with him. (pp. 2–3)

Havelock Ellis (1905/1942) differentiated individuals on the basis of sexual attractions. He saw bisexuals as a distinct category of individuals who are attracted to persons of both genders, concluding that "there would thus seem to be a broad and simple grouping of all sexually functioning persons into three comprehensive divisions: the heterosexual, the bisexual, and the homosexual" (pp. 87–88).

Freud (1937/1963) later used the term *bisexual* to refer to persons with both homosexual and heterosexual attractions or behavior:

It is well known that at all times there have been, as there still are, human beings who can take as their sexual objects persons of either sex without the one trend interfering with the other. We call these people bisexual and accept the fact of their existence without wondering much at it. . . . But we have come to know that all human beings are bisexual in this sense and that their libido is distributed between objects of both sexes, either in a manifest or a latent form. (pp. 261–262)

Most psychoanalysts maintained that the theory of bisexuality is an essential conceptual reference point for understanding psychosexual development (Stekel, 1922/1946a; 1922/1946b), masculinity and femininity (Stoller, 1972), psychopathology (Katan, 1955; Khan & Masud, 1974; Kubie, 1974; Nunberg, 1947; Weiss, 1958), and homosexuality (Alexander, 1933; Limentani, 1976; Nunberg, 1938). Some psychoanalysts challenged the utility of the concept of bisexuality, arguing that transferring the concept from evolutionary biology to psychology was inappropriate. Their position was that the individual's adaptational responses to family influences are the relevant etiological factors in the development of homosexual behavior as well as masculine and feminine characteristics (Bieber et al., 1962; Kardiner, Karesh, & Ovessey, 1959; Rado, 1940).

Other authors argued with the term *bisexual* as a descriptive category referring to individuals with both homosexual and heterosexual attractions or behavior. For example, Bergler (1956) viewed sexual orientation in strictly dichotomous terms and believed that those who consider themselves bisexual are denying their homosexual orientation:

> Bisexuality—a state that has no existence beyond the word itself—is an out-and-out fraud. . . . The theory claims that a man can be—alternatively or concomitantly—homo and heterosexual. . . . Nobody can dance at two different weddings at the same time. These so-called bisexuals are really homosexuals with an occasional heterosexual excuse. (pp. 80–81)

The polarization of sexuality into heterosexual (normal) and homosexual (abnormal) was basic to the illness model of homosexuality and lent support to the position that the diagnostic category *homosexuality* was appropriate for individuals with *any* same-gender sexual attractions or behavior. This approach was maintained and further articulated by many authors in the fields of psychoanalysis and psychiatry (Bergler, 1956; Bieber et al., 1962; Caprio, 1954, 1955; L. J. Hatterer, 1970; Ruitenbeek, 1963, 1973; Socarides, 1972, 1978). The goal of psychoanalytic psychotherapy with individuals with homosexual attractions or behavior was an exclusively heterosexual orientation.

However, traditional psychoanalytic attitudes toward homosexuality were not universally accepted in the psychiatric community (Bayer, 1981). Prominent authors in the field (Green, 1972; Hoffman, 1968; Hooker, 1956, 1965; Marmor, 1965, 1972; Szasz, 1965, 1970; G. Weinberg, 1972) challenged the prevailing position on homosexuality based on evidence from several areas: surveys of sexual behavior; ethnographic data on the incidence and integration of homosexual behavior in other cultures; criticism of clinical assessment and treatment based on the illness model; and critiques of research claiming support for hormonal, genetic, and family of origin etiologies for homosexuality. The 1973 American Psychiatric Association decision to remove homosexuality as a diagnostic category signaled a move away from the illness model and toward a more affirmative approach to homosexuality.

Bisexuality in Lesbian and Gay Identity Development Theory

The first descriptions in the literature of the lives of lesbians and gay men from other than an illness model perspective appeared in ethnographic reports on urban gay and lesbian communities (Achilles, 1967; Gagnon & Simon, 1968; Hooker, 1956, 1965; Leznoff & Westley, 1956; Ponse, 1978, 1980; Simon & Gagnon, 1967; Warren, 1974, 1980; D. G. Wolf, 1979). These and other authors found that the expression *coming out* was used to signify acknowledging one's homosexual attractions (Cory & Le-Roy, 1963; Cronin, 1974; Dank, 1971; Gagnon & Simon, 1968, 1973; Ponse, 1978, 1980; D. G. Wolf, 1979), making contact with the lesbian and gay communities (Gagnon & Simon, 1968, 1973; Hooker, 1965; Saghir & Robins, 1973), and identifying oneself to other people as being gay or lesbian (Hooker, 1965; Ponse, 1978, 1980; D. G. Wolf, 1979).

Several authors have elaborated significant events involved in *coming out* into a sequence of stages leading to the formation of positive lesbian and gay identities (Cass, 1979, 1983/1984; Coleman, 1981/1982b, Dank, 1971; de Monteflores & Schultz, 1978; Plummer, 1981; Troiden, 1979, 1988). The typical developmental sequence proceeds from a point of departure (first homosexual attractions) through a set of intermediate experiences (seeking out similar others, initiating same-gender sexual experiences and relationships, identifying oneself as gay or lesbian, and disclosing one's sexual orientation to others) to an endpoint (exclusively homosexual relationships and an integrated lesbian or gay identity). Disclosing one's sexual orientation to significant others and community participation are both seen as necessary in maintaining positive gay and lesbian identities. For these authors, the term *coming out* refers to the entire developmental process, including but not limited to disclosing one's sexual orientation to others. Troiden (1988) believed that "homosexual identities are most fully realized . . . when self-identity, perceived identity, and presented identity coincide; that is, where an accord exists among who people think they are, who they claim they are, and how others view them" (p. 31).

Cass (1984) followed up her theoretical formulation with a study designed to assess the validity of her developmental stages. Although she found evidence for the general order of milestone events, she also found that some individuals did not follow the exact sequence she had proposed, and others moved through more than one stage at the same time. These findings are in accord with similar variations found in research on lesbian identity development. (Chapman & Brannock, 1987; Sophie, 1985/1986) and support the perspective that stage theories give a general rather than exact outline of events involved in the coming out process (Coleman, 1981/1982b; Troiden, 1988).

As with other developmental models, theorists have explained deviations from the proposed direction or sequence of events. For example, in her first formulation, Cass (1979) considered a bisexual self-identification as an example of identity foreclosure, delaying or preventing the development of a positive homosexual identity. From this point of view, a bisexual self-identification and persistent heterosexual attractions, behavior, or relationships are all transitional phenomena some individuals experience as they proceed toward permanent monosexual lesbian and gay identities. More recently, however, Cass (1990) has described a bisexual identity differently, as a viable sexual identity, with a separate developmental pathway distinct from that characteristic of a homosexual identity. Coleman (1981/1982b) suggested that the developmental stages he articulated for the coming out process might apply to bisexuals as well. Troiden (1988) also saw bisexuality as a valid sexual orientation category. However, he believed that the general lack of recognition of bisexuality affects the individual's ability to sustain a bisexual identity:

> The unwillingness of people in general, and significant others in particular, to acknowledge bisexual preferences makes it more difficult to maintain and validate these preferences than heterosexual identities, which are supported continuously by sociocultural institutions, or homosexual identities, which are recognized and reinforced by institutional arrangements within the homosexual community. (p. 82)

In summary, the emergence of lesbian and gay identity theory represented an important shift in emphasis in developmental theory, away from the concern with etiology and psychopathology characteristic of the illness model toward articulation of the factors involved in the formation of positive gay and lesbian identities. While theories of lesbian and gay identity development initially saw bisexuality as a transitional phenomenon, over time the focus has shifted away from a strictly dichotomous view of sexual orientation toward a more inclusive perspective in which bisexuality is regarded as a distinct sexual orientation and identity.

Bisexuality in Sexual Orientation Theory and Assessment

The theoretical and research literature on gay and lesbian identities emerged after psychiatry and psychology moved to consider homosexuality from a more affirmative point of view. The predominance of a dichotomous view of sexual orientation, however, constrained the development of a comparable theoretical and research literature on bisexuality and bisexual identities. Examination and critique of this model led to the development of a multidimensional approach to sexual orientation, which allows for more accurate representation of the complexity of sexual orientation and acknowledgment of bisexuality as a sexual orientation and sexual identity.

Kinsey and his associates (Kinsey, Pomeroy, & Martin, 1948; Kinsey, Pomeroy, Martin, & Gebhard, 1952) considered human sexuality from a descriptive rather than a clinical point of view, and they emphasized the inadequacy of dichotomous concepts for describing the diversity of human sexual experience (Kinsey et al., 1948);

> Males do not represent two discrete populations, heterosexual and homosexual. The world is not divided into sheep and goats. Not all things are black nor all things white. It is a fundamental of taxonomy that nature rarely deals with discrete categories. Only the human mind invents categories and tries to force facts into separated pigeon-holes. The living world is a a continuum in each and every one of its aspects. The sooner we learn this concerning human sexual behavior the sooner we shall reach a sound understanding of the realities of sex. (p. 639)

They were aware that the term *bisexual* had been used to refer to individuals with both heterosexual and homosexual attractions or behavior. It was their view, however, that moving from two categories (heterosexual and homosexual) to three categories (heterosexual, bisexual, and homosexual) did not represent the continuum of human sexual behavior as accurately as their 7-point scale.

Other authors have viewed heterosexuality and homosexuality as independent aspects of sexual orientation, which they saw as the individual's physical and affectional preferences for relationships with members of the same and/or opposite biological sex (Shively & De Cecco, 1977; Storms, 1980). Sexual orientation was seen as one of four components of sexual identity, along with biological sex, gender identity, and social sex role (Shively & De Cecco, 1977). The research literature included a variety of criteria for defining sexual orientation, among which the most frequently used were sexual behavior, affectional attachments (close relationships), erotic fantasies, arousal, erotic preference, and self-identification as bisexual, heterosexual, or homosexual (Shively, Jones, & De Cecco, 1983/1984).

The Klein Sexual Orientation Grid (Klein, Sepekoff, & Wolf, 1985; Klein, 1990) provided a more encompassing approach to assessing sexual orientation by including not only sexual attraction, fantasy, and behavior, but emotional preference, social preference, heterosexual–bisexual–homosexual life-style, and self-identification as well. Individuals are asked to rate themselves on a 7-point heterosexual–bisexual–homosexual scale for each of these variables for past, present, and ideal time frames, which provides a more accurate picture of the factors involved in an individual's sexual orientation over time.

The Assessment of Sexual Orientation (Coleman, 1987, 1990) was designed to facilitate clinical interviews in which the presenting issues include sexual orientation concerns. The client indicates current relationship status, sexual orientation self-identification, desired future identification, and level of comfort with present orientation. A series of circles are also marked, in terms of both "up to the present" and "ideal" time frames, to indicate physical identity, actual and fantasized gender identity, sex-role identity, as well as sexual, fantasy, and emotional aspects of sexual orientation.

In summary, a multidimensional view of sexual orientation has evolved, which takes into consideration factors such as emotional and social preferences, life-style, self-identification, and changes in identity over time, as well as sexual attraction, fantasy, and behavior. This has led to the development of more comprehensive tools for assessing sexual orientation and a wider acknowledgment of bisexuality as a distinct sexual orientation and identity.

Theoretical Perspectives on Bisexuality and Bisexual Identities

Lesbian and gay identity theory developed out of the more affirmative approach to homosexuality that followed its removal as a diagnostic category. The discourse on bisexual identities has developed out of the more positive attitude toward bisexuality that has resulted from a critique of the dichotomous view of sexual orientation and the emergence of a multidimensional perspective. Several typologies of bisexual behavior have been elaborated, and similarities and differences between the development of bisexual, gay, and lesbian identities have been examined.

Psychoanalytic theorists used the concept of bisexuality in discussing psychosexual development in terms of evolutionary theory and in explaining homosexual attractions and behavior. The viewpoint that bisexuality is an intrinsic factor in psychosexual development was shared by Wolff (1971): "We certainly are bisexual creatures, and this innate disposition is reinforced by the indelible memory of childhood attachments, which know no limitation of sex" (pp. 45–46). She also believed that the psychoanalytic assumption of an inherent bisexuality has lent support to a greater acknowledgment of bisexuality as a sexual orientation (Wolff, 1979).

Although most psychoanalytic theorists used the concept of bisexuality to account for homosexual attractions and behavior, they believed that exclusive heterosexuality is the only normal outcome of the developmental process. Klein (1978, 1993) challenged this belief, as well as the position that sexual relationships with both women and men indicate immaturity and psychopathology. He maintained that awareness and expression of both heterosexual and homosexual attractions can enhance the individual's experience of intimacy and personal fulfillment.

Other authors also have approached bisexuality from an affirmative perspective and have emphasized that bisexuality challenges several assumptions of a dichotomous view of sexual orientation: that heterosexuality and homosexuality are mutually exclusive; that gender is the primary criterion for sexual partner selection; and that sexual orientation is immutable (Fox, 1993; Hansen & Evans, 1985; Klein et al., 1985; MacDonald, 1981, 1982, 1983; Morrow, 1989; Nichols, 1988; Paul, 1983/1984, 1985; Ross & Paul, 1992; Rust, 1992, 1993; Schuster, 1987; Weise, 1992; Zinik, 1985). Stereotypes of bisexuality in the literature have been based on these assumptions. One misconception is that bisexuality is only a transition on the way to either exclusive homosexuality or heterosexuality. Another is that bisexuals are in denial, that is, they have not come out all the way and are trying to avoid the stigma of a gay identity. The impact of these stereotypes has been that many bisexual men and women feel marginal to both the heterosexual and homosexual communities.

Several typologies of bisexuality have been elaborated, based on the extent and timing of past and present heterosexual and homosexual behavior. Klein (1978, 1993) distinguished four kinds of bisexuality: transitional, historical, sequential, and concurrent. For some individuals, bisexuality represents a stage in the process of coming out as lesbian or gay, while for others, a gay or lesbian identity is a step in the process of coming out bisexual (transitional bisexuality). Some individuals, whose sexual lives are presently heterosexual or homosexual, have experienced both same- and opposite-gender sexual attractions or behavior in the past (historical bisexuality). Other individuals have had relationships with both women and men, but with only one person during a particular period of time (sequential bisexuality), while others have had relationships with both men and women during the same time period (concurrent bisexuality). Other authors (Berkey, Perelman-Hall, & Kurdek, 1990; Boulton & Coxon, 1991; Weinberg, Williams, & Pryor, 1994) have developed similar typologies. Other factors that are relevant in considering bisexual behavior and identity have also been identified (Doll, Peterson, Magana, & Carrier, 1991): the social context in which the person lives (heterosexual, homosexual, or both); the relationship(s) in which the individual is involved; and how open the person is with others about being bisexual.

Ross (1991) described several patterns of bisexual behavior relative to identity and in terms of the circumstances in which homosexual behavior takes place. For example, a person may be hiding a homosexual orientation, exploring homosexuality, or in transition to a gay or lesbian identity (defense bisexuality). When a society provides no alternatives to marriage, homosexual behavior may take place away from the family environment (married bisexuality). Homosexual behavior may be prescribed for some or all members of a society, as in Melanesia (ritual bisexuality). For some people, gender is not a criterion for sexual attraction or partner selection (equal bisexuality). In other cases, a male who takes only the insertor role in anal intercourse with another male is considered heterosexual (*Latin* bisexuality). Homosexual behavior may be circumstantial, taking place only once or a few times (experimental bisexuality) or only when there are no heterosexual outlets (secondary bisexuality). Homosexual behavior also may occur as part of male or female prostitution (technical bisexuality).

Bisexual identity formation has not been conceptualized as a linear process with a fixed outcome, as in theories of lesbian and gay identity formation. The development of bisexual identities has been viewed as a more complex and open-ended process in light of the necessity of considering patterns of homosexual *and* heterosexual attractions, fantasies, behaviors, and relationships that occur during any particular period of time and over time (Coleman, 1987, 1990; Klein et al., 1985; Shively & De Cecco, 1977; Shively et al., 1983/1984).

Several authors have examined bisexual identity development empirically and have discussed the coming out process on the basis of their research findings (Fox, 1993; Rust, 1992, 1993; Twining, 1983; Weinberg et al., 1994). Twining (1983) identified several issues that bisexual women face in the coming out process: self-acceptance, resolving societal homophobia, developing a support network, deciding to whom disclosures of sexual orientation would be made, and coping with concerns about disclosure in professional contexts. She concluded that "an initial formulation of a conceptual theory of bisexual identity development seems to call for a task model rather than a phase or stage model" (p. 158). In contrast, based on the results of their 1983, 1984/1985, and 1988 studies, Weinberg, Williams, and Pryor (1994) outlined the stages they believed were involved in the development of bisexual identities: initial confusion, finding and applying the label, and settling into the identity. They conceptualized bisexuality as an "add-on" to an already established heterosexual identity. The authors also proposed a fourth stage, continued uncertainty, which they saw as a common experience of many bisexuals. They related this to the general lack of social validation for bisexual identities, compared to lesbian and gay identities, which are more effectively supported by visible, well-established lesbian and gay communities.

Rust (1992, 1993) and Fox (1993) have emphasized that multiple factors influence the development of bisexual identities, and dichotomous and linear conceptual approaches to sexual identity formation do not adequately describe the coming out experiences of many individuals. The results of both of their studies indicate that, although many men and women develop a bisexual identity after first considering themselves heterosexual, others arrive at a bisexual identity from an established lesbian or gay identity. These findings strongly suggest that sexual identity is not as immutable for all individuals as some theorists and researchers have assumed. Rust (1993) concluded that bisexual, lesbian, and gay identities can be viewed from the point of view of a more encompassing conceptual framework in which sexual identity development is an *ongoing* process with changes in sexual identities being "a normal outcome of the dynamic process of identity formation that occurs as mature individuals respond to changes in the available social constructs, the sociopolitical landscape, and their own positions on that landscape" (p. 74).

In summary, theory on bisexuality and bisexual identities has evolved on the basis of an ongoing critique of the illness model and the dichotomous view of sexual orientation. Bisexuality has been examined in terms of the variety of contexts and circumstances in which sexual attractions and behavior occur. A multidimensional theoretical approach to bisexual identity formation has developed which acknowledges that individuals arrive at their sexual identities by several possible routes and that sexual identity may remain constant or change as a normal response to both personal and social influences.

Bisexuality in Research on Homosexuality

Information about bisexuality first appeared in the research literature in the results of anthropological studies and ethnographic and survey studies on homosexuality, which consistently included many individuals with both heterosexual and homosexual attractions and relationships. In cross-cultural research, bisexuality has been used primarily as a descriptive term referring to the sexual behavior of individuals in particular cultures. In ethnographic research on gay and lesbian communities, and in survey research on homosexuality, bisexuality has also been used to refer to sexual attractions and behavior as well as to signify sexual orientation or sexual identity.

Anthropological Perspectives

The cross-cultural incidence of homosexual behavior has been well documented (Adam, 1985; Blackwood, 1985; Carrier, 1980; Churchill, 1967; Davenport, 1977; Ford & Beach, 1951; Herdt, 1990; Mead, 1961; Opler, 1965). However, only a few anthropologists who have reported on cultures in which some individuals exhibit both homosexual and heterosexual behavior have framed the homosexual behavior as a component of the bisexuality characteristic of sexual expression in that culture.

Based on their examination of cross-cultural patterns of sexual behavior, Ford and Beach (1951) noted the human potential for bisexuality and the inadequacy of a dichotomous view of sexuality:

When it is realized that 100 per cent of the males in certain societies engage in homosexual as well as heterosexual alliances, and
when it is understood that many men and women in our own
society are equally capable of relations with partners of the same
or opposite sex, . . . then it should be clear that one cannot clas-
sify homosexual and heterosexual tendencies as being mutually
exclusive or even opposed to each other. (p. 242)

This perspective was also expressed by Mead (1975), who believed that
bisexuality is normal, but that social attitudes about sex and love con-
strain the expression of bisexual attractions in sexual behavior and relationships:

Even a superficial look at other societies and some groups in our
own society should be enough to convince us that a very large
number of human beings—probably a majority—are bisexual in
their potential capacity for love. Whether they will become exclusively heterosexual or exclusively homosexual for all their lives
and in all circumstances or whether they will be able to enter into
sexual and love relationships with members of both sexes is, in
fact, a consequence of the way they have been brought up, of the
particular beliefs and prejudices of the society they live in and, to
some extent, of their own life history. (p. 29)

The integration of bisexuality into a particular culture is exemplified
by the coexistence of heterosexual and homosexual behavior in one
Melanesian society (Davenport, 1965):

Not all [men] become exclusively heterosexual at marriage. There
is no doubt that some do, but most do not. . . . He need not
forego pederasty as long as this does not prevent him from giving
sexual satisfaction to his wife. In other words, this is a society
that quite frankly expects and accepts some bisexual behavior in
most men, although there is nothing odd or deviant about an exclusively heterosexual male. (pp. 201–202)

Concurrent homosexual and heterosexual behavior also characterizes
another Melanesian society (Herdt, 1984):

The Sambian male . . . has the opportunity for direct experience
of both homosexual and heterosexual relations and the opportunity to compare and evaluate them. Shared communications
about the relative qualities of all sexual activities are an ordinary
part of male discourse. . . . The self-esteem of bisexuals in Mel-

anesia is relatively high and their bisexuality ego-syntonic. Neither they nor their fellows are out to lobby for or against their bisexuality. Bisexuals bear no stigma. (p. 59)

Mexican bisexuality has been examined by Carrier (1985), and Tielman, Carballo, and Hendriks (1991) have provided an overview of cross-cultural patterns of bisexual behavior as part of a research effort designed to more fully understand transmission of the human immunodeficiency virus (HIV) from a global perspective and to develop more effective health intervention and prevention strategies.

Bisexuality in Research on Lesbian and Gay Male Communities

While early ethnographic reports on lesbian and gay communities focused on the coming out process and the importance of community for maintaining homosexual identities, such efforts did not address the issue of bisexual identities. Later research, however, has provided some information on attitudes in the lesbian community toward bisexual women (Golden, 1987; Ponse, 1978; Rust, 1992, 1993; D. G. Wolf, 1979). While some lesbian respondents in these studies had never experienced heterosexual attractions or behavior, others had been involved in sexual relationships with men. Ponse (1978) and Golden (1987) called the former "primary" lesbians and the latter "elective" lesbians. Some respondents were accepting of women who admitted ongoing sexual attractions to men or who considered themselves bisexual, but many believed such women were not "real" lesbians or had not yet completed the coming out process. Warren (1974) reported similar reactions toward bisexual men from respondents in her study of a gay male community.

Research has also been conducted on situational homosexual behavior, in environments where opposite-gender partners are unavailable or relatively inaccessible (e.g., in prison, or in the military) and where homosexual behavior occurs as an occupational or clandestine activity (e.g., prostitution or tearoom sex). Although respondents in such research typically identify themselves as homosexual or heterosexual, some consider themselves bisexual, in studies of sex in prison (Wooden & Parker, 1982), male prostitution (Reiss, 1961), gay bars (Read, 1980), and sex in public places (Humphreys, 1970).

Bisexuality in Survey Research on Sexuality

The results of the research conducted by Kinsey and his associates (Kinsey et al., 1948, 1952) presented an early challenge to the belief that adult homosexuality is a rare phenomenon. Furthermore, a significant proportion of participants in these studies reported both heterosexual and homosexual behavior. Many researchers since then also have found some respondents reporting adult sexual experiences with both women and men. Researchers have differed greatly, however, in their interpretations of how the sexual behavior of such individuals relates to their sexual orientation or identity.

For example, Hunt (1974) believed that only a very limited number of American males are bisexual, or potentially so, in their adult lives. His perspective on the bisexual behavior reported by some of his respondents was that "some self-styled bisexuals . . . are basically homosexual but seek to minimize their conflicts and sense of deviance by having occasional heterosexual episodes. Others have had a bisexual period, . . . though they eventually recognized that their real orientation was toward same-sex partners" (p. 324). Likewise, Saghir and Robins (1973) took the position that the previous heterosexual attractions and relationships some of their gay and lesbian respondents reported were not a sign of bisexuality. This was also the contention of Spada (1979) concerning reports of his gay male respondents' past and current relationships with women:

> It might be argued that these men are not homosexual but bisexual. It is thus significant that such a large number of men who sufficiently consider themselves gay to respond to this survey have sexual relations with women. (p. 215)

In contrast, other researchers took a more neutral or affirmative position in presenting information about the bisexual attractions and behavior of respondents. For example, Hite (1976, 1981) and Jay and Young (1976) took a descriptive approach, including respondents' comments about their bisexuality, and the Playboy Readers' Sex Survey (1983) contrasted results of respondents based on both identity and behavior.

The illness model approach toward homosexuality was rejected by Weinberg and Williams (1974), who also questioned the polarization of sexual orientation into heterosexuality and homosexuality: "By defining heterosexuality as the norm, there also has been the tendency to view persons as either heterosexual or homosexual. This . . . poses the danger of ignoring the great range and heterogeneity of homosexuals" (p. 4). One-fifth of their combined San Francisco and New York samples rated themselves other than exclusively or predominantly homosexual on the Kinsey scale. The authors differentiated between "nonexclusive homosexuals" and "exclusive homosexuals" in their data analysis. Compared with the more exclusively homosexual men, the bisexual men were more involved with heterosexuals, more concerned with passing as heterosexual, and less known about as being "homosexual." They had more frequent and enjoyable sex with women and were more likely to have been married. The authors found no support for the argument that bisexuals are confused about their sexual identities, although their bisexual respondents evidenced greater guilt, shame, and anxiety about being "homosexual," feelings that did not appear to generalize to other psychological problems.

In their survey of the sexual experiences and psychological and social adjustment of lesbians and gay men, Bell and Weinberg (1978) noted:

> [I]t would not be unreasonable to suppose that a fairly strong heterosexual element is to be found in about one-third of those homosexual men most likely to participate in surveys of this kind. Even larger numbers of comparable homosexual women are apt to exhibit a "partial bisexual lifestyle." (p. 61)

In presenting their research findings, however, the authors did not differentiate between bisexual and homosexual respondents, even though their sample included substantial proportions of men and women who rated themselves in the midrange on the Kinsey scale for sexual feelings and behavior. The criticism has been made that combining bisexual and homosexual respondents in this way obscures information specific to both components of the sample and greatly limits the ability to generalize about either component from the study results (MacDonald, 1981, 1982, 1983).

The authors of a study of lesbian and gay male psychologists found that one-fifth of their female respondents and one-third of their male respondents considered themselves bisexual (Kooden et al., 1979). While the general responses of the bisexual psychologists were similar to those of the lesbian and gay psychologists, the bisexual respondents seemed to lack the social support networks that characterized the gay and lesbian respondents. Furthermore, the authors found that "the bisexual respondents appeared to have all of the stresses of the closeted gay respondents, but did not report having the positive experiences that were reported by the gay respondents who were generally open" (p. 68). The bisexual psychologists were more likely to be heterosexually married and less likely to be involved in the gay movement.

In their study of the development of sexual preference, Bell, Weinberg, and Hammersmith (1981) classified respondents who scored in the midrange on the Kinsey scale as bisexual. They differentiated bisexuals from exclusive homosexuals in their data analysis and found that "among the bisexuals, adult sexual preference is much less strongly tied to pre-adult sexual feelings" (p. 200). The authors concluded that "exclusive homosexuality tends to emerge from a deep-seated predisposition, while bisexuality is more subject to influence by social and sexual learning" (p. 201).

In summary, the evidence provided by ethnographic and survey studies of human sexuality indicates that many participants in such research have experienced heterosexual *and* homosexual attractions, behavior, or relationships. Based on ratings of past and current sexual attractions, sexual behavior, and self-identification, at least some of these individuals could be considered bisexual. When bisexual and homosexual respondents in sexuality research have been combined for the purposes of data analysis, information about each of these groups has been obscured. When respondents have been more adequately differentiated by sexual orientation, a more accurate characterization of both groups has been possible.

Research on Bisexuality and Bisexual Identities

Research on bisexuality has been strongly influenced by the assumptions of both the illness model and a dichotomous view of sexual orientation. Early studies addressed questions about the validity and viability of bisexuality as a sexual orientation and sexual identity as researchers examined issues such as psychological adjustment, the relationship between sexual identity and sexual behavior, and bisexuality in the context of heterosexual marriage. Just as a more affirmative approach to homosexuality led to a focus on factors involved in the development of positive lesbian and gay identities, the greater acknowledgment of bisexuality resulting from the elaboration of a multidimensional approach to sexual orientation has allowed more recent research to focus on factors involved in the development of positive bisexual identities.

Psychological Adjustment

The research demonstrating that homosexuality is not associated with psychopathology in nonclinical populations was an important part of the scientific evidence that influenced the American Psychiatric Association to remove homosexuality as a diagnostic category (Bayer, 1981; Gonsiorek, 1982). While this action contributed to a more affirmative view of homosexuality, the dichotomization of sexual orientation into heterosexuality and homosexuality remained, supporting the belief that bisexuals were psychologically maladjusted. As in comparable research on lesbians and gay men, however, research on nonclinical samples of bisexual women and men found no evidence of psychopathology or psychological maladjustment (Harris, 1977; LaTorre & Wendenberg, 1983; Markus, 1981; Masters & Johnson, 1979; Nurius, 1983; Ross, 1983; Twitchell, 1974; Weinberg & Williams, 1974; Zinik, 1984). In fact, some researchers found that self-identified bisexuals were characterized by high self-esteem (Galland, 1975, Rubenstein, 1982), self-confidence and autonomy (Galland, 1975), a positive self-concept independent of social norms (Twining, 1983), assertiveness (Bode, 1976), and cognitive flexibility (Zinik, 1984).

Identity and Sexual Behavior

Another major research focus has been the relationship between identity and sexual behavior. Some researchers approached this issue with the belief that heterosexuality and homosexuality are irreconcilable opposites. Anything other than exclusively heterosexual or homosexual behavior was seen as a case of incongruence between sexual behavior and sexual orientation. Individuals who considered themselves bisexual were seen as confused about their sexual orientation, and a bisexual identity was considered a transitional phenomenon some individuals go through in coming to terms with an underlying gay or lesbian sexual orientation (Fast & Wells, 1975; H. L. Ross, 1971; Miller, 1979; Schafer, 1976).

Other researchers proceeded from a more neutral perspective and focused on collecting descriptive data on the experiences of self-identified bisexual women and men (Blumstein & Schwartz, 1976a, 1976b, 1977; Bode, 1976; Fox, 1993; Galland, 1975; George, 1993; Harris, 1977; Hurwood, 1974; Klein, 1978; Klein et al., 1985; Little, 1989; Morse, 1989; Reinhardt, 1985; Rubenstein, 1982; Rust, 1992, 1993; Saliba, 1980; Twining, 1983; Weinberg et al., 1994; Wolff, 1979). Blumstein and Schwartz (1976a, 1976b, 1977) addressed the subject of identity and sexual behavior in an interview study of bisexual and homosexual women and men. They found that a variety of sexual behaviors were associated with bisexual, lesbian, and gay identities. Although some of their self-identified bisexual respondents did have sexual relationships with both men and women during a particular period of time, others did not. Furthermore, while some respondents who considered themselves lesbian or gay had exclusively homosexual relationships, others also had heterosexual relationships. Along these lines, in examining data from the Playboy study (Playboy Readers' Sex Survey, 1983), Lever, Rogers, Carson, Kanouse and Hertz (1992) found that one-third of the male respondents with adult bisexual behavior reported a bisexual identity, but a much larger proportion considered themselves heterosexual or gay.

Several studies have found that, for some individuals, identity appears to be related to factors other than current sexual behavior: whether a person is in a heterosexual or homosexual relationship, fear of being known as gay or bisexual, or political reasons such as loyalty to the gay or lesbian communities (Blumstein & Schwartz, 1976a, 1976b, 1977; Golden, 1987; Rust, 1992, 1993). The research literature also indicates that bisexual women and men arrive at their sexual identities by several possible sequences. While some individuals move from a heterosexual identity to a bisexual identity, others first consider themselves lesbian or gay before they consider themselves bisexual (Golden, 1987; Fox, 1993; Rust, 1992, 1993). These findings suggest that self-ratings of sexual attractions, fantasy, and behavior may vary significantly for bisexual individuals *and* for lesbian, gay, and heterosexual individuals and that ratings on these factors, including self-identification, change over time.

On the other hand, several researchers have found that most self-identified bisexuals rated themselves in the middle of the Kinsey scale for ideal behavior but tended to fall at either the heterosexual or homosexual ends of the scale when rating themselves on actual current behavior (Fox, 1993; George, 1993; Klein et al., 1985; Reinhardt, 1985). Sexual behavior appears to be constrained by the structure and dynamics of the current relationships in which individuals are engaged. This suggests that, although identity does change for some individuals, there is continuity in identity for *many* individuals, whether or not bisexual attractions are expressed in terms of sexual behavior or relationships during a particular period of time.

Homosexuality and Bisexuality in Heterosexual Marriages

The homosexual attractions and behavior of heterosexually married men and women have been the subject of extensive discussion in the literature. The traditional psychiatric position was that homosexual attractions or behavior in heterosexually married men are an indication of psychopathology (Allen, 1961; Bieber, 1969; Imielinski, 1969; L. J. Hatterer, 1970; Thornton, 1948). One writer viewed the spouses of such individuals as disturbed as well (M. S. Hatterer, 1974).

Several authors have portrayed mixed-orientation marriages as problematic at best, with separation as the typical outcome, and a necessary step for the husband in the process of coming out as a gay man (Bozett, 1982; H. L. Ross, 1971; Hill, 1987; Maddox, 1982; Malone, 1980; Miller, 1979). Some authors have described the adjustments that some couples have made in order to continue their marriages (Deabill, 1987; Gochros, 1989; Latham & White, 1978; Nahas & Turley, 1979; M. W. Ross, 1979; Whitney, 1990). The argument that married men who consider themselves bisexual are actually gay, and are attempting to avoid the stigma of a homosexual label, was examined by M. W. Ross (1983). He concluded that there was not sufficient evidence to support the assertion that the bisexual self-identification reported by some such men does not accurately reflect their sexual orientation.

Other authors who have viewed bisexuality as a valid sexual orientation and identity, rather than solely as a transitional state, have described typical characteristics of the marriages of bisexual men

(Brownfain, 1985; Coleman, 1981/1982a, 1985b; D. Dixon, 1985; Matteson, 1985; T. J. Wolf, 1985) and bisexual women (Coleman, 1985a; J. K. Dixon, 1984, 1985; Reinhardt, 1985). Several researchers have identified factors that contribute to a successful marriage with a bisexual partner: open communication between partners (Coleman, 1981/1982a, 1985b; Reinhardt, 1985; T. J. Wolf, 1985); acceptance of and discussion about the bisexual partner's homosexual feelings (Coleman, 1981/1982a; T. J. Wolf, 1985); commitment to making the relationship work (Coleman, 1981/1982a, T. J. Wolf, 1985); the spouse's maintenance of a sense of worth outside the context of the relationship; and agreement by both partners to some degree of open relationship, if sexual contact outside the relationship was desired by the bisexual partner (Coleman, 1981/1982a). The impact that the husband's disclosure of sexual orientation may have on his spouse and the marriage relationship also has been examined (Buxton, 1994; Gochros, 1989; Hays & Samuels, 1989).

The degree to which bisexuals disclose their homosexual attractions or behavior to their spouses varies widely. Brownfain (1985) found that most respondents in his nonclinical sample of bisexual married men were able to sustain a fulfilling family life, whether or not they disclosed their bisexuality to their spouses and whether or not they acted on their sexual attractions to other men. Matteson (1985) found that respondents who had disclosed to their spouses were more accepting of their homosexual experiences and bisexuality than those who had not disclosed, regardless of whether the couple was together or separating. He also found that husbands in together couples already had substantial homosexual experience and felt less need to act on current attractions to men. Husbands in separating couples had less homosexual experience and/or were more interested in relationships with men and involvement in the gay community. Reinhardt (1985) found that lack of sexual satisfaction with their husbands was not a significant factor in the decision of her bisexual respondents to pursue sexual relationships with women in addition to their marital relationships.

Research on Milestone Events in Bisexual Identity Development

Extensive data have been collected for lesbians and gay men on the "developmental milestone events" described in theoretical formulations of homosexual identity formation: first sexual attractions, behavior, and relationships; self-identification as gay or lesbian; and disclosure of sexual orientation to other people. Data have also been collected on these aspects of the process of coming out bisexual. This information allows for identification of patterns particular to bisexual identity development and clarifies similarities and differences in the formation of bisexual, lesbian, and gay identities.

First Heterosexual Attractions, Behavior, and Relationships

Bisexual men and women both experience their first heterosexual attractions at about the same ages, in their early teens, as shown in Table 3.1. This is somewhat earlier than for gay men and lesbians who have experienced heterosexual attractions, as shown in Table 3.2 and as found by Saghir and Robins (1973) and Bell et al. (1981).

Bisexual women have their first sexual experiences with men somewhat earlier than bisexual men have their first sexual experiences with women, in their middle to late teens, as Table 3.1 indicates. This is about the same as for lesbians and gay men who have had sexual experiences with persons of the opposite gender, as shown in Table 3.2 and as found by Saghir and Robins (1973) and Bell et al. (1981).

Bisexual women have their first heterosexual relationships about 2 years earlier than bisexual men, in their late teens, as Table 3.1 shows. The ages for bisexual men are about the same as for gay men who have had a heterosexual relationship (Table 3.2). No comparable data on the ages of first heterosexual relationships were found for lesbians.

First Homosexual Attractions, Behavior, and Relationships

Bisexual men experience their first sexual attractions toward other men in their early to middle teens, while bisexual women experience their first sexual attractions toward other women in their middle to late teens (Table 3.1). This is later, by about 2 to 3 years, than for gay men and lesbians (Table 3.2). The earlier ages for bisexual men compared to bisexual women are strikingly parallel to the earlier ages for gay men compared to lesbians, as shown in Tables 3.1 and 3.2 and as found by Saghir and Robins (1973) and Bell et al. (1981).

Bisexual men have their first sexual experiences with other men in their middle to late teens, while bisexual women have their first sexual experiences with other women in their early twenties (Table 3.1). This is somewhat later than for gay men and lesbians (Table 3.2). As with homosexual attractions, the earlier ages for homosexual behavior in bisexual men compared to bisexual women are strikingly parallel to the earlier ages for gay men compared to lesbians, as shown in Tables 3.1 and 3.2 and as found by Saghir and Robins (1973), Bell and Weinberg (1978), and Bell et al. (1981).

Bisexual women and men have their first homosexual relationships at about the same ages, in their early twenties (Table 3.1). This is about the same as for lesbians and gay men (Table 3.2).

Table 3.1
Average Ages at Milestone Events in Research on Bisexual Identity Development

Research	Date	N	Age	First Opposite Gender			First Same Gender			Identity as	
				Attraction	Behavior	Relationship	Attraction	Behavior	Relationship	Gay	Bi
Bisexual Women											
Harris	1977	10	28.0	—	21.1	—	17.0	22.2	—	—	25.8
Klein	1978	41	28.5	11.3	15.5	—	16.0	23.0	—	—	24.4
Kooden et al.	1979	17	—	—	—	—	16.9	22.0	24.9	27.9	—
Zinik	1984	63	31.8	10.8	—	—	—	—	—	—	23.7
Morse	1989	16	35.0	11.5	16.5	—	—	21.6	—	—	23.2
George	1993	121	30.6	—	—	—	—	—	—	24.5	25.0
Rust	1993	60	32.5	11.1	15.1	—	18.1	20.0	—	22.8	22.5
Fox	1993	486	30.3	11.6	14.7	18.0	15.8	21.4	22.4	—	26.8
Weinberg et al.	1994	44[a]	—	10.9	15.1	—	16.9	23.5	—	—	27.0
		96[a]					18.5				
Bisexual Men											
Harris	1977	15	34.9	—	20.1	—	16.0	14.5	—	—	27.3
Klein	1978	103	32.4	13.1	16.0	—	12.6	17.8	—	—	24.2
Kooden et al.	1979	64	—	—	—	—	16.2	13.9	19.1	22.3	—
Zinik	1984	72	36.2	11.9	—	—	—	—	—	—	—
Wayson	1985	21	—	—	19.8	—	13.7	18.6	—	—	—
Fox	1993	349	34.8	11.4	16.6	20.0	13.5	16.4	23.5	21.6	22.6
Weinberg et al.	1994	49[b]	—	11.7	17.3	—	17.1	16.3	—	—	27.2
		116[b]		12.8	15.9	—		17.2	—	—	29.0

[a]These figures are from the authors' 1983 study.
[b]These figures are from the authors' 1984/1985 study.

Average Ages at Milestone Events in Research on Lesbian and Gay Identity Development

| Research on | Date | N | Age | First Opposite Gender | | | First Same Gender | | | Identity as |
				Attraction	Behavior	Relationship	Attraction	Behavior	Relationship	Lesbian/Gay
Lesbians										
Kenyon	1968	123	36.4	—	—	—	16.1	21.5	—	—
Schafer	1976	151	26.2	—	18.5	—	14.5	19.8	—	20.7
Vance	1977	43	27.7	—	15.5	—	14.2	18.5	—	—
Califia	1979	286	27.5	—	—	—	—	20.0	—	20.5
Kooden et al.	1979	63	—	—	—	—	13.8	19.9	22.8	23.2
Ettore	1980	201	30.3	—	—	—	13.1	21.8	—	22.6
Fitzpatrick	1983	112	37.4	—	—	—	13.9	23.1	—	22.0
Zinik	1984	54	29.0	13.2	—	—	14.0	—	—	—
Chapman/Brannock	1987	197	34.0	—	16.8	—	—	20.6	—	22.5
Rust	1993	342	31.2	—	—	—	15.4	—	—	21.7
Weinberg et al.	1994	94[a]	—	14.3	16.4	—	16.4	20.5	—	22.5
Gay Men										
Dank	1971	182	32.5	—	—	—	13.5	—	—	19.3
Danneker/Reiche	1974	581	27.5	—	—	—	—	16.7	—	19.0
Weinberg, T.S.	1977	30	22.8	—	18.3	—	—	14.1	—	19.9
Lehne	1978	47	—	—	—	—	—	16.0	—	—
Kooden et al.	1979	138	30.0	—	—	—	12.8	14.9	21.9	21.1
Troiden	1979	150	31.0	—	—	—	—	14.9	23.9	21.3
McDonald	1982	199	29.5	—	—	—	13.0	15.0	21.0	19.0
Sommers	1982	97	—	—	—	—	10.8	—	—	18.4
Benitez	1983	178	32.0	—	18.9	20.3	12.3	19.5	23.2	20.2
Cohen-Ross	1985	93	27.9	—	14.7	—	9.0	14.4	—	16.8
Wayson	1985	58	—	—	20.6	—	—	11.0	—	—
Zinik	1984	61	27.5	14.3	—	—	11.4	—	—	—
Edgar	1987	148	35.4	—	—	—	12.1	16.9	—	—
Prine	1987	51	35.1	—	—	—	15.2	17.7	—	—
Weinberg et al.	1994	186[a]	—	14.5	17.7	—	11.5	14.7	—	21.1

[a] These figures are from the authors' 1984/1985 study.

First Bisexual, Lesbian, and Gay Self-Identifications

Most research has found that bisexual men and women first consider themselves bisexual at about the same ages, in their early to middle twenties (Table 3.1). This is about 2 to 3 years later than first homosexual self-identification for gay men and lesbians (Table 3.2). For those bisexual men and women who have considered themselves gay or lesbian, the men self-identified as gay earlier than the women self-identified as lesbian, in their early twenties (Table 3.1). This parallels the earlier homosexual self-identification of gay men compared to lesbians (Table 3.2).

Age Cohort Group Differences

Differences in the average ages at which younger and older persons first self-identify as bisexual or gay have been addressed in one study of bisexual men and women (Fox, 1993) and in three studies of gay men (Dank, 1971; McDonald, 1982; Troiden & Goode, 1980). Significant differences for bisexual men and women in four age cohort groups (under 25, 25 through 34, 35 through 44, and 45 and older) were found for first bisexual self-identification (Fox, 1993). These results parallel similar differences found between different age cohort groupings of gay men: for men under and over 30 years of age (Dank, 1971); for men in their twenties, thirties, and forties (McDonald, 1982); and for men in their early twenties, late twenties, early thirties, and late thirties (Troiden & Goode, 1980). Significant age cohort differences were also found for other typical coming out milestone events for bisexual women and men, suggesting that the entire coming out process is occurring earlier for younger bisexuals (Fox, 1933). These kinds of age group differences in samples of gay men and bisexual men and women have been seen as being related to the increased accessibility of information on sexuality and sexual orientation and the development of visible bisexual and gay communities as support systems for individuals involved in the coming out process.

Self-Disclosure of Sexual Orientation

Lesbian and gay identity theory emphasizes the importance of disclosure of sexual orientation for the development of integrated lesbian or gay identities. Information on the ages of first disclosures to other people has been collected in two studies of bisexual men and women and several studies of gay men and lesbians. Bisexual women and men first disclose their sexual orientation to another person at about the same ages, at about the same time they first consider themselves bisexual. Respondents in one large sample first disclosed their bisexuality in their early twenties (Fox, 1993), whereas respondents in two smaller samples first disclosed their bisexuality in their middle to late twenties (Weinberg et al., 1994). Lesbians first disclose in their middle twenties (Fitzpatrick, 1983), and gay men first disclose in their early to middle twenties (Benitez, 1983; Bilotta, 1987; Cody, 1988; Edgar, 1987; McDonald, 1982). Bisexual women and men first disclose to a family member in their middle twenties (Fox, 1993), as do gay men (Benitez, 1983; Bilotta, 1987; Edgar, 1987). Bisexual men and women first disclose to their father, mother, brother, or sister, in their middle twenties (Fox, 1993), while gay men first disclose to these family members in their late twenties (Cody, 1988). No comparable information on the ages of first self-disclosures to family members was found for lesbians.

Fox (1993) and Weinberg et al. (1994) found that the persons to whom the greatest proportions of respondents had disclosed their bisexuality were friends and relationship partners, including spouses. Fox (1993) found that a substantial proportion of respondents had also disclosed to a therapist, while smaller proportions of respondents had disclosed to individual family members (mother, father, sister, or brother) or to people at work or school. A greater proportion of women than men had disclosed to a female friend or male relationship partner, or to a family member, a therapist, or someone at work or at school. These disclosure patterns are similar to those found in research on lesbians (Bell & Weinberg, 1978; Chapman & Brannock, 1987; Etorre, 1980; Fitzpatrick, 1983; Hencken, 1984; Jay & Young, 1979; Kooden et al., 1979; Loftin, 1981; Weinberg et al., 1994) and gay men (Bell & Weinberg, 1978; Benitez, 1983; Cody, 1988; Cramer & Roach, 1988; Edgar, 1987; Hencken, 1984; Jay & Young, 1979; Kooden et al., 1978; Weinberg et al., 1994). The proportions of bisexual respondents who had disclosed their sexual orientation to persons other than friends and relationship partners, were smaller than those of lesbian and gay male respondents who had done so in comparable research.

Gender Differences in Coming Out Bisexual

The data for first sexual attractions, behavior, and bisexual self-identification, as shown in Table 3.1, reveal what appear to be different normative patterns for bisexual women and men. Most bisexual women experience their first heterosexual attractions and behavior *before* their first homosexual sexual attractions and behavior. In contrast, a greater proportion of bisexual men than bisexual women experience their first homosexual attractions and behavior earlier or at about the same ages as their first heterosexual behavior. Most bisexual women move from their first homosexual attractions to a bisexual identity more quickly than bisexual men, many of whom experience concurrent heterosexual and homosexual attractions and behavior at an earlier age than bisexual women and for a longer period of time before their first bisexual self-identification.

Counseling Issues

For bisexual men and women, the predominance of a polarized view of sexual orientation and the relative lack of a visible bisexual community complicate the task of coming to terms with concurrent heterosexual and homosexual attractions. As for many lesbians and gay men, psychotherapy has been helpful for many bisexual women and men in facing the issues involved in the coming out process. Several issues that bisexual women and men typically bring into psychotherapy have been identified (Coleman, 1981/1982a; Lourea, 1987; Matteson, 1987; Nichols, 1988; T. J. Wolf, 1987, 1992): uncertainty about how to interpret their sexual attractions to both women and men; isolation, based on not knowing other bisexual women or men; alienation, feeling different from both heterosexuals and gay men or lesbians; apprehension about disclosure of their bisexuality to other people in their lives; and concerns about relationships and how to proceed with new or existing relationships while being open about sexual orientation issues. Psychotherapy can assist an individual in coming to terms with these issues by facilitating greater self-acceptance and the courage to move from isolation to connection with a community of similar others. Autobiographical accounts also can be helpful by illustrating how other bisexual women and men have experienced and successfully moved through the coming out process (Falk, 1975; Geller, 1990; Hutchins & Kaahumanu, 1991; Kohn & Matusow, 1980; Norris & Read, 1985; The Off Pink Collective, 1988; Scott, 1978; Weise, 1992; Wolff, 1979).

Community

Gay and lesbian identity theory has emphasized that friendships and relationships with other gay men and lesbians, and participation in the gay and lesbian communities, are important factors in developing integrated gay and lesbian identities. While numerous descriptive accounts of gay and lesbian communities appeared in the early literature, such has not been the case regarding bisexuality. Until recently, the only information in the literature on bisexuality in the context of community was found in research on homosexuality and lesbian and gay male communities. However, a few accounts of bisexual groups in urban communities do exist (Barr, 1985; Mishaan, 1985; Rubenstein & Slater, 1985). Although the literature does not yet reflect the current growth of bisexual community groups and organizations on local, regional, and national levels, the development of community suggested by the emergence of these groups and organizations is indicated by a dramatic increase in the number of entries in successive editions of the *Interna-*

tional Directory of Bisexual Groups (Ochs, 1994). This represents a major increase in the degree of access for bisexual women and men to a community of similar others during the coming out process and on an ongoing basis.

Discussion

The illness model of homosexuality made a sharp distinction between normal (heterosexual) and abnormal (homosexual) sexual attractions and behavior. When homosexuality was removed as a diagnostic category, homosexual attractions and behavior were no longer officially considered an indication of psychopathology. This allowed for an important shift in emphasis in psychiatry and psychology away from the etiology of homosexuality and toward the development of theory and research on the formation of positive lesbian and gay identities.

Thinking about sexual orientation and sexual identity, however, continued to be based on the assumption of monosexuality, or exclusivity of heterosexual or homosexual "object choice." Looking through the lens of this dichotomous model, bisexuality appeared anomalous. For some authors, bisexuality and bisexuals simply didn't exist. They believed that few people, if any, had equal attractions to men and women, and even a slight preference for one gender or the other was taken as "evidence" that the "real" orientation was homosexual *or* heterosexual. For others, *any* homosexual attractions or behavior indicated a homosexual orientation, and individuals who claimed a bisexual identity were seen as psychologically and socially maladjusted just as lesbians and gay men were considered maladjusted from the point of view of the illness model.

At the same time, the results of research on human sexuality clearly indicated that many individuals have experienced both heterosexual and homosexual attractions and behavior. Furthermore, research found no indication of psychopathology in nonclinical samples of bisexual women and men, just as prior research had found no evidence of psychopathology in nonclinical samples of lesbians and gay men.

No single pattern of homosexual and heterosexual attractions, behavior, and relationships characterizes self-identified bisexual men and women. Individuals arrive at their sexual identities by various routes. For some women and men, sexual identity remains constant, while for others, sexual identity varies in response to changes in sexual and emotional attractions, behavior, and relationships and the social and political contexts in which these occur. Finally, one of the main differences between bisexual men and women and gay men and lesbians is in the degree to which a visible community of similar others exists and serves to support the individual in the coming out process. The extensive support networks that have developed in many communities have served this purpose for lesbians and gay men. While bisexual men and women often have looked to gay and lesbian communities for support and understanding regarding their homosexual interests and sexual minority status, the bisexual groups and organizations now emerging may be able to more effectively support them in the process of coming out bisexual and in their efforts to affiliate with other bisexual women and men.

Directions for Future Research

Multiple factors influence the development of bisexual identities, just as for heterosexual, gay, and lesbian identities. Gender, age, ethnicity, social class, and environment affect the experience and presentation of bisexual identities as well as other factors that theory and research have found to be relevant to identity: biological sex; gender identity; social sex roles; sexual attractions, fantasies, and behavior; emotional and social preferences; and life-style as well as prior lesbian, gay, and heterosexual identities.

As has been the case with most research on gay men and lesbians, research on bisexual men and women has been based on retrospective reports. Furthermore, in any particular study, respondents differ in age and in their qualitative experience of bisexuality and the coming out process. In-depth longitudinal research is needed to better understand how bisexual identities develop over time.

Questions also remain regarding the representativeness of samples in existing research on bisexual, lesbian, and gay identities which are particular to surveys of stigmatized and partly invisible populations. The largest proportion of participants in most studies have been young, middle-class, white women and men. Research is needed on older bisexuals, working-class bisexuals, and bisexual people of color, who have been underrepresented, as have been people with bisexual behavior but other sexual orientation self-identifications.

Extensive research has been conducted on relationships in which one partner is heterosexual and the other is bisexual; however, research on relationships in which the partners are bisexual and gay or lesbian or both bisexual would add to our understanding of the relationships in which bisexual women and men are involved, as would research on triad and other multiple-partner relationships. Likewise, while research has been done on the transition from heterosexual to bisexual identity and on the transition from heterosexual to bisexual to gay identity, little research exists on the transition from lesbian and gay identities to a bisexual identity or on transitions involving multiple sexual orientation self-identification sequences.

While research has been conducted on attitudes of heterosexuals toward gay men and lesbians and on homophobia, there is very little research on attitudes of heterosexuals, gay men, and lesbians toward bisexuals or on biphobia. Finally, research on how the coming out process and the maintenance of a positive bisexual identities are affected by the emergence and presence of a visible bisexual community could certainly augment our understanding of changes in the process of coming out bisexual that have occurred as a function of time and the development of community.

Conclusion

The evolution of theory and research on homosexuality and bisexuality has involved significant shifts in perspective. The movement from the heterocentric illness model to a more affirmative approach to homosexuality, and the movement from a dichotomous model to a multidimensional model of sexual orientation, both have refocused the discourse on homosexuality and bisexuality toward examination of factors involved in the development of positive lesbian, gay, and bisexual identities.

The results of research on bisexuality indicate that there are similarities and differences in coming out bisexual and coming out gay or lesbian. Like lesbians and gay men, bisexual women and men need to acknowledge and validate their homosexual attractions and relationships to achieve positive and integrated sexual identities. In this respect, current models of gay and lesbian identity development are particularly helpful in understanding the homosexual component of bisexual identity development. Bisexual women and men, however, need to acknowledge and validate both the homosexual and the heterosexual components of their identities, regardless of the degree to which either or both of these are actualized in sexual behavior or relationships.

The development of a theoretical perspective which takes into consideration the diverse patterns of homosexual and heterosexual attractions and relationships of bisexual men and women has been essential in accurately conceptualizing bisexual identity development. The multidimensional view of sexual orientation and sexual identities on which this is based can further inform theory and research and contribute to a fuller understanding of lesbian, gay, and bisexual identities.

References

Achilles, N. (1967). The development of the homosexual bar as an institution. In J. Gagnon & W. Simon (Eds.), *Sexual deviance* (pp. 228–244). New York: Harper & Row.

Adam, B. D. (1985). Age, structure, and sexuality: Reflections on the anthropological evidence on homosexual relations. *Journal of Homosexuality, 11*(3/4), 19–34.

Alexander, F. (1933). Bisexual conflict in homosexuality. *Psychoanalytic Quarterly, 2*, 197–201.

Allen, C. (1961). When homosexuals marry. In I. Rubin (Ed.), *The third sex* (pp. 58–62). New York: New Book Co.

Barr, G. (1985). Chicago bi-ways: An informal history. *Journal of Homosexuality, 11*(1/2), 231–234.

Bayer, R. (1981). *Homosexuality and American psychiatry: The politics of diagnosis.* New York: Basic Books.

Bell, A. P., & Weinberg, M. S. (1978). *Homosexualities: A study of diversity among men and women.* New York: Simon & Schuster.

Bell, A. P., Weinberg, M. S., & Hammersmith, S. K. (1981). *Sexual preference: Its development in men and women.* Bloomington: Indiana University Press.

Benitez, J. C. (1983). The effect of gay identity acquisition on the psychological adjustment of male homosexuals. (Doctoral dissertation, Northwestern University, 1982). *Dissertation Abstracts International, 43*(10), 3350B.

Bergler, E. (1956). *Homosexuality: Disease or way of life.* New York: Collier.

Berkey, B., Perelman-Hall, T., & Kurdek, L. A. (1990). Multi-dimensional scale of sexuality. *Journal of Homosexuality, 19*(4), 67–87.

Bieber, I. (1969). The married male homosexual. *Medical Aspects of Human Sexuality, 3*(5), 76–84.

Bieber, I., Dain, H. J., Dince, P. R., Drellich, M. G., Gunlach, R. H., Kremer, M. W., Rifkin, A. H., Wilbur, C. B., & Bieber, T. B. (1962). *Homosexuality: A psychoanalytic study.* New York: Random House.

Bilotta, G. J. (1987). Gay men coming out to their families or origin: An exploratory-descriptive investigation. (Doctoral dissertation, United States International University, 1987). *Dissertation Abstracts International, 48*(4), 1026A.

Blackwood, E. (1985). Breaking the mirror: The construction of lesbianism and the anthropological discourse on homosexuality. *Journal of Homosexuality, 11*(3/4), 1–18.

Blumstein, P., & Schwartz, P. (1976a). Bisexuality in men. *Urban Life, 5*(3), 339–358.

Blumstein, P. W., & Schwartz, P. (1976b). Bisexuality in women. *Archives of Sexual Behavior, 5*(2), 171–181.

Blumstein, P. W., & Schwartz, P. (1977). Bisexuality: Some social psychological issues. *Journal of Social Issues, 33*(2), 30–45.

Bode, J. (1976). *View from another closet: Exploring bisexuality in women.* New York: Hawthorne Books.

Boulton, M., & Coxon, T. (1991). Bisexuality in the United Kingdom. In R. A. P. Tielman, M. Carballo, & A. C. Hendriks (Eds.), *Bisexuality and HIV/AIDS: A global perspective* (pp. 65–72). Buffalo, NY: Prometheus Books.

Bozett, F. W. (1982). Heterogeneous couples in heterosexual marriages: Gay men and straight women. *Journal of Marital and Family Therapy, 8*(1), 81–89.

Brownfain, J. J. (1985). A study of the married bisexual male: Paradox and resolution. *Journal of Homosexuality, 11*(1/2), 173–188.

Buxton, A. P. (1994). *The other side of the closet: The coming out crisis for straight spouses and families.* New York: John Wiley & Sons.

Califia, P. (1979). Lesbian sexuality. *Journal of Homosexuality, 4*(3), 255–266.

Caprio, F. S. (1954). *Female homosexuality: A psychodynamic study of lesbianism.* New York: Grove Press.

Caprio, F. S. (1955). *The adequate male.* New York: Medical Research Press.

Carrier, J. M. (1980). Homosexual behavior in cross-cultural perspective. In J. Marmor (Ed.), *Homosexual behavior: A modern reappraisal* (pp. 100–122). New York: Basic Books.

Carrier, J. M. (1985). Mexican male bisexuality. *Journal of Homosexuality, 11*(1/2), 75–86.

Cass, V. C. (1979). Homosexual identity formation: A theoretical model. *Journal of Homosexuality, 4*(3), 219–235.

Cass, V. C. (1983/1984). Homosexual identity: A concept in need of definition. *Journal of Homosexuality, 9*(2/3), 105–126.

Cass, V. C. (1984). Homosexual identity formation: Testing a theoretical model. *Journal of Sex Research, 20*(2), 143–167.

Cass, V. C. (1990). The implications of homosexual identity formation for the Kinsey model and scale of sexual preference. In D. P. McWhirter, S. A. Sanders, & Reinisch, (Eds.), *Homosexuality/heterosexuality: Concepts of sexual orientation* (pp. 239–266). New York: Oxford University Press.

Chapman, B. E., & Brannock, J. C. (1987). Proposed model of lesbian identity development: An empirical examination. *Journal of Homosexuality, 14*(3/4), 69–80.

Churchill, W. (1967). *Homosexual behavior among males: A cross-cultural and cross-species investigation.* New York: Hawthorn Books.

Cody, P. J. (1988). The personal development of gay men: A study of the relationship of length of time "out of the closet" to locus of control, self-concept, and self-actualization. (Doctoral dissertation, California Institute of Integral Studies, 1988). *Dissertation Abstracts International, 49*(7), 2847B.

Cohen-Ross, J. L. (1985). An exploratory study of the retrospective role of significant others in homosexual identity development. (Doctoral dissertation, California School of Professional Psychology, Los Angeles, 1984). *Dissertation Abstracts International, 46*(2), 628B.

Coleman, E. (1981/1982a). Bisexual and gay men in heterosexual marriage: Conflicts and resolutions in therapy. *Journal of Homosexuality, 7*(2/3), 93–104.

Coleman, E. (1981/1982b). Developmental stages of the coming out process. *Journal of Homosexuality, 7*(2/3), 31–44.

Coleman, E. (1985a). Bisexual women in marriages. *Journal of Homosexuality, 11*(1/2), 87–100.

Coleman, E. (1985b). Integration of male bisexuality and marriage. *Journal of Homosexuality, 11*(1/2), 189–208.

Coleman, E. (1987). Assessment of sexual orientation. *Journal of Homosexuality, 14*(1/2), 9–24.

Coleman, E. (1990). Toward a synthetic understanding of sexual orientation. In D. P. McWhirter, S. A. Sanders, & Reinisch, (Eds.), *Homosexuality/heterosexuality: Concepts of sexual orientation* (pp. 267–276). New York: Oxford University Press.

Cory, D. W., & LeRoy, J. P. (1963). *The homosexual and his society: A view from within.* New York: Citadel Press.

Cramer, D. W., & Roach, A. J. (1988). Coming out to mom and dad: A study of gay males and their relationships with their parents. *Journal of Homosexuality, 15*(3/4), 79–91.

Cronin, D. M. (1974). Coming out among lesbians. In E. Goode & R. R. Troiden (Eds.), *Sexual deviance and sexual deviants* (pp. 268–277). New York: William Morrow.

Dank, B. M. (1971). Coming out in the gay world. *Psychiatry, 34,* 180–197.

Dannecker, M., & Reiche, R. (1974). *Der gewohnliche Homosexuelle.* Frankfurt: Fisher.

Davenport, W. (1965). Sexual patterns and their regulation in a society of the Southwest Pacific. In F. A. Beach (Ed.), *Sex and behavior* (pp. 164–207). New York: John Wiley & Sons.

Davenport, W. (1977). Sex in cross-cultural perspective. In F. A. Beach (Ed.), *Human sexuality in four perspectives* (pp. 115–163). Baltimore: Johns Hopkins University Press.

Deabill, G. (1987). *An investigation of sexual behaviors in mixed sexual orientation couples: Gay husband and straight wife.* Unpublished doctoral dissertation, Institute for Advanced Study of Human Sexuality, San Francisco.

de Monteflores, C., & Schultz, S. J. (1978). Coming out: Similarities and differences for lesbians and gay men. *Journal of Social Issues, 34*(3), 59–72.

Dixon, D. (1985). Perceived sexual satisfaction and marital happiness of bisexual and heterosexual swinging husbands. *Journal of Homosexuality, 11*(1/2), 209–222.

Dixon, J. K. (1984). The commencement of bisexual activity in swinging married women over age thirty. *Journal of Sex Research, 20,* 71–90.

Dixon, J. K. (1985). Sexuality and relationship changes in married females following the commencement of bisexual activity. *Journal of Homosexuality, 11*(1/2), 115–134.

Doll, L., Peterson, J., Magana, J. R., & Carrier, J. M. (1991). Male bisexuality and AIDS in the United States. In R. A. P. Tielman, M. Carballo, & A. C. Hendriks (Eds.), *Bisexuality and HIV/AIDS: A global perspective* (pp. 27–40). Buffalo, NY: Prometheus Books.

Edgar, T. M. (1987). The disclosure process of the stigmatized: Strategies to minimize rejection (Doctoral dissertation, Purdue University, 1986). *Dissertation Abstracts International, 47*(9), 3238A.

Ellis, H. (1905/1942). *Studies in the psychology of sex (Vol. I).* New York: Random House.

Ettore, E. M. (1980). *Lesbians, women, and society.* London: Routledge and Kegan Paul.

Falk, R. (1975). *Women loving: A journey toward becoming an independent woman.* New York: Random House.

Fast, J., & Wells, H. (1975). *Bisexual living.* New York: Pocket Books.

Fitzpatrick, G. (1983). Self-disclosure of lesbianism as related to self-actualization and self-stigmatization (Doctoral dissertation, United States International University, 1982). *Dissertation Abstracts International, 43*(12), 4143B.

Ford, C. S., & Beach, F. A. (1951). *Patterns of sexual behavior.* New York: Harper & Row.

Fox, R. C. (1993). *Coming out bisexual: Identity, behavior, and sexual orientation self-disclosure.* Unpublished doctoral dissertation, California Institute of Integral Studies, San Francisco.

Freud, S. (1905/1962). *Three essays on the theory of sexuality.* (J. Strachey, Trans.). New York: Basic Books.

Freud, S. (1925/1963). *An autobiographical study.* (J. Strachey, Trans.; rev. ed.). New York: Norton.

Freud, S. (1937/1963). Analysis terminable and interminable. In P. Rieff (Ed.), *Therapy and technique* (pp. 233–272). New York: Collier.

Gagnon, J. M., & Simon, W. (1968). Homosexuality: The formulation of a sociological perspective. In M. Lefton, J. K. Skipper, Jr., & C. H. McGaghy (Eds.), *Approaches to deviance: Theories, concepts and research findings* (pp. 349–361). New York: Appleton-Century-Crofts.

Gagnon, J. M., & Simon, W. (1973). *Sexual conduct: The social sources of human sexuality.* Chicago: Aldine.

Galland, V. R. (1975). Bisexual women (Doctoral dissertation, California School of Professional Psychology, San Francisco, 1975). *Dissertation Abstracts International, 36*(6), 3037B.

Geller, T. (Ed.). (1990). *Bisexuality: A reader and sourcebook.* Ojai, CA: Times Change Press.

George, S. (1993). *Women and bisexuality.* London: Scarlet Press.

Gochros, J. S. (1989). *When husbands come out of the closet.* New York: Harrington Park Press.

Golden, C. (1987). Diversity and variability in women's sexual identities. In The Boston Lesbian Psychologies Collective (Ed.), *Lesbian psychologies: Explorations and challenges* (pp. 18–34). Urbana: University of Illinois Press.

Gonsiorek, J. C. (1982). Results of psychological testing on homosexual populations. *American Behavioral Scientist, 25*(4), 385–396.

Green, R. (1972). Homosexuality as a mental illness. *International Journal of Psychiatry, 10,* 77–128.

Hansen, C. E., & Evans, A. (1985). Bisexuality reconsidered: An idea in pursuit of a definition. *Journal of Homosexuality, 11*(1/2), 1–6.

Harris, D. A. I. (1977). Social-psychological characteristics of ambisexuals (Doctoral dissertation, University of Tennessee; 1977). *Dissertation Abstracts International, 39*(2), 574A.

Harwell, J. L. (1976). Bisexuality: Persistent lifestyle or transitional state? (Doctoral dissertation, United States International University, 1976). *Dissertation Abstracts International, 37*(4), 2449A.

Hatterer, L. J. (1970). *Changing homosexuality in the male: Treatment for men troubled by homosexuality.* New York: Dell Publishing.

Hatterer, M. S. (1974). The problems of women married to homosexual men. *American Journal of Psychiatry, 131*, 275–278.

Hays, D., & Samuels, A. (1989). Heterosexual women's perceptions of their marriages to bisexual or homosexual men. *Journal of Homosexuality, 18*(1/2), 81–100.

Hencken, J. D. (1984). Sexual-orientation self-disclosure (Doctoral dissertation, University of Michigan, Ann Arbor, 1984). *Dissertation Abstracts International, 45*(7), 2310B.

Herdt, G. (1984). A comment on cultural attributes and fluidity of bisexuality. *Journal of Homosexuality, 10*(3/4), 53–62.

Herdt, G. (1990). Developmental discontinuities and sexual orientation across cultures. In D. P. McWhirter, S. A. Sanders, & Reinisch (Eds,), *Homosexuality/heterosexuality: Concepts of sexual orientation* (pp. 208–236). New York: Oxford University Press.

Hill, I. (Ed.). (1987). *The bisexual spouse: Different dimensions in human sexuality.* New York: Harper & Row.

Hite, S. (1976). *The Hite report: A nationwide study of female sexuality.* New York: Dell.

Hite, S. (1981). *The Hite report on male sexuality.* New York: Knopf.

Hoffman, M. (1968). *The gay world: Male homosexuality and the social creation of evil.* New York: Basic Books.

Hooker, E. (1956). A preliminary analysis of group behavior of homosexuals. *Journal of Psychology, 42*, 217–225.

Hooker, E. (1965). Male homosexuals and their "worlds." In J. Marmor (Ed.), *Sexual inversion: The multiple roots of homosexuality* (pp. 83–107). New York: Basic Books.

Humphreys, L. (1970). *Tearoom trade: Impersonal sex in public places.* Chicago: Aldine.

Hunt, M. (1974). *Sexual behavior in the 1970's.* New York: Dell.

Hurwood, B. J. (1974). *The bisexuals.* Greenwich, CT: Fawcett.

Hutchins, L., & Kaahumanu, L. (Eds.) (1991). *Bi any other name: Bisexual people speak out.* Boston: Alyson.

Imielinski, K. (1969). Homosexuality in males with particular reference to marriage. *Psychotherapy and Psychosomatics, 17*, 126–132.

Jay, K., & Young, A. (1979). *The gay report: Lesbians and gay men speak out about sexual experiences and lifestyles.* New York: Summit Books.

Kardiner, A., Karesh, A., & Ovessey, L. (1959). A methodological study of Freudian theory: Narcissism, bisexuality, and the dual instinct theory. *Journal of Nervous and Mental Disease, 129*(3), 207–221.

Katan, M. (1955). Those wrecked by success, bisexual conflicts, and ego defense. *The Psychoanalytic Quarterly, 24*, 477–478.

Kenyon, F. E. (1968). Studies in female homosexuality IV: Social and psychiatric aspects. *British Journal of Psychiatry, 114*, 1337–1350.

Khan, M., & Masud, R. (1974). Ego orgasm and bisexual love. *International Review of Psychoanalysis, 1*, 143–149.

Kinsey, A. C., Pomeroy, W. B., & Martin, C. E. (1948). *Sexual behavior in the human male.* Philadelphia: W. B. Saunders.

Kinsey, A. C., Pomeroy, W. B., Martin, C. E., & Gebhard, P. H. (1952). *Sexual behavior in the human female.* Philadelphia: W. B. Saunders.

Klein, F. (1978). *The bisexual option: A concept of one hundred percent intimacy.* New York: Arbor House.

Klein, F. (1990). The need to view sexual orientation as a multivariable dynamic process: A theoretical perspective. In D. P. McWhirter, S. A. Sanders, & Reinisch, (Eds.), *Homosexuality/heterosexuality: Concepts of sexual orientation* (pp. 277–282). New York: Oxford University Press.

Klein, F. (1993). *The bisexual option* (2nd ed.). New York: Harrington Park Press.

Klein, F., Sepekoff, B., & Wolf, T. J. (1985). Sexual orientation: A multi-variable dynamic process. *Journal of Homosexuality, 11*(1/2), 35–50.

Kohn, B., & Matusow, A. (1980). *Barry and Alice: Portrait of a bisexual marriage.* Englewood Cliffs, NJ: Prentice-Hall.

Kooden, H. D., Morin, S. F., Riddle, D. I., Rogers, M., Sang, B. E., & Strassburger, F. (1979). *Removing the stigma: Final report of the Board of Social and Ethical Responsibility for Psychology's Task Force on the Status of Lesbian and Gay Male Psychologists.* Washington, DC: American Psychological Association.

Krafft-Ebing, R. v. (1886/1965). *Psychopathia sexualis: A medico-forensic study* (H. Wedeck, Trans.). New York: G. P. Putnam's Sons.

Kubie, L. S. (1974). The drive to become both sexes. *Psychoanalytic Quarterly, 43*, 349–426.

Latham, J. D., & White, G. D. (1978). Coping with homosexual expression within heterosexual marriages: Five case studies. *Journal of Sex and Marital Therapy, 4*(3), 198–212.

LaTorre, R. A., & Wendenberg, K. (1983). Psychological characteristics of bisexual, heterosexual, and homosexual women. *Journal of Homosexuality, 9*(1), 87–97.

Lehne, G. K. (1978). Gay male fantasies and realities. *Journal of Social Issues, 34*(3), 28–37.

Lever, J., Rogers, W. H., Carson, S., Kanouse, D. E., & Hertz, R. (1992). Behavior patterns and sexual identity of bisexual males. *Journal of Sex Research, 29*(2), 141–168.

Leznoff, M. M., & Westley, W. A. (1956). The homosexual community. *Social Problems, 3*(4), 257–263.

Limentani, A. (1976). Object choice and actual bisexuality. *International Journal of Psychoanalytic Psychotherapy, 5*, 205–218.

Little, D. R. (1989). Contemporary female bisexuality: A psychological phenomenon. (Doctoral Dissertation, The Union for Experimenting Colleges and Universities, 1989). *Dissertations Abstracts International, 50* (11), 5379B.

Loftin, E. C. (1981). The study of disclosure and support in a lesbian population (Doctoral dissertation, University of Texas at Austin, 1981). *Dissertation Abstracts International, 42*(3), 1348A.

Lourea, D. R. (1987). Psycho-social issues related to counseling bisexuals. *Journal of Homosexuality, 11*(1/2), 21–34.

MacDonald, A. P., Jr. (1981). Bisexuality: Some comments on research and theory. *Journal of Homosexuality, 6*(3), 21–35.

MacDonald, A. P., Jr. (1982). Research on sexual orientation: A bridge that touches both shores but doesn't meet in the middle. *Journal of Sex Education and Therapy, 8*(1), 9–13.

MacDonald, A. P., Jr. (1983). A little bit of lavender goes a long way: A critique of research on sexual orientation. *Journal of Sex Research, 19*(1), 94–100.

Maddox, B. (1982). *Married and gay: An intimate look at a different relationship.* New York: Harcourt Brace Jovanovich.

Malone, J. (1980). *Straight women and gay men: A special relationship.* New York: Dial Press.

Markus, E. B. (1981). An examination of psychological adjustment and sexual preference in the female (Doctoral dissertation, University of Missouri, Kansas City, 1980). *Dissertation Abstracts International, 41*(10), 4338A.

Marmor, J. (Ed.). (1965). *Sexual inversion: The multiple roots of homosexuality.* New York: Basic Books.

Marmor, J. (1972). Homosexuality—Mental Illness or moral dilemma? *International Journal of Psychiatry, 10,* 114–117.

Masters, W. H., & Johnson, V. E. (1979). *Homosexuality in perspective.* Boston: Little, Brown and Company.

Matteson, D. R. (1985). Bisexual men in marriage: Is a positive homosexual identity and stable marriage possible? *Journal of Homosexuality, 11*(1/2), 149–172.

Matteson, D. R. (1987). Counseling bisexual men. In M. Scher, M. Stevens, G. Good, & G. A. Eichenfeld (Eds.), *Handbook of counseling and psychotherapy with men* (pp. 232–249). Newbury Park, CA: Sage Publications.

McDonald, G. J. (1982). Individual differences in the coming out process for gay men: Implications for theoretical models. *Journal of Homosexuality, 8*(1), 47–60.

Mead, M. (1961). Cultural determinants of sexual behavior. In W. C. Young (Ed.), *Sex and internal secretions (Vol. II)* (3rd ed.) (pp. 1433–1479). Baltimore: Williams & Wilkins.

Mead, M. (1975, January). Bisexuality: What's it all about? *Redbook,* pp. 6–7.

Miller, B. (1979). Gay fathers and their children. *The Family Coordinator, 28,* 544–552.

Mishaan, C. (1985). The bisexual scene in New York City. *Journal of Homosexuality, 11*(1/2), 223–226.

Moll, A. (1897/1933). *Libido sexualis: Studies in the psychosexual laws of love verified by clinical sexual case histories* (D. Berger, Trans.). New York: American Ethnological Press.

Morrow, G. D. (1989). Bisexuality: An exploratory review. *Annals of Sex Research, 2,* 283–306.

Morse, C. R. (1989). Exploring the bisexual alternative: A view from another closet (Master's thesis, University of Arizona, 1989). *Master's Abstracts, 28*(2), 320.

Nahas, R., & Turley, M. (1979). *The new couple: Women and gay men.* New York: Seaview Books.

Nichols, M. (1988). Bisexuality in women: Myths, realities, and implications for therapy. In E. Cole, & E. Rothblum (Eds.), *Women and sex therapy: Closing the circle of sexual knowledge* (pp. 235–252). New York: Harrington Park Press.

Norris, S., & Read, E. (1985). *Out in the open: People talking about being gay or bisexual.* London: Pan Books.

Nunberg, H. (1938). Homosexuality, magic and aggression. *International Journal of Psychoanalysis, 19,* 1–16.

Nunberg, H. (1947). Circumcision and problems of bisexuality. *International Journal of Psychoanalysis, 28,* 145–179.

Nurius, P. S. (1983). Mental health implications of sexual orientation. *Journal of Sex Research, 19*(2), 119–136.

Ochs, R. (1994). *The International Directory of Bisexual Groups* (11th ed.). Cambridge Ma: Bisexual Resource Center.

Off Pink Collective. (1988). *Bisexual lives.* London: Off Pink Publishing.

Opler, M. (1965). Anthropological and cross cultural aspects of homosexuality. In J. Marmor (Ed.), *Sexual inversion: The multiple roots of homosexuality* (pp. 108–123). New York: Basic Books.

Paul, J. P. (1983/1984). The bisexual identity: An idea without social recognition. *Journal of Homosexuality, 9*(2/3), 45–64.

Paul, J. P. (1985). Bisexuality: Reassessing our paradigms of sexuality. *Journal of Homosexuality, 11*(1/2), 21–34.

Playboy readers' sex survey (Part three). (1983, May). *Playboy Magazine,* pp. 126–128, 136, 210–220.

Plummer, K. (1981). Going gay: Identities, life styles and life cycles in the male gay world. In J. Hart & D. Richardson (Eds.), *The theory and practice of homosexuality* (pp. 93–110). London: Routledge & Kegan Paul.

Ponse, B. (1978). *Identities in the lesbian world: The social construction of self.* Westport, CT: Greenwood Press.

Ponse, B. (1980). Lesbians and their worlds. In J. Marmor (Ed.), *Homosexual behavior: A modern reappraisal* (pp. 157–175). New York: Basic Books.

Prine, K. A. (1987). Gay men: The open behavioral expression of sexual orientations and descriptions of psychological health (Doctoral dissertation, University of Cincinnati, 1987). *Dissertation Abstracts International, 48*(4), 1185B.

Rado, S. (October, 1940). A critical examination of the concept of bisexuality. *Psychosomatic Medicine, II*(4), 459–467.

Read, K. E. (1980). *Other voices: The style of a male homosexual tavern.* Novato, CA: Chandler & Sharp Publishers.

Reinhardt, R. U. (1985). Bisexual women in heterosexual relationships: A study of psychological and sociological patterns (Doctoral dissertation, The Professional School of Psychological Studies, San Diego, 1985). *Research Abstracts International, 11*(3), 67.

Reiss, A. J. (1961). The social integration of queers and peers. *Social Problems, 9,* 102–120.

Ritvo, L. B. (1990). *Darwin's influence on Freud: A tale of two sciences.* New Haven, CT: Yale University Press.

Ross, H. L. (1971). Modes of adjustment of married homosexuals. *Social Problems, 18,* 385–393.

Ross, M. W. (1979). Heterosexual marriage of homosexual males: Some associated factors. *Journal of Sex and Marital Therapy, 5,* 142–150.

Ross, M. W. (1983). *The married homosexual man: A psychological study.* London: Routledge & Kegan Paul.

Ross, M. W. (1990). Toward a synthetic understanding of sexual orientation. In D. P. McWhirter, S. A. Sanders, & Reinisch (Eds.), *Homosexuality/*

heterosexuality: Concepts of sexual orientation (pp. 267–276). New York: Oxford University Press.

Ross, M. W. (1991). A taxonomy of global behavior. In R. A. P. Tielman, M. Carballo, & A. C. Hendriks (Eds.), *Bisexuality and HIV/AIDS: A global perspective*, (pp. 21–26). Buffalo, NY: Prometheus Books.

Ross, M. W., & Paul, J. P. (1992). Beyond gender: The basis of sexual attraction in bisexual men and women. *Psychological Reports, 71*, 1283–1290.

Rubenstein, M. (1982). *An in-depth study of bisexuality and its relationship to self-esteem.* Unpublished doctoral dissertation, The Institute for Advanced Study of Human Sexuality, San Francisco.

Rubenstein, M., & Slater, C. A. (1985). A profile of the San Francisco Bisexual Center. *Journal of Homosexuality, 11*(1/2), 227–230.

Ruitenbeek, H. M. (1963). The male homosexual and the disintegrated family. In H. M. Ruitenbeek (Ed.), *The problem of homosexuality in modern society,* (pp. 80–93). New York: E. P. Dutton.

Ruitenbeek, H. M. (1973). The myth of bisexuality. In H. M. Ruitenbeek (Ed.), *Homosexuality: A changing picture* (pp. 199–204). London: Souvenir Press.

Rust, P. C. (1992). The politics of sexual identity: Sexual attraction and behavior among lesbian and bisexual women. *Social Problems, 39*(4), 366–386.

Rust, P. C. (1993). "Coming out" in the age of social constructionism: Sexual identity formation among lesbian and bisexual women. *Gender and Society, 7*(1), 50–77.

Saghir, M. T., & Robins, E. (1973). *Male and female homosexuality: A comprehensive investigation.* Baltimore: Williams & Wilkins.

Saliba, P. A. (1980). *Variability in sexual orientation.* Unpublished master's thesis, San Francisco State University.

Schafer, S. (1976). Sexual and social problems of lesbians. *Journal of Sex Research, 12*(1), 50–79.

Schuster, R. (1987). Sexuality as a continuum: The bisexual identity. In The Boston Lesbian Psychologies Collective (Ed.), *Lesbian psychologies: Explorations and challenges* (pp. 56–71). Urbana, IL: University of Illinois Press.

Scott, J. (1978). *Wives who love women.* New York: Walker and Company.

Shively, M., & De Cecco, J. (1977). Components of sexual identity. *Journal of Homosexuality, 3*(1), 41–48.

Shively, M. G., Jones, C., & De Cecco, J. P. (1983/1984). Research on sexual orientation: Definitions and methods. *Journal of Homosexuality, 9*(2/3), 127–136.

Simon, W., & Gagnon, J. H. (1967). The lesbians: A preliminary overview. In J. H. Gagnon & W. Simon (Eds.), *Sexual deviance* (pp. 247–284). New York: Harper & Row.

Socarides, C. W. (1972). Homosexuality: Basic concepts and psychodynamics. *International Journal of Psychiatry, 10*(1), 118–125.

Socarides, C. W. (1978). *Homosexuality,* New York: Jason Aronson.

Sommers, M. A. (1982). The relationship between present social support networks and current levels of interpersonal congruency of gay identity (Doctoral dissertation, California School of Professional Psychology, Los Angeles, 1982). *Dissertation Abstracts International, 43*(6), 1962B.

Sophie, J. (1985/1986). A critical examination of stage theories of lesbian identity development. *Journal of Homosexuality, 12*(2), 39–51.

Spada, J. (1979). *The Spada report: The newest survey of gay male sexuality.* New York: New American Library.

Stekel, W. (1922/1946a). *Bi-sexual love.* New York: Emerson Books.

Stekel, W. (1922/1946b). *The homosexual neurosis.* New York: Emerson Books.

Stoller, R. J. (1972). The "bedrock" of masculinity and femininity: Bisexuality. *Archives of General Psychiatry, 26,* 207–212.

Storms, M. D. (1980). Theories of sexual orientation. *Journal of Personality and Social Psychology, 38*(5), 783–792.

Sulloway, F. J. (1979). *Freud, biologist of the mind: Beyond the psychoanalytic legend.* New York: Basic Books.

Szasz, T. S. (1965). Legal and moral aspects of homosexuality. In J. Marmor (Ed.), *Sexual inversion: The multiple roots of homosexuality* (pp. 124–139). New York: Basic Books.

Szasz, T. S. (1970). *The manufacture of madness: A comparative study of the inquisition and the mental health movement.* New York: Dell.

Thornton, N. (1948). Why American homosexuals marry. *Neurotica, 1*(1), 24–28.

Tielman, R. A. P., Carballo, M., & Hendriks, A. C. (Eds.), (1991). *Bisexuality and HIV/AIDS: A global perspective.* Buffalo, NY: Prometheus Books.

Troiden, R. R. (1979). Becoming homosexual: A model of gay identity acquisition. *Psychiatry, 42,* 362–373.

Troiden, R. R. (1988). *Gay and lesbian identity: A sociological analysis.* Dix Hills, NY: General Hall.

Troiden, R. R., & Goode, E. (1980). Variables related to the acquisition of a gay identity. *Journal of Homosexuality, 5*(4), 383–392.

Twining, A. (1983). Bisexual women: Identity in adult development (Doctoral dissertation, Boston University School of Education, 1983). *Dissertation Abstracts International, 44*(5), 1340A.

Twitchell, J. (1974). Sexual liberality and personality: A pilot study. In J. R. Smith & L. G. Smith (Eds.), *Beyond monogamy: Recent studies of sexual alternatives in marriage* (pp. 230–245). Baltimore: Johns Hopkins University Press.

Vance, B. K. (1977). Female homosexuality: A social psychological examination of attitudinal and etiological characteristics of different groups (Doctoral dissertation, Oklahoma State University, 1977). *Dissertation Abstracts International, 39,* 451B.

Warren, C. A. B. (1974). *Identity and community in the gay world.* New York: John Wiley & Sons.

Warren, C. (1980). Homosexuality and stigma. In J. Marmor (Ed.), *Homosexual behavior: A modern reappraisal* (pp. 123–141). New York: Basic Books.

Wayson, P. D. (1985). Personality variables in males as they relate to differences in sexual orientation. *Journal of Homosexuality, 11*(1/2), 63–74.

Weinberg, G. (1972). *Society and the healthy homosexual.* New York: St. Martin's Press.

Weinberg, M. S., & Williams, C. J. (1974). *Male homosexuals: Their problems and adaptations.* New York: Penguin Books.

Weinberg, M. S., Williams, C. J., & Pryor, D. W. (1994). *Dual attraction: Understanding bisexuality.* New York: Oxford University Press.

Weinberg, T. S. (1977). Becoming homosexual: Self-discovery, self-identity, and self-maintenance (Doctoral dissertation, University of Connecticut, 1977). *Dissertation Abstracts International, 38*(1), 506A.

Weininger, O. (1903/1908). *Sex and character.* London and New York: W. Heinemann & G. P. Putnam's Sons.

Weise, E. R. (Ed.). (1992). *Closer to home: Bisexuality and feminism.* Seattle: Seal Press.

Weiss, E. (1958). Bisexuality and ego structure. *International Journal of Psychoanalysis, 39,* 91–97.

Whitney, C. (1990). *Uncommon lives: Gay men and straight women.* New York: Plume Books.

Wolf, D. G. (1979). *The lesbian community.* Berkeley: University of California Press.

Wolf, T. J. (1985). Marriages of bisexual men. *Journal of Homosexuality, 11*(1/2), 135–148.

Wolf, T. J. (1987). Group counseling for bisexual men. *Journal for Specialists in Group Work, 11,* 162–165.

Wolf, T. J. (1992). Bisexuality: A counseling perspective. In S. H. Dworkin & F. J. Gutierrez (Eds.), *Counseling gay men and lesbians: Journey to the end of the rainbow* (pp. 175–187). Alexandria, VA: American Association for Counseling and Development.

Wolff, C. (1971). *Love between women.* New York: St. Martin's Press.

Wolff, C. (1979). *Bisexuality: A study.* London: Quarter Books.

Wooden, W., & Parker, J. (1982). *Men behind bars: Sexual exploitation in prison.* New York: Plenum Press.

Zinik, G. A. (1984). The relationship between sexual orientation and eroticism, cognitive flexibility, and negative affect (Doctoral dissertation, University of California, Santa Barbara, 1983). *Dissertation Abstracts International, 45*(8), 2707B.

Zinik, G. A. (1985). Identity conflict or adaptive flexibility? Bisexuality reconsidered. *Journal of Homosexuality, 11*(1/2), 7–19.

4

Issues of Sexual Identity
in an Ethnic Minority:
The Case of Chinese American
Lesbians, Gay Men,
and Bisexual People

Connie S. Chan

This chapter concerns sexual identity formation in the context of a bicultural background in which one of the cultures is non-Western. Much contemporary thinking about identity comes from psychology, anthropology, sociology, and more recently, cultural studies and focuses on identity as a self-definition and as a social construction. Theoretical models of sexual identity development have come from a Western tradition and have not accounted for cultural differences in approaches to sexuality (including sexual expression) and sexual identity. It is inaccurate to generalize about people of color as a homogeneous group, or to group non-Western cultures together; however, the issues addressed in this chapter, focusing on one bicultural group of Chinese Americans, may apply to other ethnic minority groups.

Since so little research has been done on the issue of sexual identity and sexuality in a non-Western cultural context, this chapter raises questions which can be addressed by social scientists and cultural historians in pursuit of understanding sexual identity formation. This chapter summarizes the historical background of the development of the concept of sexual identity in the West and examines psychological models of homosexual/ethnic minority identity development. Exploring cultural differences in sexual expression, sexuality, and sexual identity for Chinese Americans and other ethnic minority groups, it also raises questions to be addressed in future research.

Although identity is a fluid concept in psychological and sociological terms, we tend to speak of fixed identities. In particular, those aspects of identity which characterize observable physical characteristics, such as race or gender, are viewed as unchanging ascribed identities. Examples of these include identifications such as a Chinese woman or an African-American man, or even broader terms such as woman of color and man of color. These constructions of identity are based on physical appearance and an individual's declaration of identity. However, even these seemingly clear distinctions are not definitive. In the context of identities based on racial and physical characteristics, ascribed identities will, rightly or wrongly, continue to be attributed to individuals by others. It is left up to the individual to assert personal identity and demonstrate it to others.

The definition of *sexual* identity is more ambiguous still, whether taken as a concept by itself or in context with cultural, racial, ethnic, or gendered identities. With sexual identity, it is generally those individuals who are considered "sexual minorities," such as lesbians, gay men, and bisexual persons, who define and declare their sexual identities. Unless there is a specific focus on sexual orientation, few in the "majority" self-consciously identify as heterosexuals. Given the assumption of heterosexuality in American society, acknowledging a sexual identity is an inherently political statement.

Even if it is one identity among several, and it is not given priority over racial, ethnic, or gendered identities, individuals who declare a nonmajority sexual identity become identified primarily in terms of this sexual identity. It is because of this "primacy effect" of transgressive sexual identity that lesbians, gay men, and bisexuals of color may be reluctant to take on a sexual identity. A declaration of lesbian/gay/bisexual identity can overshadow their racial/ethnic identity, and the latter identity generally affords a powerful sense of social belonging and group affiliation.

In research on Latina lesbians, and on Asian–American lesbians and gay men, respectively, Espin (1987) and Chan (1989) found that most preferred to be validated for both their ethnic and their lesbian/gay identities. Nonetheless, they were perceived as being primarily lesbian/gay once their sexual identities became known. These respondents felt that their ethnic/racial identities as Latina or Asian–American, as well as their gendered identities, were negated following disclosure of sexual orientation. Cultural background plays a major role in determining how an individual integrates sexuality into his or her sense of identity. Non-Western cultures such as East Asian cultures do not have the same concept of sexual identity as the European–American tradition. The models of sexual identity development and the paradigms of identity for the individual self may not be applicable for individuals who have non-Western cultural backgrounds. Indeed, one can ask whether Western sexual identity paradigms are applicable to people of color at all. Some researchers have already questioned whether the categories of sexual identity and sexual behavior are accurate in describing people of color, noting that black and hispanic men who are categorized as "homosexual" or "bisexual" by Anglos do not necessarily identify themselves as such (Alonso & Koreck, 1993; Hammonds, 1987; Morales, 1989; Worth & Rodriguez, 1987). Anthropologists Alonso and Koreck (1993) note that,

> Anglo-American sexual distinctions—"heterosexual", "bisexual", and "homosexual"—which have been reified . . . are neither universal nor natural but instead socio-culturally and historically produced categories which cannot be presumed to be applicable to U.S. minority groups or to other societies. (p. 114)

A framework will be presented which can be used to examine sexual expression and the formation of a sexual identity for people of color within the specificity of a particular ethnic group's cultural norms and values. Since sexuality is related to the meanings given to erotic feelings and actions in a specific culture, the range of sexual behaviors which are considered acceptable, the forms of sexual expression, who may express which forms of sexuality, as well as what is perceived as deviation are all factors that must be considered in understanding the formation of sexual identity (Greene, 1994).

The Western Model of Sexual Identity

The concept of sexual identity first emerged in the work of European physicians in the late nineteenth century. Their observations and subsequent categorizations of sexual behaviors—previously the province of religious and moral authorities—moved the study of sexual behaviors into a "science." It was von Krafft-Ebing's *Psychopathia Sexualis*, published in many editions between 1886 and 1901, which first described extensive categories of sexualities (von Krafft-Ebing, 1965).

Krafft-Ebing's main contribution was to stimulate much interest in examining sexual "perversions," including homosexuality. Homosexuality was defined as a sexual condition that affects some individuals who engage in sexual activity with others of the same sex.

As interest in the existence of homosexuality developed among sexologists and others in the medical profession, it became necessary to describe the norms from which homosexuality represented a deviation. Thus, the concept of heterosexuality was invented to describe normality. This also generated some interest in other sexual behaviors outside of the male heterosexual norm, including female sexuality, child and adolescent sexuality, and bisexuality, among others. The development of sexology as a field of inquiry into sexual behavior gained acceptance as it became medicalized, creating medical norms about "proper" sexual activity, interest, and expression. This attention helped legitimize the study of sexual activity, but also restricted "normal" sexual activity to male heterosexual expression. Even more restrictive norms for heterosexual female sexuality emerged, representing a precursor to future efforts at controlling women's bodies, including access to birth control and abortion. Weeks (1989) points out that,

> Sexology, then, is not merely descriptive. It is at times profoundly prescriptive, telling us what we ought to be like, what makes us truly ourselves and "normal." It is in this sense that the sexological account of sexual identity can be seen as an imposition, a crude tactic of power designed to obscure a real sexual diversity within the myth of a sexual destiny. (p. 37)

Sexual Identity versus Sexual Activity in the Context of Culture

Erotic activity between men and between women was known prior to the late nineteenth century, but it had never been explicitly named and defined before. Previously, homosexual activity existed as simple action. Not until the emergence of a homosexual identity did individuals perceive their behavior as reflecting a core part of their personhood. Foucault's (1990) famous analysis illustrates the transition:

> The nineteenth-century homosexual became a personage, a past, a case history, and a childhood, in addition to being a type of life, a life form, and a morphology, with an indiscreet anatomy and possibly a mysterious physiology. Nothing that went into his total composition was unaffected by his sexuality. It was everywhere present in him: at the root of all his actions because it was their

insidious and indefinitely active principle; written immodestly on this face and body because it was a secret that always gave itself away. It was consubstantial with him, less as a habitual stance than as a singular nature. (p. 17)

The Male Homosexual

Among men, there has long been some differentiation between men who were exclusively homosexual, men who were exclusively heterosexual, and those who maintained a heterosexual appearance while engaging in sex with other men. Studies of American and European homosexuality from the eighteenth century to the middle of the twentieth century suggest that it was gender identity—whether one looks like and acts like a man or a woman—that marked one as being "odd" or "queer." Clear signs of a distinctive homosexual life-style and identity could be identified in the latter part of the nineteenth century in part of Europe and America (Bray, 1982; Weeks, 1977). Living in a separate clandestine society of male homosexual contact in bars, clubs, and other meeting places, such men did recognize themselves as "sexual outlaws" afflicted, perhaps, with a medical and pathological condition. Unlike lesbians, their existence was always acknowledged.

The Female Homosexual

European and American women, on the other hand, had no publicly acknowledged sexuality beyond that of their roles as wives and mothers. It was not until the rise of the New Woman (first generation born between the late 1850s and the early 1900s) that bourgeois women could leave home, become educated, establish careers, and make alternative family lives with a woman companion or female friends. However, since women did not have sexual identities—and indeed some saw their purity as an example of the superior morality of their sex—it is unlikely that their deep friendships included sexual contact. It was the New Women of the post-World War I generation of the 1920s who were able to rebel and to assert their sexuality. Heterosexuals bobbed their hair and became the infamous flappers. Women who desired members of their own sex had a different problem: how to assert a sexuality when no models of lesbian sexuality existed. The most obvious way to be sexual as well as independent was to take on a masculine identity, dressing and behaving as a Mannish Woman (Newton, 1989; Smith-Rosenberg, 1989). These women, whom Newton describes as "our bourgeois women ancestors," defined a new sexual identity based on the idea that women, apart from men, could have autonomous sexual feeling. These women set the stage for a future lesbian woman's identity.

As the mid-1940s brought about increased urbanization and meeting places for homosexuals, the homophile movement of the 1950s and 1960s arose. Later still, the women's liberation movement and the Stonewall rebellion of the late 1960s created a social and political gay political movement in the United States and Europe. In the 1960s and 1970s, along with a new literature describing the male gay and lesbian experiences (written by openly identified gay men and lesbians), a lesbian and male gay identity began to develop along with a political group identification (see D'Augelli & Garnets in this volume).

A Lesbian and Gay Identity Model

Defining and declaring one's homosexual identity has been likened to "discovering a map to explore a new country" (D'Emilio, 1983). Choosing an out-of-the-norm sexual identity by identifying as lesbian or gay, individuals declare a separateness and individuality as a member of a self-defined sexual minority group. These declarations of identity are internal in a psychological sense, but also external and group-based in a political and social sense. These identifications created an identity politics which were crucial in the making of a gay/lesbian movement as well as a civil rights movement. Much as ethnic minority people of color defined themselves in the 1960s and 1970s, lesbians and gay men, by identifying and declaring a sexual minority status, defined themselves in a new category as a means of empowerment and group cohesion. To achieve this empowerment, both sexual minorities and racial minorities accentuate aspects of their lives which had been viewed as negative and stigmatized (one's race or one's homosexuality), and express pride, not shame, in their formerly devalued status.

Individuals who accept a previously stigmatized identity generally pass through several stages of development en route to embracing their new identities. Cass' (1979) model of homosexual identity formation has been frequently cited as describing the developmental process through which an individual develops an integrated lesbian or gay identity. Cass' six stages start with the premise that an individual begins with an initial self-awareness that some of his/her feelings and behaviors can be defined as homosexual, creating conflict with a previous sexual (and perhaps social) identity that had been defined as heterosexual. From this basic premise of self-awareness, an individual goes through stages of accepting, having pride in, and finally, integrating a lesbian/gay identity with other aspects of self. This model, while presented as a general framework, does not exist within a vacuum, and it presupposes favorable social conditions which allow for the affiliation and identification to occur. In stages four and five, for instance, individuals seeking identity acceptance have increased contact with other homosexuals and immerse themselves in homosexual culture and community. A lesbian/gay presence in some urban areas allows this to occur far more readily than in places where neither a homosexual culture nor a lesbian/gay community exists.

Investigators of ethnic minority sexual identity question whether the Western model of sexual identity implicit in such stages is applicable to non-Western cultures. Morales (1983, 1992) proposes that *states* rather than *stages* may be more useful to reflect the experiences of Latino gay men and Latina lesbians, who may experience several different states at the same time, unlike a stage model where resolution of one stage leads to another. Morales' model (1992) describes five states, which start with a denial of conflicts (in sexual and racial identities), and expresses a preference for a bisexual rather than gay/lesbian identity. In Cass' model, this may be viewed as a conflict of sexual identity formation; for ethnic minorities, a bisexual identity has different meanings, even for an individual who may have sex exclusively with same-sex partners. Since the lesbian/gay community is often perceived as exclusively white, a Latino or Latina may self-identify as bisexual rather than as gay or lesbian (Morales, 1992). In the latter states of Morales' model, Latino gays or Latina lesbians attempt to shift the conflict from a monocultural perspective (either Latino *or* lesbian and gay) to a multicultural dimension in which their lives can be viewed as containing multiple identities. For other nonhegemonic cultural groups such as African–Americans or Chinese–Americans, these identities do not appear to be as specifically defined. Attempts may be made to integrate different behaviors into a sense of self, but the integration of a sexual *identity* may not exist as it does for members of the dominant culture.

Moreover, a sexual identity is not merely the naming of one's perception of one's own sexuality or sexual expression, but is also a political identity. There are individuals who do not consider themselves lesbian or gay who engage in sexual activity with same-sex partners; there are also individuals who consider themselves lesbian or gay who do not have sexual contact with same-sex partners. What was once known as a homosexual identity has developed into a lesbian/gay identity as sexual orientation became a strategy for group formation, cohesion, and addressing discrimination. In the context of identity politics, a lesbian and gay identity developed into a form of resistance against conformity and restriction. The trend toward queer theory and culture takes this resistance one step further by refusing to fit into the fixed categories of heterosexual, homosexual, or bisexual and creating a greater flexibility in sexual politics and naming sexual identity.

The Question of Sexuality Identity
for Chinese–Americans

The significance of the naming is crucial to the construction of a sexual identity. The following analysis of Chinese–Americans is intended to demonstrate the complexities of this process of naming. In their Asian cultures of origin, Chinese–American lesbians, gay men, and bisexuals do not have the semantic categories available to Western women and men to define themselves. The development of a gay/lesbian identity and movement has been hindered not only by the lack of categories but also by a fundamental difference in the construction of sexuality, sexual expression, and sexual identity, as well as identity itself, in Chinese culture. This conceptual difference may explain why there is no concept of a sexual identity as we know it in the Western sense.

What do we know of homosexual practice in Chinese culture? There is evidence of male homosexual activity within traditional Chinese and East Asian culture, both in literature and in governmental policy. Third- and fourth-century B.C. texts include numerous biographies of major figures of the period that make plain their homosexuality. It was not until the seventeenth century, however, that homoerotic literature came into its own and flourished in China. Historian Vivien Ng describes how, during the seventeenth century, many references were made to homosexuality in erotic literature as well as in scholarly works. These works described male homosexual activity as between "bond brothers" where the younger "brother" lives with his elder "brother" and is provided for, including expenses incurred when the younger brother marries (Ng, 1989). Ng states that "It appears that male homosexuality was tolerated as long as it was not an exclusive sexual expression and the men fulfilled their procreative duties. On the other hand, tolerance meant, at best, a neutral attitude. Biographies of the period do not celebrate homosexual relationships in any way" (p. 77). In the mid-seventeenth century, as the Manchus established the Qing dynasty in China, they believed in using the penal code to shape the state and control behavior. Following the Confucian values of each member of society knowing her/her role and performing it accordingly, they insisted that men and women must follow their prescribed roles as husbands and fathers, wives and mothers, without deviation. Homosexuality was seen as a violation of this Confucian principle, and a law prohibiting consensual sodomy between adults was enacted to bolster traditional gender roles. While it is unclear whether this law was effective in regulating male sexuality, it did serve notice to the public that homosexuality was no longer considered a private matter (Ng, 1989). There is little mention of female homosexuality during this same time period. Ng suggests that the state regarded male homosexuality as, a worse evil than unchaste female behavior—probably because only males could carry on the family name and it was considered imperative that they fulfill their filial duty to sire sons. Seen in this light, male homosexuality (that is, nonprocreative sexual activity) was viewed as a direct challenge to the requirements of filial piety. Unchaste women, on the other hand, did not threaten the continuation of family name; they could be replaced and their reproductive function taken over by other women. (p. 89)

While sexism and different standards of behavior account for less interest in female homosexuality, it is possible that some sexual activity between women occurred in private, with no written evidence.

Private and Public Expressions of Self and Sexuality

A crucial distinction between traditional Chinese culture and Western culture is the concept of sexuality and sexual expression as a private matter. Any direct and open discussion of sexuality is unusual in Chinese culture. Even among one's closest friends, a discussion about sexuality is highly embarrassing at best and, at worst, strictly taboo (Tsui, 1985). This extreme discomfort with open and direct discussion of sexuality among Chinese–Americans is sometimes misconstrued by Westerners as asexuality or repression of sexual interest. However, what is presented publicly is very different from what is tolerated and expressed in private with sexual intimates.

The distinction between a private and public self is a core concept in Chinese culture. The public self conforms to gendered and familial role expectations and seeks to avoid actions that would bring shame not only on oneself but also on one's family. Within the Chinese part of a Chinese–American's culture, there is little support for an *individual* public identity of any kind beyond the role one is expected to play within the family. As a psychological concept of self-definition, an individual's identity, forged against a backdrop of societal forces may be perceived as being universal but is, in fact, a Western concept. In East Asian cultures such as Chinese, Japanese, and Thai, the concept of individual identity, whether by self-definition or ascribed, may not exist. Instead there is only a group identification and an identity as a family member, a social role which is related to an assignment of one's place in society. A linguistic example of this lack of individuality outside of the family role may best illustrate this point. In both Cantonese and Mandarin, the main languages of China, individuals are rarely called or referred to by their given names but are consistently named only by their family role of first daughter, second son, big sister, little brother, or fourth paternal aunt, to the extent that an individual's exact position in the hierarchy of the family structure is described by what she or he is called. A relative's exact relationship is signified by his or her "name," with different terms for relatives on the maternal and paternal side along with attached numbers indicating birth order from eldest to youngest.

Much as there is no identity outside of the family role, there is no concept of a sexual identity or of external sexual expression in Chinese culture beyond the familial expectation of procreation. Sexuality is rarely expressed in the context of one's public self, only within the private self. The private self is never seen by anyone other than an individual's most intimate family and friends (in some cases, a person may choose to never reveal a private self to anyone). The dichotomous nature of the public and private selves is far more distinct than in Western culture, where more fluidity exists between the two. The relevance of this public/private split within Chinese culture is that there is not only very little public expression of sexuality, but the private expressions of sexuality may take on different forms for Chinese–Americans than would be the norm in Western culture. One example of this is in erotic behavior, which may be expressed only privately and in far more indirect ways. Many such behaviors might be misperceived as nonerotic by Westerners unaccustomed to very subtle nuances such as a change in the register of two people having a conversation, minimal physical contact with the brush of a hand against another person, language patterns which might reflect affection but is nondiscernable to the casual observer, and quick visual glances perhaps holding the gaze just a second longer than might be expected. With private sexual expression, what one sees is not necessary what is being conveyed, unless one is familiar with the cultural nuances.

Sexual Expression in Asian Culture

The paradigms of Western sexual identity formation and sexuality must be adapted to understand the Chinese cultural influence on sexual expression in Chinese–Americans. While the lack of public expression of sexuality may be perceived as sexual conservatism, the roots of this conservative expression are not based on a philosophical rejection of the body (versus reason and intellect) or on religious morality, as is often the case in Western culture. Instead they are founded on the traditional Asian values of familial unity, which stresses family cohesion over individual desire or needs. Sexuality and homosexuality can be expressed only if they do not disrupt an individual's prescribed role within the family. As anthropologist Murray (1992) explains about men in Thailand,

> emotional relationships with women are not demanded—nor even expected—but heirs should be produced, and this is a sig-

nificant bar against exclusive homosexuality, especially in Asian cultures. . . . The tolerance for homosexual behavior so long as it does not become too consuming an interest or passion, and so long as it does not involve public gender deviance is far from acceptance of homosexual relations as being equal to or as important as procreative/familial relationships. There is no attempt in Thai law or in less formal means of social control to extirpate homosexual behavior, but to some extent this is because homosexuality is not taken seriously as a way of life. . . . (p. 33)

Murray illustrates this concept further by explaining that, in Pakistan, family life is the *only* way of life, and if a man takes care of his family's needs and produces children, what he may do for personal sexual satisfaction is irrelevant and is tolerated as long as it is kept private. He asserts that gay relationships (between men) are never the most important relationship for either partner—the family occupies that position—but can be satisfying if kept quiet and private (Murray, 1992).

These two examples illustrate non-Chinese Asian cultures (Thai and Pakistani); however, the cultural values are very similar, in terms of the importance of the family role, for a Chinese–American individual. With an uncertain identity as a person distinct from family membership, having a sexual identity or identifying with an alternative lifestyle may be literally inconceivable except to those who are much more acculturated into Western identity concepts. As a result, there is a common perception that proportionately fewer lesbian, gay, and bisexual Asian–Americans are "out" than non-Asians.

Asian–Americans who openly identify as being lesbian, gay, or bisexual, are likely to be more acculturated and to have been more influenced by American or Western culture. A study of lesbian/gay Asian–Americans supports this view, indicating that Asian–American lesbians and gay men, while preferring to be affirmed for both (sexual and ethnic) aspects of their identity, if forced to choose between affiliations, identified more closely with the lesbian/gay as well as American cultural aspects of their selves (Chan, 1989). This study's sample population of self-identified Asian–American lesbians and gay men was already skewed toward a more assimilated and Westernized population, since they considered themselves lesbian or gay. Even so, the results indicate that Asian–American lesbians and gay men respond to pressures from both their Asian and their American cultures. Respondents were more likely to come out to non-Asians than to other Asians (reflecting the pressure to maintain privacy within the Asian culture), and many had not disclosed their sexual identity to their parents, even though they had been out an average of six years. Responding to American expectations, some did report wanting to belong to a gay and lesbian community, and even sought out dates with white lesbians or gay men.

Other researchers have also found that it can be more difficult for ethnic minority individuals to come out as lesbian/gay, even if they self-identify as such (Espin, 1987; Greene, 1994; Morales, 1989) because of the perception that homosexuality is viewed as a "white" phenomenon. Loiacano (1989) observes that tasks related to gay identity development, such as choices about coming out to others, being involved with same-sex partners, and becoming politically active in the sexual minority community may be complicated by one's status as a black American. It follows that this process may be different for black Americans and other people of color than it is for white Americans.

Moreover, the lack of a discourse in which to explore sexual identity has been noted in African–American communities as well as Asian–American communities. One example is that of the response to AIDS in the African–American community, where there is a "profound silence regarding actual sexual practice, either heterosexual or homosexual, . . . largely because of the suppression of talk about sexuality generally and about male homosexuality in particular than that is enacted in Black communities through the discourses that constitute them" (Harper, 1993). Given the sexual myths and stereotypes about African–American men and women, one reaction might be an exaggerated need to demonstrate normality and to fit into the dominant culture's image of virile heterosexual models, while downplaying deviant images of effeminate men or masculine women (Greene, 1994).

Sexual Identity Formation for Ethnic Minority Individuals

Sexual identity is not an essential fixed given for any individual, nor is it developed within a vacuum. Concepts of lesbian and gay identity have evolved over a 200-year span in the West, heavily influenced by social and political conditions, from the initial sexual categories in sexology, to a male homosexual identity, to the New Woman, to lesbians, gays, bisexuals, and most recently "queer" identity. The modern homosexual identity remains a Western construct. There is no comparable sexual identity in Chinese culture.

For a Chinese woman in Beijing to have a lesbian identity, she has to define herself through Western cultural concepts. For a Chinese–American who is defining a sexual identity, she or he also must adapt Western models of sexuality and sexual expression to meet her/his own needs. At the same time, this individual will have to respond to Chinese cultural influences, which require a different set of demands on family responsibilities, privacy, and the forms of sexual expression that are considered to be acceptable. Weighing the Western pressure to come out and be openly gay against the Chinese cultural demand for privacy requires a balance among opposing forces. While some individuals may never openly admit or act on their homosexuality, others will embrace the Western model enthusiastically; still others will be openly lesbian/gay only in safe (generally non-Asian) environments.

However, the Chinese cultural restrictions on open expression of sexuality may create a diminished dichotomization of heterosexual versus homosexual behavior. Given the importance of the concept of having only a private expression of sexuality, there could actually be more allowance of fluidity within a sexual behavioral continuum. The cultural prohibition against having a definition or declaration of sexual orientation/identity may ironically result in a broader range of acceptable behaviors even as the public identities are more narrowly defined.

Social science research on lesbian and gay issues has focused on the evolution of people whose primary political and ethnic identification is as lesbian or gay, and who have been able to organize a multidimensional way of life on the basis of their sexual orientation. But we need to focus on *other* forms of homosexuality—other ways in which homosexual desire and behavior have been organized, understood, named, or left deliberately unnamed (Chauncey, 1989). We need to be careful not to view the evolution of a homosexual identity only through a Western lens, expecting that non-Western cultures, with modernization, will eventually follow the same course in achieving greater openness with homosexual behavior. Cultural differences in the construction of identity and in the expression of sexuality have to be taken into account. We are just beginning to know which questions to ask.

There is still little empirical information about sexuality, sexual identity, and sexual expression for Chinese–Americans and other non-Western ethnic minority groups. Future research questions will address important factors, specific to each cultural group, examining (1) modes of sexual expression, (2) constructions of sexual identity, (3) attitudes toward sexuality in the context of measuring cultural values and generational differences, (4) assimilation to majority values, (5) gender roles, (6) expectations of one's family of origin, (7) the economic role of the family, particularly for women and immigrants, (7) importance of procreation, (8) ties to the ethnic community, (9) assimilation and acculturation, and (10) the history of discrimination and oppression specific to that cultural group. By exploring sexuality in the context of these factors, the discourse is broadened for all individuals, as silences are broken and the range of sexual expression is more carefully articulated.

Since the issue of sexuality has been so private within many non-Western cultures, there is little knowledge of how ethnic minority individuals, forging identities within a Western culture, experience or express their homosexuality. The expression of sexuality in ethnic minority literature, film, and art gives us some clues, but we also need to study the attitudes and experiences of ethnic minority individuals across the lifespan, from adolescents developing an emergent sexuality to elders reflecting on their personal experiences. The very privateness of the concept of Chinese–American and other cultural groups about homosexuality has kept us in silence. We are now asking the questions, and it is also up to us to find the answers.

References

Alonso, A. M., & Koreck, M. T. (1993). Silences: "Hispanics," AIDS, and sexual practices. In H. Abelove, M. A. Barale, & D. M. Halperin (Eds.), *The lesbian and gay studies reader* (pp. 110–126). New York: Routledge.

Bray, A. (1982). *Homosexuality in Renaissance England.* London: Gay Men's Press.

Cass, V. C. (1979). Homosexual identity formation: A theoretical model. *Journal of Homosexuality, 4,* 219–235.

Chan, C. S. (1992). Cultural considerations in counseling Asian American lesbians and gay men. In S. Dworkin & F. Guitierrez (Eds.), *Counseling gay men and lesbians: Journey to the end of the rainbow* (pp. 115–124). Alexandria, VA: American Association for Counseling and Development.

Chan, C. S. (1989). Issues of identity development among Asian–American lesbians and gay men. *Journal of Counseling and Development, 68,* 16–20.

Chauncey, G. (1989). Christian brotherhood or sexual perversion? Homosexual identities and the construction of sexual boundaries in the World War I era. In M. Duberman, M. Vicinus, & G. Chauncey (Eds.), *Hidden from history: Reclaiming the gay and lesbian past* (pp. 294–317). New York: Meridian.

Cochran, S., Mays, V., & Leung, L. (1991). Sexual practices of heterosexual Asian–American young adults: Implications for risk of HIV infection. *Archives of Sexual Behaviors, 20,* 381–391.

D'Emilio, J. (1983). *Sexual politics, sexual communities. The making of a homosexual minority in the United States 1940–76.* Chicago and London: University of Chicago Press.

Espin, O. (1987). Issues of identity is the psychology of Latina lesbians: Explorations and challenges. In Boston Lesbians Psychologies Collective (Eds.), *Lesbian psychologies* (pp. 35–51). Urbana: University of Illinois Press.

Faderman, L. (1981). *Surpassing the love of men. Romantic love between women from the Renaissance to the present.* London: Junction Books.

Foucault, M. (1990). The perverse imagination. In E. Stein (Ed.), *Forms of desire: Sexual orientation and the social construction controversy* (pp. 11–23). New York: Routledge.

Greene, B. (1994). Ethnic-minority lesbians and gay men: Mental health and treatment issues. *Journal of Consulting and Clinical Psychology, 62,* 243–251.

Hammonds, E. (1987). Race, sex, AIDS: The construction of "Other." *Radical America, 20*(6), 28–36.

Harper, P. B. (1993). Eloquence and epitaph: Block nationalism and the homophobic impulse in responses to the death of Max Robinson. In E. Abelove, M. Bavole, & D. Halperin (Eds.), *The Lesbian and Gay Studies Reader.* (pp. 159–175). New York: Routledge.

Morales, E. S. (1989). Ethnic minority families and minority gays and lesbians. *Marriage and Family Review, 14,* 217–239.

Murray, S. (1992). The "underdevelopment" of modern/gay homosexuality in Mesoamerica. In K. Plummer (Ed.), *Modern homosexualities: Fragments of lesbian and gay experience* (pp. 29–38). London and New York: Routledge.

Newton, E. (1989). The mythic mannish lesbian: Radcliffe Hall and the new woman. In M. Duberman, M. Vicinus, & G. Chauncey (Eds.), *Hidden from history: Reclaiming the gay and lesbian past* (pp. 281–293). New York: Meridian.

Ng, V. (1989). Homosexuality and the state in late imperial China. In M. Duberman, M. Vicinus, & G. Chauncey (Eds.), *Hidden from history: Reclaiming the gay and lesbian past* (pp. 76–89). New York: Meridian.

Smith-Rosenberg, C. (1989). Discourses of sexuality and subjectivity: The new woman, 1870–1936. In M. Duberman, M. Vicinus, G. Chauncey (Eds.), *Hidden from history: Reclaiming the gay and lesbian past* (pp. 264–280). New York: Meridian.

Tsui, A. (1985). Psychotherapeutic considerations in sexual counseling for Asian immigrants. *Psychotherapy, 22,* 357–362.

von Krafft-Ebing, R. (1965). *Psychopathia sexualis.* New York: Stein and Day.

Weeks, J. (1977). *Coming out: Homosexual politics in Britain from the nineteenth century to the present.* London: Quartet.

Weeks, J. (1989). Questions of identity. In P. Caplan (Ed), *The cultural construction of sexuality* (pp. 31–51). London and New York: Routledge.

Worth, D., & Rodriguez, R. (1987). Latina women and AIDS. *Radical America, 20,* (6), 63–67.

5

Biological Perspectives on Sexual Orientation

J. Michael Bailey

The question of "biological" influences on human sexual orientation remains immensely controversial (see Barinaga, 1991). This stems, in part, from the inconclusive nature of the empirical evidence; however, the ambiguity of the scientific answers is only part of the problem. The question "Is homosexuality 'biological'?" has been subjected to many interpretations, often not clearly specified. Thus, this chapter has two main goals: first, to clarify some different meanings that have been attached to "biological" in the context of research on human sexual orientation, and second, to summarize research findings for the most pertinent meanings.

Before we consider alternative meanings of "biological," it is important to specify what is meant by sexual orientation and related terms such as heterosexual and homosexual. I use the term "sexual orientation" to refer to one's pattern of sexual attraction, to men or to women. Thus, men who are sexually attracted to women and women who are sexually attracted to men are "heterosexual" in their sexual orientation. Men who are attracted to men and women who are attracted to women have a "homosexual" orientation. Those who are attracted to both men and women have a "bisexual" orientation. Note that these are psychological rather than behavioral definitions. Thus, for example, the behaviorally heterosexual man who is attracted to both his wife and her brother is considered bisexual, and the teenage male prostitute who sells his body only for the purpose of buying gifts for his female love interest is heterosexual in orientation.

This is not the only possible meaning of sexual orientation. Some men who are sexually attracted to other men call themselves heterosexual. Some women who are less sexually attracted to women than to men call themselves lesbians. They are using these words to label what I call their "sexual identity," which I understand to be the identity that they desire for reasons other than the relative intensity of the sexual feelings for men versus women. For instance, a man who prefers sex with men may still identify himself as heterosexual, because he prefers heterosexual marriage or other aspects of life-style more common to heterosexuals (e.g., rearing children). A woman who prefers sex with men may adopt a lesbian identity as an expression of her emotional and political solidarity with lesbian feminists. In these cases sexual orientation and sexual identity, as these terms are used herein, are discordant. Some writers have emphasized the frequency of discordance between sexual identity, sexual orientation, and sexual behavior (Klein, 1990). In my research experience, however, men and women who label themselves "heterosexual" have almost always admitted to far greater sexual feelings toward and activity with the opposite sex. The opposite pattern has been true for those who call themselves "homosexual," particularly regarding recent patterns of feelings and behavior (as opposed, e.g., to feelings and behavior during adolescence). Nevertheless, these observations are based only on my own research experiences. The degree of concordance between sexual orientation, sexual identity, and sexual behavior is an important question that deserves far more systematic attention that it has received. I chose a psychological definition of sexual orientation for this chapter because it seems likely that sexual attraction is more closely linked to potential biological mechanisms than either sexual identity or sexual behavior, which are more susceptible to social processes (Le Vay, 1993). It also seems plausible that sexual orientation is more longitudinally stable than either sexual identity or sexual behavior; however, this remains an uninvestigated empirical question.

Alternative Construals of the "Biological" Question

Biological Determinism versus Free Will

The argument over whether homosexuality is "biological" or "freely chosen" is perhaps the most common and least productive version of the biology debate. It is common because participants on both sides believe that crucial moral answers hinge on its outcome. For instance, they argue that if homosexuality is biologically determined, and hence homosexuals could not have chosen heterosexuality, then it is unfair to judge their sexual behavior morally. The argument is unproductive for at least two reasons. First, its resolution is primarily a philosophical rather than an empirical matter, and scholars who have considered it at length generally (and legitimately) take a strong position independent of evidence (e.g., Money, 1988; Le Vay, 1993). Second, the rational link between the position that homosexuality is biologically determined and a sympathetic view of homosexuality is much more tenuous than commonly assumed. This is because all behavior is biologically determined, in one fundamental sense. Thus, if homosexuality (or heterosexuality) is excused on the grounds that it is biologically determined, all behavior, must be excused including behavior that should not be excused, such as dishonesty, theft, homophobia, or even genocide. These behaviors are also biologically determined, in the sense I now elaborate.

Most scientists are both (strict) determinists and materialists. Determinism, in its strict sense, implies that all present events (including mental states and behaviors) are completely caused by past events. Equivalently, given a configuration of events at Time A, there can be exactly one configuration of events at later Time B. Materialists believe that all causes and effects obtain in the material world, as opposed, for instance, to a nonmaterial "soul." Thus, a materialistic determinist acquainted with modern neuroscience believes (as I do) that all behavior is most proximately caused by brain states, and thus behavioral differences must be caused by brain differences. This is true even for socially acquired traits. For instance, there must be relevant brain differences between the group of people who have learned the quadratic theorem and the group who has not yet acquired this knowledge, though of course those brain differences are undoubtedly subtle. Future recitation of the theorem depends on activating the brain's "representation" of it. Thus, all behaviors are "biologically determined" in the sense that all events are caused, and behavioral events are caused by brain states, which are "biological." By these assumptions, the mere fact that Le Vay (1991) found a brain difference between homosexual and heterosexual men was unsurprising; such a difference has to exist. Because we are biological organisms, everything about us is traceable to biology. As John Money (1988) incisively noted: "The postnatal determinants that enter the brain through the senses by way of social communication and learning are also biological, for there is a biology of learning and remembering. That which is not biological is occult, mystical, or, to coin a term, spookological" (p. 50). To be sure, there are some more meaningful and interesting construals of the question "Is homosexuality 'biological'?," some of which are considered in the following. To encourage more responsible usage, I recommend referring to "biological" causes, influences, theories, or explanations (i.e., with quotation marks). This draws attention to the problematic term that has both numerous connotations and an uninformative literal meaning.

Innate versus Acquired

Most people participating in the "biology" debate have this version of the issue in mind, at least part of the time. As Lehrman (1970) noted, there are at least two interpretations of "innate." The interpretation of innate as genetic or heritable is the more restrictive of the two, and a discussion of that sense is deferred to the next section. A behavior is also said to develop innately to the extent that it develops in a uniform or fixed pattern without being learned. In this sense, innate signals an independence from, or perhaps a resistance to, psychosocial influences.

Studies in comparative psychology and ethology have shown that behaviors cannot simply be divided into those which are innate versus those which are acquired. For instance, Mineka et al. (1984) showed that rhesus monkeys acquired a fear of snakes by observing other monkeys react fearfully to a snake, and thus the fear is acquired. However, another study (Cook & Mineka, 1989) demonstrated that the monkeys did not acquire a fear of flowers, even though they had observed monkeys reacting fearfully to them (through videotape manipulation). They suggested that because snakes are dangerous to monkeys and flowers are not, rhesus monkeys have become "evolutionarily prepared" to learn fear of snakes easily through observation. Furthermore, since snakes are common in the monkeys' natural habitat, they are virtually guaranteed to acquire snake fear. Thus, in a sense, snake fear in rhesus monkeys is highly innate.

Given these complications, it is tempting to dismiss discussion of whether a characteristic such as homosexuality is "innate" or "acquired" as misguided, and instead to focus on elaborating the process of development. While it is certainly true that obtaining a full picture of development is more illuminating than determining the degree of innateness, the latter goal is also useful for organizing research to accomplish the former. Thus, diverse processes of acquisition such as operant and classical conditioning, imitation, and persuasion can be theoretically and empirically pitted against innate processes such as heredity and prenatal neuroendocrine development.

Genes versus Environment

The question "Is homosexuality 'biological'?" is often asked in the form "Is homosexuality genetic?" That the question is often not meant literally was recently evidenced on an American talk show in which a gay man with a heterosexual identical twin argued emphatically that sexual orientation is "genetic," seemingly oblivious to the contradictory nature of his own personal evidence. In fact, many people say "genetic" when they mean "innate," a problematic equation. For instance, if massive androgen injections given prenatally to a female fetus altered her sexual orientation, this would be an innate influence, but it would be entirely environmental. Conversely, there are conceivable developmental routes that involve the genes, but that most people would not consider innate. For instance, suppose a gene existed for feminine beauty, and furthermore, that boys with this trait were relatively likely to be treated in a way that fostered homosexuality. A quantitative genetic analysis would find homosexuality to be heritable, but the necessary developmental step would be psychosocial. A phenotypic (observable) difference between organisms is genetic, or heritable, to the extent that it is attributable to genetic differences between them, regardless of the intervening steps from genotype to phenotype.

Essentialism Versus Social Constructionism

During the past decade perhaps the most contentious version of the "biology" debate has been whether sexual orientation is a category universal (in some way) to every culture, or merely an arbitrary categorization that says more about the observer (or constructor) than the observed (e.g., Halperin, 1989). Social constructionists make much of historical accounts of Greece and Rome, in which sexual acts between men appear to have been much more common than they are in contemporary Western societies. Furthermore, they argue that there was no equivalent categorization in the ancient societies. In contrast, those labeled by the social constructionists as essentialists argue that there have probably been people whom we could identify as homosexual, bisexual, and heterosexual in all times and places. Boswell (1980, 1989, 1990) has argued persuasively that these categories have been recognized throughout the recorded history of Western civilization.

The essentialism–constructionist debate is fueled, in part, by the different ways in which the two sides use "homosexuality." Social constructionists emphasize cultural variation in incidence of homosexual behavior and in the way sexuality is treated linguistically. These issues are actually more pertinent to the social construction of sexual identity and sexual behavior than that of sexual orientation. Boswell (1990), however, has generally emphasized homosexuality and bisexuality as psychological attraction patterns.

But even granting the social constructionist premise that homosexuality (or for that matter heterosexuality) occurs in only some societies, it does not follow, as some constructionists believe (e.g., De Cecco, 1990), that "biological" investigations into sexual orientation are misguided. Given a society that has constructed the sexual categories "heterosexual" and "homosexual," there is still the question of why people may adopt one or the other label (or are so labeled by others). The categories "priest," "Sumo wrestler," and "Fortune 500 executive" are surely more socially constructed than "homosexual" or "heterosexual," but within any society in which they are meaningful, there are probably "biological" (i.e., innate or genetic) factors that contribute to the likelihood that one will be categorized within any one of them.

"Biological" Explanations of Sexual Orientation: The Empirical Evidence

The Neuroendocrine View

BACKGROUND

The most influential "biological" theory of sexual orientation is motivated by the observation that homosexuals have a sexual orientation identical to that of opposite-sex heterosexuals. Gay men and heterosexual women are sexually attracted to men; lesbians and heterosexual men are sexually attracted to women. The neuroendocrine theory of sexual orientation then, in simplistic and general form, is that the brains of gay men have something in common with those of heterosexual women, and similarly for lesbians and heterosexual men. Furthermore, according to this view, the relevant brain differences between men-preferring and women-preferring individuals are relatively innate, depending less on postnatal experience such as parental socialization than on patterns of hormonal exposure.

Before examining the neuroendocrine theory in detail, let us consider its plausibility on a priori grounds. First, children who become homosexual adults appear to display some behaviors more typical of the opposite sex. Gay men frequently (but not invariably) remember being relatively gender nonconforming in childhood—for example, being teased for being "sissies," preferring female playmates, and shunning rough sports (Bell et al., 1981; Grellert et al., 1982; Harry, 1983; Whitam, 1977). Prospective studies have shown that this association is not due to memory bias. A majority of extremely gender atypical boys become gay or bisexual adults (Green, 1987; Zuger, 1978), a far higher proportion than would be expected by chance. Similarly, lesbians recall being more masculine during childhood compared to heterosexual women (Bell et al., 1981), though there have unfortunately been no prospective longitudinal studies of tomboys. For both men and women, the association between sexual orientation and (recalled) childhood gender nonconformity is strong (though somewhat less so for women; Bailey & Zucker, 1993). This supports the idea that homosexuals have been subject to some influences more typical of the opposite sex and is thus consistent with a neuroendocrine hypothesis.

Doubtless some readers will cringe at the implication that a sexual orientation difference mirroring a sex difference is consistent with a "biological" theory. Aren't human sex differences in behavior caused by socialization differences? In fact, an immense body of research describes differences in the ways that boys and girls are socialized by parents, other adults, and peers. However, the vast majority of these studies cannot claim to show more than that boys and girls are treated differently. They cannot claim to show that this differential treatment makes *any* difference, much less that it makes *all* the difference. (The human sex differences literature is limited primarily by the difficulty of doing definitive research on etiological questions about sex differences, since it is rarely possible to separate "biological" and social influences; e.g., typical females are both "biologically" female and treated as females.) My own intuition is that both social and "biological" factors will be found necessary to account for many behavioral sex differences. In any case, advocates of neither nature nor nurture can honestly claim to have excluded the other side's explanation for any behavioral sex difference. Hence, the possibility of innate sex differences remains viable.

Indeed, sexual orientation may be an especially strong candidate for "biological" causation. This is because the most familiar social influences cannot plausibly be operating. Homosexuals are attracted to members of their own sex despite their (usually) heterosexual parents' example, and despite the punishment that they endure from peers and many other enforcers of social norms. Furthermore, prehomosexual boys are often gender nonconforming despite being socialized to the contrary and despite the punishment which often follows such behavior in males. Although some psychological theories circumvent these problems by emphasizing subtle aspects of parenting (e.g., Lidz, 1968), these theories have generated remarkably little empirical support (Bell et al., 1981; Siegelman, 1981). Moreover, insofar as such theories have garnered support, the direction of causation is ambiguous. For instance, consistent with Freudian theory, homosexual males do appear to have poorer childhood relationships with their fathers than do male heterosexuals (Bell et al., 1981). However, as Bell et al. have pointed out, it is possible that the fathers are reacting to the atypical childhood behaviors of the prehomosexual boys.

THE THEORY

The neuroendocrine theory of sexual orientation (Byne & Parsons, 1993; Ellis & Ames, 1987; Meyer-Bahlburg, 1984) posits that the sexual differentiation of brain structures affecting sexual orientation proceeds roughly analogously to the differentiation of morphological structures such as the external genitalia. Both male and female embryos start development identically. Sexual differentiation begins when the undifferentiated gonads develop into either ovaries or testes; male development is triggered by the sex determination gene on the Y chromosome. Later, the testes of the male fetus secrete two hormones that further masculine differentiation. Müllerian inhibiting substance (MIH) prevents the growth of the uterus and related structures, and in this sense is a defeminizing substance. In contrast, testosterone and other closely related substances (generally speaking, androgens) masculinize relevant structures, forming both the internal male sex organs and the external genitalia. For the most part, masculine development requires androgens, and without the action of androgens, feminine development occurs. This is evidenced most dramatically in 46,XY androgen-insensitivity syndrome, in which genetic males lack a gene needed to utilize androgens effectively, despite normal androgen levels. Individuals with this syndrome are evidently typical females, both anatomically and psychologically, with the exception of the internal reproductive organs, whose formation was blocked by MIH (Money, 1988).

The neuroendocrine theory of homosexuality hypothesizes that there are brain structures that sexually differentiate during prenatal and possibly early postnatal development, and that these structures determine sexual orientation toward males or toward females. Presumably, masculinization of the relevant brain structures in heterosexual men and homosexual women occurs because of relatively high levels of androgens, while development in a feminine direction requires a relative dearth of androgens (or relatively low sensitivity to androgens). The neuroendocrine view stresses the role of organizational, as opposed to activational, hormones. That is, androgens are hypothesized to affect the sexual differentiation of brain structures during critical periods of development. For instance, one cannot necessarily predict that in a homosexual man the differentiation of a brain structure in a feminine direction will be associated with a low level of circulating testosterone during adulthood. Indeed, that hypothesis is untenable given a large number of studies that show otherwise (Meyer-Bahlburg, 1984). It should be noted that the neuroendocrine theory makes rather strong predictions about the existence of relevant neural structures affecting sexual orientation in men and women. While the account of morphological differentiation provided above is generally accepted, the causes and extent of sexual differentiation of the human brain remain speculative.

Fortunately, the neuroendocrine theory does not merely rest on the analogy with morphological sexual differentiation. Four general areas of research have been used to support a neuroendocrine view of homosexuality: studies manipulating the sexual behavior of nonhuman animals, studies of humans with unusual patterns of hormone exposure, studies relating sexual orientation to traits thought to be innately sexually dimorphic, and direct neurophysiological studies of human sexual orientation.

STUDIES OF NONHUMAN ANIMALS

The study of other species, particularly rodents, has been immensely important in the development of a "biological" view of homosexuality (Adkins-Regan, 1988; Byne & Parsons, 1993; Meyer-Bahlburg, 1984). Perhaps the most influential animal model has been the rat. Typical female rats exhibit a posture called "lordosis" during sexual receptivity in response to appropriate tactile stimulation; lordosis allows male rats to achieve intromission and ejaculation. Typical male rats, in contrast, show high rates of mounting behavior. However, genetic males can be made to display lordosis by (surgically or chemically) castrating them prenatally or perinatally, then administering appropriate hormones during adulthood to activate the behavior. Similarly, genetic females can be made to exhibit a male pattern of sexual behavior by the perinatal administration of androgens and subsequent replacement of sex hormones in adulthood. The sexual differentiation of these behaviors has been shown to involve the preoptic, anterior, and ventromedial portions of the hypothalamus.

There is an important limitation of the rat findings as support for a neuroendocrine model for human sexual orientation (Atkins-Regan, 1988; Byne & Parsons, 1993; Meyer-Bahlburg, 1984). Human homosexuals do not clearly display a pattern of copulatory behavior typical of the opposite sex, with the exception of their sexual orientation. Homosexual men do not appear to show decreased mounting behavior, nor homosexual women an increase in mounting behavior, compared to their heterosexual counterparts. Conversely, the large majority of the rat studies have failed to assess preference for males versus females. Thus, the rat studies have focused on a dimension of behavior that is not clearly relevant to human sexual orientation. As Byne and Parsons (1993) have noted, when a neonatally castrated rat displays lordosis in response to mounting by another male, it is the mounted animal that has provoked the interest of psychoneuroendocrinologists, not the animal that initiated the contact. Yet if rat sexual behavior were directly analagous to human sexual orientation, the male who mounted the treated animal would be equally worthy of an explanation. There have, in fact, been experimental studies of the origins of preference for males versus females in rats (Brand et al., 1991, 1992) and ferrets (Martin & Baum, 1986; Stockman, Callaghan, & Baum, 1985; see also the review of this issue by Adkins-Regan, 1988). These studies have explored the consequences of either blocking the effects of androgens in male animals or administering androgens to female animals, prenatally or perinatally. In general, treated adult animals spend less time with animals of the opposite sex and more time with animals of the same sex. Though the behaviors in these studies appear to have more relevance to human sexual orientation than do studies of mounting or lordotic behavior, they are still uncomfortably distant from establishing a consistent interest in sexual contact with same-sex conspecifics.

What then has been the value, if any, of neuroendocrine studies of rodents and other nonhuman species? As Ruse (1988) has noted, these studies have had immense heuristic value in the specification of models for human sexual orientation. It was largely results of animal work that led researchers such as LeVay (1991) to focus on the anterior hypothalamus as the most promising area of the human brain to be causally related to sexual orientation. On the other hand, some scientists argue that some researchers have assumed too close a correspondence between the sexual behavior and related brain organization of rats and humans, thus leading themselves (and the field) astray (Gooren, 1990; Byne & Parsons, 1993). The ultimate gauge of the value of animal models for human sexual orientation will be the number of theoretically interesting, replicable findings that they generate, using human subjects.

STUDIES OF PRENATAL INFLUENCES IN HUMANS

For obvious reasons experimental studies of the effects of prenatal hormonal manipulations on humans are impossible. However, in some rare circumstances humans have been inadvertently exposed to unusual patterns of hormones in utero, as a result of either medical intervention or genetic anomalies. These "natural experiments" are potentially informative regarding the effects of hormones on the development of sex-dimorphic behavior such as sexual orientation.

Perhaps the most extensively studied condition has been congenital adrenal hyperplasia (CAH). CAH is a genetic autosomal recessive condition which prevents the production of sufficient quantities of cortisol to inhibit the release of adrenocorticotropic hormone (ACTH) and subsequent adrenal steroid synthesis. Affected individuals thus are exposed to high levels of androgens. The level of androgens is sufficient to cause some degree of masculinization of genitals in most females with the condition, enough so that the sex of the child is frequently ambiguous at birth. Some of these females have been reared as males, particularly prior to the 1950s, before corrective surgery was available, or because diagnosis of the condition was late. However, the large majority of such women are now assigned as females and given early surgery to feminize their genitals and ongoing hormonal therapy to prevent virilization.

A neuroendocrine theory of sexual orientation is supported by, and indeed seems to require, a finding of increased homosexuality among CAH females reared as women. There have been several studies of this issue. Ehrhardt, Evers, and Money (1968) reported that as many as half of their twenty-three CAH female subjects were bisexual (depending on the criteria). None was exclusively homosexual. This study was problematic because it included late-treated patients, who were notably masculine in appearance. In contrast, a study of eighteen late-treated CAH women found no reports of homosexual fantasy or experience (Lev-Ran, 1974). However, subjects in this study were from the Soviet Union, where intolerance of homosexuality was particularly high, possibly making subjects less open. Money et al. (1984) studied thirty women with early-treated CAH and found results similar to those of Ehrhardt et al. Of those for whom sexual history data were available, 48 percent were bisexual with respect to fantasy or behavior, significantly higher than a control group. The largest study to date on sexuality among CAH women, by Mulaikal et al. (9187; this paper contains some subjects studied by Money et al., 1984), found a 5 percent (4/80) rate of self-identification as "homosexual" or "bisexual." Unfortunately, these authors did not report the incidence of homosexual attraction, as distinct from behavior. Furthermore, fully 38 percent of the women in this sample gave insufficient data to ascertain sexual orientation. It is possible that those with homosexual feelings may have been overrepresented in that group. Dittmann et al. (1992) found increased homosexual versus heterosexual interest in thirty-four female CAH patients, compared to fourteen control sisters. Finally, in a recent abstract, Zucker et al. (1992) reported that a sample of twenty-nine CAH women had significantly less attraction to men and significantly more attraction to women than a control group consisting of their female relatives.

There is another body of CAH research which, though not directly concerned with sexual orientation, is quite relevant. This is the study of gender atypicality of female children with CAH. Since gender atypicality or gender nonconformity is a strong predictor of adult homosexuality, a finding that girls with CAH are, for instance, more tomboyish would provide indirect support for a neuroendocrine theory of homosexuality. Several studies have provided results suggesting that CAH girls are tomboyish in certain respects, particularly with respect to play patterns (Berenbaum & Hines, 1992; Ehrhardt et al., 1968; Ehrhardt & Baker, 1974). The most methodologically rigorous of these studies, by Berenbaum and Hines, compared CAH girls and boys with young male and female relatives on a free play paradigm, in which "feminine," "masculine," and "neutral" toys were equally available. CAH girls and boys and unaffected control boys were all much more likely to play with "masculine" toys and less likely to play with "feminine" toys than were control girls.

The literature regarding CAH and sexual orientation is inconclusive. Although most of the studies have found some evidence for increased homosexuality in CAH women, the largest study (Mulaikal et al., 1987) found relatively low rates. The link between CAH and some aspects of childhood gender nonconformity is more compelling, but this provides only indirect evidence for a neuroendocrine view of homosexuality. Furthermore, some have argued that even if CAH women have higher rates of homosexuality (or childhood gender nonconformity), a neuro-endocrine interpretation is unnecessary (Byne & Parsons, 1993; Bleier, 1984). This is because CAH females are often born with masculinized genitals which might very well affect parental attitudes or self-concept in important ways. However, it should be noted that Berenbaum and Hines found the degree of masculine toy preference in their CAH girls to be unrelated to the degree of genital virilization reported at diagnosis. Furthermore, parents of CAH and normal girls did not differ in their reports of behavior toward their daughters. Although studies of CAH have provided some promising results, and therefore may eventually provide definitive data on the question, they cannot now be invoked as conclusive evidence for either nature or nurture. For more conclusive findings, it will be necessary to study large samples of CAH females (as Mulaikal et al. did), comparing them to large control samples on detailed measures of sexual attraction (as some of the smaller studies did).

I have focused on CAH because it has been studied relatively frequently and because, of all the hormonal anomalies, it is closest to the neuroendocrine model of homosexual etiology. Other conditions have been mentioned as relevant for theories of sexual orientation, including androgen insensitivity, 5-alpha reductase deficiency, and prenatal exposure to synthetic hormones with androgenizing effects. However, androgen insensitivity and 5-alpha reductase deficiency are far less convincing than CAH as "natural experiments," because they do not clearly separate hormonal and experiential influences (Byne & Parsons, 1993; Money, 1988). For instance, androgen-insensitive XY individuals are effectively female in their hormonal influences. They are also raised as females, thus confounding social and "biological" influences. Female offspring of hormonally treated pregnancies are less problematic in this interpretive respect, but the results of relevant studies have been highly inconclusive (Byne & Parsons, 1993).

SEXUALLY DIMORPHIC TRAITS AND SEXUAL ORIENTATION

Another strategy for studying neuroendocrine hypotheses has been to compare homosexuals and heterosexuals on traits that are sexually dimorphic. Findings that homosexuals are somewhat intermediate between heterosexual men and women on these traits provide some support for a neuroendocrine theory of homosexuality, particularly if the relevant traits are plausibly thought to be innately sexually dimorphic. The rationale, often unstated, is that a pattern of hormonal influences causing a brain to differentiate homosexually is likely to have more general effects. These should result in a more gender atypical pattern of neural organization in some other respects, as well.

One characteristic that seemed promising in this respect was the luteinizing hormone (LH) response. Female rats show a surge of LH following secretion of estrogen, which triggers ovulation. In contrast, estrogen inhibits LH secretion in male rats. In rats this sex difference has been found to depend on the organizational effects of prenatal androgens (Gorski, 1966). Humans also show a sex difference in LH secretion following estrogen injections. Thus, great excitement initially greeted two reports that homosexual (but not heterosexual) men show a partial LH surge to the administration of estrogen (Dörner et al., 1975; Dörner, 1988; Gladue et al., 1984). These findings supported the possibility that male homosexuals have a "feminine brain."

However, it now appears that the LH data may be problematic as support for a neuroendocrine theory of homosexuality. Other studies have failed to replicate the finding of a partial LH surge in male homosexuals (Gooren, 1986a; Hendricks et al., 1989). These failures, by themselves, are not a fatal blow to the LH data, because they were all small studies, with insufficient statistical power to guarantee replication. More problematic is the work of Gooren (1986a, 1986b), who has demonstrated that the human sex difference in LH release is unlikely to reflect differences in neural organization. In an elegant series of experiments, Gooren studied male-to-female and female-to-male transsexuals, before and after hormonal therapy and sex reassignment surgery. He found that these individuals showed a pattern of LH response appropriate to their hormonal and/or gonadal sex; thus, LH response appears to be a function of circulating androgens. That is, pretreatment female-to-male and posttreatment male-to-female transsexuals showed the LH surge, while pretreatment male-to-female and posttreatment female-to-male transsexuals did not. Indeed, the same individuals showed two different patterns of LH response in two different phases of their treatment. Gooren thus demonstrated that LH response patterns are unlikely to provide information about the masculine or feminine neural organization of homosexuals or heterosexuals. Because two independent studies found an association between sexual orientation and LH response, and since no one has convincingly explained away these findings, they cannot be entirely rejected. Nor, on the other hand, can they be considered strong evidence for a neuroendocrine theory of homosexuality.

A second line of research has focused on sexually dimorphic characteristics thought to be related to cerebral lateralization (Geschwind &

Galaburda, 1985), including spatial ability and handedness. Lateralization refers to the tendency of certain brain functions to be specialized in either the right or the left cerebral hemisphere. Males are more lateralized than females, and right-handers are more lateralized than left-handers, on average, for both verbal and spatial functions (McGlone, 1980). Somewhat paradoxically, males are more likely than females to be left-handed, but this is thought by some scientists to result from a sex difference in timing of cerebral development (Geschwind & Galaburda, 1985). Men tend to have higher spatial relative to verbal abilities, and this pattern has been hypothesized to be related to sex differences in lateralization. It is also noteworthy that CAH has been associated with both increased left-handedness (Nass et al., 1987) and higher spatial scores (Resnick et al., 1986) among women.

Several studies have reported homosexual men to have a higher incidence of left-handedness than heterosexual men (McCormick et al., 1990; Lindesay, 1987; Götestam et al., 1992). Relatedly, Watson (1991) found an increased rate of left-handedness among male-to-female transsexuals, and Gooren (1991) obtained similar results in a combined sample of male-to-female and female-to-male transsexuals. On the other hand, two recent reports on large samples both failed to find an increase in left-handedness among homosexual men (Satz et al., 1991; Marchant-Haycox et al., 1991). McCormick et al. (1990) also found an increased rate of left-handedness among homosexual women, the only report to focus on women to date, and Tkachuk and Zucker (1991) found a higher incidence of left-handedness in a combined sample of homosexual males and females. Thus, there is some indication that both male and female homosexuals have an increased rate of left-handedness. (Because high levels of fetal testosterone are hypothesized to be associated with left-handedness, it is counterintuitive that male homosexuality is associated with sinistrality. James (1989) offers an intriguing explanation of this apparent paradox, suggesting that male homosexuality may arise from a different pattern of timing of prenatal androgen surges, with high androgen levels occurring when handedness is affected, and low levels occurring when sexual orientation is affected.)

Regarding spatial ability, several studies have suggested that homosexual men score lower than heterosexual men on spatial tests (Sanders & Ross-Field, 1986; Gladue et al., 1990; McCormick et al., 1991; Tkachuk & Zucker, 1991). Similarly, gender-nonconforming boys, who are likely to become homosexual men, also have been found to perform less well than controls on spatial tests (Finegan et al., 1982; Grimshaw et al., 1991). The one study focusing on women, however, found lesbians to obtain lower scores than heterosexual women (Gladue et al., 1990), a finding difficult to reconcile with a neuroendocrine theory.

Thus, a reasonable number of studies suggest that there may be lateralization differences between homosexuals and heterosexuals, particularly among men (who have been studied more often). Nevertheless, they cannot be considered definitive proof for a neuroendocrine theory of sexual orientation. This is partly because of the mixed findings. It is troubling, for instance, that the largest studies of handedness found no association with sexual orientation. But more important, neuroendocrine theories of both sexual orientation and lateralization are currently insufficiently specified to allow strong predictions, and hence confirmations, of either. Furthermore, the causes of the sex difference in spatial ability, particularly, remain controversial, with both "biological" and psychosocial explanations being offered (Linn & Petersen, 1985).

HUMAN NEUROANATOMICAL STUDIES

Potentially the most persuasive type of evidence for a neuroendocrine theory of sexual orientation is finding neuroanatomical differences between homosexuals and heterosexuals, in areas of the brain hypothesized to be involved in sexual or related behavior. Studies of nonhuman animals have implicated the hypothalamus as the most likely site of interest. However, any part of the brain that is sexually dimorphic is of interest, given the likelihood that an influence affecting sexual differentiation of the hypothalamus would affect other areas of the brain as well.

Careful, systematic research on sex differences in the human brain has only recently begun, and studies of neuroanatomical correlates of human sexual orientation are rare indeed. Before this literature is evaluated, it is useful to put it into a methodological context. Neuroanatomical studies are typically enormously painstaking enterprises. Because of this, a research team usually investigates several brain locations of interest. Sometimes a difference is discovered after the researchers, looking at at one part of the brain, notice a potential pattern elsewhere. Both of these factors increase the probability of type 1 error, that is, the possibility that a difference occurs merely as a result of chance sample fluctuations. Hence, while replication in science is always important, replication of neurophysiological findings is especially so. By the same token, failures to replicate with small samples should not be considered definitive disconfirmation of initial findings, since small samples are associated with a high type 2 error rate.

Three highly publicized reports of brain structures are related to sexual orientation. The first, by Swaab and Hofman (1990), found the suprachiasmatic nucleus of the hypothalamus to be 1.7 times larger in homosexual than in heterosexual men. This nucleus is thought to be involved in the regulation of circadian rhythms and, as such, is a surprising location in which to find a sexual orientation difference. These authors also examined a nucleus that their research group (Swaab & Fliers, 1985) had previously found to be sexually dimorphic, but found no difference between homosexuals and heterosexuals. The sexual orientation difference in the suprachiasmatic nucleus has not yet been replicated.

The most noted finding of a brain difference between homosexuals and heterosexuals was reported by LeVay (1991). LeVay investigated two hypothalamic nuclei that had previously been reported to be sexually dimorphic (Allen et al., 1989). He studied the brains of eighteen homosexual men, all of whom had died of AIDS, a comparison group of sixteen men whose sexual orientations were unknown but presumed to be heterosexual, and a group of six women. One of the nuclei was not even found by LeVay to be sexually dimorphic. However, the third interstitial nucleus of the anterior hypothalamus (INAH-3) was less than half as large in the women as in the heterosexual men, replicating the previous researchers. Furthermore, the nuclei of the homosexual men were also less than half the size of the heterosexual men's, and were indistinguishable from those of the women.

LeVay's findings have been subjected to intense scrutiny. For instance, it has been noted that the findings could be due to the effects of AIDS rather than sexual orientation. However, LeVay demonstrated that his findings were robust even when the analysis was restricted to those heterosexual men who had died of AIDS. Another criticism has been that LeVAy did not know for certain that his "heterosexual" group contained no homosexuals. However, any misclassification of subjects would diminish the obtained effect size relative to the true effect size. Finally, it should be emphasized that LeVay was studying a nucleus that had been found *twice* (counting LeVay's own demonstration) to be sexually dimorphic. Thus, the a priori justification for his search was strong. Like all important findings, LeVay's should be replicated. The INAH-3 remains the most promising road to confirmation of a neuroendocrine theory of sexual orientation.

The most recent brain study, by Allen and Gorski (1992), demonstrated sex and sexual orientation differences in the anterior commissure (AC) of the corpus collosum, with heterosexual women's ACs being larger than heterosexual men's, but with homosexual men's the largest of all. Their search was motivated by a previous finding of a sex difference in the AC (Allen & Gorski, 1991), and thus was well justified. Though apparently sexually dimorphic, the AC is not thought to be involved in sexual behavior. Thus, this finding may reflect the generalized effects of neuroendocrine influences that also affect the areas of the brain that directly regulate sexual orientation.

The neuroendocrine theory of sexual orientation is currently the most influential etiological theory of sexual orientation. Its empirical support, however, is largely indirect. The most careful and definitive studies of hormonal influence on sexually dimorphic sexual behavior have used nonhuman animals whose species-typical mating behaviors do not map directly onto ours. Rats do not seem to have a sexual orientation in the same way that humans do, and it is controversial whether the behaviors that have been studied (primarily lordosis and mounting) are relevant at all. The most replicated relevant finding in humans, that sexual orientation is related to childhood gender atypicality, is not clearly a biological phenomenon, though it does suggest that homosexuals and opposite-sex heterosexuals have been subject to similar influences, as predicted by a neuroendocrine view. Individuals who have been exposed to atypical levels of hormones are, in principle, quite relevant to the neuroendocrine theory; however, results of research on such persons have been mixed. Studies of sexually dimorphic traits related to brain lateralization such as spatial ability and handedness have also provided a complicated empirical picture. Furthermore, the neuroendocrine theory does not make strong predictions about the relationship between these traits and sexual orientation. Perhaps the most promising findings have been the demonstrations of neuroanatomical differences between heterosexual and homosexual men. If these findings are replicated (and extended to women), they may provide the long sought-after proof of neuroendocrine routes to human sexual orientation.

Genetics and Sexual Orientation

Human behavior genetics has produced evidence for substantial genetic factors in a wide variety of behavioral traits (Plomin, 1990), from different types of psychopathology to personality and intelligence, even to characteristics such as religiosity (Waller et al., 1990). Indeed, failures to find significant heritability for well-measured traits in large sample studies have been exceedingly rare. Viewed from this perspective, it is hardly daring to hypothesize that sexual orientation may be heritable as well. However, sexual orientation is significantly different from the aforementioned characteristics. Homosexuals have presumably always been at a reproductive disadvantage compared to heterosexuals. (With respect to recent history, this disadvantage is demonstrably severe. Bell and Weinberg [1978; Tables 17.1 and 17.13] showed that both male and female homosexuals reported less than one-quarter of the number of children as same-sex heterosexuals.) If sexual orientation is somewhat heritable, this means that some genes predispose individuals to homosexuality. How have those genes resisted elimination by the inevitable engine of natural selection? Even at its lowest estimated base rates, homosexuality occurs far more frequently than the highest known mutation rates; thus mutation alone cannot account for the persistence of "gay genes," if they exist. The paradox of relatively high incidence and low fertility of homosexuals makes sexual orientation a likely candidate for low or zero heritability.

It is genuinely surprising, therefore, that the available evidence is more consistent with moderate to high heritability for both male and female sexual orientation (though relevant evidence is more plentiful for men). Before reviewing this evidence, it will be useful to explicate some basic genetic concepts.

HERITABILITY

If a trait is at least partially genetic, then it should be familial. Therefore, the first step in a behavioral genetic investigation is generally to find if the trait of interest runs in families. Although necessary, familiality is not sufficient to justify a genetic conclusion, because traits can be familial for genetic or environmental reasons. Therefore, more sophisticated approaches are needed subsequently, and these might be termed "heritability studies" because they have one common goal of providing a heritability estimate for the trait.

Heritability is the proportion of phenotypic variance that is explicable by genetic variance. Represented by a number ranging from 0 to 1, heritability is estimated in several ways, though the most intuitive is the intraclass correlation of monozygotic (MZ) twins who were reared separately in environments assigned at random. This method of estimating heritability is used infrequently, because of the extreme rarity of MZ twins who were reared apart. There are, for instance, only six separated MZ pairs with homosexuality (i.e., at least one twin is homosexual) in the literature (Eckert, Bouchard, Bohlen, & Heston, 1986).

Perhaps the most widely used design for estimating heritability of human behavioral traits is the classical twin study, in which MZ and dizygotic (DZ) twins are compared for their degree of phenotypic similarity. The rationale is as follows: MZ twins are genetically identical (with rare exceptions), but DZ twins are not. MZ and DZ twins were both reared together, and thus had equally similar rearing environments. Thus, if MZ twins are more similar than DZ twins for a trait, it must reflect the increased genetic similarity. An important assumption on which the classical twin method depends is the "equal environments assumption," that the relevant environments are no more similar for MZ than for DZ twins. Although this assumption has been criticized (e.g., Lewontin et al., 1984), it seems to be accurate for traits studied so far (Plomin et al., 1989). Unfortunately, it has not been specifically examined within the context of sexual orientation.

Because heritabilities may be different for different populations (e.g., Asians versus whites), and because heritability estimates typically have substantial standard errors around them, they should be viewed as approximations. I use the following very rough scale: less than .25 is low, .25 to .50 is moderate, and greater than .50 is high heritability. Note, however, that even a "low" heritability of .16 implies a correlation of .40 between genotype and phenotype. Furthermore, provided the assumptions required to compute heritability are valid, this correlation can be interpreted causally, that is, individual differences in genotype cause individual differences in phenotype. Given our present ignorance about causes of sexual orientation, one would be delighted to find a causal connection so large. On the other hand, if heritability were .16, environmentality would be .84, implying a correlation between relevant environment and phenotype of nearly .92. In this case environmental causes would dwarf genetic ones, though even the latter would be important enough to be interesting.

FAMILIALITY OF SEXUAL ORIENTATION

Hirschfeld (1936) remarked more than fifty years ago that homosexuality appeared to run in families. However, rigorous confirmation of Hirschfeld's informal observations has taken a long time. In a landmark study Pillard and Weinrich (1986) demonstrated the plausibility of doing family genetic studies of homosexuality. Using newspaper advertisements they recruited fifty-one homosexual male and fifty heterosexual male probands, who were blind to the purpose of the study. During the interview they asked about the sexual orientation of all siblings. Furthermore, they asked (and received, to a large degree) permission to contact siblings. This was generally done through the mail, but some phone interviews were necessary. In the sibling questionnaires or interviews, several questions were asked about sexual orientation. Pillard and Weinrich showed that probands predicted their siblings' orientations with a high degree of accuracy. They also found substantially more gay brothers among gay male probands than among heterosexual male probands, 20 to 4 percent, respectively. This is roughly consistent with another family study of male homosexuality. Bailey et al. (1991) obtained estimates of the number of brothers "known" to be homosexual from heterosexual male and female probands, as well as homosexual male probands, finding a 10 percent rate among the brothers of homosexual men compared to a 2 percent rate among the brothers of heterosexual men and women. Although brothers were not contacted to verify their sexual orientations, the results of Pillard and Weinrich suggest that this is unnecessary.

Is female sexual orientation also familial? There have now been two reasonably large studies of this question. Pillard (1990) found a 25 percent rate of homosexuality or bisexuality among 60 sisters of bisexual or homosexual female probands, compared to a rate of 11 percent for sisters of 53 heterosexual female probands. Interestingly, they also found a marginally significant elevation of homosexual brothers among their homosexual female probands. If replicated, this finding would have important implications for theories of sexual orientation: a common mechanism in the development of male and female homosexuality. Bailey and Benishay (1993) also reported significant familiality. Of the ninety-nine sisters of the homosexual probands, 12 percent were homosexual, compared to 2 percent of the eighty-three sisters of the heterosexual probands. Although a slightly higher percentage of brothers of the homosexual probands were also homosexual (7 to 1%), this difference was not significant. Both Pillard (1990) and Bailey and Benishay (1993) obtained verification of probands' reports of their siblings' sexual orientation in the majority of cases, and both found such reports to be highly accurate.

GENETIC STUDIES

The first noteworthy genetic study of sexual orientation was done by Kallmann (1952a,b), who found a 100 percent concordance rate for thirty-seven male MZ twin pairs, compared to a 15 percent rate for twenty-six dizygotic male DZ pairs. Kallmann's study has been justifiably criticized for its methodology, particularly its reliance on sampling from correctional and psychiatric institutions, its lack of detail regarding zygosity diagnosis, and its anomalous findings. Most important, results of several case studies and small twin series (reviewed by Rosenthal, 1970) suggest that the true MZ concordance rate, while appreciable, is substantially less than 100 percent. Because of these problems, the study is generally held in low regard. Nevertheless, no one has offered a plausible alternative to genetic influence to account for Kallmann's strikingly different concordance rates.

A fascinating report of MZ twins raised separately (Eckert et al., 1986) was consistent with a high heritability for male sexual orientation. Both of the two male pairs included were concordant for homosexual feelings (though one of the twins classified himself as a heterosexual anyway). In contrast, in the same study none of four female pairs was concordant. Obviously, the sample size of this study was too small to justify strong conclusions.

Given the promising results obtained by Kallmann, it is somewhat surprising that almost forty years passed before the question of heritability was again investigated using large samples. Seemingly by coincidence, four reasonably large studies have been reported in the last year. All four obtained samples through advertisements in gay publications. For instance, the first and largest, by Bailey and Pillard (1991), used advertisements that asked for gay men with either male twins or adoptive brothers. (Adoptive brothers are biologically unrelated males reared as siblings to the probands.) Eligible and interested subjects called the investigators and were interviewed, usually in person, about their sexual orientations and related traits. They were also asked about their brothers' sexual orientation and, finally, for permission to contact their cotwins or adoptive brothers. As Pillard and Weinrich (1986) found, sibling reports were highly related to proband reports. The rates of homosexuality (including bisexuality) among the relatives were: 52 percent (29/56) for MZ cotwins; 22 percent (12/54) for DZ cotwins; and 11 percent (6/57) for adoptive brothers. This pattern is consistent with moderate to strong heritability for male sexual orientation. Under varying assumptions, heritability estimates ranged from .31 to .74. The lowest estimates came from models that assumed a base rate of 10 percent for homosexuality. Recent reports suggest that the lower base rate of 4 percent is more appropriate (Johnson et al., 1992; ACSF, 1992). All heritabilities computed assuming a 4 percent rate exceeded .50. One anomalous finding of the study was a lower than expected rate of homosexuality among the biological nontwin brothers of 9 percent. Genetic theory predicts that this rate should be equal to that for DZ twins and higher than that for adoptive brothers.

Because I have defined "sexual orientation" as sexual attraction rather than either identity or behavior, it is important to address one methodological issue of this study. Both probands and relatives were classified according to sexual identity, that is, whether they called themselves "gay/bisexual" or "heterosexual." This was done for three reasons. First, this was the easiest way to write the advertisements used to recruit probands. Second, in both groups sexual identity was closely related to both sexual behavior and sexual attraction patterns, as measured by the 7-point Kinsey scale (Kinsey et al., 1948). Third, probands' ratings of their relatives were used when relatives' self-ratings were unavailable, and it was believed that the concordance between probands' ratings and relatives' self-ratings would be higher for the broader categories of sexual identity than for the more specific Kinsey scores. Indirectly supporting this belief was the finding that, while probands were almost perfect at predicting whether their relatives would identify as "heterosexual" versus "gay/bisexual," they did poorly at predicting whether a nonheterosexual relative would call himself "gay" or "bisexual." This method of classifying sexual orientation was also used in the female family study by Bailey and Benishay (1993) mentioned previously and in the genetic study of female sexual orientation by Bailey, Pillard, Neale, and Agyei (1993), discussed later.

The second genetic study, restricted to twins, was reported by King and McDonald (1992). Using recruitment methods similar to those of Bailey and Pillard, they found a sample of forty-six homosexuals with twins (38 male; 8 female). The reported concordances, 25 percent for MZ twins compared to 12 percent for DZ twins, appear to conflict with the higher rates obtained by Bailey and Pillard. However, King and McDonald's sample was considerably smaller, so that the difference might largely be due to sampling error. Furthermore, it is unclear how zygosity was diagnosed in this study, nor were cotwins contacted to verify orientations, nor were results reported separately for men and women. Finally, it is noteworthy that five of seven respondents considered their cotwins entirely heterosexual despite an apparently prolonged incestuous homosexual relationship. The third study, by Whitam et al. (1992) found even higher concordances than did Bailey and Pillard—66 percent for MZ versus 30 percent for DZ pairs.

A fourth study (Bailey et al., 1993) focused exclusively on female sexual orientation. The methodology was identical to that of Bailey and Pillard's (1991) genetic study of males. Probands were homosexual or bisexual women with twins or adoptive sisters. Of the relatives whose sexual orientation could be confidently assessed, 48 percent (34/71) of MZ cotwins, 16 percent (6/37) of DZ cotwins, and 6 percent (2/35) of adoptive sisters were homosexual. Probands also reported that 14 percent (10/73) of their nontwin biological sisters were homosexual, a rate that was quite similar both to the DZ twin rate and to the rate found by Bailey and Benishay (1993) in their family study of female sexual orientation. Heritabilities were significant under a wide range of assumptions about the population base rate of homosexuality and ascertainment bias, and they were of the same order as those obtained by Bailey and Pillard for male sexual orientation (1991).

Thus, the available genetic evidence suggests that both male and female sexual orientations are moderately heritable. However, the limitations of this literature must be recognized. All the genetic studies discussed herein used a method of subject ascertainment that may be susceptible to serious biases. That is, if gay men with gay cotwins are more likely than gay men with heterosexual cotwins to volunteer for such studies, the concordance rates will be artifactually higher. Bailey and Pillard (1991), however, demonstrated that this kind of bias cannot lead to spurious findings of heritability unless it is greater for MZ than for DZ twins. Given the general consistency of the picture obtained from family studies, the small study of twins reared apart (at least for men), and the four large twin studies, all of which found higher MZ than DZ concordance, it seems likely that the heritability findings are robust. However, large population-based twin studies (for a small version, see Buhrich et al., 1991) or systematically obtained (and hence representative) samples of gay twins are necessary to address such methodological issues.

One striking result of the more recent genetic studies is the high rate of discordance among the MZ twins. Except for Kallmann's study, concordances have been well under 100 percent. This shows that environment exerts an influence on sexual orientation. It should be remembered, however, that "environment" refers simply to all nongenetic influences, biological or social. There is presently no good candidate for an environmental factor not shared by MZ cotwins that might affect sexual orientation.

Even if it could be demonstrated with certainty that sexual orientation were substantially heritable, the question would remain of what, exactly, the relevant genes are doing. Although most genetic researchers have been influenced by the neuroendocrine theory, a finding of nonzero heritability is merely consistent with it. Such a finding does not provide direct support for a neuroendocrine view because alternative genotype-to-phenotype routes involving social environmental factors are imaginable (see, e.g., Byne & Parsons, 1993). Only if either a specific gene affecting sexual orientation or a genetic marker associated with it were identified could genetic data strongly confirm a neuroendocrine theory.

THE PARADOX OF "GAY GENES" REVISITED

I have delayed discussion of possible explanations for the persistence of genes for sexual orientation until a consideration of the genetic data. While ultimately inconclusive, the genetic data seem strong enough to justify serious consideration of mechanisms by which "gay genes" might be maintained.

Several explanations have been proposed. A necessary feature of any such explanation is that although the relevant genes detract from a gay individual's reproductive output, they facilitate reproduction in other carriers. One possible model, proposed by Hutchinson (1959), is that of heterozygote superiority, of which sickle-cell anemia is an example. Heterozygote superiority occurs when individuals homozygous for either of two alleles at a genetic locus (i.e., those who have two copies of either gene) have decreased reproductive success compared to heterozygotes (who have one copy of each). This model explains the persistence of genes for sickle-cell anemia, because heterozygotes are better protected against malaria than individuals without any sickling genes. Although plausible, this model is not very useful without a specification of the alleged advantage for heterozygotes.

The second explanation considered here is an application of an immensely important concept in evolutionary theory, kin selection (Hamilton, 1964; Wilson, 1978). Applied to sexual orientation, kin selection theory suggests that while homosexuals do not themselves reproduce at high rates, their sacrifice enables kin (most likely siblings and parents) to reproduce more than they otherwise would. Kin selection requires that this increased benefit be substantial: siblings or parents must total at least two extra children for every one forgone by the homosexual individual. What is the specific mechanism by which homosexuals aid kin in reproduction? It has been proposed that homosexuals may be particularly likely to aid in rearing and to invest resources in their nieces and nephews (Weinrich, 1987; Wilson, 1978). This theory could be supported either by demonstrating increased fertility of relatives of homosexuals or by examining specific behaviors of homosexuals toward their relatives. Unfortunately, no empirical studies of this theory have been attempted, so it remains unfounded speculation.

Related Phenotypes: Bisexuality and Transsexualism

BISEXUALITY

In "biological" studies of sexual orientation, there are generally two approaches to bisexuals: either they are classified with homosexuals or they are excluded. Which approach is more justifiable?

From the vantage of a neuroendocrine theory, bisexuality need not be particularly problematic. Attraction to women means that sexual orientation has been masculinized. However, some unknown physiological process has prevented behavioral defeminization, and thus attraction to men occurs simultaneously. In this view, it makes most sense to treat bisexuals as intermediate between heterosexuals and homosexuals. Until a neuroendocrine account of bisexuality garners scientific support, however, the etiological relationship between bisexuality and either homosexuality or heterosexuality remains an open, empirical question. Relevant evidence consists of whether bisexuals are more like homosexuals or heterosexuals with respect to relevant variables. For instance, Bell et al. (1981) found bisexual women to be intermediate between heterosexual and homosexual women in recollections of childhood gender nonconformity. No such pattern was reported for men. Consistent with the null finding for men, Freund (1974) found that men who self-labeled as bisexual were aroused to homosexual but not heterosexual erotic stimuli.

One empirical strategy, as yet untapped, would be to see whether patterns of familiality differed between bisexuals and homosexuals. For example, do bisexuals and homosexuals differ in their rates of homosexual siblings? Do MZ cotwins of bisexual probands have a different distribution of sexual orientation from MZ cotwins of homosexual probands? One problem with doing such studies is that bisexuals appear to be somewhat rare, comprising a minority of nonheterosexuals in most samples. Bailey and Pillard (1991) obtained results supporting the hypothesis that homosexuality and heterosexuality may be more categorically than dimensionally distinct, with bisexuality a relatively rare occurrence. Verifying this observation could have important implications for understanding the development of sexual orientation.

TRANSSEXUALISM

Transsexualism is a rare phenotype characterized by a persistent dissatisfaction with one's anatomical sex (gender dysphoria) and a desire to change it. Blanchard (1987, 1989) has shown that there are two independent types of transsexualism, which he distinguishes as homosexual and heterosexual transsexualism. The former is characterized by attraction to the same sex, an early history of childhood gender nonconformity, early onset of gender dysphoria, and a fairly even sex ratio. The latter type of transsexuals are heterosexual without a history of childhood gender nonconformity, and are nearly always male. Heterosexual transsexuals usually have a history of fetishistic cross-dressing (transvestism), which in adulthood evidently transforms into the desire to change sex. It is homosexual transsexualism that seems likely to be etiologically related to homosexuality. Besides the obvious similarities of a homosexual orientation and childhood gender nonconformity, Blanchard and colleagues have demonstrated other nonobvious similarities in homosexuality and homosexual transsexualism (Blanchard & Sheridan, 1992a), including a sibling sex ratio biased toward males and a relatively late average birth order. On the other hand, they failed to find a high percentage of homosexual siblings among homosexual transsexuals (Blanchard & Sheridan, 1992b).

Future Directions

There is much work to be done in articulating the "biological" mechanisms involved in the development of sexual orientation. Indeed, even most researchers who are engaged in, or otherwise sympathetic to, a biological research program freely admit that neuroendocrine or genetic hypotheses about sexual orientation have not been supported to a degree of certainty that would justify their acceptance. Nor can critics of these hypotheses reasonably claim that they have been adequately falsified. There are roughly three broad programs of research that would further illuminate both the strengths and weaknesses of "biological" theories of sexual orientation: research on basic nonbiological questions of interest to homosexology in general, research designed to replicate the most important "biological" findings, and given the results of the replication attempts, research aimed at elaborating promising "biological" findings.

All researchers studying sexual orientation are impeded by the absence of knowledge about some very basic facts. Foremost are incidence figures for sexual feelings, identification, and behavior. It is symptomatic of the sorry present state of knowledge that we still look to Kinsey's (1948, 1953) data to estimate these figures, despite the facts that those data are decades old, had severe sampling biases that Kinsey acknowledged at the time, and are cited by different writers to support a wide range of estimates. For example, many people are fond of citing a 10 percent figure for homosexuality in the general population; this figure derives from Kinsey's data. Gebhard (1972), however, used Kinsey's data to estimate the incidence of female homosexuality at 1.5 percent or less. Although these differences are partly explicable by use of different criteria for "homosexuality," Kinsey's data cannot yield trustworthy, specific current estimates. Successful future studies will attempt representative sampling, obtain high cooperation rates, and ask specific and detailed questions about both sexual feelings and behavior. Though a hostile political environment has impeded progress, at least three large relevant surveys are in progress (one American, one British, and one French). These studies were most immediately motivated by the need to obtain information relevant to the epidemiology of sex practices likely to transmit HIV. Let us hope, however, that the need to focus on specific sexual behaviors will not prevent the surveys from inquiring about sexual orientation and other psychological issues as well.

To illustrate the importance of knowing incidence figures more precisely, let us consider two examples. First, suppose one interviewed a large cohort of gay men and found the rate of homosexuality among their brothers to be 12 percent. If one accepts the high estimate of 10 percent for the base rate of homosexuality in the general population, then one will conclude that familial factors make only a trivial contribution to the development of sexual orientation in men. This is because brothers of gay men, in this case, do not have much of an increased rate of homosexuality. They are only 1.2 times more likely to be gay than is a man sampled randomly from the general population. In contrast, if one accepts Gebhard's (1972) estimate of 4 percent, then this is triple the expected rate, a fairly substantial increase. As a second example, consider the possibility suggested by unsystematic research (e.g., Friday, 1991) that homosexual fantasies may be quite common among women who identify themselves as heterosexuals. If such fantasies were similar in nature, frequency, and intensity to those of homosexually identified women, then it would seem unlikely that sexual identity merely reflected sexual feelings, per se. Why would only a relatively small minority of the women capable of homosexual arousal call themselves "lesbian" and mate more or less exclusively with other women? I emphasize that this example is hypothetical, and many of us who take a biological approach believe that heterosexual and homosexual women's sexual feelings differ in important respects. But we do not know this.

Another kind of research that is needed in homosexology, generally, is a systematic study of homosexuality across many diverse cultures. The research with which I am most familiar (e.g., Bailey & Pillard, 1991; Bailey et al., 1993) primarily used white Americans as subjects, because they volunteered most frequently. Cross-cultural differences in the causes of sexual orientation are certainly conceivable and could illuminate the role of the social environment. Alternatively, it is possible, as Whitam and Mathy (1986) have suggested, that homosexuality develops similarly across cultures that seem to differ in important respects. If so, this would provide more support for a "biological" view.

The second broadly defined research program previously endorsed concerns replication. Many of the findings considered important for "biological" research were obtained in studies that had important methodological limitations. I have attempted to note the most serious limitations in the relevant sections of this chapter. My purpose here is merely to emphasize that it is crucial to demonstrate beyond a reasonable doubt the validity of findings on which a theory rests. As Zubin (1987) pithily expressed it, "It ain't ignorance that causes all the trouble. It's knowing things that ain't so!" The most important study to replicate, in my view, is LeVay's (1991). If possible, it would be highly desirable to examine brains of lesbians as well. Furthermore, areas with mixed findings, such as the CAH literature, could greatly benefit from a large, controlled, and hopefully definitive study.

Provided that careful studies replicate the most promising findings supporting the neuroendocrine and genetic theories of sexual orientation, such as LeVay's neuroanatomical study and Bailey and Pillard's genetic study of male sexual orientation, the next phases of research should attempt to elaborate their deeper meanings. Thus, for example, does the INAH-3 affect sexual orientation or is it noncausally associated with sexual orientation but masculinized along with causally relevant brain structures? A number of techniques from contemporary neuroscience may be useful in answering such questions, including immunohistochemistry, hybridization histochemistry, PET, and MRI scanning. Assuming that careful studies replicate the heritability findings, the questions of which genes are involved and what they are doing remains. Methodologies such as linkage analysis are useful in theory for the identification of genes affecting a trait, and there is reason to hope that they will someday illuminate sexual orientation. As our knowledge of the genome progresses exponentially, so will the power of these techniques. However, to date they have not been very useful in studying behavioral characteristics, perhaps because these characteristics are typically etiologically complex (Plomin, 1990). Even so, behavior genetics methods can be used to study genetic and environmental mechanisms indirectly.

For example, as I have noted previously, the high rate of discordance among the MZ twins shows that environment must exert an influence on sexual orientation. Furthermore, the effective environment for sexual orientation largely appears to include aspects of experience (social or biological) that differ between MZ twins who have been reared together. No current theories of sexual orientation would predict frequent discordance between MZ cotwins. Given the possibility of prenatal influences on sexual orientation, it would be useful to know whether aspects of the prenatal environment such as hormonal exposure often differ between MZ cotwins. The equivalent question on the psychosocial side is whether parental treatment of twins differs in ways likely to foster differences in sexual orientation.

Genetic mechanisms can be illuminated by identifying differences between probands of concordant MZ pairs and those of discordant MZ pairs. Probands of concordant pairs should have relatively high genetic loadings compared to those of discordant pairs. Bailey and Pillard (1991), for example, found that male MZ probands who had been gender atypical during childhood were neither more nor less likely than other probands to have gay cotwins. Hence, childhood gender atypicality does not appear to be a marker of genetic influence on sexual orientation. This finding should be replicated, and other candidate markers should be investigated in this manner.

Future research should also attempt to integrate different "biological" approaches. For example, neuroanatomical studies of MZ twins discordant for homosexuality could illuminate the nature of environmental influences, while analogous studies comparing MZ homosexual probands from concordant versus discordant pairs could provide valuable information about the routes by which genes exert their influence.

Conclusion

The present state of biological research on biological influences on sexual orientation is one of inconclusive complexity. My own view is that the general area is an exciting and promising one. A theory can be considered promising for only a limited time, however. Without conclusive results, it will eventually be dismissed as disappointing, having failed to fulfill its original promise. The time is ripe for biological theories of sexual orientation to fulfill theirs.

Acknowledgment

I thank Sheri Berenbaum, Tony D'Augelli, Joan Linsenmeier, Charlotte Patterson, and Miriam Wolfe for their insightful comments on a previous version of this chapter.

References

ACSF Investigators (1992). AIDS and sexual behaviour in France. *Nature, 360,* 407–409.

Adkins-Regan, E. (1988). Sex hormones and sexual orientation in animals. *Psychobiology, 16,* 335–347.

Allen, L. S., Hines, M., Shryne, J. E., & Gorski, R. A. (1989). Two sexually dimorphic cell groups in the human brain. *Journal of Neuroscience, 9,* 497–506.

Allen, L. S., & Gorski, R. A. (1991). Sexual dimorphism of the anterior commissure and massa intermedia of the human brain. *Journal of Comparative Neurology, 312,* 97–104.

Allen, L. S., & Gorski, R. A. (1992). Sexual orientation and the size of the anterior commissure of the human brain. *Proceedings of the National Academy of Sciences, 89,* 7199–7202.

Bailey, J. M., & Benishay, D. (1993). Familial aggregation of female sexual orientation. *American Journal of Psychiatry, 150,* 272–277.

Bailey, J. M., & Zucker, K. J. (1993). Childhood gender identity/role and sexual orientation: A conceptual analysis and quantitative review. Unpublished manuscript.

Bailey, J. M., Willerman, L., & Parks, C. (1991). A test of the maternal stress hypothesis of human male homosexuality. *Archives of Sexual Behavior, 20,* 277–293.

Bailey, J. M., & Pillard, R. C. (1991). A genetic study of male sexual orientation. *Archives of General Psychiatry, 48,* 1089–1096.

Bailey, J. M., Pillard, R. C., Neale, M. C., & Agyei, Y. (1993). Heritable factors influence female sexual orientation. *Archives of General Psychiatry, 50,* 217–223.

Barinaga, M. (1991). Is homosexuality biological? *Science, 253,* 956–957.

Bell, A. P., & Weinberg, M. S. (1978). *Homosexualities: A study of diversity among men and women.* New York: Simon & Schuster.

Bell, A. P., Weinberg, M. S., & Hammersmith, S. K. (1981). *Sexual preference: Its development in men and women.* Bloomington: Indiana University Press.

Berenbaum, S. A., & Hines, M. (1992). Early androgens are related to childhood sex-typed toy preferences. *Psychological Science, 3,* 203–206.

Blanchard, R. (1987). Heterosexual and homosexual gender dysphoria. *Archives of Sexual Behavior, 16,* 139–152.

Blanchard, R. (1989). The classification and labeling of nonhomosexual gender dysphorias. *Archives of Sexual Behavior, 18*, 315–334.

Blanchard, R., & Sheridan, P. M. (1992a). Sibling size, sibling sex ratio, birth order, and parental age in homosexual and nonhomosexual gender dysphorics. *Journal of Nervous and Mental Disorders, 180*, 40–47.

Blanchard, R., & Sheridan, P. M. (1992b). Proportion of unmarried siblings of homosexual and non homosexual gender-dysphoric patients. *Canadian Journal of Psychiatry, 37*, 163–167.

Bleier, R. (1984). *Science and gender: A critique of biology and its theories on women.* New York: Pergamon Press.

Boswell, J. (1980). *Christianity, social tolerance and homosexuality: Gay people in Western Europe from the beginning of the Christian era to the Fourteenth Century.* Chicago: University of Chicago Press.

Boswell, J. (1989). Revolutions, universals, and sexual categories. In M. B. Duberman, M. Vicinus, & G. Chauncey, Jr. (Eds.), *Hidden from history: Reclaiming the gay and lesbian past* (pp. 17–36). New York: New American Library.

Boswell, J. (1990). Sexual categories, sexual universals: A conversation with John Boswell. In L. D. Mass (Ed.), *Homosexuality as behavior and identity* (pp. 202–233). Binghamton, NY: Harrington Park Press.

Brand, T., Houtsmuller, E. J., & Slob, A. K. (1992). Organization of adult "sexual orientation" in male rats. Paper presented at Annual Meeting, International Academy of Sex Research, Prague, Czechoslovakia.

Brand, T., Kroonen, J., Mos, J., Slob, A. K. (1991). Adult partner preference and sexual behavior of male rats affected by perinatal endocrine manipulations. *Hormones and Behavior, 25*, 323–341.

Buhrich, N. J., Bailey, J. M., & Martin, N. G. (1991). Sexual orientation, sexual identity, and sex-dimorphic behaviors in male twins. *Behavior Genetics, 21*, 75–96.

Byne, W., & Parsons, B. (1993). Human sexual orientation: The biologic theories reappraised. *Archives of General Psychiatry, 50*, 228–239.

Cook, M., & Mineka, S. (1989). Observational conditioning of fear to fear-relevant versus fear-irrelevant stimuli in rhesus monkeys. *Journal of Abnormal Psychology, 98*, 448–459.

De Cecco, J. P. (1990). Confusing the actor with the act: Muddled notions about homosexuality. *Archives of Sexual Behavior, 19*, 409–412.

Dittmann, R. W., Kappes, M. E., & Kappes, M. H. (1992). Sexual behavior in adolescent and adult females with congenital adrenal hyperplasia. *Psychoneuroendocrinology, 17*, 153–170.

Dörner, G. (1988). Neuroendocrine response to estrogen and brain differentiation in heterosexuals, homosexuals, and transsexuals. *Archives of Sexual Behavior, 17*, 57–75.

Dörner G., Rohde W., Stahl F., Krell L., & Masius W. G. (1975). A neuroendocrine predisposition for homosexuality in men. *Archives of Sexual Behavior, 4*, 1–8.

Eckert, E. D., Bouchard, T. J., Bohlen, J., & Heston, L. L. (1986). Homosexuality in monozygotic twins reared apart. *British Journal of Psychiatry, 148*, 421–425.

Ehrhardt, A. A., Evers, K., & Money, J. (1968). Influence of androgen and some aspects of sexually dimorphic behavior in women with late-treated adrenogenital syndrome. *Johns Hopkins Medical Journal, 123,* 115–122.

Ehrhardt, A. A., & Baker, S. W. (1974). Fetal androgens, human central nervous system differentiation and behavior sex differences. In R. C. Friedman, R. M. Richart, & R. L. Vande Wiele (Eds.), *Sex differences in behavior* (pp. 33–51). New York: Wiley.

Ellis, L., & Ames, M. A. (1987). Neurohormonal functioning and sexual orientation: A theory of homosexuality–heterosexuality. *Psychological Bulletin, 101,* 233–258.

Finegan, J. K., Zucker, K. J., Bradley, S. J., & Doering, R. W. (1982). Patterns of intellectual functioning and spatial ability in boys with gender identity disorder. *Canadian Journal of Psychiatry, 27,* 135–139.

Freund, K. W. (1974). Male homosexuality: An analysis of the pattern. In J. A. Loraine (Ed.), *Understanding homosexuality: Its biological and social bases* (pp. 25–81). New York: Elsevier.

Friday, N. (1991). *Women on top.* New York: Simon & Schuster.

Gebhard, P. (1972). Incidence of overt homosexuality in the United States and western Europe. In Livingood J. M. (Ed.), *National Institute of Mental Health Task Force on Homosexuality: Final report and background papers.* Washington, DC: U.S. Government Printing Office (DHEW Publication No. HSM 72-9116), 22–29.

Geschwind, N., & Galaburda, A. M. (1985). Cerebral lateralization, Part I. *Archives of Neurology, 42,* 428–459.

Gladue, B. A., Beatty, W. W., Larson, J., & Staton, R. D. (1990). Sexual orientation and spatial ability in men and women. *Psychobiology, 18,* 101–108.

Gladue B. A., Green R., & Hellman R. E. (1984). Neuroendocrine response to estrogen and sexual orientation. *Science, 225,* 1469–1499.

Gooren, L. (1986a). The neuroendocrine response of luteinizing hormone to estrogen administration in heterosexual, homosexual, and transsexual subjects. *Journal of Clinical Endocrinology and Metabolism. 63,* 583–588.

Gooren, L. (1986b). The neuroendocrine response of luteinizing hormone to estrogen administration in humans is not sex specific but dependent on the hormonal environment. *Journal of Clinical Endocrinology and Metabolism. 63,* 589–593.

Gooren, L. (1990). Biomedical theories of sexual orientation: A critical examination. In D. P. McWhirter, S. A. Sanders, & J. M. Reinisch (Eds.), *Homosexuality/heterosexuality: Concepts of sexual orientation* (pp. 71–87). New York: Oxford University Press.

Gooren, L. (1991). New pathways into the biological research of gender dysphoria. Paper presented at Annual Meeting, International Academy of Sex Research, Barrie, Ontario.

Gorski, R. A. (1966). Localization and sexual differentiation of the nervous structures which regulate ovulation. *Journal of Reproduction and Fertility, 1* (Suppl), 67–88.

Götestam, K. O., Coates, T. J., & Ekstrand, M. (1992). Handedness, dyslexia and twinning in homosexual men. *International Journal of Neuroscience, 63,* 179–186.

Green, R. (1987). *The "sissy boy syndrome" and the development of homosexuality.* New Haven, CT: Yale University Press.

Grellert, E. A., Newcomb, M. D., & Bentler, P. M. (1982). Childhood play activities of male and female homosexuals and heterosexuals. *Archives of Sexual Behavior, 11,* 451–478.

Grimshaw, G., Zucker, K. J., Bradley, S. J., Lowry, C. B., & Mitchell, J. N. (1991). Verbal and spatial ability in boys with gender identity disorder. Paper presented at the International Academy of Sex Research, Barrie, Ontario.

Halperin, D. M. (1989). Sex before sexuality: Pederasty, politics, and power in classical Athens. In M. B. Duberman, M. Vicinus, & G. Chauncey, Jr. (Eds.), *Hidden from history: Reclaiming the gay and lesbian past* (pp. 37–53). New York: New American Library.

Hamilton, W. D. (1964). The genetical evolution of social behavior I. In G. C. Williams. (Ed.), *Group selection* (pp. 23–43). Chicago: Aldine.

Harry, J. (1983). Defeminization and adult psychological well-being among male homosexuals. *Archives of Sexual Behavior, 12,* 1–19.

Hendricks, S. E., Graber, B., & Rodriguez-Sierra, J. F. (1989). Neuroendocrine responses to exogenous estrogen: No differences between heterosexual and homosexual men. *Psychoneuroendocrinology. 14,* 177–185.

Hirschfeld, M. (1936). Homosexuality. In I. Bloch I & M. Hirschfeld (Eds.), *Encyclopaedia sexualis* (pp. 321–334). New York: Dingwall-Rock.

Hutchinson, G. E. (1959). A speculative consideration of certain possible forms of sexual selection in man. *American Naturalist, 93,* 81–91.

James, W. H. (1989). Foetal testosterone levels, homosexuality and handedness: A research proposal for jointly testing Geschwind's and Dörner's hypothesis. *Journal of Theoretical Biology, 136,* 177–180.

Johnson, A. M., Wadsworth, J., Wellings, K., Bradshaw, S., & Field, J. (1992). Sexual lifestyles and HIV risk. *Nature, 360,* 410–412.

Kallmann, F. J. (1952a). Twin and sibship study of overt male homosexuality. *American Journal of Human Genetics, 4,* 136–146.

Kallmann, F. J. (1952b). Comparative twin study on the genetic aspects of male homosexuality. *Journal of Nervous and Mental Disease, 115,* 283–298.

Kinsey, A. C., Pomeroy, W. B., & Martin, C. E. (1948). *Sexual behavior in the Human Male.* Philadelphia: Saunders.

Kinsey, A. C., Pomeroy, W. B., Martin, C. E., & Gebhard, P. H. (1953). *Sexual behavior in the human male.* Philadelphia: Saunders.

King, M., & McDonald, E. (1992). Homosexuals who are twins: A study of 46 probands. *British Journal of Psychiatry, 160,* 407–409.

Klein, F. (1990). The need to view sexual orientation as a multivariable dynamic process: A theoretical perspective. In D. P. McWhirter, S. A. Sanders, & J. M. Reinisch (Eds.), *Homosexuality/heterosexuality: Concepts of sexual orientation* (pp. 277–282). New York: Oxford University Press.

Lehrman, D. S. (1970). Semantic and conceptual issues in the nature-nurture problem. In L. R. Aaronson & E. Tobach (Eds.), *Development and evolution of behavior* (pp. 17–52). San Francisco: W. H. Freeman & Company.

LeVay, S. (1991). A difference in hypothalamic structure between heterosexual and homosexual men. *Science, 253,* 1034–1037.

LeVay, S. (1993). *The sexual brain.* Cambridge, MA: MIT Press.

Lev-Ran, A. (1974). Sexuality and educational levels of women with the late-treated adrenogenital syndrome. *Archives of Sexual Behavior, 3,* 27–32.

Lewontin, R. C., Rose, S., & Kamin, L. J. (1984). *Not in our genes.* New York: Pantheon Books.

Lidz, T. (1968). *The person: His development throughout the life cycle.* New York: Basic Books.

Lindesay, J. (1987). Laterality shift in homosexual men. *Neuropsychologia, 25,* 965–969.

Linn, M. C., & Petersen, A. C. (1985). Emergence and characterization of sex differences in spatial ability: A meta-analysis. *Child Development, 56,* 1479–1498.

Marchant-Haycox, S. E., McManus, I. C., & Wilson, G. D. (1991). Left-handedness, homosexuality, HIV infection and AIDS. *Cortex, 27,* 49–56.

Martin, J. T., & Baum, M. T. (1986). Neonatal exposure of female ferrets to testosterone alters sociosexual preferences in adulthood. *Psychoneuroendocrinology, 11,* 167–176.

McCormick, C. M., Witelson, S. F., & Kingstone, E. (1990). Left-handedness in homosexual men and women: Neuroendocrine implications. *Psychoneuroendocrinology, 15,* 69–76.

McGlone, J. (1980). Sex differences in human brain asymmetry: A critical survey. *The Behavioral and Brain Sciences, 3,* 215–227.

Meyer-Bahlburg, H. (1984). Psychoendocrine research on sexual orientation. Current status and future options. In De Vries, G. J., De Bruin, J. P. C., Uylings, H. M. B., Corner, M. A. (Eds.), *Progress in brain research* (vol. 61; pp. 375–398). Amsterdam: Elsevier.

Mineka, S., Davidson, M., Cook, M., & Keir, R. (1984). Observational conditioning of snake fear in rhesus monkeys. *Journal of Abnormal Psychology, 93,* 355–372.

Money, J. (1988). *Gay, straight, and in-between.* Oxford: Oxford University Press.

Money, J., Schwartz M., & Lewis V. G. (1984). Adult erotosexual status and fetal hormonal masculinization and demasculinization. *Psychoneuroendocrinology, 9,* 405–414.

Mulaikal, R. M., Migeon, C. J., & Rock, J. A. (1987). Fertility rates in female patients with congenital adrenal hyperplasia due to 21-hydroxylase deficiency. *New England Journal of Medicine, 316,* 178–182.

Nass, R., Baker, S., Speiser, P., Virdis, R., Balsamo, A., Cacciari, E., Loche, A., Dumic, M., & New, M. (1987). Hormones and handedness: Left-hand bias in female congenital adrenal hyperplasia patients. *Neurology, 37,* 57–77.

Pillard, R. C. (1990). The Kinsey Scale: Is it familial? In D. P. McWhirter, S. A. Sanders, & J. M. Reinisch (Eds.), *Homosexuality/heterosexuality: Concepts of sexual orientation* (pp. 88–100). New York: Oxford University Press.

Pillard, R. C., & Weinrich, J. D. (1986). Evidence of familial nature of male homosexuality. *Archives of General Psychiatry, 43,* 808–812.

Plomin, R. (1990). The role of inheritance in behavior. *Science, 248,* 183–188.

Plomin, R., DeFries, J. C., & McClearn, G. E. (1989). *Behavioral genetics: A primer.* New York: W. H. Freeman & Company.

Resnick, S., Berenbaum, S. A., Gottesman, I. I., & Bouchard, T. J. (1986). Early hormonal influences on cognitive functioning in congenital adrenal hyperplasia. *Developmental Psychology, 22,* 191–198.

Rosenthal, D. (1970). *Genetic theory and abnormal behavior.* New York: McGraw-Hill, Inc.

Ruse, M. (1988). *Homosexuality.* Oxford: Basil Blackwell Ltd.

Sanders, G., & Ross-Field, L. (1986). Sexual orientation and visuo-spatial ability. *Brain and Cognition, 5,* 280–290.

Satz, P., Miller, E. N., Selnes, O., Van Gorp, W., D'Elia, L. F. (1991). Hand preference in homosexual men. *Cortex, 27,* 295–306.

Siegelman, M. (1981). Parental backgrounds of homosexual and heterosexual men: A cross national replication. *Archives of Sexual Behavior, 10,* 505–520.

Stockman, E. R., Callaghan, R. S., & Baum, M. J. (1985). Effects of neonatal castration and testosterone propionate treatment on sexual partner preference in the ferret. *Physiology and Behaviour, 34,* 409–414.

Swaab, D. F., & Fliers, E. (1985). A sexually dimorphic nucleus in the human brain. *Science, 228,* 1112–1115.

Swaab, D. F., & Hofman, M. A. (1990). An enlarged suprachiasmatic nucleus in homosexual men. *Brain Research, 537,* 141–148.

Tkachuk, J., & Zucker, K. J. (1991). The relation among sexual orientation, spatial ability, handedness, and recalled childhood gender identity in women in men. Paper presented at Annual Meeting, International Academy of Sex Research, Barrie, Ontario.

Waller, N. G., Kojetin, B. A., Bouchard, T. J., Lykken, D. T., & Tellegen, A. (1990). Genetic and environmental influences on religious interests, attitudes, and values: A study of twins reared apart and together. *Psychological Science, 1,* 138–142.

Watson, D. B. (1991, Spring). Laterality and handedness in adult transsexuals. *SIECCAN Journal, 6,* 22–26.

Weinrich, J. D. (1987). *Sexual landscapes.* New York: Charles Scribner's Sons.

Whitam, F. L. (1977). Childhood indicators of male homosexuality. *Archives of Sexual Behavior, 6,* 89–96.

Whitam, F. L., Diamond, M., & Martin, J. (1992). Homosexual orientation in twins: A report on 61 pairs and three triplet sets. Paper presented at Annual Meeting, International Academy of Sex Research, Prague, Czechoslovakia.

Whitam, F. L., & Mathy, R. M. (1986). *Male homosexuality in four societies: Brazil, Guatemala, the Philippines, and the United States.* New York: Praeger.

Wilson, E. O. (1978). *On human nature.* Cambridge, MA.: Harvard University Press.

Zubin, J. (1987). Closing comments. In H. Häfner, W. F. Gattaz, & W. Janzarik (Eds.), *Search for the causes of schizophrenia* (pp. 359–365). Berlin: Springer-Verlag.

Zucker, K. J., Bradley, S. J., Oliver, G., Hood, J. E., Blake, J., & Fleming, S. (1992). Psychosexual assessment of women with congenital adrenal hyperplasia: Preliminary analyses. Paper presented at Annual Meeting, International Academy of Sex Research, Prague, Czechoslovakia.

Zuger, B. (1978). Effeminate behavior in boys from childhood: Ten additional years of follow-up. *Comprehensive Psychiatry, 19,* 363–369.

6

Social Constructionism: Implications for Lesbian and Gay Psychology

Celia Kitzinger

In 1987, the theme of the International Scientific Conference on Gay and Lesbian Studies (Free University of Amsterdam, December 15–18) was what was then known as the "essentialism/ social constructionism debate," seen as "the hottest philosophical controversy to hit psychology in years" (Weinrich, 1987). It is a debate which no longer attracts the same passion it did then—not because one theory has gained precedence, but rather because the adversaries apparently became weary of the argument, and the debate itself came to be seen as impeding developments within each paradigm. The key protagonists in "essentialism" and "social constructionism" today tend to pursue their scholarly endeavors with little more than token reference to researchers in the other camp. This chapter, written from my perspective as a lesbian feminist and psychologist who has participated in the debate from a social constructionist perspective (e.g., Kitzinger, 1987, 1989a, 1989b, 1992), is an overview of that debate and its implications.

The essentialism/ social constructionism debate was dogged with problems from the start, not the least among them difficulties over terminology. Both sides in the debate were named by the social constructionists, and "essentialist" quickly became a term of abuse, with scholars so labeled eager to defend themselves against the charge. According to essentialists, their views were misrepresented in a deliberately naive fashion, and caricatured as "intellectual[ly] Neanderthal" (Dynes, 1990: 217). Perhaps in the hope of fostering an illusory unity, virtually everyone became a social constructionist (of a sort) overnight, often without repudiating any of their essentialist beliefs. Consequently, to distinguish their own views from those of yesterday's essentialists, most of whom claimed the social constructionist label without making any significant adjustments to their theory, some social constructionists adopted the prefix "strong" or "radical," in opposition to the "weak" social constructionism of their opponents. The latter (who accepted neither the label "weak social constructionist" nor "essentialist") then accused the former of extremism, of "throwing the baby out with the bathwater" (Stein, 1990c: 349). Scholarly discussion degenerated into confusion and argument over the "proper" definition of social constructionism, as social constructionists levied accusations against those of their (newly inflated) number allegedly infected with the taint of "essentialism." Most recently, some of the central figures of social constructionism have begun to harness the terminology and concepts of the more fashionable postmodernism (cf. Plummer, 1992; Gergen, 1994). The theoretical underpinnings of postmodernism—its rejection of the "grand narrative" of science or of any "reality" unmediated by human experience; its refusal of "the unitary self" and concomitant characterization of people's shifting, multiple, fragmented identities constructed through "performance"; its reliance on texts or discourses that don't reflect or reveal reality but take meaning from their audiences—have proved very attractive to erstwhile "strong" social constructionists. Moreover, this new label serves to clearly differentiate them from the "weak" social constructionists whose position was increasingly conflated with their own in the psychological literature and, ultimately, has removed them from the increasingly stale social constructionist/ essentialist debate.

This chapter's structure is as follows: in the next section I discuss the emergence of the debate and its historical origins within research on sexuality, and in the second section I distinguish between what is now often known as "weak" versus "strong" social constructionism. I move on, in the third section, to identify a key aspect of social constructionism, often ignored in the research on sexuality: its challenge to empirical psychology—and, indeed, to science itself. With social constructionism clarified, examples of essentialist research on homosexuality are given in the fourth section. The next section discusses the impossibility of resolving the essentialism/social constructionism debate, and the chapter ends with a consideration of the implications of the debate for lesbian and gay politics and for the future of psychological research on lesbian and gay issues.

It should be noted that social constructionism (like the postmodernism that is replacing it) was always an interdisciplinary movement. For those who believe that realities are socially constructed, psychology is often a frustratingly narrow discipline which tends to privatize, individualize, and depoliticize the phenomena it studies (cf. Kitzinger & Perkins, 1993). Social constructionist psychologists have always drawn heavily from work by sociologists, historians, political scientists, and, lately, by literary, communication, and media theorists to make their claims about the social, historical, political, and discursive construction of psychological phenomena. For that reason, and because social constructionism within psychology cannot be understood without reference to the social constructionism outside its boundaries, the reader will find many nonpsychologists cited in this chapter: their work has been integral to the development of a social constructionist psychology.

The Emergence of Social Constructionist Research on Sexuality

Social constructionist research on sexuality is often said to have begun with a paper by British sociologist Mary McIntosh (1968) on "the homosexual role." Described as "one of the earliest social constructionist papers" (Tiefer, 1987), and "a landmark article" (Plummer, 1981b: 23), this paper is frequently cited in social constructionist considerations of sexuality and has been reprinted many times (e.g., Plummer, 1981a; Stein, 1990a). Celebrated as a "chief pioneer" (Dynes, 1990: 210) in applying a social constructionist framework to homosexuality, Mary McIntosh drew on the sociological approach of labeling theory to propose that "the homosexual should be seen as playing a social role rather than as having a condition." The assumption that homosexuality is a condition (like cancer or diabetes) has led, she says (McIntosh, 1968), to inappropriate questions about its etiology, and specifically to the innate/acquired debate which dominated pre-1970s research:

> The failure of research to answer the question has not been due to lack of scientific rigour or to any inadequacy of the available evidence; it results rather from the fact that the wrong question has been asked. One might as well try to trace the aetiology of "committee chairmanship" or "Seventh Day Adventism" as of "homosexuality." (p. 187)

The homosexual role, she argues, does not exist in many societies, only emerged in England toward the end of the seventeenth century, and (as Kinsey's 1948 and 1953 figures show) is adopted by only a small percentage of those who engage in same-sex sexual behavior. "It is not until he sees homosexuals as a social category, rather than a medical or psychiatric one," she concludes, "that the sociologist can begin to ask the right questions about the specific content of the homosexual role and about the organization and functions of homosexual groups" (p. 192).

The major contribution of this article was, as social constructionist historian Jeffrey Weeks (1981: 81) says, to pinpoint as a significant problem: "the emergence of the notion that homosexuality is a condition peculiar to some people and not others." This is, he argues, a particularly modern notion of homosexuality: "the historical evidence points to the latter part of the nineteenth century as the crucial period in the conceptualisation of homosexuality as the distinguishing characteristic of a particular kind of person" (Weeks, 1981; see also 1977). The same argument is developed by Foucault in volume one of *The History of Sexuality* (1979), a book which "has become for many social constructionists, the *locus classicus* of their program" (Stein, 1990b: 6). "The nineteenth-century homosexual," says Foucault (1979):

> became a personage, a past, a case history, and a childhood, in addition to being a type of life, a life form, and a morphology, with an indiscreet anatomy and possibly a mysterious physiology. . . . The sodomite had been a temporary aberration; the homosexual was now a species. (p. 15)

British sociologist Ken Plummer, whose edited book *The Making of the Modern Homosexual* (1981a) opens with the preceding quotation from Foucault in the frontispiece, makes a similar claim:

> At base, all the contributors to this book would argue that the homosexual is *not* a type of person that has been with us—in various guises—throughout time and space; he and she are not simply "beings" that we are slowly discovering and understanding better. . . . The "homosexual" then is an invention. . . . [This book] persistently strains to debunk the category of "homosexual." . . . (pp. 12, 29)

My own book, *The Social Construction of Lesbianism* (Kitzinger, 1987a), similarly argues that "the lesbian" as a type of being does not exist, but is rather actively constructed in a society which (according to the radical feminist analysis developed in the book) is predicated on male subordination of women through prevailing ideas of "femininity," including the requirement that the "feminine" woman be heterosexual.

In general terms, then, this refusal to view the homosexual as a type of person characterized by a potentially definable essence is pursued from a variety of perspectives in many social constructionist texts and

is probably the single most frequently cited aspect of social constructionist theory, set in contrast to the essentialist belief in the homosexual person (Stein, 1990a):

> . . . essentialists think that the categories of sexual orientation
> (e.g., heterosexual, homosexual and bisexual) are appropriate cat-
> egories to apply to individuals. According to essentialists, is it
> legitimate to inquire into the origin of heterosexuality or homo-
> sexuality, to ask whether some historical figure was a heterosex-
> ual or homosexual etc. This follows from the essentialist tenet that
> there are objective, intrinsic, culture-independent facts about
> what a person's sexual orientation is. In contrast, the social con-
> structionist denies that there are such facts about people's sexual
> orientation and would agree with the exhortation that it is mis-
> taken to look at an individual as being of a particular sexual orien-
> tation in the absence of a cultural construction of that orientation.
> (pp. 4–5)

From Mary McIntosh, through the writings of other (largely British)
authors (Hart & Richardson, 1981; Kitzinger, 1987a; Plummer, 1981a;
Weeks, 1977) the concept of "the homosexual" (and "the lesbian") was
revealed as socially, historically, and politically constructed.

The other researchers frequently cited (cf. Epstein, 1990: 246; Plummer, 1981a: 23) as originators of social constructionism are two North
American sociologists, John Gagnon and William Simon, who were
writing at about the same time as McIntosh, and drawing on the symbolic interactionist tradition to develop what they called script theory
(Simon & Gagnon, 1967a; Gagnon & Simon, 1967a, 1967b, 1973). Central to this theory (heavily cited in the British texts; cf. Plummer, 1981a;
Kitzinger, 1987a) was the refusal to privilege sexuality as a core aspect
of the self. Rather, "people become sexual in the same way they become everything else. Without much reflection, they pick up directions
from their social environment. They acquire and assemble meanings,
skills and values from the people around them" (Gagnon, 1977). Sex is
not an instinctive force or biological drive, controled by inner psychic
forces or hormonal fluctuations, but rather a social construct, regulated
by "sexual scripts." Unlike drives, which are fixed essences destined to
seek particular expression, "scripts" can be highly variable and fluid,
subject to constant revision and editing. This theory is obviously compatible with Mary McIntosh's concept of "the homosexual role."
Whereas ways of doing and experiencing sexuality had previously con-
solidated the person into a type of "being" with a sexual orientation,
now the person, far from expressing an "essential self" through sexuality, is conceptualized as an actor, fulfilling a role, complying with a

(socially constructed) script. The historian Michel Foucault (1979) is also routinely cited by (particularly "strong") social constructionists for his observation that sexual scripts (or discourses) are organized not simply by repression (e.g., banning homosexual behavior), but through definition and regulation (e.g., through sexological definition of what homosexuality is and psychological description of what "healthy" gay men and lesbians are like). Social control of sexuality not only represses lesbian and gay identities, but also produces them.

Social constructionism, then, includes the belief that societies do not simply ban homosexual activities and identities, they also actively produce and shape them in accordance with their own political and ideological requirements. It involves, too, exploration of the disjuncture between homosexual (same-sex) sexual *activities* and homosexual *identities*, that is, people "doing homosexual things" without developing a homosexual identity (e.g., some rent boys for sex only; some women are "in love with a person who *just happens to be* a woman"; cf. Kitzinger, 1987a) and others maintaining a "homosexual," "lesbian," or "gay" identity without "doing homosexual things" (e.g., celibates and some "political lesbians"). Although some theorists point to "bisexuality" (activity or identity) as an example of refusal to conform to the essentialist and dichotomous categories of "gay" and "straight," others theorize bisexuality in a way that renders it as essential an identity as any other: some people are "really" lesbian/gay; others "really" heterosexual; and some "really" bisexual (cf. Norris & Read, 1985). Just as hermaphoditism does not necessarily disrupt notions of masculinity and femininity (and may even be used to reinforce them), so bisexuality does not necessarily disrupt notions of homo- and heterosexuality. Rather, it is used to reinforce them, as in the common assumption that bisexuals are "in transition" between one sexual orientation and another, often countered by the equally essentialist declaration from bisexuals that they are neither heterosexual nor homosexual, but are bisexual. The notion of a "natural" bisexuality—as in "we're all bisexual really"—is equally essentializing in its assumption of a basic human nature. In sum, the assumption that humans have no basic, fundamental sexual nature that is transhistorical and transcultural, and to which labels such as "heterosexual", "homosexual," and "bisexual" can unproblematically be applied, is a key feature of social constructionist theory.

"Weak" versus "Strong" Forms of Social Constructionist Research

The increasingly wide use of the term "social constructionism" in lesbian and gay studies conceals an important distinction between those who argue simply that society influences and controls who we are as people and those who make much stronger claims. The weak form of social constructionism is the familiar argument that socialization, conditioning, media, advertising, and social arrangements, which encourage heterosexuality and prohibit homosexuality make it impossible to begin to understand lesbian or gay existence without reference to its social, historical, and political context. This argument is relatively unproblematic and is consistent with most psychological views that argue for, and document the role of, learning in human development. The strong form of social constructionism takes this idea further. At its most fundamental, it looks at the ways in which the taken-for-granted categories we use are themselves social constructions: the notions of "the homosexual" and "sexual drive" are seen as social categories or linguistic devices for ordering the world, which modern Western culture reifies as "natural," "universal," and "the way things have to be."

The distinctions between these so-called strong and weak forms of social constructionism is perhaps best illustrated by example. Many people accept that maleness and femaleness are social constructions in the (weak) sense that "sex-role stereotypes" and "gender socialization" determine acceptable models of masculinity and femininity, and that these models are historically and culturally variable. Psychologists researching sex or gender differences do so by comparing the performance of men and women, boys and girls, across a variety of tasks. Irrespective of whether they find categorical differences or large areas of statistical overlap between the sexes, they have predicated their work on and reinforced the notion that people are divided into two sexes. The notion that (apart from anomalies such as transsexuals and hermaphrodites) there are two, and only two, sexes is taken for granted as a basic and intransigent fact of life. Some social constructionists have begun to ask why it seems so obvious to us that people are either male or female, and whether it is possible to imagine that we do not "naturally" exist as women and men—that these are fundamentally ideological not biological categories. Although weak social constructionists accept (to varying degrees) the existence of an ideological overlay to "maleness" and "femaleness," and point to the differing constructions of masculinity and femininity in different social and ethnic groups, they nonetheless retain the notion of fundamental anatomical cross-cultural differences between the sexes. To argue that even these supposed anatomical differences are socially constructed seems bizzare and counter to common sense, yet this is precisely what some strong social constructionists propose (cf. Unger, 1988; Kitzinger, 1989b). In developing this argument it is possible to draw upon the writings of some French feminists (e.g., Wittig, 1981) who propose jettisoning the concept of "woman" altogether: it is, they say, not a natural given, but a political category. Just as the concept of race was constructed only with the socioeconomic reality of black slavery (Guillaumin, 1977), so the concept of woman functions only as a marker of otherness and subordination. To describe woman as a natural category is to biologize the historical situation of domination. Clearly, this strong social constructionist argument goes well beyond notions about the social conditioning of maleness and femaleness and challenges the very categories themselves.

Similarly, many researchers on homosexual and lesbian identities have taken a broadly sociocultural approach, arguing that the meanings attached to being gay and lesbian are socially constructed in the (weak) sense that, for example, the experience and consequences of male same-sex sexual behavior is likely to be rather different in a classical Greek pedagogic relationship, in a modern London urinal between two married men, among the *berdache* Native Americans, and in contemporary San Francisco between two Queer activists. Weak social constructionists point out that, whatever the apparent similarity of the acts involved (e.g., genital stimulation), there are clearly vast dissimilarities in the implications of such acts for the person's identity, the way in which he explains his actions to himself, and the meanings they acquire in a social context. Again, this argument is relatively unproblematic. By contrast, the strong form of social constructionism takes issue with the notion that homosexuality (or heterosexuality or bisexuality) are natural givens and challenges the idea that some people "are" or can discover themselves to be gay or lesbian, while others are "really" heterosexual (or bisexual, or whatever other categories of sexual orientation the culture has spawned). Historian Sheila Jeffreys (1987) traces the development of the category "lesbian" with turn-of-the-century sexology. She argues that the function of the label was, as men faced the threat of emerging first-wave feminism, to pathologize women who refused to submit to men. In my own social constructionist research (Kitzinger, 1987a; 1989a), I explored the social and psychological implications of the invention of the lesbian category and the meanings ascribed to it.

Weak social constructionists often point to diversity as evidence for social constructionism—"diversity" generally functioning in this context as code for people of subordinated groups such as lesbians and gay men of color, of working-class backgrounds, old people, disabled lesbians and gays, and so on. For political reasons it is important that such groups are represented (and represent themselves) in social science, in society, and in policymaking; clearly, research and theory based only on white, middle-class, middle-aged, able-bodied gays and lesbians is severely limited in scope and applicability and should never be presented as if it reflected the universal experience of lesbians and gays as a whole. There are good *political* reasons for ensuring that we do not perpetuate invisibility and oppression in our own work. From a purely logical standpoint, however, it is neither necessary nor sufficient to illustrate diversity of this type in support of (strong) social constructionism. It is not necessary because, convenient as it is to be able to point to actual instances of diverse social constructions between members of different social and ethnic groups, failure to find any such differences does not disprove or in any way present a problem for social constructionism. Social constructionism does not rely on evidence for the existence of different social constructions, because doing so is already to rely on assumptions about what constitutes "evidence," what counts as similarity or difference, and—worse still—to accept that the way the world *is* sets limits on what could be. Even if, for example, every known group in the world incorporates the distinction to varying degrees (however inflected, however variously conceived) between "male" and "female," this does not mean that such a distinction (however universal it actually is) is *essential* in the very nature of things. Moreover, the existence of diversity is not *sufficient* to prove social constructionism correct, because there is a range of many equally logically valid interpretations of diversity of which the social constructionist thesis is only one. Diversity can equally illustrate the essential similarity of human beings despite the superficial trappings of culturally induced differences, or documents white Western man's evolutionary development from "primitive" societies to his present-day pinnacle (cf. Kitzinger, 1992, for a more detailed discussion of this point).

The strong social constructionist position is not, then, simply (or even) that "homosexual/lesbian" people have different experiences, opportunities, and self-concepts in different cultures, socioeconomic, and ethnic groups or at different ages, but rather that categories of sexual orientation are themselves socially constructed. Just as "male" and "female" can be dereified, so too the categories of "gay," "lesbian," "bisexual," and "heterosexual" can be seen not as reflecting "natural" realities (determined by genes, hormones, early conditioning, or the dark forces of the unconscious), but rather as constituted by socially meaningful ways of organizing experience, by the repertoires available to us in Western culture, by common forms of discursive practice. Unless otherwise specified, I refer to this (strong) form of social constructionism in the rest of this chapter.

There is, however, another key aspect of social constructionism—one which figures large within social constructionist research in psychology more generally but is curiously absent from most of the social constructionist studies focusing on the lesbian and/or gay experience—and it is to this that I now turn.

Social Constructionism as a Challenge
to Empirical Science

The essentialist/social constructionist debate is not specific to the issue
of homosexuality, and although psychologists working on questions of
sexuality were among the first to adopt social constructionist perspectives, they were not alone in so doing. There had been earlier challenges to psychology's failure to take seriously the influence of the social (notably Mischel, 1968); however, the origins of social
constructionism in psychology are usually traced to Gergen's (1973) paper "Social Psychology as History," which sought to undermine psychology's claims to discovering "facts" about the world, documenting
the extent to which those "facts" rely on their social, historical, and
political context. As one of the main proponents of a social constructionist (now postmodernist; Gergen, 1992) psychology, Gergen (1985)
identifies as key to social constructionism this assumption that the categories we study are social rather than "natural" products. Over the last
few decades, psychology as a discipline has been forced to confront
questions about the socially constructed versus essential nature of not
just homosexuality but, potentially, every other category, including the
notion of gender (maleness and femaleness; Kessler & McKenna, 1978),
the concept of "the individual" (Sampson, 1983; Kitzinger, 1992), the
emotions (Averill, 1982; 1985; Harré, 1986), and the concepts of mental
health and mental disorder (Szasz, 1971). For each, "the objective criteria for identifying such 'behaviors,' 'events' or 'entities' are shown to
be either highly circumscribed by culture, history or social context or
altogether nonexistent" (Gergen, 1985). This aspect of social constructionism should be familiar from earlier discussions in this chapter.

But Gergen (1985) identifies a second key aspect of social constructionism: the deconstruction of science itself. Drawing on sociology and
philosophy of science (e.g., Deutscher, 1968; Knorr-Cetina & Mulkay,
1983; Garfinkel, 1981; Mitroff, 1974; Rorty, 1980), social constructionism
represents the taken-for-granted category of "science" as socially constituted and historically determined, arguing that our notions about
what it is to "do" science, what "count" as scientific facts, and what
constitutes "good" scientific practice are the products of the particular
place, time, and culture in which they are embedded. If science is
merely a local custom, it cannot purvey "objective truths" and cannot
be warranted empirically. Rejection of the notion of scientific objectivity was a feature of (radical or strong) social constructionism from the
outset (cf. Gergen, 1973, 1982, 1985) and has become particularly prominent in the postmodern accounts, now popular with those who earlier
identified themselves with social constructionism. In such accounts,
the notion of a logical, linear, and rational science is identified as part

of the "modernist" project—a "grand narrative" that now gives way to radical doubt, contingency, and irony. Modernism in psychology, according to Gergen (1992), involved

> belief in a knowable world . . . a belief in universal properties . . . principles, possibly laws that may be discovered about the properties of the subject matter . . . a belief in truth through method. In particular, the pervasive belief that, by using empirical methods and most particularly the controlled experiment, one could derive obdurate truths about the nature of the subject matter and the causal networks in which it is embedded . . . a belief in the progressive nature of research. As empirical methods are applied to the subject matter of psychology, we learn increasingly about its fundamental character. False beliefs can be abandoned, and we move toward the establishment of reliable, value-neutral truths about the various segments of the objective world. (pp. 19–20)

In Ken Plummer's words, this "quest for the grand truth, the scientific solution, . . . the linear progression, and the theoretical purity are now all seen as flawed" (Plummer, 1992: 14). Social constructionists tend to focus instead on discussing the role of power in the social making of meanings, rhetoric, and narrative in establishing sciences, reflexivity in method and theorizing, and the processes by which human experiences, common sense, and scientific knowledge are both produced in, and reproduce, human communities (e.g., Semin & Gergen, 1990; Steier, 1991; Nencel & Pels, 1991; Edwards & Potter, 1992; McNamee & Gergen, 1993—all books in the "Inquiries in Social Construction Series" edited by Gergen and Shotter). The first chapter of *The Social Construction of Lesbianism* (Kitzinger, 1987a) is devoted to an analysis of "Rhetoric in Research on Lesbianism and Male Homosexuality."

Social constructionist theory, then, means more than (although it includes) the concept of a homosexual or lesbian identity as socially constituted and historically determined. The argument that the terms "homosexual" and "lesbian" (as nouns) are of relatively recent origin, that they are "social" rather than "natural" or "essential" categories; that historically and cross-culturally same-sex sexual activity has a range of different (or no) implications for identity; and that labels and categories of sexuality are invented as part of a concern to regulate and control is well represented in the social constructionist literature on homosexuality. But the concept of social science itself as a form of rhetoric or discourse, and its implications for gay and lesbian psychology, is less often appreciated in lesbian and gay studies, even those that purport a social constructionist perspective.

Another indication of incomprehension of (strong) social constructionism's challenge to science is the frequency with which researchers present social constructionism and essentialism as though they were two competing explanations for sexual identity: homosexuality is either an "essential" or a "socially constructed" identity, and the research task is then conceptualized as the gathering of evidence to determine which of these two explanations is "right," or, indeed, to assess the relative contributions of essentialism and social constructionism in forming lesbian and gay identities. But to attempt to arbitrate on this question, and to assume that the gathering of empirical evidence can potentially resolve the matter objectively, is already to work within an essentialist framework. Those who argue, for example, that "in the last analysis, the theoretical revisions of constructionism will be of little value if there is no empirical basis for them" (Boswell, 1990: 150) attempt to use the methods of essentialism to interrogate a theoretical framework which fundamentally challenges those very methods.

Outing Closet Essentialisms

Historian John Boswell (1990), identified by many as an arch essentialist, has claimed that "no reasonable person would disagree with the proposition implicit in the constructionist critique" (p. 135) and that "no one deliberately identifies himself as an essentialist." The claim has even been made that there are virtually no essentialists left and that essentialism is a straw man, constructed by the social constructionists as a foil for their own theory (cf. Boswell, 1990: 134; Stein, 1990c: 326). In fact, from the perspective of (strong) social constructionism, what is remarkable is not how few, but how many essentialists there are, both within and beyond psychology.

Given the definition of social constructionism advanced by Ken Gergen and other strong social constructionists, essentialism is an accurate description of (1) claims that there is (or could be) scientific evidence offering accurate facts about homosexuality against which our theories and beliefs can be judged; and (2) claims that there are (or could be) specific "causes" of sexuality, such that some individuals are homosexual (or heterosexual, or bisexual) and others are not. Lesbian historian Lillian Faderman (1991), for example, despite her self-designation as "social constructionist," qualifies as "essentialist" by both criteria in the following extract:

> My own research has caused me to align myself on the side of the social constructionists. While I believe that some women, statistically very few, may have been "born different," i.e. genetically or hormonally "abnormal," the most convincing research I have been able to find indicates that such an anomaly is extremely

rare among lesbians. Perhaps in the future studies will emerge
that present compelling support for the essentialist position with
regard to lesbianism, but such work does not exist at present.
(p. 8)

Similarly, Edward Stein (1990c) states that "if one's sexual orientation
is caused by having a certain gene, then social constructionism is
wrong" (p. 352), and John Boswell (1990) claims that "if a predilection
for sexual activity with one gender could be shown to be innate in all
humans or fixed in childhood in all (or even many) known cultures,
then it would be rather pointless to argue that all 'sexuality' is socially
constructed" (p. 138). Such notions overlook the important body of research on the social construction of "maleness" and "femaleness,"
which flourishes despite our knowledge of the existence of X and Y
chromosomes and ignores the epistemological challenge of social constructionism. As Ken Gergen (1992) puts it, "the very idea of scientific
progress is a literary achievement" (p. 25). As a final example, contrast
this essentialist plea for "better science" with the social constructionist
rejection of the grand metanarrative of scientific progress:

> The process of eliminating bias from the scientific exercise is an
> ongoing one. . . . We all, scientists included, see the world
> through filters containing degrees of distortion. It is the profes-
> sional and ethical responsibility of scientists and scholars to main-
> tain an ongoing process of recognising and reducing such distor-
> tions. There is little question that this is an exceptionally difficult
> undertaking. There is also little question that scientists and schol-
> ars are obliged to undertake it. (Gonsiorek, 1991: 244)

Other examples of views that are essentialist because of their concept
of "the homosexual" as a natural given include the following:

> . . . most research findings indicate that homosexual feelings are
> a basic part of an individual's psyche. (Gonsiorek & Weinrich,
> 1991: 2)

> . . . sexual status or orientation, whatever its genesis, may be-
> come assimilated and locked into the brain as monosexually ho-
> mosexual or heterosexual or as bisexually a mixture of both. . . .
> Overall, it would appear that the most important formative years
> for homosexuality, bisexuality and heterosexuality are those of
> late infancy and prepubertal childhood. (Money, 1988: 12, 124)

> . . . a chemical imbalance in the womb can also alter sexual incli-
> nations in the eventual adult. We know how to make homosexual
> rats and monkeys. (Moir & Jessel, 1989: 36)

Essentialist views of both the scientific endeavour and lesbian/gay identities are very common throughout gay and lesbian studies. Far from being a straw person, essentialism is the dominant paradigm for most psychological studies of sexuality, and with the publicity given to biological determinist studies like Simon LeVay's (1991), it is enjoying renewed popularity.

The Impossibility of Resolving the Essentialist/ Social Constructionist Controversy

Many scholars have hoped for a "resolution" of the essentialist/social constructionist controversy, some wanting "science" to decide which is "right," others believing in the possibility of uniting the two perspectives. Given the preceding discussion, it should be clear why neither resolution is possible. If social constructionism meant only that homosexual identity is constructed in and influenced by its social context, then indeed it might be possible to explore the relative contributions of "nature" and "social context" to the making of a homosexual identity, and for those researchers who have interpreted social constructionism in this very limited (weak) sense, that is certainly a possible resolution. But insofar as (strong) social constructionism embodies a fundamental critique of social science itself, and insofar as it rejects a priori the notion of "nature" and sees society not as influential on but as constitutive of the homosexual identity, no resolution can be achieved.

This is not to say that resolution cannot be achieved within some of the debates that have flourished under the banners of essentialism versus constructionism. Arguments about the contribution of cultural influences in gay/lesbian/bisexual development; disputes about when, historically, it became possible to define oneself as "a homosexual"; disagreements about the extent to which people have (or feel they have) a "choice" in their sexual identity/orientation are all debates that are at least potentially resolvable. In fact, there are internal disagreements within both the essentialist and the social constructionist camps. But in theory, essentialists could discover the right answers, and social constructionists could use rhetorical force to persuade each other one way or the other. Moreover, there is no a priori reason why essentialists and constructionists shouldn't arrive at the *same* answers. In his ruthlessly logical analysis of potential social constructionist and essentialist answers to such questions, Edward Stein (1990c: 325–353) points out the ease with which concordance can be achieved by both sides on peripheral questions of this type. For example, it is entirely possible to believe that people have no "choice" about their sexuality from both a social constructionist and an essentialist position: whereas the essentialist might argue for biological determination or very early social determinants (cf. Money and Moir & Jessel, quoted earlier), the social constructionist might argue that, just as one is unable to choose membership in a social or economic class even though such membership is a cultural artifact, so sexual identity might be determined despite its socially constructed nature (cf. Halperin, 1990; Kitzinger, 1988). But such apparent agreements between social constructionists and essentialists serve only to conceal the fundamental differences between them.

Social constructionism does not offer alternative answers to questions posed by essentialism: it raises a wholly different set of questions. Instead of searching for "truths" about homosexuals and lesbians, it asks about the discursive practices, the narrative forms, within which homosexuals and lesbians are produced and reproduced. In its opposition to, and deconstruction of, both "homosexuals" and "science" itself, it can never be rendered compatible with the essentialist project.

Scientific and Political Implications of the Debate

The essentialist/social constructionism debate has been valuable for posing new questions and generating lively exchanges which have revitalized the field of lesbian and gay psychology. It has served, in particular, to invigorate the theory of an area of psychology that was in danger of becoming little more than continually reiterated demonstrations of lesbian and gay mental health and the descriptions of different homosexual life-styles. Controversy is useful in developing any area of inquiry, and the essentialist/social constructionist controversy has had the additional benefit of placing research on homosexuality within the main current of developing social constructionist (and, now, postmodernist) research both within and beyond the discipline. I want to suggest here that the apparent outcome of the debate, the persistence and continuing parallel development of *both* logically incompatible theoretical frameworks, is advantageous for the growth and vitality of both lesbian and gay psychology and the lesbian and gay movements.

It should be immediately obvious that both the essentialist commitment to science and the essentialist concept of "the homosexual" have proved valuable in establishing lesbian and gay civil and political rights—from Havelock Ellis' characterization of "the third sex" (used by Radcliffe Hall in her impassioned plea for lesbians in *The Well of Loneliness*) to contemporary expert witness statements about the mental health of lesbians involved in child custody cases or the influence of gay teachers on their pupils. Because essentialists retain the notion of, and aspire toward, an objective psychology, potentially uncontaminated by personal or social values, they are able to point out the scientific failings of psychological or common-sense accounts branding us sick and perverted. At the same time, their acceptance of the diagnostic enterprise in principle (cf. Gonsiorek, 1991: 115) enables them to dismiss the diagnosis of homosexuality as sickness as "bad science" (Gonsiorek, 1991: 115), because homosexuality is not a priori evidence of pathology. Many essentialists diagnose pathology in those who fear and hate homosexuals ("homophobes"; cf. Kitzinger, 1987b and Kitzinger & Perkins, 1993, for an overview and critique of homophobia research), and this has been seen by some gay liberationists as useful in combating antigay and antilesbian values. The essentialist belief in the existence of the homosexual can, says Margaret Cruikshank (1992: 28), "be interpreted as a validation of gay people, in the sense that a fixed and permanent identity is a desirable counterweight to arguments that homosexuals are just 'going through a phase.' " The biological theories of homosexual development favored by some essentialists enable a kind of moral neutrality "because it seems pointless to judge the outcome of a biological process in moral terms. It would be equally absurd to disapprove of the fact that tadpoles turn into frogs" (Moir & Jessel, 1989: 112). In claiming that we are in some way fundamentally, essentially homosexuals, we also claim that it is beyond our conscious control. We did not "chose" to be homosexual, and because no choice or act of free will is involved, we cannot be held personally responsible or judged morally culpable. For example, an American bishop, drawing on essentialist findings about the etiology of homosexuality, supported the demand for church blessings on gay partnerships, saying "homosexuality isn't immoral because it is caused by a chemical process in the brain" (Spong, 1988). In this way, essentialism, despite its earlier uses to "prove" lesbian and gay pathology, is often helpful to the lesbian and gay causes, in demonstrating lesbian and gay mental health and so vindicating those who seek equality and acceptance with heterosexuals.

The relationship between social constructionism and the gay and lesbian liberation movements has been more problematic. The critique of science is generally popular only when it is "bad" science which is under consideration (science allegedly demonstrating our pathology). Early feminist critiques of psychology, such as the groundbreaking article "Psychology Constructs the Female" by Naomi Weisstein (1971), argued quite simply that "psychology has nothing to say about what women are really like, what they need and what they want, essentially because psychology does not know," and the same arguments were made by lesbians and gay men. However, such critiques were rarely a call for the end of scientific authority per se; rather they functioned as calls for *more* and *better* science, science that respects the evidence, based on more than social stereotype, myth, and prejudice. Today, Naomi Weisstein describes the postmodern refusal of science as "a deeply conservative retreat." The rejection of the modernist project is characterized as leaving us without any firm ground on which to stand to describe our "realities."

> *Of course,* there is paralysis: once knowledge is reduced to insurmountable personal subjectivity, there is no place to go; we are in a swamp of self-referential passivity. Sometimes I think that, when the fashion passes, we will find many bodies, drowned in their own wordy words, like the Druids in the bogs. Meanwhile, the patriarchy continues to prosper. (Weisstein, 1993, pp. 243–244)

The other key problem which arises for social constructionist politics centers on the deconstruction of the category "homosexual," a move which has sometimes been seen to run counter to the political interests of lesbians and gays—even, on occasion, by social constructionist researchers themselves. Debates about the political relevance of scientific theories are commonplace today (cf. Green, 1992; Luker, 1993), but such concerns were prominent from the very beginning of social constructionist theory. When Mary McIntosh (1981) was writing her germinal article, "The Homosexual Role," opposing the notion of the transcultural and transhistorical existence of the homosexual, male homosexuality was illegal in the United Kingdom, and the Homosexual Law Reform Society was campaigning for law reform on a thoroughly essentialist basis:

> They were putting forward the view that homosexuals could not help being homosexual; it was just how nature made them, or at least something that happened in very early childhood and that all societies have their homosexuals, so there should be no laws against homosexual behaviour. . . . So I felt very diffident about actually publishing anything, because I thought I was right but, on the other hand, this was not the moment to be going round talking about it. It would not contribute to the political developments of the time to say that sort of thing. I think that may be partly why I submitted it to an American journal rather than an English one, because the debates did not have quite the same form there." (p. 44)

The Wolfenden Report, which recommended the UK 1967 law reforms on male homosexuality, used deterministic arguments about homosexuality as an innate and permanent condition. Basically the same arguments were resurrected twenty years later in the campaign against Section 28 of the Local Government Act (now law in the United Kingdom), which makes it illegal for local government funds to be used to "promote" homosexuality as a "pretended family relationship"—a ruling with potentially serious implications for state schools, libraries, arts centers, and advice-giving organizations. The opponents of Section 28 often resorted to essentialist arguments, backed up by personal experience, data from the literature on conversion therapies, or simply the belief that this was the rhetorical form most likely to succeed against the Conservative government's data. The key argument was that no amount of proslytizing can change someone's sexual orientation, represented as a fixed and essential part of their identity. "We are what we are. It is impossible to force or encourage someone into a different sexuality from that which pertains to them," said Labour MP Chris Smith.

The social constructionist alternative advanced by some lesbian feminists (e.g., Alderson & Wistrich, 1988; Kitzinger, 1988) was predicated on the judgment that these essentialist arguments signaled political disaster. First, they are defensive and apologetic: homosexuality must be tolerated because "we can't help it"; our sexuality is beyond our control and outside our responsibility. The plea is that our homosexuality be excused on the grounds of diminished responsibility and accepted on condition that it's not contagious—cannot be spread by seduction or indoctrination. Second, it involves a tacit acceptance of the view that we are a "minority" of one in ten (or thereabouts) who have always existed and will always exist as an "alternative life-style" or "sexual variation," thus reinforcing belief in the validity of the heterosexual norm (of nine in ten) to which we constitute the alternative or variation. This directly contradicts the feminist analysis of heterosexuality, which presents it not as a natural, instinctive, and numerically normative sexual orientation, but rather as a coercive patriachal institution (e.g., Rich, 1980; Wilkinson & Kitzinger, 1993). Third, arguing that we were born that way (or might as well have been) is intended to suggest that homosexuality is "natural" (as natural as heterosexuality!), the assumption being that what is natural is both ethically acceptable and politically unchangeable. Feminists have spent more than a century challenging concepts of the natural which relegate women to the kitchen and the bedroom and justify and condone male subjugation of women. The use of the "gay seagulls" argument by some gay liberationists (like the use, by some feminists, of the female spider that bites off the head of the male in the act of copulation) is an attempt to redefine and problematize the natural. But arguing about the proper definition of nature only evades and obscures the political context defining the terms of the debate.

From the late 1960s on, while gay men in the United Kingdom were campaigning for law reform using the argument that homosexuality is a natural sexual orientation (and that our personal lives are our own private concern), second-wave feminists were beginning to analyze the oppressive role of heterosexuality and to explore the radical political implications of lesbianism (arguing that the personal is political). Unlike most gay men, who had a vested interest in essentialist arguments about homosexuality as an innate or very early developed form of being, lesbian feminists began to develop a theory that reflects *our* own interests—that lesbianism can potentially be chosen by all women in opposition to patriarchal oppression: "any woman can be a lesbian." Lesbian feminists then went on to explore why, under heteropatriarchy, so few women are able to choose lesbianism, why it is so hard for heterosexual women to change their erotic and sexual desires even when they consciously wish to do so, and to find political explanations for these social realities to replace the individualized approaches of essentialism (Kitzinger et al, 1992; Wilkinson & Kitzinger, 1993). Social constructionist approaches, then, overlap and fit well with aspects of radical lesbian feminist theory.

Given this apparent fit between radical lesbian feminist theory and social constructionist approaches, the political opposition to social constructionism and postmodernism from lesbian and feminist academics (psychologists included) (e.g., Burman, 1990; Jeffreys, 1993) is perhaps surprising at first. Part of this opposition stems, as we have seen, from the epistemological challenge to science itself—indeed to any notion of a fixed, objective reality (such as "patriarchy" or "oppression") which is encountered as an already-existing fact. Another important concern shared with gay men arises out of a need to self-define as an oppressed group: how, after all, do you protest a socially imposed categorization except by organizing around that category? Lesbianism may be a historically and culturally specific category, but when Adrienne Rich (1980) took our modern notion of lesbianism and extended it to form a "lesbian continuum," linking the resisters of heteropatriarchy across cultures and throughout history, she inspired political action. By contrast, being told that lesbians "don't really exist" inhibits and stultifies. If lesbianism doesn't exist, people fail to "see it." To be seen demands some identity, even if culturally scripted. Just when lesbian feminism and the gay movement made it possible for us to speak confidently for ourselves as lesbians, or as gay men, we are told that such a stance is theoretically suspect, and charges of essentialism are now used to scare lesbians and gays away from making any political claims on behalf of a group called "lesbian" or "gay." There has also been some concern about the extent to which early social constructionist research focused on the analysis of "the lesbian" as a socially constructed category, without, until very recently, an explicit analogous consideration of the socially constructed nature of *heterosexuality*. This led some lesbian feminists to reject social constructionism with the retort, "We'll deconstruct when they deconstruct" (MacDonald, 1990: 89). Other lesbians and gay men have taken the opportunity social constructionism offers to deconstruct heterosexuality itself (cf. Katz, 1990; Wilkinson & Kitzinger, 1993, 1994). Finally, some social constructionists (e.g., McIntosh, 1992; Faderman, 1991) use postmodern concepts of category transgression to express support for sadomasochism and other forms of sexual and fashion "adventures," which are rigorously criticized by radical lesbian feminists (e.g., Kitzinger & Kitzinger, 1993; Jeffreys, 1993). This, too, has led to distrust of social constructionism in radical lesbian feminist circles.

To sum up the political implications, then, it is not obvious that either essentialism or social constructionism is intrinsically best suited to be the theoretical precursor to lesbian and gay liberation. *Both* have been used successfully by lesbians and gay men in advancing their own causes. *Both* have led their proponents to political positions which they, or other activists, find uncomfortable or downright offensive. It seems that the oppression of lesbians and gay men can be effected by both essentialist and social constructionist alike; and, equally, the struggle against that oppression, can make use of both (albeit logically incompatible) frameworks. My own solution is to be a radical lesbian feminist first, a social constructionist (or essentialist) when it suits my radical feminist purposes (and a "psychologist," as conventionally defined, virtually never, because of the tremendous problems in uniting psychology with social constructionist and radical lesbian feminist perspectives; this is further explored in Kitzinger, 1990, and Kitzinger & Perkins, 1993).

The implication of this discussion for the development of lesbian and gay psychology is to encourage both essentialism *and* social constructionism. Most of psychology retains a strong commitment to essentialism (cf. Gergen, 1992), such that essentialist research on lesbian and gay issues has a firm foundation within the discipline. No other area of psychology lacks proponents of the essentialist standpoint, and it would augur ill for lesbian and gay psychology were this area alone in eschewing essentialist research and theory. In terms of securing (outside the United States) and maintaining (within it) a firm foothold for lesbian and gay issues within the discipline of psychology as a whole, then, essentialist perspectives are a vital necessity. Essentialist perspectives are also important in furthering civil rights. As long as the legal and political apparatus by which we are governed is (or affects to be) responsive to scientific "evidence" or "data" in making decisions about who is allowed to teach what in state schools, who is permitted to adopt or foster children or to use medically provided artificial insemination services, who is imprisoned, and what acts of violence count as crimes, one can argue that it is important for gay and lesbian psychologists not to vacate the field. (Note, however, that I have also advanced the opposite argument—that we should abandon empirical research forthwith; Kitzinger, 1992). If one accepts this argument, it becomes important to identify those areas of research most likely to have an impact on social change: contemporary research on violence and hate crimes against lesbians and gay men (e.g., Herek & Berrill, 1992, Plasek & Allard, 1985) seems a promising candidate.

It is equally important to point out that *not* developing social constructionist (and, now, postmodernist) perspectives would have left research in this area looking quaintly old-fashioned, both within psychology and (especially) within the interdisciplinary field of lesbian and gay studies. In evolving social constructionist and postmodernist approaches, lesbian and gay research is seen to advance in line with theoretical developments within (and beyond) psychology as a whole, and sometimes to be on the cutting edge of those developments, for example, in so-called queer theory (cf. de Lauretis, 1991; Smyth, 1992; Smith, 1992), which—whatever criticisms we might advance from a lesbian feminist perspective (and these are many)—at least succeeds more often than do social constructionism or postmodernism in uniting academic theory with political activism. For social constructionists, empirical work with a potentially political impact is often frustratingly problematic because of social constructionism's own critique of empiricism. Increasingly, research from this perspective points reflexively to its own socially constructed nature and thus loses the potential rhetorical impact of "empirically verified facts."

The social constructionist/essentialist debate is ultimately irresolvable, because these two positions are not commensurate. Social constructionism and essentialism not only offer different answers, but also ask different questions and rely on different approaches to finding the answers (empiricism versus rhetoric). In many ways, social constructionism can be seen as a kind of metatheory, because it can incorporate essentialism as a form of rhetoric. On the whole I have generally (though not always; cf. Comely et al., 1990) aligned myself with the social constructionist perspective. But for social constructionists there is always the option of using essentialist arguments as a rhetorical form on a par with any other. The extent to which social constructionists should self-consciously and in their own (on their groups') interest use a rhetorical form (such as that of empirical science) in which they do not personally believe is a matter of ethical and political debate (cf. Hall et al., 1992; Kitzinger, 1990). Contemporary moral values stressing sincerity and the individualistic concept of "being true to oneself" denounce such choices as "inauthentic" and mendacious. But social constructionism has revealed these very values as socially constructed: notions of "sincerity" and "authenticity" depend on a peculiarly modern and culturally specific concept of "selfhood" (Trilling, 1972; see also

Kitzinger, 1992). In any event, it is hard to argue for the moral or political superiority of a refusal to attest to the mental health of a lesbian mother in a custody case on the grounds that the concept of "mental health" is a socially constructed one. At such times, the "moral purity" of social constructionists is a luxury sustained only because of the existence of their theoretical opponents, the unreconstructed essentialists who can truthfully, and without bad faith, enter the witness stand. Both politically, and theoretically (because much of it is critique), social constructionism depends on the continuing existence of essentialism.

Hence, whatever the problems for individual psychologists who feel forced to make a choice between opposing perspectives, it can only be a sign of the vitality of lesbian and gay psychology as a discipline, and of its potential for continuing contribution to lesbian and gay politics, that the unresolvable essentialist/constructionist debate has now been transcended and that research continues within both traditions.

References

Alderson, L., & Wistrich, H. (1988). Clause 29: Radical feminist perspectives. *Trouble and Strife 13*: 3–8.

Averill, J. (1982). *Anger and aggression*. New York: Springer-Verlag.

Averill, J. (1982). The social construction of the emotions: With special reference to love. In K. J. Gergen & K. E. Davis (Eds.), *The social construction of the person* (pp. 89–109). New York: Springer-Verlag.

Boswell, J. (1990). Categories, Experience and Sexuality. In Stein, Edward (Ed.), *Forms of desire: Sexual orientation and the social constructionist controversy* (pp. 133–173). New York: Routledge.

Burman, E. (1990). Differing with deconstruction. In I. Parker & J. Shotter (Eds.), *Deconstructing social psychology* (pp. 208–220). London: Routledge.

Comely, L., Kitzinger, C., Perkins, R., & Wilkinson, S. (1990). Proposal for a Psychology of Lesbianism Section within the British Psychological Society.

Cruikshank, M. (1992). *The gay and lesbian liberation movement*. London: Routledge.

Deutscher, I. (1968). On social science and the sociology of knowledge, *American Sociologist 3*: 291–292.

Dynes, W. R. (1990). Wrestling with the Social Boa Constrictor. In E. Stein (Ed.), *Forms of desire: Sexual orientation and the social constructionist controversy* (pp. 209–238). New York: Routledge.

Edwards, D., & Potter, J. (1992). *Discursive psychology*. London: Sage.

Epstein, S. (1990). Gay politics, ethnic identity: The limits of social constructionism. In E. Stein (Ed.), *Forms of desire: Sexual orientation and the social constructionist controversy* (pp. 239–294). New York: Routledge.

Faderman, L. (1991). *Odd girls and twilight lovers: A history of lesbian life in twentieth-century America*. London: Penguin.

Foucault, M. (1979). *The history of sexuality: Vol I*. London: Allen Lane.

Gagnon, J. H. (1977). *Human sexualities*. Glenview, IL: Scott, Foresman & Co.

Gagnon, J. H., & Simon, W. S. (Eds.), (1967a). *Sexual deviance*. New York: Harper & Row.

Gagnon, J. H., & Simon, W. S. (1967b). Femininity in the lesbian community, *Social Problems 15*: 212–211.

Gagnon, J. H., & Simon, W. S. (1973). *Sexual conduct: The social sources of human sexuality*. Chicago: Aldine.

Garfinkel, A. (1981). *Forms of explanation: Rethinking the questions in social theory*. New Haven: Yale University Press.

Gergen, K. J. (1973). Social psychology as history, *Journal of Personality and Social Psychology, 26*: 309–320.

Gergen, K. J. (1985). The social constructionist movement in modern psychology, *American Psychologist, 40*: 266–275.

Gergen, K. J. (1982). *Toward transformation in social knowledge*. New York: Springer-Verlag.

Gergen, K. J. (1992). Toward a postmodern psychology. In S. Kvale (Ed.), *Psychology and postmodernism* (pp. 17–30). London: Sage.

Gergen, K. J. (1994). Exploring the Postmodern: Perils and potentials, *American Psychologist, 49*: 412–416.

Gonsiorek, J. C. (1991). Conclusion. In J. C. Gonsiorek & J. D. Weinrich (Eds.), *Homosexuality: Research implications for public policy* (pp. 244–248). London: Sage.

Gonsiorek, J. C., & Weinrich, J. D. (Eds.) (1991). *Homosexuality: Research implications for public policy*. London: Sage.

Green, R. (1992). *Sexual science and the law*. Cambridge, MA: Harvard University Press.

Guillaumin, C. (1977). Race et native: système des marques, idée de groupe naturel et rapport sociaux, *Pluriel*, 11.

Hall, M., Kitzinger, C., Loulan, J., Perkins, R. (1992). Lesbian psychology, lesbian politics, *Feminism & Psychology 2*(1): 7–25.

Halperin, D. M., & Schneider, R. (1990). "Homosexuality": A cultural construct. In D. M. Halperin *One hundred years of homosexuality and other essays on Greek love* (pp. 41–53). New York: Routledge.

Hart, J., & Richardson, D. (Eds.) (1981). *The theory and practice of homosexuality*. London: Routledge and Kegan Paul.

Harré, R. (1986). *The social construction of emotions*. Oxford: Blackwell.

Herek, G. M., & Berrill, K. T. (1992). *Hate crimes: Confronting violence against lesbians and gay men*. London: Sage.

Jeffreys, S. (1987). *The spinster and her enemies*. London: Pandora.

Jeffreys, S. (1993). The lesbian heresy, Talk given for The Lesbian Idea series of the London Lesbian History Group, January 22, 1993.

Katz, J. (1990). The invention of heterosexuality, *Socialist Review 21*: 7–34.

Kessler, S., & McKenna, W. (1978). *Gender: An ethnomethodological approach*. New York: Wiley.

Kitzinger, C. (1987a). *The social construction of lesbianism*. London: Sage.

Kitzinger, C. (1987b). Heteropatriarchal language: The case against "homophobia," *Gossip: A Journal of Lesbian Feminist Ethics, 5*: 15–20.

Kitzinger, C. (1988). Sexuality: Nature, choice or construction, *Lesbian and Gay Socialist, 15*: 18–19.

Kitzinger, C. (1989a). Liberal humanism as an ideology of social control. In K. Gergen & J. Shotter (Eds.), *Texts of identity* (pp. 82–98). London: Sage.

Kitzinger, C. (1989b). Deconstructing sex differences, *British Psychological Society Psychology of Women Section Newsletter, 4*: 9–17.

Kitzinger, C. (1989c). The rhetoric of pseudoscience. In I. Parker & J. Shotter (Eds.), *Deconstructing social psychology* (pp. 61–75). London: Routledge.

Kitzinger, C. (1990). Resisting the discipline. In E. Burman (Ed.), *Feminists and psychological practice* (pp. 119–136). London: Sage.

Kitzinger, C. (1992). The individuated self concept: A critical analysis of social constructionist writing on individualism. In G. Breakwell (Ed.). *Social psychology of identity and the self concept.* London: Surrey University Press.

Kitzinger, C., Wilkinson, S., & Perkins, R. (Eds.), (1992). Heterosexuality, *Feminism & Psychology* 2(3): 293–509.

Kitzinger, C., & Perkins, R. (1993). *Changing our minds: Lesbian feminism and psychology.* New York: New York University Press; London: Onlywomen Press.

Kitzinger, J., & Kitzinger, C. (1993). Doing it: Representations of lesbian sex. In G. Griffin (Ed.), *Outwrite: popularizing lesbian texts.* London: Pluto Press.

Knorr-Cetina, K., & Mulkay, M. (Eds.) (1983). *Science observed.* London: Sage.

de Lauretis, T. (Ed.) (1991). Queer theory: Lesbian and gay sexualities, *Differences* 3(2).

LeVay, S. (1991). A difference in hypothalamic structure between heterosexual and homosexual men. *Science, 253,* 1034–1037.

Luker, K. (1993). Review of Sexual Science and the Law, by Richard Green, *New York Times Book Review,* 1/31/93: 33.

MacDonald, I. (1990). We'll deconstruct when they deconstruct. In M. L. Adams, H. Lenskyj, P. Masters, & M. Randall (Eds.), Confronting heterosexuality, *Resources for Feminist Research* 19(3/4): 89–90.

McIntosh, M. (1968). The homosexual role, *Social Problems* 16(2): 182–192. (Reprinted in Edward Stein (Ed.) (1992). *Forms of desire: Sexual orientation and the social constructionist controversy* (pp. 25–42). New York: Routledge; and, with a postscript, in Ken Plummer (Ed.) (1981). *The making of the modern homosexual* (pp. 30–49). London: Hutchinson.

McIntosh, M. (1981). Interview in K. Plummer (Ed.) (1981). *The making of the modern homosexual* (pp. 44–49). London: Hutchinson

McIntosh, M. (1992). Liberalism and the contradictions of sexual politics. In L. Segal & M. McIntosh (Eds.). *Sex exposed* (pp. 155–168). London: Virago.

McNamee, S., & Gergen, K. J. (1993). *Therapy as social construction.* London: Sage.

Mischel, W. (1968). *Personality and assessment.* New York: Wiley.

Mitroff, I. I. 91974). *The subjective side of science.* Amsterdam: Elsevier.

Moir, A., & Jessel, D. (1989). *Brainsex: The real difference between men and women.* London: Mandarin/Octopus.

Money, J. (1988). *Gay, straight, and in-between: The sexology of erotic orientation.* Oxford: Oxford University Press.

Nencel, L., & Pals, P. (1991). *Constructing knowledge: Authority and critique in social science*. London: Sage.

Norris, S., & Read, E. (Eds) (1985). *Out in the open: People talking about being gay or bisexual*. London: Pan Books.

Plasek, J. W., & Allard, J. (1985). Misconceptions of homophobia. In J. P. De Cecco (Ed.), *Bashers, baiters and bigots: Homophobia in American society*. New York: Harrington Park Press.

Plummer, K. (1981a). (Ed.), *The making of the modern homosexual*. London: Hutchinson.

Plummer, K. (1981b). Building a sociology of homosexuality. In K. Plummer (Ed.), *The making of the modern homosexual* (pp. 17–29). London: Hutchinson.

Plummer, K. (1992). (Ed.), *Modern homosexualities*. London: Routledge.

Rich, A. (1980). Compulsory heterosexuality and lesbian existence, *Signs: Journal of Women in Culture and Society 5*(4), 631–657.

Rorty, R. (1980). *Philosophy and the mirror of nature*. Oxford: Blackwell.

Sampson, E. E. (1983). Deconstructing psychology's subject, *Journal of Mind and Behavior, 4*: 135–164.

Samin, G. R., & Gergen, K. J. (1990). (Eds.), *Everyday understandings: Social and scientific implications*. London: Sage.

Simon, W., & Gagnon, J. H. (1967). Homosexuality: The formulation of a sociological perspective, *Journal of Health and Social Behaviour 8*: 177–184.

Smith, A. M. (1992). Resisting the erasure of lesbian sexuality: A challenge for queer activism. In K. Plummer (Ed.), *Modern homosexualities: Fragments of lesbian and gay experience*. London: Routledge.

Smyth, C. (1992). *Lesbians talk queer notions*. London: Scarlet Press.

Spong, J. (1988). Quoted in *The Pink Paper*, July 28, 1988.

Steier, F. (Eds.) (1991). *Research and reflexivity*. London: Sage.

Stein, E. (Ed.), (1990a). *Forms of desire: Sexual orientation and the special constructionist controversy*. New York: Routledge.

Stein, E. (1990b). Introduction. In E. Stein (Ed.), *Forms of desire: Sexual orientation and the social constructionist controversy* (pp. 3–10). New York: Routledge.

Stein, E. (1990c). Conclusion: The essentials of constructionism and the construction of essentialism. In E. Stein (Ed.), *Forms of desire: Sexual orientation and the special constructionist controversy* (pp. 325–354). New York: Routledge.

Szasz, T. (1971). *The manufacture of madness*. London: Routledge & Kegan Paul.

Tiefer, L. (1987). Social constructionism and the study of human sexuality. In P. Shaver & C. Hendrick (Eds.), *Sex and gender*. London: Sage.

Trilling, L. (1972). *Sincerity and authenticity*. Cambridge, MA: Harvard University Press.

Unger, R. (1988). Psychological, feminist and personal epistemology. In M. Gergen (Ed.), *Feminist thought and the structure of knowledge* (pp. 124–141). New York: New York University Press.

Weeks, J. (1977). *Coming out: Homosexual politics in Britain from the nineteenth century to the present*. London: Quartet.

Weeks, J. (1981). Discourse, desire and sexual deviance: Some problems in a history of homosexuality. In K. Plummer, (Ed.), *The making of the modern homosexual* (pp. 76–111). London: Hutchinson.

Weinrich, J. (1987). *Sexual landscapes: Why we are what we are, why we love who we love.* New York: Charles Scribner's Sons. (Chapter 5 reprinted in Stein, E. (Ed.), (1990). *Forms of desire: Sexual orientation and the special constructionist controversy.* New York: Routledge.)

Weisstein, N. (1971). Psychology constructs the female. Reprinted in C. Kitzinger (Ed.), Psychology constructs the female: A reappraisal, *Feminism & Psychology* 3(2): 211–226.

Weisstein, N. (1993). Power, resistance and science: A call for a revitalized feminist psychology. In C. Kitzinger (Ed.), Psychology constructs the female: A reappraisal, *Feminism & Psychology* 3(2): 239–245.

Wilkinson, S., & Kitzinger, C. (Eds.), (1993). *Heterosexuality: A "Feminism & Psychology" reader.* London: Sage.

Wilkinson, S., & Kitzinger, C. (1944). The social construction of heterosexuality, *Journal of Gender Studies* 3(3); 305–314.

Wittig, M. (1981). One is not born a woman. In S. L. Hoagland & J. Penelope (Eds.), *For lesbians only: A separatist anthology* (pp. 439–447). London: Onlywomen Press.

II

Personal Development Over the Lifespan

7

Lesbian, Gay Male, and Bisexual Adolescents

Ritch C. Savin-Williams

This chapter[1] reviews psychological research on North American gay male, lesbian, and bisexual youth, giving voice to many of the concerns of adolescents who find that, by simply being themselves, they are sexual outcasts in the eyes of their families, peers, and culture. The neglect of sexual minority youth by professionals is of concern because those who should be responsive to the needs of lesbian, bisexual, and gay male adolescents continue to write, publish, teach, counsel, and establish public policy as if such youths did not or should not exist. Despite the fact that mature, healthy sexual functioning in adulthood has its origins in childhood and adolescence, North American culture is ignorant and neglectful of sexual and erotic development during adolescence (Money, 1987). A prevailing cultural assumption is that homosexuality is the province of adulthood; what these adults were as children and adolescents is a mystery. Although researchers may have great difficulty finding and naming these youths, they exist. This unre-

[1] This chapter articulates basic premises and principles which are more fully elaborated in other writings. The first (Savin-Williams, 1990), an empirical survey of 317 lesbian, bisexual, and gay male youths between the ages of 14 and 23 years, describes basic characteristics, coming out status, and levels of self-esteem. The second (Savin-Williams, 1993) is an interview study of the influence that childhood and adolescent sexual behavior has on the formation of a sexual identity among forty-four gay and bisexual male youths. The third (Savin-Williams & Cohen, in press) is a book for practitioners and policymakers. Portions of this chapter were previously published in Savin-Williams (1994) and Savin-Williams and Rodriguez (1993).

sponsiveness by psychologists is particularly consequential because sexual minority youth are disproportionately at risk for various physical, emotional, cognitive, and mental health problems.

The invisibility of sexual minority youth was illustrated at the 1990 meetings of the interdisciplinary Society for Research in Adolescence. Not a single presentation, among literally hundreds of posters, symposiums, and invited addresses, focused on lesbian, bisexual, or gay male youth. When textbooks on adolescence discuss "homosexuality," it is in a separate, usually short, section located in the latter half of the adolescent sexuality chapter, near the end of the book, and sandwiched around topics such as self-stimulation, contraceptive use, and sexually transmitted diseases. The discussion is primarily devoted to adolescent homosexual behavior, the prevalence and causes of homosexuality, and societal attitudes toward homosexuality. Readers will discover relatively little regarding the life and concerns of an "average" lesbian, bisexual, or gay male teenager.

In this chapter I review fundamental dilemmas that bisexual, gay male, and lesbian youths face as they confront the unique tasks involved in being a sexual minority in a society that assumes all of its members are heterosexual. The focus is limited to the recognition, establishment, and expression of sexual identity; peer harassment; and heterosexual and homosexual dating. First, problems inherent in defining a gay male, bisexual, and lesbian adolescent, and thus the importance of distinguishing between sexual behavior and sexual identity, are discussed.

Sexual Behavior and Sexual Identity

A pervasive assumption held by researchers is that all children and adolescents are heterosexual. One difficulty may be uncertainty and confusion over distinctions between sexual behavior and identity. We recognize that children and adolescents engage in homosexual behavior, but we have great difficulty understanding how individuals can be so certain of their sexuality before adulthood that they call themselves lesbian, gay, or bisexual.

Sexual identity is the enduring sense of oneself as a sexual being which fits a culturally created category and accounts for one's sexual fantasies, attractions, and behaviors. Self-definition need not be static or publicly declared, although there are developmental presses in North American culture toward consistency in sexual impulses, images, attractions, and activities. A youth may have a same-sex sexual identity but engage in heterosexual behavior and feel attractions for both sexes, but in different ways (e.g., lust toward males and emotional love for females). With advancing age through adolescence and young adulthood, however, an increasingly high correspondence is likely among these aspects of sexual identity.

The fact that sexual identity is often unsettled at the onset of adolescence regardless of sexual orientation may reflect the sexual experimentation of many early adolescents. Various forms of sexual activity occur independent of one's attractions or identity, as a result of curiosity, peer or familial pressure, or opportunities that emerge. For example, a significant number, perhaps a majority of youths who have identified or will eventually identify as lesbian, bisexual, or gay engage in heterosexual sex during their childhood and adolescence (Boxer, Cook, & Herdt, 1989; D'Augelli, 1991; Remafedi, 1987a, 1987b; Roesler & Deisher, 1972; Rotheram-Borus, Rosario, Meyer-Bahlburg, Koopman, Dopkins, & Davies, in preparation; Savin-Williams, 1990, 1993; Sears, 1991).

In a comprehensive research survey of nearly 35,000 junior and senior high school students in Minnesota (Remafedi, Resnick, Blum, & Harris, 1992), less than 1 percent of those who were sure about their sexual orientation *identified* themselves as lesbian or gay. Another 10 percent were "unsure" of their sexual orientation; these youths were more likely than self-identified heterosexual teens to have homoerotic attractions and fantasies and less likely to have engaged in heterosexual sex. The percentage of adolescents who labeled themselves lesbian or gay was fairly constant across the ages. When questioned regarding *homosexual attractions,* adolescents were more likely to report homosexual attractions than to label themselves "homosexual": 2 percent at age 12 years and 6 percent at 18 years. The question most frequently left blank was how frequently they were involved in homosexual *sexual activity.* The number of youths who engaged in homosexual behavior increased from less than 1 percent at age 12 years to almost 3 percent at 18 years. A minority of these youths (27%) identified themselves as gay, lesbian, or bisexual. Those who did were just as likely as "heterosexual" adolescents to report having had heterosexual sexual encounters. Nearly 3 percent of all youths said they had same-sex *sexual fantasies;* 30 percent of the 3 percent identified themselves as gay or lesbian and had same-sex sexual experiences. Thus, youths were most likely to report having homosexual attractions and fantasies; engaging in homosexual sex was third. Least reported was the identification of oneself as lesbian or gay.

Other research supports Remafedi et al.'s findings. For example, a number of studies document that (1) homosexual sex is not the exclusive domain of adolescents who later identify as bisexual, lesbian, or gay, and (2) many youths realize a same-sex identity without the benefit of same-sex activity (Bell, Weinberg, & Hammersmith, 1981; Boxer, 1988; Boxer, Cook, & Herdt, 1991; Coles & Stokes, 1985; Fay, Turner,

Klassen, & Gagnon, 1989; Hedblom, 1973; Manosevitz, 1970; Remafedi, 1987a; Roesler & Deisher, 1972; Saghir & Robins, 1969, 1973; Sanders, 1980; Savin-Williams, 1990, 1993; Sorensen, 1973). Most youths are loathe to report themselves as being lesbian, bisexual, or gay. In a 1985 survey, only one of over 1,000 youths checked the "homosexual identity" box (Coles & Stokes, 1985). Five times as many acknowledged same-sex sexual behavior. Of more than 500, 16- to 18-year-olds attending Cornell University's summer high school program in 1985 and 1986, 8 said they were lesbian, bisexual, or gay. Four times as many had adolescent same-sex encounters (Savin-Williams, unpublished data). Thus, relatively few adolescents who report same-sex attractions, fantasies, or activities acknowledge that they are gay, lesbian, or bisexual.[2]

The developmental processes that lesbian, bisexual, and gay male adolescents experience in recognizing, accepting, and affirming their sexual identity are difficult to determine because little research has addressed these issues. The meaning of sexual attractions, fantasies, and behaviors, however, does become clearer with age. Remafedi et al. (1992) noted that "sexual orientation and perceptions of bisexuality gradually give way to heterosexual or homosexual identification with the passage of time and/or with increasing sexual experience" (p. 720). Young adolescents may be more willing than older youths to conform to classifications of sexuality defined by adult society and imposed by peers, media, and social institutions. The low (1–3%) percentages reported by surveys are almost certainly not an accurate reflection of the number of youths who are lesbian, bisexual, or gay or who will later define themselves as such.

Bisexual, gay male, and lesbian adolescents exist; sometimes they have heterosexual sex, homosexual sex, both heterosexual and homosexual sex, or no sex. Sexual identity may be clear or ambivalent, but eventually most bisexual, lesbian, and gay male youths emerge as healthy adults. The process of recognizing and expressing this sexual identity is referred to as "coming out."

Coming Out to Self and Others

One of the most important developments in the life of a lesbian, bisexual, or gay male youth is how she or he comes to the point of self-identification. What are the important events or processes that lead to

[2]These findings may be applicable to other countries as well. For example, Breakwell and Fife-Schaw (1992) studied over 2,000 English youths between the ages of 16 and 20 years. Relatively few, less than 2 percent, reported engaging in same-sex sexual activities. When adjusted for missing data, however, the percentages increase in several categories to nearly 8 percent.

this conclusion? Is the sexual identity present before or after sexual behavior or enlightened by it? What are the consequences of the profound fears and anxieties associated with this realization? There are relatively few answers to these difficult questions because theoretical and empirical attention has been devoted to the process of disclosing or concealing one's sexual identity rather than to the earlier process of self-realization that one is bisexual, lesbian, or gay.

Several coming out models describe the various stages that an individual undergoes in moving from first realization to an integrated same-sex identity. These models reflect the theoretical orientations of their authors: psychoanalytic (Isay, 1989), ego psychological (Minton & McDonald, 1983/1984), symbolic interactional (Weinberg, 1983), interpersonal congruency (Cass, 1979, 1984), sexual scripts (Troiden, 1989), and classical and social learning (Storms, 1981). These models provide a sketch of the feelings and thoughts that an adolescent might have regarding the emergence of homoerotic attractions into consciousness (see review of seven coming-out sequences in Minton & McDonald, 1983/1984). The models, however, are often based on the retrospective reflections of adult lesbians and gay men and thus do not necessarily apply to adolescents.

Initial Awareness

From an early age, usually before adolescence, many sexual minority youths report that they "feel different" or consider themselves to be outsiders (Hunter & Schaecher, 1987). One example in popular culture is Idgie, in the movie, "Fried Green Tomatoes." She had little interest as a child in traditional feminine activities. She enjoyed climbing trees, fishing, and wearing "boy" clothes; she was assertive, stubborn, and resilient. Isay (1989) described these feelings among gay males:

> They saw themselves as more sensitive than other boys; they cried more easily, had their feelings more readily hurt, had more aesthetic interests, enjoyed nature, art, and music, and were drawn to other "sensitive" boys, girls, and adults. (p. 23)

In retrospective adult studies, over three-quarters of lesbians and gay men reported having experienced this feeling of differentness during their childhood and adolescence (Bell et al., 1981; Troiden, 1979). The origins and meanings of this sensation are seldom clear to the individual. With age, the feeling of "apartness" or "isolation" becomes increasingly prevalent and is given new meaning during adolescence (Hunter & Schaecher, 1987; Martin, 1982; Robertson, 1981). This could be a "bolt of lightening" or, more likely, a series of small realizations, sandwiched around efforts to deny or suppress the knowledge from one's consciousness. Malyon (1981) noted the importance of puberty in the realization process. The physical changes of these years eroticize and place new meanings on familiar feelings. It is biology with an existential meaning because the adolescent frequently feels as if she or he is in an uncharted, uninhabited country.

Bisexual, lesbian, and gay male youths frequently recognize that they do not have the erotic, sexual interest in the other sex that their peers appear to have. They may possess that which society defines as inappropriate interest in activities, behaviors, and characteristics of the other sex. Although peers may label these as "homosexual," sexual minority youth are likely to reject the definition of these feelings and themselves as bisexual, lesbian, or gay. These conflicts are nearly universal features of coming out stories (Adair & Adair, 1978; Curtis, 1988; Eichberg, 1990; Hall Carpenter Archives, 1989; Heron, 1983; Marotta, 1982; Penelope & Wolfe, 1989). Many fears emerge, most prominent of which is being emotionally and socially rejected or isolated. Youths may doubt their ability to meet heterosexual obligations; not having the same sexual motivations as peers becomes a source of great anxiety.

Coming to Terms with Self-Recognition

Most coming out models propose that after early feelings of alienation, confusion, and uneasiness emerges a growing realization that these feelings have a sexual component. From that point through the course of adolescence it becomes increasingly more difficult to deny same-sex attractions. Boxer, Herdt, and associates (1988, 1989) reported the following landmarks in their Chicago sample of lesbian, bisexual, and gay male youths (averages are in years; standard deviations are in parentheses):

	Males	Females
First homosexual attraction	9.6 (3.6)	10.1 (3.7)
First homosexual fantasy	11.2 (3.5)	11.9 (2.9)
First homosexual activity	13.1 (4.3)	15.2 (3.1)
First heterosexual activity	13.7 (3.6)	13.6 (3.6)
Age at first disclosure	16.0 (2.4)	16.0 (1.8)

The sexes varied significantly on one dimension; onset of same-sex activity was later in girls. Also noteworthy is the relatively young ages at which these milestones were reached; this is in contrast with earlier research conducted with adult gay men and lesbians (see Boxer, 1988; Boxer et al., 1991; Dank, 1971; Harry & DeVall, 1978; Kooden et al., 1979; McDonald, 1982; Remafedi, 1987a, 1987b; Riddle & Morin, 1978;

Savin-Williams, 1990; Troiden, 1979, 1989). This may reflect a retrospective bias or a true change; that is, current generations are coming out at younger ages.

Lesbian, gay male, and bisexual youths most often first share the secret of their sexual identity with a best friend, usually a girl. For example, among lesbian, bisexual, and gay male youths in Chicago, two-thirds of the boys and over half of the girls first revealed their sexual identity to a same-aged peer (Boxer, 1988). Currently this coming out occurs in high school or the first years of college (Savin-Williams, 1990).

The research of Rotheram-Borus and colleagues (in preparation, 1991) with gay and bisexual African–American and Hispanic male youths from the Hetrick-Martin Institute in New York City highlights major stressors faced by sexual minority youths when they come out. The youths most feared peer ridicule and arguments with parents. Much to the surprise of many, disclosure to friends was usually a positive event, more so than if their friends discovered the information on their own. Thus, not to disclose to friends and family may be more stressful than evading, hiding, and remaining in the closet, because of the anxiety associated with being "found out." In either case (Rotheram-Borus et al., 1991),

> Whether gay youths disclose or others discover their sexual orientation, they have little control over others' reactions, i.e., will they be accepted or rejected? Perhaps it is this inability to predict the outcome that makes gay events stressful in their contemplation and actual occurrence, and explains cover-up of a gay sexual orientation. (p. 192)

A youth's reaction to self-awareness ranges from relief and joy to depression and self-destructive behavior. A number of defenses against self-recognition and self-labeling delay the process of coming out to others.

Coming Out to Self and Self-Esteem

Empirical evidence suggests a positive association between coming out to one's self and feelings of self-worth. The psychologically well-adjusted bisexual, lesbian, or gay male individual is out to self and has integrated a sexual identity with her or his overall personal identity (see reviews in Savin-Williams, 1990; Troiden, 1989).

Gender differences have been reported in the association between age of self-recognition and self-esteem. One of the best predictors of self-esteem among lesbian youths found in one study was an early recognition of homoerotic attractions (Savin-Williams, 1990). Gay male youths who were aware of same-sex attractions at an early age did not differ, however, in terms of current self-esteem level from those who became aware of such feelings later. Other findings suggest that girls who know they are lesbian at an early age are a special group with particularly high self-esteem.

Unanswered, however, is whether high self-esteem or the recognition of homosexuality emerges first. Those with a positive sense of self may be better equipped to recognize this aspect of their personality; such girls may be generally more insightful and self-accepting than those who are unaware of their homosexuality until late adolescence or young adulthood. Or the longer developmental period that these women have to come to terms with what it means to be a lesbian gives them sufficient time to integrate and accept this aspect of their lives. They can thus seek psychological and social resources and services that further enhance their sense of self.

Similar dynamics may not operate with bisexual and gay males. Recognition of homoerotic attractions at an early age are perhaps developmentally too early for the psychological skills and maturity that many early adolescent males possess. Or coming out at an early age may be the result of the most "feminine" boys being brought to awareness by peers because their gender-atypical behaviors and mannerisms violate sex-role expectations. Dank (1973) noted that because male adolescents are particularly sensitive to how they are perceived by peers, terms used to label a nonheterosexual orientation become especially destructive for a healthy sense of self. To preserve self-worth, a boy in our culture is not likely to place himself into such a category. The prohibition for females to behave in a gender-atypical manner is less severe, and such behavior may even be rewarded, thus having positive effects on their self-esteem level. Before these questions can be adequately answered, however, longitudinal data are necessary.

Diversity among Lesbian, Bisexual, and Gay Male Youth

Few investigators have systematically studied individual or group differences in sexual identity milestones. Considerable variations exist in the development of a sexual identity across individuals, groups, and historic time, based in part on the sex of the youth, community size and location, religiosity, social class, and race or ethnicity. An excellent example of diversity among female youth is a small-scale study conducted with college women who had at least one homosexual experience (Goode & Haber, 1977). Some women were labeled "sexual adventurers" because they had an array of sexual experiences with both men and women; others with same-sex experiences were expected to eventually identify as lesbian. As a group, the women were "not, by any means, uniformly turned off to sex with men, nor do they uniformly sing its praises" (p. 19). Researchers' awareness of variability among lesbian, gay male, and bisexual youth has recently increased as a result of empirical studies of lesbian, gay male, and bisexual youths of African–American and Hispanic descent (Rotheram-Borus et al., 1991), those from the South (Sears, 1991), and youths living in rural and small town communities (D'Augelli, 1991; Savin-Williams, 1990).

Rodriguez (Savin-Williams & Rodriguez, 1993) argued that lesbian, gay male, and bisexual youth of color face formidable tasks in developing a mature identity because they must integrate their ethnic, cultural, and racial background with their sexual orientation and identity. The racial or ethnic background of a youth may present both an impediment and an advantage in forming a bisexual, gay, or lesbian identity and a positive sense of self-worth. The youth of color who identifies with both ethnic or racial and gay male, bisexual, or lesbian communities can gain a rich array of knowledge and social support. He or she is likely to garner support from sexual minority communities that the cultural community is not able to give, including affirmation of his or her sexuality; a place in which he or she can feel relaxed and open about same-sex desires, activities, and relationships; and identification of institutions that will meet needs based on sexual identity. Similarly, familial, racial, ethnic, and cultural ties provide a youth of color a cultural or racial identification, a unique heritage, and a sense of self as a person of color (Morales, 1983). All too often, however, institutions within these communities, such as families, peer groups, and religious organizations, present youth with information that handicaps the development of a positive identity based on an acceptance and integration of one's racial/ethnic and sexual identities. The information may contain ideas that differ from positions advocated by lesbian, bisexual, and gay male communities, including that which is "appropriate" sex-role behavior, the importance of choosing one identity over the other, and what it means to be a sexual or an ethnic minority.

Sears (1991) and D'Augelli (1991) reported that the milestones noted by Boxer and Herdt in Chicago were reached at a later age in their samples of lesbian, bisexual, and gay male youths living in the South and in rural communities. For example, the gay male college youths D'Augelli (1991) surveyed became aware of same-sex feelings, on average, at age 11, had their first homosexual sex 4.5 years later, labeled themselves gay just before high school graduation, and first disclosed their homosexuality 2 years later at age 19 years. More interesting than these averages, however, is the interindividual diversity within the sample in reaching these landmarks. One youth was first aware of homoerotic feelings at age 1 year; another at 20 years. First sexual experience occurred at age 5 years for one individual and at 22 years for another. Labeling one's self as gay spanned the years from preadolescence to young adulthood, with much variety in the sequencing of events. One youth immediately labeled himself gay after becoming aware of his attractions; another took 14 years to make the same connection. While the group averaged 8 years between awareness of attractions and disclosure to another, one youth waited 18 years. Eleven percent of the youths had same-sex encounters before self-labeling as gay, 8 percent simultaneously, and 75 percent afterwards. One youth had sex with another male 4 years before self-acknowledgment; another waited 15 years after self-recognition for his first same-sex experience.

Conclusion

Lesbian, bisexual, and gay male youth share many of the developmental concerns that other adolescents experience, as well as those which are the direct result of being a sexual outcast in North American culture. Because a primary developmental task of adolescence is the consolidation of personal identity, the growing awareness of homoerotic desires during this time, along with the knowledge that these feelings are condemned by others, may lead to considerable intrapsychic conflict and anxiety. For the youth struggling with a stigmatizing sexual identity, adolescence can be a time of conflict and distress. With pressures from family and peers to be heterosexual, gay male, lesbian, and bisexual youths face unique hurdles in their efforts to forge a healthy sense of self.

Disclosing sexual identity to others may be counterproductive to a healthy outcome (Malyon, 1981). Too often the self-acknowledged lesbian, bisexual, or gay male adolescent does not receive the necessary support to overcome family and peer ridicule, abuse, and alienation (Hunter & Schaecher, 1987; Rotheram-Borus et al., 1991). The psychological consequences of these conditions are little understood, in part because of the dearth of social science research investigating these concerns.

Harassment and Violence from Peers

One of the most difficult issues for bisexual, lesbian, and gay male adolescents is being harassed by peers. The Harvey Milk School in New York City was created by the Hetrick-Martin Institute, a social service agency established to enhance the well-being of sexual minority youth, in response to the peer harassment that gay male, lesbian, and bisexual youth receive in other public schools. Research with these youths indicates that most frequently abused are youths who fail to live up to cultural ideals of sex-appropriate, masculine and feminine behaviors and roles (Martin & Hetrick, 1988). Gonsiorek (1988) noted that the consequences of being gender atypical are particularly problematic during adolescence:

> Males experience intense peer pressure to be "tough" and "macho," and females to be passive and compliant. Although social sex roles are not intrinsically related to sexual orientation, the distinction is poorly understood by most adolescents, as well as by most adults. Adolescents are frequently intolerant of differentness in others and may castigate or ostracize peers, particularly if the perceived differentness is in the arena of sexuality or sex roles. (p. 116)

The rules of socially appropriate behavior and the consequences of nonconformity are known by many youths. Over 95 percent of the youths who sought the services of the Hetrick-Martin Institute reported that they frequently felt separated and emotionally isolated from peers because of their differentness (Martin & Hetrick, 1988).

Bisexual, gay male, and lesbian adolescents may thus monitor their interpersonal interactions. Hetrick and Martin (1987: 31) reflected, "They may feel afraid to show friendship for a friend of the same sex for fear of being misunderstood or giving away their secretly held sexual orientation." If erotic feelings become aroused and threaten expression, youths often seek to terminate same-sex friendships rather than reveal their secret. Other-sex friendships may be easier because they avoid the issue of physical and sexual intimacy, are viewed as heterosexual "interest," and enhance peer status.

Peer rejection can be expressed in direct ways, such as in verbal and physical abuse. A significant number of sexual minority youths report that they have been physically assaulted, robbed, raped, and sexually abused (Martin & Hetrick, 1988; Remafedi, 1987b; Rotheram-Borus et al., 1991). In Sears' (1991) study, 97 percent of the interviewed lesbian, gay male, and bisexual youths recalled negative attitudes that were held by classmates, and more than half feared harassment, especially if they came out in high school. Only two of thirty-six found a peer group that was supportive of lesbian and gay people. As a result, most passed as heterosexual until graduation. Over one-half of Latino and African–American gay and bisexual male adolescents and 40 percent of the Hetrick-Martin youths said they had been ridiculed because of their sexuality (Martin & Hetrick, 1988; Rotheram-Borus et al., 1991). A survey of the Los Angeles County school system found that the high prevalence of antigay abuse inflicted by classmates on gay male, bisexual, and lesbian youths is apparently premeditated, rather than a chance occurrence, and that the incidence is escalating dramatically (Peterson,

1989). The most frequent abusers are fellow teenagers. Fear of being verbally or physically harassed is related to hiding one's homosexuality (D'Augelli, 1991). These data correspond to the documented antigay violence occurring on college campuses (D'Augelli, 1992).

As a result of emotional, social, and cognitive isolation and verbal and physical abuse, many lesbian, bisexual, and gay male youths have school- and home-related problems. These include poor school performance, truancy, failing a grade, and dropping out of school. Bisexual, gay male, and lesbian youth may desire to avoid abuse and maintain the family secret but by coming out to their family they are often "rejected, mistreated, or become the focus of the family's dysfunction" (Gonsiorek, 1988: 116). If these abused youths run away they face a world that is all too ready to exploit them. They are thus at extreme risk for substance abuse, prostitution, and suicide (Burnison, 1987; Coleman, 1989; Gibson, 1989; Remafedi, 1987b; Rotheram-Borus et al., 1991).

Dating

Romantic relationships serve important developmental functions in the lives of not only heterosexual youth but sexual minority youth as well. Dating those to whom one is sexually attracted is often considered to be a means by which one experiments with intimacy and sexuality. However, dating someone who is erotically attractive is seldom an option for gay male and lesbian youths. The possibility of dating someone of the same sex is so remote that most youths never consider it a reasonable expectation. This separation of the erotic from the socially and emotionally acceptable (heterosexual dating) may produce self-doubt, anger, resentment, and distortion in development during the adolescent years. If lesbian, bisexual, and gay male youths have opportunities to explore their sexuality, it may be confined to sexual encounters, with either same- or other-sex individuals, which often lack romance, affection, and intimacy.

Because little information exists in mainstream scientific writings regarding same-sex romance and dating among gay male, bisexual, and lesbian youth, there is little to help us understand the lives of sexual minority youth struggling with issues of identity and intimacy. Although there is also little research focusing on heterosexual dating among bisexual, gay male, and lesbian youth, convincing data indicate that these youths engage in heterosexual sex.

Heterosexual Sex and Dating

Retrospective data from adult gay men and lesbians reflecting on their adolescence and young adulthood reveal the extent to which heterosexual dating and sex are commonplace (Bell & Weinberg, 1978; Gundlach & Riess, 1968; Saghir & Robins, 1973; Schafer, 1976; Spada, 1979; Troiden & Goode, 1980; Weinberg & Williams, 1974). Motivations include denial of same-sex feelings, fun and curiosity, internalization of pressures to conform with society's insistence on heterosexual norms and behaviors, and a desire to reduce the personal strains of coming out.

Heterosexual activity among lesbian and gay male youth has been well documented. A large percentage of lesbian adolescents have engaged in heterosexual sexual experiences—two of every three in one study (Boxer et al., 1989), three of every four in a second (Sears, 1991), and eight of ten in a third (Savin-Williams, 1990). In five samples, over one-half of the male youths had past heterosexual experiences (Boxer, Cook, & Herdt, 1989; Remafedi, 1987a, 1987b; Roesler & Deisher, 1972; Savin-Williams, 1990; Sears, 1991). Few of these youths, however, had extensive heterosexual sex; most typically, they had two or three partners. Some youths reported they could not really know that they are lesbian, bisexual, or gay without first trying heterosexual sex. But these activities often became " 'sex without feelings' which the youths 'kept trying' to enjoy without success" (Boxer et al., 1989: 19). The sexual experiences felt unnatural, lacking in emotional intensity. Many gay male youths used heterosexual sex to deny homoerotic attractions; lesbian youths often reported that heterosexual sex resulted from peer pressure and coercion. Heterosexual sex and dating may thus serve as a cover for an emerging sexual identity, allowing youths to "pass" as straight and thus mask their homosexuality.

Romantic Relationships among Lesbian and Gay Male Youth

Living with a partner of the same gender for life is a goal endorsed by most lesbian, bisexual, and gay male youth (D'Augelli, 1991; Harry & DeVall, 1978; Remafedi, 1987b; Sanders, 1980; Savin-Williams, 1990). Establishing a romance with a same-sex partner helps one resolve issues of sexual identity and thus feel more "complete" and "chosen" (Silverstein, 1981). Research with adults documents that those in a love relationship have high levels of self-esteem and self-acceptance, but the causal pathway is unclear (Savin-Williams, 1990). Being in a same-sex romance could increase and build positive self-image, but it may also be that those with high self-esteem are more likely to form relationships and to stay in them.

Few published studies with lesbian, bisexual, and gay male teenagers focus on their dating relationships. There are suggestive data from several studies. In one, fewer than 20 percent had a "first homosexual sexual experience" occur in the context of dating or romance. Lesbians were more likely than gay males to have their first same-sex experience while dating (Pratch, Boxer, & Herdt, in preparation). In Sears's (1991) study of late adolescent and young adult lesbians, gay males, and bisexuals in the South, almost 90 percent had heterosexually dated while in high school. Although 25 percent reported that they "dated" a member of the same sex, these dates seldom involved emotional commitment, were of a short duration, and were filled with turmoil and secrecy. None was overt.

Among 29 Minnesota youths (Remafedi, 1987a & 1987b), 10 had a steady male partner at the time of the interview. Of the other 19, 11 had been in a gay relationship. Most tellingly, all but 2 of the 29 hoped for a steady male partner in their future. D'Augelli (1991) reported that one-half of his sample of 61 college males were "partnered." Relationships were begun, on average, at age 19 years; the range was from 12 to 24 years of age. Almost one-half of these relationships lasted longer than 6 months; most youths were not living with their partner. Many of these relationships, however, were turbulent, which is often characteristic of first relationships. The most troubling mental health concern the gay men had was termination of a close relationship, which ranked just ahead of telling parents about one's homosexuality.

In my research, two-thirds of the males and over 80 percent of the females reported having a romantic relationship during their high school or college years (Savin-Williams, 1990). Lesbians and bisexual women had more relationships, romances that began at an earlier age, longer lasting relationships, and more relationships at the time of data collection than did gay and bisexual men. Men were slightly more likely to begin their romantic career with a same- rather than an other-sex partner. Lesbians and bisexual females who had a high proportion of same-sex romances were most likely to be in a current romantic affair and to be "out" to others. Their self-esteem level was essentially the same as those who had a high percentage of heterosexual relationships. If they began romances early, during adolescence, they also tended to be in a current relationship and to experience long-lasting romances. Gay and bisexual male youths who had a large percentage of romantic relationships with boys rather than with girls also had a large number of love affairs, were in a current relationship, and had high self-esteem. But, counter to intuition, they were not more likely to be publicly "out." Boys who initiated romances at an early age had long-term and multiple relationships. Finally, those who had many romances also tended to have high self-esteem and were publicly out.

Conclusion: Psychological Repercussions

The difficulties of dating same-sex partners during adolescence are monumental. First is the difficulty of finding each other. Most bisexual, gay male, and lesbian youth are closeted—not out to themselves, let alone to others. A second barrier is the consequences of same-sex dating, such as family and peer harassment, both verbal and physical. A third impediment is the lack of public recognition or celebration of those who are romantically involved with a member of the same gender. Youth learn that emotional intimacy should be achieved only with members of the other sex.

> For the homosexual-identified student, high school is often a lonely place where, from every vantage point, there are couples: couples holding hands as they enter school; couples dissolving into an endless wet kiss between school bells; couples exchanging rings with ephemeral vows of devotion and love. (Sears, 1991, pp. 326–327)

Adolescents may never realize that sexual and emotional intimacy can be merged within a same-sex relationship. The consequences for gay male youths have been articulated by Remafedi (1990). They may have sex with other boys or men, but the two may never kiss because to do so would be too meaningful. This escape from intimacy can be very damaging: "Without appropriate opportunities for peer dating and socialization, gay youth frequently eschew intimacy altogether and resort to transient and anonymous sexual encounters with adults" (p. 1173). Consequences include being at increased risk for sexually transmitted diseases (e.g., HIV), especially if youths turn to prostitution to meet their intimacy needs (Coleman, 1989).

The unique effects of being deprived of dating opportunities have not been articulated for lesbian adolescents. Rothblum's (1990) review of depression among adult lesbians suggests that being involved in a lesbian relationship is highly correlated with self-esteem, self-acceptance, and social support. The lack of true intimacy and the considerable social and emotional isolation may be an instigating factor for some lesbian and bisexual teenagers to become pregnant or to marry heterosexually (Martin & Hetrick, 1988).

Bisexual, gay male, and lesbian youths may give up hope that they will ever have the opportunity to develop committed, loving relationships with members of their gender. Denied the opportunity to be romantically involved with someone of the same sex, youth often suffer impaired feelings of self-esteem that reinforce the belief that one is unworthy of receiving love and affection. This may increase the risk for self-destructive behaviors, including suicide (Bell & Weinberg, 1978; Gibson, 1989; Remafedi, Farrow, & Deisher, 1991).

Research Recommendations

Relatively little is known concerning the developmental processes or experiences that are critical when a youth realizes that she or he is lesbian, gay, or bisexual. The paucity of social science research reflects the bias that youth can be heterosexual or uncertain, but not gay, bisexual, or lesbian. At the most basic level, the behavioral sciences must reject this false assumption and proceed to conduct critically needed empirical studies. Cultural heterosexism, which reflects ignorance, biases, and prejudices, must be overcome (Herek, Kimmel, Amaro, & Melton, 1991):

> Overcoming these prejudices will lead to better science, as researchers recognize the many ways in which heterosexist bias has influenced formulation of research questions, sampling procedures, methods and measures, and the interpretation of results. (p. 963)

Modifications are needed in terms of both research methodology and content areas. Because Herek et al. (1991) have recently reviewed the heterosexist biases in psychological research, more space in this chapter is devoted to content areas than research methodology.

Research Methodology

Social scientists should use research instruments that do not assume all youths are heterosexual or engage only in heterosexual behavior. Herek et al. (1991) noted, "Unfortunately, the bulk of scientific research has ignored sexual orientation and behavior or has uncritically adopted societal prejudices against gay and bisexual people" (p. 957). For example, questionnaires can be written so that both heterosexual and homosexual behavior, attractions, fantasies, and orientation are presented as normative. It should be assumed that girls can be attracted to girls, boys to boys, and girls and boys to both sexes.

Special efforts should be made to include sexual minority youth in our research. This suggestion applies both to lesbian, gay male, and bisexual researchers—many of whom need to be reminded that homosexuality does not begin in adulthood—and to others who study adolescence. Until recently, the largest sample of gay male, bisexual, and lesbian youths studied was 29, and few of these individuals could be considered "typical" gay male youths. Research on urban, white gay males must be balanced by attention to those who are severely underrepresented in research conducted to date—lesbians, bisexuals (of both sexes), racial minorities (especially Asian–Americans and Native Americans), Jews and Catholics, the physically challenged, young adolescents, and rural and low socioeconomic youths. The variability thus produced would generate new insights, as Goode and Haber (1977) discovered almost two decades ago in their research with college women:

> It is in the very fact that this group contains women with strikingly different experiences and inclinations—seemingly a drawback—that its informative strength lies. . . . Samples of homosexuals have typically been preselected on the assumption that the various dimensions and traits assumed to characterize homosexuality inevitably hang together . . . it is probabalistic rather than certain, and cannot be assumed in the first place. (p. 19)

The existence of sexual minority youth should be publicized in our journals, books, conferences, courses, and research. Courses on adolescence should integrate data about sexual minorities across all domains discussed; adolescent textbooks should strike their "homosexual behavior" sections and refer to sexual minority youth issues throughout the volume; special issues on sexual minority youth should be on the agenda for professional journals in the area of adolescence; and local, regional, and national conferences should actively recruit speakers and programs on sexual minority youth.

Content Areas

A large selection of content areas should be explored to better understand sexual minority youth. As noted earlier, researchers either ignore the topic of sexual minority youth or explore homosexual behavior among youth, leaving untouched information other than sexual behavior that pertains to the lives of bisexual, gay, and lesbian individuals.

It is generally assumed that because of their genetic proclivities, heterosexual youth are attracted to the other sex. A similar assumption is rarely taken with regard to sexual minority youth—that they are naturally attracted to same-sex individuals. The prevailing belief is that something went "wrong" to make them the way they are.

An understanding of all youth would be enhanced by careful investigation of the sequencing of sexual orientation, fantasies, behavior, and identity. Longitudinal research designs would be most useful, although retrospective techniques can generate helpful data as well (see example in Savin-Williams, 1993). Two models are most frequently articulated by theoreticians. In one, the sequence proposes that sexual orientation is genetic (or, if environmental, then established during prenatal life), which gives expression to or motivates sexual fantasies and, sometimes, sexual behavior during childhood and adolescence. Sexual behavior serves to confirm or disconfirm the fantasies and orientation, although sexual behavior need not be present for sexual identity to develop (e.g., lesbian, bisexual, and gay male virgins). Sexual identity evolves to make sense of these sexual processes and events. An alternative model essentially denies the existence of sexual orientation and posits that sexual identity is the accumulation of sexual experiences and learning that an individual undergoes during her or his lifetime. If a sexual orientation is proposed, it is assumed to be bisexual or ambiguous. In either model, the sexual identity adopted can be articulated and understood only within a cultural context. Much more needs to be known regarding the cognitive and emotional processes that lead an individual to recognize, understand, accept, and express her or his sexuality before either model of sexual identity can be verified.

The processes of coming out to self and to others need to be distinguished and then studied in their own right. The critical factors that lead to denial or acceptance of a sexual minority status remain unexplored. Among many possible factors are the degree to which one conforms to stereotypic cultural definitions of masculinity and femininity, awareness and knowledge about sexuality in general and homosexuality/bisexuality in particular, possession of a family support system, and positive self-esteem. Most coming out models need extensive empirical documentation, especially regarding their applicability to lesbians, bisexual individuals, people of color, and various religious groups.

The research reviewed on dating among sexual minority youth suggests that it may be particularly important to consider the experience of the sexes and bisexuals separately. Also helpful would be an investigation of when same-sex romantic relationships are desired and an exploration of the natural history of romances, such as how the youths found each other, what impediments to forming a relationship were faced and how they were overcome, and why they broke up. The connection between romances and psychological health, identity formation, self-disclosure, and coming out to others needs to be examined.

Empirical research on lesbian teenagers is practically nonexistent, for reasons that are not difficult to imagine (e.g., the sexist nature of psychological research). Questions which should be addressed include: What is unique about the lesbian experience of adolescence? Is it easier for her to hide from herself and others? If so, what are the effects on her psychological health and sexual identity? What are the differences between females who come out early versus late? What is the relationship between feminism and coming out as lesbian for a teenager?

Another long neglected area of research is adolescent bisexuality. In the first edited book on gay and lesbian youth in the social sciences (Herdt, 1989), bisexuality is noted only in passing. Bisexuality poses a unique opportunity for researchers because bisexual youth have their own set of hurdles to face. For example, it may be difficult for heterosexual persons to understand why anyone would choose to be involved with a member of the same sex when she or he is erotically and emotionally attracted to someone of the other sex. Lesbians and gay males may feel that the heterosexually involved bisexual person is "selling out." The impact of "bi-phobia" from heterosexual, gay male, and lesbian communities can be devastating. Also unknown is whether recognizing and accepting one's bisexuality are similar to the processes among gay male and lesbian adolescents regarding their homosexuality. A major complication for a bisexual youth is how to understand her or his sexual feelings and desires if gender is not the deciding issue, as it is for heterosexual, lesbian, and gay male youths.

A critical need is information on methods to enhance the mental health of bisexual, lesbian, and gay male youth. This is particularly important to investigate because far too many youths end their lives prematurely; devote their sexuality to the service of others rather than to themselves; and exhibit self-destructive behavior through substance abuse, running away, school failure, and infection with HIV. How do youth with these problems differ from other sexual minority youths? What led them to this point and how can this process be reversed or prevented?

Finally, another topic in need of study is the special needs of gay male, bisexual, and lesbian youth of color. The dual identities, multiple roles, emotional conflicts, and psychological adjustments that result from the complex situations in which lesbian, bisexual, and gay male youth of color find themselves must be acknowledged in research strategies.

Any list of underresearched topics in this area must be long. In relation to the major issues addressed in this chapter, research is needed to examine the impact of other identities (e.g., religious, economic, and political identities) and the effects of cultural and historical change on sexual behavior, sexual identity, coming out, receiving peer harassment, and dating. There is a long agenda for the next generation of researchers.

Final Reflections

One of the primary tasks of adolescence is to explore and consolidate an identity. The reality of growing up as lesbian, gay, or bisexual in North American culture handicaps that process. It is difficult for youths to totally rid themselves of the incorporation of biases against homosexuality and bisexuality that are prevalent in the social world. Defenses against self-recognition may be so entrenched, the stigmatization of homosexuality so severe, and the adolescent ego so fragile and

diffuse that offering assistance to adolescents may be extremely difficult. An adult or another youth can be the perfect role model and be
patient, open, and sensitive; but it may not be the "right time" for
adolescents who resist the unwanted attractions and present to the
world a socially acceptable heterosexuality while maintaining the secrecy of their inner homoerotic life ("passing").

Passing may be a destructive strategy because it fosters low self-
regard, inner turmoil, acting-out behavior, and low levels of interpersonal intimacy. How long can a gay male, bisexual, or lesbian adolescent pretend before he or she begins to have difficulty separating the
pretensions from the realities? For personal authenticity and self-worth
to develop, a youth needs self-validation; passing as something one is
not is hypocritical and self-alienating (Colgan, 1987; Lee, 1977; Martin,
1982). Many youths "use" heterosexual dating to blind themselves and
others. When they are dating, the name-calling lessens and peer status
and prestige increase.

The isolation and sense of alienation that many sexual minority
youths experience is compounded by their inability to meet others similar to themselves. The result may be despair, which leads to suicidal
feelings or suicide attempts. Healthy personality development requires
being "true to yourself." Aware of this, some youths try to blend their
emerging sexual identity with a life in the normative culture of high
school. They are willing to accept the trade-off of social ostracism for
feeling authentic to their sexual self. They need validation as they attempt, like other adolescents, to find those similar to themselves.

These issues may very well be compounded for the sexual minority
adolescent of color who perceives that she or he faces yet a second
stigma, her or his race or ethnicity (Morales, 1983). Such youths may
be able to pass as heterosexual, but not as white. The double stigmatization frequently exists in the heterosexual, white adolescent world;
the adolescent of color may also encounter racism in gay male, bisexual, and lesbian communities and homophobia in her or his cultural
community. Some find sources of support and encouragement from
nonwhite, nonheterosexual communities, but it is a risky venture
(Savin-Williams & Rodriguez, 1993).

Most research attention has focused on the problems of sexual minority youth rather than the promises. Social scientists need to listen
to these youths, to hear their concerns, insights, and solutions. But by
so doing we must not ignore the fact that many if not most lesbian,
gay male, and bisexual youths persevere and cope with their hostile
world to lead happy, productive lives with a healthy sense of self. For
this to occur they must have opportunities to meet other sexual minority youths, develop intimate and sexual relationships, and come out to
self and others.

The invisibility of sexual minority youth is quickly becoming a part of our past as bisexual, lesbian, and gay male youth across the country are refusing to allow their sexual identities to be suppressed. Many are now coming out to themselves and others while in junior and senior high school. This is probably largely due to the increased visibility of same-sex identified people in our culture. What this means for youths is relatively simple and yet profound. It is more difficult for homoerotically inclined youths to ignore the reality of their attractions, impulses, and desires than in previous generations. It still happens, but efforts to repress or deny them are more likely to fail. The results of this process are striking. The age of coming out to self and others is falling. Studies conducted in the 1970s and early 1980s reported that the age of coming out to nongays averaged early to mid-20s. Current research places this same event in the late teenage years (see review in Savin-Williams, 1990). The match among sexual impulses, cognitive abilities, and sexual behavior during puberty is such that youths today are better able to realize that their sexual desires, attractions, and activities fit the definition of a gay, bisexual, or lesbian identity.

What happens when a youth decides not to pass and to come out? Despite the progress, it can be a physical and psychological nightmare if the youth suffers verbal and physical abuse. Positive alternatives to a heterosexual existence are not readily apparent to most sexual minority youths. There are few models and even fewer avenues of assistance. As a result, many return to the closet, to reemerge in safer times, frequently in college. This delay, this living a lie, is unfair and potentially destructive. It can also be changed, in part by a devotion to empirical research which lifts the veil from the experience of growing up lesbian, gay, or bisexual in North American culture.

References

Adair, N., & Adair, C. (1978). *Word is out*. New York: Dell.

Bell, A. P., & Weinberg, M. S. (1978). *Homosexualities: A study of diversity among men and women*. New York: Simon & Schuster.

Bell, A. P., Weinberg, M. S., & Hammersmith, S. K. (1981). *Sexual preference: Its development in men and women*. Bloomington: Indiana University Press.

Boxer, A. M. (1988). Betwixt and between: Developmental discontinuities of gay and lesbian youth. Paper presented at the Society for Research on Adolescence, Alexandria, VA.

Boxer, A. M., Cook, J. A., & Herdt, G. (1989). First homosexual and heterosexual experiences reported by gay and lesbian youth in a urban community. Paper presented at the Annual Meeting of the American Sociological Association. San Francisco, August.

Boxer, A. M., Cook, J. A., & Herdt, G. (1991). Double jeopardy: Identity transitions and parent-child relations among gay and lesbian youth. In K. Pillemer & K. McCartney (Eds.), *Parent-child relations throughout life* (pp. 59–92). Hillsdale, NJ: Lawrence Erlbaum.

Breakwell, G. M. & Fife-Schaw, C. (1992). Sexual activities and preferences in a United Kingdom sample of 16 to 20-year-olds. *Archives of Sexual Behavior, 21,* 271–293.

Burnison, M. (1987). Runaway youth: Lesbian and gay issues. Paper presented at the Symposium on Gay and Lesbian Adolescents, Minneapolis, MN.

Cass, V. (1979). Homosexual identity formation: A theoretical model. *Journal of Homosexuality, 4,* 219–235.

Cass, V. (1984). Homosexual identity formation: Testing a theoretical model. *The Journal of Sex Research, 20,* 143–167.

Coleman, E. (1989). The development of male prostitution activity among gay and bisexual adolescence. *Journal of Homosexuality, 17,* 131–149.

Coles, R., & Stokes, G. (1985). *Sex and the American teenager.* New York: Harper & Row.

Colgan, P. (1987). Treatment of identity and intimacy issues in gay males. *Journal of Homosexuality, 14,* 101–123.

Curtis, W. (Ed.) (1988). *Revelations: A collection of gay male coming out stories.* Boston: Alyson.

Dank, B. M. (1971). Coming out in the gay world. *Psychiatry, 34,* 180–197.

Dank, B. M. (1973). The homosexual. In D. Spiegel & P. Keith-Spiegel (Eds.), *Outsiders USA* (pp. 269–297). San Francisco: Rinehart.

D'Augelli, A. R. (1991). Gay men in college: Identity processes and adaptations. *Journal of College Student Development, 32,* 140–146.

D'Augelli, A. R. (1992). Lesbian and gay male undergraduates' experiences of harassment and fear on campus. *Journal of Interpersonal Violence, 7,* 383–395.

Eichberg, R. (1990). *Coming out: An act of love.* New York: Dutton.

Fay, R. E., Turner, C. F., Klassen, A. D., & Gagnon, J. H. (1989). Prevalence and patterns of same-gender sexual contact among men. *Science, 243,* 338–348.

Gibson, P. (1989). Gay male and lesbian youth suicide. In ADAMHA, *Report of the Secretary's Task Force on Youth Suicide.* Vol. 3 (pp. 110–142). (DHHS Pub. No (ADM) 89–1623). Washington, DC: U.S. Government Printing Office.

Goode, E., & Haber, L. (1977). Sexual correlates of homosexual experience: An exploratory study of college women. *The Journal of Sex Research, 13,* 12–21.

Gonsiorek, J. C. (1988). Mental health issues of gay and lesbian adolescents. *Journal of Adolescent Health Care, 9,* 114–122.

Gundlach, R. H., & Riess, B. F. (1968). Self and sexual identity in the female: A study of female homosexuals. In B. F. Riess (Ed.), *New directions in mental health* (pp. 205–231). New York: Grune & Stratton.

Hall Carpenter Archives (1989). *Walking after midnight: Gay men's life stories.* London: Routledge.

Harry, J., & DeVall, W. B. (1978). *The social organization of gay males.* New York: Praeger.

Hedblom, J. H. (1973). Dimensions of lesbian sexual experience. *Archives of Sexual Behavior, 2,* 329–341.

Herdt, G. (Ed.) (1989). *Gay and lesbian youth.* New York: Harrington Park Press.

Herek, G. M., Kimmel, D. C., Amaro, H., & Melton, G. B. (1991). Avoiding heterosexist bias in psychological research. *American Psychologist, 46,* 957–963.

Heron, A. (Ed.) (1983). *One teenager in ten.* Boston: Alyson.

Hetrick, E. S., & Martin, A. D. (1987). Developmental issues and their resolution for gay and lesbian adolescents. *Journal of Homosexuality, 14,* 25–44.

Hunter, J., & Schaecher, R. (1987). Stresses on lesbian and gay adolescents in schools. *Social Work in Education, 9,* 180–189.

Isay, R. A. (1989). *Being homosexual: Gay men and their development.* New York: Farrar-Straus-Giroux.

Kooden, H., Morin, S., Riddle, D., Rogers, M., Sang, B., & Strassburger, F. (1979). *Removing the stigma. Final report. Task force on the status of lesbian and gay male psychologists.* Washington, DC: American Psychological Association.

Lee, J. A. (1977). Going public: A study in the sociology of homosexual liberation. *Journal of Homosexuality, 3,* 47–78.

Malyon, A. K. (1981). The homosexual adolescent: Developmental issues and social bias. *Child Welfare, 60,* 321–330.

Manosevitz, M. (1970). Early sexual behavior in adult homosexual and heterosexual males. *Journal of Abnormal Psychology, 76,* 396–402.

Marotta, T. (1982). *Sons of Harvard: Gay men from the class of 1967.* New York: Quill.

Martin, A. D. (1982). Learning to hide: The socialization of the gay adolescent. *Adolescent Psychiatry, 10,* 52–65.

Martin, A. D., & Hetrick, E. S. (1988). The stigmatization of the gay and lesbian adolescent. *Journal of Homosexuality, 15,* 163–183.

McDonald, G. J. (1982). Individual differences in the coming out process for gay men: Implications for theoretical models. *Journal of Homosexuality, 8,* 47–60.

Minton, H. L., & McDonald, G. J. (1983/1984). Homosexual identity formation as a developmental process. *Journal of Homosexuality, 9,* 91–104.

Money, J. (1987). Introduction. In T. Sandfort (Ed.), *Boys on their contacts with men: A study of sexually expressed friendships* (pp. 5–7). Elmhurst, NY: Global Academic.

Morales, E. S. (1983). *Third World gays and lesbians: A process of multiple identities.* Paper presented at the Ninety-First Annual Convention of the American Psychological Association, Anaheim, CA.

Penelope, J., & Wolfe, S. J. (Eds.) (1989). *The original coming out stories.* Freedom, CA: Crossing Press.

Peterson, J. W. (1989). Gay runaways are in more danger than ever, and gay adults won't help. *The Advocate,* April 11, pp. 8–10.

Pratch, L., Boxer, A. M., & Herdt, G. (in preparation). First sexual experiences among gay and lesbian youth: Person, age, and context.

Remafedi, G. (1987a). Male homosexuality: The adolescent's perspective. *Pediatrics, 79*, 326–330.

Remafedi, G. (1987b). Adolescent homosexuality: Psychosocial and medical implications. *Pediatrics, 79*, 331–337.

Remafedi, G. (1990). Fundamental issues in the care of homosexual youth. *Adolescent Medicine, 74*, 1169–1179.

Remafedi, G., Farrow, J. A., & Deisher, R. W. (1991). Risk factors for attempted suicide in gay and bisexual youth. *Pediatrics, 87*, 869–875.

Remafedi, G., Resnick, M., Blum, R., & Harris, L. (1992). Demography of sexual orientation in adolescents. *Pediatrics, 89*, 714–721.

Riddle, D. I., & Morin, S. F. (Eds.) (1978). Psychology and the gay community. *Journal of Social Issues, 34*, 1–138.

Robertson, R. (1981). Young gays. In J. Hart & D. Richardson (Eds.), *The theory and practice of homosexuality* (pp. 170–176). London: Routledge & Kegan Paul.

Roesler, T., & Deisher, R. (1972). Youthful male homosexuality. *Journal of the American Medical Association, 219*, 1018–1023.

Rothblum, E. D. (1990). Depression among lesbians: An invisible and unresearched phenomenon. *Journal of Gay & Lesbian Psychotherapy, 1*, 67–87.

Rotheram-Borus, M. J., Rosario, M., & Koopman, C. (1991). Minority youths at high risk: Gay males and runaways. In M. E. Colten & S. Gore (Eds.), *Adolescent stress: Causes and consequences* (pp. 181–200). New York: Aldine DeGruyter.

Rotheram-Borus, M. J., Rosario, M., Meyer-Bahlburg, H. F. L., Koopman, C., Dopkins, S. C., & Davies, M. (in preparation). Sexual and substance use behaviors among homosexual and bisexual male adolescents in New York City.

Saghir, M. T., & Robins, E. (1969). Homosexuality I: Sexual behavior of the female homosexual. *Archives of General Psychiatry, 20*, 192–201.

Saghir, M. T., & Robins, E. (1973). *Male and female homosexuality*. Baltimore: Williams & Wilkins.

Sanders, G. (1980). Homosexualities in the Netherlands. *Alternative Lifestyles, 3*, 278–311.

Savin-Williams, R. C. (1990). *Gay and lesbian youth: Expressions of identity*. Washington, DC: Hemisphere.

Savin-Williams, R. C. (1994). Dating those you can't love and loving those you can't date. In R. Montemayor, G. R. Adams, & T. P. Gullotta (Eds.), *Personal relationships during adolescence. Advances in adolescent development* (pp. 196–215). Newbury Park, CA: Sage.

Savin-Williams, R. C. (1993). *Sex and sexual identity among gay and bisexual male youths*. Unpublished manuscript.

Savin-Williams, R. C., & Cohen, K. M. (Eds.) (in press), *The lives of lesbians, gays, and bisexuals: Developmental, clinical, and cultural issues*. Fort Worth: Harcourt Brace Jovanovich.

Savin-Williams, R. C., & Rodriguez, R. G. (1993). A developmental, clinical perspective on lesbian, gay male, and bisexual youths. In T. P. Gullotta, G. R. Adams, & R. Montemayor (Eds.), *Adolescent sexuality. Advances in adolescent development. Volume 5* (pp. 77–101). Newbury Park, CA: Sage.

Schafer, S. (1976). Sexual and social problems of lesbians. *The Journal of Sex Research, 12,* 50–69.

Sears, J. T. (1991). *Growing up gay in the South: Race, gender, and journeys of the spirit.* New York: Harrington Park Press.

Silverstein, C. (1981). *Man to man: Gay couples in America.* New York: William Morrow.

Sorensen, R. (1973). *Adolescent sexuality in contemporary society.* New York: World Book.

Spada, J. (1979). *The Spada report: The newest survey of gay male sexuality.* New York: New American Library.

Storms, M. D. (1981). A theory of erotic orientation development. *Psychological Review, 88,* 340–353.

Troiden, R. R. (1979). Becoming homosexual: A model of gay identity acquisition. *Psychiatry, 42,* 362–373.

Troiden, R. R. (1989). The formation of homosexual identities. *Journal of Homosexuality, 17,* 43–73.

Troiden, R. R., & Goode, E. (1980). Variables related to the acquisition of a gay identity. *Journal of Homosexuality, 5,* 383–392.

Weinberg, M., & Williams, C. J. (1974). *Male homosexuals: Their problems and adaptations.* New York: Penguin Books.

Weinberg, T. S. (1983). *Gay men, gay selves.* New York: Irvington.

8

Lesbians and Gay Men in Midlife

Douglas C. Kimmel and Barbara E. Sang

Research on middle-aged gay men and lesbians today is best understood when viewed in its cultural and historical context. First, persons who are between age 40 and 60 today reached sexual maturity before the impact of the 1969 protest demonstrations following a police raid on the Stonewall bar. That event began to change the social construction of homosexuality from a personal pathology to minority group membership. Some middle-aged persons were active participants in the historical events that brought about those changes. Second, middle-aged lesbians and gay men were in the prime of middle adulthood when the AIDS epidemic emerged. Many have been personally touched by the AIDS epidemic. Survivors of this cohort will enter old age and be followed by a cohort of middle-aged lesbians and gay men with different historical and cultural experiences. Therefore, to review characteristics of midlife today, we must recall the context in which this cohort of gay men and lesbians constructed their identity and the beliefs they held about their lives as a result. It is difficult to delimit the precise age range for these cohort effects, however, because of individual variation, socioeconomic status, geographical location, able-bodiedness, gender, race, and ethnicity.

Historical Background

In general, middle-aged lesbians and gay men today were isolated from one another in their youth. There were few books or magazines, especially for lesbians. As the baby boom followed World War II, the roles of housewife and mother with several children were emphasized, and education for women was discouraged. For gay men and lesbians, the climate was one of secrecy, very few positive role models, and great fear of exposure (D'Emilio, 1983). However, in the 1950s, organizations such as the Daughters of Bilitis and the Mattachine Society emerged despite the "witch hunts" of homosexuals and Communists led by Senator Joseph McCarthy. Research studies and occasional books began to question the pathology model of homosexuality, but most portrayed it negatively. A few novels such as *The Well of Loneliness* and *Another Country* were available and provided a sense of identification. Some gay men found ways to meet sexually, but lesbians often remained isolated. Many living in rural areas moved to brighter prospects in urban areas, where social networks could be found at least for gay men. The view of the future was not positive: relationships were thought to be short-lived, exposure and arrest were feared, and aging was seen as lonely. Nonetheless, many ignored these stereotypes and coped with whatever difficulties came along, formed long-term relationships, and led lives of quiet nonconformity.

The historical changes of the 1970s had effects on all cohorts of lesbians and gay men and demonstrated the effects a younger generation can have on older ones. As a pioneer in the homophile movement noted, what had once been a personal identity for gay men and lesbians became a collective identity, and the stigma of homosexuality as mental illness dissolved into the possibility of an open and proud minority status (Hay, 1990). Other historical influences have also had significant effects on this group of midlife lesbians and gay men. For example, the feminist movement had such profound effects on some women that Faderman (1984) coined the term "new gay lesbians" to describe those women who came out after the feminist emergence in contrast to those who came out before. Likewise, Kitzinger (1987) has argued that, for some women, the radical lesbian movement redefined the nature of sexual orientation from a psychological characteristic to a political ideology.

The AIDS epidemic of the 1980s also brought profound changes to gay men and lesbians. With the AIDS crisis now in its second decade, most midlife gay men have been confronted with the premature deaths of friends their age or younger. Some, of course, are infected with the virus thought to cause AIDS, a status that can result in unusual awareness of mortality. Many middle-aged gay men have partners who are experiencing AIDS-related illnesses, or who have died. Unlike many other fatal diseases, AIDS can be transmitted to the sexual partner, so caring for a lover who is ill may be a rehearsal for one's own dying. The direct impact of the AIDS epidemic has been greater among gay men than among lesbians. Thus, historical events have affected the psychology of middle age in markedly different ways for lesbians and gay men today.

Overview of Midlife Theories

Development during adulthood, especially during the midlife years, has been described in three different ways (Kimmel, 1990). Although often seen as contradictory, these perspectives are complementary: (1) adult development is a relatively continuous process of maturation or unfolding of personality themes that were laid down early in life; (2) adult development consists of a series of predictable stages or periods when significant change or crisis may occur; (3) social age norms, historical effects, and idiosyncratic transitions combine to provide the pattern of adult lives.

Research on adult development has been almost exclusively heterosexual in its focus. Women have typically been viewed in terms of their biological time clocks and traditional family or relationship roles such as care giving. Men have been assumed to be highly involved in work. With few exceptions (Fertitta, 1984; Kimmel, 1978; Lee, 1989; Sang, Warshow, & Smith, 1991), lesbian and gay midlife development has not been included in theories of adult development (Cornett & Hudson, 1987). One implication of this omission is that gays and lesbians have had few developmental models for conceptualizing their own life course or interpreting normative crises they may experience. This may enhance the opportunity for creating individual norms and roles (Brown, 1989).

One contribution of research on lesbian and gay male midlife has been to add the dimension of sexual orientation to these models of adult development. Several new variables are added in this way: coming out as a lesbian or gay man as a developmental event; integrating one's sexual orientation into broader developmental themes; creating self-relevant norms and expectations for the order and timing of developmental events or periods; and fitting one's relatively unique life into the progression of developmental events of significant others, such as one's parents, children, and lovers. Moreover, adult development overlaps for many people with the development of long-term relationships, which sometimes follow a developmental sequence of their own (see Chapter 10). Also, for some gay men and lesbians, parenting is a major theme in adult development (see Chapter 11).

Our task in this chapter is to integrate these various themes into an overview of the diversity of midlife experiences among gay men and lesbians. We begin with a focus on central aspects for lesbians: changes in the self, working life, relationships, menopause, and sexuality. In the following section we focus on gay men. We conclude with a discussion of what we know and what we hope to learn about lesbians and gay men in midlife.

Lesbians at Midlife

Sense of Self

Children leaving home is frequently cited as the central event that marks the beginning of midlife changes for traditional heterosexual women. At this time many women go back into the work force, if they are not already working. Women whose lives have been oriented around care-taking and performing the role of the "other" have begun to search for their own identity, separate from children and husbands (Junge & Maya, 1985; Rubin, 1979). In contrast, a study by Fertitta (1984) of 68 white, child-free lesbian women, never legally married, 40 to 55 years of age, highly educated, all from the west coast reported that finding an identity separate from others and proving themselves as independent persons were not central issues for these women. Many lesbians have spent a lifetime learning to define themselves independent of other people's reactions. Some midlife lesbians reported that in fighting their oppression as lesbians they have developed a stronger sense of self (Sang, 1991). Moreover, there is reason to believe that lesbians place less emphasis on youth and traditional standards of beauty than heterosexual women, and are therefore less threatened by the aging process (Kirkpatrick, 1989; Posin, 1991).

Another characteristic that distinguishes lesbians and nonconventional women from traditional middle and upper middle class midlife women is the continuity of their work lives (Fertitta, 1984; Sang, 1991). Although their careers or the nature of their work may change in midlife, most lesbians work out of economic necessity, for stimulation, and as part of their identity throughout adult life (Hall & Gregory, 1991; Fertitta, 1984; Sang, 1991). The observation that women's employment histories seem to be more fluid and less linear than men's employment histories (Baruch & Brooks-Gunn, 1984) may thus not apply to most lesbians. A major theme that emerged for midlife lesbians in a questionnaire study by Sang (1991) of 110 self-identified lesbians, age 40 to 59, who were generally well-educated and white, was the desire to have more fun and to be less achievement oriented. Many reported not wanting to push or strive as much as they did when younger. Work was described as easier, less stressful, and consequently more enjoyable and satisfying. There was a new sense of freedom; women described themselves as more open, playful, and spontaneous. Thus, midlife appears to be a particularly creative time for lesbians (Sang, in press).

Affluent college-educated heterosexual women in their early 50s whose children had just left home have been reported to be in their "prime" (Mitchell & Helson, 1990). These women describe their lives in very positive terms at this time. Midlife lesbians also appear to be in their "prime" despite the fact that, in the Sang study, about half (46%) the respondents reported they had or were going through a "midlife crisis" (Sang, 1991; in press). These midlife lesbians felt this to be the best time in their life (76%) and felt more self-directed and self-confident than they remembered having felt at younger ages. One respondent wrote, "Each year seems to get better despite some of the seemingly endless struggles. Generally, I feel better about myself and my life than I ever have . . . more focused yet more diverse in my interests and activities." Lesbians in the Fertitta (1984) study also reported a variety of positive internal changes such as gaining perspective, resolution of conflicts, self acceptance, and wisdom when asked what the meaning of middle age was for them. Specific questions about worries and stressors, however, elicited concerns about finances and time pressures in other studies on midlife lesbians (Bradford & Ryan, 1991; Woodman, 1990). If there are times that are better than others, they do not appear to be triggered by such predictable markers as children leaving the home. The qualities that Mitchell and Helson (1990) posit for enhancing the quality of life for midlife women, autonomy and intimacy, appear to be characteristic of lesbians throughout their adult development.

In Sang's (1991) study it is not clear to what extent children leaving home affected the lives of midlife lesbians with children. In the accounts of midlife respondents with children, there was no spontaneous mention of this issue. It is conceivable that children leaving the home is not as great a change in the lives of lesbian mothers as it is for traditional heterosexual women because of the existence and continuity of many other significant roles and interests. Because their identities may be derived from many other sources as well, the meaning and significance of motherhood may also be different for lesbians than for heterosexual women. Further research is needed in this area.

One factor that may contribute to midlife being viewed as such a positive time among lesbians studied by Sang (1991) is the feeling that they have attained greater wisdom, power, and freedom. As a result of the gay and women's movements, more midlife lesbians and feminists are coming into contact with each other for the first time and are feeling a need to find new rituals and new ways of expressing their "midlife passage" (Downing, 1987; Gauding, 1991; Walker, 1985). In our culture the wisdom and maturity that comes with aging has traditionally been attributed to midlife men. Gentry and Seifert (1991) describe the "Croning Celebration," a special birthday party, typically for a woman who is 50 or older or who is postmenopausal. This celebration is a public rite of passage that recognizes the wisdom that comes to women from life experience. For the past seven years lesbians in the Washington, D.C., area have also been holding a yearly weekend conference entitled "Passages," which is a multicultural, multiracial conference on aging and ageism for all lesbians. Events such as these emphasize positive aspects of aging for lesbians.

Work and Income

Midlife lesbians have been found to derive meaning and identity from both work and relationships throughout their adult lives (Fertitta, 1984; Sang, 1990; 1991). Midlife lesbians also reported a significant number of personal interests—an average of ten each, in addition to political and spiritual activities (Sang, 1991). A major midlife issue for these lesbians is the striving for balance and wholeness. Each woman, in her own way, described her efforts to accommodate relationships, work, and personal interests. Because of perceived pressure to spend long hours at work, finding a balance between work life and home life was difficult for many lesbians. This issue also emerged as a major theme for lesbians in other studies and is further discussed in the next section.

Fertitta (1984) and Turner (1987) suggested that it is never-married lesbians who are most comparable to men in terms of commitment to careers. Men in our society know from childhood that they are expected to be self-supporting. Some lesbians are also aware from an early age that they will have to support themselves. Lesbians who are in midlife today, however, grew up at a time when girls were discouraged from having careers and taking an active part in the world. Lesbians who came out in their teens and twenties were more likely to report having had career expectations as teenagers (79%) compared to lesbians who came out in their thirties (59%) or older (over 40; 44%) (Sang, 1990; 1991). Of the women who did have career aspirations, a little more than half (64%) were of a nontraditional nature, for example, scientist, doctor, professor, business owner, and athlete. It was the women who came out in their teens, twenties, and thirties who were more likely to envision themselves in nontraditional careers (74%) compared to women who identified themselves as lesbians at midlife (44%). The majority of lesbians who came out at midlife had been married heterosexually (96%). It is significant that lesbians in this sample became self-supporting on the average at 26 years old. Lesbians who came out earlier, however, were self-supporting in their early twenties

(Sang, 1991). In summary, evidence suggests that work has greater salience and is a more significant part of the midlife lesbian's identity than is reported for traditional midlife heterosexual women (Fertitta, 1984; Sang, 1991).

The career achievements of lesbians, like those of other women, are limited by sex discrimination in hiring, promotion, pay, and access to informal networks (Riddle & Sang, 1978). Data from the *National Lesbian Health Care Survey* (Bradford & Ryan, 1991) revealed that the earned income of middle-aged lesbians in this sample was not commensurate with their educational preparation and professional experience. Reasons for this discrepancy between training and income are not clear. It is possible that to feel comfortable, lesbians may work outside the mainstream in jobs that do not pay well. Further study of this issue is clearly in order.

With few exceptions, lesbians in the Sang (1991) study did not express anguish over their career achievements the way traditional midlife men are reported to do. Other studies also found no such concerns. Although it is possible that these studies failed to inquire about such issues, lesbians also may not be as concerned with making it to the "top." Prestigious, high-level positions may actually be avoided by lesbians because to survive in them, they must keep home and work lives separate and hide more than they would like to (Woodman, 1990; Woods & Harbeck, 1991). It is also likely that, because lesbians find meaning and self-esteem from many other areas, work does not assume such all-consuming importance. Eighty-six percent of the sample described their work as satisfactory or very good. These findings may not apply to working-class women, and more research is needed in this area.

Relationships

Are lesbian relationships different at midlife from those at earlier ages? There are no longitudinal studies that make such comparisons; however, a few studies on midlife lesbians' relationships suggest developmental differences. Hall and Gregory (1991) interviewed nine mostly white midlife professional lesbian couples from the San Francisco Bay area who were between 35 and 50 and who had been in their relationships on an average of 6 years. All interviewees had previous significant relationships and most had more than one. Due to separations, infidelity, illness, and so on, the original expectation that they would find one partner with whom they would live "forever after" had been tempered among these women. These midlife lesbians tended to see romance, if not relationships, as transitory.

A number of midlife lesbians were found to be single, that is, not in a committed couple relationship (Bradford & Ryan, 1991, 40%; Fertitta,

1984, 43%; Sang, 1991, 33%). Based on the available data, reasons for being single or not cannot be determined, nor can one tell how relationship status affected women's quality of life. Midlife lesbians who do not define themselves as part of a couple relationship may be seeing one woman, many, or none. Raphael and Robinson (1984) found single midlife lesbians to have more lesbian friends than coupled lesbians of the same age. They also reported that a few single midlife lesbians were experimenting with alternative forms of bonding and intimacy that might or might not have sexual components, such as communal living.

Midlife lesbians were reported (Bradford & Ryan, 1991) to be nearly twice as likely to be living alone (27% vs. 17%) as women in the general population, even if they were in a relationship. By the time one arrives at midlife it may not be economically feasible to move in with a new lover, especially if one has done this several times in the past. Another possible reason that midlife lesbians are more likely to live alone is suggested by a small study conducted by Coss (1991). Based on intensive interviews with eight women between 24 and 61, she found that women who grew up in the 1950s never considered living openly as lesbians the way younger lesbians do today. In addition, a few of these single midlife lesbians said that they would welcome a relationship but only if it "fit" in and was not disruptive to the satisfying balance they had achieved in their work and social lives.

One of the biggest problems midlife lesbian couples report is finding sufficient time for each other and for friends, that is, finding a balance between work and intimacy (Fertitta, 1984; Sang, 1991; Woodman, 1990). Problems also arise when one member of a couple is less busy than the other. Not only do lesbians provide support for one another's work, but work itself seems to affect the couples' experience of intimacy; partners report spending more time together conferring about career projects, problem-solving, arguing about and debriefing from their jobs than in any other activity.

Midlife lesbians, whether in couples or single, tended to derive support and a sense of connection from friends, family, and the lesbian community (Bradford & Ryan, 1991; Fertitta, 1984; Sang, 1991; Woodman, 1990). One of their greatest sources of support they reported, however, was lesbian women friends around the same age. Fertitta (1984) found that 81 percent of her midlife sample of lesbians were more likely to get support from their "new family"—that is, lovers, ex-lovers, and friends—than from their family of origin. She also reported that twice as many lesbians (50%) as heterosexual women (25%) in her sample reported being close to ex-lovers. Tully (1989) reported that the majority of midlife lesbians (89%) in her sample turned to their women friends for care-giving support rather than their biological family or community health institutions. A large percentage of middle-aged lesbians were found to be hiding their lesbianism from most or all of their family members (Bradford & Ryan, 1991), and this might be one reason why midlife lesbians are less involved with their family of origin. Raphael and Robinson (1984) found that midlife lesbians with high self-esteem tended to have weak sibling ties and strong friendship ties.

The extent of a midlife lesbian's connection to the lesbian community is related to many variables, some of which are the age at which she came out, her need for secrecy, and her geographical area (Bradford & Ryan, 1991; Woodman, 1990). All 68 of the mostly professional midlife lesbians in Fertitta's study (1984) were actively involved in the lesbian community. This affiliation played an important role in their self-acceptance and in their maintenance of a positive gay identity. In contrast, fewer than half (34%) of the midlife lesbians in Woodman's study (1990) were affiliated with lesbian and gay organizations. Fear of disclosure was the primary reason given among those who were not affiliated. One of the primary concerns for this socially isolated group of midlife lesbians was finding other lesbian their own age with whom to socialize. This sample of midlife lesbians differs from other samples of professional midlife women in terms of geographical region (64% are from the Southwest, South, and Midwest), relationship status (all were in couple relationships), and age when they came out (30s and 40s).

In addition to lovers, ex-lovers, and friends, midlife lesbians may also have significant relationships with their own children and grandchildren and those of their partners. Kirkpatrick (1989), Rothschild (1991), and Sang (1992) describe some of the dynamics of midlife lesbian mothers dealing with adolescent children. Such relationships can be particularly difficult if the mother is first coming out as a lesbian at midlife.

Another significant role for many midlife lesbians is that of care-giver to aging parents. Warshow (1991) pointed out that 75 percent of care-givers are women, and the "unmarried" daughter has historically been considered the best candidate for this position. Her career and relationships have often been considered expendable. It is not known what percentage of midlife lesbians are care-givers, nor is there much information about the impact of such care-giving on the lives of lesbian care-givers.

Menopause and Sexuality

Cole and Rothblum (1990; 1991) conducted the first systematic survey of sexual attitudes and behaviors of lesbian women at menopause. Their sample consisted of 41 women (38 self-identified lesbians, one bisexual, and two whose sexual orientation was not indicated). The average age of this entirely white nonclinical sample was 51.5 years. The majority of respondents (56%) were postmenopausal, that is, had ceased to menstruate for at least one year. An additional 16 percent had a hysterectomy. In contrast to menopausal heterosexual women who expressed a great deal of worry about their changing sexuality (e.g., were concerned about being able to please their partner, arousal time, dry vaginas, and loss of clitoral sensitivity; Cole, 1988; Leiblum, 1990; Morokoff, 1988), 75 percent of lesbians reported that their sex lives were as good as or better than ever. For lesbians, the emphasis was firmly on the quality of their *relationships* instead of on their sexual functioning (Cole & Rothblum, 1991).

Sang[1] (1993) reported similar findings for her sample of midlife women (average age 47), 22 percent of whom were postmenopausal or had hysterectomies (15%). Half (50%) of these midlife respondents reported that their sex life was more open and exciting than in the past. Better sex was attributed to being able to be more open and vulnerable, to enhanced communication, and to less pressure about orgasms as well as to the greater importance of touching, loving, and sharing. Many of the women who came out as lesbians at midlife reported being sexual for the first time. The majority of midlife lesbians reported being sexually active with a partner (71% in the Cole & Rothblum study and 74% in the Sang study). There was little change since the onset of menopause in the types of sexual activities lesbians enjoyed (Cole & Rothblum, 1991).

The reasons for the differences reported in sexual satisfaction between lesbians and heterosexual women during menopause are not clear and deserve additional research. Cole and Rothblum suggested that one reason is that lesbian women are not as focused on intercourse or penetration as heterosexual women, and therefore the physiological changes of menopause might not be so disruptive. A variety of other factors including a dependence on male sexual performance, interest, and attraction may interfere with sexual satisfaction for midlife heterosexual women.

Menopause may not have the same psychological significance for lesbians and nontraditional women as it does for women whose main role and identity has been connected to child-rearing. For some midlife lesbians, however, the approach of menopause can be a time of loss and conflict. Lesbians who grew up in the 1950s and 1960s did not have the options of parenting in the same way that some lesbians do today. At midlife, lesbians who do want children are faced with the decision of whether or not to have them. Lesser (1991) explains that choosing whether or not to become a mother today is an often grueling process of sifting through contradictory personal feelings and cultural beliefs in an effort to identify one's own preferences and desires.

---

[1] The specific question on menopause was introduced later in the study and, therefore, only 75 women were asked this question instead of 110.

Lesser interviewed fifteen mostly white professional women between the ages of 36 and 47 who were childless to explore their experiences. A third of the women reported a clear sense that having children was not something they wanted to do and that they experienced no regrets. At the other extreme, a few women reported wanting children but changing their minds when they considered the difficulties that children of lesbians would encounter. The rest of the sample were ambivalent about wanting children.

A significant midlife change reported by 25 percent of the women in the Sang (1991) sample was identifying themselves as "lesbians" for the first time, that is, "coming out." Thirty-nine percent of these women had their first same-sex sexual experience before midlife but had not labeled themselves lesbian until midlife. Some of these respondents reported being aware of same-sex sexual feelings in childhood (26%) and adolescence (37%). Charbonneau and Lander (1991) reported on another sample of midlife women (thirty women ranging in age from the mid-30s to the mid-50s) who, with few exceptions, never considered the possibility that they could be lesbians and were initially quite surprised to find that they had fallen in love with a woman. Lesbians who came out at midlife also sometimes reported feeling sexual for the first time. These findings attest to the fact that sexual development does not necessarily proceed according to one defined path.

Summary

Midlife lesbians who have been studied to date have been mainly white, professional, able-bodied middle- and upper-middle-class women. The majority of midlife lesbians were found to feel good about themselves and to report that midlife was the best period in their life. Both work and relationships were integral parts of the midlife lesbians' sense of identity. They also reported numerous personal interests in addition to political and spiritual involvement. Financial worry was a source of stress for many midlife lesbians; there was often considerable discrepancy between their level of education and their income.

Unlike traditional heterosexual women, who at midlife are returning to work or are working for the first time after children leave home, midlife lesbians were found to have been self-supporting since early adulthood. Midlife lesbians reported changes at work such as not striving as hard as they did when younger and the feeling of being knowledgeable and at "maximum capacity" in their field.

The majority of midlife lesbians studied reported being in a "couple" relationship. Close women friends were also reported to be important sources of support and intimacy. Some midlife lesbians were involved in the lesbian and gay community, but others from this generation remained closeted for fear of losing their jobs. The majority of midlife lesbians reported being active sexually and enjoyed sex more at this time because of better interpersonal communication. Midlife was also a time for some women to come out as lesbians.

Based on the studies that have been done on midlife lesbians, it appears possible that the lives of midlife lesbians are in some ways more diverse and complex than those reported for other midlife adults. Midlife lesbians certainly have many roles to integrate and balance. It may be that the complexity of their lives contributes to the sense of life satisfaction expressed by many lesbians at midlife.

Gay Men at Midlife

No research similar to the studies just described on lesbians at midlife has been reported for gay men. Prior to the 1970s, the study of gay men was largely confined to research on psychopathology (Morin, 1977). Lifespan developmental psychologists and gerontologists did not focus on gay men growing older until a few pioneering studies emerged (Francher & Henkin, 1973; Kelly, 1977; Kimmel, 1977; 1978; 1979; Weinberg, 1969; Weinberg & Williams, 1974). Despite continued research attention to older gay men since 1980 (e.g., Berger, 1980; 1982; 1984; Gray & Dressel, 1985; Lee, 1987; Quam & Whitford, 1992), little research has focused specifically on middle-aged men. It was not uncommon in these studies to include persons over age 40 or 45 in the "aging" group; for example, 26 percent of Berger's (1982) sample of 112 "older homosexual men" were between ages 40 and 49, and 44 percent were between ages 50 and 59. Others compared younger and "older" groups (over age 45 or 50), with no specific attention to the middle-aged respondents (Gray & Dressel, 1985; Weinberg & Williams, 1974).

One study did focus on the age at which middle age is thought to begin (Bennett & Thompson, 1990). It found that gay men perceived their middle age as beginning at 41 and old age as beginning at 63, on the average, which was consistent with Minnigerode's (1976) finding for gay men and also similar to findings from studies based on general samples (e.g., Neugarten, Moore, & Lowe, 1965). However, the study also found that gay male respondents perceived middle age and old age as beginning earlier for gay men in general (ages 39 and 54, respectively) than for themselves—a phenomenon described as "accelerated aging" that is consistent with ageist stereotypes within the gay male community. Kooden (unpublished) in a discussion of middle-aged gay men has given a useful definition of ageism: "The man is measured by how much of his youth he has retained, which devalues his present age."

Thus, in the absence of specific research, we have few road maps of adult development for gay men; those maps that do exist are based primarily on the interplay of heterosexual family models, work trajectories, and personal maturation. In the next section we seek to identify a few themes that may be unique for gay men.

Themes of Midlife

It is clear that there is great diversity in patterns of adult development among gay men. For example, those men who do not come out as gay until midlife experience these years as a prolonged search for identity, especially in terms of sexuality. Guilt, secrecy, heterosexual marriage, conflicted relationships with both women and men, and tentative forays into gay social life often characterize this struggle. The result can be delayed social development, traumatic family crises, and a dramatic change in life when one comes out. In contrast, a second pattern is the gay man who recognizes that he is gay early in life and takes advantage of the benefits this identity offers, such as an opportunity to cross social boundaries of race, class, and age. Others use opportunities for education and travel as steppingstones out of rural areas into urban centers with extensive gay communities.

Within this perspective of diversity, we focus on four aspects of midlife that are important for many gay men: education, work, and retirement; intimate relationships; social networks; and sexuality. For many gay men, this phase of development is similar to the phase described by Vaillant (1977) in his longitudinal study of adult development among men: *intimacy and career consolidation*. One strives to focus on occupational development and to establish loving relationships with friends and, in many cases, with a special companion.

Education, Work, and Retirement

Several questions about the interaction of gay identity, socioeconomic status, occupational choice, and work need further investigation. For example, most samples of gay men studied in empirical research tend to be more affluent and better educated than average men of the same age (Adams & Kimmel, 1991; Berger, 1982; Lee, 1987; Quam & Whitford, 1992; Weinberg & Williams, 1974). However, it is clear that this finding could be a sampling artifact, since there is evidence of a hidden gay male population. Harry (1990) reported on the characteristics of a nationwide telephone survey by the American Broadcasting Company–Washington Post poll in 1985 that included a question about sexual orientation. The characteristics of gay males in this sample (3.7% of all men surveyed) contrast sharply with those of samples studied in research to date: 42 percent of the self-identified homosexual or bisexual group were currently married; they were underrepresented in the highest income groups and overrepresented in the lower income groups; over half lived in small towns; and a sizable minority were African– or Hispanic–American. Harry concluded that there is a substantial married homosexual or bisexual population that is disproportionately minority and low in educational status. This group is difficult to locate, and is undoubtedly overlooked in most studies of urban gay white males that have been reported to date.

Several research questions are raised by the usual studies that find relatively high levels of education and income in samples of gay men compared with the general male population. Is it that freedom from family responsibilities and expenses allows greater educational and financial opportunities for these gay men who are not married or are open? Perhaps success at work and the stimulation, income, and power it can provide is a significant aspect of identity and feelings of success for some gay men because other traditional sources of male success, such as family roles, are often unavailable. It might also be that some gay men strive to compensate for feelings of inadequacy or inferiority or to create positions of relative invulnerability by means of their achievements. For example, based on his 4-year longitudinal study of forty-seven gay male respondents over age 50, Lee (1987) observed that the level of life satisfaction was associated with the respondent's social class and perception that he was above the average standard of living for his age. Moreover, Lee concluded that the gay men who were aging most successfully were also those who remained "in the closet." This finding contrasts sharply with the idea that being open about one's sexuality or active in the gay community is associated with satisfaction in aging (Quam & Whitford, 1992). It also contradicts the idea that an individual's experience in coping competently with an earlier crisis, such as coming out, is associated with satisfaction later in life (Kimmel, 1978). Whether this result will replicate among younger cohorts of gay men is a question that cannot be resolved without further research.

Another line of research is suggested by the report that gay men experience a "glass ceiling" to job promotion within many companies that prevents gay workers from advancing to the highest ranks (Stewart, 1991). A dissertation by Woods (cited in Stewart, 1991) reported that a typical response for lesbians and gay men is to "cap their ambitions and watch the clock, or find a ghetto in the company." One respondent in this study who was blatantly harassed changed jobs at Pacific Gas & Electric and retreated to the closet: "I just sit very quietly in my office and do my job. I am not interested in advancing. It's just not worth it" (p. 46). Another reported changing jobs so that he would not have to relocate, since he had to consider his long-term partner but believed his employer would not understand. For this reason, some gay men in midlife opt out of the corporate world into business for themselves, a style Woods termed "entrepreneurial flight." Thus, the "career ladder" may differ for gay men as a result of discrimination, some of which may be based on marital status or social networks instead of sexual orientation per se. Today, of course, some gay men are also retiring early, or going on disability leave because of AIDS-related health problems.

The importance of self-employment for gay men was suggested in earlier studies of "aging" gays. Weinberg and Williams (1974) and Berger (1982) reported that self-employed gay men were less concerned than those who worked for others with concealment and were more integrated into the gay community, respectively: "It is the self-employed who stand out the most. As a group, they anticipate the least discrimination, and . . . are the least concerned with passing" (Weinberg & Williams, 1974, p. 228). Russo (1982) likewise found that gay leaders were typically self-employed. Recent changes by a few major employers (such as Levi Strauss and Lotus) to respond openly to the concerns of their lesbian and gay employees might reduce the need for midlife gays to seek self-employment in the future.

Finally, patterns of retirement and activities in the early years of retirement deserve study. It may be that gay men express creativity in this sphere also (Brown, 1989). Conversely, in the absence of biological children and other traditional contributions to future generations, work may take on added importance for many gay men and they may choose not to retire as early as they might otherwise. Work may also be one sphere where gay men have meaningful contact with older and younger generations—an important theme for some older gay men (Kimmel, 1978). Research has also begun examining the retirement housing preferences of gay men and lesbians, finding that a large majority do have an interest in living arrangements that are sensitive to their needs (Lucco, 1987; Quam & Whitford, 1992).

In summary, our understanding of midlife gay men would benefit greatly from research that focuses on the importance, development, and patterns of education, career or occupation, and retirement for gay men. Useful comparisons could be made with lesbians and with general samples. Variations by socioeconomic status, ethnicity, and race would be expected.

Intimate Relationships

Although some research has focused on gay male relationships (see Chapter 10), little attention has been given to special issues for long-term or middle-aged couples. For example, studies of aging have reported lovers who have been together for 30 to 40 or more years. It would be useful to examine the issues and strengths these couples identify. Also, age differences between partners have rarely been examined (Lee, 1987; Steinman, 1990). Another issue that has been described primarily in response to the AIDS epidemic is the impact of bereavement on gay male partners (Geis, Fuller, & Rush, 1986; Klein & Fletcher, 1986).

A particular concern for some couples is relations with each partner's family, especially if the care of aged parents or other relatives falls on either partner's shoulders. For example, coming out to one's family and extended relatives may become moot after a certain number of years as a couple. How do gay couples manage these relationships, especially as care-giving becomes more intense? Likewise, what roles do gay men seek with members of younger generations in the family of origin, including nieces and nephews? Ethnic and racial differences are likely to be especially important for studies of these family relationships (Adams & Kimmel, 1991).

Another important dimension that deserves research attention is the way in which gay male couples negotiate career decisions and balance each other's occupational development, as well as retirement choices. It is likely that some parallel patterns exist to those identified for heterosexual couples or lesbian couples. However, Blumstein and Schwartz (1983), in their sample of couples, noted that 51 percent of the gay men (average age 35 years) and 61 percent of the lesbians (average age 32 years) were predominately relationship-centered—a higher level than among heterosexual groups of the same gender and comparable ages; conversely, 16 and 18 percent, respectively, were predominately work-centered—lower than among the heterosexual groups, especially for men. Thus, gay males may opt out of the career competition ladder not only because of discrimination, but also because of a desire to balance career and a relationship more equally.

In addition, little is known about the ways in which two male partners maintain commitment to one another and to two separate career ladders. For example, is the decision to relocate made on a "your turn, my turn" pattern or on the basis of relative income or power in the relationship? Blumstein and Schwartz found that one partner tends to be work-centered and the other tends to be the caretaker in the relationship, regardless of sexual orientation or gender. They also found that couples who are both relationship-centered were the happiest, and those in which both were career-centered were the least happy. Age differences, and developmental differences based on the length of the relationship, may also be relevant.

Social Networks

Various studies of aging gay men have noted the importance of self-created friendship networks that replace or supplement the biological family (Friend, 1987). An important aspect of the friendship network is that younger friends need to be found and maintained, since the family does not necessarily provide contact with younger generations for gay men (Kimmel, 1979).

It is especially important to note the significance of long-term friends, for it becomes impossible to replace relationships spanning several decades later in life. Thus, the diabolical impact of AIDS has robbed many middle-aged gay men of their compatriots who experienced with them the persecution of the 1960s, the struggle and sexual freedom of the 1970s, and AIDS epidemic of the 1980s. In many parts of the country, the depletion of surviving midlife gay men's social networks because of losses to AIDS is extreme.

Research on gay male social networks also needs to consider their volunteer roles both in the gay and lesbian community and outside of it. Many middle-aged gay men were involved and some played leading roles in creating the services and supports that presently exist. Religious, social service, social, and AIDS-related organizations provide significant social networks and contacts for some gay men (see Chapter 12). Others have little interest, but may have benefited indirectly and applaud their existence (Adams & Kimmel, 1991).

Sexuality

Patterns of aging male sexual response are well known (Friend, 1987; Kimmel, 1990). For example, slower and less firm erections result from a variety of factors, both psychosocial and physical; the sense of impending ejaculation tends to disappear; and the need for ejaculation at each sexual occasion is reduced. Some gay men report that these changes are associated with an increase in sexual pleasure, since they focus less on orgasm and more on generalized sexual pleasure (Kimmel, 1979). It may also be that reduced sexual activity, which is expected based on studies of general samples of aging men, may increase the perception of pleasure as the act becomes less frequent. A study by Pope and Schulz (1990) reported that nearly all of the 87 gay males (aged 40–70) in the sample said they were sexually active (91%); most reported no change in sexual enjoyment (69%) and 13 percent reported an increase in enjoyment. Gray and Dressel (1985) reported that there was no significant difference by age group (16–29 years, 30–49 years, 50+ years) in number of sexual partners or in the amount of sexual activities for the sample studied by Jay and Young (1979). Berger (1982) reported that over 60 percent of his respondents (age 40–79) had engaged in sex once a week or more often during the 6 months prior to the study; moreover 73 percent reported that they were "somewhat or very satisfied" with their sex lives. However, Weinberg and Williams (1974) found that older homosexuals (age 45+) reported less frequent sex than the younger respondents. Blumstein and Schwartz (1983) noted that the length of the relationship was associated with a decrease in sexual activity for gay men and lesbians greater than the effect of age alone, although the latter was important also.

It is likely that gay men place great importance on sexual activity, including masturbation, since homosexuality (and, to a large extent, masculinity) may be seen as socially constructed and based on sexuality. Therefore, gay males in midlife are likely to be more sexually active than heterosexuals or lesbians of the same age; Blumstein and Schwartz (1983) reported similar findings for a younger sample of gay men, lesbians, and heterosexuals. We would expect that the AIDS epidemic, use of VCRs for pornography, and norms about safe sex would each have important effects on the frequency of, satisfaction with, and role of sex in the lives of middle-aged gay men today. All of these areas deserve empirical study.

Summary

A great deal of attention has been given to the midlife crisis or transition (Kimmel, 1990). One could argue that gay men are likely to experience a midlife crisis for two reasons. First, Livson (1981) found that well-adjusted men and women at age 50 who had been nontraditional earlier in life were more likely than traditional men and women to have experienced a period of change and reassessment in midlife. Second, several studies and theories of the midlife crisis have suggested that certain factors might intensify a midlife crisis for gay men, regardless of their traditional or nontraditional personality: concerns about issues of mortality and a search for meaning and wholeness in life within a heterosexist society, fear of physical illness, occupation-related stress or being passed over for a promotion, family issues including care of aging parents, concerns about one's family lineage, and a feeling that one has lost some masculine prowess with advancing age. The literature on "accelerated aging" and the feared loss of sexual attractiveness noted earlier might also intensify the threat of a midlife crisis. In addition, Kooden (unpublished) suggested that the tasks of midlife gay men involve other specific issues, including shedding internalized negative and ageist attitudes. He suggests that this process requires confronting the fact that one's physical persona has changed so that one cannot be loved for physical attributes alone, taking responsibility for the choices one has made so far, and finding one's own voice. This latter concept refers to the idea that gay men often hide part of themselves from others and develop a guarded stance toward the world associated with hiding their gayness from significant others. In contrast, middle-aged gay men have the opportunity to begin "writing the book of one's life while being its central character"—taking authorship of one's past and future goals.

Also, given the concurrent development of the gay community, middle-aged gay men have the opportunity to choose whether and how to connect themselves with circles of influence and power, whereas before they felt it was important to remain secretive and unconnected with others. Potentially, according to Kooden, this prospect allows them to recognize individual diversity among their peers, and also to acknowledge the family they may have created over the years.

On the other hand, gay men could be less likely than others to experience a midlife crisis because they tend to be socially outside the mainstream of normative developmental events. Thus, they would be expected to experience midlife in a way that is similar to other periods of their lives; that is, determined more by previous patterns of coping with individualized cultural, social, and personal influences than by any of the generalized patterns described here. Those who developed competence in coping with crises earlier in life and who are in a position to take advantage of a creative stance toward midlife may find that it yields high levels of developmental potential.

Conclusions

This discussion of midlife has been an exploration of the experiences of a pioneer generation. Many have been positive role models and were among the creators and activists of the emerging gay and lesbian community. They were substantially less closeted than older generations. Some are actively challenging ageism (Copper, 1988; Macdonald & Rich, 1983). Thus, this generation will have an impact on patterns of aging for gays and lesbians in the future. It is important that this generation be studied now, because their lives have spanned a unique period of history.

It is also important to examine gay and lesbian midlife samples to expand our understanding of and theories about midlife. For example, are the issues associated with intimacy and generativity (Erikson, 1968) different for gay men and lesbians? How do the coping skills that enable the transitions of middle age differ by socioeconomic status, race, ethnicity, gender, and marital status for lesbians and gay men? What are the differences between early and late midlife (the 40s versus age 55+)? Since aging is generally occurring later because of improved physical health, and age norms are becoming less salient in many areas of life (Brooks-Gunn & Kirsch, 1984; Kimmel, 1990), what effect is this having on the experience of middle age for gays and lesbians? Finally, what questions are important to ask differently for lesbians and gay men in order to understand this period of the lifespan?

Our review here has suggested four overarching themes that are relevant for lesbians and gay men at midlife. Each of these points is also a call for additional research, because very little relevant data exist with which to evaluate these tentative conclusions.

First, there are several examples of greater diversity and more fluidity in developmental patterns for gay men and lesbians in comparison with heterosexual samples.

Second, parallels may be noted in work and career issues for lesbians and gay men, including limitations placed on promotions by the "glass ceiling," reactions to discrimination on the job such as withdrawing from competition or the choice of self-employment, and attitudes toward retirement.

Third, lesbians and gay men seem to be similar in their styles of more equal balance of career and relationship commitments, especially compared with heterosexual men. Choosing a partner whose focus on the relationship or on the career is complementary to one's own may also be a characteristic shared by many lesbians and gay men.

Fourth, differences in ethnicity and race, as well as in socioeconomic status, prior and current heterosexual experiences, and marital status, may be expected to influence patterns of midlife for lesbians and gay men. Almost no data exist on these variations, but there are emerging signs that such data may soon become available, as telephone surveys and studies of ethnic and racial groups become more frequent.

Virtually all research approaches in this area have been limited to interviews and questionnaires with cross-sectional samples. More longitudinal and observational forms of research need to be undertaken. For a variety of reasons, longitudinal studies are problematic, including issues of confidentiality, funding, and continued accessibility over time. However, a study that compared over time, for example, lesbians and gay men who came out pre-Stonewall with post-Stonewall cohorts would be a welcome advance in the field. Several alternative approaches also might be suggested. Observation of selected behavior variables at a social gathering sponsored by a lesbian and gay aging program could be used to compare age groups. Reactions of coworkers to middle aged versus younger and older gay and lesbian workers could be assessed. A dating service type of questionnaire could be used to compare respondents by age group; also, ratings by young and older raters of the questionnaire responses could be compared. A variety of attitude studies related to age discrimination by gender would be of interest. For example, videotaped interactions of lesbians and gay men in prearranged situations could be studied by age group according to selected variables related to concepts such as ageism. Measures of social distance in seating arrangements between college-age research subjects and confederates who differ by age and gender could be assessed. An innovative type of study would be to employ a beeper signal to alert the participant several times each day to enter into a log book the type of activity currently underway, and related variables such as affect and involvement in the activity; age, gender, and sexual orientation might be relevant independent variables (cf. Csikszentmihalyi & Larson, 1984). It is important to study this midlife population now since the pre-Stonewall cohort of lesbians and gay men will soon be chronologically in old age, making only retrospective studies of middle age possible. Attention also needs to be given to issues of able-bodiedness, socioeconomic status, ethnicity, and race in this population.

One underlying theme of this review is that middle age is more complex than either adolescence or aging: it involves more roles, greater diversity in daily tasks and commitments, and few general themes or markers. Perhaps for this reason, midlife has often been overlooked in empirical research. But, for the same reason, it offers a rich variety of relevant opportunities for studies on a remarkable population of lesbians and gay men.

References

Adams, C. L., & Kimmel, D. C. (1991, November). Older African–American gay men. Paper presented at the annual meetings of the Gerontological Society of America, San Francisco, CA.

Baruch, G., & Brooks-Gunn, J. (1984). The study of women in midlife. In G. Baruch & J. Brooks-Gunn (Eds.), *Women in midlife* (pp. 1–8). New York: Plenum Press.

Bennett, K. C., & Thompson, N. L. (1990). Accelerated aging and male homosexuality: Australian evidence in a continuing debate. *Journal of Homosexuality, 20* (3/4), 65–75.

Berger, R. M. (1980). Psychological adaptation of the older homosexual male. *Journal of Homosexuality, 5*(3), 161–175.

Berger, R. M. (1982). *Gay and gray: The older homosexual man.* Urbana: University of Illinois Press.

Berger, R. M. (1984). Realities of gay and lesbian aging. *Social Work, 29*(1), 57–62.

Blumstein, P., & Schwartz, P. (1983). *American couples: Money, work, sex.* New York: William Morrow.

Bradford, J., & Ryan, C. (1991). Who we are: Health concerns of middle-aged lesbians. In B. Sang, J. Warshow, & A. Smith (Eds.), *Lesbians at midlife: The creative transition* (pp. 147–163). San Francisco: Spinsters.

Brooks-Gunn, J., & Kirsch, B. (1984). Life events and the boundaries of midlife for women. In G. Baruch, & J. Brooks-Gunn (Eds.), *Women in midlife* (pp. 11–30). New York: Plenum Press.

Brown, L. S. (1989). New voices, new visions: Toward a lesbian/gay paradigm for psychology. *Psychology of Women Quarterly, 13*, 445–458.

Charbonneau, C. & Lander, P. (1991). Redefining sexuality: Women becoming lesbian in midlife. In B. Sang, J. Warshow, & A. Smith (Eds.), *Lesbians at midlife: The creative transition* (pp. 35–43). San Francisco: Spinsters.

Csikszentmihalyi, M., & Larson, R. (1984). *Being adolescent: Conflict and growth in the teenage years.* New York: Basic Books.

Cole, E. (1988). Sex at menopause: Each in her own way. In E. Cole & E. Rothblum (Eds.), *Women and sex therapy* (pp. 159–168). New York: Harrington Park Press.

Cole, E., & Rothblum, E. (1990). Commentary on "Sexuality and the Midlife Woman." *Psychology of Women Quarterly, 14,* 509–512.

Cole, E., & Rothblum, E. (1991). Lesbian sex after menopause: As good or better than ever. In B. Sang, J. Warshow, & A. Smith (Eds.), *Lesbians at midlife: The creative transition* (pp. 184–193). San Francisco: Spinsters.

Copper, B. (1988). *Over the hill: Reflections on ageism between women.* Freedom, CA: Crossing Press.

Cornett, C. W., & Hudson, R. A. (1987). Middle adulthood in the theories of Erikson, Gould, and Vaillant: Where does the gay man fit? *Journal of Gerontological Social Work, 10* (3/4), 61–73.

Coss, C. (1991). Single lesbians speak out. In B. Sang, J. Warshow, & A. Smith (Eds.), *Lesbians at midlife: The creative transition* (pp. 132–140). San Francisco: Spinsters.

D'Emilio, J. (1983). *Sexual politics, sexual communities.* Chicago: University of Chicago Press.

Downing, C. (1987). *Journey through menopause—a personal rite of passage.* New York: Crossroad.

Erikson, E. H. (1968). *Identity: Youth and crisis.* New York: Norton.

Faderman, L. (1984). The "new gay" lesbians. *Journal of Homosexuality, 10* (3/4), 85–95.

Fertitta, S. (1984). Never married women in the middle years. A comparison of lesbians and heterosexuals. Unpublished doctoral dissertation. Wright University, Los Angeles.

Francher, J. S., & Henkin, J. (1973). The menopausal queen: Adjustment to aging and the male homosexual. *American Journal of Orthopsychiatry, 43,* 670–674.

Friend, R. A. (1987). The individual and social psychology of aging: Clinical implications for lesbians and gay men. *Journal of Homosexuality, 14* (1/2), 307–331.

Gauding, M. (1991). Meditation on the goddess Kali. In B. Sang, J. Warshow, & A. Smith (Eds.), *Lesbians at midlife: The creative transition* (pp. 215–222). San Francisco: Spinsters.

Geis, S. B., Fuller, R. L., & Rush, J. (1986). Lovers of AIDS victims: Psychosocial stresses and counseling needs. *Death Studies, 10*(1), 43–53.

Gentry, J., & Seifert, F. (1991). A joyous passage: Becoming a crone. In B. Sang, J. Warshow, & A. Smith (Eds.), *Lesbians at midlife: The creative transition* (pp. 225–233). San Francisco: Spinsters.

Gray, H., & Dressel, P. (1985). Alternative interpretations of aging among gay males. *The Gerontologist, 25,* 83–87.

Hall, M., & Gregory, A. (1991). Subtle balances: Love and work in lesbian relationships. In B. Sang, J. Warshow, & A. Smith (Eds.), *Lesbians at midlife: The creative transition* (pp. 122–133). San Francisco: Spinsters.

Harry, J. (1990). A probability sample of gay males. *Journal of Homosexuality, 19*(1), 89–104.

Hay, H. (1990, April 22–28). Identifying as gay—there's the key. *Gay Community News*, p. 5.

Jay, K., & Young, A. (1979). *The gay report: Lesbians and gay men speak about sexual experiences and lifestyles.* New York: Summit Books.

Junge, M., & Maya, V. (1985). Women in their forties: A group portrait and implications for psychotherapy. *Women & Therapy, 4,* 3–19.

Kelly, J. (1977). The aging male homosexual: Myth and reality. *The Gerontologist, 17,* 328–332.

Kimmel, D. C. (1977). Psychotherapy and the older gay man. *Psychotherapy: Theory, Research and Practice, 14,* 386–393.

Kimmel, D. C. (1978). Adult development and aging: A gay perspective. *Journal of Social Issues, 34*(3), 113–130.

Kimmel, D. C. (1979). Life-history interviews of aging gay men. *International Journal of Aging and Human Development, 10,* 239–248.

Kimmel, D. C. (1990). *Adulthood and aging: An interdisciplinary, developmental view* (3rd ed.). New York: Wiley.

Kirkpatrick, M. (1989). Lesbians: A different middle-age? In J. Oldham & R. Liebert (Eds.), *New psychoanalytic perspectives: The middle years* (pp. 135–148). New Haven, CT: Yale University Press.

Kitzinger, C. (1987). *The social construction of lesbianism.* London: Sage.

Klein, S. J., & Fletcher, W. (1986). Gay grief: An examination of its uniqueness brought to light by the AIDS crisis. *Journal of Psychosocial Oncology, 4*(3), 15–25.

Kooden, H. (unpublished). The excitement of being a middle-aged gay man. Unpublished manuscript.

Lee, J. A. (1987). What can homosexual aging studies contribute to theories of aging? *Journal of Homosexuality, 13*(4), 43–71.

Lee, J. A. (1989). Invisible men: Canada's aging homosexuals. Can they be assimilated into Canada's "liberated" gay communities? *Canadian Journal on Aging, 8*(1), 79–97.

Leiblum, S. (1990). Sexuality and the midlife woman. *Psychology of Women Quarterly, 14,* 495–508.

Lesser, R. (1991). Deciding not to become a mother. In B. Sang, J. Warshow, & A. Smith (Eds.), *Lesbians at midlife: The creative transition* (pp. 84–90). San Francisco: Spinsters.

Livson, F. B. (1981). Paths to psychological health in the middle years: Sex differences. In D. H. Eichorn, J. A. Clausen, N. Haan, M. P. Honzik, & P. H. Mussen (Eds.), *Present and past in middle life* (pp. 195–221). New York: Academic Press.

Lucco, A. J. (1987). Planned retirement housing preferences of older homosexuals. *Journal of Homosexuality, 14*(3/4), 35–56.

Macdonald, B., & Rich, C. (1983). *Look me in the eye: Old women, aging and ageism.* San Francisco: Spinsters.

Minnigerode, F. A. (1976). Age-status labeling in homosexual men. *Journal of Homosexuality, 1,* 273–276.

Mitchell, V., & Helson, R. (1990). Women's prime of life: Is it the 50s? *Psychology of Women Quarterly*, 14, 451–470.

Morin, S. (1977). Heterosexual bias in psychological research on lesbianism and male homosexuality. *American Psychologist*, 32, 629–637.

Morokoff, P. (1988). Sexuality in premenopausal and postmenopausal women. *Psychology of Women Quarterly*, 12, 489–511.

Neugarten, B. L., Moore, J. W., & Lowe, J. C. (1965). Age norms, age constraints, and adult socialization. *American Journal of Sociology*, 70, 710–717.

Pope, M., & Schulz, R. (1990). Sexual attitudes and behavior in midlife and aging homosexual males. *Journal of Homosexuality*, 20(3/4), 169–177.

Posin, R. (1991). Ripening. In B. Sang, J. Warshow, & A. Smith (Eds.), *Lesbians at midlife: The creative transition* (pp. 143–146). San Francisco: Spinsters.

Quam, J. K., & Whitford, G. S. (1992). Adaptation and age-related expectations of older gay and lesbian adults. *The Gerontologist*, 32, 367–374.

Raphael, S., & Robinson, M. (1984). The older lesbian: Love relationships and friendship patterns. In T. Darty & S. Potter (Eds.), *Women–identified women* (pp. 67–82). Palo Alto: Mayfield.

Riddle, D., & Sang, B. (1978). Psychotherapy with lesbians. *Journal of Social Issues*, 34(3), 84–100.

Rothschild, M. (1991). Life as improvisation. In B. Sang, J. Warshow, & A. Smith (Eds.), *Lesbians at midlife: The creative transition* (pp. 91–98). San Francisco: Spinsters.

Rubin, L. (1979). *Women of a certain age: The midlife search for self*. New York: Harper & Row.

Russo, A. J. (1982). Power and influence in the homosexual community: A study of three California cities. *Dissertation Abstracts International*, 43, 561B. (University Microfilms No. DA8215211.)

Sang, B. (1990). Reflections of midlife lesbians on their adolescence. In E. Rosenthal, (Ed.), *Women, aging and ageism* (pp. 111–117). New York: Haworth Press.

Sang, B. (1991). Moving towards balance and integration. In B. Sang, J. Warshow, & A. Smith (Eds.), *Lesbians at midlife: The creative transition* (pp. 206–214). San Francisco: Spinsters.

Sang, B. (1992). Counseling and psychotherapy with midlife and older lesbians. In S. Dwolkin & F. Gutierrez (Eds.), *Counseling gay men and lesbians: Journey to the end of the rainbow* (pp. 35–48). Alexandria, VA: American Association for Counseling and Development.

Sang, B. (1993). Some existential issues of midlife lesbians. In L. D. Garnets & D. C. Kimmel (Eds.), *Psychological perspectives on lesbian and gay male experiences* (pp. 500–516). New York: Columbia University Press.

Sang, B. (in press). Midlife as a creative time for lesbians. In G. Vida (Ed.), *Our right to love*. New York: Penguin Books.

Sang, B., Warshow, J., & Smith, A. (Eds.) (1991). *Lesbians at midlife: The creative transition*. San Francisco: Spinsters.

Steinman, R. (1990). Social exchanges between older and younger gay male partners. *Journal of Homosexuality*, 20(3/4), 179–206.

Stewart, T. A. (1991, December 16). Gay in corporate America. *Fortune*, 42–56.

Tully, C. (1989). Caregiving: What do midlife lesbians view as important? *Journal of Gay & Lesbian Psychotherapy, 1*, 87–103.

Turner, B. (1987, August). Developmental perspectives on issues for lesbians at midlife. Paper presented at the meeting of the American Psychological Association, Atlanta, GA.

Vaillant, G. (1977). *Adaptation to life*. Boston: Little, Brown.

Walker, B. (1985). *The crone: Women of age, wisdom and power*. San Francisco: Harper & Row.

Warshow, J. (1991). Eldercare as a feminist issue. In B. Sang, J. Warshow, & A. Smith (Eds.), *Lesbians at midlife: The creative transition* (pp. 65–72). San Francisco: Spinsters.

Weinberg, M. S. (1969, December). The aging male homosexual. *Medical Aspects of Human Sexuality*, 66–67, 71–72.

Weinberg, M. S., & Williams, C. J. (1974). *Male homosexuals: Their problems and adaptations*. New York: Oxford University Press.

Woodman, N. (1990). Twenty five women: Their perspectives on oppression and the relationships which sustain them. Unpublished paper.

Woods, S. E., & Harbeck, K. M. (1991). Living in two worlds: Identity management strategies used by lesbian physical educators. *Journal of Homosexuality, 22* (3/4), 141–166.

9

Development in Late Life: Older Lesbian and Gay Lives

James D. Reid

This chapter provides an introduction to the major issues involved in the study of lesbian, gay, and bisexual older adults, with an emphasis on directing attention away from myths of inevitable decline in late life. The assumption that aging is synonymous with decline becomes particularly negative when generalized to older lesbians, gay men, and bisexuals who have been incorrectly portrayed as lonely and pathetically miserable. Such myths and stereotypes are not substantiated by research on the lives of older gay men and lesbians. Lifespan developmental perspectives are reviewed in order to place the lives of older bisexuals, gay men, and lesbians within an ongoing developmental context. A major theme of the chapter will be the considerable ability of older adults to adapt and adjust to the challenges of aging. This capacity has directed theoretical and empirical inquiry toward the concept of successful aging. It is argued that the unusual challenges experienced by older bisexuals, lesbians, and gay men place them at an advantage and, hence, promote successful aging. Attention is then turned to gaps in the existing literature as well as critical areas of future inquiry regarding the lives of older lesbians, gay men, and bisexuals.

As the percentage of the American population age 65 and over has grown (from 5% in 1900 to 12% in 1988; Department of Health and Human Services, 1988), a number of changes have occurred in the conceptualization of development in later life. Only recently has the field of gerontology begun to accumulate a body of knowledge concerning the physical, psychological, and social realities of the elderly. Because of the paucity of empirical data, researchers, clinicians, and the lay public are often confronted with myths and stereotypes about older adult lives. Indeed, ageist beliefs that late life is synonymous with inevitable physical and mental decline, isolation, and depression are still common. Despite the assumption that most older adults are abandoned by their families and live a lonely existence in nursing homes, most older adults (95%) live in their own homes (Kermis, 1986), with frequent contacts with family members and friends (Aizenberg & Treas, 1985). Although most older adults (85%) ultimately experience one or more chronic illnesses, these illnesses are not debilitating (Sloan, 1986).

The combination of gradual and abrupt changes that occur over the course of later life illustrates the importance of individual differences in aging. Older adults are not a homogeneous group. In fact, with advancing age, biological, psychological, and social variability increases (Baltes & Baltes, 1990). The increase in variability during late life makes discussion of the "typical" older adult exceedingly difficult. In conjunction with increasing variability is the reality of physical health problems and increasing needs for medical and social services for the very old. Gerontologists draw distinctions between older adults based on chronological age. Typically, "middle age" is thought of as occurring between the ages of 35 and 55. Late life is divided into periods of "young old" (65 to 75 or 80), "old old" (75 or 80 to about 90), and "oldest old" (90+). These age groupings allow for more precise conclusions about age-related processes affecting development in late life.

Because the aging process is characterized by gradual change, most older adults continually adapt and adjust to physical limitations, changing social networks, and other challenges. Observation of the fact that most older adults do adapt and adjust has begun to positively influence a number of myths and stereotypes about aging. As myths about aging have been dispelled, an evolution has occurred in our thinking about the full range of possibilities in late life. Whereas the early gerontological literature focused on populations of older adults who were institutionalized with physical and mental disabilities, more recent gerontological inquiry has focused on a continuum of developmental outcomes in late life. Thus, in the 1970s and 1980s emphasis shifted away from sick or pathological aging, to the study of the "typical or usual" older adult, not living in an institution, but rather living and functioning in the community with little or no impairment (Rowe & Kahn, 1987). A major result of the shift in focus to the full range of human functioning in late life has been the introduction of the concept of "successful aging," which is addressed in this chapter. The study of successful aging has increased attention to those processes of adaptation which contribute to optimal development in late life.

The study of older adults typically involves age comparisons in which older and younger groups are compared on a variable of interest. However, age comparisons lead to conclusions about age-related developmental change that are confounded by the influence of the historical period in which the individual lives. Historical events, such as changes in technology, attitudes, behaviors, and beliefs, interact with true age-related changes. As a result, the study of developmental processes is intimately linked to the historical period in which development takes place.

The lives of older gay men, lesbians, and bisexuals have been shaped in important ways by the historical period in which they have grown and developed, lived, and worked. These history-graded influences (Baltes & Willis, 1979) on development have differentially affected different cohorts of lesbians, bisexuals, and gay men. For example, an individual born in 1930 was nearly 40 years of age at the time of the 1969 Stonewall Inn riots, which sparked the gay civil rights movement. During the pre-Stonewall era individuals experienced the developmental tasks of childhood, adolescence, and young adulthood in a very different social climate than would prevail later in history. In those years, homosexuals were viewed as "perverted" by society, "evil" by the church, "sick" by the medical and psychiatric professions, and "criminals" by the police. As Lee (1987) notes, "The Life," a code word used by pre-Stonewall homosexuals to identify and describe their secret identity, evolved into the present-day "gay community." Examination of the lives of older bisexuals, lesbians, and gay men illustrates how age, personal characteristics, and social context continually interact to shape identity.

Whereas at one time in recent history homosexuals were ignored by social scientists, today the increased visibility and demands for civil rights by the gay, lesbian, and bisexual community have directed increasing attention to the sizable numbers of older bisexuals, lesbians, and gay men living, working, and contributing to the society in which they live. We do not know the exact percentage of gay men, lesbians, and bisexuals in the United States population, although it has been estimated that there are some 3.5 million older lesbians and gay men (Dawson, 1982). As the body of literature concerning the lives of older lesbians and gay men accumulates, stereotypes which were once held by gerontologists are giving way to a greater understanding of not only gay and lesbian aging, but older adults in general. Previously, social scientists believed that single adults, straight or gay, were doomed to a lonely existence, divorced from family and without friends (cf. Lee, 1987). We now know that older gay men and lesbians are not inevitably alone and despondent. Many older gay men and lesbians have children as the result of previous heterosexual unions. For instance, 27 percent of the older lesbians in Kehoe's (1989) study, and 20 percent of gay men in Berger's (1982a) study reported previous marriages. Alternately, older gays and lesbians have reconstituted families in the form of friendship and support networks, which serve as substitutes for traditional families (Friend, 1980; Raphael & Robinson, 1980). Thus, research on older gay, lesbian, and bisexual identities has added diversity and complexity to simplistic conceptualizations of aging.

This brief introduction to the field of gerontology should sensitize the reader to the social context of myths and stereotypes about older adults held by the larger society. The subsequent discussion of the lives of older bisexuals, lesbians, and gay men focuss on those conditions associated with optimal development in late life. The unique adaptations made by gay men, lesbians, and bisexuals serve to illustrate concepts of optimal adult development and aging.

Theoretical Perspectives on Human Aging

Developmental Approaches to Adult Development and Aging

Theories of adult development and aging have focused on progressive developmental change from birth to death. Using studies of biographies and autobiographies recorded in the 1930s, Buhler (1968) proposed five characteristic phases of the lifespan based on biological growth of the organism. Jung's (1933) analytical psychology outlined general periods in the life cycle. Whereas in the first half of life, an individuals' goals and pursuits required an investment in expansion of consciousness and experience, the second half of life was a time of consolidation and turning inward. The psychodynamic theory of Erikson (1950; 1968; 1976) postulates eight distinct life stages. As the individual encounters each stage of life, he or she experiences the ascendance of a particular crisis or conflict. As a result of the various conflicts, characteristic ego strengths develop. For example, the crisis that becomes ascendent in late-life is ego integrity versus despair. Wisdom is believed to develop as a result of a successful resolution of this crisis in the final stage of life.

Levinson's (1977; 1978; 1986) theory of adult development, though not explicitly addressing development in late life, postulates that adult development is characterized by a predictable sequence of alternating periods of growth, stability, and transitions in the life course. What develops is the *life structure*, the "underlying pattern or design of a person's life at a given time" (Levinson, 1986, p. 6). The life structure is not static. Rather, it is dynamic and sequential, undergoing alternating periods of growth and development, followed by periods of stability, then periods of developmental change. At each transition point, the individual will terminate the old life structure, initiate a new life structure, and move to a new level of psychological individuation (Levinson, 1986).

The life structure, as proposed by Levinson, is perhaps the best suited theoretical construct to illustrate the dynamic complexity of developmental change. When an individual asks "What is my life like now"?, he or she is asking "How have my physical characteristics, my developmental history, my psychological positions and personality traits, my current interpersonal relationships, and the historical context in which I live combined to produce the life structure that I am experiencing at this moment?" Thus, the individual's conceptualization of the self is thought to be a continually evolving process of adaptation to developmental influences which are both abrupt and gradual. Adjusting to transitions in the life structure may be a source of psychological distress, or a major step in living more fully.

COMING OUT AS A MAJOR DEVELOPMENTAL TRANSITION

From a developmental perspective, coming out of the closet is a life-structure transition that may take many years. The unique identity that develops takes many forms, depending on the individual and his or her life circumstances. In the most private form, coming out may entail the individual's first conscious consideration that he or she has feelings for persons of the same sex. The private psychological experiences and conflicts that result may lead the individual to share her or his feelings with family and friends and seek support from informal organizations, or professional services. Coming out is not a normative developmental event that is anticipated by the individual. Nor is coming out an event that is recognized as a developmental marker by the larger culture. Rather, it is a minority developmental experience which the individual often faces alone. Furthermore, coming out may occur at any age. Some individuals come out during adulthood, after having formed heterosexual unions and led very different lives.

Despite the age at which an individual comes out, or the amount of time that the process may take, coming out is a developmental transition which involves a major expansion of the self. In Levinsonian terms, the individual must terminate his or her previous life structure and initiate a new self-concept as a lesbian, gay man, or bisexual person. In addition, the individual must examine, to some extent, the fundamental polarities of the self, including issues of young versus old, creation versus destruction, and masculinity versus femininity (Levinson, 1978). By doing so, the individual may move to a new level of integration, incorporating the new identity and life structure as a gay man, lesbian, or bisexual person into the previous sense of self. The

outcome of this developmental transition has profound implications for
self-worth, self-esteem, coping mechanisms, and mental health. As a
result, there is tremendous potential for personal growth and development. Conversely, the changes may be overwhelming and tax the individual's coping resources.

The major expansion of the self that occurs as a result of adaptation
to the developmental transition of coming out is thought to result in
the formation of a distinct characterological attribute or ego strength.
Kimmel (1978) recognizes the emergence of a unique ego strength as a
result of the identity crisis of coming out as a buffer against the stressful effects of later life crises. The suggestion that adaptation to the
stress of coming out results in the development of greater personal
resources for the individual also appears in Friend's (1980) conceptualization of "crisis competence" and Berger's (1980) "mastery of crisis."

Adjustment and adaptation to an identity as a gay male, lesbian, or
bisexual can be viewed as a developmental transition which results in
unique strengths and character formation in the individual. Previously
held stereotypes associated being homosexual with distinct disadvantages that compounded with advancing age (Simon & Gagnon, 1967);
however, today researchers suggest that coming out holds clear advantages. Francher and Henkin (1973) were first to suggest that successful
adaptation to the alienation and aloneness imposed by a homophobic
culture was associated with coping skills and interpersonal experiences
that would be advantageous in later life. Berger (1982a) noted that successful resolution of the major crisis experienced when coming out provides the individual with unusual stamina, energy that is not available
to heterosexual women and men. As is addressed next, numerous
studies of older gay men and lesbians conclude that psychological well-
being and self-respect are the resultant prizes that grow out of successful adaptation of a positive identity.

These emergent aspects of character are believed to place the individual at an advantage for meeting the challenges of aging. Featherman,
Smith, and Peterson (1990) have suggested that successful aging requires continued "adaptive competence" (p. 53) as the older adult is
faced with inevitable change, challenge, and opportunities for development. As Featherman and colleagues (1990) point out, adaptive
competence becomes increasingly challenging with aging, because previously well-structured developmental tasks of adolescence and young
adulthood (i.e., graduation, education, intimacy, etc.) are associated
with clear roles and rule-based behaviors. In late life, however,
developmental tasks become increasingly ill-structured (generativity,
ego-integrity, wisdom) and individualized. The highly individualized
nature of development in late life draws our attention to individual

differences in adaptation to varying developmental conditions, events, and outcomes. Such concepts of variability and plasticity are crucial components in our understanding of successes and difficulties in the lives of older lesbians, gay men, and bisexuals.

Theories of Successful Aging

The concept of successful aging is becoming popular in current literature on aging. Rowe and Kahn (1987) have dimensionalized a broad continuum of aging processes, ranging from pathological aging, through usual or normal aging, to successful aging. Recent volumes devoted to the subject (i.e., Baltes & Baltes, 1990) have directed attention to theoretical perspectives and reviewed the small but growing number of empirical studies. Baltes and Baltes (1990) suggest a multicriteria approach for assessing successful aging, including length of life, biological health, mental health, cognitive efficacy, social competence and productivity, personal control, and life satisfaction. Baltes and Baltes (1990) argue that successful aging requires adaptation to changing biological, psychological, and social circumstances. Their model of successful aging, "selective optimization with compensation," argues that optimal aging requires that the individual *select* behaviors and experiences which will *optimize* his or her personal control, life goals, activities, and interests. Optimization reflects adjustment to the reality of loss and restricted functioning in late life while remaining engaged in those relationships and behaviors which are fulfilling to the individual. Because of the reality of loss and restricted roles in late life, an additional component of the Baltes' theory includes changing ones' body or environment to *compensate* for limitations and difficulties.

Friend (1991) has articulated a theory of successful aging in gay men and lesbians which has as its defining feature the achievement of a positive lesbian or gay identity. Friend's theory of successful aging rests on the achievement of a positive identity as an openly gay man or lesbian. As such, Friend's theory complements and extends Baltes and Baltes' (1990) theory of successful aging by arguing that achievement of a positive identity as a lesbian or gay man places the individual at a distinct advantage for continued adaptation to the challenges of aging. From this perspective, an individual's identity is heavily determined by the social context in which she or he develops for the following reasons. Individuals assign meaning to experience by mutual consent, and labels are applied to persons and forms of experience. Ultimately, these labels come to define the identity of a person in a group. Because of the social stigma assigned to the label and experience of same-sex relationships, individuals who are lesbian or gay develop in an atmosphere of negative evaluation by society. As Friend points out, negative evaluation by the larger social group places the individual at risk of assimilating these attitudes and values, and feeling negative about himself or herself.

Within this social-developmental context, Friend postulates two distinct outcomes in terms of identity formation. Optimally, the individual will reject the larger group value held by a homophobic culture and reconstruct a new meaning for the feelings and experiences associated with being lesbian or gay. Such women and men are called "affirmative" older lesbians and gay men, because they have actively constructed a positive gay or lesbian identity and have attained a "high level of self-acceptance and psychological adjustment, even within the hostile historical periods in which they were raised" (Friend, 1991, p. 108). The less optimal outcome described by Friend (1991) involves acquiescence to the beliefs and attitudes of the larger social group and incorporation of negative beliefs and feelings about the self. This outcome is seen in two characteristic forms of identity formation: (1) The "stereotypic" older lesbian or gay man who internalizes the homophobia of the larger culture and conforms to those images by keeping his or her sexual orientation secret, living with shame and self-loathing; and (2) the "passing" older gay man or lesbian who incorporates the homophobia of the larger culture and enters heterosexual relationships, or remains closeted in order to "pass" as a heterosexual person. The cornerstone of Friend's theory of successful aging rests on the achievement of a positive identity based on rejection of the bias and stereotypes of the larger group and reconstruction of a set of attitudes, feelings, and values which allow for an affirmative identity as a lesbian or gay person. The process of deconstructing the previously learned stereotypes and reconstructing a new identity has concomitant effects in other areas of life. According to Friend's theory, one result of developing an affirmative identity as a gay or lesbian is the emergence of the psychological attributes of "crisis competence" and flexible gender roles. These abilities are a powerful adaptive attribute that allows the older lesbian or gay person to deal successfully with the many challenges of aging.

Research on Older Lesbians, Gay Men, and Bisexuals

The body of research addressing psychological development in older gay men, lesbians, and bisexuals is small. Indeed, as a discipline, gerontology has essentially ignored sexual orientation in its major journals, handbooks, and reviews. The general conclusions from the available data on the lives of older gay men and lesbians support the contention that those individuals who have made optimal adaptations as a result of achieving a positive self-identity as lesbians, gay men, or bisexuals are at an advantage for continued growth and adaptation in late life. More studies of older gay men are found in the literature than of lesbians. There are no published studies of older individuals who define themselves as bisexual, quite probably because no one has thought to ask the question.

Research on Older Gay Men

Francher and Henkin (1973) were the first to publish data contradicting the stereotype of lonely, isolated, and sad older gays living exceptionally stressful lives, lacking the structural supports provided by community, church, and family. Although based on a small sample of nine highly educated and economically advantaged older gay men living in New York City, Francher and Henkin's data suggest that, as a result of coping with the crisis of coming to terms with ones' identity as a gay male in a homophobic culture, the individual acquired advantageous adaptive capacities for dealing with other stressors in later life.

In a sample of gay men over the age of 45, Weinberg and Williams (1974) found that positive adjustment to a gay identity was associated with higher self-esteem and self-acceptance. In another study, Weinberg and Williams (1974) sampled 2,500 gay men living in Europe and the United States. This study found that older gay men were more likely to live alone and have sex less frequently than younger gay men. However, young and old did not differ in personal adjustment. Similarly, a study conducted by Kimmel (1978) of a sample of fourteen white, educated, economically advantaged gay men living in New York City ranging in age from 55 to 81 years supported Weinberg and Williams' (1974) findings. In general, although their sexual activity was less frequent than when they were younger, sex was still important in the lives of the respondents. One-half of the respondents felt that sex was more satisfactory in later life than it was when they were younger. However, there seemed to be a distinctly different quality to the sexual experience. Older men reported that they placed "less accent on genitals, and more on the total person" (Kimmel, 1978, p. 119).

Attitudes about aging were studied by Minnigerode (1976) in a sample of ninety-five gay men ranging in age from 25 to 68 years. In this study, gay men were asked at what age they believed middle age and old age began. Respondents reported that, on average, an individual reached middle age at 41 years and old age at 64 years. These age-status norms are virtually identical to figures found in a sample of (presumably) heterosexuals (Neugarten, Moore, & Lowe, 1965). Kelly's (1977) study of 261 gay men ages 16 to 79 (193 completed questionnaires while another 48 participants completed interviews) refuted a number of negative stereotypes held in the popular and scientific literature concerning older gay men. Of the total sample of 261, 30 participants were between the ages of 65 and 75. The data were collected from questionnaires and interviews conducted in the Los Angeles gay community during 1973–1974. In general, the participants in this sample continued to be engaged in the gay world, had many gay friends, maintained a satisfactory sex life, and did not consider themselves effeminate. However, Kelly's data document a number of problems that confront older individuals. The most important problems were stigmatization because of age, loss of people who are emotionally important to them, and fear of institutionalization. In addition, these data reveal a number of problems unique to older gay men, including discriminatory social practices; rules, laws, and attitudes; absence of children to provide emotional support, physical security, and economic assistance; being prevented from visiting or being visited by life partner in hospitals and nursing homes; and legal discrimination in terms of being prevented from inheriting a life partner's properties and assets.

Berger's (1980, 1982b) research remains one of the most extensive surveys of older gay men in the literature. These data are based on 122 questionnaires and 10 interviews of gay men ages 44 to 72 sampled from a "four-county area in one locale" in the midwestern United States. Thirty percent of Berger's sample were over 60 years of age. The major findings from the older respondents' data were that a strong self-identity as a homosexual was associated with high self-acceptance and life-satisfaction, although most respondents admitted that the process of acquiring these attributes had been difficult. Furthermore, contrary to the popular stereotype, the older gay men in this sample were not particularly concerned about their identity as gay men. These men were "out" to 95 percent of their friends, they were not particularly distressed by growing old, and they were not experiencing mental or emotional difficulties. What emerged from these data was a picture of positive adjustment among gay men who had achieved a positive identity and renewed freedom in late life. Among those variables that contributed to their adjustment was having and maintaining a satisfactory close relationship. Berger's (1980; 1982b) data concludes that the problems for gay men come not from negative attitudes the respondents held about aging, because the respondents' attitudes were positive. Rather, Berger concludes that the problems of older gay men are a result of inadequate and insensitive institutional policies, legal discrimination, social services neglect, and medical oversight.

In a major review of sociological theories, Lee (1987) examines the contribution that gay and lesbian studies can make to theories of aging. He suggests that optimal development in late life requires that older gays and lesbians adjust their previously idealistic perceptions and develop a "perspective on life." These newly acquired expectancies and attitudes are accompanied by concomitant wisdom in selection of experiences designed to enhance continued optimal adaptation. Based on data from a 4-year longitudinal study of forty-seven Canadian gay men ranging in age from 50 to 80, Lee (1987) found wealth, health, and lack of loneliness were associated with high life satisfaction. Lee's data dispute Berger's (1980) conclusion that the various crises gay men have endured equip them to age successfully. Indeed, Lee (1987) suggests that, "sailing to a happy homosexual old age may be more a matter of steering clear of storms, rather than weathering them" (p. 57). Thus, Lee's conclusions also challenge Friend's (1991) theory of successful aging, which posits that achievement of an affirmative and public gay identity is the defining feature of successful aging. Citing his repeated interviews, Lee (1987) concludes that successful aging involves being fortunate and/or skillful enough to avoid stressors, including the stress of coming out. In Lee's cohort of men, it is understandable that avoidance of the stress associated with adopting a public identity as a gay man may have been very adaptive. Pre-Stonewall cohorts learned to accommodate to the prevailing heterosexual world by hiding their homosexuality (Grube, 1991). Such accommodations are well described in the biographies of older gay men edited by Vacha (1985).

Finally, in a sample of thirty-nine lesbians and forty-one gay men over the age of 50 living in a midwestern metropolitan area, Quam and Whitford (1992) found that both older gay men and lesbians reported high levels of life satisfaction and acceptance of the process of aging. The participants in this study indicated that they maintained high levels of involvement in the gay community, and such involvement was an asset to accepting the realities of aging.

Research on Older Lesbians

The research literature focusing on the lives of older lesbians is sparse (for review, see Cruikshank, 1991). Commenting on the difficulty of recruiting older lesbians in research, Martin and Lyon (1992) reported that older lesbians were highly concerned about privacy and uncomfortable about being identified as lesbian. Meyer (1979) studied twenty community-dwelling older lesbians, ranging in age from 50 to 73 years. Her data corroborate studies of older gay men and refute myths and stereotypes held about older homosexuals. For example, Meyer's (1979) results revealed that whereas most older lesbians remained sexually active and were not lonely or isolated, these women had adjusted to aging in diverse ways. For these lesbians, attitudes about aging reflect a continuum ranging from feeling well adjusted and holding positive attitudes, to holding negative views of aging and being concerned with health, illness, and dying (Meyer, 1979).

Conclusions from the West Coast Old Lesbian Conference (Meyer & Raphael, 1988) suggest a range of adjustment outcomes as older lesbians negotiate the reality of discrimination and lack of social services, and empower themselves to mold social organizations to meet their needs. Similarly, a report by Poor (1982) documents concerns held by older lesbians as they negotiate the realities of a homophobic and discriminatory culture, particularly lack of sensitivity by the medical establishment.

A study of adjustment to aging in a sample of twenty-five lesbians (mean age 64) and twenty-seven gay men (mean age 65) revealed that adjustment to a positive identity as a lesbian or gay male was achieved after years of struggle in the face of intense discrimination and homophobia in the larger society (Adelman, 1991; Minnigerode, Adelman, & Fox, 1980). Adelman discusses the damaging effects on older lesbians who were forced to live with fear of disclosure and had to keep their sexual orientation secret from coworkers and family members for extended periods of time. In subsequent analyses, Adelman (1991) reported that psychological adjustment to aging (as measured by high life satisfaction, low self-criticism, and few psychosomatic complaints) was predicted by the sequence of early gay developmental events. Results showed that experimentation with same-sex partners *before* self-definition as lesbian or gay was related to greater life satisfaction in late life. These data support developmental expectations of developing a lesbian or gay identity, which prescribe a sequence of (a) awareness of same-gender attraction; (b) sexual experimentation with members of the same gender; and (c) self-definition as lesbian or gay (Cass, 1984; Dank, 1971). In addition, Adelman's study found that high life satisfaction was positively associated with having both gay/lesbian and heterosexual friendships.

In a collection of twenty-two biographical statements, Adelman (1986) allows readers to explore the lives of older lesbians as they recount their own experiences. Adelman reports that older lesbians are not inevitably depressed and alone; indeed, many describe late life as a time of happiness and freedom. A key conclusion of the report, which cannot be stressed strongly enough, is "the most important factor for determining psychological well-being in lesbians in late life is the level of homophobia in society and ourselves" (p. 11).

Results from a study of twenty-five lesbians over age 60 suggest that many older lesbians remain deeply closeted, choosing to selectively disclose their lesbian identities to few friends and family members (Almvig, 1982). Kehoe's (1986) study of seventy-eight women ranging in age from 65 to 85 years was an attempt to gather data on an estimated population of greater than one million older lesbians living in the United States. Nearly half of the women in this sample had previously been in heterosexual marriages. Over half (52%) rated their self-image or mental health as good or excellent; they described their relationships with other women as highly emotional, caring, gentle, and spiritual. The most frequently mentioned difficulties reported by these women were health problems, financial stressors, isolation and loneliness, and aging. The results suggest a composite profile of an older woman who is physically and mentally healthy and feels positive about herself. In a later study of older lesbians, Kehoe (1989) obtained questionnaire data from 100 women over 60 years of age living in all regions of the United States. The participants who completed the 87-item questionnaire were predominantly white and middle-class. In general, the findings suggest that the older lesbian accepts aging, is in good or excellent health, feels very positive about being a lesbian, and has high life satisfaction.

Taken together, the available literature suggests that the stereotypes of lonely, alienated, and despondent older lesbians and gay men are incorrect. Rather, what emerges is picture of older gay men and lesbians who are active, selectively engaging in activities and interests of their choosing. There is, apparently, considerable variability in how the lesbian or gay man has adapted her or his identity to varying contexts of discrimination. Some older gay men and lesbians prefer to keep their sexual orientation private, while others are open and highly engaged in public organizations and activities. These data underscore the reality of unique and individual adaptations as a result of different developmental experience and personal needs.

Special Considerations in the Study of Older Lesbian and Gay Lives

Development in the Context of Hate, Intolerance, and Discrimination

As a result of the experience of being different from the heterosexual majority and the social atmosphere of intolerance and discrimination, the older lesbian, gay man, and bisexual person must confront, negotiate, and adapt to the complexities associated with exceptional experiences in life (cf. Adelman, 1991). The exceptional nature of development stems in large part from the hostile context in which development takes place (Almvig, 1982; Dunker, 1987; Martin & Lyon, 1992; Raphael & Robinson, 1980). In childhood, sex-role socialization is grounded in sexism and ensures that development will occur in a context of the tyranny of normative expectations regarding those modes of behavior deemed appropriate by dominating social forces. This tyranny of normative expectations applies to gender roles, and is apparent not only among the lay public, but within the profession of psychology. Although the American Psychiatric Association dropped homosexuality as a pathology in 1973 and deleted "ego-dystonic homosexuality" by 1987, "Gender Identity Disorder of Childhood" remains an official diagnostic category. Hence, feminine behavior in boys and masculine behavior in girls may be seen as an indication of mental illness by professionals. In late life the sexism inherent in normative gender roles translates directly into power and access to power. Adelman (1986) notes there are twice as many women as men over the age of 65, however, most older women live at or below the poverty line.

Ageism, the suspicion and disregard for the aged, adds yet another layer of fear and uncertainty to the lives of older lesbian, gay, or bisexual persons. A common stereotype of older persons is that they are sick, depressed, and cranky. On the opposite end of the spectrum, well-intentioned researchers, students, and service providers may view older adults as quaint relics or cute anomalies. Ageism interacts with homophobia to create particularly negative stereotypes of the older lesbian (Deevey, 1990) and gay man (Kelly, 1977). A particularly insidious aspect to ageism is the invisibility of older persons in our cultural experience. Old persons are, for the most part, simply ignored. The message to old people is that they do not matter. As a result, many old persons are silenced, and kept from developing their full potential. The invisibility of older persons stems from our cultures' isolation of the aged. Older persons are often left alone, ignored, and placed in facilities designed to serve only part of the needs of older adults.

There continues to be considerable ageism within the lesbian and gay community. The gay subculture is particularly youth-oriented (Weinberg & Williams, 1974), attributing value and status to the young and attractive. The extent of ageism in the gay community can be seen in research on "accelerated aging" in gay men (Bennett & Thompson, 1991; Friend, 1980; Kelly, 1977; Laner, 1978; Minnigerode, 1976). In these studies, gay men were asked at what age middle age begins and at what age one becomes "old." The debate centers largely on the age at which gay men reported themselves and other gays as middle-age or old. The fact that some gay men believed they entered middle age or old age earlier than men in Neugarten et al.'s (1965) classic study of age-status norms was taken as evidence of "accelerated aging" in gay men. These findings also reflect age norms in the gay community. Bennett and Thompson (1991) found that most gay men denied that they themselves were ageist, although respondents did recognize that chronological age is regarded as a meaningful marker of status in the larger gay community.

Social change associated with the gay rights movement has destabilized the way older and younger gay men previously interacted and communicated. Grube (1991) argues that, prior to 1969, older and younger gay men interacted in a "mentor/protege" tradition, with older established and respected gay men introducing younger gay men to social circles that remained closeted. Such social situations provided a welcome and respected place for gay men to grow old. In the post-1969 organized gay community, radical and institution-building reformists rejected the "mentor/protege" tradition as reflecting internalized homophobia by supporting remaining in the closet. Younger, gay liberationists then formed their own social, political, and economic organizations, which tended to ignore older gay men and deny them positions of leadership.

Major Issues Facing Older Lesbians and Gays in Late Life

The major concerns of all older people center on issues related to physical health, managing finances, and coping with isolation and loneliness. What is unique to older bisexuals, gay men, and lesbians is the challenge of pursuing and maintaining social and emotional attachments in the face of intolerance, stigma, and discrimination. Adelman (1986) reports that older lesbians are not inevitably depressed and alone. She concludes that the major determinant of psychological well-being in late life is the level of homophobia in society. As a result of the forces of hate in our culture, family relationships may be strained, support groups may be nonexistent, and the older gay man or lesbian may be reluctant to seek out those existing support groups that are available.

Because of the pervasive level of homophobia in our culture, lesbians, gay men, and bisexuals are in need of socially supportive networks. A component of successful adaptation to aging involves purposive exits (Featherman et al., 1990) from nonsupportive and hostile contexts. The lesbian or gay man may create new, supportive relationships to fulfill needs for social connection and intimacy. Many gay men and lesbians adopt children and create homes, which fulfill important needs for social connection, intimacy, and generativity.

Services for the Aged

As noted earlier, there are an estimated 3.5 million older lesbian and gay men in the United States (Dawson, 1982). However, the actual number of older gay men and lesbians that use programs and services specifically aimed at this population is far below population parameters. It is important to keep in mind that many older gay and lesbian persons have adapted to the stresses associated with hate and fear by "passing" as heterosexual persons. As a result, they may not want to be identified to service agencies and may refuse to participate in programs and services. In addition, the older person may actually be harmed by being dismissed by members of the younger gay community who hold ageist stereotypes or view old lesbians and gays as the lucky ones who survived the current ravages caused by the AIDS epidemic.

Because of the advances made by the gay and lesbian communities in expecting and receiving a share of public services, we can expect to observe greater use of services designed to meet the needs of subsequent cohorts of older gay males, lesbians, and bisexuals. In addition, organizations developed to meet the needs of older lesbians and gay men are growing in size and scope. Noted among such organizations are Senior Action in a Gay Environment (SAGE) in New York City and Gay and Lesbian Outreach to Elders (GLOE) in San Francisco. Agencies that offer gerontological programs and services specifically targeted for older gays, lesbians, and bisexuals need to be ever mindful of individuals' desire for privacy. Outreach programs must be understanding and respectful of the reality of isolated and fearful individuals. Some older persons may have never come out of the closet. Instead they may have suffered in silence all their lives, experiencing shame at being and feeling different, fearing for their personal safety, and suffering from very real discrimination. Service providers should welcome those individuals who wish to participate while respecting the choices of those who do not. As noted earlier, successful aging is a process of selecting those environments and behaviors which an individual believes will optimize his or her life choices. Many lesbians and gays may perceive that staying in the closet is the best way for them to steer clear of storms and stressors (Lee, 1987).

Finally, service providers need to be aware of the considerable variability among older bisexual persons, gay men, and lesbians. The recipe for a successful program is not the same for all individuals. Gay men and lesbians may be interested in and want different activities and programs. Services should be tailored to the needs and desires of the older person, not what the agency or individual staff members assume older persons want. What is needed is an increasing variety of choices of programs and services within the community. Increasing the choices will better serve populations with various needs and interests. Above all, outreach service providers must listen to the needs and desires of old people. The goal of service providers should be to listen respectfully while older lesbians, bisexual persons, and gay men define themselves, their needs, and their interests. Professionals need to work with older people toward their own empowerment.

HEALTH CARE

One of the major issues faced by all older persons is the availability of affordability of appropriate health care. The older lesbian, gay man, or bisexual shares similar concerns and may experience unique health care needs. For example, people over age 65 account for 10 percent of reported AIDS cases, and many of these individuals are gay or bisexual men (Centers for Disease Control, 1989). Health care concerns among older lesbians (Meyer, 1979) and gay men (Berger, 1982) may be compounded by reluctance to reveal one's sexual orientation to physicians or fear of homophobia in service institutions. Physical and mental health clinics, physicians' offices, hospitals, and nursing homes may be particularly unfriendly places for gay men, bisexuals, and lesbians. Providers of social and medical services often hold the same ageist and homophobic views (Poor, 1982). For example, older lesbians and gay men have been prevented from visiting their life partner in the hospital or nursing home, excluded from important decisions regarding his or her care, and ignored at funeral services. Hence, physicians and other health care professionals at every level need to receive training in how to be respectful of the lesbian, gay man, or bisexual patient and how to be sensitive to their relationships.

Of particular concern within health care settings is the medicalization of aging by some health care professionals, which has reduced the aging process to a "condition" which needs to be "treated." As such the older adult may be approached not as an individual, but as a condition to be treated, medicated, or dismissed as hopeless. Conversely, health care professionals may overlook treatable conditions because they assume the condition is an inevitable outcome of the aging processes. For example, memory impairments may be attributed to dementia, a condition for which there is no known cure, when the impairment is actually the result of depression, a condition which responds favorably to treatment (Beck, Rush, Shaw, & Emery, 1979; Gallagher & Thompson, 1983).

MENTAL HEALTH

The adaptive competencies acquired with successful negotiation of psychological and social stressors associated with coming to terms with one's sexual orientation may give the older lesbian, gay male, or bisexual an advantage (Weinberg & Williams, 1974). The data on mental health reported by Ryan and Bradford (1987) suggest that older lesbians were less troubled by the pressures of life than were younger lesbians. Seventy-three percent of their sample reported seeing a professional counselor at some point during their life. Most reported seeking treatment for feelings of sadness or depression (36%), having interpersonal problems with a partner/lover (22%), or being gay (14%). The most commonly reported problems for all age groups were money problems, problems with lover(s), and job worries. Respondents over the age of 55 reported less intensity and frequency in these concerns than did younger lesbians. For example, 69 percent of lesbians 17 to 24 reported money problems, but only 15 percent of lesbians 55 years or older reported being particularly troubled by financial concerns. Berger's (1980) study of 112 gay men 40 years of age or older found that positive adjustment and life satisfaction was related to having an exclusive relationship, a satisfactory sex life, integration in the gay community, and openness about sexual orientation. Similarly, Quam and Whitford (1992) report that adjustment in both gay men and lesbians during later life involves acceptance of aging, maintenance of high levels of life satisfaction, and being active in the gay and lesbian community. Nevertheless, older gay men, lesbians, and bisexuals are faced with a number of unique stressors during the course of development. Social and emotional losses may be invisible to others and, hence, fail to receive others' recognition or support. Thus, feelings of grief and loss which are usually expected and supported in the larger community may be ignored when they involve relationships not sanctioned as legitimate by the heterosexist larger community. In addition, the lesbian or gay male is faced with the very real fear of being the victim of verbal and physical abuse. In these ways, the challenges of life and barriers to successful aging are compounded for many older gay men, lesbians, and bisexual persons.

LEGAL ISSUES

Legal services are another source of concern of the aging bisexual, lesbian, or gay man. Because lesbian and gay relationships are not sanctioned by law, troublesome legal issues can arise that may have severe consequences. The older lesbian, bisexual, or gay man needs to take steps to ensure that his or her legal affairs are in order. He or she must take responsibility to ensure that legal documents are prepared exactly according to his or her wishes. Legal advisers must be trained to be sensitive to issues associated with sexual orientation and held accountable when they fail to do so. Finally, boards of directors of hospitals, nursing homes, senior citizens centers, and other agencies that serve the needs of older adults must write policy statements with inclusive language regarding sexual orientation. Public recognition of the existence of older gay men, bisexuals, and lesbians begins a process of sensitization to gay and lesbian issues in staff, other residents, and the community. The addition of inclusive language in policies, stating that lesbians and gays are welcome, is an important message.

Future Directions for Research

A significant contribution to the literature on older lesbians and gay men was made with the publication of *Gay Midlife and Maturity* (Lee, 1991), which first appeared as a special issue of the *Journal of Homosexuality* (1990, vol. 20). This collection reviews and extends the current literature focused on the lives of older lesbians and gay men. Lee (1991) outlines a number of key areas in which research is needed. These include (1) the gay or lesbian couple aging together; (2) the "gay widow"; (3) "married" or "bisexual" gays/lesbians aging; (4) the single older gay/lesbian; (5) aged gays and lesbians in the "gay community"; (6) special therapy and counseling needs of the elder gay and lesbian; (7) gay/lesbian death and dying; and (8) empowerment of older lesbian and gay adults.

In addition to these recommendations, to more fully understand developmental processes and meet the diverse and changing needs of lesbians, gay men, and bisexual persons, researchers must attend to a number of key methodological issues.

SAMPLING ISSUES

Kinsey's data (Kinsey, Pomeroy, & Martin, 1948; Kinsey, Pomeroy, Martin, & Gebhard, 1953) on human sexuality continues to be an important source of estimates of the percentage of lesbians, gay men, and bisexuals in the U.S. population. However, no studies of older lesbian, gay, or bisexual persons have systematically sampled from this larger population, in part because older lesbians and gay men may be justifiably reluctant to identify themselves. A number of studies cited in current literature use samples of convenience, recruited from agencies that specifically serve older gays and lesbians (i.e., senior centers, bars, or selected organizations with primarily lesbian or gay memberships), or use "snowball" sampling procedures (i.e., selective referral of friends and people known to be gay or lesbian in the community). As a result, the samples in these studies have been predominantly white, well-educated, and economically advantaged. Kelly's (1977) study attempted to avoid bars and establishments which might systematically exclude the poor while obtaining a wider cross-section of the gay community. Kelly employed participant observers who were active in the gay community in Los Angeles and recruited study participants from a popular gay beach, the Los Angeles Metropolitan Community Church congregation, advertisements in gay-oriented newspapers, and use of friendship networks. Similarly, in Kehoe's (1989) nationwide sample of older lesbians, announcements were placed in lesbian/feminist newsletters and periodicals, feminist bookstores, and women's centers, and letters were sent to directors of women's studies programs in colleges and universities. Despite the attempts to reach a large segment of the lesbian and gay communities, the samples remained predominately white, urban, and middle class.

COHORT EFFECTS

It is well recognized that generational differences exist as a result of the historical period in which an individual develops. These cohort effects limit the generalizability of existing data on the lives of lesbians and gay men. For example, the process and implications of coming out of the closet were much different in 1930 than they are in 1990. Pre-Stonewall generations of gays and lesbians ventured out of the closet at tremendous physical and social risk. As noted in a number of studies of older gay men and lesbians, many older persons remain deeply closeted. Baltes and Baltes (1990) report that early adulthood is the era of the lifespan in which historical changes are most observable. Hence the social revolutions of the Stonewall riots, the women's movement, and the AIDS epidemic are important historical events that account for age-related intergenerational differences. As noted by Adelman (1991), "For future generations of gay people who grow up in a more accepting and more supportive environment, postponement of self-definition may no longer be either necessary or adaptive" (p. 28). As the struggle for social equality continues, generational differences will be of major importance for those investigating the lives of gay men, lesbians, and bisexual persons. Indeed, observation of social and psychological attributes of subsequent cohorts of persons identified as bisexual, gay, or lesbian may represent a potent measure of the effects of social and cultural change.

AGE AS A VARIABLE

Age differences between younger and older gay men or lesbians have been introduced in very few studies. Bell and Weinberg (1978) sampled 686 gay men of varying ages and made comparisons based on sexual behavior and psychological adjustment. The major finding was that older men had fewer sexual partners than did younger men, although the level of sexual interest did not decrease with age. In addition, younger and older men did not differ on levels of psychological adjustment. Kelly's (1977) study of 241 gay men between the ages of 16 and 79 reported that older gay men were less likely than younger ones to participate in activities of the gay community. Similarly, Weinberg and Williams' (1974) study of 2,500 gay men in Europe and the United States found that older men were more likely to live alone and had sex less frequently than younger gay men. However, young and old did not differ on measures of personal adjustment. Few studies make finer age distinctions such as comparing "young old" with "old old." One exception is Quam and Whitford's (1992) study of older lesbians and gay men over 50, which compared men and women less than 60 years old with those over 60 on a number of social/demographic variables. Although few statistically significant differences were found, age differences were found among lesbian and gay senior citizens for participation in religious activities, interest in special social organizations, and interest in housing.

At this point, we have no data on age differences between the "young old" lesbian or gay man and her or his "oldest old" counterpart. Such cross-sectional comparisons are only a small portion of the story of development in late life. Furthermore, studies designed to measure developmental changes will greatly improve our understanding of the lives of older gay men, bisexual persons, and lesbians. Longitudinal studies of the process of adaptation across the lifespan promise to be a rich area of inquiry for future researchers.

Sex and Gender Differences

Comparisons of men and women in late life can highlight individual differences and variability associated with aging. Also, studies of individuals who vary in their enactment of traditional gender roles would be useful. Few studies compare older gay men and lesbians on biological, psychological, and social variables. In their study of twenty-six older lesbians and twenty-seven older gay men (Adelman, 1991; Minnigerode et al., 1980), no significant differences were found between the gay men and lesbians in their sample on fifteen indicators of psychological adjustment. As noted earlier, Adelman (1991) reports that adjustment in late life is related to the sequence of early gay/lesbian developmental events. Interestingly, although Adelman reports no differences between men and women on predictor variables, there is no discussion of whether gay men and lesbians differed on outcome measures (i.e., the sequence of early developmental events). Quam and Whitford (1992) investigated sex differences in their sample of eighty older lesbians and gay men. Although few significant differences between men and women were found, men reported that they frequented bars more often and were more interested in engaging in social organizations catering to both men and women than did the women in the sample. The older lesbians were more interested in attending exclusive lesbian organizations and living in retirement housing sensitive to the needs of gay men or lesbians than were the men in the sample. Adelman (1980) has recommended investigation of individuals who violate socially prescribed gender roles (i.e., the masculine lesbian and the feminine gay man). Comparisons of styles of adjustment and adaptation of gay men and lesbians who can pass for straight with individuals whose appearance and behavior makes them easily identifiable as an older gay or lesbian will expand the scope and diversity of studies of aging. Systematic investigation of sex and gender differences and similarities on psychological and social variables will provide important information for more fully understanding and appreciating the lives of gay men and lesbians.

Race/Ethnicity

Few studies of sexual orientation in older adults have included race/ethnicity as a variable of interest. One exception is the work of Bell and

Weinberg (1978), who found few differences in their sample of African–American and Caucasian older gay men. A major problem with studies that compare samples of Caucasians with samples drawn from other racial or ethnic groups is similar to the issue raised when heterosexuals are compared with gays or lesbians. We know there are differences. The major issue involved is not to make ethnocentric comparisons in which a Caucasian sample is used as a referent group against which other groups are judged to be deficient.

It is surprising that, given the large numbers of Asian and Hispanic persons living in a number of U.S. cities, no studies of older Asian or Hispanic lesbians, bisexuals, or gay men are reported in the literature. In addition, intracultural comparisons (i.e., comparisons of persons of Cuban, Mexican, and Colombian descent) of variability within an ethnic group can highlight the subtleties of cultural influences. The inclusion of participants from different racial and ethnic groups can highlight sources of individual variability associated with aging and allow service providers to tailor programs to meet the needs of different individuals.

Summary

A developmental approach is advocated for studying the lives of older lesbians, gay men, and bisexuals. The focus in on the process of continuous development across the lifespan. Coming out, and coming to terms with one's identity as a bisexual, lesbian, or gay man, is a major life transition which is associated with redefinition and consolidation of an individual's life structure. Friend's (1991) theory of successful aging suggests that the non-normative life transition associated with coming out and coming to terms with one's sexual orientation result in the emergence of psychological strengths which place the individual at an advantage when faced with subsequent life stressors and challenges of aging. For pre-Stonewall cohorts of gay men and lesbians who had to accommodate to the realities of hostile and homophobic worlds, staying in the closet was an adaptive strategy for avoiding debilitating stress (Lee, 1987). Such coping is less necessary for subsequent cohorts. Transitions, redefinitions, and consolidations of an individual's life structure become highly individualized. Current cohorts of lesbians, gay men, and bisexuals need to avoid the tyranny of the current majority Zeitgeist and respect the choices and styles of coping that older gay men and lesbians have developed. Research into the lives of older lesbians and gay men has dispelled myths and stereotypes and challenged conventional wisdom held by gerontologists regarding the conditions necessary for the maintenance of high levels of life satisfaction and a positive self-identity in late life. The results of the sparse literature focusing on psychological adaptation and adjustment among older lesbians and gay men reveal a considerable capacity to tolerate a lifetime of stressors in a homophobic environment. Optimal development in later life is described as a process of adaptation to the very real challenges and stressors associated with living in the context of hate and discrimination and developing characterological attributes that foster continued adjustment. Older gay men and lesbians proceeded through formative states of identity development in a very different cultural milieu than do current cohorts of bisexuals, gay men, and lesbians. As such, the study of older bisexuals, lesbians, and gay men's lives directs our attention to the impact of cultural context and cultural change, and the considerable variability of adjustment outcomes. Optimal identity development is a function of the degree to which cultural and contextual environments can serve as a supportive atmosphere and simultaneously challenge the individual to move toward unique growth and development. We can only hope that continued enlightenment of the larger society regarding the destructive consequences of projections of hate onto specific groups will lead to more favorable environments for all people who are different.

References

Adelman, M. (1980). Adjustment to aging and styles of being gay: A study of elderly gay men and lesbians. Unpublished doctoral dissertation, Wright Institute, Boston.

Adelman, M. (1986). *Long time passing: Lives of older lesbians.* Boston: Alyson.

Adelman, M. (1991). Stigma, gay lifestyles, and adjustment to aging: A study of later-life gay men and lesbians. In J. A. Lee (Ed.), *Gay midlife and maturity* (pp. 7–32). New York: Haworth Press.

Aizenberg, R., & Treas, J. (1985). The family in late life: Psychosocial and demographic considerations. In K. Birren & K. Schaie (Eds.), *Handbook of the psychology of aging* (pp. 169–189). New York: Van Nostrand Reinhold.

Almvig, C. (1982). *The invisible minority: Aging and lesbianism.* New York: Utica College of Syracuse University.

Baltes, P. M., & Baltes, M. M. (1990). Psychological perspectives on successful aging: The model of selective optimization with compensation. In P. Baltes & M. Baltes (Eds.), *Successful aging* (pp. 1–35). New York: Cambridge University Press.

Baltes, P. M., & Willis, S. L. (1979). The critical importance of appropriate methodology in the study of aging: The sample case of psychometric intelligence. In F. Hoffmeister & C. Muller (Eds.), *Brain functions in old age.* Heidelberg: Springer-Vertag.

Beck, A., Rush, D., Shaw, D., & Emery, G. (1979). *Cognitive therapy of depression.* New York: Guilford.

Bell, A. P., & Weinberg M. S. (1978). *Homosexualities: A study of diversity among men and women.* New York: Simon & Schuster.

Bennett, K. C., & Thompson, N. L. (1991). Accelerated aging and male homosexuality: Australian evidence in a continuing debate. In J. A. Lee (Ed.), *Gay midlife and maturity* (pp. 65–75). New York: Haworth Press.

Berger, R. (1980). Psychological adaptation of the older male homosexual. *Journal of Homosexuality, 5,* 161–175.

Berger, R. M. (1982a). *Gay and gray: The older homosexual man.* Champaign: University of Illinois Press.

Berger, R. M. (1982b). The unseen minority: Older gays and lesbian. *Social Work, 27,* 236–242.

Buhler, C. (1968). The developmental structure of goal setting in group and individual studies. In C. Buhler & F. Massarik (Eds.), *The course of human life* (pp. 26–54). New York: Springer.

Cass, V. (1984). Homosexual identity formation: Testing a theoretical model. *Journal of Sex Research, 20,* 143–167.

Centers for Disease Control. (1989). *AIDS in an aging society.* New York: Springer.

Cruikshank, M. (1991). Lavender and gray: A brief survey of lesbian and gay aging studies. In J. A. Lee (Ed.), *Gay midlife and maturity* (pp. 77–87). New York: Haworth Press.

Dank, B. (1971). Coming out in the gay world. *Psychiatry, 34,* 180–197.

Dawson, K. (1982, November). Serving the older gay community. *SIECUS Report, 17* 5–6.

Deevey, S. (1990). Older lesbian women: An invisible minority. *Journal of Gerontological Nursing, 16,* 35–39.

Dunker, B. (1987). Aging lesbians: Observations and speculations. In Boston Lesbian Psychologies Collective (Eds.), *Lesbian psychologies:* Explanations and challenges (pp. 72–82). Urbana: University of Illinois Press.

Erikson, E. H. (1950). *Childhood and society.* New York: Norton.

Erikson, E. H. (1968). *Identity, youth, and crisis.* New York: Norton.

Erikson, E. H. (1976). Reflections on Dr. Borg's life cycle. *Daedalus, 105,* 1–28.

Featherman, D. L., Smith, J., & Peterson, J. G. (1990). Successful aging in a postretired society. In P. Baltes & M. Baltes (Eds.), *Successful aging* (pp. 50–93). New York: Cambridge University Press.

Francher, J. S., & Henkin, J. (1973). The menopausal queen: Adjustment to aging and the male homosexual. *American Journal of Orthopsychiatry, 43,* 670–674.

Friend, R. A. (1980). Gayaging: Adjustment and the older gay male. *Alternative Lifestyles, 3,* 231–248.

Friend, R. A. (1991). Older lesbian and gay people: A theory of successful aging. In J. A. Lee (Ed.), *Gay midlife and maturity* (pp. 99–118). New York: Haworth Press.

Gallagher, D., & Thompson, L. W. (1983). Depression. In P. M. Lewinshon & L. Teri. (Eds.), *Clinical geropsychology: New directions in assessment and treatment* (pp. 7–37). New York: Pergamon.

Grube, J. (1991). Natives and settlers: An ethnographic note on early interaction of older homosexual men with younger gay liberationists. In J. A. Lee (Ed.), *Gay midlife and maturity* (pp. 119–135). New York: Haworth Press.

Jung, C. G. (1933). The stages of life. In J. Campbell (Ed.), *The portable Jung* (pp. 3–22). New York: Viking.

Kehoe, M. (1986). Lesbians over 65: A triple invisible minority. *Journal of Homosexuality, 12,* 139–152.

Kehoe, M. (1989). *Lesbians over sixty speak for themselves.* New York: Haworth Press.

Kelly, J. (1977). The aging male homosexual: Myths and reality. *The Gerontologist, 17,* 328–332.

Kermis, M. D. (1986). *Mental health in late life: The adaptive process.* Boston: Jones and Bartlett.

Kimmel, D. C. (1978). Adult development and aging: A gay perspective. *Journal of Social Issues, 34,* 113–130.

Kinsey, A. C., Pomeroy, W. P., Martin, C. E., & Gebhard, P. H. (1953). *Sexual behavior in the human female.* Philadelphia: W. B. Saunders.

Kinsey, A. C., Pomeroy, W. P., & Martin, C. E. (1948). *Sexual behavior in the human male.* Philadelphia: Saunders.

Laner, M. R. (1978). Growing older male: Heterosexual and homosexual. *Gerontologist, 18,* 496–501.

Lee, J. A. (1980). The social organization of sexual risk. *Alternative Lifestyles, 2,* 69–100.

Lee, J. A. (1987). What can homosexual aging studies contribute to theories of aging? *Journal of Homosexuality, 13,* 43–71.

Lee, J. A. (Ed.). (1991). *Gay midlife and maturity.* New York: Haworth Press.

Levinson, D. J. (1977). The mid-life transition. *Psychiatry, 40,* 99–112.

Levinson, D. J. (1986). A conception of adult development. *American Psychologist, 41,* 3–13.

Levinson, D. J., Darrow, C. N., Klein, E. B., Levinson, M. H., & McKee, B. (1978). *The seasons of a man's life.* New York: Knopf.

Martin, D., & Lyon, P. (1992). The older lesbian. In B. Berzon and R. Leighton (Eds.), *Positively gay* (pp. 111–120). Berkeley: Celestial Arts.

Meyer, M. (1979). The older lesbian. Unpublished master's thesis, California State University, Dominquez Hills.

Meyer, M., & Raphael, S. (1988). The old lesbian: Some observations ten years later. In M. Shernoff (Ed.), *Resource book on lesbian and gay health.* New York: National Lesbian and Gay Health Foundation.

Minnigerode, F. A. (1976). Age-status labeling in homosexual men. *Journal of Homosexuality, 1*(3), 263–276.

Minnigerode, F. A., Adelman, M. R., & Fox, D. (1980). Aging and homosexuality: Physical and psychological well-being. Unpublished manuscript, University of San Francisco.

Neugarten, B. L., Moore, J. W., & Lowe, J. C. (1965). Age norms, age constraints, and adult socialization. *American Journal of Sociology, 70,* 710–717.

Poor, M. (1982). The older lesbian. In M. Cruikshank (Ed.), *Lesbian studies* (pp. 165–173). Old Westbury, NY: Feminist Press.

Quam, J. K., & Whitford, G. S. (1992). Adaptation and age-related expectations of older gay and lesbian adults. *The Gerontologist, 32,* 367–374.

Raphael, S. M. & Robinson, M. K. (1980). The older lesbian. *Alternative Lifestyles, 3,* 207–229.

Rowe, J. W., & Kahn, R. L. (1987). Human aging: Usual and successful. *Science, 237,* 143–149.

Ryan, C., & Bradford, J. (1987). The national lesbian health care survey: Mental health implications. Report submitted to the National Institute of Mental Health.

Simon, W., & Gagnon, J. H. (1967). The lesbians: A preliminary overview. In J. H. Gagnon & W. Simon (Eds.), *Sexual deviance* (pp. 177–185). New York: Harper & Row.

Sloan, J. W. (1986). *Practical geriatric therapeutics.* Oradell, NJ: Medical Economics Books.

U.S. Department of Health & Human Services. (1988). *Vital statistics of the United States, 1985. Vol. 2. Mortality* (Part A). Hyattsville, MD.

Vacha, K. (Ed.) (1985). *Quiet fire: Memoirs of older gay men.* Trumansburg, NY: Crossing Press.

Weinberg, M. S., & Williams C. J. (1974). *Male homosexuals: Their problems and adaptations.* New York: Oxford University Press.

III

Relationships
and Families

10

Lesbian and Gay Couples

Lawrence A. Kurdek

Because there is disagreement over the estimated number of lesbian and gay Americans (Herek, 1991), no definitive data exist on the number of American lesbian and gay couples. Nonetheless, surveys indicate that between 45 and 80 percent of lesbians and between 40 and 60 percent of gay men are currently involved in a steady romantic relationship (Bell & Weinberg, 1978; Harry, 1984; Jay & Young, 1977). Further—and contrary to popular myths (Herek, 1991; Peplau, 1991)—lesbians and gay men form long-lasting cohabiting relationships. Blumstein and Schwartz (1983) reported that 8 percent of the 1,576 lesbian couples and 18 percent of the 1,938 gay couples they studied lived together 10 or more years. Bryant and Demian (1990) reported that 14 percent of the 706 lesbian couples and 25 percent of the 560 gay couples they studied lived together 10 or more years. Thus, being part of a couple is integral to the lives of many lesbians and gay men.

The limited information we have regarding lesbian and gay couples comes from two major research traditions. The first is characterized by atheoretical descriptive reports of lesbian and gay couples. These include descriptions of lesbian couples (e.g., Clunis & Green, 1988); descriptions of gay couples (e.g., McWhirter & Mattison, 1984); comparisons of lesbian and gay couples on relationship-related variables (e.g., Kurdek, 1991a); and comparisons of heterosexual, lesbian, and gay couples on relationship-related variables (e.g., Blumstein & Schwartz, 1983). The second, and more recent, research tradition is represented by studies designed to test models of close relationships based on social psychological theories (e.g., Kelley & Thibaut's, 1978 interdependence theory) using studies of lesbian and gay couples (e.g., Kurdek, 1991a) as well as studies of heterosexual, lesbian, and gay couples (e.g., Kurdek, 1993, 1994).

This chapter summarizes descriptive accounts of lesbian and gay couples, reviews theory-based findings regarding relationship satisfaction and relationship stability in lesbian and gay couples, and discusses issues raised by extant findings. In view of limited data on lesbian and gay adolescents (Boxer & Cohler, 1989), only adult lesbians and gay men are the focus of concern.

Descriptive Accounts of Lesbian and Gay Couples

Because of the social stigma surrounding homosexuality, lesbians and gay men receive little, if any, information regarding the nature of lesbian and gay couples in the course of their socialization. As a result, lesbian and gay close relationships develop without consensual norms (Laird, in press).

It should be underscored at the outset that most of the descriptive data we have on lesbian and gay couples come from relatively young, white, and well-educated volunteer respondents. Thus, the "typical couple" profiles presented here likely apply to only a select group of lesbian and gay couples. Although relevant large-scale data do not exist, descriptive accounts of relationship features are likely to vary by race, ethnicity, age, and geographical context (Laird, 1993; Peterson, 1992).

A General Ethnography of Lesbian and Gay Couples: The Bryant and Demian National Survey

One of the most detailed descriptive accounts of lesbian and gay couples is provided by Bryant and Demian's (1990) national survey of 1,749 individuals, who represented 706 lesbian couples and 560 gay couples. The mean age for lesbian and gay male respondents was 34.7 and 36.5 years, respectively. The majority of both men and women (95% apiece) in this study were white and averaged 16 years of formal education. The modal income level for both men and women was $25,001 to $40,000. Because the goal of this study was to collect descriptive data, selected findings of the study are presented by survey topic. Whenever possible, relevant findings from other studies are presented.

PREVIOUS RELATIONSHIPS

Many of the male and female respondents (38% and 32%, respectively) indicated that their current relationship was their first major lesbian/

gay relationship. Female respondents were more likely than male respondents to have been involved in a heterosexual marriage (27% vs. 19%, respectively). Consistent with the latter finding, Blumstein and Schwartz (1983) reported that 22 percent of their lesbian respondents and 15 percent of their gay male respondents were previously married.

Name Used to Identify Partner

Many (40%) male respondents called their partner "lover," whereas many (35%) female respondents referred to their partner as "partner" or "life partner." McWhirter and Mattison (1984) and Berger (1990) also reported that most members of the gay couples they studied referred to each other as "lover."

How Partner Was Met

Lesbians were likely to have met their partner through friends (28%), at work (21%), or at a social event (16%). Gay men were likely to have met their partner at a bar (22%), through friends (19%), or at a social event (13%). McWhirter and Mattison (1984) and Berger (1990) also mention that the first contact between gay couples is likely to occur in a gay establishment.

Relationship Rituals

Fifty-seven percent of the women and 36 percent of the men reported that they wore a ring or some other symbol to represent their relationship. Nineteen percent of the women and 11 percent of the men had held some ceremony to commemorate the event.

Residence

Most of the couples (82% male, 75% female) lived together during the previous year of the relationship. Thirty-six percent of the male couples and 32 percent of the female couples jointly owned their residence whereas 27 and 33 percent, respectively, jointly rented or leased their residence. Housing discrimination was reported by 15 percent of the renters and 9 percent of the homeowners. McWhirter and Mattison (1984) reported that most of the male couples they studied moved in together after about 1 month of acquaintance. Nichols (1987) has also commented on the relatively short courtship period for lesbians.

Presence of Children

Twenty-one percent of the women and 9 percent of the men reported "caring" for children, although it was not clear whether these children resided with the couple. These children were offspring from a previous marriage for 74 percent of the women and 79 percent of the men. Thirteen percent of the women were impregnated through artificial insemination. Ten percent of the women and 4 percent of the men planned to have children. Blumstein and Schwartz (1983) report that 7 percent of their lesbian couples had children living with them more than 6 months per year. Unfortunately, gay couples were not asked about children.

FINANCES

Eighty-two percent of the male couples and 75 percent of the female couples shared all or part of their incomes. Both Blumstein and Schwartz (1983) and McWhirter and Mattison (1984) report that the probability of a couple will pool finances increases with the length of time living together.

SOCIAL SUPPORT

Both men and women indicated that the major source of social support for their relationships came from other gay/lesbian friends, followed in order by siblings, mother, and father. Men and women were also most likely to turn to friends for help with their relationships. Similar findings were reported by Kurdek (1988a) and Kurdek and Schmitt (1987a).

LEGAL ARRANGEMENTS

Thirty-two percent of the female respondents and 39 percent of the male respondents had executed a will. Respective percentages for power of attorney were 28 and 27 percent, and for a partnership agreement they were 9 and 10 percent.

Homogamy in Partner Selection

One of the most consistent findings in the marriage literature is that "like marries like"; that is, spouses tend to be similar on demographic variables (South, 1991). Given the limited number of potential partners from which lesbians and gay men have to choose, however, one might expect that the homogamy principle would be less true for them.

The most extensive study of this issue (Kurdek & Schmitt, 1987b) involved comparing the degree of partner similarity in fifty gay, fifty-six lesbian, forty-four married, and thirty-five heterosexual cohabiting couples. Relative to partners in the other couples, those in gay couples had the largest discrepancies on age, personal income, and level of education. Low homogamy on demographic characteristics for gay couples has also been reported by Bell and Weinberg (1978), Harry (1984), and McWhirter and Mattison (1984). The latter authors speculate that age differences in gay partners may enhance the complementarity partners feel toward one another and facilitate how power in the relationship is established. Lesbians may be attracted to women of similar age because age homogamy is likely to facilitate a general pattern of equal power in the relationship (Blumstein & Schwartz, 1983; Reilly & Lynch, 1990).

The Normative Developmental Course of Lesbian and Gay Couples

McWhirter and Mattison (1984) and Clunis and Green (1988) have provided stage descriptions of how gay couples and lesbian couples, respectively, develop. McWhirter and Mattison (1984) derived their stage model from a cross-sectional study of 156 predominantly white, well-educated male couples. Clunis and Green (1988) modified and expanded the McWhirter and Mattison stages based on their experiences as therapists. Both sets of authors note that not all couples fit the stage model.

McWhirter and Mattison (1984) proposed that gay male couples develop in a six-stage sequence. The blending stage occurs in the first year and is characterized by merging, limerence (e.g., intense preoccupation with and longing for the partner), shared activity, and high sexual activity. Years 2 and 3 (nesting) are marked by homemaking, finding compatibility, the decline of limerence, and ambivalence about the relationship. Reappearance of the individual, expressing dissatisfactions, dealing with conflict, and establishing traditions occur during the maintaining stage (year 4 and 5). The building stage happens during years 6 through 10 and includes collaborating, increasing individual productivity, establishing independence and individual habits, and dependability of partners.

Years 11 through 20 are described as a releasing stage that involves trusting, merging of money and possessions, midlife evaluations of priorities, and taking each other for granted. Finally, the last stage of renewing occurs after 20 or more years of cohabitation and is characterized by achieving financial and emotional security; shifting perspectives regarding time, health, and loss; restoring romance in the partnership; and remembering events in the relationship history.

Unlike McWhirter and Mattison (1984), Clunis and Green (1988) begin their developmental sequence with a prerelationship stage, described as a time during which partners decide whether to invest time and energy in getting to know each other better. This is followed by a romance stage, which has many of the characteristics of McWhirter and Mattison's blending stage, and a conflict stage that is similar to McWhirter and Mattison's maintaining stage. With the acceptance stage comes a sense of stability and an awareness of the faults and shortcomings of each partner. This is followed by the commitment stage in which partners work on balancing opposing needs while accepting each other as trustworthy. In the collaboration stage, the couple works to create something together (e.g., a baby, a business venture) in the world outside of the relationship that enhances the relationship.

To date, independent empirical studies have addressed only McWhirter and Mattison's (1984) stage model. Kurdek and Schmitt (1986a) examined the relation between the quality of the relationship and the first three stages of this model (blending, nesting, and maintaining) in gay, lesbian, married, and heterosexual cohabiting couples. Generally, findings were consistent with McWhirter and Mattison's (1984) prediction that the second and third year of the relationship were likely to involve stress and disillusionment. Compared with blending and maintaining couples, nesting couples reported the lowest satisfaction with affection and sex, the lowest amount of shared activity, and the most frequent number of dysfunctional beliefs regarding sexual perfection. Because these stage differences characterized all four types of couples (i.e., stage differences did not interact with type of couple), it appears that, in many respects, the early stages of relationship development are similar for homosexual and heterosexual couples.

The Division of Household Labor in Lesbian and Gay Couples

There is ample evidence that the behavior of heterosexual couples is strongly gender-linked and that this gender specialization increases when husbands and wives becomes fathers and mothers (Thompson & Walker, 1989). Unlike heterosexual partners, who come to their marriages with strong gender-linked expectations of how household labor will be divided, homosexual partners cannot use gender to assign roles and tasks in their relationships for the obvious reason that both partners are the same gender.

In their study of gay, lesbian, and married couples, Blumstein and Schwartz (1983) reported that 30 percent of full-time employed gay partners and 27 percent of full-time employed lesbian partners did more than 10 hours of housework per week. Comparable percentages for full-time employed wives and husbands were 59 and 22 percent, respectively. Clearly, relative to husbands and gay/lesbian partners, wives do the bulk of household labor. Kurdek (1993) reached a similar conclusion in a study of gay, lesbian, and married couples.

How do partners in gay and lesbian couples assign household tasks? In their study of gay couples, McWhirter and Mattison (1984) noted that the handling of household chores varied by stage of the relationship. In the first year of the relationship, partners shared almost all chores. Later, however, routines got established as chores were assigned primarily on the basis of each partner's skill and work schedule.

In instances where each partner was skilled, partners willingly un-learned previous skills in order to create complementarity and a sense of balance in the relationship.

Blumstein and Schwartz (1983) and Kurdek (1993) noted that lesbian couples at any stage of the relationship were particularly likely to di-vide household labor equally. Blumstein and Schwartz (1983) speculate that lesbians may avoid task specialization in the area of household work because of the low status traditionally associated with the women who do it. This speculation is consistent with other reports that lesbian couples are more likely than either gay or heterosexual couples to fol-low an ethic of equality (Bell & Weinberg, 1978; Clunis & Green, 1988; Peplau & Cochran, 1990).

The Negotiation of Power in Lesbian and Gay Couples

Because conflict in intimate relationships is inevitable, strategies for re-solving conflict are critical for couple stability. In their national survey of lesbian and gay couples, Bryant and Demian (1990) stated that the percentage of women reporting verbal abuse and physical abuse from their partners was 17 and 3 percent, respectively. Corresponding val-ues for men were 15 and 3 percent. Most of the female and male re-spondents (28% and 26%, respectively) reported two small arguments per month.

Blumstein and Schwartz (1983) found that the partner with the higher income wielded more personal power in money management issues in gay, married, and heterosexual cohabiting couples but not in lesbian couples. Further, they speculated that because earning poten-tial is a central part of a man's identity, money management might be especially troublesome for gay couples. Although Berger (1990) re-ported that the most frequent area of conflict for gay couples involved finances, Kurdek (1992a) found that managing finances was a trouble-some area for *both* gay and lesbian couples. In fact, Kurdek (1992a) found that the top five areas of conflict for lesbian and gay couples were identical: finances, driving style, affection/sex, being overly criti-cal, and household tasks.

Two studies have assessed directly how lesbian and gay couples re-solve conflict, and no differences between the two types of couples emerged in either study. Falbo and Peplau (1980) found that lesbians and gay men did not differ in the types of strategies they reported using to get what they wanted. Kurdek (1991a) found that lesbians and gay men were equally likely to use positive problem-solving, with-drawal, compliance, and negative problem-solving to resolve conflict within their relationships.

Sexual Behavior in Lesbian and Gay Couples

The most extensive report on sexual behavior in lesbian and gay relationships comes from Blumstein and Schwartz (1983). Of all the areas of couplehood studied by these authors, the largest differences between lesbian and gay couples occurred in this area. Blumstein and Schwartz (1983) found that gay couples were more sexually active than lesbian, heterosexual cohabiting, or married couples in the early years of the relationship. After 10 years together, however, gay couples had sex less frequently than married couples and frequently devised explicit arrangements for sexual activity outside of the relationship. Gay couples' acceptance of sexual nonexclusivity is one of the most distinctive features of their relationships (Blasband & Peplau, 1985; Bryant & Demian, 1990; Harry, 1984; McWhirter & Mattison, 1984; Kurdek, 1991b; Kurdek & Schmitt, 1986b), although the frequency of sexual nonexclusivity may be declining due to the HIV/AIDS epidemic (Kelly, St. Lawrence, Hood, & Brasfield, 1989).

Blumstein and Schwartz (1983) reported that lesbian couples had sex less than any other type of couple, no matter how long partners had been in their relationship. Frye (1990), however, notes that because the number of times a heterosexual couple "has sex" usually means the number of times a male partner has an orgasm, lesbian couples may vary widely in how they interpret "having sex." This point is especially relevant in light of additional findings by Blumstein and Schwartz (1983) that lesbian couples prized nongenital affection (e.g., kissing, hugging, and holding) more than any other type of couple. These authors explained the relatively infrequent genital sexual activity of lesbian couples in terms of women's having internalized social messages that women should have negative feelings about sexuality in general and about their bodies in particular. They also note that initiating sexual activity may disrupt the ethic of equality that guides interpartner interactions. Nichols (1987, 1990) echoes similar themes in her discussion of sexual activities among lesbians.

Blumstein and Schwartz (1983) and McWhirter and Mattison (1984) found no evidence that lesbian partners and gay partners regularly assume "active" and "passive" roles in sexual interactions. In fact, Blumstein and Schwartz (1983) report that, in each of the four types of couples they studied, satisfaction with sex was linked to a perception of equality in initiating and refusing sex.

There is limited evidence regarding the specific types of sexual activity engaged in by gay and lesbian couples. McWhirter and Mattison (1984) reported that over 90 percent of the gay couples they interviewed engaged in kissing and hugging, body rubbing and kissing, tongue kissing, fellatio, being fellated, mutual fellatio, and mutual masturbation. Seventy-one percent of the respondents reported engaging in anal intercourse and 41 percent reported engaging in analingus. Eighty-three percent of the respondents reported they were satisfied with their sexual relationship, and 91 percent reported that their level of satisfaction had increased since the beginning of the relationship. Of the 81 respondents who reported sexual problems, the most common (43%) was erective failure.

No in-depth descriptions of the types of sexual activity engaged in by lesbian cohabiting couples could be found. However, Loulan (1987) reported the results from survey data gathered from 1,566 lesbians, 62 percent of whom were coupled. At least 80 percent of the respondents reported that they did the following activities to their partners: touching breasts, kissing breasts, licking breasts, and putting fingers in vagina. Seventy-one percent of the respondents reported that they performed oral sex on their partner; 56 percent said they put their tongue in their partner's vagina; and 55 percent said they masturbated their partners. Similar percentages were obtained with regard to the activities respondents reported their partners did to them. Finally, the percentages of respondents indicating that they were somewhat, passably, fairly well, and completely satisfied with their current sex life were 24, 8, 38, and 14, respectively.

Comparisons of Relationship Satisfaction in Lesbian and Gay Couples

Whether or not lesbians and gay men report different levels of relationship satisfaction seems to depend on the measure of relationship satisfaction. If the measure is a global one that taps overall levels of satisfaction, no differences between gay and lesbian couples emerge (Duffy & Rusbult, 1986; Kurdek, 1991a). However, if the measure includes specific appraisals of the value of the relationship and rewards derived from the relationship, then lesbians tend to report higher relationship quality than gay men (Blumstein & Schwartz, 1983; Kurdek, 1988b). Because of their more intense socialization experiences in the area of interpersonal skills (Vargo, 1987), women may be biased to value relationships more than men. Consistent with this view, Kurdek (1994) found that gay men did not differ from married men in appraisals of relationship quality and lesbians did not differ from married women.

Correlates of Relationship Satisfaction in Lesbian and Gay Couples

The most striking finding regarding the factors linked to relationship satisfaction is that they seem to be the same for lesbian couples, gay couples, and heterosexual couples. These correlates include feelings of having equal power and control; having at least one emotionally expressive partner in the couple; perceiving many attractions and few alternatives to the relationship; endorsing few dysfunctional beliefs regarding relationships; placing a value on attachment; and engaging in shared decision-making (Blumstein & Schwartz, 1983; Duffy & Rusbult, 1986; Kurdek, 1994b; Kurdek & Schmitt, 1986c, 1986d).

Because gay couples are more likely than lesbian couples to engage in sexual activities outside of the relationship, the relation between relationship satisfaction and sexual exclusivity in gay couples has received some attention. McWhirter and Mattison (1984) reported that *none* of the couples they studied who were together more than 5 years was sexually exclusive. It is important to note, however, that interviews were conducted in 1979, a pre-AIDS era, and that the sample was geographically restricted to the San Diego area. Other studies using samples from more geographically diverse areas have not found such an absolute relation between relationship longevity and sexual nonexclusivity. For example, with a sample of 65 gay couples from 22 states, Kurdek (1988b) found that of 19 couples together more than 10 years, 26 percent were sexually exclusive. It is also of note that gay partners in sexually exclusive and sexually nonexclusive relationships report equivalent levels of relationship satisfaction (Blasband & Peplau, 1985; Kurdek, 1988b, 1991a; Kurdek & Schmitt, 1986b; Silverstein, 1981).

Theoretical Models for Predicting Relationship Functioning in Lesbian and Gay Couples

In contrast to the descriptive accounts of lesbian and gay couples which extol the diversity of lesbian and gay couples, the theory-based work on lesbian and gay couples has focused on identifying fairly abstract factors that account for variability in *any* type of relationship. In short, these theories assume that despite variability in the day-to-day experience of relationships, similarities in the social psychological processes regulate how these relationships function.

The theories used to predict relationship satisfaction and relationship stability in lesbian and gay couples were originally developed from work on dating and married heterosexual couples. Taken together, these theories advance four interrelated propositions about relationship functioning: (a) The individual difference proposition: appraisals of relationship satisfaction are related to individual difference variables that filter relationship information (Bradbury & Fincham, 1988); (b) the interdependence proposition: appraisals of relationship satisfaction are a function of the rewards associated with being in the relationship, the costs involved in being in the relationship, and the extent to which the relationship meets an internal standard of what a "good" relationship is. Further, appraisals of relationship commitment are a function of not only relationship satisfaction, but also the presence of attractive alternatives to the relationship and the investment made in the relationship (Rusbult, 1983); (c) the problem-solving proposition: individual partners' appraisals of relationship satisfaction are related to the problem-solving styles the couple uses to resolve conflict (Gottman & Krokoff, 1989); and (d) the partner discrepancy proposition: appraisals of relationship satisfaction and relationship stability are related to the degree to which partners differ in their relationship needs, the importance placed on relationship values, and individual differences linked to interpersonal competence (Cowan & Cowan, 1990).

How well do these propositions account for relationship functioning in lesbian and gay couples? Relevant data regarding relationship satisfaction and relationship stability are reviewed in turn. It will be seen that the preceding set of propositions do a reasonably good job of explaining variability in these two dimensions of relationship functioning.

Relationship Satisfaction

Two studies are relevant here. In the first study, Kurdek (1992b) obtained assessments of relationship satisfaction; demographic variables; individual difference variables (dysfunctional beliefs about relationships, expressiveness, satisfaction with social support, and negative affectivity); and interdependence variables (perceived rewards from the relationship, perceived costs to the relationship, investment in the relationship, and alternatives to the relationship) over a 4-year period for thirty-one lesbian and sixty-one gay couples. Generally, regardless of type of couples, decreases in relationship satisfaction over the 4 years of study were linked to increases in dysfunctional beliefs, decreases in perceived rewards, increases in perceived costs, and decreases in investment.

In the second study (Kurdek, 1991a), the relationship satisfaction of partners from fifty-one lesbian couples and seventy-five gay couples was correlated with variables from the individual difference, interdependence, and problem-solving models. Regardless of type of couple, high relationship satisfaction was linked to few dysfunctional beliefs, high expressiveness, high satisfaction with social support, and low self-consciousness (the individual difference variables); high perceived rewards, low perceived costs, and low discrepancy between one's real and ideal relationships (the interdependence variables); and frequent compromise/negotiation, infrequent conflict engagement, and infrequent withdrawal (the problem-solving variables).

An important theoretical contribution of this study was that findings were consistent with the position that variables from the three models accounted for variability in relationship satisfaction at different levels of generality. The individual difference model is the most general because it characterizes persons as coming to an intimate relationship with preset filters through which relationship information is processed. At a more specific level is the interdependence model which focuses on evaluations of the benefits and costs of a particular relationship. Finally, at the most specific level is the problem-solving model, which taps appraisals of the specific strategies partners use to resolve conflicts within their particular relationships. The strongest evidence for this multilayered approach to conceptualizing what factors influence the appraisal of relationship satisfaction was that the effects of variables from the more specific levels mediated the effects of variables from the more general levels (Kurdek, 1991a).

Relationship Stability

Only two studies have identified factors that predict dissolution in lesbian and gay couples. In their study of lesbian, gay, heterosexual cohabiting, and married couples, Blumstein and Schwartz (1983) did an 18-month follow-up on about half of their sample. Dissolution rates were 18 percent, 13 percent, 14 percent, and 4 percent, respectively. These authors report that partners in *any* couple who experienced major difficulties in the areas of money, work, or sex were likely to dissolve their relationship.

In the 4-year study of lesbian and gay couples summarized earlier, Kurdek (1992b) reported that twelve of the fifty-three (22%) lesbian couples and ten of the eighty (12%) gay couples had separated. The difference between the two proportions was not significant. Relative to partners from intact couples, those from separated couples (in their last year of cohabitation) differed on demographic variables, individual difference variables, and interdependence variables. Specifically, they were younger, more frequently reported negative affectivity (e.g., depression and anxiety), reported lower relationship satisfaction, valued personal autonomy more highly, and invested less in the relationship. Surprisingly, discrepancies between partners on the three sets of variables did not discriminate between intact and separated couples. Interdependence variables were found to mediate the effects of the individual difference variables. That is, although the individual difference scores discriminated between intact and separated couples on their own, they lost their discriminating power once the interdependence scores were controlled. It is likely that individual difference variables directly affect appraisals of the costs and benefits associated with a particular relationship (Kurdek, 1991a).

Predicting Reactions to Relationship Dissolution

Information on factors that predict lesbians' and gay men's reactions to the end of a relationship is even more limited than that regarding relationship stability. Kurdek (1991c) obtained survey data from both partners of seven lesbian and six gay couples who had recently (about 5 months earlier) ended their relationships. There was no evidence that lesbians and gay men reacted differently to the dissolution. Further, no evidence suggested that lesbians in particular faced problems regarding being too close (i.e., merging and fusion; Krestan & Bepko, 1980). In fact, the general pattern of findings was remarkably similar to that obtained with heterosexual couples (e.g., Bloom & Hodges, 1981).

The most frequently given reasons for ending the relationship were nonresponsiveness of the partner and absence/emotional distance. The most frequently experienced emotions since the dissolution were personal growth, loneliness, and relief from conflict. The most frequent problems encountered since the dissolution were managing contact with the former partner and financial stress. Overall, respondents who were adapting well to the dissolution expected the separation and felt they were prepared for it.

Because these respondents were part of a longitudinal study, it was possible to link their experience of the separation to their appraisals of themselves and their relationship during the last year of cohabitation. Generally, the person who adjusted well to a separation had many years of education, knew and lived with the partner for few months, did not pool finances with the partner, reported little love for the partner, placed a low value on attachment, and reported infrequent psychological distress. In short—consistent with Rusbult's (1983) interdependence model—this person perceived few attractions to the relationship and few barriers to leaving, saw appealing alternatives to the relationship, and did not invest much in the relationship.

Conclusions and Unresolved Issues

Consistent Findings about Lesbian and Gay Couples

Although information regarding lesbian and gay couples is limited, six findings have been reported with some consistency. First, and most basic, many gay men and lesbians see themselves as part of a couple. Second, a major difference between lesbian and gay couples is that lesbian couples are more likely to be sexually exclusive. Third, compared to heterosexual couples, gay couples and especially lesbian couples are more likely to follow an ethic of equality, basing their interactions on what has been termed a "best friend" model (Harry & DeVall,

1978). Fourth, lesbian and gay relationships show reliable changes over time that are similar to those observed in heterosexual couples. Fifth, in comparisons of the global relationship satisfaction of lesbians, gay men, and heterosexuals few differences emerge. Finally, the predictors of relationship satisfaction and relationship stability are also similar for lesbian, gay, and heterosexual couples. In general, satisfaction and stability are linked to individual difference, interdependence, and problem-solving variables.

Needed Descriptive Information about Lesbian and Gay Couples

Although there are many gaps in our knowledge of lesbian and gay couples, five will be highlighted. First, how do lesbian and gay couples structure their relationships? In the absence of conventional partner roles, it is unclear how lesbian and gay couples create predictability in the experience of their relationships (Klinkenberg & Rose, 1992). Do they seek out "established" couples for advice? Do they construct roles on a trial-and-error basis? Are certain strategies for role formation reliably linked to satisfaction and stability? Perhaps the best way to study these issues would be to follow lesbian and gay couples from the time they meet their partner through the early period of cohabitation.

Second, what kinds of needs do lesbians and gay men seek to satisfy in their intimate relationships? Drigotas and Rusbult (1992) have argued that central elements in understanding relationship stability are identifying needs that are important to a relationship and assessing the extent to which those needs are satisfied by the current and alternative relationships. Although clinical observations have identified dependency needs as particularly problematic for lesbian couples (Krestan & Bepko, 1980), data from nonclinic samples have not (Kurdek, 1991c; Melamed, 1992). Future work on the issue of dependency needs might be anchored within the Drigotas and Rusbult (1992) framework.

Third, what kinds of relationship tensions do lesbian and gay couples experience? Because resolving conflict constructively is critical to relationship satisfaction and relationship stability, it would be useful to examine dyadic processes in conflict resolution. Do particular combinations of problem-solving styles work well or poorly for particular kinds of issues (Gottman & Krokoff, 1989; Kurdek, 1992a)? Can one expressive, accommodating partner carry the weight of conflict resolution (Rusbult, Verette, Whitney, Slovik, & Lipkus, 1991)?

Fourth, because there are few external barriers to prevent lesbians and gay men from leaving their relationships, what kinds of psychological and social processes create commitment to the relationship? Work with heterosexual couples has indicated that committed partners devalue the attraction of alternatives to the relationship as a way of maintaining commitment (Johnson & Rusbult, 1989). Future studies could examine if partners in stable lesbian and gay couples engage in similar processes.

Because commitment can also be enhanced by social forces outside of the immediate couple (Laird, in press; Rusbult, 1983), it would also be of interest to see if relationship satisfaction and relationship stability are affected by the degree to which social systems that include one or both partners support the relationship. These systems might include families of origin, friends, coworkers, neighbors, and members of the immediate heterosexual and lesbian/gay community.

Finally, how is the experience of couplehood affected by age, race, ethnicity, and geographical location? To date, the study of lesbian and gay couples has primarily attended to gender as a moderator variable; yet relationship initiation, relationship development, and relationship dissolution are affected by the social–cultural–historical context within which lesbians and gay men develop.

Although gay men and lesbians are all subject to various forms of heterosexist discrimination, there is evidence that older lesbians and gay men as well as lesbians and gay men of color are likely to experience rejection from other gays and lesbians as well (Bell & Weinberg, 1978; Clunis & Green, 1988; Friend, 1991; Peterson, 1992). Because gay and lesbian youth are growing up in the midst of the HIV/AIDS epidemic, cohort-specific external barriers to relationship development may increase. Finally, geographical location is likely to be a relevant factor, inasmuch as some areas of the country are more repressive than others. For instance, large cities are more likely than small towns or rural areas to have lesbian and gay organizations and establishments in which lesbians and gay men can meet a variety of prospective partners.

Theoretical Issues

One of the most pressing needs in the study of lesbian and gay couples is to develop conceptual frameworks that integrate current findings and generate testable predictions. Using interdependence theory as a reference, lesbians, gay men, and heterosexuals are likely to differ greatly in *what* they perceive to be the rewards, costs, comparison levels, alternatives, and investments associated with their relationships. Further, these perceptions are highly likely to be affected by cohort, age, race, ethnicity, and personal relationship history. However, despite this diversity in form, the *function* of these interdependence elements should be robust enough to make reliable predictions about relationship satisfaction and relationship stability across diverse types of couples.

Given what little information we have about the functioning of lesbian and gay couples, we need descriptive studies that put relationships in their social–cultural–historical contexts. These studies are likely to highlight the diversity of relationship-specific forms among gay men, lesbians, and heterosexuals. At a more abstract level, however, this diversity in form is likely to reflect a uniformity of function in how all couples begin, endure, and dissolve.

References

Bell, A. P., & Weinberg, M. S. (1978). *Homosexualities: A study of diversity among men and women*. New York: Simon & Schuster.

Berger, R. M. (1990). Men together: Understanding the gay couple. *Journal of Homosexuality, 19*, 31–49.

Blasband, D., & Peplau, L. A. (1985). Sexual exclusivity versus openness in gay couples. *Archives of Sexual Behavior, 14*, 395–412.

Bloom, B. L., & Hodges, W. F. (1981). The predicament of the newly separated. *Community Mental Health Journal, 17*, 277–293.

Blumstein, P., & Schwartz, P. (1983). *American couples: Money, work, sex*. New York: William Morrow and Company, Inc.

Boxer, A. M., & Cohler, B. J. (1989). The life course of gay and lesbian youth. *Journal of Homosexuality, 17*, 315–355.

Bradbury, T. N., & Fincham, F. D. (1988). Individual difference variables in close relationships: A contextual model of marriage as an integrative framework. *Journal of Personality and Social Psychology, 54*, 713–721.

Bryant, S., & Demian (Eds.) (1990, May/June). *Partners: Newsletter for gay and lesbian couples*. (Available from Partners, Box 9685, Seattle, WA 98109).

Clunis, D. M., & Green, G. D. (1988). *Lesbian couples*. Seattle: Seal Press.

Cowan, P. A., & Cowan, C. P. (1990). Becoming a family: Research and intervention. In I. Sigel & E. Brody (Eds.), *Family research*. Hillsdale, NJ: Erlbaum.

Drigotas, S. M., & Rusbult, C. E. (1992). Should I stay or should I go? A dependence model of breakups. *Journal of Personality and Social Psychology, 62*, 62–87.

Duffy, S. M., & Rusbult, C. E. (1986). Satisfaction and commitment in homosexual and heterosexual relationships. *Journal of Homosexuality, 12*, 1–23.

Falbo, T., & Peplau, L. A. (1980). Power strategies in intimate relationships. *Journal of Personality and Social Psychology, 38*, 618–628.

Friend, R. A. (1991). Older lesbian and gay people: A theory of successful aging. *Journal of Homosexuality, 20*, 99–118.

Frye, M. (1990). Lesbian "sex." In J. Allen (Ed.), *Lesbian philosophies and cultures* (pp. 305–315). Albany, NY: SUNY Press.

Gottman, J. M., & Krokoff, L. J. (1989). Marital interaction and satisfaction: A longitudinal view. *Journal of Consulting and Clinical Psychology, 57*, 47–52.

Harry, J. (1984). *Gay couples*. New York: Praeger.

Harry, J., & DeVall, W. B. (1978). *The social organization of gay males*. New York: Praeger.

Herek, G. M. (1991). Myths about sexual orientation: A lawyer's guide to social science research. *Law and Sexuality, 1*, 133–172.

Jay, K., & Young, A. (1977). *The gay report: Lesbians and gay men speak out about sexual experiences and life styles.* New York: Summit Books.

Johnson, D. J., & Rusbult, C. E. (1989). Resisting temptation: Devaluation of alternative partners as a means of maintaining commitment in close relationships. *Journal of Personality and Social Psychology, 57,* 967–980.

Kelley, H. H., & Thibaut, J. W. (1978). *Interpersonal relations: A theory of interdependence.* New York: Wiley.

Kelly, J. A., St. Lawrence, J. S., Hood, H. V., & Brasfield, T. L. (1989). Behavioral intervention to reduce AIDS risk activities. *Journal of Consulting and Clinical Psychology, 57,* 60–67.

Klinkenberg, D., & Rose, S. (1992, August). Dating scripts of gay men and lesbians. Paper presented at the meeting of the American Psychological Association, Washington, DC.

Krestan, J., & Bepko, C. S. (1980). The problem of fusion in the lesbian relationship. *Family Process, 19,* 277–289.

Kurdek, L. A. (1988a). Perceived social support in gays and lesbians in cohabiting relationships. *Journal of Personality and Social Psychology, 54,* 504–509.

Kurdek, L. A. (1988b). Relationship quality of gay and lesbian cohabiting couples. *Journal of Homosexuality, 15,* 93–118.

Kurdek, L. A. (1991a). Correlates of relationship satisfaction in cohabiting gay and lesbian couples: An integration of contextual, investment, and problem-solving models. *Journal of Personality and Social Psychology, 61,* 910–922.

Kurdek, L. A. (1991b). Sexuality in homosexual and heterosexual couples. In K. McKinney & S. Sprecher (Eds.), *Sexuality in close relationships* (pp. 177–191). Hillsdale, NJ: Erlbaum.

Kurdek, L. A. (1991c). The dissolution of gay and lesbian couples. *Journal of Social and Personal Relationships, 8,* 265–278.

Kurdek, L. A. (1992a, August). Conflict in gay and lesbian cohabiting couples. Paper presented at the meeting of the American Psychological Association, Washington, DC.

Kurdek, L. A. (1992b). Relationship stability and relationship satisfaction in cohabiting gay and lesbian couples: A prospective longitudinal test of the contextual and interdependence models. *Journal of Social and Personal Relationships, 9,* 125–142.

Kurdek, L. A. (1993). The allocation of household labor in homosexual and heterosexual cohabiting couples. *Journal of Social Issues, 49,* 127–139.

Kurdek, L. A. (1994). The nature and correlates of relationship quality in gay, lesbian, and heterosexual cohabiting couples: A test of the contextual, investment, and discrepancy models. In B. Greene G. M. Herek (Eds.), *Lesbian and gay psychology: Theory, research, and clinical applications* (pp. 133–155). Thousand Oaks, CA: Sage.

Kurdek, L. A., & Schmitt, J. P. (1986a). Early development of relationship quality in heterosexual married, heterosexual cohabiting, gay, and lesbian couples. *Developmental Psychology, 22,* 305–309.

Kurdek, L. A., & Schmitt, J. P. (1986b). Relationship quality of gay men in closed or open relationships. *Journal of Homosexuality, 12,* 85–99.

Kurdek, L. A., & Schmitt, J. P. (1986c). Relationship quality of partners in heterosexual married, heterosexual cohabiting, and gay and lesbian relationships. *Journal of Personality and Social Psychology, 51,* 711–720.

Kurdek, L. A., & Schmitt, J. P. (1986d). Interaction of sex role self-concept with relationship quality and relationship beliefs in married, heterosexual cohabiting, gay, and lesbian couples. *Journal of Personality and Social Psychology, 51,* 365–370.

Kurdek, L. A., & Schmitt, J. P. (1987a). Perceived support from family and friends in members of homosexual, married, and heterosexual cohabiting couples. *Journal of Homosexuality, 14,* 57–68.

Kurdek, L. A., & Schmitt, J. P. (1987b). Partner homogamy in married, heterosexual cohabiting, gay, and lesbian couples. *Journal of Sex Research, 23,* 212–232.

Laird, J. (1993). Lesbian and gay families. In F. Walsh (Ed.), *Normal family processes* (pp. 282–328). New York: Guilford.

Loulan, J. (1987). *Lesbian passion: Loving ourselves and each other.* San Francisco: Spinsters.

McWhirter, D. P., & Mattison, A. M. (1984). *The male couple: How relationships develop.* Englewood Cliffs, NJ: Prentice-Hall.

Melamed, D. K. (1992, August). Internalized homophobia and lesbian couple functioning. Paper presented at the meeting of the American Psychological Association, Washington, DC.

Nichols, M. (1987). Lesbian sexuality: Issues and developing theory. In Boston Lesbian Psychologies Collective (Ed.), *Lesbian psychologies: Explorations and challenges* (pp. 97–125). Urbana: University of Illinois Press.

Nichols, M. (1990). Lesbian relationship: Implications for the study of sexuality and gender. In D. P. McWhirter, S. A. Sanders, & J. M. Reinisch (Eds.), *Homosexuality/heterosexuality: Concepts of sexual orientation* (pp. 350–366). New York: Oxford University Press.

Peplau, L. A. (1991). Lesbian and gay relationships. In J. C. Gonsiorek & J. D. Weinrich (Eds.), *Homosexuality: Research implications for public policy* (pp. 177–196). Newbury Park, CA: Sage.

Peplau, L. A., & Cochran, S. D. (1990). A relational perspective on homosexuality. In D. P. McWhirter, S. A. Sanders, & J. M. Reinisch (Eds.), *Homosexuality/heterosexuality: Concepts of sexual orientation* (pp. 321–349). New York: Oxford University Press.

Peterson, J. L. (1992). Black men and their same-sex desires and behaviors. In G. Herdt (Ed.), *Gay culture in America* (pp. 147–164). Boston: Beacon.

Reilly, M. E., & Lynch, J. M. (1990). Power-sharing in lesbian relationships. *Journal of Homosexuality, 19,* 1–30.

Rusbult, C. E. (1983). A longitudinal test of the investment model: The development (and deterioration) of satisfaction and commitment in heterosexual involvements. *Journal of Personality and Social Psychology, 45,* 101–177.

Rusbult, C. E., Verette, J., Whitney, G. A., Slovik, L. F., & Lipkus, I. (1991). Accommodation processes in close relationships: Theory and preliminary empirical evidence. *Journal of Personality and Social Psychology, 60,* 53–78.

Silverstein, C. (1981). *Man to man: Gay couples in America.* New York: Morrow.

South, S. J. (1991). Sociodemographic differentials in mate selection preferences. *Journal of Marriage and the Family, 53,* 928–940.

Thompson, L., & Walker, A. J. (1989). Women and men in marriage, work,
and parenthood. *Journal of Marriage and the Family, 51,* 845–872.

Vargo, S. (1987). The effects of women's socialization on lesbian couples. In
Boston Lesbian Psychologies Collective (Ed.), *Lesbian psychologies: Explorations and challenges* (pp. 161–173). Urbana: University of Illinois Press.

11

Lesbian Mothers, Gay Fathers, and Their Children

Charlotte J. Patterson

The central heterosexist assumption that everyone is or ought to be heterosexual is nowhere more prevalent than in the area of parent–child relations. Not only are children usually assumed to be heterosexual in their orientation, but mothers and fathers are also generally expected to exemplify heterosexuality in their attitudes, values, and behavior. From this perspective, children with lesbian and gay parents seem not to exist, and the idea of lesbian or gay parenthood may be difficult even to imagine. In contrast to such expectations, however, many lesbians and gay men are parents.

Despite the multiple difficulties involved in attempting to count lesbian and gay parents and their children, a number of writers have offered estimates of the numbers of such parents and children in the United States today (Bozett, 1987; Falk, 1989; Gottman, 1990; Miller, 1979; Patterson, 1992). Estimates of gay or lesbian parents in the United States range from 2 million to 8 million; estimates of children of gay or lesbian parents range from 4 million to 14 million. Because reliable figures are not available, it is impossible to decide with certainty which estimates are correct (Patterson, 1992). Whatever the precise numbers may be, however, lesbian and gay parenting is by no means rare. Knowledgeable observers report that lesbian and gay parenting is on the rise; in fact, the growth of lesbian and gay parenting has been so rapid in recent years that some observers have described a "lesbian baby boom," or a "gayby boom" (Patterson, 1992, in 1994a, 1994c; Pennington, 1987; Steckel, 1985; Weston, 1991).

This chapter first considers some of the issues and perspectives relevant to research on lesbian and gay families with children. This is followed by an overview of research on lesbian and gay parents, and then a review of research on children of lesbian and gay parents. The chapter ends with a summary of the conclusions from existing studies and suggestions for future work.

Issues and Perspectives

Research on lesbian mothers, gay fathers, and their children has arisen in an historical context that has helped shape the issues believed to be worthy of study as well as the perspectives from which they are explored. In this section, I describe three main standpoints from which interest in lesbian and gay parenting has emerged, and I identify some of the sources of diversity within lesbian and gay parenting communities.

Perspectives on Lesbian Mothers, Gay Fathers, and Their Children

Interest in lesbian and gay parents and their children has arisen from several perspectives. First, the phenomenon of large numbers of openly lesbian and gay parents raising children represents a sociocultural innovation that is unique to the current historical era. The emergence of substantial numbers of openly self-identified gay men and lesbians is a recent historical occurrence (D'Emilio, 1983; Faderman, 1991). Because many individuals identify themselves as lesbian or gay for the first time in adulthood, many have been married and given birth to children before they assumed lesbian or gay identities. Others become parents after their lesbian or gay identities have become well established.

To what extent does growing up with lesbian or gay parents influence children's development? Lesbian and gay families with children raise questions about the kinds of home environments that can foster positive development in children (Patterson, 1992, 1994c). To the extent that parental influences are critical in psychosocial development, and to the extent that lesbians and gay men may provide distinctive socialization experiences, then the children of gay men and lesbians can be expected to develop in ways that are different from children of heterosexual parents. Because it is widely believed that family environments do exert significant influences on children, and that lesbian and gay parents provide input that is different in important ways from that provided by heterosexual parents, it has often been suggested that the experience of growing up with a gay or lesbian parent significantly affects the children involved. Although feminists sometimes speculate

on benefits that might accrue to mothers and children in a less patriarchal world (e.g., Gilman, 1915/1979), expectations based on many psychological theories are generally more negative.

Theories of psychological development have traditionally emphasized distinctive contributions of both male and female parents to the
healthy personal and social development of children. For instance, psychoanalytic theory highlights the oedipal drama, in which the presence
of both male and female parents is thought to facilitate successful resolution of children's conflicts (Bronfenbrenner, 1960). More recent feminist psychoanalytic writers also emphasize different influences of male
and female parents on child development (Chodorow, 1980). Similarly,
social learning approaches to personality development (Huston, 1983)
see children as learning distinctive lessons from the examples and the
rewards offered by both male and female parents. Although cognitive
developmental theory (e.g., Kohlberg, 1966) and gender schema theory
(Bem, 1983) do not require such assumptions, proponents of these
views have not challenged them. As a result, prominent perspectives
on individual differences in personal and social development are often
believed to predict difficulties in development among children of lesbian and gay parents. Empirical research with such families thus provides an opportunity to evaluate heterosexist theoretical assumptions
that are often taken for granted.

A third perspective from which interest in lesbian and gay families
with children has arisen is that of the law. The legal system in the
United States has long been hostile to gay men and to lesbians who
are or wish to become parents (Editors of the Harvard Law Review,
1990; Falk, 1989; Polikoff, 1990; Rivera, 1991). Because judicial and legislative bodies in some states have found lesbians and gay men to be
unfit as parents because of their sexual orientation, lesbian mothers
and gay fathers have often been denied custody or visitation with their
children following divorce (Editors of the Harvard Law Review, 1990).
Lesbians' and gay men's opportunities to become foster or adoptive
parents have similarly been curtailed by public policies and judicial decisions that embody a variety of negative expectations about the likely
influences of lesbian and gay parents on the development of children
in their care (Ricketts, 1991; Ricketts & Achtenberg, 1990). Because
such negative assumptions have often been explicit in judicial determi-
nations involving child custody and visitation, and because such assumptions are open to empirical test, they have provided an important
impetus for research in this area.

Sources of Diversity among Lesbian and Gay Families

Reasons for interest in research on lesbian and gay families with children have thus emerged from a number of perspectives. In considering

these, however, it is important not to overlook many sources of diversity among lesbian and gay families with children. To comprehend adequately the diversity that characterizes these families, it is important to examine some of the differences among them.

One important distinction among lesbian and gay families with children concerns the sexual identity of parents at the time of a child's birth or adoption. Probably the largest group of children with lesbian and gay parents today are those who were born in the context of heterosexual relationships between the biological parents, and whose parent or parents subsequently identified as gay or lesbian. These include families in which the parents divorce when the husband comes out as gay, families in which the parents divorce when the wife comes out as lesbian, families in which the parents divorce when both parents come out, and families in which one or both of the parents comes out and the parents decide not to divorce. Gay or lesbian parents may be single, or they may have same-sex partners. A gay or lesbian parent's same-sex partner may or may not take up step-parenting relationships with the children. If the partner has also had children, the youngsters may also be cast into step-sibling relationships with one another. Thus, gay and lesbian families with children born in the context of heterosexual relationships are themselves a relatively diverse group.

In addition to children born in the context of heterosexual relationships between parents, lesbians and gay men are having children (Crawford, 1987; Patterson, 1992, 1994a, 1994b; Pies, 1985, 1990; Rohrbaugh, 1988; Steckel, 1987; Weston, 1991). The majority of such children are probably conceived through donor insemination (DI). Lesbians who wish to bear children may choose a friend, relative, or acquaintance to be the sperm donor or may use sperm from an unknown donor. When sperm donors are known, they may or may not take parental, avuncular, or other roles relative to children (Patterson, 1994a, 1994b; Pies, 1985, 1990). Gay men may also become biological parents of children whom they intend to parent, whether with a single woman (who may be lesbian or heterosexual), a lesbian couple, or a gay male partner. Options pursued by gay men and lesbians also include both adoption and foster care (Ricketts, 1991). Thus, children are being brought up today in a diverse array of lesbian and gay families, many of which simply did not exist as recently as 50 years ago.

Another important distinction among lesbian and gay parents is the extent to which family members are biologically related to one another (Pollack & Vaughn, 1987; Riley, 1988; Weston, 1991). Although biological relatedness of family members is taken for granted in many heterosexual families, this is often not the case in lesbian and gay families with children. When children are born by means of DI into lesbian families, they are generally related biologically only to the birth mother, not to her partner. Similarly, when children are born to a gay couple by means of surrogacy, only the father who served as a sperm donor is biologically related to the child. In heterosexual families, heavy cultural weight is traditionally placed on biological kinship, and expectations for relationships with "blood kin" are generally different from those for relationships with others. An important issue among lesbian and gay families concerns the extent to which biological relatedness does or ought to affect the experience of kinship (Polikoff, 1990; Riley, 1988; Weston, 1991).

An additional distinction of particular importance for lesbian and gay families is living arrangements for minor children. As in heterosexual families, children may be in the sole physical custody of one or both biological parents, or they may be in joint physical custody (i.e., spending part of their time in one parent's household, and part in another's). Because of the hostility of the legal system to gay and lesbian parents, many lesbian mothers and gay fathers have lost custody of their children to heterosexual spouses following divorce, and the threat of custody litigation looms larger in the lives of custodial divorced lesbian mothers than it does in the lives of custodial divorced heterosexual ones (Lyons, 1983; Pagelow, 1980). Almost certainly, a greater proportion of gay and lesbian parents has lost custody of their children against their will than is true of the heterosexual population. For this reason, many more lesbians and gay men are noncustodial parents (i.e., do not have legal custody of their children) and nonresidential parents (i.e., do not live in the same household with their children) than might otherwise be expected.

Beyond these basic distinctions, others may also be important. In addition to difficulties in defining sexual orientation (see Brown and Gonsiorek, Chapters 1 and 2), lesbian and gay families with children may differ in a number of other important ways. These include income, education, race/ethnicity, gender, and culture. A gay professional couple whose baby was carried by a surrogate mother may have a family experience that is different in many ways from that of a divorced lesbian mother of three who is beginning to work outside the home for the first time. A single gay man who lives with an adopted teen-aged son in an urban neighborhood with many other gay and lesbian parents and children may provide a different environment than a lesbian couple who lives with their toddler twins in a rural area, where they are relatively isolated from other lesbian and gay families. Such variability undoubtedly contributes to differences in the qualities of life in lesbian and gay families.

In the next sections, I first describe research on lesbian and gay parents, followed by studies of their children. Within each of these two sections, I begin with work on families whose children were born or adopted in the context of heterosexual relationships, and then describe studies of families whose children were born or adopted by lesbian and gay parents. Within each section, I also consider questions of diversity among lesbian and gay families with children, although research on such questions is as yet very scarce.

Research on Lesbian Mothers and Gay Fathers

Despite the diversity of lesbian and gay parenting communities, most available research to date has been conducted with relatively homogeneous samples of participants. Samples of parents have generally been composed of white, middle- or upper-middle-class, well-educated individuals living in major urban centers, generally in the United States. Any studies that provide exceptions to this rule are specifically noted. In this section, I first present research on those who became parents in the context of heterosexual relationships, before coming out as lesbian or gay. Following that, I describe studies of lesbians who became parents after coming out. Other recent reviews of this material can be found in Bigner and Bozett (1990), Bozett (1989), Cramer (1986), Falk (1989), and Gibbs (1988).

Lesbians and Gay Men Who Became Parents in the Context of Heterosexual Relationships

An important impetus for research in this area has come from extrinsic sources, such as judicial concerns about the psychological health and well-being of lesbian versus heterosexual mothers. Other work has arisen from concerns that are more intrinsic to the families themselves, such as what and when children should be told about their parents' sexual orientation. In this section, the material arising from extrinsic concerns is reviewed first, followed by the material stemming from intrinsic concerns. Because studies tend to focus either on mothers or on fathers, the two research traditions are considered separately. Although some of these parents may not have been married to the heterosexual partner with whom they had children, it is likely that most were. To avoid the use of more cumbersome labels, then, I refer to "divorced lesbian mothers" and "divorced gay fathers."

DIVORCED LESBIAN MOTHERS

Because it has often been raised as an issue by judges presiding over custody disputes (Falk, 1989; Hitchens, 1979/80; Kleber, Howell, & Tibbits-Kleber, 1986), a number of studies have assessed the overall mental health of lesbian compared to heterosexual mothers. Consistent with data on the mental health of lesbians in general (Gonsiorek, 1991), research in this area has revealed that divorced lesbian mothers score at least as high as divorced heterosexual mothers on assessments of psychological functioning and adjustment. For instance, studies have found no differences between lesbian and heterosexual mothers on self-concept (Mucklow & Phelan, 1979; Rand, Graham, & Rawlings, 1982), happiness (Rand et al., 1982), or overall adjustment or psychiatric status (Golombok, Spencer, & Rutter, 1983; Thompson, McCandless, & Strickland, 1971).

Another area of judicial concern has focused on maternal sex-role behavior, and its potential impact on children (Falk, 1989). Stereotypes cited by the courts suggest that lesbians might be overly masculine, or that they might interact in inappropriate ways with their children. In contrast to expectations based on the stereotypes, however, neither lesbian mothers' reports about their own sex-role behavior (Kweskin & Cook, 1982) nor their self-described interest in child-rearing (Kirkpatrick, Smith, & Roy, 1981) have been found to differ from those of heterosexual mothers. Reports about responses to child behavior (Mucklow & Phelan, 1979) and ratings of warmth toward children (Golombok et al., 1983) have been found not to differ significantly between lesbian and heterosexual mothers. Hoeffer (1981) described lesbian mothers in her sample as more likely to choose a mixture of masculine and feminine sex-typed toys for their children, whereas heterosexual mothers were more likely to choose sex-typed toys to the exclusion of others, but there was no suggestion of inappropriate behavior on the part of any of the mothers.

Some differences between lesbian and heterosexual mothers have also been reported. Lyons (1983) and Pagelow (1980) found that divorced lesbian mothers reported greater fear about loss of child custody than did divorced heterosexual mothers. Similarly, Green, Mandel, Hotvedt, Gray, and Smith (1986) reported that lesbian mothers were more likely than heterosexual mothers to be active in feminist organizations. While findings of this sort are hardly surprising, other reported differences are more difficult to interpret. For instance, Miller, Jacobsen, and Bigner (1981) reported that lesbian mothers were more "child-centered" in their discipline techniques than heterosexual mothers. In a sample of African–American lesbian mothers and African–American heterosexual mothers, Hill (1987) found that lesbian mothers reported being more flexible about rules, more relaxed about sex play and modesty, and more likely to have nontraditional expectations for their daughters. Pending confirmation and replication with different samples, the overall significance of these findings remains unclear.

Several studies have also examined the social circumstances and relationships of lesbian mothers. Divorced lesbian mothers have consistently been reported to be more likely than divorced heterosexual mothers to be living with a romantic partner (Harris & Turner, 1985/

86; Kirkpatrick et al., 1981; Pagelow, 1980). Whether this represents a difference between lesbian and heterosexual mother-headed families or reflects sampling biases of the research cannot be determined on the basis of information in the published reports. Information is sparse about the impact of such relationships in lesbian mother families, but what has been published suggests that, like heterosexual step-parents, coresident lesbian partners of divorced lesbian mothers can be important sources of conflict as well as support in the family (Harris & Turner, 1985/86; Kirkpatrick et al., 1981).

Relationships with the fathers of children in lesbian mother homes have also been studied. Few differences in the likelihood of paternal financial support have been reported for lesbian and heterosexual families with children; Kirkpatrick and her colleagues (1981) reported, for example, that only about half of heterosexual and about half of lesbian mothers in their sample received any financial support from the fathers of their children. Findings about frequency of contact with the fathers are mixed, with some (e.g., Kirkpatrick et al., 1981) reporting no differences as a function of maternal sexual orientation and others (e.g., Golombok et al., 1983; Hare & Richards, 1993) reporting more contact among lesbian than among heterosexual mothers. In a comparison of contacts with friends and relatives among heterosexual and lesbian mothers, Green and his colleagues (1986) reported no differences.

Although most research to date has involved assessment of possible differences between lesbian and heterosexual mothers, a few studies have reported other comparisons. For instance, in a study of divorced lesbian mothers and divorced gay fathers, Harris and Turner (1985/86) found that fathers were more likely to report higher incomes and to report that they encouraged sex-typed toy play among their children than mothers, who were more likely to see benefits for their children (e.g., increased empathy and tolerance for differences) as a result of having lesbian or gay parents. In comparisons of relationship satisfaction among lesbian couples who did or did not have children, Koepke, Hare, and Moran (1992) reported that couples with children scored higher on overall measures of relationship satisfaction and of the quality of their sexual relationship. These findings are intriguing, but further research is needed before their interpretation will be clear.

Another important set of questions, as yet little studied, concerns the conditions under which lesbian mothers experience enhanced feelings of well-being, support, and ability to care for their children. Rand and her colleagues (1982) reported that the psychological health of lesbian mothers was associated with the mothers' openness about her sexual orientation with her employer, ex-husband, children, and friends, and with her degree of feminist activism. Kirkpatrick (1987) found that lesbian mothers living with partners and children had greater economic and emotional resources than those living alone with their children. Much remains to be learned about determinants of individual differences in psychological well-being among lesbian mothers.

A number of additional issues that have arisen in the context of divorced lesbian mother families also need to be studied. For instance, when a mother is in the process of coming out as a lesbian to herself and to others, at what point in that process should she address the topic with her child, and in what ways should she do so—if at all? And what role should the child's age and circumstances play in such a decision? Some writers have suggested that early adolescence may be a particularly difficult time for parents to initiate such conversations and that disclosure may be less stressful at earlier or later points in a child's development (Baptiste, 1987; Huggins, 1989; Lewis, 1980; Paul, 1986), but systematic research on these issues is just beginning. Similarly, many issues remain to be addressed regarding stepfamily and blended family relationships that may emerge as a lesbian mother's household seeks new equilibrium following her separation or divorce from the child's father.

DIVORCED GAY FATHERS

Relatively little empirical research has been done on gay fathers to date. A small handful of studies have addressed questions about possible differences between gay and heterosexual fathers in psychological adjustment, parenting behavior, and other social relationships. Much of the existing work has been devoted to efforts to conceptualize changes in gay fathers' identities over time.

Although considerable research has focused on the overall psychological adjustment of lesbian mothers compared to that of heterosexual mothers, no published studies of gay fathers make such comparisons with heterosexual fathers. It seems likely that this is attributable to the greater role of judicial decision-making as an impetus for research on lesbian mothers. In jurisdictions where the law provides for biases in custody proceedings, these are likely to favor female and heterosexual parents. Perhaps because, other things being equal, gay fathers are very unlikely to win custody battles over their children after divorce, fewer such cases seem to have reached the courts. Consistent with this view, only a minority of gay fathers have been reported to live in the same households with their children (Bigner & Bozett, 1990; Bozett, 1980, 1989; Crosbie-Burnett & Helmbrecht, 1993).

Research on the parenting attitudes of gay versus heterosexual divorced fathers has, however, been reported. Bigner and Jacobsen (1989a and 1989b) studied thirty-three gay and thirty-three heterosexual fathers, each of whom had at least two children. Their results revealed that, with one exception, there were no significant differences between gay and heterosexual fathers in their motives for parenthood. The single exception concerned the greater likelihood of gay than heterosexual fathers to cite the higher status accorded to parents than to nonparents in the dominant culture as a motivation for parenthood (Bigner & Jacobsen, 1989a). In a more recent study, Bigner and Jacobsen (1992) also concluded that divorced gay fathers and divorced heterosexual fathers were more similar than different in their attitudes toward parenting.

Bigner and Jacobsen (1989b; 1992) also asked the gay and heterosexual fathers to report on their own behavior when interacting with their children. Although no differences emerged in the fathers' reports of involvement or intimacy, gay fathers reported that their behavior was characterized by greater responsiveness, more reasoning, and more limit-setting than heterosexual fathers. These reports by gay fathers of greater warmth and responsiveness, on the one hand, and greater control and limit-setting, on the other, are strongly reminiscent of findings from research with heterosexual families, and seem to raise the possibility that gay fathers are more likely than their heterosexual counterparts to exhibit authoritative patterns of parenting behavior such as those described by Baumrind (1967; Baumrind & Black, 1967). Caution must be exercised, however, in interpreting these results, which stem entirely from parental reports about their own behavior.

In addition to research comparing gay and heterosexual fathers, a handful of studies have made other comparisons. For instance, Robinson and Skeen (1982) compared sex-role orientations of gay fathers with those of gay men who were not fathers, and found no differences. Similarly, Skeen and Robinson (1985) found no evidence to suggest that gay men's retrospective reports about relationships with their own parents varied as a function of whether or not they were parents themselves. As noted previously, Harris and Turner (1985/86) compared gay fathers and lesbian mothers, reporting that while gay fathers had higher incomes and were more likely to report encouraging their children to play with sex-typed toys, lesbian mothers were more likely to believe that their children received positive benefits such as increased tolerance for diversity from having lesbian or gay parents. Studies like these begin to suggest the possibilities for research on gender, sexual orientation, and parenting behavior, and it is clear that there are many valuable directions this research could take.

A recent study by Crosbie-Burnett and Helmbrecht (1993) identified predictors of happiness with family life among forty-eight divorced gay fathers, their gay partners, and their teen-aged offspring. Even though most of the teenagers lived primarily with their mothers and only visited in the gay fathers' households, predictors of family happiness were strongly related to the role of the fathers' partners. For teenagers as well as for their fathers and the fathers' partners, psychological inclusion of the partners into the family and the quality of partners' relationships with the teenagers were important predictors of happiness with family life.

Much research in this area has also arisen from concerns about the gay father identity and its transformations over time. Miller (1979) and Bozett (1980, 1981a, 1981b, 1987) have described the processes through which a man who considers himself to be a heterosexual father may come to identify himself, both in public and in private, as a gay father. Based on extensive interviews with gay fathers in both the United States and Canada, these authors have emphasized the pivotal nature of identity disclosure itself and of the reactions to disclosure by significant people in fathers' lives. Miller (1979) has suggested that though a number of factors such as extent of occupational autonomy and amount of access to gay communities may affect how rapidly a gay man is able to disclose his identity to others, the most important of these is likely to be the experience of falling in love with another man. It is this experience, more than any other, Miller argues, that leads a man to integrate the otherwise compartmentalized parts of his identity as a gay father. Although this hypothesis is open to empirical evaluation, such research has not yet been reported.

Overall, then, it is clear that research on gay fathers has begun. At the same time, however, much remains to be accomplished. In particular, empirical research has not yet addressed questions about the sources of diversity among gay fathers. For instance, one such question concerns variations in the amount of contact that a divorced gay man has with his children, and how his relationship with them may be affected by such variations. Another question concerns the ways in which a man's contacts with gay communities and with parenting communities can affect his views of himself as well as of his relationships with his children. The research agenda here is clearly extensive.

Lesbians and Gay Men Choosing to Become Parents

Although for many years lesbian mothers and gay fathers were generally assumed to have become parents in the context of previous heterosexual relationships, both men and women are increasingly choosing to undertake parenthood in the context of preexisting lesbian and gay identities (Crawford, 1987; Patterson, 1992, 1994a, in 1994b; Pies, 1985, 1990). A substantial body of research addresses the transition to parenthood among heterosexuals (e.g., Cowan & Cowan, 1992), examining ways in which decisions to have children are made, normative changes during the transition to parenthood, and factors related to individual differences. In contrast, very little research has explored the transition to parenthood for gay men or lesbians. While many issues that arise for heterosexuals also face lesbians and gay men (e.g., concerns about how children will affect couple relationships, economic concerns about supporting children), lesbians and gay men must also cope with many additional issues because of their situation as members of stigmatized minorities. These issues are best understood by viewing them against the backdrop of pervasive heterosexism and antigay/antilesbian prejudice.

Antigay and antilesbian prejudice is evident in institutions involved with health care, education, and employment that often fail to support, and in many cases, are openly hostile to lesbian and gay families (Casper, Schultz, & Wickens, 1992; Polikoff, 1990; Pollack & Vaughn, 1987). Prospective lesbian and gay parents may encounter antigay prejudice and bigotry even from their families of origin (Pollack & Vaughn, 1987; Weston, 1991). Many if not most of the special concerns of prospective lesbian and gay parents stem from problems created by such hostility (Patterson, in press-b).

A number of interrelated issues are often faced by prospective lesbian and gay parents (Patterson, in 1994b). One of the first needs among this group is for accurate, up-to-date information on how lesbians and gay men can become parents, how their children are likely to develop, and what supports are available to assist gay and lesbian families. In addition to these educational needs, lesbians and gay men who are seeking biological parenthood are also likely to encounter various health concerns, ranging from medical screening of prospective birth parents to assistance with DI techniques, prenatal care, and preparation for birth. As matters progress, a number of legal concerns about the rights and responsibilities of all parties emerge (Editors of the Harvard Law Review, 1990; Polikoff, 1990). In addition, there are financial issues; along with the support of a child, auxiliary costs of medical and legal assistance may be considerable. Finally, many kinds of social and emotional concerns are also likely to emerge. For instance, prospective parents may experience frustration if plans for parenthood are delayed (e.g., by infertility) or disappointment if family members and friends are not supportive of their desire to become parents (Crawford, 1987; Pies, 1985, 1990; Patterson, in 1994b; Pollack & Vaughn, 1987).

As this brief outline of issues suggests, numerous research questions are posed by the emergence of prospective lesbian and gay parents. What are the factors that influence lesbians' and gay men's inclinations to make parenthood a part of their lives, and through what processes do they operate? What effects does parenting have on lesbians or gay men who undertake it, and how do these effects compare with those experienced by heterosexuals? How effectively do special services such as support groups serve the needs of lesbian and gay parents and prospective parents? What are the elements of a supportive social climate for gay and lesbian parents and their children? As yet, little research has addressed such questions.

The earliest studies of child-bearing among lesbian couples were reported by McCandlish (1987) and by Steckel (1987). Both investigators reported research based on small samples of lesbian couples who had given birth to children by means of DI. Their focus was primarily on the children in such families, and neither investigator attempted to assess mothers systematically. McCandlish (1987, p. 28), however, noted that, regardless of their interest in parenting before the birth of the first child, the nonbiological mothers in each couple unanimously reported an "unexpected and immediate attachment" to the child. Although both mothers took part in parenting, they reported shifting patterns of care-taking responsibilities over time, with the biological mother taking primary responsibility during the earliest months, and the nonbiological mother's role increasing in importance after the child was 12 or more months of age. Couples also reported changes in their own relationships following the birth of the child, notably a reduction or cessation in sexual intimacy. Results of these pioneering studies thus raise many intriguing issues and questions for further research.

Hand (1991) examined the ways in which seventeen lesbian and seventeen heterosexual couples with children under 2 years of age shared childcare, household duties, and occupational roles. Hand's principal finding was that lesbian couples shared parenting more equally than did heterosexual couples. Lesbian nonbiological mothers were significantly more involved in childcare and regarded their parental role as significantly more salient than did heterosexual fathers. Lesbian biological mothers viewed their maternal role as more salient than did any of the other mothers, whether lesbian or heterosexual. Fathers viewed their occupational roles as more salient than did any of the mothers, whether lesbian or heterosexual.

Another recent study (Osterweil, 1991) involved thirty lesbian couples with at least one child between 18 and 36 months of age. Consistent with Hand's results for parents of younger children, Osterweil reported that biological mothers viewed their maternal role as more salient than did nonbiological mothers. In addition, although household maintenance activities were shared about equally, biological mothers reported somewhat more influence in family decisions and somewhat more involvement in childcare. Osterweil also reported that the couples in her study scored at about the mean for normative samples of heterosexual couples in overall relationship satisfaction. Taken together, results of the Hand and Osterweil studies thus suggest that lesbian couples who have chosen to bear children are likely to share household and childcare duties to a somewhat greater degree than do heterosexual couples.

Patterson (in press) studied twenty-six families headed by lesbian couples who had children between 4 and 9 years of age living at home with them. Consistent with results of other investigators (Koepke et al., 1992; Osterweil, 1991), Patterson found that lesbian parents' relationship satisfaction was generally high relative to norms for relationship satisfaction among heterosexual couples. Although they reported sharing household tasks and decision-making equally, the couples in this study reported that biological mothers were more involved in childcare and nonbiological mothers spent longer hours in paid employment. Within this context, they also reported greater satisfaction with division of labor when childcare was shared more equally between them.

Two studies of men who became fathers after identifying themselves as gay have also been reported. Sbordone (1993) studied seventy-eight gay men who had become parents through adoption or surrogacy arrangements, and compared them with eighty-three gay men who were not fathers. Consistent with earlier findings for divorced gay fathers (Skeen & Robinson, 1985), there were no differences between fathers and nonfathers on reports about relationships with the men's own parents. Gay fathers did, however, report higher self-esteem and fewer negative attitudes about homosexuality than did gay men who were not fathers.

An interesting result of Sbordone's (1993) study was that more than half of the gay men who were not fathers indicated that they would like to rear a child. Those who said that they wanted children were younger than those who said they did not, but the two groups did not otherwise differ (e.g., on income, education, race, self-esteem, or attitudes about homosexuality). Given that fathers had higher self-esteem and fewer negative attitudes about homosexuality than either group of nonfathers, Sbordone speculated that gay fathers' higher self-esteem might be a result rather than a cause of parenthood.

Another study of gay men choosing parenthood was conducted by McPherson (1993), who assessed division of labor, satisfaction with division of labor, and satisfaction with couple relationships among twenty-eight gay and twenty-seven heterosexual parenting couples. Consistent with evidence from lesbian parenting couples (Hand, 1991; Osterweil, 1991; Patterson, in press), McPherson found that gay couples reported a more even division of responsibilities for household maintenance and childcare than did heterosexual couples. Gay parenting couples also reported greater satisfaction with their division of childcare tasks than did heterosexual couples. Finally, gay couples also reported greater satisfaction with their couple relationships, especially in the areas of cohesion and expression of affection.

As this brief review has revealed, research on lesbians and gay men who have chosen to become parents is still sparse. Most research has been conducted on a relatively small scale, and many important issues have yet to be addressed. It is clear that much remains to be learned about the determinants of lesbian and gay parenting and its impact on lesbian and gay parents themselves.

Research on Children of Lesbian and Gay Parents

Like research on parents, research on children of lesbian and gay parents has, with few exceptions, been conducted with relatively homogeneous groups of white, well-educated, middle-class, largely professional families living in or around urban centers in the United States or other Western countries. Unless otherwise specifically noted, these characteristics apply to all of the research on children of lesbian and gay parents described in this section. Research on children born in the context of heterosexual relationships is presented first, followed by a description of new work with children born to or adopted by lesbian and gay parents.

Research on Children Born in the Context of Heterosexual Relationships

As with research on lesbian mothers, much of the impetus for research in this area has been generated by judicial concerns about the psychosocial development of children residing with gay or lesbian parents. Research in each of three main areas of judicial concern—namely, children's sexual identity, other aspects of children's personal development, and children social relationships—is summarized here. For other recent reviews of this material, see Falk (1989), Gibbs (1988), Green and Bozett (1991), Patterson (1992), and Tasker and Golombok (1991).

Reflecting issues relevant in the largest number of custody disputes, most of the research compares development of children with custodial lesbian mothers to that of children with custodial heterosexual mothers. Since many children living in lesbian mother–headed households have undergone the experience of parental divorce and separation, children living in families headed by divorced but heterosexual mothers are widely believed to provide the best comparison group. Although some studies focus exclusively on children of gay men or lesbians (Green, 1978; Paul, 1986), most compare children in divorced lesbian mother–headed families with children in divorced heterosexual mother–headed families.

SEXUAL IDENTITY

Following Money and Ehrhardt (1972), I consider research on three aspects of sexual identity here. Gender identity concerns a person's self-identification as male or female. Gender-role behavior concerns the extent to which a person's activities, occupations, and the like are regarded by the culture as masculine, feminine, or both. Sexual orientation refers to a person's attraction to and choice of sexual partners—heterosexual, homosexual, or bisexual. To examine the possibility that children in the custody of lesbian mothers experience disruptions of sexual identity, I describe research findings relevant to each of these three major areas of concern.

Research on gender identity has failed to reveal any differences in the development of children as a function of their parents' sexual orientation. In one of the earliest studies, Kirkpatrick, Smith, and Roy (1981) compared the development of twenty 5- to 12-year-old children of lesbian mothers to that of twenty same-aged children of heterosexual mothers. In projective testing, most children in both groups drew a same-sex figure first, a finding that fell within expected norms. Of those who drew an opposite-sex figure first, only three (one with a lesbian mother, and two with heterosexual mothers) showed concern about gender issues in clinical interviews. Similar findings have been reported in projective testing by other investigators (Green, 1978; Green, Mandel, Hotvedt, Gray, & Smith, 1986). Studies using more direct methods of assessment (e.g., Golombok, Spencer, & Rutter, 1983) have yielded similar results. No evidence for difficulties in gender identity among children of lesbian mothers has been reported.

Research on gender-role behavior has also failed to reveal difficulties in the development of children with lesbian mothers. Green (1978) reported that twenty of twenty-one children of lesbian mothers in his sample named a favorite toy consistent with conventional sex-typed toy preferences, and that all twenty-one children reported vocational choices within typical limits for conventional sex roles. Results consistent with those described by Green have also been reported for children by Golombok et al. (1983), Hoeffer (1981), and Kirkpatrick et al. (1981); and for adult daughters of lesbian mothers, by Gottman (1990). In interviews with fifty-six children of lesbians and forty-eight children of heterosexual mothers, Green et al. (1986) found no differences with respect to favorite television programs, television characters, games, or toys. These investigators did, however, report that daughters of lesbian mothers were more likely to be described as taking part in rough and tumble play or as playing with "masculine" toys such as trucks or guns, but they found no comparable differences for sons. In all of these studies, the behavior and preferences of lesbian mothers' children were seen as falling within normal limits.

Rees (1979) administered the Bem Sex Role Inventory to twelve young adolescent offspring of lesbian mothers and twelve same-aged youngsters of heterosexual mothers. Although children of lesbian and heterosexual mothers did not differ on masculinity or on androgyny, adolescent offspring of lesbian mothers reported greater psychological femininity than did their same-aged peers with heterosexual mothers. This result seems to run counter to expectations based on stereotypes of lesbians as lacking in femininity. Overall, research has failed to reveal any notable difficulties in the development of sex-role behavior among children of lesbian mothers.

A number of investigators have also studied sexual orientation, the third component of sexual identity. For instance, Huggins (1989) interviewed thirty-six youngsters who were between 13 and 19 years of age; half were the offspring of lesbian mothers and half had mothers who were heterosexual in their orientation. No children of lesbian mothers identified themselves as lesbian or gay, but one child of a heterosexual mother did; this difference was not statistically significant. Similar results have been reported by Golombok and her colleagues (1983), Gottman (1990), Green (1978), Paul (1986), and Rees (1979); a few children of lesbian mothers have identified themselves as gay, lesbian, or bisexual, but their numbers did not exceed expectations based on presumed population base rates. Studies of the offspring of gay fathers have yielded similar results (Bozett, 1980, 1982, 1987, 1989; Miller, 1979). None of the evidence to date suggests that the offspring of lesbian or gay parents are any more likely than those of heterosexual parents to become lesbian or gay themselves.

Despite the consistency of the findings, this research can be criticized on a variety of grounds. For instance, many lesbians do not self-identify as such until adulthood (see Brown, Chapter 1); for this reason, studies of sexual orientation among adolescents may count as heterosexual some individuals who will come out as lesbian later in life. Concern has also been voiced that, in many studies comparing children of divorced heterosexual mothers with children of divorced lesbian mothers, lesbian mothers were more likely to be living with a romantic partner; in these cases, variables of maternal sexual orientation and household composition have been confounded. While these and other methodological issues still await resolution, it remains true that no significant problems in the development of sexual identity among children of lesbian mothers have yet been identified.

OTHER ASPECTS OF PERSONAL DEVELOPMENT

Studies of other aspects of personal development among children of gay and lesbian parents have assessed psychiatric and behavior problems (Golombok et al., 1983; Kirkpatrick et al., 1981), personality (Gottman, 1990), self-concept (Huggins, 1989; Puryear, 1983), locus of control (Puryear, 1983; Rees, 1979), moral judgment (Rees, 1979), and intelligence (Green et al., 1986). As was true for sexual identity, studies of other aspects of personal development have revealed no significant differences between children of lesbian or gay parents and children of heterosexual parents. On the basis of existing evidence, then, hypotheses that children of gay and lesbian parents suffer deficits in personal development seem to be without empirical foundation.

SOCIAL RELATIONSHIPS

Studies assessing potential differences between children of gay and lesbian versus heterosexual parents have sometimes included assessments of children's social relationships. Because of concerns voiced by the courts that children of lesbian and gay parents might encounter difficulties among their peers, the most common focus of attention has been on peer relations. Studies in this area have consistently found that school-aged children of lesbian mothers report a predominantly same-sex peer group and that the quality of their peer relations is described by their mothers and by the investigators as good (Golombok et al., 1983; Green, 1978; Green et al., 1986). Anecdotal and first-person accounts describe children's worries about being stigmatized as a result of their parents' sexual orientation (Pollack & Vaughn, 1987; Rafkin, 1990), but available research provides no evidence for the proposition that the development of children of lesbian mothers is compromised by difficulties in peer relations. Further research would be especially valuable in this area.

Research has also been directed toward description of children's relationships with adults, especially fathers. For instance, Golombok et al. (1983) found that children of lesbian mothers were more likely than children of heterosexual mothers to have contact with their fathers. Most children of lesbian mothers had some contact with their father during the year preceding the study, but most children of heterosexual mothers had not; indeed, almost a third of the children of lesbian mothers reported at least weekly contact with their fathers, whereas only one in twenty of the children of heterosexual mothers reported this. Kirkpatrick and her colleagues (1981) also reported that lesbian mothers in their sample were more concerned than heterosexual mothers that their children have opportunities for good relationships with adult men, including fathers. Lesbian mothers' own social networks have been found to include both men and women, and their offspring as a result have contact with adults of both sexes. Hare and Richards (1993) reported that the great majority (90%) of children living with divorced lesbian mothers in their sample also had contact with their fathers. Overall, results of the meager research to date suggest that children of lesbian parents have satisfactory relationships with adults of both sexes.

Concerns that children of lesbian or gay parents are more likely than children of heterosexual parents to be sexually abused have also been voiced by judges in the context of child custody disputes. Results of research in this area show that the great majority of adults who perpetrate sexual abuse are male; sexual abuse of children by adult women is very rare (Finkelhor & Russel, 1984; Jones & MacFarlane, 1980). Lesbian mothers are thus extremely unlikely to expose their children to sexual abuse. Moreover, the overwhelming majority of child sexual abuse cases involve an adult male abusing a young female (Jones & MacFarlane, 1980). Gay men are no more likely than heterosexual men to perpetrate child sexual abuse (Groth & Birnbaum, 1978). Fears that children in custody of gay or lesbian parents might be at heightened risk for sexual abuse are thus without empirical foundation.

DIVERSITY AMONG CHILDREN WITH DIVORCED LESBIAN
OR GAY PARENTS

Despite the tremendous diversity of gay and lesbian communities (Blumenfeld & Raymond, 1988), research on differences among children of lesbian and gay parents is still very limited. Here I focus on the impact of parental psychological and relationship status as well as on the influence of other stresses and supports.

One important dimension of variability among gay and lesbian families concerns whether or not the custodial parent is involved in a romantic relationship, and if so, what implications this may have for children. Pagelow (1980), Kirkpatrick et al. (1981), and Golombok et al. (1983) all reported that divorced lesbian mothers were more likely than divorced heterosexual mothers to be living with a romantic partner. Huggins (1989) reported that self-esteem among daughters of lesbian mothers whose lesbian partners lived with them was higher than that among daughters of lesbian mothers who did not live with a partner. This finding might be interpreted to mean that mothers who are high in self-esteem are more likely to be involved in romantic relationships and to have daughters who are also high in self-esteem, but many other interpretations are also possible. In view of the small sample size and absence of conventional statistical tests, Huggins' (1989) finding should be interpreted with caution. In view of the judicial attention that lesbian mothers' romantic relationships have received during custody proceedings (Falk, 1989; Hitchens, 1979/80; Kirkpatrick, 1987), however, it is surprising that more research has not examined the impact of this variable on children.

Rand, Graham, and Rawlings (1982) found that lesbian mothers' sense of psychological well-being was related to the extent to which they were open about their lesbian identity with employers, ex-husbands, and children. In this sample, a mother who felt more able to disclose her lesbian identity was also more likely to express a greater sense of well-being. In light of the consistent finding that children's adjustment in heterosexual families is often related to maternal mental health (Rutter, Izard, & Read, 1986; Sameroff & Chandler, 1975), one might expect factors which enhance mental health among lesbian mothers also to benefit the children of these women. No research investigating this possibility has yet been reported, however.

Another area of great diversity among families with a gay or lesbian parent is the degree to which a parent's sexual identity is accepted by other significant people in children's lives. Huggins (1989) found a tendency for children whose fathers rejected maternal lesbianism to report lower self-esteem than those whose fathers were neutral or positive. Due to small sample size and absence of conventional statistical tests, however, this finding should be seen as suggestive rather than definitive. Huggins' results raise questions about the extent to which reactions of important adults in a child's environment can influence responses to discovery of a parent's gay or lesbian identity.

Effects of the age at which children learn of parents' gay or lesbian identities have also been a topic of study. Paul (1986) reported that those who were told either in childhood or in late adolescence found the news easier to cope with than did those who first learned of it during early to middle adolescence. Huggins (1989) reported that those who learned of maternal lesbianism in childhood had higher self-esteem than did those who were not informed until adolescence. Some writers have suggested that early adolescence is a particularly difficult time for children to learn of their parents' lesbian or gay identities (Baptiste, 1987; Lewis, 1980).

As this brief review reveals, research on diversity among families with gay and lesbian parents is just beginning (Freiberg, 1990; Martin, 1989). Existing data favor early disclosure of identity to children, positive maternal mental health, and a supportive milieu, but the available data are still limited. No information is yet available on differences stemming from race or ethnicity, family economic circumstances, cultural environments, or related variables. Because none of the published work has employed observational measures or longitudinal designs, little is known about behavior within these families or about any changes over time. It is clear that much remains to be learned about differences among gay and lesbian families and the impact of such differences on children growing up in these homes.

Research on Children Born to or Adopted by Lesbian Mothers

Although many writers have recently noted an increase in child-bearing among lesbians, research with these families remains very new (Patterson, 1992, in 1994a; Polikoff, 1990; Pollack & Vaughn, 1987;

Riley, 1988; Weston, 1991). In this section, I summarize the research to date on children born to or adopted by lesbian mothers. Although some gay men are also undertaking parenthood after coming out, no research has yet been reported on these families.

In one of the first systematic studies of children born to lesbians, Steckel (1985, 1987) compared the progress of separation-individuation among eleven preschool children born by means of DI to lesbian couples with that among eleven same-aged children of heterosexual couples. Using parent interviews, parent and teacher Q-sorts, and structured doll-play techniques, Steckel compared independence, ego functions, and object relations among children in the two types of families. Her main results documented impressive similarity in development among them. Similar findings, based on extensive interviews with five lesbian mother families were also reported by McCandlish (1987).

Steckel (1985, 1987) did, however, report some suggestive differences between groups. Children of heterosexual parents saw themselves as somewhat more aggressive than did children of lesbians, and they were seen by both parents and teachers as more bossy, domineering, and negativistic. Children of lesbian parents, on the other hand, saw themselves as more lovable and were seen by parents and teachers as more affectionate, more responsive, and more protective toward younger children. In view of the small sample size, and the large number of statistical tests performed, these results must be considered suggestive rather than definitive. Steckel's (1985, 1987) work is, however, worthy of special attention in that it was the first to make systematic comparisons of development among children born to lesbian and to heterosexual couples.

The first study to examine psychosocial development among preschool and school-aged children born to or adopted by lesbian mothers was conducted by Patterson (1994a). Thirty-seven 4- to 9-year-old children were studied, using a variety of standardized measures, including the Achenbach and Edelbrock Child Behavior Checklist, a measure of social competence and behavior problems, and the Eder Children's Self-View Questionnaire, a measure of self-concepts. Open-ended interviews were used to assess preferences associated with sex-role behavior.

The results showed that children scored in the normal range for all measures. On the Child Behavior Checklist, for example, children of lesbian mothers' scores for social competece, internalizing behavior problems, and externalizing behavior problems differed significantly from the scores for a large clinical sample used in norming the test, but did not differ from the scores for a large representative sample of normal children also used in norming the test (Achenbach & Edelbrock,

1983). Likewise, children of lesbian mothers reported sex-role preferences within the expected range for children of this age. On most subscales of the self-concept measure, answers given by children of lesbian
mothers did not differ from those given by same-aged children of heterosexual mothers studied in the standardization sample.

On two subscales of the self-concept measure, however, children of
lesbian mothers reported feeling more reactions to stress (e.g., feeling
angry, scared, or upset), but a greater sense of well-being (e.g., feeling
joyful, content, and comfortable with themselves) than did the same-
aged children of heterosexual mothers in the standardization sample.
One possible interpretation is that children of lesbian mothers reported
greater reactivity to stress because, in fact, they experienced greater
stress in their daily lives than other children did. Another possibility is
that, regardless of actual stress levels, children of lesbian mothers were
better able to acknowledge both positive and negative aspects of their
emotional experience. Although this latter interpretation is perhaps
more consistent with the differences in both stress reactions and well-
being, clarification of these and other potential interpretations must
await the results of further research.

While results of Patterson's (1994a) study addressed normative questions, a more recent report (Patterson, in press) based on the same
sample focused on individual differences. In particular, Patterson (in
press) studied the twenty-six families in her sample that were headed
by a lesbian couple, and assessed division of labor, satisfaction with
division of labor, and satisfaction with couple relationships as predictors of children's adjustment. Results revealed that parents' satisfaction with their relationships, though high, was not associated with outcomes for children. Parents were, however, more satisfied and children
were more well-adjusted when labor involved in childcare was more
evenly distributed between the parents. These results suggest the importance of family process variables as predictors of child adjustment
in lesbian as well as in heterosexual families (Patterson, 1992).

Conclusions

Research on lesbian mothers, gay fathers, and their children is a phenomenon of the last 15 years. Systematic study of lesbian and gay families with children began in the context of judicial challenges to the fit-
ness of lesbian and gay parents. For this reason, much of the early
research was designed to evaluate judicial presumptions about negative consequences for the psychological health and well-being of parents and children in lesbian and gay families. Although much remains
to be done to understand the conditions that foster positive mental
health among lesbian mothers, gay fathers, and their children, the re-

sults of early research are exceptionally clear. Results of the empirical research provide no reason, under the prevailing "best interests of the child" standard, to deny or curtail parental rights of lesbian or gay parents on the basis of their sexual orientation; nor do systematic studies provide any reason to believe that lesbians or gay men are less suitable than heterosexuals to serve as adoptive or foster parents.

With these conclusions in mind, researchers are now also beginning to turn their attention to areas of diversity among gay and lesbian families and starting to examine conditions that help gay and lesbian families flourish. This transition, now well under way, appears to be gathering momentum, and it justifies the conclusion that research on lesbian and gay families has reached a significant turning point (Patterson, 1992, in 1994c). Having addressed negative assumptions represented in psychological theory, judicial opinion, and popular prejudice, researchers are now in a position to explore a broader range of issues. In this regard, much work remains to be done.

From a methodological viewpoint, a number of directions seem especially promising. Longitudinal research is needed to follow families over time and illuminate how changing life circumstances affect both parents and children. There is also a clear need for observational studies, and for work conducted with larger samples. A greater focus on family interactions and processes as well as on structural variables is also likely to be valuable (Patterson, 1992).

From a substantive point of view, many issues relevant to lesbian and gay families are in need of study. First and most obvious is the need for studies representing the demographic diversity of lesbian and gay families. With few exceptions (e.g., Hill, 1987), existing research involves mostly white, well-educated, relatively affluent families who live in urban areas in the United States. More work is needed to understand differences that are based on race and ethnicity, family economic circumstances, and cultural environments. Research of this kind should elucidate differences as well as commonalities among lesbian and gay families with children.

Future research should also, insofar as possible, encompass more levels of analysis. Existing research has most often focused on children or on their parents, considered as individuals. As valuable as this emphasis has been, it is also important to consider couples and families as such. Assessments of dyadic adjustment or family climate can enhance understanding of individual-level variables such as self-esteem. When families are considered at different levels of analysis, nested within the neighborhood, regional, and cultural contexts in which they live, a more comprehensive understanding of lesbian and gay families is likely to emerge.

In this effort, it will be valuable to devote attention to family process as well as family structure. How do lesbian and gay families negotiate their interactions with institutional settings such as the school and the workplace (Casper et al., 1992)? How are family processes and interactions affected by economic, cultural, religious, and legal aspects of the contexts in which families live? How do climates of opinion that prevail in their communities affect lesbian and gay families, and how do families cope with prejudice and discrimination when these are encountered?

Gender deserves special attention in this regard. Inasmuch as lesbian and gay relationships encourage the separation of gender and behavioral roles, one might expect to find considerable variability among families in the ways they carry out essential family, household, and childcare tasks (Hand, 1991; Osterweil, 1991; Patterson, in press). In what ways do nontraditional divisions of labor affect children who grow up in lesbian and gay homes? And in what ways does the performance of nontraditional tasks affect parents themselves? In general terms, it will be valuable to learn more about the relative importance of gender and behavioral roles in lesbian and gay families with children.

One additional issue that should be given special emphasis is the conceptualization of parents' sexual identities. In the research literature on gay and lesbian parenting, scant attention has been devoted to the fluidity of sexual identities over time, or to the implications of such fluidity for children. For instance, many parents are probably bisexual to some degree, rather than exclusively heterosexual, gay, or lesbian; yet this is rarely noted, much less studied directly in the existing research literature. Increasing numbers of adults seem to be identifying themselves as bisexual (see Fox, Chapter 3). Future research might benefit from closer attention to issues in assessment of parental sexual orientation.

In conclusion, although research to date on lesbian mothers, gay fathers, and their children has been fruitful, there is yet much important work to be done. Having addressed many of the heterosexist prejudices of jurists, theorists, and others, researchers are now poised to examine a broader range of issues raised by the emergence of different kinds of lesbian and gay families with children. Results of future work in this area have the potential to increase our knowledge about gay and lesbian families, stimulate innovations in our theoretical understanding of human development, and inform legal rulings and public policies relevant to lesbian mothers, gay fathers, and their children.

References

Achenbach, T. M., & Edelbrock, C. (1983). *Manual for the Child Behavior Checklist and Revised Child Behavior Profile*. Burlington: University of Vermont, Department of Psychiatry.

Baptiste, D. A. (1987). Psychotherapy with gay/lesbian couples and their children in "stepfamilies": A challenge for marriage and family therapists. In E. Coleman (Ed.), *Integrated identity for gay men and lesbians: Psychotherapeutic approaches for emotional well-being* (pp. 223–238). New York: Harrington Park Press.

Baumrind, D. (1967). Childcare practices anteceding three patterns of preschool behavior. *Genetic Psychology Monographs, 75,* 43–88.

Baumrind, D., & Black, A. E. (1967). Socialization practices associated with dimensions of competence in preschool boys and girls. *Child Development, 38,* 291–327.

Bem, S. L. (1983). Gender schema theory and its implications for child development: Raising gender-aschematic children in a gender-schematic society. *Signs: Journal of Women in Culture and Society, 8,* 598–616.

Bigner, J. J., & Bozett, F. W. (1990). Parenting by gay fathers. In F. W. Bozett & M. B. Sussman (Eds.), *Homosexuality and family relations* (pp. 155–176). New York: Harrington Park Press.

Bigner, J. J., & Jacobsen, R. B. (1989a). The value of children to gay and heterosexual fathers. In F. W. Bozett (Ed.), *Homosexuality and the family* (pp. 163–172). New York: Harrington Park Press.

Bigner, J. J., & Jacobsen, R. B. (1989b). Parenting behaviors of homosexual and heterosexual fathers. In F. W. Bozett (Ed.), *Homosexuality and the family* (pp. 173–186). New York: Harrington Park Press.

Bigner, J. J., & Jacobsen, R. B. (1992). Adult responses to child behavior and attitudes toward fathering: Gay and nongay fathers. *Journal of Homosexuality, 23,* 99–112.

Blumenfeld, W. J., & Raymond, D. (1988). *Looking at gay and lesbian life.* Boston: Beacon.

Bozett, F. W. (1980). Gay fathers: How and why they disclose their homosexuality to their children. *Family Relations, 29,* 173–179.

Bozett, F. W. (1981a). Gay fathers: Evolution of the gay father identity. *American Journal of Orthopsychiatry, 51,* 552–559.

Bozett, F. W. (1981b). Gay fathers: Identity conflict resolution through integrative sanctioning. *Alternative lifestyles, 4,* 90–107.

Bozett, F. W. (1982). Heterogeneous couples in heterosexual marriages: Gay men and straight women. *Journal of Marital and Family Therapy, 8,* 81–89.

Bozett, F. W. (1987). Children of gay fathers. In F. W. Bozett (Ed.), *Gay and lesbian parents* (pp. 39–57). New York: Praeger.

Bozett, F. W. (1989). Gay fathers: A review of the literature. In F. W. Bozett (Ed.), *Homosexuality and the family* (pp. 137–162). New York: Harrington Park Press.

Bronfenbrenner, U. (1960). Freudian theories of identification and their derivatives. *Child Development, 31,* 15–40.

Casper, V., Schultz, S., & Wickens, E. (1992). Breaking the silences: Lesbian and gay parents and the schools. *Teachers College Record, 94,* 109–137.

Chodorow, N. (1978). *The reproduction of mothering: Psychoanalysis and the sociology of gender.* Berkeley: University of California Press.

Cowan, C. P., & Cowan, P. A. (1992). *When partners become parents: The big life change for couples.* New York: Basic Books.

Cramer, D. (1986). Gay parents and their children: A review of research and practical implications. *Journal of Counseling and Development, 64,* 504–507.

Crawford, S. (1987). Lesbian families: Psychosocial stress and the family-building process. In Boston Lesbian Psychologies Collective (Eds.), *Lesbian psychologies: Explorations and challenges* (pp. 195–214). Urbana: University of Illinois Press.

Crosbie-Burnett, M., & Helmbrecht, L. (1993). A descriptive empirical study of gay male stepfamilies. *Family Relations, 42,* 256–262.

D'Emilio, J. (1983). *Sexual politics, sexual communities: The makings of a homosexual minority in the United States, 1940–1970.* Chicago: University of Chicago Press.

Editors of the Harvard Law Review (1990). *Sexual orientation and the law.* Cambridge, MA: Harvard University Press.

Faderman, I. (1991). *Odd girls and twilight lovers: A history of lesbian life in twentieth century America.* New York: Columbia University Press.

Falk, P. J. (1989). Lesbian mothers: Psychosocial assumptions in family law. *American Psychologist, 44,* 941–947.

Finkelhor, D., & Russell, D. (1984). Women as perpetrators: Review of the evidence. In D. Finkelhor (Ed.), *Child sexual abuse: New theory and research* (pp. 171–187). New York: Free Press.

Freiberg, P. (1990). Lesbian moms can give kids empowering role models. *APA Monitor, 21,* 33.

Gibbs, E. D. (1988). Psychosocial development of children raised by lesbian mothers: A review of research. *Women and Therapy, 8,* 55–75.

Gilman, C. P. (1979). *Herland.* New York: Pantheon. (Originally published 1915).

Golombok, S., Spencer, A., & Rutter, M. (1983). Children in lesbian and single-parent households: Psychosexual and psychiatric appraisal. *Journal of Child Psychology and Psychiatry, 24,* 551–572.

Gonsiorek, J. C. (1991). The empirical basis for the demise of the illness model of homosexuality. In J. C. Gonsiorek & J. D. Weinrich (Eds.), *Homosexuality: Research implications for public policy* (pp. 115–136). Newbury Park, CA: Sage.

Gottman, J. S. (1990). Children of gay and lesbian parents. In F. W. Bozett & M. B. Sussman (Eds.), *Homosexuality and family relations* (pp. 177–196). New York: Harrington Park Press.

Green, G. D., & Bozett, F. W. (1991). Lesbian mothers and gay fathers. In J. C. Gonsiorek & J. D. Weinrich (Eds.), *Homosexuality: Research implications for public policy* (pp. 197–214). Thousand Oaks, CA: Sage.

Green, R. (1978). Sexual identity of 37 children raised by homosexual or transsexual parents. *American Journal of Psychiatry, 135,* 692–697.

Green, R., Mandel, J. B., Hotvedt, M. E., Gray, J., & Smith, L. (1986). Lesbian mothers and their children: A comparison with solo parent heterosexual mothers and their children. *Archives of Sexual Behavior, 7,* 175–181.

Groth, A. N., & Birnbaum, H. J. (1978). Adult sexual orientation and attraction to underage persons. *Archives of Sexual Behavior, 7,* 175–181.

Hand, S. I. (1991). The lesbian parenting couple. Unpublished doctoral dissertation, The Professional School of Psychology, San Francisco.

Hare, J., & Richards, L. (1993). Children raised by lesbian couples: Does the context of birth affect father and partner involvement? *Family Relations,* *42,* 249–255.

Harris, M. B., & Turner, P. H. (1985/86). Gay and lesbian parents. *Journal of Homosexuality, 12,* 101–113.

Hill, M. (1987). Child-rearing attitudes of Black lesbian mothers. In Boston Lesbian Psychologies Collective (Eds.), *Lesbian psychologies: Explorations and challenges* (pp. 215–226). Urbana: University of Illinois Press.

Hitchens, D. J. (1979/80). Social attitudes, legal standards, and personal trauma in child custody cases. *Journal of Homosexuality, 5,* 1–20, 89–95.

Hoeffer, B. (1981). Children's acquisition of sex-role behavior in lesbian-mother families. *American Journal of Orthopsychiatry, 5,* 536–544.

Huggins, S. L. (1989). A comparative study of self-esteem of adolescent children of divorced lesbian mothers and divorced heterosexual mothers. In F. W. Bozett (Ed.), *Homosexuality and the family* (pp. 123–135). New York: Harrington Park Press.

Huston, A. (1983). Sex typing. In E. M. Hetherington (Ed.), P. H. Mussen (Series Ed.), *Handbook of child psychology: Vol. 4. Socialization, personality, and social development* (pp. 387–487). New York: Wiley.

Jones, B. M., & McFarlane, K., Eds. (1980). *Sexual abuse of children: Selected readings.* Washington, DC: National Center on Child Abuse and Neglect.

Kirkpatrick, M. (1987). Clinical implications of lesbian mother studies. *Journal of Homosexuality, 13,* 201–211.

Kirkpatrick, M., Smith, C., & Roy, R. (1981). Lesbian mothers and their children: A comparative survey. *American Journal of Orthopsychiatry, 51,* 545–551.

Kleber, D. J., Howell, R. J., & Tibbits-Kleber, A. L. (1986). The impact of parental homosexuality in child custody cases: A review of the literature. *Bulletin of the American Academy of Psychiatry and Law, 14,* 81–87.

Kohlberg, L. (1966). A cognitive-developmental analysis of children's sex-role concepts and attitudes. In E. E. Maccoby (Ed.), *The development of sex differences* (pp. 82–173). Stanford, CA: Stanford University Press.

Koepke, L., Hare, J., & Moran, P. B. (1992). Relationship quality in a sample of lesbian couples with children and child-free lesbian couples. *Family Relations, 41,* 224–229.

Kweskin, S. L., & Cook, A. S. (1982). Heterosexual and homosexual mothers' self-described sex-role behavior and ideal sex-role behavior in children. *Sex Roles, 8,* 967–975.

Lewis, K. G. (1980). Children of lesbians: Their point of view. *Social Work, 25,* 198–203.

Lyons, T. A. (1983). Lesbian mothers' custody fears. *Women and Therapy, 2,* 231–240.

Martin, A. (1989). The planned lesbian and gay family: Parenthood and children. *Newsletter of the Society for the Psychological Study of Lesbian and Gay Issues, 5,* 6 & 16–17.

McCandlish, B. (1987). Against all odds: Lesbian mother family dynamics. In F. Bozett (Ed.), *Gay and lesbian parents* (pp. 23–38). New York: Praeger.

McPherson, D. (1993). Gay parenting couples: Parenting arrangements, arrangement satisfaction, and relationship satisfaction. Unpublished doctoral dissertation, Pacific Graduate School of Psychology.

Miller, B. (1979). Gay fathers and their children. *Family Coordinator, 28,* 544–552.

Miller, J. A., Jacobsen, R. B., & Bigner, J. J. (1981). The child's home environment for lesbian versus heterosexual mothers: A neglected area of research. *Journal of Homosexuality, 7,* 49–56.

Mucklow, B. M., & Phelan, G. K. (1979). Lesbian and traditional mothers' responses to adult responses to child behavior and self concept. *Psychological Reports, 44,* 880–882.

Money, J., & Ehrhardt, A. A. (1972). *Man and woman, boy and girl: The differentiation and dimorphism of gender identity from conception to maturity.* Baltimore: Johns Hopkins University Press.

Osterweil, D. A. (1991). Correlates of relationship satisfaction in lesbian couples who are parenting their first child together. Unpublished doctoral dissertation, California School of Professional Psychology, Berkeley/Alameda.

Pagelow, M. D. (1980). Heterosexual and lesbian single mothers: A comparison of problems, coping and solutions. *Journal of Homosexuality, 5,* 198–204.

Patterson, C. J. (1992). Children of lesbian and gay parents. *Child Development, 63,* 1025–1042.

Patterson, C. J. (1994a). Children of the lesbian baby boom: Behavioral adjustment, self-concepts, and sex-role identity. In B. Greene & G. Herek (Eds.), *Contemporary perspectives on lesbian and gay psychology: Theory, research, and applications* (pp. 156–175). Thousand Oaks, CA: Sage.

Patterson, C. J. (in 1994b). Lesbian and gay couples considering parenthood: An agenda for research, service, and advocacy. *Journal of Gay and Lesbian Social Services, 1,* 33–55.

Patterson, C. J. (1994c). Lesbian and gay families. *Current Directions in Psychological Science, 3,* 62–64.

Patterson, C. J. (in press). Families of the lesbian baby boom: Parents' division of labor and children's adjustment. *Developmental Psychology.*

Paul, J. P. (1986). Growing up with a gay, lesbian, or bisexual parent: An exploratory study of experiences and perceptions. Unpublished doctoral dissertation, University of California at Berkeley, Berkeley, CA.

Pennington, S. (1987). Children of lesbian mothers. In F. W. Bozett (Ed.), *Gay and lesbian parents* (pp. 58–74). New York: Praeger.

Pies, C. (1985). *Considering parenthood.* San Francisco: Spinsters/Aunt Lute.

Pies, C. (1990). Lesbians and the choice to parent. In F. W. Bozett & M. B. Sussman (Ed.), *Homosexuality and family relations* (pp. 137–154). New York: Harrington Park Press.

Polikoff, N. (1990). This child does have two mothers: Redefining parenthood to meet the needs of children in lesbian mother and other nontraditional families. *The Georgetown Law Review, 78,* 459–575.

Pollack, S., & Vaughn, J. (1987). *Politics of the heart: A lesbian parenting anthology.* Ithaca, NY: Firebrand Books.

Puryear, D. (1983). A comparison between the children of lesbian mothers and the children of heterosexual mothers. Unpublished doctoral dissertation, California School of Professional Psychology, Berkeley, CA.

Rafkin, L. (1990). *Different mothers: Sons and daughters of lesbians talk about their lives.* Pittsburgh: Cleis Press.

Rand, C., Graham, D. L. R., & Rawlings, E. I. (1982). Psychological health and factors the court seeks to to control in lesbian mother custody trials. *Journal of Homosexuality, 8,* 27–39.

Rees, R. L. (1979). *A comparison of children of lesbian and single heterosexual mothers on three measures of socialization.* California School of Professional Psychology, Berkeley, CA.

Ricketts, W. (1991). *Lesbians and gay men as foster parents.* Portland: National Child Welfare Resource Center, University of Southern Maine.

Ricketts, W., & Achtenberg, R. (1990). Adoption and foster parenting for lesbians and gay men: Creating new traditions in family. In F. W. Bozett & M. B. Sussman (Eds.), *Homosexuality and family relations* (pp. 83–118). New York: Harrington Park Press.

Riley, C. (1988). American kinship: A lesbian account. *Feminist Issues, 8,* 75–94.

Rivera, R. (1991). Sexual orientation and the law. In J. C. Gonsiorek & J. D. Weinrich (Eds.), *Homosexuality: Research implications for public policy* (pp. 81–100). Newbury Park, CA: Sage.

Robinson, B. E., & Skeen, P. (1982). Sex-role orientation of gay fathers versus gay nonfathers. *Perceptual and Motor Skills, 55,* 1055–1059.

Rohrbaugh, J. B. (1988). Choosing children: Psychological issues in lesbian parenting. *Women and Therapy, 8,* 51–63.

Rutter, M., Izard, C. E., & Read, P. B. (Eds.), (1986). *Depression in young people: Developmental and clinical perspectives.* New York: Guilford.

Sameroff, A. J., & Chandler, M. (1975). Reproductive risk and the continuum of caretaking casualty. In F. D. Horowitz (Ed.), *Review of child development research* (Vol. 4). Chicago: University of Chicago Press.

Sbordone, A. J. (1993). Gay men choosing fatherhood. Unpublished doctoral dissertation, Department of Psychology, City University of New York.

Skeen, P., & Robinson, B. (1985). Gay fathers' and gay nonfathers' relationships with their parents. *Journal of sex research, 21,* 86–91.

Steckel, A. (1985). Separation–individuation in children of lesbian and heterosexual couples. Unpublished doctoral dissertation, The Wright Institute Graduate School, Berkeley, CA.

Steckel, A. (1987). Psychosocial development of children of lesbian mothers. In F. W. Bozett (Ed.), *Gay and lesbian parents* (pp. 75–85). New York: Praeger.

Tasker, F. L., & Golombok, S. (1991). Children raised by lesbian mothers: The empirical evidence. *Family Law, 21,* 184–187.

Thompson, N., McCandless, B., & Strickland, B. (1971). Personal adjustment of male and female homosexuals and heterosexuals. *Journal of Abnormal Psychology, 78,* 237–240.

Weston, K. (1991). *Families we choose: Lesbians, gays, kinship.* New York: Columbia University Press.

IV

Community and Contextual Issues

12

Lesbian, Gay, and Bisexual Communities

Anthony R. D'Augelli and Linda D. Garnets

This chapter reviews the communities that lesbians and gay men have formed in their attempts to create settings for themselves in American society. Lesbians, gay men, and bisexual people are perhaps unique in their creation of "communities" because their invisibility and their oppressed status have hampered their efforts to find each other. Within psychology, the concept of community has represented both the literal environments in which people live and the affiliative links they develop to kindred others without regard to proximity. These communities may or may not overlap. For example, many lesbians and gay men seek out others in settings far removed from their homes and, indeed, might feel unsupported in their local neighborhoods.

Many concepts of lesbian and gay community life have been suggested. Theorists have conceptualized lesbian and gay communities as "a bounded group possessing special norms and a particular argot" (Simon & Gagnon, 1967), a "psychological kinship system" (Barnhart, 1975), a "sociopsychological unity" (Wolf, 1979), a "satellite culture" (Humphreys & Miller, 1980), a "communal sense" (Rainone, 1986), and "a range of social groups in which lesbian individuals may feel a sense of camaraderie with other lesbians" (Krieger, 1982). Lockard (1985) defines the lesbian community as

   . . . interacting social networks of lesbians, who share a group identity or consciousness based on their sexual preference along with certain basic values, and who gather together to create and maintain institutions that support their social interactions, and which also serve to support the group identity and shared values. (p. 86).

Murray (1992) argues that lesbian and gay communities meet technical criteria for the term "community" as do other social collectives, such as ethnic communities. In his view, territories with unusually large concentrations of lesbians, gay men, and bisexuals encourage the perception of community, but not all people engaging in same-sex sexual behavior would share that perception or the need for social interaction. He defines community as "a concentration of interaction among those who identify themselves as gay into gay primary groups, concentration of space (of residence, but, more important, of community institutions) in specifiable territory, learned (though not monolithic) norms, institutional completeness, collective action, and a sense of shared history" (Murray, 1992: 113). This echoes Sarason's (1974) classic definition of community:

A community is more than a political or geographical area. It contains a variety of institutions which may be formally or informally related to each other—or not related. It is made up of myriads of groups, transient or permanent, which may have similar or different purposes and vary in size, power, and composition. It possesses resources and vehicles for their disbursement. Its groups and institutions vary considerably in size, purposes, and the power they possess or seek. And a community has a distinctive history which, although it may be no longer relevant in the psychologial sense, is crucial for understanding some of its present qualities and social, political, religious, and economic characteristics. (p. 131)

In this chapter, we will not discuss how lesbians, gay men, and bisexual people live in particular geographical areas, though clearly the history of lesbian and gay life in this country is closely tied to a handful of metropolitan areas that, for one reason or another, attracted sufficient numbers of lesbians and gay men to generate communities. Much of this rich information is available in social histories (e.g., Bérubé, 1990; Cruikshank, 1992; D'Emilio, 1983; Faderman, 1991; Fitzgerald, 1986; Marcus, 1992). Nor will we describe how they live in "the community," in a general sense. We will, on the other hand, discuss general psychological processes in these "communities of creation," some of which also happen to be particular neighborhoods. We use Herrell's (1992) definition of lesbian and gay communities as deriving "not from parents and peers during childhood, but from adult participation in a network of institutions and from shared responses to the pervasive denial of social personality itself" (p. 248). That is, these communities evolve because of oppressive circumstances, and often function to direct resistance to this oppression. Because lesbian, gay, and bisexual communities reflect the cultural and historical contexts from which they emerged, we start with a brief overview of this history.

A Social History of Lesbian/Gay Communities

Prior to World War II, there were friendship networks who met in private settings and in the few gay/lesbian-oriented clubs and bars that were located in major metropolitan areas. These settings provided the principal sense of community available in that era. Faderman (1991) provides a comprehensive analysis of lesbian club culture of the 1920s through the 1940s, and Garber (1989) presents a thoughtful discussion of the lesbian/gay nature of the Harlem Renaissance of the 1920s.

The first major flourishing of lesbian and gay communities, however, occurred following World War II. The war created the conditions for the development of a collective identity—large numbers of gay men were drafted, many lesbians enlisted, and homoerotically oriented women and men could find each other in the sex-segregated military environment (Bérubé, 1990; D'Emilio, 1983).

Following the war, many who connected in the military continued their relationships. Some went on to organize social and political groups under the general rubric of "Homophile Rights." The Homophile Rights Movement initiated the beginnings of a gay/lesbian community by explicitly seeking to integrate lesbians and gay men into community life. In other words, the social settings frequented by lesbians and gay men prior to World War II provided safety, but did not encourage social change; the consequences of being seen outside of the bars or clubs were far too dangerous. In contrast, the Homophile Movement stimulated the emergence of a *public group identity*; lesbians and gay men were seen as members of a *collectively* oppressed minority. The postwar migration of lesbians and gay men to large metropolitan areas provided physical proximity; the repressive attacks on lesbians and gay men by McCarthy and other politicians provided public visibility, prompting a beginning awareness among lesbian/gay people of their commonality with others (D'Emilio, 1983). Of course, this awareness also underscored the dangers involved in public acknowledgment of membership in this hidden "community." Homosexuality was illegal in the United States at that time; not until 1962 did Illinois become the first state to decriminalize consensual same-sex behavior between adults.

In 1951, in Los Angeles, the first formal American gay rights organization, the Mattachine Society, was founded. The Mattachine Society consisted of men who formed groups in metropolitan areas like Chicago, Los Angeles, New York, and San Francisco. Despite its Marxist roots, the group developed an accommodationist philosophy which advocated treatment of lesbian/gay people like anyone else. In 1955, the Daughters of Bilitis was formed in San Francisco, providing similar social, educational, and consciousness-raising functions for lesbians. The primary focus of both groups was to help the lesbian/gay individual adjust to society by developing a positive self-image and educating the general public about the mistreatment of lesbians and gay men. The issue of homosexuality as pathology was considered the province of the "medical experts" of the time, whose conflicting, though predominantly pathologizing, opinions were presented in publications of both groups (Bayer, 1981; Esterberg, 1990).

In contrast to the accommodationist politics of the Mattachine and the Daughters of Bilitis in the 1950s, lesbian and gay communities of the 1960s relied on confrontation and protest to gain access to resources and eliminate discriminatory laws and policies, primarily in employment. Increasing information about homosexuality, especially groundbreaking empirical studies such as Hooker's (1957), which found no evidence of psychopathology in gay men, encouraged greater identification with lesbian/gay identity, although the identity remained highly socially stigmatized. A transition occurred in which negative societal attitudes about homosexuality were defined as the problem.

This transformation in cultural attitudes led to the event considered the spark that ignited the modern lesbian/gay rights movement. On June 27, 1969, the Stonewall rebellion occurred. This event consisted of several days of confrontations in which the more public segments of the local gay community rioted, following a routine police raid on a gay bar in the Greenwich Village neighborhood of New York City, the Stonewall Inn. This event marked the beginning of a period of consolidation of lesbian and gay communities in New York and other urban areas, along with the development of visible subcultures, the formation of lesbian/gay-defined settings and institutions, and intensified political mobilization.

Symbolizing active resistance to harassment and marginalization, Stonewall heralded a dramatic new phase of community-building whose ideological motto was "Out of the closets and into the streets" (Jay & Young, 1977). "Coming out"—public disclosure of sexual orientation to family, friends, and employers—developed as a strategy to attack prejudice and reduce stereotypes as well as to relieve personal isolation. Coming out not only served personal goals but also allowed lesbians and gay men to see each other, providing a foundation for increased community-building. The philosophy guiding the post-

Stonewall gay liberation movement of the early 1970s was that invisibility maintained social oppression by fueling stereotypes and allowing myths to remain unchallenged.

A crucial feature of the post-Stonewall era was the emergence of a lesbian–feminist movement, whose ideology had an important influence on many lesbian communities (Krieger, 1982; Wolf, 1979). The feminist movement challenged ideas about women's sexuality by deconstructing the concept of gender. The movement reduced stigma by defining women's affection on a broad continuum, providing a catalyst for more women to identify themselves as lesbian or bisexual (Faderman, 1984).

The development of lesbian communities was also spurred by women's experience of sexism in gay male organizations. Because of strains between lesbian and gay male communities and the ongoing development of the women's movement, many lesbians sought to eliminate patriarchal oppression in their lives. They started to view themselves as "women-identified women," whose primary emotional, erotic, and spiritual commitments are to women (Rich, 1980). Women's communities evolved around a network of nonhierarchical institutions such as coffeehouses, clinics, shelters, record companies, publishing companies, and collectives based on lesbian–feminist politics. The simultaneous rise of the male-dominated gay liberation movement and the lesbian–feminist movement intensified differences between the groups. For example, for gay men, liberation meant freedom from harassment and the power to exercise sexual freedom; for lesbian feminists, liberation meant resisting patriarchal oppression and developing new forms of intimacy and community (Pearlman, 1987; Raymond, 1986). Tensions between these different aims were often difficult to resolve. Despite these conflicts, the growing sense of community translated into visible economic, social, and political institutions during the early 1970s. Before Stonewall, fewer than 50 lesbian or gay organizations existed nationwide. By 1973, over 700 lesbian or gay organizations and groups had emerged (D'Emilio, 1983). During this period, many lesbians and gay men gravitated to a handful of large cities known to be more accepting of lesbian and gay life.

During the second half of the 1970s, the antigay backlash of the new right provided a stimulus for political solidification. Both Anita Bryant's 1977 "Save Our Children" campaign in Florida and an effort to enact legislation to ban lesbian and gay teachers in California were firmly rebuffed. A formerly isolated group of women and men emerged as a political force. In 1977, openly gay Harvey Milk was elected to the powerful Board of Supervisors in San Francisco, demonstrating the changing power of the lesbian and gay community. Milk was assassinated a year later by one of his colleagues on the Board, an act that underscored the intense threat produced in some opponents (Shilts, 1982).

The use of a "common enemy" strategy to unite the lesbian/gay community and promote group solidarity has continued through the 1980s and 1990s. During the 1980s, virulent new attacks by the religious right facilitated more cogender organizing and massive public protests. Recent examples were efforts during 1992 to defeat explicitly antigay legislative initiatives in Colorado and Oregon. While many have viewed this as an effective way to engage lesbians and gay men in political activities by increasing membership in gay/lesbian groups and facilitating greater identification with the lesbian/gay community, others have questioned whether a community bound in resistance to a common threat can sustain communal bonds (Rainone, 1987).

During the 1980s, lesbians and gay men responded to the challenge of the HIV/AIDS crisis. Intensified political organizing sought to obtain increased funding for research on HIV and for the expansion of critically needed services for those with HIV illnesses. Gay communities in New York, San Francisco, and Los Angeles rapidly constructed entire systems of care with which to respond to the range of HIV illnesses and their associated problems. These projects developed information and referral systems, support networks of "buddies" for people who needed help, counseling services, and advocacy units. They also developed models for community education to prevent new HIV infections and to maintain safer sex patterns of sexual behavior. Developed in the face of governmental indifference, many of these organizations succeeded because they were embedded in social networks in lesbian and gay communities and were administered by known members of these communities.

The scope of the HIV epidemic went beyond the capabilities of community-based groups, however. Lack of national leadership, inadequate funding, and increasing evidence of discrimination based on a combination of HIV status and sexual orientation led to greater militancy (Shilts, 1987). Groups such as the AIDS Coalition to Unleash Power (ACT-UP) and Queer Nation rejected progressivist politics for civil disobedience and self-assertion (Kramer, 1989). These groups symbolized a different kind of community power—an unwillingness to tolerate official nonresponsiveness in the face of an epidemic that was decimating gay communities. The HIV epidemic brought the lives of lesbian, gay, and bisexual people into national awareness in an unprecedented way. The community was thrust into the public eye, as was the formal and informal discrimination routinely experienced by open lesbians and gay men. As the HIV epidemic spread through all strata of American life, eroding the persistent stereotypes held about gay and lesbian life, more and more people acknowledged their sexual orientation. In addition, those who remained "closeted" or uncertain realized that there was an enormous community with which to identify. Because of the nature of the HIV epidemic, however, the identification remained an ambivalent one.

Contemporary lesbian, gay, and bisexual communities are based on shared identity derived from sexual orientation. The most well-known communities exist in geographically bounded neighborhoods in several large cities and are characterized by high visibility, many formal and informal institutions, and considerable political clout (see Herdt, 1992, for descriptions of several such communities). The many lesbian and gay community organizations and activities in these neighborhoods—for instance, bookstores, theaters, restaurants, community centers, and scores of political, recreational, and social groups—serve as cultural centers, gathering places, and forums for the expression of lesbian/gay culture. They foster a powerful psychological sense of community and facilitate socialization into the many different niches of urban lesbian/gay life.

Historically, gay male urban communities have been more highly concentrated, visible, and economically advantaged than lesbian communities. Lesbian communities have focused more intensely on philosophical issues of identity and relationships, reflecting their linkage to radical feminism (see Allen, 1990, and Hoagland, 1988, for current discussions of these issues). Contemporary lesbian communities are composed of networks connected by social and political activities. Many of these communities remain politicized, actively debating analyses by cultural feminists and sexual radicals, issues of affiliation with gay male groups, and approaches to age, racial, class, and ethnic differences (Faderman, 1991). The lesbian community has tried to define a uniquely lesbian cultural vision, which is expressed in music and literature, and disseminated at national and regional music festivals and conferences.

The important role of cultural symbols and rituals in the creation and maintenance of communities among lesbians and gay men should be noted. Coming out has been conceptualized as a rite of passage, and the ritual of telling one's coming out experiences to others "forms our tribal lore" (Zimmerman, 1984: 674). Telling these stories to one another, lesbians and gay men bond together and affirm group identity. Moreover, the community uses symbols of shared oppression (e.g., the pink triangle which Nazis affixed to gay men, who were sent to concentration camps during World War II), symbols of liberation (e.g., the lambda and the rainbow flag), and national events (lesbian/gay Pride Day parades in the spring, which commemorate the Stonewall rebellion, and National Coming Out Day in October, which marks the anniversary of the 1987 National March for Gay and Lesbian Rights). As

Herrell (1992) correctly notes, "The annual parade is, in part, a strategic response to the situation of being gay in a homophobic society" (p. 227).

Different communities vary in how lesbians and gay men collectively interact; in how ageism, classism, and racism are addressed; and in how mobilization has succeeded in confronting local problems. For example, there are ongoing debates within gay male and lesbian communities about strategies to make it safe to come out. "Outing," the exposing of public figures who are closeted lesbians or gay men, is seen by some as a necessary confrontational strategy to attack prejudice and reduce stereotypes. Others view it as a violation of the right to privacy. The debate continues as lesbian and gay communities struggle to find strategies that preserve individual freedom while at the same time encouraging greater numbers to come out, as a way of promoting a societal norm that allows for diversity of sexual orientation.

An important recent development has been the emergence of bisexuality within lesbian and gay communities (Hutchins & Kaahumanu, 1991; Weise, 1992). Although many lesbians and gay men have histories of heterosexual involvements of varying degrees, and despite the likelihood that responsiveness to both sexes is an inherent characteristic, women and men who self-identify as bisexual report feeling excluded by lesbian/gay communities as well as by mainstream society. Bisexual people seem to be less restricted by gender in their sexual and affectional attractions than either gay men or lesbians. In addition, their sexual orientation may develop differently from those of lesbians or gay men (Bell, Weinberg, & Hammersmith, 1981).

Bisexual women and men, a newly emerging political force, challenge the cultural emphasis on biological sex as the basis for sexual identity (Bennett, 1992). Pressure from bisexual activists and charges of "biphobia" leveled against lesbian and gay community leaders have led to acrimonious debates about the nature of sexual identity and the politics of self-definition. There is little doubt that many consistently define themselves as bisexual, that sexual activity with women and men is not just transitional or transitory for some—between 10 and 15 percent of the population (Reinisch, 1990: 143). It seems likely that community groups for bisexually identified women and men will increase; surely these will provide settings for some who would not define themselves as lesbian or gay, and for some who are indeed in a transitional sexual identity status. In addition to resources specifically devoted to bisexual people, it seems likely that a more inclusive nonheterosexual "community" will emerge, perhaps under the rubric of "queer community."

Despite the common ground of sexual orientation, lesbian and gay community life is highly contextual, varying tremendously across settings. Much of the historical development of lesbian and gay communities originated in certain urban areas, but communities exist in suburban and rural areas as well. Due to the nature of nonurban areas, these communities are much less visible and have far fewer formal organizations than would be found in metropolitan areas. Indeed, in many rural areas, communities take the form of small, densely connected informal networks which operate without drawing the attention of others. Often, a small gay/lesbian bar provides a hub for these networks, although women's groups typically eschew such settings. These networks have the advantage of providing secure connections with others; their disadvantage is that they cannot provide the range of recreational, social, educational, and political opportunities available in urban areas. Outside of metropolitan areas, anonymity is much more difficult to sustain, an important issue if substantial risks are attached to disclosure of sexual orientation. Unless there are state antidiscrimination laws, fewer legal protections are available in suburban and rural areas, so that loss of employment and housing could occur if sexual orientation were known or suspected. Discussion of such communities can be found in D'Augelli (1989a), D'Augelli and Hart (1987), Lynch (1992), and Krieger (1982).

There has also been documentation of the globalization of lesbian and gay community-building outside the United States (Likosky, 1992; Miller, 1992). Two international lesbian and gay organizations, the International Lesbian and Gay Association and the International Lesbian Information Service, have been formed in recent years. Their purpose is to monitor rights, sponsor international meetings, and lend assistance to lesbian and gay rights groups in different countries.

Psychological Engagement with Lesbian/Gay/Bisexual Communities

Even under the best of circumstances, affiliation with a lesbian/gay/bisexual community is difficult because of the stigma attached to non-heterosexual life. Even with the gradual erosion of the pathology model, there is a deeply felt ambivalence about identifying with a stigmatized community. Personal hesitancies are complemented by problems of accessibility of lesbian/gay/bisexual community resources. In many areas, these resources are hidden and known only to those who have already come out. There are few ways to learn about lesbian/gay/bisexual issues without self-identification (although such resources as anonymous telephone helplines provide a notable exception). Even if a person knows about local resources, decisions to access them can be fraught with anxiety. This tension diminishes with repeated efforts and contacts with others, but there is often a strong approach–avoidance dynamic. We know little about what factors spur different people in their efforts to affiliate with, explore, and become integrated into such communities. We do, however, know about inhibiting factors which provide psychological barriers from joining such communities. The most powerful barriers are (1) stresses related to coming out, (2) heterosexism, and (3) identification barriers.

The Stresses of Coming Out

Coming out is a complex sequence of events through which individuals acknowledge, recognize, and label their sexual orientation and then disclose it to others throughout their lives. Managing lesbian/gay identity usually includes developing strategies to evade the stigma associated with homosexuality, leading to boundaries between the person's heterosexual and the lesbian/gay worlds. The process of coming out is a gradual erosion of these boundaries such that one is known as lesbian or gay in all crucial life domains, including family life, work, and community life.

Lesbians and gay men maintain self-esteem most effectively when they identify with and are integrated into a larger lesbian/gay community (Crocker & Major, 1989). "Coming in" refers to this process of identifying with a larger group of lesbian and gay people (Petrow, 1990). Lesbians and gay men report more primary support from partners and friends than from family (Blumstein & Schwartz, 1983; Kurdek, 1988; Kurdek & Schmitt, 1987; Weston, 1991). Exploration of lesbian and gay subcultures and socialization into its norms facilitate learning the folkways, behavior, language, and structure of the community (Plummer, 1975). This contact helps to foster group identity, provides role models, and diminishes feelings of isolation or alienation (Harry, 1984; Kurdek, 1988). Research has documented the positive impact of acknowledging lesbian/gay feelings to others and being involved with lesbian and gay social networks and communities (Harry & Duvall, 1978; Kurdek, 1988; Weinberg & Williams, 1974). Coming out to others has been associated with enhanced personal integrity (Rand, Graham, & Rawlings, 1982; Wells & Kline, 1987), decreased feelings of isolation (Murphy, 1989), and greater acceptance from others (Olsen, 1987). The presence of a lesbian/gay support system is related to more adaptive coping strategies and lower stress (Gillow & Davis, 1987) and to better overall adjustment (Kurdek, 1988).

The diversity among lesbian and gay individuals and their life situations suggests wide variation in coming out processes; for some, coming out is especially difficult. For instance, lesbian and gay people of color have several sets of "identities" and "communities" to reconcile. To integrate their multiple identities, many lesbians and gay men of color may establish priorities as to their affiliation with their racial/ethnic community and the lesbian/gay community. Lesbians and gay men of color often turn to the primarily Anglo lesbian and gay community, at least early in their coming out process. They may not, however, obtain the support they need in these settings (see Chan, 1989; Cochran & Mays, 1986; deMonteflores, 1981; Loiacano, 1989; Morales, 1989); lesbians and gay men of color have often reported experiences of racism within the larger lesbian and gay community, making it difficult for them to feel fully accepted (Hom, 1992). One of the major ways that lesbians and gay men of color have gained integration of their multiple identities has been to form formal and informal organizations of their own (Hidalgo, 1984; Icard, 1985/86). Given that affiliation with lesbian and gay communities is more problematic, it might be expected that they would align less readily with these communities than with their White counterparts, although no research has yet addressed this issue.

Heterosexism

Heterosexism is defined as "an ideological system that denies, denigrates, and stigmatizes any nonheterosexual form of behavior, identity, relationship, or community" (Herek, 1990: 316). Heterosexism fuels the disenfranchisement of lesbians and gay men by perpetuating the view that their sexual orientation is inherently flawed. Heterosexism manifests itself on both cultural and psychological levels. On a cultural level, social customs and institutions perpetuate the assumption that heterosexuality is the only appropriate form of affectional and sexual expression. On a psychological level, individual attitudes and behaviors that reflect heterosexual norms are socially reinforced, and victimizers obtain peer approval by the expression of antilesbian/antigay views.

Heterosexism is reflected in social policies and laws in which basic rights of lesbians and gay men are unprotected. Lesbians and gay men remain excluded from lists of protected categories in most civil rights legislation, despite plentiful evidence that their rights are routinely denied or abridged (Green, 1992; Rivera, 1991). Except for a handful of statewide laws and a few dozen municipal laws, no legal protection exists from overt discrimination against lesbians and gay men in employment, housing, or access to public accommodations. Almost half of the United States still criminalize private consensual adult homosexual activity. Lesbian and gay relationships have no legal status, except in the very few locales in which domestic partnerships can be registered. If they are parents, lesbians and gay men may lose custody of their children as a result of the powerful heterosexist assumptions embedded in family law and in current judicial custom in many parts of the country. (Some states, e.g., California, have laws specifying that sexual orientation cannot be considered relevant in custody disputes.) Few institutional policies (e.g., insurance regulations, inheritance laws, and hospital visitation rules) acknowledge lesbian and gay relationships. Because of such heterosexism, untoward events can occur, often unpredictably, in lesbians' and gay men's lives in a variety of critical life domains, including child custody (Achtenberg, 1987; Falk, 1989), employment (Hall, 1989; Levine & Leonard, 1984; Levine, 1979), and education (D'Augelli, 1989b, 1989c, 1991b; Herek, 1986; Shepard, 1990).

Heterosexism stifles psychological connections to lesbian and gay communities because it encourages the belief that such groups are alien, deviant, or dysfunctional. It suggests that all aspects of lesbian, gay, or bisexual life—personal, familial, social, and civic—are discontinuous with heterosexual persons' lives. It mystifies and demonizes lesbians and gay men, creating an "other" with whom it is difficult to identify. The legal and policy correlates of heterosexism reinforce this alienating process. Treating consensual homosexual activity as a felony, for instance, the sodomy laws symbolically convey the heterosexist message; pragmatically, though seldom used, the laws are available to harass openly lesbian and gay people. We have little research investigating the impact of symbolic and distal heterosexism on identification with lesbian/gay communities. Surely, negative images of lesbians and gay men in mass media, for instance, have a chilling impact (see Gross, 1991).

Identification Barriers

Despite a far more accepting climate than in earlier years and slowly diminishing heterosexism, many lesbians and gay men still have difficulty identifying with gay or lesbian communities. Garnets and Kimmel (1991) suggest four factors that exacerbate the difficulties lesbian and gay people experience in achieving community identity: (1) invisibility; (2) the unique nature of lesbian/gay personal identity; (3) the lack of group identity from birth; (4) and low awareness of the history of lesbian and gay communities.

First, the lesbian and gay male "community" is not homogeneous but diverse in terms of gender, race, ethnicity, age, socioeconomic status, relationship status, parenthood, health status, disabilities, and politics. Lesbians share with women the institutional oppression of sexism and share with gay men the social stigma of homosexuality and the abridgement of civil rights (Eldridge, 1987; Zimmerman, 1984). The stigma attached to lesbian/gay status serves as a powerful binder for the lesbian and gay communities. However, because of their diversity and the power of stigma, and because sexual orientation is not publicly identifiable, most lesbian and gay people can "pass" as heterosexual. "Passing" hides their sexual orientation from public view and, more important, from one another. Unable to identify one another, lesbians and gay men must take specific steps to affiliate with their social group. These steps involve substantial risk; affiliation must be an active process.

Second, lesbian or gay identity is an "achieved" rather than an ascribed status; stigmatization does not occur at birth. Unlike other disenfranchised groups, lesbians and gay men are initially socialized as members of the majority group (Yearwood & Weinberg, 1979). Lesbians and gay men generally label their sexual orientation at a relatively late chronological point in the process of personal development, even though many report "feeling different" much earlier. Therefore, they learn negative attitudes about lesbians and gay men before they realize that the myths apply to themselves. Having internalized heterosexist views, they must undergo a process of identity transformation to achieve self-esteem and positive community identification. Initially, many feel that they have little in common with cultural representations of lesbians and gay men. This distancing from identification slows up affiliation and involvement with a community. Paradoxically, such involvement is needed to challenge the stereotypes.

Third, because their parents typically are heterosexual, lesbians and gay men grow up with little intergenerational continuity. Lesbians and gay men do not identify with their parents or family as members of the same minority group. Parents generally cannot provide useful role models for developmental transitions, nor do they provide buffers from conflict or protection from discrimination, especially if their offspring has not come out to them. In fact, family disruption often follows disclosure of sexual orientation. Thus, many lesbians and gay men come to terms with their sexual identity in relative isolation, deprived of the attention and affection of their close friends and family (Strommen, 1989a, 1989b).

Fourth, until recently, lesbians and gay men have had little awareness of their collective history. The rich histories of lesbian and gay communities are not passed on through family traditions, and they are hidden from our general cultural heritage. Without a shared sense of historical and cultural experience, lesbians and gay men often must recreate their communities. Few lesbians and gay men in the earlier phases of coming out appreciate that they can become part of a larger community, since they have remained isolated and assume that there are few others like themselves. With few positive cultural models of lesbians and gay men to emulate, and without accurate media portrayals of lesbian and gay communities, there is rarely realistic anticipatory socialization into lesbian and gay community life. For instance, lesbian/gay history has not been taught in schools and is often deliberately

buried. In addition, lesbians and gay men cannot readily see themselves accurately portrayed in literature or in popular media (Gross,
1991).

Steps Toward Empowerment: A Community Research Agenda

During the two decades since Stonewall, lesbians and gay men have
worked together at the local, regional, and national levels to build viable communities, to provide needed programs and services, to cope
with an unprecedented health emergency, and to build a political
power base for social change. Many have gained control over their own
lives by coming out on both individual and collective levels, and by
changing systemic conditions that perpetuate injustice, discrimination,
and violence. By identifying sources of oppression, bringing them to
awareness, mobilizing power, and changing some fundamental social
structures that maintain marginality, lesbians and gay men have translated empowerment concepts such as those described by several writers (Rappaport, 1981; Swift & Levin, 1987) into action. Nonetheless,
there are continuing efforts by conservative groups to turn back political and social progress by portraying lesbians and gay men as "threats
to the family." Violence has increased, a consequence of greater lesbian
and gay visibility and the HIV epidemic (Herek & Glunt, 1988). Lesbians and gay men who do not live near metropolitan areas still experience profound isolation, with few sources of social support. Many lesbians and gay men live with prejudice on a daily basis. Empowerment
thus has been only partially accomplished.

Psychologists are in a crucial position to contribute to continued social progress for lesbians, gay men, and bisexual people by playing
four types of roles (Swift & Lewin, 1987). First, as *conceptual analysts,*
psychologists can take the lead in the development of theory related to
all aspects of sexual orientation. In every area of lesbian/gay/bisexual
life, ranging from the ontogenesis of sexual orientation through the
nature of same-sex relationships to dimensions of community life,
much conceptual work must be done (D'Augelli, 1994). Second, as *re-
searcher/reporters,* they can document empowerment deficits, sharing
their results with the broader community. This involves, for example,
building on the growing research base documenting the prevalence of
heterosexist bias and prejudice (Comstock, 1991; Herek, 1989). Third,
as *collaborator/educators,* psychologists can increase the awareness of
those most affected by their diminished empowerment status. This is
accomplished by reducing bias and misinformation through education
and training about lesbians and gay men. Fourth, as *advocates/systems
activists,* they can mobilize resources by removing existing barriers. At

a community level, this involves redefining social norms to create institutional protections and helping in the creation of safe climates for lesbian/gay people to be open about their identity.

There are at least four community research issues for the 1990s and beyond that would greatly benefit from the assistance of applied psychologists: (1) prejudice, discrimination, and violence; (2) mental health and health enhancement; (3) the HIV/AIDS epidemic; and (4) civil rights. Community empowerment strategies used in the past are briefly reviewed, followed by recommendations for the future.

Combating Prejudice, Discrimination, and Violence

ACTION RESEARCH

Historically, a first step was to document the pervasive effects of heterosexism in society and to disseminate that information in a variety of settings. Lesbians and gay men have participated in research that (1) documents that as individuals, couples, and a social community, they do not evidence lower levels of adjustment (Gonsiorek, 1991); (2) focuses on the nature and impact of negative social attitudes (Herek, 1991); (3) documents harassment and discrimination (Comstock, 1991; Herek & Berrill, 1992); (4) provides data to challenge legal assumptions that sexual orientation is incompatible with child custody, adoption, and foster care (Falk, 1989; Patterson, 1992); and (5) documents the persistence of bias and misinformation among mental health practitioners (Garnets, Hancock, Cochran, Goodchilds, & Peplau, 1991).

COMMUNITY EDUCATION

A second strategy has been to raise the consciousness of lesbians and gay men about the sources of their oppression. Educational programs and courses about lesbian/gay life enhance affirmation of identity, relationships, and community. Community organizing and public education strategies are used by lesbian/gay communities to reduce prejudice and discrimination. Educational information has been developed and is disseminated to address stereotypes in settings such as workplaces, educational and religious institutions, and government. The National Campaign to End Homophobia, for example, a national network of people working to end heterosexism through education, holds conferences and disseminates training materials and informational brochures.

MEDIA

Public awareness and mass media campaigns aim to reduce stereotypes of lesbians and gay men, specifically through increased visibility and recognition of the diversity which exists among them (Kirk & Madsen, 1989). The Lesbian and Gay Public Awareness Project has developed a

media campaign which includes newspaper ads, billboards, and a
speakers' bureau. To confront distorted images, the Gay and Lesbian
Alliance Against Defamation (GLAAD) attempts to shape values and
public opinion through the news and entertainment media.

CAMPUS ORGANIZING

The goals of organizing in high schools, colleges, and universities are
threefold: (1) to create an environment which ensures equitable treatment and freedom from harassment (Rofes, 1989); (2) to encourage research and scholarship in the areas of lesbian and gay studies (D'Augelli, 1991b; D'Emilio, 1990; Nieberding, 1989); and (3) to increase
visibility of lesbian and gay students, faculty, and staff on campus
(D'Augelli, 1991a). Several studies have documented harassment and
discrimination on college campuses (D'Augelli, 1989b,c, 1992; D'Augelli & Rose, 1990; Herek, 1986; Nelson & Baker, 1990; Shepard, 1990)
and have documented institutional change toward campuswide antidiscrimination policies (D'Augelli, 1991a). The development of lesbian
and gay resource centers, undergraduate and graduate student support
groups and caucuses, and staff and faculty networks creates helping
communities for students, faculty, and staff. Moreover, lesbian and
gay studies have emerged and these issues are integrated in curricula
focused on human diversity and multiculturalism (D'Augelli, 1991b;
D'Emilio, 1990; Escoffier, 1990; Roscoe, 1988).

RELIGIOUS INSTITUTIONS

Discrimination in religious institutions has been confronted as well.
Antiheterosexism educators have begun a dialogue about biblical–theo-
logical views in various denominations (Balka & Rose, 1989; McCloud,
1985; McNeill, 1988). Policies restricting open lesbians and gay men
from ordination are being challenged (e.g., by Reform Jews, Episcopa-
lians, and Presbyterians). Lesbians and gay men are demanding to be
accepted as full members in churches and synagogues. Several religious organizations for lesbians and gay men have been created, such
as Affirmation (Mormons), Metropolitan Community Church (Christian nondenominational), Dignity (Catholic), and Beth Chayim Chadas-
him (Jewish).

ANTILESBIAN/ANTIGAY VIOLENCE

A multilevel approach has been used to confront violence against lesbians and gay men. The prevalence of such hate crimes has been well-
documented (Comstock, 1991; Herek & Berrill, 1992). As a result of
political lobbying, the National Hate Crimes Statistics Act was passed
in 1990. The law requires the U.S. Justice Department to collect data

on bias crimes, including prejudice based on sexual orientation. Community-based crime victim services for lesbians and gay men, such as the New York City Gay and Lesbian Anti-Violence Project, have been developed in many cities to handle the aftermath of violence (Garnets, Herek, & Levy, 1990; Wertheimer, 1990). Community organizing, self-defense training, and neighborhood patrols have conceptualized hate crimes as lesbian/gay community problems.

COLLABORATIONS TO PREVENT PREJUDICE,
DISCRIMINATION, AND VIOLENCE

Collaborative strategies to address antilesbian/antigay discrimination and violence include documentation of its incidence and patterns in a variety of contexts and settings, of its mental health consequences, of institutional responses, and of prevention efforts (Herek & Berrill, 1990). To confront antigay prejudice, efforts should involve expansion of existing mass media campaigns aimed at reducing stereotypes and bias and the development of public awareness and comprehensive programs to prevent hate-motivated violence (Herek, 1989). Education and systems change efforts are needed to confront the secondary victimization that lesbians and gay men experience after a hate crime (Herek & Berrill, 1990). Finally, research can bring to public awareness diversity within lesbian and gay male populations; refute stereotypes about lesbians and gay men; and address the impact of negative social attitudes. Increased visibility of lesbians and gay men of color, teens, and older adults, of committed couples, and of parents will help to eradicate current myths.

Mental Health and Health Enhancement

Because of the unresponsiveness of traditional health and human service systems, lesbian- and gay-operated mental health and social service (Burns & Rofes, 1988; Gonsiorek, 1982) and health service (Ratner, 1988; Vachon, 1988) agencies have proliferated. These community service centers combine professional and peer counseling, client advocacy, collaborative linkages with mainstream agencies, and consultation and education to professionals and the general public.

Lesbian and gay services are especially needed to address the problems of lesbian and gay youth (Slater, 1988). Increasing numbers of youth are recognizing their sexual orientation at earlier ages and are disclosing it to others earlier, often in high school. Teens who acknowledge they are lesbian or gay in high school experience considerable peer harassment and seldom obtain family support (Gibson, 1989). These youth, as well as those who remain undisclosed, are at high risk for mental health problems, especially self-destructive behavior, and are also at risk for academic failure (Rofes, 1989). Several important developments have occurred to reach out to lesbian and gay youth. One example is Project 10, a pioneering school-based counseling and drop-in program for lesbian and gay high school students in Los Angeles. In addition, several frameworks for lesbian and gay youth services now exist and could serve as models for program development (D'Augelli, 1993; Schneider, 1988; Whitlock, 1988).

Another group whose needs are currently poorly served are lesbian and gay older adults. Social organizations and social service agencies have emerged in the past 10 years to address some of their needs (Dunker, 1987; Kimmel, 1979/80; Raphael & Meyer, 1988). These programs include Senior Action in a Gay Environment (SAGE) in New York City, Project Rainbow in Los Angeles, and Gay and Lesbian Outreach to Elders (GLOE) in San Francisco. These organizations offer a variety of social activities and social support, assist with managing chronic health problems, provide transportation for homebound older adults, offer bereavement counseling, and help with institutional heterosexism (e.g., discriminatory policies in nursing homes and hospital care) and legal problems. In addition, regional conferences of older lesbians have occurred in the past few years (e.g., the West Coast Old Lesbian Conference and the Passages conference in Washington, D.C.), expanding women's networks.

Self-help and mutual aid groups have also proliferated in lesbian and gay communities to support coming out, offer education about lesbian and gay life, and support lesbian and gay parents as well as parents and children of lesbians and gay men (Eller & King, 1990; Piersol, 1988). Perhaps the best known groups are Federation of Parents and Friends of Lesbians and Gay Men (PFLAG), organized for parents whose offspring have come out, and the Gay and Lesbian Parents Coalition, an international association of lesbian mothers, gay fathers, and their children.

COLLABORATIONS FOR MENTAL HEALTH ENHANCEMENT

Psychologists could help in the expansion of accessible lesbian and gay-affirming services in mental health, social service, and health settings. One focus could be on evaluation of programs to assist gay men, lesbians, their families, and friends to deal with conflicts and stresses associated with coming out. Expansion of social networks, self-help groups, support groups for coming out, and group and individual efforts to strengthen coping skills are also needed. Moreover, the development of human service programs for lesbian and gay couples and their families is another important collaborative activity. Service programs for victims of hate crimes are also needed. Psychologists can provide organizational consultation to lesbian and gay community service centers aimed at strengthening the structure and efficiency of their work.

Confronting the HIV/AIDS Crisis

The HIV/AIDS crisis has mobilized the lesbian/gay community to confront attitudes, develop programs, and challenge political roadblocks with strategies familiar to community psychologists. They have confronted the ongoing impact of HIV in the gay male community by developing approaches and services to care for the ill, providing early identification of HIV status, and developing primary prevention approaches emphasizing safer sex. A "People with AIDS" self-empowerment movement has grown from local efforts to a nationally coordinated one (Callen & Turner, 1988). Grassroots advocacy organizations such as ACT-UP and Queer Nation have used civil disobedience to highlight heterosexist policies and delayed bureaucratic response to the epidemic.

COLLABORATIVE POSSIBILITIES IN THE HIV EPIDEMIC

Strategies to address the ongoing impact of HIV/AIDS and the prevention of further HIV infections could include coordinated community planning (e.g., HIV helping networks; D'Augelli, 1990); training and consultation to increase knowledge and to reduce bias about AIDS among health and human service systems that deal with AIDS-affected individuals; strategies to prepare community systems for the long-term impact of the health crisis; further development and expansion of AIDS prevention models (e.g., to promote safer sex); and research and education to address AIDS-related stigma and antigay attitudes.

Promotion of Civil Rights

Community organizing and legislative lobbying strategies have been used to promote civil rights for lesbians and gay men. Political Action Committees have been formed at local, state, and national levels. Gay and lesbian political clubs have formed to influence partisan politics. The National Gay and Lesbian Task Force (NGLTF), formed in 1973, was the first truly national civil rights organization. Its activities include lobbying, advocacy, community organizing, media projects, antiviolence efforts, and leadership development for lesbian and gay activists.

National and local gay legal organizations (such as the Lambda Legal Defense and Education Fund and the National Center for Lesbian Rights) have worked for nondiscrimination policies in housing, health care, employment, personnel benefits, and access to public accommodations. They have targeted the institutional homophobia of the military (Dyer, 1990). Moreover, they have attempted to change laws to accord legal recognition to domestic partners (i.e., heterosexual and homosexual couples in long-term committed relationships). Success occurred recently in several cities such as San Francisco, when lesbians and gay men registered as domestic partners at the County Clerk's office, in a process analogous to obtaining a marriage license. In New York City, lesbian and gay municipal employees have been extended benefits previously reserved for heterosexually married couples. This trend has extended to higher education, with universities (such as the University of Chicago, the University of Iowa, and Stanford University) extending employee benefits to domestic partnerships.

Collaborative Possibilities for Civil Rights Protection

Collaborative strategies to address civil rights of lesbians and gay men could include further research documenting the inequities in civil rights experienced by lesbians and gay men; promotion of public and organizational policies that provide legal protection and nondiscrimination and foster legal recognition; research focused on the impact of social, legal, and political influences on lesbian and gay lives (e.g., effects of antidiscrimination legislation or the restrictiveness of child custody legislation); and development of information programs on antidiscrimination policies and legal rights to disseminate to the lesbian and gay communities both locally and nationally.

Conclusion

Until comparatively recently, a lesbian, gay, or bisexual sexual orientation was not considered a reflection of human diversity but of pathology. An important step toward creating safe and supportive settings for lesbians, gay men, and bisexual people took place in the decades following World War II. The Homophile Rights and Gay Liberation movements stimulated the emergence of a group identity as members of a collectively oppressed minority in American society. This led to the development of the increasingly complex social, political, and cultural collectives that are the lesbian/gay/bisexual communities of contemporary American society.

This chapter has documented the primary means by which lesbians, gay men, and bisexual people have created their communities. These are (1) empowerment strategies aimed at gaining control over their own lives and influencing norms through personal disclosure of sexual orientation at both individual and collective levels; (2) identification with and integration into larger lesbian/gay social networks and communities; (3) changing systemic conditions that perpetuate injustice, discrimination, and violence; and (4) promotion of public and organizational policies that provide equal status and legal protection against discrimination.

Challenges and barriers created by the heterosexist norms of mainstream society have inhibited many lesbian, gay, and bisexual people from identifying with and joining their communities. Because of this, they have been denied access to crucial emotional support and affirmation and have been unable to take advantage of the richness of lesbian/gay/bisexual communities. Lesbians, gay men, and bisexual people constitute a large disenfranchised population which has been rendered invisible, marginalized, and deprived of basic civil rights. As a result, they lose control of many aspects of their personal, family, and community life, and must cope with ongoing fear. Lesbians, gay men, and bisexual people must continually assert their existence in society, confront multiple forms of bigotry, and deal with increasing victimization. Despite progress, the risks of disclosure of sexual orientation as nonheterosexual remain great in American society.

There are unique aspects of lesbian, gay, and bisexual sexual orientation which impede identification with a community. Consolidation of a distinctive identity is a difficult personal challenge for lesbians, gay men, and bisexual people. Many lack the experience of belonging to a cohesive social group and are not accustomed to group membership. The rich histories of gay and lesbian communities are not passed along to potential members by the usual mechanisms of socialization; indeed, these histories are hidden from the general historical record. Without a shared sense of culture, lesbians, gay men, and bisexual people often have found bonding and community development to be an arduous process. Many barriers, both practical and psychological, real and imagined, stand in the way.

With sexual orientation the only common ground, lesbian, gay, and bisexual community life is highly heterogeneous. Thus, to create a safe setting for people to be open about their identity requires adhering to the principle of "diversity-within-unity" (Faderman, 1991). This model of community building encourages lesbian, gay, and bisexual people who differ in race, socioeconomic status, gender, age, religion, and so on to find a place within the same social collective, however large and diverse.

By applied research and action, psychologists can continue the empowerment and community-building that has been started by members of lesbian, gay, and bisexual communities. Psychologists can collaborate with these communities in many ways. Social norms must be redefined to create institutional protections for lesbian, gay, and bisexual people, and to create a safe climate for openness about personal identity. This includes creating environments in which (1) on both individual and group levels, divergence from the heterosexual norm is not used to justify denial of personal and civil rights; (2) lesbian, gay, and bisexual people are free from fear, harassment, and violence; (3) everyday language and custom recognize and value diversity in sexual orientation; and (4) lesbians, gay men, and bisexual people have equal access to social and other resources.

References

Achtenberg, R. (1987). Preserving and protecting the families of lesbians and gay men. In M. Shernoff & W. A. Scott (Eds.), *The sourcebook on lesbian/gay health care* (pp. 237–245). Washington, DC: National Lesbian and Gay Health Foundation.

Allen, J. (Ed.) (1990). *Lesbian philosophies and cultures.* Albany: State University of New York Press.

Balka, C., & Rose, A. (Eds.) (1989). *Twice blessed: On being lesbian, gay, and Jewish.* Boston: Beacon Press.

Barnhart, E. (1975). Friends and lovers in a lesbian counterculture community. In N. Glazer-Malbin (Ed.), *Old family/new family* (pp. 3–23). New York: D. Van Nostrand.

Bayer, R. (1981). *Homosexuality and American psychiatry: The politics of diagnosis.* New York: Basic.

Bell, A. P., Weinberg, M. S., & Hammersmith, S. K. (1981). *Sexual preference: Its development in men and women.* Bloomington: Indiana University Press.

Bennett, K. (1992). Feminist bisexuality: A both/and option for an either/or world. In E. R. Weise (Ed.), *Closer to home: Bisexuality and feminism* (pp. 205–232). Seattle: Seal Press.

Bérubé, A. (1990). *Coming out under fire: The history of gay men and women in World War II.* New York: Free Press.

Blumstein, P., & Schwartz, P. (1983). *American couples: Money, work, sex.* New York: Morrow.

Burns, R., & Rofes, E. (1988). Gay liberation comes home: The development of community centers within our movement. In M. Shernoff & W. A. Scott (Eds.), *The sourcebook on lesbian/gay health care* (pp. 24–29). Washington, DC: National Lesbian and Gay Health Foundation.

Callen, M., & Turner, D. (1988). AIDS self-empowerment movement. M. Shernoff & W. A. Scott (Eds.), *The sourcebook on lesbian/gay health care* (pp. 187–192). Washington, DC: National Lesbian and Gay Health Foundation.

Chan, C. S. (1989). Issues of identity development among Asian American lesbians and gay men. *Journal of Counseling and Development, 68,* 16–20.

Cochran, S. D., & Mays, V. M. (1986). The Black Lesbian Relationship Project: Relationship experiences and the perception of discrimination. Paper presented at the annual meeting of the American Psychological Association, Washington, DC.

Comstock, G. D. (1991). *Violence against lesbians and gay men.* New York: Columbia University Press.

Crocker, J., & Major, B. (1989). Social stigma and self-esteem: The self-protective properties of stigma. *Psychological Review, 96,* 608–630.

Cruikshank, M. (1992). *The gay and lesbian liberation movement.* New York: Routledge.

D'Augelli, A. R. (1989a). The development of a helping community for lesbians and gay men: A case study in community psychology. *Journal of Community Psychology, 17,* 18–29.

D'Augelli, A. R. (1989b). Homophobia in a university community: Views of prospective resident assistants. *Journal of College Student Development, 30,* 546–552.

D'Augelli, A. R. (1989c). Lesbians' and gay men's experiences of discrimination and harassment in a university community. *American Journal of Community Psychology, 17,* 317–321.

D'Augelli, A. R. (1990). Community psychology and the HIV epidemic: The development of helping communities. *Journal of Community Psychology, 18,* 337–346.

D'Augelli, A. R. (1991a). Lesbians and gay men on campus: Visibility, empowerment, and educational leadership. *Peabody Journal of Education, 66,* 124–142.

D'Augelli, A. R. (1991b). Teaching lesbian/gay development: From oppression to exceptionality. *Journal of Homosexuality, 22,* 213–227.

D'Augelli, A. R. (1992). Lesbian and gay male undergraduates' experiences of harassment and fear on campus. *Journal of Interpersonal Violence, 7,* 383–395.

D'Augelli, A. R. (1993). Preventing mental health problems among lesbian and gay college students. *Journal of Primary Prevention, 13*(4), 1–17.

D'Augelli, A. R. (1994). Lesbian and gay male development: Steps toward an analysis of lesbians' and gay men's lives. In B. Greene & G. M. Herek (Eds.), *Lesbian and gay psychology: Theory, research and clinical applications.* (pp. 118–132). Thousand Oaks, CA: Sage.

D'Augelli, A. R., & Hart, M. M. (1987). Gay women, men, and families in rural settings: Toward the development of helping communities. *American Journal of Community Psychology, 15,* 79–93.

D'Augelli, A. R., & Rose, M. L. (1990). Homophobia in a university community: Attitudes and experiences of white heterosexual males. *Journal of College Student Development, 31,* 484–491.

D'Emilio, J. (1993). *Sexual politics, sexual communities: The making of a homosexual minority in the United States, 1940–1970.* Chicago: University of Chicago Press.

D'Emilio, J. (1990). The campus environment for gay and lesbian life. *Academe, 76,* 16–19.

deMonteflores, C. (1981). Conflicting allegiances: Therapy issues with Hispanic lesbians. *Catalyst, 12,* 31–36.

Dunker, B. (1987). Aging lesbians: Observations and speculations. In The Boston Lesbian Psychologies Collective (Eds.), *Lesbian psychologies: Explorations and challenges* (pp. 72–82). Urbana: University of Illinois Press.

Dyer, K. (Ed.) (1990). *Gays in uniform: The Pentagon's secret reports.* Boston: Alyson.

Eldridge, N. S. (1987). Gender issues in counseling same-sex couples. *Profes-sional psychology: Research and practice, 18,* 567–572.

Eller, M., & King, D. J. (1990). Self-help groups for gays, lesbians, and their loved ones. In R. Kus (Ed.), *Keys to caring: Assisting your gay and lesbian clients* (pp. 330–339). Boston: Alyson.

Escoffier, J. (1990). Inside the ivory closes: The challenges facing lesbian and gay studies. *Out/look, 9,* 40–48.

Esterberg, K. G. (1990). From illness to action: Conceptions of homosexuality in *The Ladder,* 1956–1965. *The Journal of Sex Research, 27*(1), 65–80.

Faderman, L. (1984). The "new gay" lesbian. *Journal of Homosexuality, 10,* 85–95.

Faderman, L. (1991). *Odd girls and twilight lovers: A history of lesbian life in twentieth-century America.* New York: Columbia University Press.

Falk, P. J. (1989). Lesbian mothers: Psychosocial assumptions in family law. *American Psychologist, 44,* 941–947.

Fitzgerald, F. (1986). *Cites on a hill: A journey through contemporary American cul-tures.* New York: Simon & Shuster.

Garber, E. (1989). A spectacle in color: The lesbian and gay subculture of Jazz Age Harlem. In M. B. Duberman, M. Vicinus, & G. Chauncy (Eds.), *Hidden from history: Reclaiming the gay and lesbian past* (pp. 318–331). New York: New American Library.

Garnets, L., Hancock, K. A., Cochran, S. D., Goodchilds, J., & Peplau, L. A. (1991). Issues in psychotherapy with lesbians and gay men: A survey of psychologists. *American Psychologist, 46,* 964–972.

Garnets, L., Herek, G. M., & Levy, B. (1990). Violence and victimization of lesbians and gay men: Mental health consequences. *Journal of Interper-sonal Violence, 5,* 366–383.

Garnets, L., & Kimmel, D. (1991). Lesbian and gay male dimensions in the psychological study of human diversity. In J. Goodchilds (Ed.), *Psycho-logical perspectives on human diversity in America* (pp. 143–192). Washing-ton, DC: American Psychological Association.

Gibson, P. (1989). Gay male and lesbian youth suicide. In ADAMHA, *Report of the Secretary's Task Force on Youth Suicide* (Vol. 3, pp. 110–142). Washing-ton, DC: U.S. Government Printing Office (DHHS Pub. No. [ADM] 89-1623).

Gillow, K. E., & Davis, L. L. (1987). Lesbian stress and coping methods. *Journal of Psychosocial Nursing, 25,* 28–32.

Gonsiorek, J. (1982). Organizational and staff problems in gay/lesbian mental health agencies. *Journal of Homosexuality, 7,* 193–208.

Gonsiorek, J. C. (1991). The empirical basis for the demise of the illness model of homosexuality. In J. C. Gonsiorek & J. D. Weinrich (Eds.), *Homosexu-ality: Research implications for public policy* (pp. 115–136). Newbury Park, CA: Sage.

Green, R. (1992). *Sexual science and the law.* Cambridge: Harvard University Press.

Gross, L. (1991). Out of the mainstream: Sexual minorities and the mass media. *Journal of Homosexuality, 21,* 19–46.

Hall, M. (1989). Private experiences in the public domain: Lesbians in organiza-tions. In J. Hearn, D. L. Sheppard, P. Tancred-Sheriff, & G. Burrell

(Eds.), *The sexuality of organization* (pp. 125–138). Newbury Park, CA: Sage.

Harry, J. (1984). *Gay couples*. New York: Praeger.

Harry, J., & Duvall, W. B. (1978). *The social organization of gay males*. New York: Praeger.

Herdt, G. (1992). *Gay culture in America: Essays from the field*. Boston: Beacon.

Herek, G. M. (1986). Sexual orientation and prejudice at Yale: A report on the experiences of lesbian, gay, and bisexual members of the Yale community. Unpublished report.

Herek, G. M. (1989). Hate crimes against lesbians and gay men: Issues for research and policy. *American Psychologist, 44,* 948–955.

Herek, G. M. (1990). The context of anti-gay violence: Notes on cultural and psychological heterosexism. *Journal of Interpersonal Violence, 5,* 316–333.

Herek, G. M. (1991). Stigma, prejudice, and violence against lesbians and gay men. In J. C. Gonsiorek & J. D. Weinrich (Eds.), *Homosexuality: Research implications for public policy* (pp. 60–80). Newbury Park, CA: Sage.

Herek, G. M., & Berrill, K. T. (1990). Anti-gay violence and mental health: Setting an agenda for research. *Journal of Interpersonal Violence, 5,* 414–423.

Herek, G. M., & Berrill, K. T. (Eds.) (1992). *Hate crimes: Confronting violence against lesbians and gay men*. Newbury Park, CA: Sage.

Herek, G. M., & Glunt, E. K. (1988). An epidemic of stigma: Public reactions to AIDS. *American Psychologist, 43,* 886–891.

Herrell, R. K. (1992). The symbolic strategies of Chicago's Gay and Lesbian Pride Day Parade. In G. Herdt (Ed.), *Gay culture in America* (pp. 225–252). Boston: Beacon.

Hidalgo, H. A. (1984). The Puerto Rican lesbian in the United States. In T. Darty & S. Potter (Eds.), *Women-identified women* (pp. 105–115). Palo Alto, CA: Mayfield.

Hoagland, S. L. (1988). *Lesbian ethics: Toward new value*. Palo Alto, CA: Institute of Lesbian Studies.

Hom, A. Y. (1992). Family matters: A historical study of the Asian Pacific Lesbian Network. University of California, Los Angeles, unpublished mater's thesis.

Hooker, E. (1957). The adjustment of the male overt homosexual. *Journal of Projective Techniques, 21,* 18–31.

Humphreys, L., & Miller, B. (1980). Identities in the emerging gay culture. In J. Marmor (Ed.), *Homosexual behavior: A modern reappraisal* (pp. 142–156). New York: Basic Books.

Hutchins, L., & Kaahumanu, L. (Eds.) (1991). *Bi any other name*. Boston: Alyson.

Icard, L. (1985/86). Black gay men and conflicting social identities: Sexual orientation versus racial identity. *Journal of Social Work and Human Sexuality, 4,* 83–92.

Jay, K., & Young, A. (Eds.). (1977). *Out of the closets: Voices of gay liberation*. New York: Jove.

Kimmel, D. (1979/80). Life-history interviews of aging gay men. *International Journal of Aging and Human Development, 10,* 239–248.

Kirk, M., & Madsen, H. (1989). *After the ball: How America will conquer its fear and hatred of gays in the 90's.* New York: Doubleday.

Kramer, L. (1989). *Report from the holocaust: The making of an AIDS activist.* New York: St. Martin's Press.

Krieger, S. (1982). Lesbian identity and community: Recent social science literature. *Signs, 8,* 91–108.

Kurdek, L. A. (1988). Perceived social support in lesbians and gays in cohabiting relationships. *Journal of Personality and Social Psychology, 54,* 504–509.

Kurdek, L. A., & Schmitt, J. P. (1987). Perceived emotional support from family and friends in members of gay, lesbian, and heterosexual cohabiting couples. *Journal of Homosexuality, 14,* 57–68.

Levine, M. P. (1979). Employment discrimination against gay men. *International Review of Modern Sociology, 9,* 151–163.

Levine, M. P., & Leonard, R. (1984). Discrimination against lesbians in the workforce. *Signs, 9,* 700–710.

Likosky, S. (1992). *Coming out: An anthology of international gay and lesbian writings.* New York: Pantheon.

Lockard, D. (1985). The lesbian community: An anthropological approach. *Journal of Homosexuality, 11,* (3–4), 83–95.

Loiacano, D. K. (1989). Gay identity issues among Black Americans: Racism, homophobia, and the need for validation. *Journal of Counseling and Development, 68,* 21–25.

Lynch, F. R. (1992). Nonghetto gays: An ethnography of suburban homosexuals. In G. Herdt (Ed.), *Gay culture in America: Essays from the field* (pp. 165–201). Boston: Beacon.

Marcus. E. (1992). *Making history: The struggle for gay and lesbian equal rights, 1945–1990.* New York: Harper Collins.

McCloud, J. O. (1985). *Breaking the silence, overcoming the fear: Homophobia education.* New York: Presbyterian Church Education Series.

McNeill, J. J. (1988). *Taking a chance on God: Liberating theology for gays, lesbians, and their lovers, families, and friends.* Boston: Beacon.

Miller, N. (1992). *Out in the world.* New York: Simon & Shuster.

Morales, E. S. (1989). Ethnic minority families and minority gays and lesbians. *Marriage and Family Review, 14,* 217–239.

Murphy, B. (1989). Lesbian couples and their parents: The effects of perceived parental attitudes on the couple. *Journal of Counseling and Development, 68,* 46–51.

Murray, S. O. (1992). Components of gay community in San Francisco. In G. Herdt (Ed.), *Gay culture in America* (pp. 107–146). Boston: Beacon.

Nelson, R., & Baker, H. (1990). The educational climate for gay, lesbian, and bisexual students at the University of California at Santa Cruz. Santa Cruz: University of California at Santa Cruz.

Nieberding, R. A. (Ed.) (1989). In every classroom: The report of the President's Select Committee for Lesbian and Gay Concerns. Office of Student Life Policy and Services, Rutgers University, New Jersey.

Olsen, M. R. (1987). A study of gay and lesbian teachers. *Journal of Homosexuality, 13,* 73–81.

Patterson, C. J. (1992). Children of lesbian and gay parents. *Child Development,* 63, 1025–1042.

Pearlman, S. F. (1987). The saga of continuing clash in lesbian community, or will an army of ex-lovers fail? In The Boston Lesbian Psychologies Collective (Eds.), *Lesbian psychologies: Explorations and challenges* (pp. 313–326). Urbana: University of Illinois Press.

Petrow, S. (1990, May). Together wherever we go. *The Advocate,* pp. 42–44.

Piersol, C. W. (1988). A support group for gay and bisexual married men: A guide to organization and planning. In M. Shernoff & W. A. Scott (Eds.), *The sourcebook on lesbian/gay health care* (pp. 78–85). Washington, DC: National Lesbian and Gay Health Foundation.

Plummer, K. (1975). *Sexual stigma: An interactionist account.* London: Routledge & Kegan Paul.

Rainone, F. L. (1987). Beyond community: Politics and spirituality. In Boston Lesbian Psychologies Collective (Eds.), *Lesbian psychologies: Explorations and challenges* (pp. 344–353). Chicago: University of Illinois Press.

Rand, C., Graham, D. L., & Rawlings, E. (1982). Psychological health and factors the court seeks to control in lesbian mother custody trials. *Journal of Homosexuality, 8,* 27–39.

Raphael, S., & Meyer, M. (1988). The old lesbian: Some observations ten years later. In M. Shernoff & W. A. Scott (Eds.), *The sourcebook on lesbian/gay health care* (pp. 68–72). Washington, DC: National Lesbian and Gay Health Foundation.

Rappaport, J. (1981). In praise of paradox: A social policy of empowerment over prevention. *American Journal of Community Psychology, 9,* 1–26.

Ratner, E. F. (1988). Treatment issues for chemically dependent lesbians and gay men. In M. Shernoff & W. A. Scott (Eds.), *The sourcebook on lesbian/gay health care* (pp. 162–168). Washington, DC: National Lesbian and Gay Health Foundation.

Raymond, J. G. (1986). *A passion for friends: Toward a philosophy of female affection.* Boston: Beacon.

Reinisch, J. M. (1990). *The Kinsey Institute new report on sex.* New York: St. Martin's Press.

Rich, A. (1980). Compulsory heterosexuality and lesbian existence. *Signs, 5,* 631–660.

Rivera, R. R. (1991). Sexual orientation and the law. In J. C. Gonsiorek & J. D. Weinrich (Eds.), *Homosexuality: Research implications of public policy* (pp. 81–100). Newbury Park, CA: Sage.

Rofes, E. (1989). Opening up the classroom: Responding to the educational needs of gay and lesbian youth. *Harvard Educational Review, 59,* 444–453.

Roscoe, W. (1988). Making history: The challenge of gay and lesbian studies. *Journal of Homosexuality, 15,* 1–40.

Sarason, S. B. (1974). *The psychological sense of community: Prospects for a community psychology.* San Francisco: Jossey-Bass.

Schneider, M. S. (1988). *Often invisible: Counseling gay and lesbian youth.* Toronto: Central Toronto Youth Services.

Shepard, C. F. (1990). Report on the quality of campus life for lesbian, gay, and bisexual students. Student Affairs Information and Research Office, University of California, Los Angeles.

Shilts, R. (1982). *The mayor of Castro Street: The life and times of Harvey Milk*. New York: St. Martin's Press.

Shilts, R. (1987). *And the band played on: Politics, people, and the AIDS epidemic*. New York: St. Martin's Press.

Simon, W., & Gagnon, J. H. (1967). Homosexuality: The formulation of a sociological perspective. *Journal of Health and Social Behavior, 8,* 177–185.

Slater, B. R. (1988). Essential issues in working with lesbian and gay male youths. *Professional Psychology, 19,* 226–235.

Strommen, E. F. (1989a). Hidden branches and growing pains: Homosexuality and the family tree. *Marriage and Family Review, 14,* 9–34.

Strommen, E. F. (1989b). "You're a what?": Family members' reactions to the disclosure of homosexuality. *Journal of Homosexuality, 18,* 37–58.

Swift, C., & Levin, G. (1987). Empowerment: An emerging mental health technology. *Journal of Primary Prevention, 8,* 71–94.

Vachon, R. (1988). Lesbian and gay public health: Old issues, new approaches. M. Shernoff & W. A. Scott (Eds.), *The sourcebook on lesbian/gay health care* (pp. 20–23). Washington, DC: National Lesbian and Gay Health Foundation.

Weinberg, M. S., & Williams, C. J. (1974). *Male homosexuals: Their problems and adaptations*. New York: Oxford University Press.

Weise, E. R. (Ed.) (1992). *Closer to home: Bisexuality and feminism*. Seattle: Seal Press.

Wells, J. W., & Kline, W. B. (1987). Self-disclosure of homosexual orientation. *Journal of Social Psychology, 127,*191–197.

Wertheimer, D. M. (1990). Treatment and service interventions for lesbian and gay male crime victims. *Journal of Interpersonal Violence, 5,* 384–400.

Weston, K. (1991). *Families we choose: Lesbians, gays, kinship*. New York: Columbia University Press.

Whitlock, K. (1988). *Bridges of respect: Creating support for lesbian and gay youth*. Philadelphia: American Friends Service Committee.

Wolf, D. G. (1979). *The lesbian community*. Berkeley: University of California Press.

Yearwood, L., & Weinberg, T. (1979). Black organizations, gay organizations: Sociological parallels. In M. P. Levine (Ed.), *Gay men: The sociology of male homosexuality* (pp. 301–316). New York: Harper & Row.

Zimmerman, B. (1984). The politics of transliteration: Lesbian personal narratives. *Signs, 9,* 663–682.

13

Psychological Heterosexism in the United States

Gregory M. Herek

Lesbians and gay men have made tremendous social and political gains since the 1969 Stonewall rebellion. These advances include securing passage of protective state and local legislation and obtaining widespread legitimation as a minority community in American society. Nevertheless, institutional intolerance and personal hostility toward lesbians and gay men remain a fact of life in the United States today. In this chapter, the term *heterosexism* is used to describe this phenomenon. Heterosexism is defined as the ideological system that denies, denigrates, and stigmatizes any nonheterosexual form of behavior, identity, relationship, or community.[1]

Heterosexism is manifested at both the cultural and the individual

---

[1]I avoid the term *homophobia*, which has often been used to describe hostility toward gay men, lesbians, and bisexuals (Herek, 1984; Smith, 1971; Weinberg, 1972). Any single word is necessarily limited in its adequacy for characterizing a phenomenon that encompasses issues of morality, legality, discrimination, civil liberties, violence, and personal discomfort. *Homophobia* is particularly ill-suited to this purpose, however, for three reasons. First, it is linguistically awkward; its literal meaning is something like "fear of sameness." Second, antigay prejudice is not truly a phobia; it is not necessarily based on fear; nor is it inevitably irrational or dysfunctional for individuals who manifest it (Fyfe, 1983; Herek, 1986b; Nungesser, 1983; Shields & Harriman, 1984). Third, using the term homophobia can easily mislead us into thinking of antigay prejudice in exclusively individual terms, as a form of mental illness rather than as a pattern of thought and behavior that can actually be adaptive in a prejudiced society.

levels. Cultural heterosexism, like institutional racism and sexism, pervades societal customs and institutions. It operates through a dual process: homosexuality is usually rendered invisible and, when people who engage in homosexual behavior or who are identified as homosexual become visible, they are attacked by society. Examples of cultural heterosexism include the widespread lack of legal protection from anti-gay discrimination in employment, housing, and services; the continuing ban against lesbian and gay military personnel; the absence of legal recognition for lesbian and gay committed relationships; and the existence of sodomy laws in nearly one-half of the states (e.g., Herek, 1989, 1990, 1993b, 1994a; Melton, 1989; Rivera, 1991; Rubenstein, 1993).

Psychological heterosexism is the individual manifestation of cultural heterosexism. It is reflected in feelings of personal disgust, hostility, or condemnation of homosexuality and of lesbians and gay men, which continue to be widespread (e.g., Herek, 1994b; Herek & Glunt, 1993; Marsiglio, 1993; Schneider & Lewis, 1984). Psychological heterosexism is also expressed behaviorally. Empirical research indicates that significant numbers of gay men and lesbians have been the targets of verbal abuse, harassment, discrimination, or physical assault because of their sexual orientation (Berrill, 1992; Gross & Aurand, 1992; Herek, 1993a; Levine, 1979; Levine & Leonard, 1984; "Results of poll," 1989).

The present chapter uses social science theory and empirical research to describe and explain psychological heterosexism in the United States today. The first section addresses the attitudinal and belief components of psychological heterosexism, with special attention to cognitive and motivational processes. In the second section, behavioral aspects of psychological heterosexism—specifically, acts of violence against lesbians and gay men—are discussed. In the third section, the consequences of psychological heterosexism are considered. The final section includes suggestions for empirical research on psychological heterosexism.

Attitudinal and Belief Components of Psychological Heterosexism[2]

Although racism, antisemitism, and heterosexism (as well as other forms of prejudice against minority groups) each has its own unique history and content, each can be understood by the same social scientific theories and measured by the same methodologies (e.g., Bierly, 1985; Gergen & Gergen, 1981; Herek, 1984, 1987a, 1988). In the following section, psychological heterosexism is discussed in terms of two constructs central to the social psychological analysis of prejudice: be-

[2]Portions of this section were adapted from Herek (1991).

liefs (probabilistic statements about relationships between phenomena) and attitudes (evaluations of persons, issues, and objects on such dimensions as good–bad, like–dislike, or favorable–unfavorable).

Beliefs, Stereotypes, and Cultural Ideologies

THE CONTENT OF ANTIGAY STEREOTYPES

Negative stereotypes are exaggerated, fixed, and derogatory beliefs (e.g., Allport, 1954). Like negative stereotypes about other minority groups, those about lesbians and gay men reflect the internalization of historically evolved cultural ideologies, or belief systems, that justify the subjugation of minorities. Because these ideologies are ubiquitous in popular culture (e.g., through mass media), individuals' stereotypes are continually reinforced.

Some stereotypes reflect ideologies that are specific to a particular out-group. One of the most widespread stereotypes is that a homosexual orientation is inherently related to gender-role nonconformity, such that lesbians uniformly manifest characteristics culturally defined as "masculine" and gay men manifest "feminine" qualities (e.g., Herek, 1984; Kite & Deaux, 1986, 1987). This belief is sufficiently strong that men and women whose behavior and appearance are inconsistent with cultural gender prescriptions are more likely than others to be labeled homosexual (Deaux & Lewis, 1984; Storms, Stivers, Lambers, & Hill, 1981). Lesbians and gay men who violate stereotypical expectations, as many do, may actually be disliked (Laner & Laner, 1979; Storms, 1978), and a heterosexual who is perceived as being able to identify and label a nonobvious homosexual may subsequently be better liked by other heterosexuals (Karr, 1978).

Other stereotypes reflect cultural ideologies about outsiders in general, typically portraying out-group members as simultaneously threatening and inferior to members of the dominant in-group. Adam (1978) documented some of the themes common to cultural images of gay people, blacks, and Jews alike. These include being animalistic, hypersexual, overvisible, heretical, and conspiratorial (see also Gilman, 1985). Yet another ideology ascribes disease (physical and mental) to all three groups. Just as being black or Jewish was equated historically with mental illness (Erikson, 1963; Gilman, 1985; Szasz, 1970), so was homosexuality officially labeled a mental illness by the American Psychiatric Association until 1973 (Bayer, 1987; see also Bérubé, 1990; Gonsiorek, 1991).

COGNITIVE PROCESSES UNDERLYING STEREOTYPES

Stereotyping represents an undesirable outcome of an otherwise adaptive psychological process. The world constantly bombards us with an overwhelming amount of sensory stimulation. Interpreting and responding to each separate item of information is beyond human mental capabilities. Yet individual survival requires that we be able to detect important occurrences in the environment, make reasonably accurate predictions about how they will affect us, and behave accordingly. Consequently, we use a variety of strategies for judging the importance of information and for integrating it with our past experiences. These strategies enable us to perceive the world as reasonably stable, fairly predictable, and generally manageable (e.g., Snyder, 1981).

One such strategy is *categorization*, whereby we mentally group different objects (including people) according to some characteristic they all share. Once an object is grouped with others, we can access a considerable amount of information about it simply by recalling the category's defining features. A stereotype represents the inappropriate application of categorization to a social group (e.g., Hamilton, 1981). Stereotypes result when we (1) categorize people into groups on the basis of some characteristic; (2) attribute additional characteristics to that category; (3) then attribute those other characteristics individually to all of the group's members (e.g., Snyder, 1981). Rather than being based on features that actually define the group (e.g., the belief that all gay people have a primary sexual or romantic attraction to others of their own sex), a stereotype involves characteristics that are unrelated to criteria for group membership (e.g., the belief that all gay men are child molesters or that all lesbians hate men).

Stereotypes about lesbians and gay men are resistant to change for the same reasons that all stereotypes tend to persist. Heterosexuals often notice only those characteristics that are congruent with their stereotypes about gay people *(selective perception)*, fail to recall incongruent characteristics retrospectively *(selective recall)*, and use the content of stereotypes as the basis for *illusory correlations*. Each of these phenomena is discussed here briefly.

People often perceive the world selectively, attending to information that supports their stereotypes and ignoring information that contradicts them. This process of selective perception influences heterosexuals' responses to gay men and lesbians. For example, Gross and his colleagues (Gross, Green, Storck, & Vanyur, 1980) found that students on their campus believed gay men generally to be theatrical, gentle, and liberated, whereas heterosexual men were perceived as more aggressive, dominant, competitive, strong, and stable. The same students believed lesbians generally to be dominant, direct, forceful, strong, liberated, and nonconforming, whereas heterosexual women were perceived as more likely to be conservative and stable. The researchers asked a separate sample of students to watch a brief videotaped interview with a man or woman and then to describe the interviewee in terms of these characteristics. Gross et al. (1980) found that students who were told that the target person was gay rated her or him higher on "gay traits" and lower on "heterosexual traits" than those who received no information about the interviewee's sexual orientation. Using only a gay male stimulus person, Gurwitz and Marcus (1978) replicated this finding at a different university.

Stereotypical beliefs not only distort perceptions of current interactions; they also can affect an individual's memory of past events. Snyder and Uranowitz (1978), for example, provided undergraduates with a 750-word case study of the life history of a woman named "Betty K." After reading the file, some students were told that Betty later became involved in a lesbian relationship and went on to a satisfying career as a physician living with her female lover. Other students learned that Betty married and went on to a satisfying career as a physician living with her (male) husband. On subsequent factual questions, students tended to remember events that fit with their knowledge about Betty's sexual orientation. Those who learned that Betty became a lesbian tended to remember that she did not have a steady boyfriend in high school, for example, whereas students who learned that she married heterosexually recalled that she dated boys (see also Snyder, 1981).

Heterosexuals' observations of gay people as a group are likely to be distorted by illusory correlations, that is, the erroneous perception that a particular characteristic occurs with disproportionate frequency among gay men and lesbians. Chapman and Chapman (1969) found that illusory correlations influenced perceptions of homosexuality among clinicians and lay people alike. In one study (Chapman & Chapman, 1969), clinicians responding to a survey were asked to describe their own observations of the kinds of responses "prominent in the Rorschach protocols of men with problems concerning homosexual impulses" (p. 273).[3] The clinicians reported having observed a variety of such responses, including human/animal anal content, feminine clothing, and humans with sex confused. Empirical research, however, had already demonstrated that these responses were *not* more common among homosexuals than among heterosexuals. The clinicians' impressions thus appear to have been shaped by cultural ideologies about homosexuality rather than by their own unbiased observations. (The Chapmans found that the signs incorrectly listed by the clinicians closely matched those associated with homosexuality by members of the lay public.)

In a follow-up experiment, the Chapmans presented college students

---

[3] This study was conducted before the 1973 decision by the American Psychiatric Association to remove homosexuality as a diagnosis from the Diagnostic and Statistical Manual.

with various types of responses to a series of Rorschach cards, each response attributed to a person manifesting particular "symptoms." Although each kind of response was paired with each symptom exactly the same number of times, the students incorrectly perceived that particular responses were given more frequently by homosexual men. These were the *same* responses that clinicians in the first study had also believed to be associated with homosexuality. The Chapmans concluded that the students' observations, like those of the clinicians, had been influenced by their preexisting ideas about homosexuality; they erroneously remembered a correlation between certain Rorschach signs and homosexuality because of their stereotypical beliefs.

Because of illusory correlations, and the selective perception and recall of stereotype-confirming information, antigay stereotypes are very resistant to change, even when reality contradicts them. Thus, many heterosexuals erroneously "observe" (or remember observing) a disproportionate number of gay men and women who are maladjusted, obsessed with sex, and incapable of committed relationships. They fail to notice gay people who violate these stereotypes or heterosexuals who fulfill them.

Attitudinal Correlates of Psychological Heterosexism

Empirical research has demonstrated that heterosexuals' attitudes toward gay men and lesbians are consistently correlated with various psychological, social, and demographic variables. In contrast to heterosexuals with favorable attitudes toward gay people, those with negative attitudes are (1) more likely to support traditional gender roles; (2) less likely to report having themselves engaged in homosexual behavior or to self-identify as lesbian or gay; (3) more likely to perceive their peers as manifesting negative attitudes; (4) less likely to have had personal contact with gay men or lesbians; (5) likely to be older and less well-educated; (6) more likely to have resided in geographic areas where negative attitudes represent the norm (e.g., rural areas; the midwestern and southern United States); and (7) more likely to be strongly religious and to subscribe to a conservative religious ideology (for reviews, see Herek, 1984, 1991; Kite, 1994).

In addition, heterosexual males tend to manifest higher levels of prejudice than do heterosexual females, especially toward gay men (Kite, 1984, 1994; Herek, 1984, 1988; Herek & Glunt, 1993). This sex difference results in part from heterosexual females' greater likelihood of personal contact with openly gay people, which is strongly correlated with greater acceptance of lesbians and gay men (Herek & Glunt, 1993). This differential contact, in turn, may be a product of the strong linkage in American culture between masculinity and heterosexuality, which creates considerable pressures (both social and psychological) for males to affirm their masculinity through rejection of that which is not culturally defined as masculine (male homosexuality) or perceived as negating the importance of males (lesbianism). Because heterosexual women are less likely to perceive rejection of homosexuality as integral to their own gender identity, they may experience fewer pressures to be prejudiced and, consequently, have more opportunities for personal contact with gay people (Herek, 1986a, 1987a, 1988).

Some individuals display a pattern of personality traits associated with general intolerance for stigmatized groups, often labeled *authoritarianism* (e.g., Adorno et al., 1950; Altemeyer, 1988). A significant correlation has been observed consistently between antigay attitudes and high scores on measures of authoritarianism (Altemeyer, 1988; Herek, 1988; Hood, 1973; Karr, 1978; Larsen, Reed & Hoffman, 1980; MacDonald & Games, 1974; Smith, 1971; Sobel, 1976).

Given this propensity for some individuals to express intolerant attitudes toward a variety of out-groups, it is not surprising that antigay prejudice has been found in some studies to correlate with racism (Bierly, 1985; Henley & Pincus, 1978). This correlation appears to be affected by religious orientation (Herek, 1987b). White heterosexual college students tended to score high on both antiblack racism and antigay prejudice if their religious beliefs were extrinsically motivated (i.e., if their religion functioned primarily as a means for fitting in with a social group). In contrast, those with intrinsically motivated religious beliefs (i.e., beliefs that provide an overarching framework by which all life is understood) tended to score low on racism and high on antigay attitudes. This pattern probably reflects the norms and values associated with each orientation: Instrinsics conformed to religious ideals (which generally condemned racism but not antigay prejudice), whereas Extrinsics conformed to community norms (which fostered both racism and antigay prejudice; Herek, 1987b).

The Psychological Functions of Heterosexism

As indicated by the previously mentioned study of religious orientation (Herek, 1987b), different heterosexuals hold negative attitudes toward lesbians and gay men for different reasons. In my own empirical research, I have explored these differences using the *functional approach* to attitudes, a perspective that earlier researchers applied to whites' attitudes toward blacks and Americans' attitudes toward Russians (e.g., Katz, 1960; McClintock, 1958; Smith, Bruner, & White, 1956). The central assumption of the functional approach is that people hold and express particular attitudes because they derive psychological benefit from doing so. According to the functional approach, two individuals can have very different motivations for expressing what appears to be the same attitude, or they can express opposing opinions yet share a similar motivation. Attitude change is most likely to occur when an individual's attitudes stop being functional.

Using this perspective, I analyzed essays about homosexuality written by 205 heterosexual college students (Herek, 1987a) and found three principal psychological functions underlying the students' attitudes. I labeled the first of these the *experiential* function.[4] Attitudes serving an experiential function assisted the students in making sense of their previous interactions with gay people. Those who had experienced pleasant interactions with a gay man or lesbian generalized from that experience and accepted gay people in general. Others reported negative attitudes resulting from their unpleasant experiences with gay men or lesbians. Whether favorable or unfavorable, experiential attitudes help an individual to make sense of past experiences and fit them into a larger worldview, one that is organized primarily in terms of her or his own self interest.

Because only about one-third of American adults personally know someone who is openly gay (Herek & Glunt, 1993), most heterosexuals' attitudes necessarily are not experiential. For them, homosexuality and gay people are primarily symbols. Whereas attitudes toward people with whom one has direct experience function primarily to organize and make sense of those experiences, attitudes toward symbols serve a different kind of function. Such attitudes help people to increase their self-esteem by expressing important aspects of themselves—by declaring (to themselves and to others) what sort of people they are. Affirming who one *is* often is accomplished by distancing oneself from, or even attacking, people who represent the sort of person one *is not* (or does not want to be).

Many respondents in my study wrote essays that manifested a *social identity* function.[5] The opinions expressed in these essays appeared to help the authors increase their feelings of self-esteem in two ways: by expressing important values and by aligning themselves with an important reference group. Consequently, I divided the social identity function into two interrelated components. The first of these is the *value-expressive* function. Attitudes serving a value-expressive function enable people to affirm their belief in and adherence to important values that are closely related to their self-concepts.

---

[4]In my earlier papers (Herek, 1986b, 1987a), I used the term *experiential-schematic*. This somewhat cumbersome term has been shortened for this chapter.

[5]In my earlier papers (Herek, 1986b, 1987a), I used the term *social expressive*. For greater clarity, I have substituted the term *social identity* in this chapter.

In one essay, for example, the author expressed her personal philosophy of "live and let live." For her, being gay was a personal matter, and her values dictated that people should not be condemned for what they do in their personal lives so long as they do not force themselves on unwilling others. Expressing her views about gay people allowed her to express her personal values about individual liberties, which were fundamental to her perception of herself as an open-minded person. In another essay, the author expressed her need to perceive herself in terms of her religious faith. In her view, opposing homosexuality was an integral part of being a good Christian, which was of central importance to feeling good about herself. It was not homosexuality per se that was important; homosexuality was a symbol for all that is immoral and contrary to her religious views. If her religion were to define left-handedness as it now defines homosexuality, she would probably express similar attitudes toward left-handed people.

The second component of the social identity function is *social expression*. With this function, expressing an attitude strengthens one's sense of belonging to a particular group and helps an individual to gain acceptance, approval, or love from other people whom she or he considers important (e.g., peers, family, neighbors). When gay people are perceived as the epitome of outsiders and denigrating them solidifies one's own status as an insider, the attitude serves a negative social-expressive function. When lesbians and gay men are regarded favorably by one's group (or are members of that group) and supporting them strengthens one's group affiliations, the attitude serves a positive social-expressive function. In both cases, the approval that is won through expressing these attitudes increases the individual's own self-esteem, which is of central importance to her or him. Sometimes social support for attitudes is experienced directly, as when others tell us that they agree with our opinions or approve of our actions, that they accept us and like us. At other times, the support is indirect or imagined, as when we experience satisfaction because we feel others would approve of us if they knew what we were saying or doing.

I observed one additional attitude function that also treats lesbians and gay men as symbols: the *ego-defensive* function. Defensive attitudes lower a person's anxiety resulting from her or his unconscious psychological conflicts, such as those surrounding sexuality or gender. This function is summarized in the popular notion that heterosexuals who express antigay prejudice do so out of fear that they themselves are latent homosexuals. In the last 20 years, as "homophobia" has been increasingly defined as a social problem, this explanation for antigay prejudice has become widespread (Herek, 1994b; Weinberg, 1972). Although it does not explain all prejudice against lesbians and gay men (or even most of such prejudice), it does appear to fit some people for whom lesbians or gay men symbolize unacceptable parts of themselves (e.g., "effeminacy" for some men, "masculinity" for some women). For them, expressing antigay hostility represents an unconscious strategy through which they can avoid an internal conflict by externalizing it—projecting it onto a suitable symbol apart from themselves. By rejecting (or even attacking) gay people, the defensive individual can deny that unacceptable aspect of him- or herself while also symbolically attacking it. Defensive attitudes are often expressed through strong feelings of disgust toward homosexuality or perceptions of danger from gay people of one's own gender.

It is important to recognize the nexus between psychological and cultural heterosexism. Psychological heterosexism can serve the functions described here only when an individual's psychological needs converge with the culture's ideology. Antigay prejudice can be value-expressive only when an individual's self-concept is closely tied to values that also have become socially defined as antithetical to homosexuality. It can be social-expressive only insofar as an individual strongly needs to be accepted by members of a social group that rejects gay people or homosexuality. It can be defensive only when lesbians and gay men are culturally defined in a way that links them to an individual's own psychological conflicts.

Violence Against Lesbians and Gay Men[6]

The previous section focused on attitudes and beliefs. As already noted, however, psychological heterosexism is often manifested through violence against lesbians and gay men. In a review of twenty-four separate questionnaire studies with convenience samples, Berrill (1992) reported that a median of 9 percent of respondents had been assaulted with a weapon because of their sexual orientation. For simple physical assault, the median was 17 percent. For vandalism of property, it was 19 percent. Across the studies, a median of 44 percent of respondents had been threatened with violence; 33 percent had been chased or followed; 25 percent had had objects thrown at them; 13 percent had been spat upon; and 80 percent had been verbally harassed. These were all incidents that resulted from the victim's perceived sexual orientation. Violence and property crimes of the sort routinely experienced by all Americans were not included.

Because none of the studies reviewed by Berrill (1992) used probability samples, the percentages he reported cannot be generalized to the

[6]Portions of this section were adapted from Herek (1989) and Herek (1992).

entire U.S. gay and lesbian population. They are consistent, however, with the results of a national telephone survey of a probability sample of 113 lesbians and 287 gay men commissioned by the San Francisco *Examiner*. In that survey, 5 percent of the men and 10 percent of the women reported having been physically abused or assaulted in the previous year because they were gay. Nearly half (47%) reported experiencing some form of discrimination (job, housing, health care, or social) at some time in their life based on their sexual orientation (Results of poll, 1989).

The problem of antigay victimization and harassment has received scant attention from social and behavioral scientists. Only a few published studies document the prevalence of antigay victimization (e.g., Berrill, 1992; Comstock, 1989, 1991; D'Augelli, 1992; Dean, Wu & Martin, 1992; Herek, 1993a; Hunter, 1992; von Schulthess, 1992). This lack results in part from the indifference to antigay violence that has historically dominated American society. It also reflects the difficulty of obtaining accurate data about the phenomenon of antigay violence and victimization. Empirical inquiry into antigay hate crimes must overcome all of the methodological problems associated with other types of research on crime and victimization, as well as the problems created by the stigma attached to homosexuality in American society.

For example, underreporting is a problem with all categories of crimes in the United States; National Crime Surveys indicate that only 60 percent of aggravated assaults with injury and 40 percent of simple assaults were reported in 1980 (O'Brien, 1985). For antigay hate crimes, the problem is even more serious: Perhaps as few as 10 percent are reported (Berrill, 1992; Gross & Aurand, 1992; Herek, 1993a). Underreporting of antigay victimization is especially widespread because lesbians and gay men often do not trust local law enforcement personnel and fear additional harassment and recriminations (e.g., job discrimination) if their sexual orientation becomes public. When antigay violence takes the form of sexual assault, the problem of underreporting may be especially serious, with male sexual assault victims being even less likely to report than female victims (Kaufman, DiVasto, Jackson, Voorhees, & Christy, 1980). These problems necessitate a multimethod approach to data collection, including case studies, surveys of victim populations, and surveys of perpetrator populations (Herek, 1989).

Data currently available suggest that the bulk of reported attacks are perpetrated by males, usually juveniles or young adults in groups, who are not known by the victim (Berrill, 1992). This is consistent with the pattern observed for most assaults (O'Brien, 1985). This tentative profile of attackers should not lead researchers to ignore other manifestations of antigay hate crimes, including victimization of lesbians and gay men at the hands of hate groups (e.g., Segrest & Zeskind, 1989), family members (Gross & Aurand, 1992; Hunter, 1992), and law enforcement officials (Berrill, 1992; Comstock, 1991).

The Psychological Functions of Antigay Violence

Earlier in this chapter, I discussed the motivations that underlie heterosexist attitudes. In the following section, I consider how the functional approach can be applied to hate crimes against lesbians and gay men.

VALUE-EXPRESSIVE VIOLENCE

Value-expressive violence provides a way for perpetrators to express values that are central to their self concepts. The value-expressive motivation was illustrated in an interview conducted by journalist Michael Collins (1992) with members of a Los Angeles gang called the Blue Boys. At one point in Collins's interview, the gang's leader justified their actions in value-expressive terms. Characterizing homosexuality as a serious societal problem, he stated that the gang members would not "sit back and watch the poisoning of America" (Collins, 1992). He further portrayed the group members as upholding important values when he compared their violent assaults on gay men to "the work of Batman or some other masked avenger" (pp. 195–196). His comments are consistent with the rhetoric of hate groups such as the Ku Klux Klan, which regularly appeal to moral authority (Segrest & Zeskind, 1989). As Harry (1992) observed, value-based justifications for antigay violence often derive from societal norms surrounding the institution of gender. Although disengaged from the conventional moral order, perpetrators may develop rationalizations that designate gay people as worthy of punishment and allow attackers to see themselves as "rendering gender justice and reaffirming the natural order of gender-appropriate behavior" (Harry, 1992; 116).

SOCIAL-EXPRESSIVE VIOLENCE

Membership in a social group often is a central component of one's identity (Hamner, 1992). By clearly differentiating and then attacking an out-group, antigay violence can help in-group members feel more positive about their group and, consequently, about themselves as well. For example, Weissman (1992) interviewed several young men who had harassed gay men in Greenwich Village. They generally described their behavior as a practical joke, but it appears also to have strengthened their sense of group solidarity. The informal leader explained, "Peer pressure has a lot to do with it. Sometimes you're forced into doing something to prove yourself to others" (p. 176). Another group member described his feelings after the incident: "Relief. A kind of high. There was also a strong, close feeling that we were all in something together" (p. 176).

Social-expressive motivations also were apparent among the previously mentioned Blue Boys (Collins, 1992). They had a clearly formed in-group, signified by their "uniform" of blue baseball jackets, their use of blue bats in their assaults, and their framed "Statement of Principals," which they claimed to have signed in blood. In addition, the Blue Boys' leader also seemed to seek recognition and acceptance from a larger audience; he fantasized that people who read about the group's exploits would cheer them on, much the way baseball fans cheer a home run (Collins, 1992).

Perpetrators in antigay sexual assaults may also be motivated by needs to maintain status and affiliation with their peers. From a series of interviews with perpetrators of male–male rapes, Groth and Burgess (1980) concluded, "Some offenders feel pressured to participate in gang rape to maintain status and membership with their peers. . . . [A]cceptance and recognition by one's peers becomes a dynamic in group rape, and mutual participation in the assault serves to strengthen and confirm the social bond among the assailants" (p. 808).

EGO-DEFENSIVE VIOLENCE

Antigay assaults can provide a means for young males to affirm their heterosexuality or masculinity by attacking someone who symbolizes an unacceptable aspect of their own personalities (e.g., homoerotic feelings or tendencies toward effeminacy). This process may be partly conscious, as evidenced in comments by the Blue Boys (Collins, 1992). Their leader repeatedly affirmed that they were "real men" who were "out there fucking chicks every night" (p. 194) and explained that they "chose the blue baseball bats because it's the color of the boy. The man is one gender. He is not female. It is male. There is no confusion. Blue is the color of men, and that's the color that men use to defeat the anti-male, which is the queer" (p. 194).

In many cases, the ego-defensive motivations of antigay attacks are likely to be hidden from the perpetrators themselves. A dramatic example can be found in the brutal murder of Robert Hillsborough by a gang of young men in San Francisco in the summer of 1977 (Shilts, 1982). One of the men convicted of the murder, 19-year-old John Cordova, stabbed Robert Hillsborough fifteen times, while shouting "faggot, faggot." What makes this story a possible example of defensive attitudes is the interesting fact that Cordova was also sexually attracted to men but he could not admit it to himself. He had an occasional sexual relationship with a male construction contractor, who said that Cordova often initiated sexual encounters but "never wanted to act like he knew what he was doin' " during them (Shilts, 1982; 168). Cordova would always wake up as if he were in a daze, insisting he had no idea what had happened the night before. When he stabbed Robert

Hillsborough over and over, Cordova may have been unconsciously attacking and striking out at his own homosexual desires.

Ego-defensive motives also can underlie sexual assaults in which the perpetrator apparently wished to punish the victim as a way of dealing with his own unresolved and conflicting sexual interests. From their interviews with perpetrators, Groth and Burgess (1980) speculated that assailants in male–male rape who were conflicted about their own homosexual attraction may have seen their victim as a temptation and subsequently have used rape in an attempt to punish him for arousing them.

Violence with Multiple Motivations

In many antigay assaults, the perpetrators probably act out of several motives simultaneously. Multiple motivations may be especially likely in street assaults by young male perpetrators. Such assailants are at a chronological age when establishing their adult identity, including their manhood, is of considerable importance (Erikson, 1963). Many of them strongly embrace what the culture has defined as "masculine" characteristics, while rejecting "feminine" characteristics (Horwitz & White, 1987). Identity formation is both a personal and a social process; it must be done for oneself, for one's peers, and for the larger society. Consequently, gay men and lesbians may serve simultaneously as multiple symbols for young male gangs. They may represent (1) unacceptable feelings or tendencies experienced privately by each gang member (for example, deviations from heterosexuality or culturally prescribed gender roles); (2) the out-group; and (3) what society has defined as evil. At the same time, such attacks may be based in part on past experiences with gay people. The perpetrator, for example, may have had an unpleasant interaction with an individual who incidentally was gay and may seek vengeance by attacking a proxy for that individual. Consequently, gang attacks may simultaneously serve experiential, ego-defensive, social-expressive, and value-expressive functions for the perpetrators.

Other perpetrators also are likely to have multiple motives for their antigay attacks. Police officers, for example, work to uphold societal values in an institution where the sense of the in-group is strong and masculinity has traditionally been revered (Niederhoffer, 1967). Some of them have interacted with an openly gay person only in a crime situation. Especially for young policemen, who may still be solidifying their adult identities, antigay violence may serve psychological functions quite similar to those previously discussed for street gangs. Similarly, parents who assault their lesbian daughters or gay sons may have multiple motivations. They may be trying to banish unacceptable feelings from a child whom they consider to be an extension of their own identity (an ego-defensive function), while fulfilling their culturally defined parental role of imparting society's values to their children (a value-expressive function), and while seeking to protect the integrity of their family from what they perceive as outside, perhaps alien influences (a social-expressive function). The assault also may result in part from the parent's feelings of anger and frustration that have built up during a long series of unpleasant interactions (an experiential function).

Consequences of Antigay Prejudice

Like members of other stigmatized groups, gay people face numerous psychological challenges as a result of society's hostility toward them. In addition to the psychological consequences of antigay prejudice, three topics warrant brief elaboration here: consequences of hiding one's sexual orientation, consequences of overt victimization, and consequences of antigay prejudice for heterosexuals (see also Garnets, Herek, & Levy, 1990).

Lesbians and gay men must traverse a sequence of events through which they recognize their own homosexual orientation, develop an identity based on it, and disclose their orientation to others. This process is usually termed *coming out* (a shortened form of *coming out of the closet*). Conversely, being *in the closet* or *closeted* refers to passing as heterosexual. Because of cultural heterosexism, people generally are presumed to be heterosexual. Coming out, therefore, is an ongoing process, and different gay people are out of the closet to varying degrees.

Most children internalize society's ideology of sex and gender at an early age. As a result, gay women and men usually experience some degree of negative feeling toward themselves when they first recognize their own homosexuality in adolescence or adulthood. This sense of what is usually called *internalized homophobia* often makes the process of identity formation more difficult (Malyon, 1982). In the course of coming out, most lesbians and gay men successfully overcome the threats to psychological well-being posed by heterosexism. They manage to reclaim disowned or devalued parts of themselves, developing an identity into which their sexuality is well integrated. Psychological adjustment appears to be highest among men and women who are committed to a gay or lesbian identity and who do not attempt to hide their homosexuality from others. Conversely, people with a homosexual orientation who have not yet come out, who wish that they could become heterosexual, or who are isolated from the gay community may experience greater psychological distress (Bell & Weinberg, 1978; Hammersmith & Weinberg, 1973; Malyon, 1982; Weinberg & Williams, 1974).

As a result of heterosexism, many individuals feel compelled to hide their homosexuality or "pass" as heterosexual (e.g., Humphreys, 1972; see also Goffman, 1963). Respondents to the San Francisco *Examiner's* 1989 national survey of lesbians and gay men, for example, waited an average of 4.6 years after knowing they were gay before they came out (which presumably involved disclosing their homosexual orientation to another person). Depending on the area of the country, between 23 and 40 percent had *not* told their family that they were gay; between 37 and 59 percent had *not* disclosed their sexual orientation to coworkers (Results of poll, 1989).

Hiding one's sexual orientation can create a painful discrepancy between public and private identities. Because they face unwitting acceptance of themselves by prejudiced heterosexuals, gay people who are passing may feel inauthentic, that they are living a lie, and that others would not accept them if they knew the truth (Goffman, 1963; Jones et al., 1984). The need to pass is likely to disrupt longstanding family relationships and friendships as lesbians and gay men create distance from others in order to avoid revealing their sexual orientation. When contact cannot be avoided, they may keep their interactions at a superficial level as a self-protective strategy. Passing also creates considerable strain for gay partnerships. As already noted, even openly gay people are deprived of institutional support for their long-term relationships (e.g., insurance benefits). Those who are passing must, in addition, actively hide or deny their relationship to family and friends; consequently, the problems and stresses common to any relationship must be faced without the social supports typically available to heterosexual lovers or spouses.

Once they come out, lesbians and gay men risk rejection by others, discrimination, and even violence, all of which can carry psychological consequences that endure long after their immediate physical effects have dissipated (Garnets, Herek, & Levy, 1990). Being the target of discrimination, for example, often leads to feelings of sadness and anxiety (Dion, 1986); it can also lead to an increased sense that life is difficult and unfair, and dissatisfaction with one's larger community (Birt & Dion, 1987).

Lesbian and gay male victims of hate crimes may face special psychological challenges. Because antigay hate crimes represent an attack on the victim's gay identity and her or his community, it is likely that the psychological consequences of such crimes include effects on the victim's feelings about herself or himself as a gay person and on her or his feelings toward the gay community. The victim's homosexuality may become directly linked to the heightened sense of vulnerability that normally follows victimization (Norris & Kaniasty, 1991). One's homosexual orientation consequently may be experienced as a source of danger, pain, and punishment rather than intimacy, love, and community. Internalized homophobia may reemerge or be intensified. Attempts to make sense of the attack, coupled with the common need to perceive the world as a just place, may lead to feelings that one has been justifiably punished for being gay (Bard & Sangrey, 1979; Lerner, 1970). Such characterological self-blame can lead to feelings of depression and helplessness (Janoff-Bulman, 1979), even in individuals who are otherwise comfortable with their sexual orientation (for further elaboration of these points, see Garnets et al., 1990; Herek, 1994a).

Further, a gay or lesbian crime survivor may experience increased discrimination or stigma from others who have learned about her or his sexual orientation as a consequence of the victimization. Such *secondary victimization* (Berrill & Herek, 1992), which can further intensify the negative psychological consequences of victimization, is often expressed explicitly by representatives of the criminal justice system, including police officers and judges (Berrill & Herek, 1992). It also extends outside the criminal justice system. If their sexual orientation becomes publicly known as a result of a crime, for example, some lesbians and gay men risk loss of employment or child custody. Even in jurisdictions where statutory protection is available, many gay people fear that disclosure of their sexual orientation as a result of victimization will result in hostility, harassment, and rejection from others. Secondary victimization may be experienced as an additional assault on one's identity and community, and thus an added source of stress. The threat of secondary victimization often acts as a barrier to reporting a crime or seeking medical, psychological, or social services (Berrill & Herek, 1992).

Although not often discussed, heterosexism also has negative consequences for heterosexuals. Because of the stigma attached to homosexuality, many heterosexuals monitor and constrict their own behavior to avoid being labeled gay; this pattern appears to be especially strong among American males (e.g., Herek, 1986a; Lehne, 1976; Pleck, 1981). For example, many men avoid clothing, hobbies, and mannerisms that might be labeled "effeminate." Antigay prejudice also interferes with same-sex friendships. Males with strongly antigay attitudes appear to have less intimate nonsexual friendships with other men than do males with tolerant attitudes (Devlin & Cowan, 1985).

Implications for Research

Empirical research is needed on all facets of psychological heterosexism, including its scope and prevalence in the population, its underlying motivations, its mental health consequences, and its prevention and reduction. Because describing a comprehensive research agenda in this area is beyond the scope of the present chapter, I briefly discuss here three questions around which I believe empirical inquiry is especially important. Obviously these are only a few of the many areas in which research should be conducted (for a more detailed discussion, see Herek & Berrill, 1990).

How can heterosexist attitudes and beliefs be changed or eliminated? The principal focus of past work has been describing the direction, intensity, and correlates of heterosexuals' attitudes toward lesbians and gay men. Many studies have explored the psychological processes that underlie antigay hostility but have been limited in their generalizability because of their reliance on convenience samples of college undergraduates. Other studies have used probability samples and survey methodology but have not been informed by psychological theory (for reviews, see Herek, 1984, 1991; Kite, 1994; Morin & Garfinkle, 1978). A task for future research, therefore, is to collect data from probability samples to address theoretically sophisticated questions.

One of the most important topics to be examined in such studies is the psychological processes that underlie changes in heterosexuals' attitudes toward lesbians and gay men. Even while most Americans continue to condemn homosexuality morally and to reject or feel uncomfortable about gay people personally, national survey data indicate that they are increasingly reluctant to condone discrimination on the basis of sexual orientation (e.g., Herek, 1994c; Hugick, 1992). This shift may reflect heterosexuals' increased opportunities for personal contact with an openly gay or lesbian individual (Herek & Glunt, 1993; Schneider & Lewis, 1984) or increased exposure to information about homosexuality and the gay and lesbian community (Anderson, 1981; Cerny & Polyson, 1984; Goldberg, 1982; Lance, 1987; Pagtolun-An & Clair, 1986; Stevenson, 1988). Such experiences may reduce prejudice by causing heterosexuals to perceive gay men and lesbians as individuals rather than a homogeneous group (Brewer & Kramer, 1985; Brewer & Miller, 1984; Wilder, 1978; but see also Rothbart & John, 1985). A complementary hypothesis is that acquiring new information or personal contact experiences may make previously negative attitudes less functional for meeting psychological needs (Herek, 1987b). Future research should explore these and other possible explanations for attitude change among heterosexuals.

How do lesbians and gay men cope successfully with problems created by psychological and cultural heterosexism? Empirical research is also needed on the mental health impact of heterosexism. We need to develop a better understanding of the negative psychological consequences of prejudice, discrimination, and violence for lesbians and gay men (e.g., Garnets et al., 1990). In particular, data are needed for understanding the aftermath of violent victimization and the factors that affect coping among lesbian and gay male survivors. Three types of factors should be examined. First, the impact of previctimization (background) variables, such as demographic characteristics, prior life stressors, and personality factors, should be assessed. Second, characteristics of the victimization itself should be examined. Data are needed, for example, about how psychological outcomes are affected by the type of attack, the severity of physical or psychological injury suffered, whether or not the the victims knew the assailant(s), whether or not the attack occurred in a gay-identified setting, whether or not the attack was perpetrated by an organized hate group, and whether or not the antigay nature of the attack was ever disclosed by the victim to others. Third, the effect of postvictimization experiences on coping should be examined. Possible variables to be considered here include the different cognitive strategies used by victims to make sense of their experience, and the different forms of social interaction and support available to survivors.

Given that most lesbians and gay men demonstrate normal psychological adjustment (Gonsiorek, 1991), it is also important to study how they successfully survive heterosexist stigma and function well in society. One hypothesis for possible exploration is that involvement with the gay community assists lesbians and gay men in coping with heterosexism. Community resources might aid individuals in making adaptive attributions about the causes of their discrimination or victimization as well as self-enhancing evaluations of their current status (Janoff-Bulman, 1979, 1982; Taylor, Wood, & Lichtman, 1983). For example, hate-crime victims who are integrated into the gay community may be better able than others to bolster their self-esteem by attributing victimization to societal heterosexism rather than to their own merits or abilities, or by comparing their own victimization experiences to the experiences of other lesbians and gay men who have suffered more serious injuries or losses (Crocker & Major, 1989).

What variables underlie overt expressions of heterosexism, such as acts of violence against lesbians and gay men? More data are needed to understand the processes through which behavioral expressions of heterosexism occur. In the area of antigay violence, for example, most information to date has been derived from small-scale surveys with convenience samples of lesbians and gay men and from reports of community-based social service agencies (e.g., Berrill, 1992). Data from perpetrators of violence are almost entirely absent from the literature (for interviews with perpetrators, see Collins, 1992; Comstock, 1991; Weissberg, 1992).

Future research should explore the social and psychological dynamics of antigay attacks using large and diverse samples of victim and perpetrator populations. One strategy is to describe victims' and perpetrators' experiences before, during, and after the attack. Studies with victims, for example, could describe the frequency with which various categories of victimization occur (e.g., homicide, physical assault, sexual assault, vandalism, threat) among various subgroups of the lesbian and gay community (e.g., racial, sexual, and geographic). Studies of perpetrators could describe motivations. To what extent were perpetrators driven by deep-seated hostility toward gay men and lesbians, for example, and to what extent did they succumb to peer pressure and situational factors?

Conclusion

In 1993, the American public was swept up in an unprecedented controversy about the status of lesbians and gay men in the United States military (Herek, 1993b). One of the least noted but perhaps most significant features of the public discussion was that, rather than questioning the loyalty or ability of gay men and lesbians, the policy debate primarily concerned heterosexuals' antigay prejudices. Although the military's exclusionary policies had been justified earlier on the basis of presumed performance deficits by gay male and lesbian personnel, the 1993 discourse eventually focused on the ability of heterosexuals to tolerate openly gay comrades in arms (Herek, 1993b).

Whether this shift in the terms of debate represents a fundamental advance by gay men and lesbians in their struggle for civil liberties remains to be seen. It seems clear, however, that the cultural, social, and psychological roots of heterosexism warrant increasing attention from social scientists, policymakers, and the lay public throughout the 1990s and into the new millennium.

References

Adam, B. D. (1978). *The survival of domination: Inferiorization and everyday life.* New York: Elsevier.

Adorno, T., Frenkel-Brunswik, E., Levinson, D. J., & Sanford, R. N. (1950). *The authoritarian personality.* New York: Harper & Row.

Allport, G. (1954). *The nature of prejudice.* New York: Addison Wesley.

Altemeyer, B. (1988). *Enemies of freedom: Understanding right-wing authoritarianism.* San Francisco: Jossey-Bass.

Anderson, C. L. (1981). The effect of a workshop on attitudes of female nursing students toward homosexuality. *Journal of Homosexuality, 7* (1), 57–69.

Bard, M., & Sangrey, D. (1979). *The crime victim's book.* New York: Basic Books.

Bayer, R. (1987). *Homosexuality and American psychiatry: The politics of diagnosis* (2nd Ed.). Princeton, NJ: Princeton University Press.

Bell, A. P., & Weinberg, M. S. (1978). *Homosexualities: A study of diversity among men and women.* New York: Simon & Schuster.

Berrill, K. T. (1992). Anti-gay violence and victimization in the United States: An overview. In G. M. Herek & K. T. Berrill (Eds.), *Hate crimes: Confronting violence against lesbians and gay men* (pp. 19–45). Newbury Park, CA: Sage.

Berrill, K. T., & Herek, G. M. (1992). Primary and secondary victimization in anti-gay hate crimes: Official response and public policy. In G. M. Herek & K. T. Berrill (Eds.), *Hate crimes: Confronting violence against lesbians and gay men* (pp. 289–305). Newbury Park, CA: Sage.

Bérubé, A. (1990). *Coming out under fire: The history of gay men and women in World War II.* New York: Free Press.

Bierly, M. M. (1985). Prejudice toward contemporary outgroups as a generalized attitude. *Journal of Applied Social Psychology, 15* (2), 189–199.

Birt, C. M., & Dion, K. L. (1987). Relative deprivation theory and responses to discrimination in a gay male and lesbian sample. *British Journal of Social Psychology, 26,* 139–145.

Brewer, M. B., & Kramer, R. M. (1985). The psychology of intergroup attitudes and behavior. *Annual Review of Psychology, 36,* 219–243.

Brewer, M. B., & Miller, N. (1984). Beyond the contact hypothesis: Theoretical perspectives on desegregation. In N. Miller & M. B. Brewer (Eds.), *Groups in contact: The psychology of desegregation* (pp. 281–302). San Diego: Academic Press.

Cerny, J. A., & Polyson, J. (1984). Changing homonegative attitudes. *Journal of Social and Clinical Psychology, 2* (4), 366–371.

Chapman, L. J., & Chapman, J. P. (1969). Illusory correlation as an obstacle to the use of valid psychodiagnostic signs. *Journal of Abnormal Psychology, 74,* 271–280.

Collins, M. (1992). The gay bashers. In G. M. Herek & K. T. Berrill (Eds.), *Hate crimes: Confronting violence against lesbians and gay men* (pp. 191–200). Newbury Park, CA: Sage.

Comstock, G. D. (1989). Victims of anti-gay/-lesbian violence. *Journal of Interpersonal Violence, 4,* 101–106.

Comstock, G. D. (1991). *Violence against lesbians and gay men.* New York: Columbia University Press.

Crocker, J., & Major, B. (1989). Social stigma and self-esteem: The self-protective properties of stigma. *Psychological Review, 96,* 608–630.

D'Augelli, A. (1992). Lesbian and gay male undergraduates' experiences of harassment and fear on campus. *Journal of Interpersonal Violence, 7,* 383–395.

Dean, L., Wu, S., & Martin, J. L. (1992). Trends in violence and discrimination against gay men in New York City: 1984 to 1990. In G. M. Herek & K. T. Berrill (Eds.), *Hate crimes: Confronting violence against lesbians and gay men* (pp. 46–64). Newbury Park, CA: Sage.

Deaux, K., & Lewis, L. L. (1984). Structure of gender stereotypes: Interrelationships among components and gender label. *Journal of Personality and Social Psychology, 46,* 991–1004.

Devlin, P. K., & Cowan, G. A. (1985). Homophobia, perceived fathering, and male intimate relationships. *Journal of Personality Assessment, 49,* 467–473.

Dion, K. L. (1986). Responses to perceived discrimination and relative deprivation. In J. M. Olson, C. P. Herman, & M. P. Zanna (Eds.), *Relative depri-*

vation and social comparison: The Ontario Symposium, Volume 4 (pp. 159–179). Hillsdale, NJ: Lawrence Erlbaum.

Erikson, E. H. (1963). *Childhood and society* (2nd Ed.). New York: W. W. Norton.

Fyfe, B. (1983). "Homophobia" or homosexual bias reconsidered. *Archives of Sexual Behavior, 12,* 549–554.

Garnets, L., Herek, G. M., & Levy, B. (1990). Violence and victimization of lesbians and gay men: Mental health consequences. *Journal of Interpersonal Violence, 5* (3), 366–383.

Gergen, K. J., & Gergen, M. M. (1981). *Social psychology.* New York: Harcourt Brace Jovanovich.

Gilman, S. L. (1985). *Difference and pathology: Stereotypes of sexuality, race, and madness.* Ithaca, NY: Cornell University Press.

Goffman, E. (1963). *Stigma: Notes on the management of spoiled identity.* Englewood Cliffs, NJ: Prentice-Hall.

Goldberg, R. (1982). Attitude change among college students toward homosexuality. *Journal of American College Health, 30* (6), 260–268.

Gonsiorek, J. C. (1991). The empirical basis for the demise of the illness model of homosexuality. In J. C. Gonsiorek & J. D. Weinrich (Eds.), *Homosexuality: Research implications for public policy* (pp. 115–136). Newbury Park, CA: Sage.

Gross, A. E., Green, S. K., Storck, J. T., & Vanyur, J. M. (1980). Disclosure of sexual orientation and impressions of male and female homosexuals. *Personality and Social Psychology Bulletin, 6,* 307–314.

Gross, L., & Aurand, S. K. (1992). *Discrimination and violence against lesbian women and gay men in Philadelphia and the Commonwealth of Pennsylvania.* Philadelphia: Philadelphia Lesbian and Gay Task Force. (Available from PLGTF, 1616 Walnut Street, #1005, Philadelphia, PA 19105-5313.)

Groth, A. N., & Burgess, A. W. (1980). Male rape: Offenders and victims. *American Journal of Psychiatry, 137* (7), 806–810.

Gurwitz, S. B., & Marcus, M. (1978). Effects of anticipated interaction, sex, and homosexual stereotypes on first impressions. *Journal of Applied Social Psychology, 8,* 47–56.

Hamilton, D. L. (Ed.) (1981). *Cognitive processes in stereotyping and intergroup behavior.* Hillsdale, NJ: Lawrence Erlbaum.

Hammersmith, S. K., & Weinberg, M. S. (1973). Homosexual identity: Commitment, adjustment, and significant others. *Sociometry, 36* (1), 56–79.

Hamner, K. A. (1992). Gay-bashing: A social identity analysis of violence against lesbians and gay men. In G. M. Herek & K. T. Berrill (Eds.), *Hate crimes: Confronting violence against lesbians and gay men* (pp. 179–190). Newbury Park, CA: Sage.

Harry, J. (1992). Conceptualizing anti-gay violence. In G. M. Herek & K. T. Berrill (Eds.), *Hate crimes: Confronting violence against lesbians and gay men* (pp. 113–122). Newbury Park, CA: Sage.

Henley, N. M., & Pincus, F. (1978). Interrelationships of sexist, racist, and antihomosexual attitudes. *Psychological Reports, 42,* 83–90.

Herek, G. M. (1984). Beyond homophobia: A social psychological perspective on attitudes toward lesbians and gay men. *Journal of Homosexuality, 10* (1/2), 1–21.

Herek, G. M. (1986a). On heterosexual masculinity: Some psychical consequences of the social construction of gender and sexuality. *American Behavioral Scientist, 29* (5), 563–577.

Herek, G. M. (1986b). The instrumentality of attitudes: Toward a neofunctional theory. *Journal of Social Issues, 42* (2), 99–114.

Herek, G. M. (1987a). Religion and prejudice: A comparison of racial and sexual attitudes. *Personality and Social Psychology Bulletin, 13* (1), 56–65.

Herek, G. M. (1987b). Can functions be measured? A new perspective on the functional approach to attitudes. *Social Psychology Quarterly, 50,* 285–303.

Herek, G. M. (1988). Heterosexuals' attitudes toward lesbians and gay men: Correlates and gender differences. *Journal of Sex Research 30,* 239–244.

Herek, G. M. (1989). Hate crimes against lesbians and gay men: Issues for research and policy. *American Psychologist, 44* (6), 948–955.

Herek, G. M. (1990). The context of anti-gay violence: Notes on cultural and psychological heterosexism. *Journal of Interpersonal Violence, 5* (3), 316–333.

Herek, G. M. (1991). Stigma, prejudice, and violence against lesbians and gay men. In J. Gonsiorek & J. Weinrich (Eds.), *Homosexuality: Research implications for public policy* (pp. 60–80). Newbury Park, CA: Sage.

Herek, G. M. (1992). Psychological heterosexism and antigay violence: The social psychology of bigotry and bashing. In G. M. Herek, & K. T. Berrill (Eds.), *Hate crimes: Confronting violence against lesbians and gay men* (pp. 149–169). Newbury Park, CA: Sage.

Herek, G. M. (1993a). Documenting prejudice against lesbians and gay men on campus: The Yale Sexual Orientation Survey. *Journal of Homosexuality, 25* (4), 15–30.

Herek, G. M. (1993b). Sexual orientation and military service: A social science perspective. *American Psychologist, 48,* 538–549.

Herek, G. M. (1994a). Heterosexism, hate crimes, and the law. In M. Costanzo & S. Oskamp (Eds.), *Violence and the Law* (pp. 89–112). Thousand Oaks, CA: Sage.

Herek, G. M. (1994b). Assessing attitudes toward lesbians and gay men: A review of empirical research with the ATLG scale. In B. Greene & G. M. Herek (Eds.) *Lesbian and gay psychology: Theory, research, and clinical applications* (pp. 206–228). Thousand Oaks, CA: Sage.

Herek, G. M. (in press). The HIV epidemic and public attitudes toward lesbians and gay men. In M. P. Levine, P. Nardi, & J. Gagnon (Eds.), *The impact of the HIV epidemic on the lesbian and gay community.* Chicago: University of Chicago Press.

Herek, G. M., & Berrill, K. (1990). Anti-gay violence and mental health: Setting an agenda for research. *Journal of Interpersonal Violence, 5* (3), 414–423.

Herek, G. M. & Berrill, K. T. (Eds.) (1992). *Hate crimes: Confronting violence against lesbians and gay men.* Newbury Park, CA: Sage.

Herek, G. M., & Glunt, E. K. (1993). Interpersonal contact and antigay prejudice: Results from a national survey. *The Journal of Sex Research, 30,* 239–244.

Hood, R. W., Jr. (1973). Dogmatism and opinions about mental illness. *Psychological Reports, 32,* 1283–1290.

Horwitz, A. V., & White, H. R. (1987). Gender role orientations and styles of pathology among adolescents. *Journal of Health and Social Behavior, 28,* 158–170.

Hugick, L. (1992, June). Public opinion divided on gay rights. *Gallup Poll Monthly,* 2–6.

Humphreys, L. (1972). *Out of the closets: The sociology of homosexual liberation.* Englewood Cliffs, NJ: Prentice-Hall.

Hunter, J. (1992). Violence against lesbian and gay male youths. In G. M. Herek, & K. T. Berrill (Eds.), *Hate crimes: Confronting violence against lesbians and gay men* (pp. 76–82). Newbury Park, CA: Sage.

Janoff-Bulman, R. (1979). Characterological versus behavioral self-blame: Inquiries into depression and rape. *Journal of Personality and Social Psychology, 37,* 1798–1809.

Janoff-Bulman, R. (1982). Esteem and control bases of blame: "Adaptive" strategies for victims versus observers. *Journal of Personality, 50,* 180–192.

Jones, E. E., Farina, A., Hastorf, A. H., Markus, H., Miller, D. T., & Scott, R. A. (1984). *Social stigma: The psychology of marked relationships.* New York: W. H. Freeman.

Karr, R. (1978). Homosexual labeling and the male role. *Journal of Social Issues, 34* (3), 73–83.

Katz, D. (1960). The functional approach to the study of attitudes. *Public Opinion Quarterly, 24,* 163–204.

Kaufman, A., DiVasto, P., Jackson, R., Voorhees, D., & Christy, J. (1980). Male rape victims: Noninstitutionalized assault. *American Journal of Psychiatry, 137* (2), 221–223.

Kite, M. E. (1984). Sex differences in attitudes toward homosexuals: A meta-analytic review. *Journal of Homosexuality, 10* (1/2), 69–81.

Kite, M. E. (1994). When perceptions meet reality: Individual differences in reactions to gay men and lesbians. In B. Greene & G. Herek (Eds.), *Lesbian and gay psychology: Theory, research, and clinical applications* (pp. 25–53). Thousand Oaks, CA: Sage.

Kite, M. E., & Deaux, K. (1986). Attitudes toward homosexuality: Assessment and behavioral consequences. *Basic and Applied Social Psychology, 7* (2), 137–162.

Kite, M. E., & Deaux, K. (1987). Gender belief systems: Homosexuality and the implicit inversion theory. *Psychology of Women Quarterly, 11* (1), 83–96.

Lance, L. M. (1987). The effects of interaction with gay persons on attitudes toward homosexuality. *Human Relations, 40* (6), 329–336.

Laner, M. R., & Laner, R. H. (1979). Personal style or sexual preference: Why gay men are disliked. *International Review of Modern Sociology, 9,* 215–228.

Larsen, K. S., Reed, M., & Hoffman, S. (1980). Attitudes of heterosexuals toward homosexuality: A Likert-type scale and construct validity. *Journal of Sex Research, 16* (3), 245–257.

Lehne, G. K. (1976). Homophobia among men. In D. S. David & R. Brannon (Eds.), *The forty-nine percent majority: The male sex role* (pp. 66–88). Reading, MA: Addison-Wesley.

Lerner, M. J. (1970). The desire for justice and reactions to victims. In J. Macaulay & L. Berkowitz (Eds.), *Altruism and helping behavior* (pp. 205–229). New York: Academic Press.

Levine, M. P. (1979). Employment discrimination against gay men. *International Review of Modern Sociology, 9* (5–7), 151–163.

Levine, M. P., & Leonard, R. (1984). Discrimination against lesbians in the work force. *Signs, 9* (4), 700–710.

MacDonald, A. P., Jr., & Games, R. G. (1974). Some characteristics of those who hold positive and negative attitudes toward homosexuals. *Journal of Homosexuality, 1* (1), 9–27.

Malyon, A. K. (1982).Psychotherapeutic implications of internalized homophobia in gay men. *Journal of Homosexuality, 7* (2/3), 59–69.

Marsiglio, W. (1993). Attitudes toward homosexual activity and gays as friends: A national survey of heterosexual 15–19-year-old males. *The Journal of Sex Research, 30,* 12–17.

McClintock, C. (1958). Personality syndromes and attitude change. *Journal of Personality, 26,* 479–492.

McClosky, H., & Brill, A. (1983). *Dimensions of tolerance: What Americans believe about civil liberties.* New York: Russell Sage.

Melton, G. B. (1989). Public policy and private prejudice: Psychology and law on gay rights. *American Psychologist, 44,* 933–940.

Morin, S. F., & Garfinkle, E. M. (1978). Male homophobia. *Journal of Social Issues, 34* (1), 29–47.

Niederhoffer, A. (1967). *Behind the shield: The police in urban society.* Garden City, NY: Doubleday.

Norris, F. H., & Kaniasty, K. (1991). The psychological experience of crime: A test of the mediating role of beliefs in explaining the distress of victims. *Journal of Social and Clinical Psychology, 10,* 239–261.

Nungesser, L. G. (1983). *Homosexual acts, actors, and identities.* New York: Praeger.

O'Brien, R. M. (1985). *Crime and victimization data.* Beverly Hills, CA: Sage.

Pagtolun-An, I., & Clair, J. M. (1986). An experimental study of attitudes toward homosexuals. *Deviant Behavior, 7,* 121–135.

Pleck, J. H. (1981). *The myth of masculinity.* Cambridge: MIT Press.

Results of poll. (1989, June 6). *San Francisco Examiner,* p. A19.

Rivera, R. R. (1991). Sexual orientation and the law. In J. C. Gonsiorek & J. D. Weinrich (Eds.), *Homosexuality: Research implications for public policy.* (pp. 81–100). Newbury Park, CA: Sage.

Rothbart, M., & John, O. P. (1985). Social categorization and behavioral episodes: A cognitive analysis of the effects of intergroup contact. *Journal of Social Issues, 41* (3), 81–104.

Rubenstein, W. (Ed.) (1993). *Lesbians, gay men, and the law.* New York: New Press.

Schneider, W., & Lewis, I. A. (1984, February/March). The straight story on homosexuality and gay rights. *Public Opinion, 7,* 16–20, 59–60.

Segrest, M., & Zeskind, L. (1989). *Quarantines and death: The far Right's homophobic agenda.* Atlanta: Center for Democratic Renewal.

Shields, S. A., & Harriman, R. E. (1984). Fear of male homosexuality: Cardiac responses of low and high homonegative males. *Journal of Homosexuality,* 10 (1/2), 53–67.

Shilts, R. (1982). *The mayor of Castro Street: The life and times of Harvey Milk.* New York: St. Martin's.

Smith, K. T. (1971). Homophobia: A tentative personality profile. *Psychological Reports, 29,* 1091–1094.

Smith, M. B., Bruner, J. S., & White, R. W. (1956). *Opinions and personality.* New York: Wiley.

Snyder, M. (1981). On the self-perpetuating nature of social stereotypes. In D. Hamilton (Ed.), *Cognitive processes in stereotyping and intergroup behavior* (pp. 183–212). Hillsdale, NJ: Erlbaum.

Snyder, M., & Uranowitz, S. W. (1978). Reconstructing the past: Some cognitive consequences of person perception. *Journal of Personality and Social Psychology, 36,* 941–950.

Sobel, H. J. (1976). Adolescent attitudes toward homosexuality in relation to self concept and body satisfaction. *Adolescence, 11* (43) 443–453.

Stevenson, M. R. (1988). Promoting tolerance for homosexuality: An evaluation of intervention strategies. *Journal of Sex Research, 25* (4), 500–511.

Storms, M. D. (1978). Attitudes toward homosexuality and femininity in men. *Journal of Homosexuality, 3* (3), 257–263.

Storms, M. D., Stivers, M. L., Lambers, S. M., & Hill, C. A. (1981). Sexual scripts for women. *Sex Roles, 7,* 699–707.

Szasz, T. S. (1970). *The manufacture of madness.* New York: Harper & Row.

Taylor, S. E., Wood, J. V., & Lichtman, R. R. (1983). It could be worse: Selective evaluation as a response to victimization. *Journal of Social Issues, 39* (2), 19–40.

Von Schulthess, B. (1992). Violence in the streets: Anti-lesbian assault and harassment in San Francisco. In G. M. Herek, & K. T. Berrill (Eds.), *Hate crimes: Confronting violence against lesbians and gay men* (pp. 65–75). Newbury Park, CA: Sage.

Weinberg, G. (1972). *Society and the healthy homosexual.* New York: St. Martin's.

Weinberg, M. S., & Williams, C. J. (1974). *Male homosexuals: Their problems and adaptations.* New York: Oxford University Press.

Weissman, E. (1992). Kids who attack gays. In G. M. Herek & K. T. Berrill (Eds.), *Hate crimes: Confronting violence against lesbians and gay men* (pp. 170–178). Newbury Park, CA: Sage.

Wilder, D. A. (1978). Reduction of intergroup discrimination through individuation of the out-group. *Journal of Personality and Social Psychology, 36,* 1261–1374.

14

The Impact of the HIV Epidemic on U.S. Gay Male Communities

Jay P. Paul, Robert B. Hays, and Thomas J. Coates

By the end of December 1993, over 360,000 cases of AIDS had been reported in the United States, and over 220,200 people reportedly died of AIDS (Center for Disease Control and Prevention, 1994). Gay and bisexual men continue to be the U.S. population hardest hit by AIDS, with almost 60 percent of AIDS cases in the United States being in this group.[1] Certain urban centers with large gay populations have been especially hard hit, with cumulative totals of reported AIDS cases by the end of 1993 running to over 58,000 in New York City, over 18,000 in San Francisco, and 23,000 in Los Angeles (Centers for Disease Control and Prevention, 1994). Both the last decade's history and immediate future of the collective gay/lesbian/bisexual[2] community have been dramatically altered in the face of this disaster.

More than a medical issue, AIDS has wrought a major political, social, and psychological sea change in gay communities. In the history of gay communities in the United States, the point dividing the world

---

[1] This percentage is based on the total number of men who reported sex with men as an exposure category, divided by the total number of cases reported to the Centers for Disease Control and Prevention by the end of 1993, and it therefore includes men with multiple exposure categories.

[2] For brevity and clarity, we occasionally use the term "gay" to refer to all who self-identify as part of a gay/lesbian/bisexual collectivity (for example, in talking about "gay community" and "gay activism") rather than its more restrictive common usage referring to homosexually active men who identify as "gay." When using it in its more restrictive meaning, we will refer to "gay men."

"pre-AIDS" and "post-AIDS" seems likely to eclipse the significance of the date of the so-called Stonewall riots (the night of June 27–28, 1969, popularly viewed as the birth of modern gay activism in the United States). The HIV epidemic has affected practically every aspect of gay life: sexuality, the meaning of being gay, the social structures and modes of participation in the community, the creative output of a generation facing its mortality, and alliance-building between gay activists and other political/social activist groups. Urban gay male culture has shifted from one that exulted in youth, freedom, and pleasure to one in which illness, death, and loss are omnipresent. Urban gay communities have met the tremendous challenges of the HIV epidemic with ingenuity, resilience, unparalleled behavior changes and an outpouring of volunteerism and giving. The previous decade of community organization and development laid the groundwork to adapt programs to deal with this crisis over a prolonged period of governmental neglect and persistent attacks by right-wing political and religious leaders.

In this chapter, we discuss research findings and our observations of ways in which this epidemic has affected gay and bisexual men, gay communities, and public perceptions of homosexuality. The impact of AIDS has reverberated through gay communities at four levels: (1) the individual level, in terms of changes in gay and bisexual men's behavior, attitudes, and emotional well-being; (2) the social level, in terms of changes in interpersonal relations, social networks, and norms; (3) the community level, in terms of changes in the gay community's structure, institutions and direction; and (4) the societal level, in terms of changes in the gay community's relationship with the larger society.

Much of the empirical work to date has been done with white male samples (primarily in large American cities), although the information available on people of color is increasing. We will, nonetheless, acknowledge the diversity of circumstances and responses among various subgroups of the so-called gay male community, and point to the need for further research in a variety of areas. Describing the impact of an ongoing major historical phenomenon like the HIV epidemic risks distortions that only the passage of time can correct (Pressman, 1990), but we hope our speculations can generate hypotheses for future research.

The Context of Change: The U.S. Gay Community Before AIDS

The modern gay community and gay activism in the United States has developed in an ongoing fashion since the period after World War II (Adam, 1987; Bérubé, 1990; D'Emilio, 1983; see also Garnets & D'Augelli, in this volume). During the 1950s, existing gay and lesbian groups attempted to gain some degree of "acceptability" within a society that repressed and stigmatized diversity. The gay liberation movement following the Stonewall riots was one of a series of social movements that shook the United States in the 1960s and 1970s. Gay liberation challenged the social order rooted in the heterosexual nuclear family, with its institutionalized sexism, entrenched primacy of procreative sexuality, and stigmatization of homosexuality.

As gay-identified gathering places in many larger U.S. cities became less subject to police raids and repression, neighborhoods developed with distinct clusterings of gay-related businesses and gay populations (Levine, 1979). From a clandestine bar-oriented world that offered a limited refuge from societal discrimination, the urban gay community developed a broader and more open infrastructure of meeting places, businesses, institutions, political associations, religious groups, social clubs, newspapers, resorts, and special interest groups (Humphries, 1979; Newman, 1978). Gay men, lesbians, and bisexuals were no longer as socially invisible and isolated as they had been prior to 1969. Being part of a visible collective entity helped generate new community-level responses to such problems as antigay stigmatization, discrimination, and violence. The newly emerging political and economic clout of the gay constituency was tested by the first wave of openly gay community leaders.

With the emergence of urban gay communities, came the development of a unique gay male bathhouse culture (Brodsky, 1987; Judell, 1978; Lauritsen, 1987; Weinberg & Williams, 1979). Gay male liberation of the 1970s emphasized the celebration of gay male sexuality, the avoidance of constrictive gender roles, and the exploration of new ways of bonding. Sexual experimentation was a means whereby gay and bisexual men could free themselves of societally imposed notions of guilt and shame around homoeroticism (Marks, 1988). This led to a debate within the urban gay male community even before AIDS about the emphasis on sexuality by some men, with critics charging that gay male bonding patterns were being reduced to the mutual pursuit of orgasm (Kramer, 1978).

Rates of sexually transmitted diseases within urban gay male communities skyrocketed (Peyton, 1988; Shilts, 1987). Among a 1970s national convenience sample of over 1,000 gay men (Spada, 1979), 44 percent had contracted a sexually transmitted disease (STD) and 53 percent had been infested by "crabs" (body lice). Thirty-five percent of a San Francisco gay male sample (Bell & Weinberg, 1978) reported one or two previous STDs; 28 percent reported at least three episodes of an STD. Rectal gonorrhea rates among asymptomatic San Francisco gay/

bisexual men using on-site or outreach services of one STD clinic peaked at 9.1 percent in 1981 and have declined to 0.9 percent in 1990 (Pickering, Sharpton, Thornhill, & Di Milia, 1991). The spread of hepatitis B among urban gay men in the late 1970s led to greater public education and awareness of health dangers, the recruitment of gay male volunteers to participate in vaccine trials, and the first attempts to define what would come to be known as "safer sex." The vaccine trials were the first collaboration between groups within the gay community and the Centers for Disease Control, and represented a forerunner of the community-based responses to the advent of the HIV epidemic.

Growing gay visibility also stimulated a serious backlash; in a number of ballot initiatives, the religious Right challenged the growing political power and presence of the gay community in the late 1970s. This coalition of fundamentalist and conservative Christian groups pursued a political remedy to their discomfort with the social upheavals of the previous decades, which led to an increasingly secular American culture in which religious dogma's moral absolutism no longer prevailed. The reactionary response of the New Right preceded any public awareness of AIDS, but the emergence of the HIV epidemic provided additional fuel for their attacks on homosexuality as an illness and a sin.

On the eve of the HIV epidemic, lesbians, gay men, and bisexuals had achieved increased public visibility, but were also facing increasing schisms and uncertainty within the gay political movement. This visibility was primarily limited to those large U.S. urban centers (e.g., New York, San Francisco, Los Angeles) that had established gay neighborhoods with gay-specific groups, institutions, social structures, and political clout. These same cities would become the epidemic's early epicenters. In a cruel twist, the sexual mores emphasizing erotic exploration and experimentation in the name of sexual liberation contributed to the rapid spread of HIV among urban gay and bisexual males. However, the developing sense of gay community in those areas would enable the mobilization and initiation of community-based responses to the crisis. The shared threat of the HIV epidemic and political attacks of the Right drew together disparate groups, and contributed to a renewed sense of community.

Impact on Individual Life-Styles

Changes in Sexual Behavior

Dramatic changes have occurred in gay men's sexual behavior since the advent of the AIDS crisis (Coates et al., 1988; Ekstrand & Coates, 1990; Martin et al., 1989; McCusker et al., 1989), perhaps the most ex-

tensive behavioral shifts ever documented in the public health literature (Coates, 1990). Most pronounced have been declines in rates of
unprotected anal intercourse and in the number of male sexual partners, two factors which were identified early on as related to developing AIDS (Martin, 1987; Schechter et al., 1988). The incorporation of
condom use into gay male sexual practices has certainly been a striking
change noted in research (Catania et al., 1991). One longitudinal survey of 624 New York City gay men (Martin et al., 1989) found reports
of condom use to skyrocket from 2 percent in 1981 to 62 percent in
1987. Oral-genital sex remains widely practiced by gay men; Martin
and his associates (1989) found that 85 percent of respondents had engaged in fellatio in 1987. However, swallowing semen has greatly declined, with less than 10 percent reporting this activity in 1987. Likewise, rimming and fisting appear to have decreased (Ekstrand &
Coates, 1990; Johnson & McGrath, 1987). Corresponding with these
changes are sharp declines in the incidence of rectal gonorrhea (Coates
et al., 1988; Schulz, Friedman, Kristal, et al., 1984). Increases in the
percentages of urban gay men who practice celibacy and monogamy
have also been reported (Martin et al., 1989). Findings from the San
Francisco Men's Health Study (SFMHS; Ekstrand & Coates, 1990), a
population-based sample of 686 gay men interviewed at 6-month inter-
vals since 1984, show that the percentage of men with multiple sex
partners steadily decreased from 80 percent in 1984 to slightly over 50
percent in 1988. Similarly, the percentage of men engaging in sex with
anonymous partners declined from 50 percent in 1984 to 30 percent
in 1988.

Since the first indication that substance use in concert with sexual
activity was associated with greater sexual risk among gay and bisexual
men (Stall et al., 1986), public health messages have emphasized the
desirability of avoiding sex under the influence. Evidence suggests that
the use of a variety of drugs (e.g., nitrite inhalants, cocaine, marijuana)
in combination with sexual activity has declined over the last decade
(Leigh, 1990; Martin, 1990).

Unfortunately, these patterns of behavioral change are uneven:
much less sexual risk reduction has been observed in gay and bisexual
men who are outside AIDS epicenters (Ames & Beeker, 1990; Kelly et
al., 1990; St. Lawrence et al., 1989; Ruefli et al., 1992), ethnic minorities
(Peterson et al., 1989), substance abusers (Paul et al., 1993), and
younger (Hays, Kegeles, & Coates, 1990; Stall et al., 1992). For example, younger gay men are consistently found to engage in higher rates
of unsafe sex than older gay men (Hays, Kegeles, & Coates, 1990; Stall
et al., 1992), resulting in a disproportionate number of new HIV sero-
conversions within the gay community among younger men. One 1992
population-based survey of San Francisco gay men aged 18 to 29,

found 17 percent to be HIV+, with seroprevalence rates ranging from 5 percent among 18- to 23-year-olds to 28 percent in 27- to 29-year-olds (Winkelstein et al., 1993). In response to these findings, a number of AIDS organizations are developing AIDS prevention programs tailored to the specific needs and subcultures of gay and bisexual men who are young (Kegeles et al., 1992; Hays, Kegeles, & Coates, 1993), from rural areas or small towns (Beadnell & Roffman, 1992; Kelly et al., 1991; Roffman et al., 1991), and men of color (Peterson, Coates, et al., 1992).

Even in urban areas which have shown substantial declines in rates of unprotected anal sex, many gay and bisexual men appear to be having difficulty consistently following sexual risk-reduction guidelines (Adib et al., 1991; Ekstrand & Coates, 1990; Stall et al., 1990). Nineteen percent of the respondents in one longitudinal survey of San Francisco gay men (Stall et al., 1990) had "relapsed" to unprotected anal sex with a nonmonogamous partner at least once between 1984 and 1987. A considerable body of literature now exists detailing individual, situational, and social variables associated with whether or not gay and bisexual men engage in safer sex, including such factors as perceived risk of HIV infection, perceived peer norms regarding safer sex, sexual communication skills, self-efficacy regarding condom use, enjoyment levels of safer versus unsafe sex, and combining drug or alcohol use with sex (e.g., Aspinwall et al., 1991; Bahr, et al., 1993; McCusker et al., 1989; Offir, Fisher, Williams, & Fisher, 1993).

After a period of sexual constraint and reappraisal, the gay community has generated new forms of sexual expression within somewhat safer contexts. Though we cannot locate published data on this, it appears that there has been an increase in risk-free expressions of gay sexuality that involve a greater use of fantasy, such as "phone sex" or participating in computer bulletin boards focused on gay male sex. In addition, a number of gay male "sex clubs" have opened in many urban communities. In an exploratory ethnographic study of San Francisco sex clubs, Frutchey and Williams (1992) found that patrons report an increasing popularity of such sites due to dissatisfaction with gay bars as a place to socialize and meet sex partners. According to Frutchey and Williams, these clubs provide strong environmental reinforcement for safer sex and are enjoyed by patrons not only for the availability of sexual partners, but for their social atmosphere, their affirmation of gay sexuality, and the sense of safety as a gay site. Since disagreement continues over whether commercial sex venues such as sex clubs and bathhouses promote safer or unsafe sex (Bolton, Vincke, & Mak, 1992) and over how prevention efforts can be more effective in these establishments, empirical data on these issues would be valuable.

It has been suggested that concern about AIDS contributes to increases in sexual dysfunctions among gay men, including erectile and orgasmic difficulties, diminished sexual interest, and aversion to sex (Gochros, 1992; Harowski, 1987; Odets, 1991). The lack of comparable data sets on the sexual functioning of gay and bisexual men prior to and since the advent of AIDS makes it difficult to test these hypotheses. Bell and Weinberg (1978) provide a rare glimpse of the sexual functioning of urban gay men in the pre-AIDS era; further research comparing those incidence rates to rates of sexual problems in a comparable sample today is needed. Nevertheless, using a convenience sample of 205 New York City gay and bisexual men, Meyer-Bahlburg and his colleagues (1991) found HIV+ men experienced more problems with lack of sexual interest, diminished sexual pleasure, and erectile difficulties than did HIV− men; no differences were found in orgasmic dysfunction. As these problems were not linked to medical status, the authors suggested they may be mediated by affective responses to the epidemic. Similarly, Catalan and his colleagues (1992) found that infection with HIV had adverse sexual effects in a population of gay men attending STD clinics in England, irrespective of medical status, and suggested that the incidence of delayed ejaculation (a relatively infrequent problem in the general population) was related to concerns about infecting sexual partners. However, Cohen, Salit, and Emmott (1993) found sexual dysfunction was related to increasing severity of HIV illness. In a convenience sample of 180 (96 HIV+; 84 HIV−) gay men recruited in medical settings in Toronto, rates of erectile disorder and hypoactive sexual desire disorder were, respectively 50 and 42 percent among those with an AIDS diagnosis, and 10 and 20 percent among mildly symptomatic HIV+s, but 0 percent for those who were either HIV− or asymptomatic HIV+. However, half of the asymptomatic HIV+ gay men reported dissatisfaction with their sex life, which may be a consequence of reported declines in sexual activity (apparently related to fear of disclosure of HIV status and of rejection). Only 11 percent of the HIV− men reported problems in their sex life, and all of them felt that *excessive* sexual activity was a problem—commonly regarded as a behavioral addiction.

Redefining Gay Sexuality

The threat of HIV has led gay and bisexual men, collectively and individually, to reexamine and redefine their sexuality over the last decade. This questioning goes beyond the evaluation of specific sexual practices to an exploration of the place and significance of sex in gay life. Sexuality was a primary focus and common bonding experience for gay men in the 1970s; AIDS forcibly altered this sexual expression of identity and affiliation in the gay community. Nowadays, the potentially mortal dangers of unrestrained passion are all too clear; illness and death have invaded the realm of the erotic.

Gay and bisexual men have two major tasks before them in adapting to sex in the era of AIDS: first, to revitalize gay male sexuality and overcome its negative associations; second, to revise the symbology of eroticism, love, and commitment based on "safer sex" guidelines. Gay men have had to work hard for years to affirm the positive meanings of sex in the face of contrary messages from a culture that is uncomfortable with sex generally and specifically stigmatizes homosexuality. Risk reduction messages tread an uneasy line between advocating necessary public health guidelines and imposing a code of morality under the rubric of public health (e.g., see discussion of "sexual promiscuity" in Bolton, 1992). Significantly, research indicates that campaigns using gay-sensitive, sex-positive risk reduction messages are more effective than fear-based prevention campaigns (Quadland & Shattls, 1987; Rosser, 1991).

However, the gay community has only begun to articulate an amended "vocabulary" of sexual expression that accommodates to this new age of sexual caution. To some degree, continuing high-risk sexual practices may be a result of the positive meanings attached to unsafe sex and the negative connotations of safer sex. Sex between men serves strong social affiliative needs as well as sexual needs, and qualitative research suggests that high-risk sexual practices may serve as an expression of love, affection, commitment, acceptance, or passion (Hickson et al., 1992; Levine & Siegel, 1992). As Prieur et al. (1989) noted, "There can lie a good deal of longing and love in unsafe sex—and that is why the whole problem is so extremely difficult." Research has consistently indicated that unprotected anal sex is more common among men in primary relationships than among those who have no steady partner (Martin, Dean, Garcia, & Hall, 1989; McKirnan et al., 1991; McKusick, Horstman, & Coates, 1985). Many HIV seroconcordant couples choose to have sex without condoms as they believe they are not at further sexual risk, but this trend also reflects a perceived conflict between an emotional allegiance and risk-reduction guidelines. Pollack and his colleagues' (1990) study of the gay men in the San Francisco AIDS Behavioral Research Project [ABRP] cohort found that men practicing unsafe sex within primary relationships were likely to describe themselves as having the same serostatus as their partner, being in love, and responding to partners' requests. Among a San Francisco sample of gay men entering substance abuse treatment, 51 percent of those reporting unprotected anal sex said that on "most" or "all" occasions they were in love; 70 percent reported thinking most or every time that it would please their sex partner (Paul, Stall, Crosby, Barrett, & Midanik, 1993).

A condom may represent an emotional as well as physical barrier for some gay men. While implying a concern for the other partner, it may suggest a fear of his potential infectivity, and serve as an ever-present reminder of disease. Further, limiting one's repertoire to safer sex may lead to decreases in physical satisfaction, emotional gratification, and a sense of intimacy between partners (Gold et al., 1991; Martin, 1986). Further research in this arena examining the complex subjective meanings of sexual behaviors and what determines the level of satisfaction associated with given activities may help us to understand the difficulties of maintaining low-risk sexual practices once a gay or bisexual man has learned to initiate such behaviors.

Impact on Health Habits

The AIDS epidemic has led to changes in health promotion activities within the gay community. Many who are HIV-infected may see health habits (such as careful diet, exercise, stress reduction, and rest) as part of a sensible program of secondary prevention. Such changes may also serve important intrapsychic functions for men under the shadow of HIV, by providing a sense of control over one's health. Studies of sexual risk reduction, secondary prevention, and the natural history of HIV disease in gay men have also provided opportunities to learn about gay men's participation in other health behaviors. After sexual practices, the area that has probably received the most research focus is alcohol and drug use.

Decrease in Alcohol and Drug Use

Longitudinal studies of gay men have suggested an abatement in substance use over the last decade. Martin and his colleagues (1989) reported declines in alcohol abuse and recreational drug use in a cohort of New York City gay men. Approximately one-half of the 12 percent of the sample diagnosed as alcohol abusers in 1986 did not meet the criteria for alcohol abuse upon follow-up in 1987. Use of inhalant nitrites, barbiturates, amphetamines, and hallucinogens declined 80 percent between the pre-AIDS baseline of 1981 and follow-up in 1987. Declines were also observed for cocaine and opiate use, but these were not statistically significant. The percentage of abstainers from all drug use more than doubled, from 16 percent in 1981 to 39 percent in 1987. Ostrow and his colleagues (1990) also reported substantial reductions between 1984 and 1988 in drug use within a Chicago cohort of gay men, although the prevalence of heavy drinking (at least 60 drinks per month) remained constant (between 12 and 16%). Using DSM-III-R diagnostic criteria, Remien and his associates (1990) found high lifetime rates of alcohol and drug abuse/dependence (36 and 48%, respectively) but low *current* rates (3.4 and 6.7%, respectively) in a sample of 208 New York City gay men, supporting Martin's findings of a pattern of remission from alcohol and other drug abuse among gay men.

Remien and his coworkers (1990) also examined respondents' reasons for ending their problematic use of alcohol or drugs since 1982 (when the HIV epidemic had begun). Commonly given reasons included fear of AIDS (39%), non-HIV–related health problems (29%), changes in other risky behaviors that led to a reduction in alcohol/drug use (37%), and a general change in norms within the gay community regarding substance use (24%). HIV+ men commonly mentioned as motivators a fear of AIDS (46%) and knowledge of HIV status (39%). The data from this study suggest new norms of substance use within the gay community,[3] with the HIV epidemic adding some urgency to the resolution of problems with alcohol and drug use.

Increased Spiritual Focus

Religion can be a major support for people in crisis, both by helping to reframe the nature of the problem and by providing emotional support to deal with the crisis (Pargament, 1990). Although there are little data to confirm this, it is our impression that AIDS has stimulated many gay people to reexamine their lives and spiritual beliefs. Those facing a terminal illness often shift their emphasis from the future and external areas of achievement (such as one's career) to a more introspective or contemplative approach, searching for meaning or a sense of purpose in their own lives (Belcher, Dettmore, & Holzemer, 1989). Spirituality has been defined as "that part of the self where the search for meaning takes place" (Taylor & Ferszt, 1990). Those dealing with death within their intimate social network may find some consolation in spiritual beliefs. Such beliefs may aid in coping with a crisis of mysterious origins, for which conventional problem-solving strategies are ineffectual (Spilka, Shaver, & Kirkpatrick, 1985). Spiritual and religious beliefs may help individuals overcome feelings of meaninglessness and alienation by furnishing a transcendent universal order to all events (Ambrosio & Sheehan, 1991). As some religious groups have seized upon the HIV epidemic to denounce certain groups and behaviors as "sinful" (Jakobi, 1990), those with HIV disease may feel alienated from traditional religious institutions and initiate a quest for alternative spiritual resources (Johnson, 1988). In a survey of sixty-three self-identified gay men, Somlai (1993) found that most saw traditional religions as unsympathetic; the HIV+ respondents were more likely to focus on alternative spiritual practices with immediate and tangible benefits, including spiritual readings, guides, body therapy, and native rituals.

---

[3] Alcohol use within the lesbian community is thought to have declined during roughly the same period in which the HIV epidemic became a predominant concern in the gay male community (Hastings, 1982; Rubin, 1989); the changes that men made in that time period may be viewed as part of a broader shift in gay community norms and health behaviors.

Spirituality may not provide only a means of coping, but a strategy of self-healing within the gay community. Some of the alternative therapies with which many gay men with HIV have experimented incorporate spiritual beliefs (e.g., metaphysical self-healing or holistic approaches of Bernie Siegel and Louise Hay). The increase in spirituality in the gay community may also be linked to the phenomenal growth of the 12 Step movement among lesbians, gays, and bisexuals in the past decade, paralleling the described reductions in alcohol and drug abuse mentioned previously (Paul, Bloomfield, & Stall, 1991).

In a survey of 648 readers of a gay periodical (Lee & Busto, 1991), 20 percent noted an increase in their belief in God or a spiritual force as a consequence of AIDS. The following comment epitomizes how many respondents viewed the AIDS/spirituality connection: "People whose lives are touched by AIDS may find some spiritual meaning in their lives that they did not have before, but that does not mean that the spiritual meaning is in AIDS itself. I think our response to AIDS in our own lives is where the meaning may be found, not in the disease" (p. 84). Belcher and her colleagues (1989) interviewed 35 persons diagnosed with HIV disease about their spiritual beliefs, and found their constructs of spirituality varied widely (including those centered on organized religion, 12 Step constructs of a "Higher Power," and metaphysical concepts). All noted that their experiences of living with HIV disease had altered their spiritual perspective, sometimes deepening or intensifying that spiritual focus.

Impact on the Gay Male Identity

Broadening the Construct of Gay Identity

Since AIDS first emerged, gay and bisexual men have faced changes in what it means both to be gay and to participate in the gay community. In the 1970s and early 1980s, sex was a clear common bond for an otherwise quite heterogeneous group. The significance of sexuality for many gay men's identities in the seventies (Connell & Kippax, 1990; Vicini et al., 1991) meant that the changes in sexual practices demanded by AIDS left some men in a quandary over how to reconstruct their sense of self as gay. Activists in the 1970s had substituted the term "gay" for "homosexual," to broaden the identity beyond sexual behavior and avoid a term tainted by medical science's imputations of pathology. Nonetheless, the relative novelty of both this more-than-sexual construction of "gayness" and emergent gay institutions meant that some found this identity construct intangible. While this has not led to a new consensually validated configuration of gayness, it appears that a broader set of gay "roles" may be emerging.

Today men can choose among many avenues of entry to and social participation in the gay community other than gay bars and sexual environments. Their sense of belonging to a gay community may be defined in terms of commitments to the collectivity (e.g., political activism, volunteerism in AIDS service organizations), as much as sexual or emotional commitments to individuals. Their "gayness" (or "queerness") may be articulated by their aesthetic or their politics as much as by their carnality. This greater dimensionality to "gay life" has the potential of imparting a greater richness to the gay identity, giving it multiple reference points on which to draw. Those with a broader understanding of gay identity may also be more resilient in this crisis. Based on analyses of longitudinal data from the Chicago MACS (Multicenter AIDS Cohort Study), Joseph and his colleagues (1991) concluded that

> homosexual men who experience their gay identity as more than simply a matter of sexual preference and sexual expression may find it easier, in the long run, to not only change their sexual behavior but participate in their "gayness" in such a way as to sustain such changes while satisfying their identity needs as gay men. In essence, these men draw from a wider array of experiences, attitudes, and means of expression to bolster their personal identities. (p. 295)

Coming Out Issues for Youth

It has been suggested that as a result of the AIDS epidemic, many gay male adolescents may delay the development of their gay identities and postpone homosexual relationships, since denial of same-sex erotic and affectional feelings appears easier to cope with than antigay hostility, stigma, and the possibility of terminal illness (Feldman, 1989). The gap between privately identifying as gay and disclosing this sense of self to another has been reported in previous surveys: a 1989 Teichner national survey of lesbians and gay men found that people reported an average lapse of 4.6 years after identifying as gay before coming out to another person (cited in Herek, 1991). However, this does not distinguish between those coming out prior to and those coming out in the "age of AIDS." On the other hand, the consensus of a series of informal interviews with both gay therapists and gay men (Marks, 1988) was that AIDS did not appear to inhibit the coming out process. AIDS is only one of a myriad of barriers facing those coming out, and the danger embodied by HIV may be outweighed by other considerations, including an increase in positive public images of both gay and bisexual men and the gay community. In fact, a trend has been noted for the coming out process to occur at an earlier age than ever before, at least in urban areas (Herdt, 1989).

Social changes associated with gay political activism have provided those who are coming out with a more stable and diversified lesbian, gay, and bisexual world with which youths can identify and within which they can integrate. The maturation and growing public presence of the U.S. gay community has allowed adolescents and young adults to feel both less isolated in the coming out process and more aware that such an identity acquisition forecloses fewer options than was previously assumed. In addition, a new perception of the gay community has been engendered by its response to the HIV epidemic: the demonstrations of concern and caring for its members, political activism, and sense of social responsibility may be more attractive to some than its previous public image as an intensely sexual culture.

The Impact of HIV Status

HIV Antibody Testing

The development of the HIV antibody test in the mid-1980s immediately presented a series of dilemmas to gay and bisexual men. Initially, there were more potential costs to testing than apparent benefits. Suspicions about the validity and reliability of the test were understandable, given high proportions of false positives for other screening tests for sexually transmitted diseases (Brandt, 1988). Some were uneasy about how governmental agencies would use test results, with fear that a positive test result would become the new "pink triangle" to identify members of the gay community (Siegel et al., 1989). In addition, there were many potential costs to testing as HIV+, including psychological distress in dealing with the test result's implications (McCusker et al., 1988; Ostrow, et al., 1989), and concern over whom might gain access to one's HIV test findings (Siegel et al., 1989). Being identified as HIV+ could potentially result in job loss, loss of insurance coverage, social isolation or rejection by partners, peers, and family, or loss of civil liberties. Western medicine could offer little, initially, to those identified as HIV+ to prevent the progression of HIV illness. Not until the development of antiviral therapies and prophylaxes for such opportunistic infections as pneumocystis carinii pneumonia (PCP) did a stronger rationale exist for gay and bisexual men to be serotested.

Siegel et al. (1989) explored the reasons for antibody testing given by a sample of 120 New York City gay men. They found that men were typically motivated by several factors: (1) to relieve the stress of not knowing their HIV antibody status, (2) to motivate the initiation and maintenance of health and life-style changes, (3) to make more informed and responsible decisions about sexual practices, (4) to clarify a potentially HIV-related medical condition, and (5) to take advantage of existing medical treatments for HIV infection. Data suggest that test results have sometimes been helpful in motivating individuals to take action and make life-style changes; however, the evidence is equivocal in terms of the impact of knowledge of serostatus on sexual risk practices among gay and bisexual men (Coates, Morin, & McKusick, 1987; Doll, O'Malley, et al., 1990; Higgins, et al., 1990; McCusker et al., 1988; Ostrow et al., 1989). As the epidemic continues, people will go through the testing process many times. The meaning of getting retested, and the needs of those who return for HIV "status reports" have not been researched to our knowledge, and it is possible that existing pre- and posttest counseling programs may be better oriented toward those who are tested for the first time than to those who are retested periodically.

Concern over loss of confidentiality of test results continues to be highly salient. One study of those seeking HIV antibody tests at an anonymous testing site (Kegeles, et al., 1990) found that two-fifths of the respondents stated they would not go for antibody testing without the protection of anonymity. Those without adequate social supports, lacking an empathic and informed health care provider, or living in geographic regions that mandate case reporting (or simply lack anonymous antibody-testing sites) may find the costs of identifying their HIV serostatus continue to outweigh the potential benefits of testing and early intervention if they are seropositive.

Issues for HIV-Infected Men

BEING HIV POSITIVE

Being HIV+ changes a gay or bisexual man's life in profound ways. Individuals often experience extreme anxiety and/or depression, at least in the short-term, when informed of their positive antibody status (Coates & Lo, 1990; Ostrow et al., 1989). Learning that one is HIV+ is a confrontation with mortality that may trigger a reexamination of one's priorities, goals, and relationship to the universe (Belcher et al., 1989; Remien, Rabkin, Williams, & Katoff, 1992; Schaefer & Coleman, 1992). For some, this may mean increased attention to interpersonal relationships; for others, increased spirituality; for others, radical changes in career plans. Some have speculated that living with HIV accelerates one's adult development, as individuals are prematurely confronted with major life transitions (e.g., the death of friends, physical deterioration, retirement from work), and the demands of completing the unfinished business of one's life within a sharply constricted time frame.

In qualitative interviews with fifty-five predominantly asymptomatic

HIV+ gay men, Siegel and Krauss (1991) identified three major adaptive challenges confronting HIV+ gay men: (1) dealing with the likelihood of a curtailed lifespan (feeling an urgency to attain life goals, deciding to what extent to invest in the future); (2) dealing with reactions to a stigmatizing illness (deciding whom to tell, coping with feelings of shame and contamination); and (3) developing strategies for maintaining physical and emotional health (feeling the need to monitor and exert control over one's health, maintaining emotional equilibrium). Many HIV+ individuals embark on self-help regimens such as dietary changes, stress management, spiritual development, and exercise programs in the hope that their efforts can halt or slow the progression of the disease. For example, Lovejoy et al. (1992) found that HIV+ gay men increased their use of self-care behaviors and developed information networks to acquire HIV-related information once aware of their HIV status.

Maladaptive responses, such as fatalism and social withdrawal, are also common. Furthermore, HIV+ men must deal not only with the realization that they are infected, but with the awareness of being *infectious*. This may promote positive behavior changes (e.g., safer sex), but it may also trigger irrational responses, such as giving up sex completely or withdrawing from social contact. Cohen, Salit, and Emmott (1993) found that their HIV+ gay men not in relationships were more likely than HIV− single gay men to express no interest in having a partner and fear of involvement (most pronounced among HIV+ asymptomatics, with rates of 44 and 25%, respectively). A variety of individual factors may affect the way gay men respond to their HIV status. For example, HIV+ men who have less internal control of control are more likely to be severely depressed (Murphy et al., 1991). Likewise, less psychological distress has been found to be related to the use of active behavioral coping strategies, such as finding out more about HIV, eating a healthier diet, and seeking social support, versus avoidance strategies such as refusing to think about or take action regarding HIV (Namir et al., 1987; Wolf et al., 1991). The use of avoidant coping strategies by HIV+ men has been found to be predicted by internalized homophobia and low self-esteem (Nicholson & Long, 1990). Of a nonrandom sample of fifty-eight HIV+ German and Swedish gay men, the fifteen men who occasionally had either unprotected anal or oral sex with ejaculation were typically more depressed, more likely to blame themselves for being infected, used avoidant coping styles, and relied on external professional control more than internal controls (Clement, 1992).

Response to being HIV+ is also influenced by the stage of HIV infection. A longitudinal study of San Francisco gay men (Hays, Turner, &

Coates, 1992) found that HIV+ gay men were likely to become depressed when they began to experience physical symptoms of HIV illness. Other research has shown that individuals with AIDS-related conditions experience greater distress than AIDS-diagnosed individuals, perhaps because of the greater uncertainties about the course of their illness, anticipations of negative effects such as pain, rejection and social isolation, general fear of the unknown, and fewer available institutional resources (Chuang et al., 1989; Goldmeir, 1987; Tross & Hirsch, 1988). An actual AIDS diagnosis may lower one's anxiety, since it resolves some of the ambiguity about one's condition and "sets the battle strategy" for one's future plans (L. McKusick, personal communication).

As medical advances are made in the treatment of HIV, HIV-infected individuals face a growing array of options that may halt or slow HIV disease progression. A vital area for further research, therefore, is the examination of factors that influence the decision-making process of HIV+ men about their medical treatment. In a qualitative study of factors associated with treatment decisions, Siegel and colleagues (1992) found that men were prompted to initiate treatment by the desire to exert mastery and control over one's health, to closely monitor one's health status, and to buy time until medical breakthroughs occur. Reluctance to formally acknowledge one's illness, fear of disrupting the body's biological balance, anticipation of potential negative side effects, fear of financial strain, and distrust of the medical establishment were associated with avoiding treatment. Todak and associates (1992) studied psychosocial factors related to the use of AZT by HIV+ gay men and found that men who elected to take AZT scored higher on measures of personal affirmation and social support than did men who declined AZT. Further research that examines factors which influence HIV+ men's coping process and treatment decisions would be valuable.

Dealing with HIV Illness

HIV illness affects virtually every area of a person's life, not only because of the physical and psychological impact of having a life-threatening illness, but also because of the increased likelihood of discrimination, ostracism, abandonment, and loss of employment and financial resources. Due to the slow progressive deterioration involved in this illness, individuals with AIDS experience a series of losses over time, including loss of physical attractiveness, loss of mobility and physical functions, loss of work and a standard of living, and loss of social roles. Furthermore, some treatments for HIV-related symptoms are quite disruptive or unpleasant in themselves and may have unpredictable side effects. It is understandable that gay men experiencing symptoms of HIV disease are more likely than HIV-negative men to see their health as being controlled by powerful others and by chance (Waller, 1992). It is not surprising that depression, anxiety, confusion, anger, and suicidal tendencies are common among gay men with HIV disease. A considerable proportion of PWAs experience levels of anxiety and depression severe enough to warrant DSM-III diagnoses of adjustment disorder or major depression (Dilley et al., 1985; Frierson, Lippman, & Johnson, 1987; Tross & Hirsch, 1988). Depression among HIV+ gay men has been linked to higher levels of sexual risk-taking and use of a variety of illicit drugs (Murphy et al., 1991); furthermore, it has been suggested that psychological distress may contribute to clinical progression of HIV infection. Elevated suicide rates have also been found for men with HIV disease (Coté, Biggar, & Dannenberg, 1992; Kizer et al., 1988; Marzuk et al., 1988). For example, Marzuk and colleagues (1988) found that the suicide rate was 36 times higher among men with AIDS diagnoses than among nondiagnosed men in New York City; Coté and his colleagues (1992) found the rate among men with AIDS to be 7.4 times the national figure between 1987 and 1989.

Most gay men with HIV disease are 25 to 49 years old[4] and typically at fairly vulnerable points in their adult development in areas such as career, personal life, family relations, and financial achievement. Meeting the developmental challenges of early adulthood—establishing a career, forming enduring relationships, solidifying one's sense of identity—is daunting enough for a gay man in a homophobic society without having to also cope with a life-threatening illness. Furthermore, because of the social stigma associated with HIV illness and its etiology, those with AIDS tend to be denied some of the psychological benefits of the sick role derived by other seriously ill patients (Herek & Capitano, 1992; Larsen, Serra, & Long, 1990; Pleck et al., 1988). Instead, they are often socially rejected and have difficulty obtaining insurance, employment, housing, and medical care. HIV illness may also impel gay men to disclose their homosexuality to family, friends, and colleagues for the first time, which may pose additional risks and challenges. Individuals with HIV illness may experience guilt or regret over their past sexual behaviors or life-style, and anguish at the thought of other individuals whom they may have unknowingly infected (Christ, Wiener, & Moynihan, 1985; Nichols, 1983). The design and evaluation of interventions that help gay men with HIV meet these difficult challenges should be a high priority for social scientists interested in alleviating the negative effects of this epidemic.

---

[4]By the end of December 1993, 85 percent of the cumulative total of reported male AIDS cases in the United States were between the ages of 25 and 49 (Centers for Disease Control and Prevention, 1994).

Issues for HIV-Negative Men

AIDS has also had an impact on the mental health of those gay and bisexual men who are HIV-negative. The focus on the health-care concerns of those who are HIV+ in the gay community has sometimes obscured the toll that this epidemic is taking on those who are not HIV-infected. Hays, Catania, and their colleagues (1990) found that a San Francisco gay male cohort scored approximately one-and-a-half standard deviations above the norm on measures of depression and anxiety and that scores did not vary based on HIV antibody status (although HIV+ and AIDS-diagnosed men reported more AIDS-related worry). Gorman, Wiley, and their colleagues (1992) found suicide to be the leading cause of non-AIDS mortality in the SFMHS/San Francisco General cohorts followed since 1984; this was distributed among both HIV+ and HIV− groups.

Several dynamics may lead to distress among uninfected gay and bisexual men (Odets, 1990). First, they share the experience of the entire community of caring for others with HIV and dealing with multiple losses. HIV-negative men may be burdened by "survivor's guilt," a sense that their serostatus is somehow a betrayal or an abandonment of those who are HIV-infected. Fears of infection may lead to distancing from those who are ill with HIV disease; the desire to avoid those who are ill may also be due to emotional exhaustion and fear of facing yet another loss. There is also an element of ambiguity and fragility with HIV-negative serostatus—the possibility of seroconversion remains a threatening subtext in all future sexual encounters. Finally, it must be acknowledged that *all* gay and bisexual men are confronted with an increasing tide of discrimination, violent attacks (gay-bashings), and all are identified as possible sources of contagion, due to the continued perception of HIV illness as a "gay disease." Clinical reports of distress among HIV-negatives (e.g., Harowski, 1987; Moon, 1991; Odets, 1990) are from gay communities with estimated 30 to 50 percent HIV seroprevalence rates. The generalizability of such reports is only slowly being tested by research, although data from several longitudinal cohort studies do not confirm pervasive malais among HIV-negative gay and bisexual men. However, a recent report (Lackner, Caumartin, Joseph, & Ostrow, 1992) using 526 gay men from two longitudinal Chicago cohorts found that depression on follow-up was associated with prior reports of gay-related discrimination experiences. In a Canadian sample of over 2,300 gay men from 35 cities (Calzavara et al., 1993), 20 percent of the HIV-seronegative men reported that "discrimination because of AIDS" and "uncertainty about the future" were "big problems" for them (in addition to loneliness).

Wayment, Kemeny, and Silver (1990) examined the presence of "survivor syndrome" (manifested by survivor guilt, chronic death anxiety, and psychic numbing as measured on the Affects Balance Scale) among 129 HIV-negative gay and bisexual men participating in the UCLA Multicenter AIDS Cohort Study and the UCLA Natural History of AIDS–Psychosocial Study. Using path model analysis, they found those who had higher lifetime totals of sexual partners were more likely to report feeling survivor guilt and death anxiety. Having more lifetime sexual partners was also associated with having more intimates and close friends who had died of AIDS, which may heighten the sense of being uniquely saved. Satisfaction with social support from gay friends (and indirectly, group involvement) served to protect these men from experiencing survivor guilt and death anxiety. This suggests that social support interventions may be effective in dealing with this phenomenon.

Impact on Gay Relationships and Social Networks

Primary Relationships

Developing and maintaining gay relationships in a society that actively opposes them has always been challenging. The HIV epidemic has introduced new complexities to that process, but has also heightened the importance of interpersonal relationships for gay men. As a consequence of the HIV crisis, gay men have increased motivation to form relationships and changed their priorities concerning relationships (Marks, 1988). This is reflected in the increased campaigns to establish laws in various communities protecting and affirming stable forms of gay relationships (e.g., "domestic partner" legislation), in addition to continuing the legal battles to remove antisodomy laws (Beauchamp, 1991). The increased emphasis on finding a primary romantic relationship may be due to both shifts in values in the gay male community and its use as a strategy for dealing with fears about AIDS. Being a single gay man today means having to deal more seriously with the health implications of each new sexual encounter, and having a large number of sexual partners may be viewed as less desirable (Kyle, 1989).

In a national survey of its gay male readers, the *Partners Newsletter for Gay and Lesbian Couples* found that 29 percent of the respondents said that the AIDS epidemic had contributed to their decision to form a relationship, and 48 percent believed that AIDS had a role in the continuation of the relationship (Bryant & Damiam, 1990). Hoff and her colleagues (1992b) interviewed men from the San Francisco AIDS Behavioral Research Project [ABRP] cohort about their relationship histories pre- and post-AIDS, to investigate the influence of the AIDS epidemic on gay relationships. The percentage of men who reported being in a primary relationship was found to steadily increase from 26 percent in 1970 to 59 percent in 1990, and remained fairly stable at levels of 47 to 59 percent throughout the epidemic years. The authors attribute the overall increase to societal changes resulting from the gay liberation movement. In contrast, Nardi (1992) reviewed the percentages of gay men in relationships in various surveys conducted between the late 1960s and 1991, and found that the reported rates have been fairly stable, fluctuating between 40 and 50 percent. While AIDS may have motivated some to enter or maintain relationships, it also terminated many relationships due to deaths of partners. The majority of men agreed with the statement "Having a lover or regular sex partner would reduce my chances of getting AIDS" (87% in 1984; 65% in 1991). Although the men expressed consistent support for the statement "It's best to be monogamous" (64% in 1984; 66% in 1991), the percentage of relationships that were monogamous remained less than 10 percent at most times.

Disclosing HIV Status

Deciding whom to tell that one is HIV+ can be extremely difficult and agonizing. Disclosing such information is a double-edged sword: while disclosure may provide opportunity for the HIV+ individual to receive valuable social support, it may also lead to added stress because of stigmatization, discrimination, and disruption of personal relationships. Conversely, hiding one's HIV+ status from important others may be a source of stress and can interfere with initiating or adhering to potentially critical medical treatments. An examination of San Francisco's ABRP data (Hays et al., 1993) revealed that 95 percent of the HIV+ gay men reported disclosing their status to their lovers and closest gay friends. Relatives and colleagues were much less likely to be told, and typically were not informed until the men began to develop symptoms of HIV illness. Ambivalence and conflict about disclosure to loved ones was common; men wished to be open with them and draw on their support but did not want to worry them or disrupt the existing relationships. High ratings of the helpfulness of loved ones in response to disclosure were associated with less depression and anxiety among the men.

HIV Status and Dating

For gay men, HIV status has added a new complexity to the process of forming and developing relationships. HIV status does appear to influence partner selection, according to an analysis from San Francisco's AIDS Behavioral Research Project (Hoff et al., 1992a). Both HIV− gay men and men who had not been tested for the HIV antibody showed a strong tendency to prefer HIV− men for romantic partners, whereas HIV+ men demonstrated no pronounced preference. A content analysis of gay personals ads in the *Village Voice* placed within successive 3-month periods in 1978, 1982, 1985, and 1988 (Davidson, 1991) showed a similar rise in health-related partner preferences. Davidson found much more concern about health in the language of the ads (found in only about 2% of ads in 1978, but in over 36% of ads in 1988). He also found over time that men showed an increased likelihood to present sexual exclusivity as a condition of establishing a relationship, rather than as an issue to be negotiated once a relationship began (from little more than 2% in 1978 to over 13% of ads in 1988).

HIV status is an issue that gay men who are dating must confront at some point. How do gay men handle this? Using ABRP data, Hays and colleagues (in preparation) found that 22 percent of the men said they asked men they were dating about their HIV status "right away." In fact, 22 percent said they only dated men with the same status as themselves. Eighty-six percent said they discussed HIV status if they felt the relationship was getting serious; 79 percent said they would discuss it if the relationship became sexual. There are inconsistencies, however, between stated intent and practice with regard to sharing an HIV+ test result. Although the vast majority of gay and bisexual men surveyed at alternative testing sites in California said they intended to tell both their primary partners (88%) and nonprimary sexual partners (73%) if they tested positive (Kegeles, Catania, & Coates, 1988), 52 percent of the HIV+ gay and bisexual male sample recruited at a Los Angeles HIV clinic said they had not told at least one of their sexual partners that they were HIV+ prior to having sex with them (Marks, Richardson, & Maldonado, 1991). It appears that HIV status is acknowledged as having important ramifications for the growth of intimate relationships, but the potentially disruptive consequences of disclosing an HIV+ status inhibit total candor. The impact of HIV issues on dating and relationship formation is an extremely important topic that unfortunately has received scant research attention.

Help-Seeking and Social Support

As we have discussed, the AIDS crisis presents the gay community with a wide range of profound stressors. Social support—the comfort, information, and assistance provided informally by friends and family—has been found to buffer the impact of stressful life experiences (Caplan, 1990). Social support has been recognized as specifically important for gay men's psychological well-being (Hammersmith & Weinberg, 1973; Jacobs & Tedford, 1980; Schmitt & Kurdek, 1987; Weinberg & Williams, 1974). Social support research on gay men consistently shows that gay men tend to rely on friends and partners for many of

the support functions typically filled by biological families for heterosexuals (Hays, Catania, McKusick, & Coates, 1990; Kurdek & Schmitt,
1987).

In coping with AIDS-related concerns, gay men report a high rate of
help-seeking from their social networks. Of the San Francisco gay men
surveyed in the ABRP, 96 percent of those diagnosed with AIDS, 82
percent of those who were HIV+, 77 percent of those who were HIV−,
and 72 percent of those who were untested reported seeking help from
others for AIDS-related concerns during the previous year (Hays, Catania, McKusick, & Coates, 1990). High percentages of AIDS-diagnosed
men sought help from all categories of sources (peers, professionals,
relatives), whereas HIV+, HIV−, and untested men were more likely
to seek help from peers (friends and partners). Regardless of the men's
HIV status, peers were perceived as the most helpful. Furthermore,
peers appeared to be the most effective source of support for gay men;
their helpfulness was associated with less anxiety and depression. An
examination of the social networks of gay men with AIDS showed similar findings: networks with a high percentage of gay friends (versus
relatives) and with other individuals with AIDS were associated with
less depression and anxiety (Hays, Chauncey, & Tobey, 1990). Social
support appears to serve a buffering role for gay men dealing with HIV
illness. In a longitudinal study of San Francisco gay men, those who
were more satisfied with the social support they received, particularly
informational support, were less likely to be depressed 1 year later
(Hays, Turner, & Coates, 1992). Other studies have found lower perceived availability or quality of social support to be associated with
negative psychosocial outcomes, including mood disturbance, depression, and poorer quality of life for persons with HIV infection in general (Eich, Frick, Dobler-Mikola, & Lüthy, 1991; Flynn, Hedge, Slaughter, & Green, 1993; Lamping et al., 1992).

Social support from one's peers has also been found to be related to
gay men's adoption of safer sex practices (Emmons et al., 1986; McKusick et al., 1990). A survey of gay and bisexual men in Portland, Oregon (O'Brien, 1992), found that men who reported higher levels of peer
support for practicing safer sex reported lower levels of risk behavior
and fewer depressive symptoms than men who felt they could not talk
about HIV with their gay or bisexual friends (also Stall et al., 1992).

The AIDS crisis has highlighted how important and critical gay peers
are in influencing the behavior, attitudes, and psychological well-being
of gay men; yet AIDS has already decimated entire social networks
within the gay community, thereby depriving gay men of many of the
benefits of social support. Community programs that promote the development of new social ties or provide alternative sources of support
are especially valuable. A variety of psychotherapy group formats are

being tested for efficacy in bolstering the coping of those dealing with HIV infection (Emmott, 1991; Mulder et al., 1992; Murphy et al, 1993). However, not everyone is willing to participate in traditional support groups (Hedge & Glover, 1990), so alternatives must be developed. Investigations of community-level interventions to reduce isolation and rebuild support networks for gay men would also be beneficial.

Caring for Loved Ones with AIDS

Large numbers of gay and bisexual men care for loved ones with AIDS. In a telephone survey using a probability sample of gay men living in major U.S. cities, 54 percent reported that they had provided informal care to a lover, friend, or relative with AIDS (Turner, Catania, & Gagnon, 1993). Whereas relatives tend to be the most likely care-givers with most illnesses (Brody, 1985), gay peers tend to provide many of the functions provided by relatives for heterosexuals. For example, in an interview study of gay men with AIDS, McCann and Wadsworth (1992) found that their care-givers were mostly close male friends (45%) or partners (42%). Only 8 percent of the men named a parent or sibling as their care-taker.

Caring for someone with AIDS can be highly draining and stressful (e.g., Peabody, 1987). Studies of care-giving for those with other serious, chronic illnesses show that care-givers often experience detrimental effects on their psychological well-being, physical health, interpersonal relations, social life, and financial status (Rabins, Mace, & Lucas, 1982; Stewart, Haley, & Saag, 1993; Zarit, Todd, & Zarit, 1986). Care-giving for PWAs poses unique challenges, given the stigmatizing nature of HIV illness, its unpredictable course, and the relative youthfulness of both those afflicted and their care-givers, who most likely never anticipated having to deal intimately with serious illness at this stage in their lives (and may have little preparation for doing so). Because AIDS care-givers are often reluctant to acknowledge to others that they are caring for someone with AIDS, to protect confidentiality or avoid stigma and discrimination by others (Powell-Cope & Brown, 1992), they often carry out their care-giving role in relative secrecy and isolation, with insufficient emotional support (Hart, Mann, & Stewart, 1991). One-third of the care-givers interviewed by McCann and Wadsworth (1992) reported that they would have liked more help with their care-giving duties. Fifteen percent said they had received insufficient emotional support from others. Care-givers who are themselves HIV+ face added challenges since they may overidentify with those they care for (Pearlin et al., 1988), seeing in them a frightening foreshadowing of their own future. Care-givers may also sacrifice their own health in their efforts to help others. On the other hand, care-giving may serve a coping function for HIV+ men by focusing their activities and concerns away from their own infection (Folkman, Chesney, Boccellari, et al., 1992). There may be times when care-givers themselves are ill and alternate between offering support and needing it.

As AIDS cases continue to rise within the gay community, increasing numbers of gay men will find themselves in care-giving roles. Further, as medical advances emerge which prolong the lifespan of people with AIDS, the length of time individuals serve in care-giving roles will increase. Many communities have developed special services to help care-givers cope with the demands of their roles. For example, San Francisco's Kairos House offers support groups and counseling for care-givers. Further research investigating the care-giving process and factors related to effective care-giving for persons with AIDS—especially research that develops and evaluates interventions to promote effective care-giving—would be beneficial.

Death of Loved Ones

By 1987, approximately two-thirds of two different San Francisco cohorts of gay men had experienced the death of one or more lovers, friends, or acquaintances (Coates, Kegeles, Ekstrand, & Stall, unpublished data). Martin and his colleagues (1989) noted the substantial increases in AIDS-related loss in their cohort of New York gay men over the history of the epidemic:

> In 1981 the annual incidence of AIDS-related bereavement was less than 2%. By 1985 the non-cumulative annual incidence had reached 18%. That figure continued to increase to 23% in 1987. These rates do not reflect the fact that of those who are bereaved, over one third have lost two or more close individuals within the same year. Some men have reported as many as six close losses in 1 year . . . whereas others have been chronically bereaved of close loved ones for 3 or more consecutive years of the epidemic. . . . In addition, AIDS-related bereavement is not a random event. . . . but is disproportionately concentrated among those aged 35 to 45, who are HIV antibody positive, and who have experienced one or more clinically significant signs of AIDS-related illness. (p. 287)

We are still in the early stages of understanding the process of AIDS-related bereavement in the gay community. Earlier bereavement research focusing on either the individual or a community typically involved a single episode of loss whose impact could be noted, followed by a progression of discrete psychological tasks necessary to resolve the grief. AIDS-related bereavement within the gay community is far more complex. We are dealing with the premature deaths of many young men who go through a lengthy, progressively debilitating illness. Many have lost numerous people to AIDS, and each loss is compounded by those preceding it (Carmack, 1992). Some individuals report that their entire gay social network has been decimated by AIDS. Many of those who experience losses are themselves threatened by HIV disease, and thus each experience of losing a friend or lover involves anticipating their own course of illness and death. The relentless pace of the epidemic allows no time to work through one loss before another either occurs or is anticipated (Klein, 1992). Many in the gay community have experienced continuous, ongoing losses and felt little support or acknowledgment by society at large (Biller & Rice, 1990). We cannot say what the long-term consequences of such a series of losses will be. A number of studies show that the risk of psychiatric morbidity is great when dealing with bereavement. Martin (1988) found that the level of psychological distress (as indicated by symptoms of traumatic stress response, demoralization, sleep problems, sedative use, and recreational drug use) increased directly with the number of AIDS-related bereavements in his New York gay sample. An initial follow-up report (Martin et al., 1989) noted that posttraumatic stress disorder–related symptoms increased significantly annually from 1985 to 1987, although other symptoms (demoralization, sleep problems, guilt, and suicidal ideation) decreased over those years. When the sample was followed through 1991, however, the intensity and duration of the measured effects of loss were found to diminish over time (Martin & Dean, 1993). Martin and Dean concluded that the impact of such losses was mediated by the HIV status and health of the gay male respondents.

The importance of these findings on the scope of the problem of AIDS bereavement and its consequences is twofold. First, the mental health of the members of the gay community at large is at risk and health promotion interventions are necessary. The number of AIDS cases and AIDS-related deaths continues to soar, more than quadrupling since mid-1987 (Centers for Disease Control and Prevention, 1994). We need to test what kinds of programs might be effective on both an individual and a community level. Some have suggested that rituals may be important devices for the community to deal with its grief, and several have already developed within the gay community: the Names Quilt, the annual candlelight marches, and frequent memorial services. We need to learn more about how people manage to balance "functional engagement" with "functional detachment" to deal with the impact of multiple loss, and how to avoid unhealthy overinvolvement or "shutting down" (Carmack, 1992). Second, those who are HIV-infected need special interventions as depression, stress, the number of close individuals one has lost to AIDS, distress due to AIDS loss, and social support can influence disease progression (Burack et al., 1992; Coates, 1990; Coates, Temoshok, & Mandel, 1984; Coates et al., 1989; Kiecolt-Glaser & Glaser, 1988; Persson et al., 1991).

Impact of the HIV Epidemic
on a Community Level

The New Gay Activism

AIDS has in some ways been a catalyst for the political coming-of-age of the gay community. The U.S. government's inadequate response to the HIV crisis brought home the prevalence of discriminatory, homophobic attitudes in contemporary American society, and the danger created by such attitudes are far more palpable to most gay men today than prior to the epidemic.[5] Those who had previously led relatively privileged lives as white men have been painfully confronted with the realization that equal treatment for all in our society is a myth. Spurred by circumstances created by the epidemic, many in the gay community now have a heightened awareness of the need for legal protections and recognition of gay relationships, in areas such as bereavement time off, hospital visitation rights, and insurance. A new impetus exists for the securing of "gay rights," and anger and negative perceptions of the U.S. government and society have increased in connection to the perceived lack of response to the HIV crisis (Hart et al., 1990). Many attempts to confront antigay discrimination on a national level have resulted, within the government, businesses, and other institutions (e.g., the Boy Scouts of America).

The AIDS crisis has created a new sense of urgency and militancy in the gay community, and the success of groups such as ACT-UP (AIDS Coalition to Unleash Power) has politicized many in the gay community and led to a revitalized gay activism (Altman, 1986). Anger over the AIDS crisis has energized the gay community and led to many embracing the confrontational political tactics of ACT-UP. In turn, ACT-UP provided a model for the organization Queer Nation, founded in New York City in 1990, to address gay issues other than AIDS (e.g., gay-related hate crimes). The highly visible "actions" of these groups recollect the Gay Liberation Front and Gay Activist Alliance "zaps" of the early 1970s. In addition, activist groups are increasingly involved in more sophisticated advocacy works as well as direct street actions. A survey of 549 *OUT/LOOK* readers (Escoffier & Rocchio, 1991) indicated

---

[5]In contrast, Spada (1979) asked a national convenience sample of primarily middle-class white gay men ($n = 1038$) if they had ever been denied any of their rights because they were gay; over 72 percent responded in the negative, and only 18 percent responding in the affirmative.

overwhelming approval of most controversial AIDS activist tactics (e.g., blocking rush-hour traffic on San Francisco's Golden Gate Bridge; heckling former President Bush; demonstrating outside of New York City's St. Patrick's Cathedral). In part, this may be because so many respondents considered themselves to be AIDS activists (68%). Those whose involvement was spurred by their own HIV infection or illness were more likely than other self-identified AIDS activists to have engaged in civil disobedience, to have lobbied on AIDS issues, and to approve of controversial actions—even ones that might destroy or harm public or private property. It appeared that the more personal the threat epitomized by HIV, the less weight is given to social conventions of propriety.

It was in a climate of outrage and radicalized gay politics that the debate about "outing" (publicly announcing the sexual orientation of covert gays who are in influential positions, through either their public stature or their political power) developed (Cain, 1991; DeRanleau, 1990; Huston, 1990; Outweek, 1990). The gay community debated the sanctity of an individual's right to privacy counterbalanced by the individual's responsibility to the lesbian, gay, and bisexual collectivity. To activists forcibly outed by AIDS, the right to privacy appeared to be largely a matter of social privilege rather than a legal guarantee, and activists were furious that those with the most social power apparently were ignoring their putative responsibility. This argument is still strong, as outing was a tactic approved of by a vast majority of those polled in the *OUT/LOOK* survey mentioned previously in all cases where elected or appointed officials obstruct the fight against AIDS (68%) or support policies that perpetuate homophobia and obstruct gay/lesbian rights (73%). In any event, the debate about outing has led to an unparalleled public discussion of "the closet," and that process may be linked to the increasing numbers of "out" public figures. An article in the June 1993 *San Francisco Sentinel* listed 120 openly gay and lesbian publicly elected officials in the United States.

The Emergence of CBOs for Prevention and Care

The slow response of governmental agencies to the HIV epidemic resulted in an enormous need for a broad range of health, social, and educational services. This led to the initiation by the gay community of a variety of community-based organizations (CBOs) that filled the gap by providing services to the gay community (Arno, 1991). The response that the gay community has shown—forming a variety of nonprofit, grassroots agencies to deliver services (e.g., The Gay Men's Health Crisis in New York, The San Francisco AIDS Foundation in San Francisco, The AIDS Project Los Angeles)—is an outgrowth of the gay community's ability to mobilize cadres of volunteers and organize itself politically and financially. San Francisco's much-touted "model of care" was developed in a context of the gay community's increasing political clout, given its gay political clubs and the inclusion of gay, lesbian, and bisexual staff on various levels of the city's bureaucracy. The community-based organizations that have emerged do face problems— typically a combination of funding shortages, volunteer burnout, and difficulties in penetrating the nongay, nonwhite, nonmale communities into which the epidemic has spread. But they have achieved a measure of legitimacy previously unheard of for gay-defined organizations, providing an array of crucial services in prevention, advocacy, and health care. As such, they have not only provided a new set of community leaders and representatives, but they have given the gay community a greater sense of control over key issues in their lives and provided a model of community-based response to a crisis.

The Emergence of New Leaders

The HIV epidemic has been responsible for the loss of many political leaders and role models in the gay community (Krieger, 1991), although it has also provided a context in which new heroes have been recognized for their contributions to the fight against HIV. In the contemporary gay community, lesbian, gay, and bisexual leaders have emerged not just through participation in activist groups, but through their participation in AIDS service organizations. The leaders of these organizations have had to cultivate a variety of relationships both with the community and with the political system to meet the expanding needs for their services. The training in management, political lobbying, and organization-building that involvement in these organizations has provided has given the gay community a whole new way of developing leaders outside of previously existing gay churches and political clubs (Jernigan, 1988: 49). Although these leaders may be sophisticated in dealing with some issues, a concern has been raised that they lack the expertise in gay political activism and are effective only in the AIDS arena (Rofes, 1990).

Volunteerism within the Gay Community

The tremendous needs within the gay community as a consequence of the AIDS crisis have inspired an enormous number of gay men and lesbians to volunteer for AIDS-related causes. All across the United States, thousands of gay men and lesbians have volunteered their services in a wide variety of community organizations. A survey estimated that volunteers provided over 530,000 hours of labor to AIDS agencies in the San Francisco Bay Area alone (AIDS Service Providers Association of the Bay Area, 1990). Over 3,000 volunteer staff were reported by these agencies in the spring of 1990, primarily providing direct services either in prevention efforts or to people with HIV disease. In their research on AIDS volunteerism, Snyder and Omoto (1992) identified five major motivations for volunteering: personal values, desire for information or understanding, community concern, personal development, and esteem enhancement. They found that AIDS volunteers motivated by more "self-oriented" desires, such as esteem enhancement and personal development, were more likely to continue to volunteer over a one-year period of the study.

We suspect that the wave of volunteerism has impacted the gay community in many positive ways beyond the accomplishment of the immediate goals of the volunteer work. Volunteer experiences can provide opportunities to enhance self-esteem and a sense of personal empowerment. They also provide gay men and lesbians a chance to interact with each other in significant ways that are less likely in other gay settings such as bars. Thus, they may foster the development of social networks within the gay community that might otherwise never exist. Further, by witnessing the altruistic behaviors of so many of its members, the gay community as a whole can derive a tremendous sense of pride and community spirit. As Snyder and Omoto (1992) suggest, "action research" examining strategies for recruiting and retaining AIDS volunteers would provide both practical information to community organizations' management of volunteer programs and further our psychological understanding of prosocial behavior.

Dealing with Diversity in the Gay Community

Social psychological research shows that the presence of an outside threat greatly influences intragroup functioning and cohesiveness. The AIDS crisis has influenced the interrelationships of the various subgroups that comprise the gay community. Unresolved differences between subgroups lost their immediacy in the face of this pandemic and the response of the larger society to the gay community as a whole.

RELATIONS BETWEEN MEN AND WOMEN

An important area of change in the gay community has been the change in the relationship between gay/bisexual men and the women's community. In many ways, by the end of the 1970s, lesbians and gay men were on very different tracks and their alliance was an uneasy one. But the emergence of the AIDS crisis, and the challenges that created in the areas of health care, antigay violence and discrimination, led many lesbians to respond rapidly and combat this epidemic alongside gay men. Rapprochement was also possible on some of the issues that generated antagonism in the prior decade, as many lesbians began to recognize the need to be involved in a joint "gay movement" as well as the feminist movement. More gay men were willing to learn about

the specific concerns women have about health care, economic discrimination, and sexism and to commit to political action on behalf of
women's issues as well as their own. This is not to say that all antagonism has ceased. Women have expressed concern over the numbers of
lesbians taking on the gender-typed caretaker role for gay men with
AIDS, fearing a lack of reciprocity. Justifiable resentments exist about
the recognition and energy given to what has largely been a disease of
men in the gay community, while women's health concerns have taken
a backseat (Winnow, 1989). The new cosexual atmosphere in many
groups and gathering places in the gay community has promoted the
beginnings of a dialogue between women and men.

RELATIONS BETWEEN YOUNGER AND OLDER GAY MEN

Historical changes in the gay community as a consequence of the AIDS
epidemic have contributed to a "generation gap" between older and
younger gay men. Every generation feels the need to assert its independence from previous generations (Erickson, 1968), yet the highly
threatening nature of AIDS may have intensified the younger generation's motivation to separate themselves from their gay elders. In some
communities, this was exemplified by the emergence of age-segregated
social groups (e.g., San Francisco's "Boy Clubs"). This has also been
evident in the development of a new aesthetic among younger gay
men, who created both a new look and a new club scene that may feel
quite alien to those who came out in the seventies period of the gay
male "clone" (Leger, 1989; Vollmer, 1990). With the decline of bathhouses and other hallmarks of the pre-AIDS gay life-style, young gay
men today live in a very different world from the previous generation
of gay men. Young men have expressed feelings ranging from envy to
bewilderment to disgust in reconciling the differences between their
experience and that of the earlier generation. The older generation has
passed on a mixed inheritance to the younger generation. Concern
about the future of the gay community may provide the impetus for
those confronted with their own mortality to share the history and political education they have experienced with those representing the
hope for the future.

RELATIONS BETWEEN GAYS AND BISEXUALS

The AIDS crisis brought a new visibility to the emerging bisexual
movement and bisexuals within the larger gay community. The CDC's
recognition of gay *and bisexual* men among its risk groups for HIV infection—as well as the use of the broad term "men who have sex with
men"—focused more academic attention on the issue of bisexuality
(Doll, Peterson, White, & Ward, 1990), concerns about bisexual men
serving as a vector of transmission into the general population (McKir-

nan et al., 1993) and the inadequacies in existing empirical research on the topic (Boulton & Weatherburn, 1990). This recognition of bisexuals by both the general public and the gay community as a distinct subgroup (although they might be denigrated as either sexual anarchists or diseased pariahs) coincided with the development of a more organized bisexual movement protesting the enforced invisibility and the stereotyping of bisexuals both in society at large and in the gay community. The growing acceptance of this life-style and label within the gay community is evidenced by the number of organizations that have shifted to the more inclusive term "lesbian, gay, and bisexual" versus "lesbian and gay," as well as the broader meanings given to the term "queer."

RELATIONS BETWEEN GAY RACIAL AND ETHNIC GROUPS

AIDS was originally seen as a white man's disease by ethnic minority gays, though this belied the fact that ethnic minority communities tended to have a disproportionately high percentage of AIDS cases (Kingsley et al., 1991; Mays & Cochran, 1993; Peterson, & Marin, 1988; Selik, Castro, & Pappaioanou, 1988). As with the case of younger men, the threat of AIDS may have initially contributed to increased social separation of nonwhite gay men from white gay men. However, ethnic minority gay communities slowly recognized the need to mobilize themselves with regard to HIV issues or they would likely be ignored or ineffectively addressed by the existing community AIDS organizations. Likewise, issues of cultural appropriateness and minority representation became increasingly salient as AIDS service providers designed and implemented programs. One can speculate that the experience of confronting the AIDS crisis has stimulated the mobilization of ethnic gay communities around health issues, furthered the dialogue on issues of cultural diversity within the gay community as a whole and reinforced the commitment of gay community leaders to a policy of inclusiveness in designing and implementing community services. These discussions offer white gay men an opportunity to learn what it means to be a gay man of color, how the identity issues differ, and the competing allegiances that arise out of affiliations to one's respective ethnic community, to the (white) "gay community," and to one's network of other gay men of color.

Society Responds to the Gay Community

AIDS-Related Stigma and Homophobia

The association of AIDS with the gay community has shaped discourse on both AIDS and homosexuality in our society over the last decade.

The response to AIDS shares many features with American society's responses to other deadly epidemics, such as the cholera epidemics of the nineteenth century (Rosenberg, 1987). Plagues have been interpreted as the response of either nature or god to a stigmatized out-group. Gay men are more likely to be blamed for their HIV illness than are heterosexuals (Herek & Glunt, 1988; St. Lawrence et al., 1990). St. Lawrence and her colleagues (1990) found college students' attitudes toward persons with AIDS and toward gay men with a critical illness to overlap on many variables, including seeing them both as more responsible for their illness, more deserving of their illness, more deserving to die, and people without whom the world would be better off. Blaming the victim both preserves a sense of order and justice to the universe (Lerner, 1966) and alleviates fears of personal vulnerability for those who are not members of such disliked minorities. Thus, fear of AIDS contagion may be contained by intensifying the negative attributions made about affected groups and reinforcing the sense of personal distance between oneself and those who are HIV-infected.

Fear of AIDS also justifies the continued institutional subjugation or oppression of certain groups. Several studies have found pervasive evidence of broad patterns of stigmatization of those who are at risk or already infected with HIV. Many HIV-infected persons have been the object of harassment or violence (National Association of People With AIDS, 1992). There have been many examples of discrimination against those with HIV illness by employers, insurance companies, and the judicial system (Schulman, 1991). This tendency toward stigmatization and avoidance has been found even among professional care-givers and health care providers (see, for example, Kelly et al., 1987; Pleck et al., 1988).

The association of the entire gay community with AIDS and continued fears about casual contagion held by the general public have influenced general attitudes toward gay men, lesbians, and bisexuals. AIDS stigma has reintensified some of the homophobic attitudes in our society. As Feldman (1989) noted, "Male homosexuals, who in the past had been seen by the wider society as sinners, criminals or mentally ill, were now seen as diseased and dangerously infectious. The homophobia and antigay bias which had begun to wane in the United States was reemerging under the guise of this growing fear of AIDS" (p. 187). This has been a presumed contributory factor in the rise of antigay violence and discrimination in many U.S. cities (National Gay & Lesbian Task Force, 1987). A number of studies have shown links between the stigmatization of those with AIDS and homophobic attitudes (Chapdelaine & Cohn, 1988; Herek & Capitano, 1992; Herek & Glunt, 1991; Larsen, Serra, & Long, 1990; Pleck et al., 1988; Stipp & Kerr, 1989).

The perception of gay men as diseased and the carriers of a biological, if not moral, contagion has intensified the antigay political rhetoric of the religious right. Their apparent strategy has included preaching a doctrine of AIDS as divine or natural retribution for the "perversity" of gay male sexuality. Over the course of the 1992 presidential elections, the Republican Party used the term "family values" as a thinly disguised code for justifying antigay policies.

Increased Visibility of the Gay Community

At the same time, the HIV epidemic has also afforded the general public more opportunities to understand and associate with lesbians, gay men, and bisexuals. The urgency of this public health crisis has demanded that sexuality be treated with a candor that would otherwise never be permissible on news programs or television shows. Homosexuality and bisexuality are no longer the taboo subjects they once were for legitimate public debate. The HIV epidemic has meant that male homosexual behavior and the gay community has been discussed and scrutinized more intensively by health care professionals, educators, researchers, the media, and the lay public. The HIV crisis not only has increased the visibility of gays, but has been associated with changes in how gay themes are presented in the media. A number of AIDS diagnoses and deaths have prompted public awareness that many prominent celebrities were gay—Rock Hudson being a historic example—thus providing examples of gay men that run counter to previous media stereotypic portrayals of gays as weak, passive inverts (see Russo, 1991). Such memorable examples can be powerful aids in reducing antigay prejudice and stigma (Herek, 1991).

There is now a new openness about the diversity of the gay experience and the diversity of those who identify as gay, lesbian, or bisexual, in part because of the HIV epidemic. First of all, this disease has robbed many men of their privacy and their power to determine what others may learn about their sexual and personal lives. The creation of AIDS service agencies has provided an environment in which many in the gay community feel comfortable being "out" for the first time on the job. In addition, assumptions about the relative safety of being "in the closet" versus being openly gay have been challenged by the fact that many men have been propeled by this epidemic to disclose their sexual orientation. Recent polls reveal a shift toward greater openness, as 43 percent of Americans now say that they know someone who is homosexual—double the number of only 7 years before (Schmalz, 1992). Prejudicial attitudes can be altered by regular interaction with individuals from stigmatized groups. This may help explain why public opinion surveys have shown a shift since the 1970s toward greater willingness to guarantee the basic civil rights of the gay community

(Herek, 1991). The public has also been exposed to new images of the gay community through its response to the HIV epidemic: men and women joining together to fight AIDS, developing an array of supportive community resources, and showing character, maturity, and strength by caring for those who are sick.

Future Directions for Research

In trying to summarize the impact of HIV on gay communities in the United States, we have reviewed some of the major areas of investigation by social scientists and indicated some areas for further exploration. Although it is possible that one may extrapolate too far and ascribe too much as direct consequences of the HIV pandemic, it is clear that the brutal force of this epidemic—whether by itself or in concert with other determinants—has dramatically altered the gay community in a host of ways that will be felt for generations. Sexual activity has new implications and concerns in this era of AIDS, particularly for gay and bisexual men. The last decade has seen changes not only in gay men's sexual behavior, but also in the ways gay and bisexual men socialize, in the importance and functions of both primary relationships and friendships, and in the emotional and psychological impact of dealing with the constant facts of dying and death in one's community. On a broader level, HIV has contributed to shifts in the institutions and rituals that define participation in the gay community, in the divisions and linkages of different subgroups within that abstract monolithic entity we term the "gay community," in the political and social concerns of gay activists and the larger gay community, and in the relationship of the larger society to the gay community. Several areas of research needing attention are described by the following questions.

How can we develop effective primary and secondary HIV prevention programs? As noted, gay and bisexual men have generally been remarkably adaptive in modifying their sexual behaviors in response to the threat of HIV, reducing their frequency of engaging in high-risk sexual behavior while exploring new varieties of "safer sex." However, studies done over the last few years indicate that considerable difficulty is involved in *sustaining* sexual risk-reduction behavior, and much work has gone into understanding what have been termed unsafe sex "relapses." There is a need to develop and evaluate more innovative prevention programs, such as community-level interventions that work to change norms and mobilize the resources of existing social groups to combat the spread and impact of HIV. Such community-level interventions also require developing different methods of evaluation.

We also need to learn much more about how to delay disease progression and promote psychological well-being among HIV-infected gay and bisexual men. Understanding the issues influencing the health-care decision-making of HIV-infected men is imperative for the development of interventions to encourage their use of available health-care resources and to adapt these resources to most effectively meet their needs.

What interventions might help gay and bisexual men cope with the impact of the epidemic? As HIV has spread through the gay community, it has confronted people with illness and death on a monumental scale, creating an apparently unceasing grieving process. The need to investigate how people cope under this siege, and to implement and evaluate mental health services and prevention programs, cannot be overstated. Gay men have traditionally relied on friends and partners for many of the functions filled by relatives for heterosexuals, yet AIDS has decimated many of those gay social networks. It is critical that both group and community-level interventions be developed to reduce alienation and isolation created by friendship networks' fragmentation, and to encourage the growth of new social networks and supportive relationships.

How can the gay community continue to provide needed services for those who are HIV-infected? Many AIDS-related organizations arose as an immediate response to a clear crisis; they could not anticipate that the urgent demands of the moment would continue to grow and that their services would be needed for years. Evaluating organizational structures and the overall provision of services is necessary to ensure that agencies adapt with the shifts in the epidemic, avoid duplication of efforts, and continue to meet the needs of their clients as efficiently as possible. Effective AIDS-related community-based organizations rely heavily on the use of volunteers to provide direct services. As the epidemic continues, the pool of potential recruits has not expanded at a rate commensurate to the numbers of those needing services. Identifying the issues related to both recruitment and burnout among volunteers and paid staff workers is imperative to the survival of these organizations.

How has AIDS changed what it means to be gay? In the era of AIDS, gay and bisexual men are also faced with formulating a new construct of gay identity that is broader than sex and AIDS, and identifying new ways of feeling a part of the gay community. More research would be useful to understand the impact of the HIV epidemic on the paths of gay or bisexual identity formation, as well as how it has influenced the life-course developmental issues for gay and bisexual men. HIV antibody testing has created a new milestone in a gay man's development, with profound consequences for virtually all aspects of his life. What can we say about how HIV status contributes to identity and what ways it influences a sense of affiliation to the broader gay community? The HIV epidemic has provided the impetus for a variety of changes in the organization of the gay community, the relationships between subgroups, and the available routes of participation in the gay community. To varying degrees, it has helped provoke greater recognition of the need for alliances within an extremely heterogeneous population. The need to unify to meet the threat of HIV (as well as the religious right), and the mobilization and creation of HIV-related services may have helped create a sense of "gay community" in areas outside major metropolitan centers that had not previously experienced that sense of visibility and unification.

In what ways can we reduce widespread prejudices and antipathy to gays, lesbians, and bisexuals? The response evoked by AIDS in U.S. society is inseparable from American perceptions of the gay male community. Fear of AIDS has provoked a wave of antigay discrimination and violence; narrow-minded attitudes toward those who have HIV illness are shaped by the stigma attached to the behaviors that provide a route of HIV transmission. At the same time, counterpoised against this is the fact that increased public awareness of AIDS has led to increased visibility of lesbians, gay men, and bisexuals, and the dissemination of more realistic and sympathetic portrayals of the gay community in the mass media. Research is necessary to understand the fears and negative attitudes held by many in American society toward gays, lesbians, and bisexuals, and to help develop programs to challenge stereotypes, reduce prejudice, and foster acceptance. Public opinion has a very direct impact on the course of the HIV epidemic, on both the macro-level, in terms of shaping public health policy, and the micro-level, in terms of altering the experience of individuals who must cope with stigmatization, harassment, and inequities in our health care system and priorities.

In the second decade of the HIV epidemic, we are confronted with many challenges. As behavior change remains the surest means of slowing the spread of HIV infection, we must make sure prevention programs are empirically evaluated and then broadly disseminated. To this end, researchers must collaborate more closely with those community-based organizations that provide services. We must also find ways to maximize the coping resources and emotional resilience of individuals and gay communities struggling with the toll of HIV. Future historians will note how well we all responded to these demands.

Acknowledgments

This work was supported in part by the National Institute of Mental Health/National Institute of Drug Abuse (MH42459—The Center for

AIDS Prevention Studies), and by grants from the National Institute on Alcohol Abuse and Alcoholism (R01-AA08233-04) and the National Institute of Mental Health (MH46816).

References

Adam, B. (1987). *The rise of a gay and lesbian movement.* Boston, MA: Twayne Publishers.

Adib, S., Joseph, J., Ostrow, D., Tal, M., & Schwartz S. (1991). Relapse in sexual behavior among homosexual men: A 2-year follow-up from the Chicago MACS/CCS. *AIDS, 5* (6), 757–760.

AIDS Service Providers Association of the Bay Area. (1990). *Report on AIDS volunteers in San Francisco.* AIDS Service Providers Association of the Bay Area, San Francisco, California.

Altman, D. (1986). *AIDS in the mind of America.* Garden City, NJ: Doubleday.

Ambrosio, A., & Sheehan, E. (1991). The just world belief and the AIDS epidemic. *Journal of Social Behavior and Personality, 6*(1), 163–170.

Ames, L., & Beeker, C. (1990). Gay men in small cities: How risky are they? Poster presentation at the Sixth International Conference on AIDS, San Francisco, CA, June 20–24.

Arno, P. (1991). An expanded role for community-based organizations. In N. F. McKenzie (Ed.), *The AIDS reader: Social, political, and ethical issues* (pp. 497–504). New York, NY: Meridien Books.

Aspinwall, L., Kemeny, M., Taylor, S., Schneider, S., & Dudley, J. (1991). Psychosocial predictors of gay men's AIDS risk-reduction behavior. *Health Psychology, 10* (6), 432–444.

Bahr, G., Sikkema, K., Kelly, J., Fernandez, M., Stevenson, L., Koob, J., Miller, J., Rompa, D., Morgan, M., Multhauf, K., & Adair, V. (1993). Attitudes and characteristics of gay men who remain at continued risk for contracting HIV infection. Poster presentation at the Ninth International Conference on AIDS, Berlin, Germany, June 6–11.

Beadnell, B., & Roffman, R. (1992). Reducing treatment barriers: Using the telephone to provide services to hard-to-reach populations. *Social Work.*

Beauchamp, D. (1991). Morality and the health of the body politic. In N. McKenzie (Ed.), *The AIDS reader: Social, political, and ethical issues* (pp. 408–421). New York: Meridian Books.

Belcher, A., Dettmore, D., & Holzemer, S. (1989). Spirituality and sense of well-being in persons with AIDS. *Holistic Nursing Practioner, 3*(4), 16–25.

Bell, A., & Weinberg, M. (1978). *Homosexualities: A study of diversity among men and women.* New York: Simon & Schuster.

Bérubé, A. (1990). *Coming out under fire: The history of gay men and women in World War II.* New York: Free Press.

Biller, R., & Rice, S. (1990). Experiencing multiple loss of persons with AIDS: Grief and bereavement issues. *Health and Social Work, 15*(4), 283–290.

Bolton, R. (1992). AIDS and promiscuity: Muddles in the models of HIV prevention. *Medical Anthropology, 14,* 145–223.

Bolton, R., Vincke, J., & Mak, R. (1992). Gay saunas: Venues of HIV transmission or AIDS prevention? Poster presentation at the Eighth International Conference on AIDS, Amsterdam, The Netherlands, July 19–24.

Boulton, M., & Weatherburn, P. (1990, June). *Literature review on bisexuality and HIV transmission.* Report commissioned by the Social & Behavioral Research Unit, World Health Organization's Global Programme on AIDS.

Brandt, A. (1988). AIDS in historical perspective: Four lessons from the history of sexually transmitted diseases. *American Journal of Public Health, 78*(4), 367–371.

Brody, E. (1985). Patient care as a normative family stress. *The Gerontologist, 25,* 19–29.

Brodsky, J. (1987). A retrospective ethnography of the Mineshaft. Paper presented at the *Homosexuality, Which Homosexuality?* Conference, Amsterdam, The Netherlands, December 15–18.

Bryant, S., & Damian (1990). *Partners newsletter for gay and lesbian couples.* Seattle: Sweet Corn Productions.

Burack, J., Stall, R., Barrett, D., & Coates, T. (1992). Depression predicts accelerated CD4 decline among gay men in San Francisco. Paper presented at the Eighth International Conference on AIDS, Amsterdam, The Netherlands, July 19–24.

Cain, R. (1991). Disclosure and secrecy among gay men in the United States and Canada: A shift in views. *Journal of the History of Sexuality, 2*(1), 25–45.

Calzavara, L., Myers, T., Godin, G., Lambert, J., Locker, D., Ennis, M. & The Canadian AIDS Society. (1993). Psychosocial problems reported by gay and bisexual men in Canada: Do problems vary with known HIV antibody and clinical status? Poster presentation at the Ninth International Conference on AIDS, Berlin, Germany, June 6–11.

Caplan, G. (1990). Loss, stress, and mental health. *Community Mental Health Journal, 26*(1), 27–48.

Carmack, B. (1992). Balancing engagement/detachment in AIDS-related multiple losses. *Image: Journal of Nursing Scholarship, 24*(1), 9–14.

Catalan, J., Klimes, I., Day, A., Garrod, A., Bond, A., & Gallwey, J. (1992). The psychosocial impact of HIV infection in gay men: A controlled investigation and factors associated with psychiatric morbidity. *British Journal of Psychiatry, 161,* 774–778.

Catania, J., Coates, T., Stall, R., Bye, L., Kegeles, S., Capell, F., Henne, J., McKusick, L., Morin, S., Turner, H., Pollack, L. (1991). Changes in condom use among homosexual men in San Francisco. *Health Psychology, 10*(3), 190–199.

Centers for Disease Control and Prevention (1994). *HIV/AIDS Surveillance Report, 5*(4), 1–33. U.S. Department of Health and Human Services.

Chapdelaine, A., & Cohn, E. (1988). Predictors of attitudes toward acquired immune deficiency syndrome (AIDS). Presented at the Annual Meeting of the American Psychological Association, Atlanta, Georgia, August.

Christ, G., Wiener, L., & Moynihan, R. (1985). Psychosocial issues in AIDS. In V. DeVita, S. Hellman, & S. Rosenberg (Eds.), *AIDS: Etiology, diagnosis, treatment and prevention* (pp. 275–297). Philadelphia: Lippincott.

Chuang, H., Devins, G., Hunsley, J., & Gill, M. (1989). Psychosocial distress and well-being among gay and bisexual men with human immunodeficiency virus infection. *American Journal of Psychiatry, 146,* 876–880.

Clement, U. (1992). Psychological correlates of unprotected intercourse among HIV-positive gay men. *Journal of Psychology and Human Sexuality, 5*(1/2), 133–155.

Coates, T. (1990). Strategies for modifying sexual behavior for primary and secondary prevention of HIV disease. *Journal of Consulting and Clinical Psychology, 58*(1), 57–69.

Coates, T., & Lo, B. (1990). Counseling patients seropositive for human immunodeficiency virus: An approach for medical practice. *Western Journal of Medicine, 153*(6), 629–634.

Coates, T., Morin, S., & McKusick, L. (1987). Behavioral consequences of AIDS antibody testing among gay men. *Journal of the American Medical Association, 258,* 1889.

Coates, T., Stall, R., Ekstrand, M., Lang, W., Solomon, G., & Hauck, W. (1989). Behavioral and psychological predictors of progression of HIV disease: The San Francisco Men's Health Study. Paper presented at the Fifth International Conference on AIDS, Montreal, Canada, June 4–9.

Coates, T., Stall, R., Kegeles, S., Lo, R., Morin, S., & McKusick, L. (1988). AIDS antibody testing: Will it stop the AIDS epidemic? Will it help people infected with HIV? *American Psychologist, 43,* 859–864.

Coates, T., Temoshok, L., & Mandel, J. (1984). Psychosocial research is essential to understanding and treating AIDS. *American Psychologist, 39,* 1309–1314.

Cohen, M., Salit, I., & Emmott, S. (1993). Sexual dysfunctions in HIV-positive gay men. Poster presentation at the 9th International Conference on AIDS, Berlin, Germany, June 6–11.

Connell, R., & Kippax, S. (1990). Sexuality in the AIDS crisis: Patterns of sexual practice and pleasure in a sample of Australian gay and bisexual men. *Journal of Sex Research, 27*(2), 167–198.

Coté, T., Biggar, R., & Dannenberg, A. (1992). Risk of suicide among persons with AIDS: A national assessment. *Journal of the American Medical Association, 268*(15), 2066–2068.

Davidson, A. (1991). Looking for love in the age of AIDS: The language of gay personals, 1978–1988. *Journal of Sex Research, 28*(1), 125–137.

D'Emilio, J. (1983). *Sexual politics, sexual communities: The making of a homosexual minority in the United States, 1940–1970.* Chicago: University of Chicago Press.

DeRanleau, M. (1990, May 10). Truth and soul: Why I outed a "prominent local official" (Editorial). *San Francisco Sentinel,* pp. 7–9.

Dilley, J., Ochitill, H., Perl, M., & Volberding, P. (1985). Findings in psychiatric consultations with patients with acquired immune deficiency syndrome. *American Journal of Psychiatry, 142,* 82–85.

Doll, L., O'Malley, P., Pershing, A., Darrow, W., Hessol, N., & Lifson, A. (1990). High-risk sexual behavior and knowledge of HIV antibody status in the San Francisco City Clinic cohort. *Health Psychology, 9*(3), 253–265.

Doll, L., Petersen, L., White, C., & Ward, J. (1990). Homosexually and nonhomosexually identified men who have sex with men: A behavioral comparison. Oral presentation at the Sixth International Conference on AIDS, San Francisco, California, June 20–24.

Eich, D., Frick, G., Dobler-Mikola, A., & Lüthy, R. (1991). Psychological well-being in asymptomatic HIV-positive individuals is associated with age and social network. Poster presentation at the Seventh International Conference on AIDS, Florence, Italy, June 16–21.

Ekstrand, M., & Coates, T. (1990). Maintenance of safer sex behaviors and predictors of risky sex: The San Francisco Men's Health Study. *American Journal of Public Health, 80*(8), 973–977.

Ekstrand, M., Coates, T., Guydish, J., Hauck, W., Collette, L., & Hulley, S. (1992). Bisexual men in San Francisco are not a common vector for spreading HIV infection to women: The San Francisco Men's Health Study. Unpublished manuscript.

Emmons, C., Joseph, J., Kessler, R., Wortman, C., Montgomery, S., & Ostrow, D. (1986). Psychosocial predictors of reported behavior change in homosexual men at risk for AIDS. *Health Education Quarterly, 13* (4), 331–345.

Emmott, S. (1991). Cognitive group therapy for coping with HIV infection. Poster presentation at the Seventh International Conference on AIDS, Florence, Italy, June 16–21.

Erikson, E. (1968). *Identity: Youth and crisis.* New York: W.W. Norton & Co.

Escoffier, J., & Rocchio, G. (1991, Winter). Queery results: AIDS activism: Where we stand. *OUT/LOOK, 11* 87–88.

Feldman, D. (1989). Gay youth and AIDS. *Journal of Homosexuality, 17*(1/2), 185–913.

Flynn, R., Hedge, B., Slaughter, J., & Green, J. (1993). Social support and psychological well-being in persons with HIV infection. Poster presentation at the Ninth International Conference on AIDS, Berlin, Germany, June 6–11.

Folkman, S., Chesney, M., Boccellari, A., Cooke, M., Collette, L., & Christopher, A. (1992). Death of partner affects mood of HIV + and HIV − caregiving men differently. Poster presentation at the Eighth International Conference on AIDS, Amsterdam, The Netherlands, July 19–24.

Folkman, S., Chesney, M., Pollack, L., & Phillips, C. (1992). Stress, coping, and high-risk sexual behavior. *Health Psychology, 11*(4), 218–222.

Frierson, R., Lippman, S., & Johnson, J. (1987). AIDS: Psychological stresses on the family. *Psychosomatics, 28*(2), 65–68.

Frutchey, C., & Williams, A. (1992). Cultural factors in gay male group sexual interactions: Findings and implications for planning HIV prevention strategies. Poster presentation at the Eighth International Conference on AIDS, Amsterdam, The Netherlands, July 19–24.

Gochros, H. (1992). The sexuality of gay men with HIV infections. *Social Work, 37*(2), 105–109.

Gold, R., Skinner, M., Grant, P., & Plummer, D. (1991). Situational factors and thought processes associated with unprotected intercourse in gay men. *Psychology and Health, 5*(4), 259–278.

Goldmeier, D. (1987). Psychosocial aspects of AIDS. *British Journal of Hospital Medicine, 37*, 232–240.

Gorman, M., Wiley, J., Winkelstein, W., Shiboski, S., & Moss, A. (1992). Suicide as the leading cause of non-AIDS mortality in a cohort of men in San Francisco. Poster presentation at the Eighth International Conference on AIDS, Amsterdam, The Netherlands, July 19–24.

Grothe, T., & McKusick, L. (1992). Coping with multiple loss. *FOCUS: A Guide to AIDS Research and Counseling, 7*(7), 5–6.

Hammersmith, S., & Weinberg, M. (1973). Homosexual identity: Commitment, adjustment and significant others. *Sociometry, 36*, 56–79.

Harowski, K. (1987). The worried well: Maximizing coping in the face of AIDS. *Journal of Homosexuality, 14*(1/2), 299–306.

Hastings, P. (1982). Alcohol and the lesbian community: Changing patterns of awareness. *Drinking and Drug Practices Surveyor, 18*, 3–7.

Hart, C., Taylor, S., Kemeny, M., & Dudley, J. (1990). Positive and negative changes in response to the threat of AIDS: Psychological adjustment as a function of severity of threat and area of life. Poster presentation at the Sixth International Conference on AIDS, San Francisco, California, June 20–24.

Hart, G., Mann, K., & Stewart, M. (1991). The support need of persons with hemophilia and AIDS or HIV-related illness and their family caregivers: An exploratory study. Ottawa, Canada: Government of Canada, Health and Welfare.

Hays, R., Catania, J., McKusick, L., & Coates, T. (1990). Help-seeking for AIDS-related concerns: A comparison of gay men with various HIV diagnoses. *Americna Journal of Community Psychology, 18*(5), 743–755.

Hays, R., Chauncey, S., & Tobey, L. (1990). The social support networks of gay men with AIDS. *Journal of Community Psychology, 18*, 374–385.

Hays, R., Kegeles, S., & Coates, T. (1990). High HIV risk-taking among young gay men. *AIDS, 4*(9), 901–907.

Hays, R., Kegeles, S., & Coates, T. (1993). Community mobilization promotes safer sex among young gay and bisexual men. Oral presentation at the Ninth International Conference on AIDS, Berlin, Germany, June 6–11.

Hays, R., McKusick, L., Pollack, L., Hilliard, B., Hoff, C., & Coates, T. (1993). Disclosing HIV seropositivity to significant others. *AIDS, 7*(3), 425–431.

Hays, R., Turner, H., & Coates, T. (1992). Social support, AIDS-related symptoms and depression among gay men. *Journal of Consulting and Clinical Psychology, 60*(3), 463–469.

Hedge, B., & Glover, L. (1990). Group intervention with HIV seropositive patients and their partners. *AIDS Care, 2*(2), 147–154.

Herdt, G. (1989). Introduction: Gay and lesbian youth, emergent identities, and cultural scenes at home and abroad. *Journal of Homosexuality, 17*(1/2), 1–42.

Herek, G. (1991). Stigma, prejudice, and violence against lesbians and gay men. In J. C. Gonsiorek & J. D. Weinrich (Eds.), *Homosexuality: Research implications for public policy* (pp. 60–80). Newbury Park, CA: Sage Publications, Inc.

Herek, G., & Capitano, J. (1992). AIDS-related stigma persists in the United States. Poster presentation at the Eighth International Conference on AIDS, Amsterdam, The Netherlands, July 19–24.

Herek, G., & Glunt, E. (1988). An epidemic of stigma: Public reactions to AIDS. *American Psychologist, 43*(11), 886–891.

Herek, G., & Glunt, E. (1991). AIDS-related attitudes in the United States: A preliminary conceptualization. *Journal of Sex Research, 28*(1), 99–123.

Hickson, F., Weatherburn, P., Davies, P., Hunt, A., Coxon, A., & McManus, T. (1992). Why gay men engage in anal intercourse. Poster presentation at the Eighth International Conference on AIDS, Amsterdam, The Netherlands, July 19–24.

Higgins, D., Galavotti, C., O'Reilly, K., Schnell, D., Rugg, D., & Johnson, R. (1990). The effect of HIV antibody counseling and testing on risk behaviors: Are the studies consistent? Poster presentation at the VI International Conference on AIDS, San Francisco, CA, June 20–24.

Hoff, C., McKusick, L., Hilliard, B., & Coates, T. (1992a). The impact of HIV antibody status on gay men's partner preferences: A community perspective. *AIDS Education and Prevention, 4*(3), 197–204.

Hoff, C., McKusick, L., Hilliard, B., Ekstrand, M., & Coates, T. (1992b). Changes in gay relationships before the AIDS epidemic and now. Poster presentation at the Eighth International Conference on AIDS, Amsterdam, The Netherlands, July 19–24.

Humphries, L. (1979). Exodus and identity: The emerging gay culture. In M. Levine (Eds), *Gay Men: The sociology of male homosexuality* (pp. 134–147). New York: Harper & Row.

Huston, B. (1990, May). Crosstalk: "The secret gay life of . . .". *San Francisco Bay Times*, p. 14.

Jacobs, J., & Tedford, W. (1980). Factors affecting self-esteem of the homosexual individual. *Journal of Homosexuality, 5*, 373–382.

Jakobi, P. (1990). Medical science, Christian fundamentalism and the etiology of AIDS. *AIDS Public Policy Journal, 5*(2), 89–93.

Jernigan, D. (1988). Why gay leaders don't last. *OUT/LOOK, 1*(2), 33–49.

Johnson, T. (1988). Spiritual questions in gay counseling. In M. Shernoff & W. Scott (Eds.), *The sourcebook on lesbian/gay health care, (2nd ed.)* (pp. 137–141). Washington, DC: National Lesbian/Gay Health Foundation.

Johnson, D., & McGrath, H. (1987). Perceived changes in sexual practices among homosexual men. Poster presentation at the Third International Conference on AIDS, Washington, DC, June 1–5.

Joseph, K., Adib, S., Joseph, J., & Tal, M. (1991). Gay identity and risky sexual behavior related to the AIDS threat. *Journal of Community Health, 16*(6), 287–297.

Judell, B. (1978). Sexual anarchy. In K. Jay & A. Young (Eds.), *Lavender culture* (pp. 135–139). New York: Jove Publications (HBJ).

Kaal, H. (1992). Grief counseling for gay men. *FOCUS: A Guide to AIDS Research and Counseling, 7*(7), 1–4.

Kegeles, S., Catania, J., & Coates, T. (1988). Intentions to communicate positive HIV antibody status to sex partners. *Journal of the American Medical Association, 259*, 216–217.

Kegeles, S., Catania, J., Coates, T., Pollack, L., and Lo, B. (1990). Many people who seek anonymous HIV-antibody testing would avoid it under other circumstances. *AIDS, 4,* 595–588.

Kegeles, S., Coates, T., Christopher, T., & Lazarus, J. (1989). Perceptions of AIDS: The continuing saga of AIDS-related stigma. *AIDS, 3*(Suppl 1), S253–S258.

Kegeles, S., Hays, R., & Coates, T. (1992). A community-level risk reduction intervention for young gay and bisexual men. Poster presentation at the Eighth International Conference on AIDS, Amsterdam, The Netherlands, July 19–24.

Kelly, J., & Murphy, D. (1992). Psychological interventions with AIDS and HIV: Prevention and treatment. *Journal of Consulting and Clinical Psychology, 60*(4), 576–585.

Kelly, J., St. Lawrence, J., Brasfield, T., Stevenson, L., Diaz, Y., & Hauth, A. (1990). AIDS risk behavior patterns among gay men in small Southern cities. *American Journal of Public Health, 80,* 416–418.

Kelly, J., St. Lawrence, J., Diaz, Y., Stevenson, L., Hauth, A., Brasfield, T., Kalichman, S., Smith, J., & Andrew, M. (1991). HIV risk behavior reduction following intervention with key opinion leaders of population: An experimental analysis. *American Journal of Public Health, 81*(2), 168–171.

Kelly, J., St. Lawrence, J., Smith, S., Hood, H., & Cook, D. (1987). Stigmatization of AIDS patients by physicians. *American Journal of Public Health, 77,* 789–791.

Kiecolt-Glaser, J., & Glaser, R. (1988) Psychological influences on immunity: Implications for AIDS. *American Psychologist, 43*(11), 892–898.

Kingsley, L., Zhou, S., Bacellar, H., Rinaldo, C. Jr., Chmiel, J., Detels, R., Saah, A., VanRaden, M., Ho, M., Muñoz, A., & Multicenter AIDS Cohort Study Group (1991). Temporal trends in Human Immunodeficiency Virus type 1 seroconversion 1984–1989. *American Journal of Epidemiology, 134*(4), 331–339.

Kizer, K., Green, M., Perkins, C., Doebbert, G., & Hughes, M. (1988). AIDS and suicide in California. *Journal of the American Medical Association, 260*(13), 1881.

Kowalewski, M. (1988). Double stigma and boundary maintenance: How gay men deal with AIDS. *Journal of Contemporary Ethnography, 17,* 211–228.

Klein, S. (1992). AIDS-related gay grief: An update including multiple loss syndrome. Poster presentation at the Eighth International Conference on AIDS, Amsterdam, The Netherlands, July 19–24.

Kramer, L. (1978). *Faggots.* New York: Random House.

Krieger, L. (1991, December 29). A lost generation of AIDS activists. *Sunday San Francisco Chronicle/Examiner,* pp. A1, A14.

Kurdek, L., & Schmitt, J. (1987). Perceived emotional support from family and friends in members of gay, lesbian and heterosexual cohabiting couples. *Journal of Homosexuality, 14,* 57–68.

Kyle, G. (1989). Philosophos: AIDS and the new social order. *Journal of Sex Research, 26*(2), 276–278.

Lackner, J., Caumartin, S., Joseph, J., & Ostrow, D. (1992). The effects of daily stressors and life events on mental health in a cohort of gay men at risk for AIDS. Poster presentation at the Eighth International Conference on AIDS, Amsterdam, The Netherlands, July 19–25.

Lamping, D., Gilmore, N., Grover, S., Tsoukas, C., Falutz, J., Hamel, M., & Di Meco, P. (1992). Social support and health-related outcomes in persons with HIV infection. Poster presentation at the Eighth International Conference on AIDS, Amsterdam, The Netherlands, July 19–25.

Larsen, K., Serra, M., & Long, E. (1990). AIDS victims and heterosexual attitudes. *Journal of Homosexuality, 19*(3), 103–116.

Lauritsen, J. (1987). Political-economic construction of gay male identities. Paper presented at the *Homosexuality, Which Homosexuality?* Conference, Amsterdam, The Netherlands, December 15–18.

Lee, K., & Busto, R. (1991, Fall). Queery results: When the spirit moves us. *OUT/LOOK, 14,* pp. 83–85.

Leger, M. (1989, Winter). The boy look. *OUT/LOOK, 1*(4), 44–45.

Leigh, B. (1990). The relationship of substance use during sex to high-risk sexual behavior. *Journal of Sex Research, 27*(2), 199–213.

Lerner, M. (1966, August). The unjust consequences of a need to believe in a just world. Presentation at the 74th Annual Convention of the American Psychological Association, New York.

Levine, M. (1979). Gay ghetto. In M. Levine (Ed.), *Gay men: The sociology of male homosexuality* (pp. 182–204). New York: Harper & Row.

Levine, M., & Siegel, K. (1992). Unprotected sex: Understanding gay men's participation. In J. Huber & B. Schneider (Eds.), *The social context of AIDS* (pp. 47–71). Newbury Park, CA: Sage Publications.

Lovejoy, N., Morgenroth, B., Paul, S., Freemen, E., & Christianson, B. (1992). Potential predictors of information-seeking behavior by homosexual/bisexual (gay) men with a human immunodeficiency virus seropositive health status. *Cancer Nursing, 15*(2), 116–124.

Marks, R. (1988). Coming out in the age of AIDS: The next generation. *OUT/LOOK, 1*(1), 66–74.

Marks, G., Richardson, J., & Maldonado, N. (1991). Self-disclosure of HIV infection to sexual partners. *American Journal of Public Health, 81*(10), 1321–1322.

Martin, J. (1986). Sexual behavior changes, psychological distress and appraised vulnerability to AIDS among gay men. Paper presented at the 12th Annual Meeting of the International Academy of Sex Research, Amsterdam, The Netherlands, September 6–20.

Martin, J. (1987). The impact of AIDS on gay male sexual behavior patterns in New York City. *American Journal of Public Health, 77*(5), 578–581.

Martin, J. (1988). Psychological consequences of AIDS-related bereavement among gay men. *Journal of Consulting and Clinical Psychology, 56*(6), 856–862.

Martin, J. (1990). Drug use and unprotected anal intercourse among gay men. *Health Psychology, 9*(4), 450–465.

Martin, J., & Dean, L. (1993). Effects of AIDS-related bereavement and HIV-related illness on psychological distress among gay men: A 7-year longitudinal study, 1985–1991. *Journal of Consulting and Clinical Psychology, 61*(1), 94–103.

Martin, J., Dean, L., Garcia, M., & Hall, W. (1989). The impact of AIDS on a gay community: Changes in sexual behavior, substance use, and mental health. *American Journal of Community Psychology, 17*(3), 269–293.

Marzuk, P., Tierney, H., Tardiff, K., Gross, E., Morgan, E., Hsu, M., & Mann, J. (1988). Increased risk of suicide in persons with AIDS. *Journal of the American Medical Association, 259*, 1333–1337.

Mays, V., & Cochran, S. (1993). High risk HIV-related sexual behaviors in a national sample of U.S. black gay and bisexual men. Oral presentation at the Ninth International Conference on AIDS, Berlin, Germany, June 6–11.

McCann, K., & Wadsworth, E. (1992). The role of informal carers in supporting gay men who have HIV-related illness: What do they do and what are their needs? *AIDS Care, 4*(1), 25–34.

McCusker, J., Stoddard, A., Mayer, K., Zapka, J., Morrison, C., & Saltzman, S. (1988). Effects of HIV antibody test knowledge on subsequent sexual behaviors in a cohort of homosexually active men. *American Journal of Public Health, 78*, 462–467.

McCusker, J., Stoddard, A., McDonald, M., Zapka, J., & Mayer, K. (1992). Maintenance of behavioral change in a cohort of homosexually active men. *AIDS, 6*, 861–868.

McCusker, J., Stoddard, A., Zapka, J., Zorn, M., & Mayer, K. (1989). Predictors of AIDS-preventive behavior among homosexually-active men: A longitudinal study. *AIDS, 3*, 443–448.

McKenzie, N. (Ed.) (1991). *The AIDS reader: Social, political, and ethical issues.* New York: Meridian Books.

McKirnan, D., Doll, L., Harrison, J., Delgado, W., Doetsch, J., Mendoza, G., & Burzette, R. (1991). Primary relationships confer risk for HIV exposure among gay men. Poster presentation at Seventh International Conference on AIDS, Florence, Italy, June 16–21.

McKirnan, D., Stokes, J., Vanable, P., Burzette, R., & Doll, L. (1993). Predictors of unsafe sex among bisexual men: The role of gay identification. Poster presentation at the Ninth International Conference on AIDS, Berlin, Germany, June 6–11.

McKusick, L., Coates, T., Morin, S., Pollack, L., & Hoff, C. (1990). Longitudinal predictors of reductions in unprotected anal intercourse among gay men in San Francisco: The AIDS Behavioral Research Project. *American Journal of Public Health, 80*(8), 978–983.

McKusick, L., Horstman, W., & Coates, T. (1985). AIDS and sexual behavior reported by gay men in San Francisco. *American Journal of Public Health, 75*(5), 493–496.

Meyer-Bahlburg, H., Exner, T., Lorenz, G., Gruen, R., Gorman, J., & Ehrhardt, A. (1991). Sexual risk behavior, sexual functioning, and HIV-disease progression in gay men. *Journal of Sex Research, 28*(1), 3–27.

Moon, T. (1991). Survivor guilt in HIV negative men. Unpublished manuscript.

Morin, S., Charles, K., & Malyon, A. (1984). The psychological impact of AIDS on gay men. *American Psychologist, 39*(11), 1288–1293.

Mulder, C., Emmelkamp, P., Mulder, J., Antoni, M., Sandfort, T., & de Vries, M. (1992). The immunological and psychosocial effects of group intervention for asymptomatic HIV-infected homosexual men. Poster presentation at the Eighth International Conference on AIDS, Amsterdam, The Netherlands, July 19–24.

Murphy, D., Kelly, J., Bahr, G., Stevenson, L., Kalichman, S., Koob, J., Morgan, M., Brasfield, T., & Berstein, B. (1993). Comparison of cognitive-behavioral and social support group psychotherapies for HIV-infected persons. Poster presentation at the Ninth International Conference on AIDS, Berlin, Germany, June 5–11.

Murphy, D., Kelly, J., Brasfield, T., Koob, J., Bahr, R., & St. Lawrence, J. (1991). Predictors of depression among persons with HIV infection. Presentation at the Seventh International Conference on AIDS, Florence, Italy, June 16–21.

Namir, S., Wolcott, D., Fawzy, F., & Alumbaugh, M. (1987). Coping with AIDS: Psychological and health implications. *Journal of Applied Social Psychology, 17*(3), 309–328.

Nardi, P. (1992). Lovers, friends and other strangers: The impact of AIDS on gay and lesbian relationships. Unpublished manuscript.

National Association of People with AIDS (1992). HIV in America: A profile of challenges facing Americans living with HIV. Report by the National Association of People with AIDS.

National Gay and Lesbian Task Force (1987). *Anti-gay violence: Victimization and defamation in 1986.* New York: National Gay and Lesbian Task Force.

Newman, F. (1978). Why I'm not dancing. In K. Jay & A. Young (Eds.), *Lavender culture* (pp. 140–145). New York: Jove Publications (HBJ).

Nichols, S. (1983). Psychiatric aspects of AIDS. *Psychosomatics, 24*(12), 1083–1089.

Nicholson, W., & Long, B. (1990). Self-esteem, social support, internalized homophobia, and coping strategies of HIV + gay men. *Journal of Consulting and Clinical Psychology, 58*(6), 873–876.

O'Brien, K. (1992). Social ties affect mental health and risk behavior. Paper presented at the 145th Annual Meeting of the American Psychiatric Association, Washington, DC.

Odets, W. (1990). The psychological epidemic: The impact of AIDS on uninfected gay and bisexual men. Unpublished manuscript.

Odets, W. (1991, Fall). The secret epidemic. *OUT/LOOK, 14,* 45–49.

Odets, W. (1992). Unconscious motivations for the practice of unsafe sex among gay men in the United States. Poster presentation at the Seventh International Conference on AIDS, Amsterdam, The Netherlands, July 19–24.

Offir, J., Fisher, J., Williams, S., & Fisher, W. (1993). Reasons for inconsistent AIDS-preventive behaviors among gay men. *Journal of Sex Research, 30*(1), 62–69.

Ostrow, D., Beltran, E., Joseph, J., Wesch, J., & Chmiel, J. (1990). Recreational drugs and condom use patterns in the Chicago MACS/CCS cohort of homosexually active men. Paper presented at The 143rd Annual Meeting of the American Psychiatric Association, New York, NY.

Ostrow, D., Joseph, J., Kessler, R., Soucy, J., Tal, M., Eller, M., Chmiel, J., &

Phair, J. (1989). Disclosure of HIV antibody status: Behavioral and mental health correlates. *AIDS Education and Prevention, 1*, 1–11.

Outweek. (1990, May 16). Smashing the closet: The pros and cons of outing. Essays by S. Beery, V. Brownworth, A. Folayan, H. Madsen, A. Miller, S. Pettit, G. Rotello. pp. 40–53.

Pargament, K. (1990). God help me: Toward a theoretical framework of coping for the psychology of religion. *Research in the Social Scientific Study of Religion, 2*, 195–224.

Paul, J., Bloomfield, K., & Stall, R. (1991). Gay and alcoholic: Epidemiologic and clinical issues. *Alcohol Health and Research World, 15*(2), 151–160.

Paul, J., Stall, R., Crosby, G., Barrett, D., & Midanik, L. (1993). Correlates of sexual risk-taking among gay male substance abusers. Unpublished manuscript.

Peabody, B. (1987). *The screaming room.* New York: Avon.

Pearlin, L., Semple, S., & Turner, H. (1988). The stress of AIDS caregiving: A preliminary overview of the issues. In I. Corliss & M. Pittman (Eds.), *AIDS: Principles, practices and policies.* Washington, DC: Hemisphere Corp.

Persson, L., Hanson, B., Ostergren, P., Moestrup, T., & Isacsson, S. (1991). Social network, social support and the amount of CD-4 lymphocytes in a representative urban Swedish population of HIV seropositive homosexual men. Poster presentation at the Seventh International Conference on AIDS, Florence, June 16–21.

Peterson, J., Coates, T., Catania, J., Middleton, L., Hilliard, B., & Hearst, N. (1992). High-risk sexual behavior and condom use among gay and bisexual African–American men. *Americal Journal of Public Health, 82*(11), 1490–1494.

Peterson, J., Fullilove, R., Catania, J., & Coates, T. (1989). Close encounters of an unsafe kind: Risky sexual behaviors and predictors among black gay and bisexual men. Poster presentation at the Fifth International Conference on AIDS, Montreal, Canada, June 4–9.

Peterson, J., & Marin, G. (1988). Issues in the prevention of AIDS among Black and Hispanic men. *American Psychologist, 43*(11), 871–877.

Peyton, H. (1988). AIDS prevention for gay men: A selected history and analysis of the San Francisco experience 1982–1987. Unpublished paper. San Francisco AIDS Foundation.

Pickering, J., Sharpton, T., Thornhill, J., & Di Milia, J. (1991). Sexually transmitted diseases among San Francisco Bay Area men. Poster presentation at the Seventh International Conference on AIDS, Florence, Italy, June 16–21.

Pleck, J., O'Donnell, L., O'Donnell, C., & Snarey, J. (1988). AIDS-phobia, contact with AIDS, and AIDS-related job stress in hospital workers. *Journal of Homosexuality, 15*(3/4), 41–54.

Pollack, L., Ekstrand, M., Stall, R., & Coates, T. (1990). Current reasons for having unsafe sex among gay men in San Francisco: The AIDS Behavioral Research Project. Poster presentation at the Sixth International Conference on AIDS, San Francisco, California, June 20–24.

Powell-Cope, G. & Brown, M. (1992). Going public as an AIDS family caregiver. *Social Science and Medicine, 34*(5), 571–580.

Pressman, J. (1990). Review Essay: AIDS and the burden of historians. *Journal of the History of Sexuality, 1*(1), 137–143.

Prieur, A., Anderson, A., Frantzsen, E., Hanssen, A.-H., Høigård, C., & Valberg, A. (1989). Gay men: Reasons for continued practice of unsafe sex. Presented at the Eleventh National Lesbian and Gay Health Conference, San Francisco, CA, April 5–9.

Quadland, M., & Shattls, W. (1987). AIDS, sexuality, and sexual control. *Journal of Homosexuality, 14*(1/2), 277–298.

Rabins, P., Mace, N., & Lucas, M. (1982). Impact of dementia on the family. *Journal of the American Medical Association, 243,* 333–335.

Remien, R., Rabkin, J., Williams, J., Bradbury, M., Ehrhardt, A., & Gorman, J. (1990). Cessation of substance use disorders in gay men. Paper presented at the 143rd Annual Meeting of the American Psychiatric Association New York, NY.

Remien, R., Rabkin, J., Williams, J., & Katoff, L. (1992). Coping strategies and health beliefs of AIDS longterm survivors. *Psychology and Health, 6,* 335–345.

Richwald, G., Morisky, D., Kyle, G., Kristal, A., Gerber, M., & Friedland, J. (1988). Sexual activities in bathhouses in Los Angeles County: Implications for AIDS prevention education. *Journal of Sex Research, 25*(2), 169–180.

Rofes, E. (1990, Spring). Gay groups vs. AIDS groups: Averting civil war in the 1990s. *OUT/LOOK, 8,* 8–17.

Roffman, R., Beadnell, B., Stern, M., Gordon, J., Downey, L., & Siever, M. (1991). Phone counseling in reducing barriers to AIDS prevention. Paper presented at the 99th Annual Meeting of the American Psychological Association, San Francisco, CA, August 16–20.

Rosenberg, C. (1987). *The cholera years* (2nd. ed.). Chicago: University of Chicago Press.

Ross, M., Tebble, W., & Viliunas, D. (1992). Staging of reactions to AIDS virus infection in asymptomatic homosexual men. Unpublished manuscript.

Rosser, B. (1991). The effects of using fear in public AIDS education on the behavior of homosexually active men. *Journal of Psychology & Human Sexuality, 4*(3), 123–134.

Rubin, S. (1989, May 24). The end of the lesbian "Cheers." *San Francisco Chronicle,* p. B5.

Ruefli, T., Yu, O., & Barton, J. (1992). Sexual risk-taking in smaller cities: The case of Buffalo, New York. *Journal of Sex Research, 29*(1), 95–108.

Russo, V. (1991) *The celluloid closet: Homosexuality in the movies.* New York: Borgo Press.

St. Lawrence, J., Hood, H., Brasfield, T., & Kelly, J. (1989). AIDS risk knowledge and risk behavior among homosexual men in high- and low-AIDS prevalence cities. *Public Health Reports, 104,* 391–395.

St. Lawrence, J., Husfeldt, B., Kelly, J., Hood, H., & Smith, S. Jr. (1990). The stigma of AIDS: Fear of disease and prejudice toward gay men. *Journal of Homosexuality, 19*(3), 85–101.

San Francisco AIDS Foundation Education Department & Cooper, C. (1992, May). Oral sex activity and safe sex behaviors in a highly HIV-educated sample of gay and bisexual men. Report prepared by the San Francisco AIDS Foundation, San Francisco, CA.

San Francisco Sentinel (1993, June 23). Our gay and lesbian elected officials. *San Francisco Sentinel*, p. 25.

Schaefer, A., Paar, G., Siedenbiedel, W., Breukel, M., Noack, R., & Stäcker, K.-H. (1993). Psychosocial correlates of a four-month group therapy in HIV-positive homosexual and bisexual men. Poster presentation at the Ninth International Conference on AIDS, Berlin, Germany, June 7–11.

Schaefer, S., & Coleman, E. (1992). Shifts in meaning, purpose, and values following a diagnosis of human immunodeficiency virus (HIV) infection among gay men. *Journal of Psychology and Human Sexuality*, 5(1/2), 13–29.

Schechter, M. (1988). Patterns of sexual behavior and condom use in a cohort of homosexual men. *American Journal of Public Health*, 78(12), 1535–1538.

Schmalz, J. (1992, October 11). Gay politics goes mainstream. *New York Times Magazine*, pp. 18–21, 29, 41–42, 50–53.

Schmitt, K., & Kurdek, L. (1987). Personality correlates of positive identity and relationship involvement in gay men. *Journal of Homosexuality*, 13(4), 101–109.

Schulman, D. (1991). AIDS discrimination: Its nature, meaning, and function. In N. McKenzie (Ed.), *The AIDS reader: Social, political, and ethical issues* (pp. 463–490). New York: Meridian Books.

Schulz, S., Friedman, S., Kristal, A. et al. (1984). Declining rates of rectal and pharyngeal gonorrhea among men—New York City. *Journal of the American Medical Association*, 252, 327–328.

Shilts, R. (1987). *And the band played on: Politics, people, and the AIDS epidemic.* New York: St. Martin's Press.

Selik, R., Castro, K., & Pappaioanou, M. (1988). Racial/ethnic differences in the risk of AIDS in the United States. *American Journal of Public Health*, 78(12), 1539–1545.

Siegel, K., Bauman, L., Christ, G., & Krown, S. (1988). Patterns of change in sexual behavior among gay men in New York City. *Archives of Sexual Behavior*, 17(6), 481–497.

Siegel, K. & Krauss, B. (1991). Living with HIV infection: Adaptive tasks of seropositive gay men. *Journal of Health and Social Behavior*, 32, 17–32.

Siegel, K., Raveis, S., & Krauss, B. (1992, March). Factors associated with urban gay men's treatment initiation decisions for HIV infection. *AIDS Education and Prevention*, 4(2), 135–142.

Siegel, K., Levine, M., Brooks, C., & Kern, R. (1989). The motives of gay men for taking or not taking the HIV antibody test. *Social Problems*, 36(4), 368–383.

Snyder, M., & Omoto, A. (1992). Volunteerism and society's response to the HIV epidemic. *Current Directions in Psychological Science*, 1(4), 113–116.

Somlai, A. (1993). The spiritual practices and needs of people living with HIV and AIDS. Poster presentation at the Ninth International Conference on AIDS, Berlin, Germany, June 6–11.

Spada, J. (1979). *The Spada report: The newest survey of gay male sexuality.* New York: Signet Books.

Spilka, B., Shaver, P., & Kirkpatrick, L. (1985). A general attribution theory for the psychology of religion. *Journal for the Scientific Study of Religion, 24*(1), 1–20.

Stall, R., Barrett, D., Bye, L., Catania, J., Frutchey, C., Henne, J., Lemp, G., & Paul, J. (1992). A comparison of younger and older gay men's HIV risk-taking behaviors: The Communications Technologies 1989 cross-sectional survey. *Journal of Acquired Immune Deficiency Syndromes, 5,* 682–687.

Stall, R., Ekstrand, M., Pollack, L., McKusick, L., & Coates, T. (1990). Relapse from safer sex: The next challenge for AIDS prevention efforts. *Journal of Acquired Immune Deficiency Syndromes, 3,* 1181–1187.

Stall, R., McKusick, L., Wiley, J., Coates, T., & Ostrow, D. (1986). Alcohol and drug use during sexual activity and compliance with safe sex guidelines for AIDS: The AIDS Behavioral Research Project. *Health Education Quarterly, 13*(4), 359–371.

Stewart, K., Haley, W., & Saag, M. (1993). Effects of caregiving tasks, social network, and patient functioning on informal caregivers of HIV-infected men. Poster presentation at the Ninth International Conference on AIDS, Berlin, Germany, June 6–11.

Stipp, H., & Kerr, D. (1989). Determinants of public opinion about AIDS. *Public Opinion Quarterly, 53,* 98–106.

Taylor, P., & Ferszt, G. (1990). Spiritual healing. *Holistic Nursing Practicitioner, 4*(4), 32–38.

Todak, G., Kertzner, R., Remien, R., Lin, S., Williams, J., Friedman, R., Ehrhardt, A., & Gorman, J. (1992). Psychosocial factors in the decision to decline zidovudine (AZT) treatment in HIV seropositive gay men. Poster presentation at the Eighth International Conference on AIDS, Amsterdam, The Netherlands, July 19–24.

Tross, S., & Hirsch, D. (1988). Psychological distress and neuropsychological complications of HIV infection and AIDS. *American Psychologist, 43,* 929–934.

Turner, H., Catania, J., & Gagnon, J. (1993). The prevalence of informal caregiving to persons with AIDS in the United States. Unpublished manuscript under review.

Turner, H., Hays, R., & Coates, T. (1993). Determinants of social support among gay men: The context of AIDS. *Journal of Health and Social Behavior, 34*(3), 37–53.

Vicini, M., Meraviglia, P., & Valsecchi, L. (1991). AIDS as identity crisis: A research on the symbolic meaning of AIDS through drawing and Rorschach tests. Poster presentation at the Seventh International Conference on AIDS, Florence, Italy, June 16–21.

Vollmer, T. (1990, May 10). Young gays long on style, short on substance. *San Francisco Sentinel,* p. 7.

Waller, P. (1992). Health-promoting behavior and health locus of control among gay men. Poster presentation at the Seventh International Conference on AIDS, Florence, Italy, June 16–21.

Wayment, H., Kemeny, M., & Silver, R. (1990). Survivor syndrome in the gay community. Poster presentation at the Sixth International Conference on AIDS, San Francisco, CA, June 20–24.

Weinberg, M. S., & Williams, C. J. (1974). *Male homosexuals: Their problems and adaptations*. New York: Oxford University Press.

Weinberg, M., & Williams, C. (1979). Gay baths and the social organization of impersonal sex. In M. Levine (Ed.), *Gay men: The sociology of male homosexuality*. (pp. 165–181). New York: Harper & Row.

Winkelstein, W. Jr., Wiley, J., Osmond, D., et al. (1993). The San Francisco Young Men's Health Study. Oral presentation at the Ninth International Conference on AIDS, Berlin, Germany, June 6–11.

Winnow, J. (1989, Summer). Lesbians working on AIDS: Assessing the impact on health care for women. *OUT/LOOK, 5*, 10–18.

Wolf, T., Balson, P., Morse, E., Simon, P., Gaumer, R., Dralle, P., & Williams, M. (1991). Relationship of coping style to affective state and perceived social support in asymptomatic and symptomatic HIV-infected persons: Implications for clinical management. *Journal of Clinical Psychiatry, 52*, 171–173.

Zarit, S., Todd, P., & Zarit, J., (1986). Subjective burden of husbands and wives as caregivers: A longitudinal study. *The Gerontologist, 26*, 260–272.

15

Psychotherapy with Lesbians and Gay Men

Kristin A. Hancock

Lesbians and gay men refer themselves for psychotherapy in sizable proportions compared to their heterosexual counterparts (Bell & Weinberg, 1978; National Lesbian & Gay Health Foundation, 1987). In a comprehensive study by Bell and Weinberg (1978), the utilization of mental health services by lesbians and gay men was compared to that of heterosexual women and men. Fifty-eight percent of the white homosexual males and 48 percent of the African–American homosexual males had consulted a mental health professional at least once in their lives compared to only 30 percent of the white heterosexual males and 23 percent of the African–American heterosexual males in the study. Furthermore, although women have traditionally used mental health services in greater numbers than men, the Bell and Weinberg data show the same trend for white (68%) and African–American (58%) lesbians compared with white (40%) and African–American (42%) heterosexual women. Unfortunately, the quality of service provision to gay and lesbian clients varies dramatically.

Evidence indicates that services provided to lesbians and gay men may not be optimal. In 1986, Garnets, Hancock, Cochran, Goodchilds, and Peplau (1991) conducted a national survey of American Psychological Association members on the quality of psychotherapy services to lesbian and gay clients. While the study notes that some providers demonstrate knowledge and sensitivity to the special problems and concerns of these clients, it also uncovered inadequate and inappropriate care. Not only did some psychotherapists still view homosexuality as psychopathology, some were continuing to "prescribe" heterosexuality as a remedy. In addition, the Garnets et al. (1991) data indicate that some providers continue to discourage, change, and demean lesbian and gay clients; others trivialize and disregard gay and lesbian relationships, refusing to provide couples therapy to them. Not surprisingly, this report also shows that some practitioners are uninformed or misinformed about fundamental issues facing lesbians and gay men such as the psychological consequences of prejudice and discrimination. Another investigation of the attitudes of psychotherapists toward gay and lesbian clients by Graham, Rawlings, Halpern, and Hermes (1984) found that the two major concerns of providers were (1) the ability to maintain objectivity and (2) a lack of knowledge about homosexuality. The authors relate these deficits to the tendency to assume a "blame-the-victim" perspective on the part of the therapist. They suggest that the problems and concerns of lesbian and gay clients were viewed by the practitioners as having been created by the client's sexual orientation rather than society's response to it.

In the survey by Garnets et al. (1991), nearly all of the providers reported having seen at least one gay or lesbian client in psychotherapy at least once, knowingly. In this light, the need for the basic education and training of all psychotherapy service providers in gay and lesbian issues is readily apparent. Without it, incompetence in this area is perpetuated as these service providers supervise or teach students or interns who are or will be practicing psychotherapy with lesbian and gay clients.

This chapter is organized into three sections on psychotherapy with gay men and lesbians: (1) therapy shown to be inappropriate and counterproductive with lesbian and gay clients, (2) major issues in the treatment of these clients, and (3) suggestions for further education, training, and research regarding psychotherapeutic service provision to lesbians and gay men.

Inappropriate and Counterproductive Service Provision

Assessment

In spite of the fact that there is no empirical basis for the notion that homosexuality per se is indicative of mental illness, psychological disturbance, or maladjustment (Gonsiorek, 1991), some practitioners continue to view homosexuality as psychopathology, developmental arrest, or other psychological disorder. In Garnets et al.'s (1991) study, many problems of gay and lesbian clients were attributed to a homosexual orientation without evidence that it was so. There were also descriptions of psychologists who believe that homosexuality necessarily indicates the presence of psychopathology. The approach taken by these providers opposes the ethical responsibility of psychologists to maintain an awareness of and to use "current scientific and professional information" in their professional activities (in this case, the treatment of lesbians and gay men; American Psychological Association, 1992, Section 1.05). Other assessment errors made by practitioners include the assumption (on the provider's part) that the client is heterosexual (Garnets et al., 1991). If the client says nothing, he or she is assumed to be heterosexual or asexual rather than gay or lesbian (Glenn & Russell, 1986). There is also a tendency to discount a client's self-identification as lesbian or gay when she or he does mention sexual orientation (Garnets et al., 1991). Each of these problems are examples of heterosexist bias, the belief that heterosexuality is the only acceptable or most acceptable sexual orientation.

Another assessment error described in the survey conducted by Garnets et al. (1991) was a failure to recognize the extent to which gay or lesbian clients' own negative attitudes, feelings, and ideas regarding homosexuality influence their symptoms or distress. These negative attitudes, often referred to as "internalized homophobia," involve the incorporation of antigay prejudice into the self-image of a lesbian or gay individual (Malyon, 1981, 1982). This results from developing in a society which condones prejudice against gay men and lesbians. Gonsiorek and Rudolph (1991) summarize this model as follows:

> Children who will eventually be bisexual or homosexual often develop an awareness of being different at an early age. They may not understand the nature or precise meaning of their differentness, but they soon learn it is negatively regarded. As these individuals develop and mature, they reach a fuller understanding of the nature of this difference and the considerable negative societal reaction to it. These negative feelings may be incorporated into the self-image resulting in varying degrees of *internalized homophobia*. Negative feelings about one's sexual orientation may be overgeneralized to encompass the entire self. Effects of this may range from a mild tendency toward self-doubt in the face of prejudice to overt self-hatred and self-destructive behavior. (p. 166)

Internalized homophobia is a major issue in treating gay and lesbian clients. To underestimate its importance can have serious consequences.

The most common example of assessment error is the presumption of heterosexuality. When heterosexuality is presumed or heterosexist attitudes prevail, it is indeed very difficult for a client to broach the subject of bisexuality or homosexuality. To have one's self-identification as lesbian, gay, or bisexual discounted on disclosure to therapist is even worse. Often therapists do this by providing gay, lesbian, and bisexual clients with interpretations or explanations for their identity. Garnets et al. (1991) found instances in which lesbian and gay clients were told their identity was a manifestation of problems with parents and an instance in which a man's gay self-identification was dismissed on the basis of insufficient heterosexual experience. Bisexual clients have been frustrated by the way in which clinicians rigidly and simplistically treated their sexual orientation. Klein and his associates (1990) have noted that major studies comparing homosexual with heterosexual populations (e.g., Bell & Weinberg, 1978; Masters & Johnson, 1979; Saghir & Robbins, 1973) have generally placed the bisexuals with the homosexual participants, which suggests that there are no differences between homosexuals and bisexuals or that the differences are insignificant.

Intervention

The efforts of psychotherapy service providers to change the sexual orientation of clients from homosexual or bisexual to heterosexual are referred to as "conversion therapy." Specific techniques reflect different theoretical frameworks (e.g., psychoanalytic, behavioral, social learning, etc.). Davison (1976, 1978, 1991), a well-known behavioral psychologist and former president of the Association for the Advancement of Behavior Therapy, maintains that therapies designed to change sexual orientation are unethical; by their very existence, they reaffirm societal and professional biases against homosexuality, and should therefore be eliminated. Reviews by Haldeman (1991) and Silverstein (1972, 1977, 1991) concur. Haldeman (1991) examined empirical research of sexual orientation conversion treatments originating from religious organizations as well as those put forth by psychology and psychiatry, finding no credible evidence that sexual orientation can be changed.

Many therapists indicate, at least verbally, that they accept homosexuality. Yet, as psychotherapy proceeds, these therapists tend to focus on the sexual orientation of a lesbian, gay, or bisexual client when it is inappropriate and irrelevant to do so (Garnets et al., 1991). One therapist mentioned in the survey conducted by Garnets and her associates wanted to focus on sexual orientation issues with a lesbian client rather than issues relating to her mastectomy, even though the client was quite comfortable with her lesbianism. It is likely that such responses are often unconscious in nature. There are also times when the disclosure of a homosexual orientation is more consciously disturbing to a psychotherapist. Garnets et al. (1991) found instances in which a client's revelation of homosexual feelings or homosexual identity was followed by abrupt termination of care without appropriate referral.

Identity

One of the most prominent difficulties psychotherapy service providers have is an inadequate understanding of gay and lesbian identity development (Garnets et al., 1991). Some therapists might tend to treat homosexuality as though it were a developmental phase through which one might have to pass on the way to heterosexuality. Others might view it merely as sexual activity without any accompanying associated sense of identity at all. Related problems include failing to understand the extent to which a client's gay or lesbian identity can be effected by his or her own negative views of homosexuality (i.e., internalized homophobia) and underestimating the difficulty of negotiating that identity in a society in which antigay sentiment is encouraged (Garnets et al., 1991).

Those individuals who identify themselves as bisexual must face negative evaluations and perceptions which seem to stem from inconsistent usage of the term "bisexuality" and from conflicts within psychology regarding the nature of bisexuality. Zinik (1985) describes what he refers to as the "conflict" model from which psychology and psychiatry has traditionally viewed bisexuality. This model approaches bisexuality as identity confusion or conflict, as a temporary phase or transitional stage between heterosexuality and homosexuality, or as a defense against a homosexual identity. This older perspective of human sexuality is essentially dichotomous in nature and assumes that heterosexuality and homosexuality cannot coexist without serious psychological conflict. For this reason, service providers who subscribe to this view may perceive conflict where there is none and, as is often the case with homosexuality, attempt to fix something which does not require repair. If bisexuality is approached in such a manner, the psychotherapist is destined not to understand or even perceive the unique difficulties encountered by a bisexual client in negotiating his or her feelings and identity in our society.

Ethnic and racial minority identity issues have also been traditionally neglected and are therefore often not addressed in psychotherapy with gay, lesbian, and bisexual clients. In this case, the psychotherapy service provider may *not* perceive conflicts or issues where they exist. Prominent among the issues lesbian, gay, and bisexual individuals face is that of double or even triple minority status in society. The need for and conflicts between various identifications is important to consider in working with members of ethnic and racial minorities (cf. Espin, 1987; Gock, 1885; Gutierrez & Dworkin, 1992; Loiacano, 1989; Morales, 1992). Gonsiorek and Rudolph (1991) note the importance of such factors as sex-role socialization and sex differences within culturally diverse populations to understanding identity issues of clients from these populations.

Relationships

Garnets et al. (1991) found a number of instances in which lesbian and gay relationships were discounted and discouraged by psychotherapists who were insensitive to or uninformed about the nature of such relationships. Couples therapy, a common treatment modality used by therapists for heterosexual couples, was not provided or recommended when it would have been appropriate to do so. Consider the gay male couple described in the survey who sought treatment regarding the inhibited sexual desire of one partner and who were told by a therapist that this problem meant that the partner manifesting the difficulty was probably not gay and the couple should break up (Garnets et al., 1991).

When the gay or lesbian relationship is acknowledged as valid by a psychotherapist, a problem then arises regarding the therapist's sensitivity to the unique aspects of both lesbian and gay relationships. Garnets and her associates (1991) found that therapists sometimes relied on a heterosexual frame of reference to formulate the interventions with gay and lesbian clients. For example, in one situation described in the study, a lesbian client was told by her therapist to read a book about heterosexual marriage problems because these difficulties were the same as those in her lesbian relationship. This was prescribed without taking into account the differences a relationship between two women might have from a relationship between a woman and a man.

The situations that develop in a relationship in which one or both members are bisexual have been largely unnoticed by psychology until fairly recently (e.g., Blumenstein & Schwartz, 1976; Brownfain, 1985; Coleman, 1985a, 1985b). Bisexual members of such couples are often viewed by psychotherapy service providers as conflicted and/or in transition from one side of a dichotomous model of sexuality to the other. Lourea (1985) suggests that bisexuals become aware of their orientation later in life than most gay, lesbian, or heterosexual individuals and are therefore more likely to be in a couple when they confront the issues and conflicts raised by a bisexual orientation. While these issues are discussed at greater length later, it is worth mentioning here that information on bisexual relationships has been ignored by those who educate and train psychotherapists to a far greater degree than information on the relationships of gay men and lesbians. This means psychotherapists essentially operate with little or no scientific information on the issues.

Family and Parenting Issues

Two areas of concern were described by Garnets et al. (1991) regarding the treatment of family and parenting issues. The first concern is the assumption that lesbians and gay men are inadequate parents simply because of their sexual orientation. The interventions which follow from such a view can be damaging to the families of gay and lesbian clients as well as to the clients themselves. For example, one lesbian described in the survey was told by a therapist that her "friend" should move out because her "friend's" presence was harmful to her son's sexual identity. Consider, too, the lesbian couple with two grammar school–aged boys who sought family therapy regarding parenting concerns. The therapist told one of the women that, if her sons were to see her dating a man, they would be more obedient. This therapist also suggested that the man spend the night and have breakfast with her and the boys and that this would cure their masculinity crisis. In this case, deception, rather than honesty, was regarded as therapeutic in the "professional judgment" of this provider.

The second concern expressed by Garnets et al. (1991) has to do with the inability of psychotherapists to understand or ascertain the effects of antigay prejudice and discrimination on gay and lesbian parents and their children. When one client told his therapist that his son was being teased at school because he (the father) was gay, the therapist responded by telling him that he should pay no attention to it because all children get teased (Garnets et al., 1991). Ariel and Stearns (1992) point out that as children of lesbian and gay parents deal with the issues of adolescence, problems involving discrimination can take on added significance. Needless to say, the issues confronting the adolescent children of lesbians and gay men as they strive to establish their identities against peer pressures to conform to heterosexual familial norms are important and should not be dismissed as trivial.

Major Issues in the Treatment of Gay, Lesbian, and Bisexual Clients

The discussion of major treatment issues is divided into six sections: (1) coming out, (2) antigay and other prejudice, (3) relationship issues, (4) the concerns of lesbian and gay youth, (5) gay and lesbian parenting, (6) family of origin concerns, and (7) therapist issues.

Coming Out

"Coming out" is an issue unique to gay men and lesbians. Gonsiorek and Rudolph (1991) summarize the process as follows:

> . . . gay individuals progress through a series of stages. . . . There is an initial stage where individuals block recognition of same-sex feelings through a variety of defensive strategies that may exact a high psychological price for their maintenance. Some individuals maintain these defensive strategies indefinitely and constrict their same-sex feelings. Usually, they consume in the process much psychological energy and incur constriction in general functioning style and damage to self-esteem. For many individuals, however, a gradual recognition of same-sex interests emerges. The individual, by stages, begins to gradually tolerate that significant same-sex feelings are present.
>
> This is usually followed by a period of emotional and behavioral experimentation with homosexuality and often an increasing sense of normalcy about same-sex feelings. Some models postulate a second crisis after the dissolution of a first relationship in which a reemergence of negative feelings about being gay or lesbian occurs. As the individual again begins to accept his or her same-sex feelings, a sense of identity as gay or lesbian is successfully integrated and accepted as a positive aspect of the self. (p. 164)

They emphasize that coming out involves a major shift in an individual's identity, which often includes emotional distress. How well the individual facing such change fares with this process depends on his or her psychological disposition as well as the kind, quality, and extent of interpersonal support available. It is important to note that the development of lesbian, gay, and bisexual self-identification can cease at any point in this process, an outcome Cass (1979) calls "identity foreclosure." There may be any number of reasons for the cessation of lesbian or gay identity development. The negative attitudes of society, those of significant others, and the extent to which the person has internalized them have much to do with inhibited gay or lesbian development.

Service providers must explore the many attitudes and feelings of the individual struggling with identifying him/herself as gay/lesbian. The toll taken by delayed identity development should also be carefully assessed and explored with the client. Therapists must evaluate the strength and resilience of the client going through the coming out process. A person with a more rigid character style is likely to have more difficulty than one who can more readily accommodate intrapsychic change. For those who are religious, coming out is an identity shift that conflicts with a deep-seated Judeo-Christian tradition for which the punishment can include the loss of one's family and friends.

Gonsiorek and Rudolph (1991) also report sex differences in coming out: "this process for males appears more abrupt and more likely to be associated with psychiatric symptoms, whereas the process for women appears characterized by greater fluidity and ambiguity" (p. 165). The reasons for the differences are related to gender-role socialization differences. Basow (1992) notes that boys receive more intense socialization pressure to behave in gender-appropriate ways than girls, with more punishment for not doing so. As a result, females have greater gender-role flexibility than males. Another difference has to do with the meaning that is ascribed to homosexual feelings and behavior. Because women's relationships are generally characterized by greater emotional expressiveness and intimacy, strong feelings or attachments to another woman may not be immediately interpreted as erotic. It is not until the feelings are identified as sexual and sexual behavior occurs that a woman is confronted with identifying herself as lesbian or bisexual (Gramick, 1984). It is this latter aspect of a woman's feelings that she is apt to repress or deny even after other strong emotions have existed for some time. For men, the process tends to be more abrupt, manifesting in sexual behavior without the emotional intimacy which characterizes female relationships. Similarly, men are then apt to repress or deny the significance of this behavior.

Coming out is also heavily influenced by culture, class, and ethnicity (Gonsiorek & Rudolph, 1991). Generalizations of current information about this process to various racial and ethnic populations should be done cautiously. Complex interactions between a culture's views of homosexuality and gender roles result in double or even triple minority status for some gay or lesbian individuals. Members of minority populations are often faced with complicated and difficult decisions regarding personal identity in which considerable dissonance is experienced between cultural identity and lesbian or gay identity (e.g., Gock, 1985; Morales, 1983; Sears, 1989). Further, minority group members differ in how and why they experience difficulties. For example, Chan (1989) found that Asian gay men experience more discrimination regarding their sexual orientation than Asian lesbians. On the other hand, Asian lesbians experience more discrimination for being Asian. These findings point to the need for a serious examination of the ways in which discrimination interacts with a culture's gender-role socialization and its attitudes toward homosexuality.

Antigay Prejudice

The most serious and prevalent problem gay men and lesbians continue to face is antigay prejudice. The National Gay and Lesbian Task Force Policy Institute (1992) reports that gay men and lesbians are subject to harassment and threats of violence, bomb threats, phychical assault, police abuse, vandalism, arson, and homicide. Among the most frequent forms of victimization are harassment and threats of violence and physical assault (National Gay & Lesbian Task Force Policy Institute, 1992). Verbal harassment is by far the most common form of victimization. When antigay attitudes or feelings are internalized by lesbians and gay men, they take a tremendous toll on self-esteem, causing considerable psychological distress. Therapists must realize that it is impossible to grow up in a culture in which such sentiments are pervasive and not internalize them to a certain extent.

There are many manifestations of internalized homophobia, including the tendency to put normal adolescent social behaviors such as dating and romantic involvements on hold and the tendency to act on same-sex feelings without taking responsibility for them or to compartmentalize homoerotic feelings. The psychotherapist must be in a position to explore the internalized negativity about homosexuality so that identity development can resume. Appropriate treatment views homosexuality as a normal variant of human sexuality. Malyon (1982) refers to such help as "gay-affirmative" psychotherapy. Such treatment

> . . . challenges the traditional view that homosexual desire and fixed homosexual orientations are pathological. . . . This approach regards homophobia, as opposed to homosexuality, as a major pathological variable in the development of certain symptomatic conditions. . . . The special complications and aberrations of identity formation . . . are considered to be the result of social values and attitudes, not as inherent to the issue of object-choice. (p. 69)

Garnets, Herek, and Levy (1992) describe the unique difficulties for victims of antigay violence. Most critically, the victim's sexual orientation becomes associated with the vulnerability which normally follows in such situations (Garnets et al., 1992; Janoff-Bulman & Frieze, 1983). A victim is likely to attribute the attack to his or her sexual orientation. Internalized homophobia is thereby exacerbated, and attempts to comprehend the meaning of the violence may lead to the conclusion that it was a consequence of (or punishment for) one's homosexuality.

The consequences of verbal assault can be as severe as those of physical assault (Garnets et al., 1992). In addition to finding it difficult to understand the emotional aftermath of a verbal assault, the victim may tend to minimize the feelings he or she does experience. Victims do, however, tend to restrict their behavior as a result of this kind of harassment because they fear physical assault may take place (Garnets et al., 1992).

The response to antigay victimization is affected by the degree to which the survivor has come out. The individual who has gone through the coming out process has more tools to assist him/her in coping with this crisis (e.g., social support systems, resources in the community, and a positive association with being gay or lesbian). On the other hand, the person who is in the early stages of the coming out process may have far fewer resources to assist in recovering from victimization. The result is likely to be the attribution of blame to sexual orientation ("bad things happen to me because I am gay") and associated depression and feelings of helplessness (Garnets et al., 1992). The therapist who works with survivors of antigay violence should be sensitive to his/her own heterosexist biases and have accurate information regarding gay and lesbian identity development, community resources, and the mental health issues of victims.

Relationship Issues

Gay and lesbian relationships are both different from and similar to those of heterosexuals. The psychosocial stressors faced by lesbian and gay couples are greater than those experienced by heterosexual couples. The societal stigma against homosexuality prevents many gay and lesbian couples from being open about their relationships. There is also far less social and familial support for gay and lesbian couples than for heterosexual couples (Kurdek, 1988; Kurdek & Schmidt, 1987b). The relationships of lesbians and gay men also do not enjoy the legal recognition that heterosexual marriages are given. The contracts and legal ties of marriage have been shown to serve as barriers to leaving a relationship (Kurdek & Schmidt, 1986). In addition, gay and lesbian couples are also more likely to be interracial than heterosexual couples and have consequently a greater potential for associated cultural conflict (Garcia et al., 1987).

Gay and lesbian couples share a number of similarities with heterosexual couples. All three desire attachment and autonomy in their relationships, are generally satisfied with their relationships, and use similar power strategies (Falbo & Peplau, 1980; Howard et al., 1986; Kurdek & Schmidt, 1986; Peplau, 1981). Heterosexual and homosexual couples tend to go through similar stages in their relationships (i.e., from early infatuation and high sexual activity through settling down and conflicting feelings, to activities which serve to maintain the relationship;

Kurdek & Schmidt, 1987a). Conflicts common to heterosexual relationships are also common to lesbian and gay relationships (Blumstein & Schwartz, 1983). For example, issues regarding money and conflicts over the ways in which a partner's career interferes with the relationship are typical sources of difficulties for both homosexual and heterosexual couples.

The dynamics of gay and lesbian couples do, in fact, differ because of the influence of gender-role socialization (Basow, 1992). In other words, gay men and heterosexual men tend to resemble one another in their relationships more than gay men resemble lesbians in theirs, while lesbians and heterosexual women are more similar to one another in relationships than gay men and lesbians. For males, according to Gilligan (1982), separation and individuation are crucial for gender identity. To be masculine, a boy must separate from his mother and be different from her. This identity is threatened by attachment and intimacy, since these are traditionally viewed as characteristic of femininity. Gender-role socialization trains men to separate sex from love, to be dominant, sexually active, and reluctant to express emotion, which inhibits the development of intimacy (Basow, 1992; Hawkins, 1992). When two men couple, these attributes are prominent. Blumstein and Schwartz (1983, 1990) found that relationships between gay men were the most sexually active and the least monogamous compared to lesbian relationships and heterosexual marital and cohabiting relationships. Gay men were also found to engage in power struggles more often than lesbians (Kurdek & Schmidt, 1987a). Hawkins (1992) advises the psychotherapist working with gay male couples to be observant:

. . . without training in how to deal with their feelings and, even more basically, in how to recognize an area of emotional conflict, [gay men] frequently do not present themselves with some of the problems that actually trouble them the most. The helping professional then has to keep an ear open for the deeper, usually shame-laden, problem areas that the couple may not recognize or may be avoiding. (p. 83)

Thus, the psychotherapy service provider must assess the problems of the gay male couple carefully while keeping in mind the ways in which gender-role socialization acts on each partner. Forstein (1986), for instance, cites gender-role expectations as crucial to understanding the ways in which a gay couple negotiate their intimacy and distance needs. Important, too, is the extent to which each man has established a positive gay identity. McWhirter and Mattison (1982), Forstein (1986), and Hawkins (1992) are several investigators who describe psychotherapy with gay male couples at length.

The issues of lesbian couples have much to do with the fact that each partner is a woman. While gender-role socialization fosters distance in males, the same process promotes attachment in females, teaching them to place relationship before autonomy (Basow, 1992; Gilligan, 1982). Femininity is associated with relationship, attachment, and intimacy (Gilligan, 1982). Just as gay male couples experience difficulty with intimacy and emotion, lesbian couples tend to have difficulty retaining separate identities. This problem is referred to as "merging" or "fusion." Psychological merger is a theme that has dominated the literature on psychotherapy with lesbian couples for over a decade (e.g., Burch, 1982, 1986, 1993; Clunis & Green, 1988; Hancock, 1984; Krestan & Bepko, 1980). Burch (1993) describes fusion as

> . . . the merger of couples who have difficulty feeling or being separate from each other, who have to think in terms of each other with every move, who in fact feel guilty or anxious about interests, thoughts, and feelings that are not shared. Their individual selves have been given over to fusion, and they may feel it is a necessity of the relationship not to retrieve them. (p. 95)

Lesbian couples who have not been successful in establishing a workable balance between autonomy and intimacy may have difficulties as one partner attempts to reestablish a sense of self (Burch, 1993). Differences are apt to be highlighted, fights and/or affairs tend to be initiated, and a partner may sexually or emotionally withdraw or leave the relationship. Lesbian fusion was previously regarded as problematic in the literature because separation has been viewed as an essential developmental task (e.g., Chodorow, 1978; Mahler et al., 1975). Current thought on the subject emphasizes the importance of relatedness for women and argues against pathologizing it (Miller, 1991; Mitchell, 1989; Surrey, 1991). These theorists assert that the psychological development of women profoundly differs from that of men, and to measure a woman's mental health by a masculine standard (separation) is inappropriate. Thus, in assessing the autonomy and intimacy needs of a lesbian couple, the therapist should be aware of the sex differences in the psychological development between women and men, to look more closely at the lesbian relationship, and not to pathologize the couple's capacity for closeness without evaluating the quality of that closeness.

Just as it contributes to the psychological distress of the individual, antigay prejudice exacerbates and creates problems for the lesbian or gay couple. The responses of a homophobic society to gay and lesbian couples—often hostile and dramatic—are a chronic source of stress not experienced by heterosexual married or cohabiting couples. Societal rejection of homosexuality bends a lesbian couple in on itself and isolates the couple from the society at large, which creates a phenomenon referred to as the "two against the world" posture (Krestan & Bepko, 1980). The psychotherapist must be aware of the fact that gay men and lesbians in couples and alone face antigay prejudice or the prospect of it daily in our society. Further, as he or she works with a lesbian or gay couple, the provider must also be vigilant for internalized homophobia in either or both members.

Unique and often difficult problems confront couples in which one or both members are bisexual. Coleman (1985a) found that women who later developed bisexual feelings were not likely to be aware of these feelings at the time they married. They were also more likely to end their marriages earlier over the conflicts the issue of their sexual orientation brought to the surface (including what was viewed as chronic sexual dissatisfaction in the marriage). On the other hand, men in an earlier study by Coleman (1981/1982) tended to be more aware of their feelings toward the same sex when they married. Disclosures regarding bisexuality tended to be more of a general description of feelings and attraction than of actual behavior or relationships (Coleman, 1981/1982, 1985b; Wolf, 1985). Generally, disclosure of bisexuality produced the crisis for which the couple sought treatment. The one problem studies on married bisexual people reported was intense conflict about sexual behavior outside the relationship (Coleman, 1981/1982, 1985a; Wolf, 1985). Lourea (1985) argues that bisexual individuals become conscious of their orientation at a later age than heterosexual, gay, and lesbian individuals. For this reason, the issues they face are usually addressed within the context of a relationship. According to Lourea (1985), before the work can proceed with the integration of the bisexual into the relationship, the therapist must work with feelings of anger, hurt, betrayal, and trust in the couple—especially on the part of the individual who is not bisexual.

Lourea (1985) delineates six concerns which commonly surface as the couple struggles with the issue of bisexuality: (1) antigay prejudice, (2) the perception of sexual attraction as a choice, (3) spousal fear of losing his or her partner to someone of the same sex, (4) issues of nonmonogamy or extramarital sexual relationships, (5) the effect of a parent's bisexual orientation on his or her children, and (6) the effect of coming out as a bisexual on one or both members of the couple. Any of these concerns can create feelings of insecurity, stress, and/or confusion in one or both members of the couple. The therapist should be prepared to explore any irrational fears, myths, and stereotypes as they arise. As concerns surface, it is imperative the therapist facilitate ongoing communication and expression of feelings with the couple through treatment.

Gay and Lesbian Youth

Theorists and researchers have found that the identity development of lesbian and gay youth can be arrested or slowed by factors directly related to antigay prejudice (e.g., Cass, 1979; Coleman, 1981/1982; Gonsiorek & Rudolph, 1991; Malyon, 1981; Troiden, 1988). Societal homophobia deprives these young people of the socialization structures heterosexual youth enjoy as they make the difficult and often tumultuous transition between childhood and adulthood. The most obvious support heterosexual youth enjoy is parental support to one degree or another. Few parents provide support for a child's budding interest in members of the same sex. In a study of 329 gay and lesbian adolescents between the ages of 12 and 21, Hetrick and Martin (1987) found that the two most important problems reported by participants were isolation and rejection. Forty percent of the adolescents in this study reported that they had experienced violence—often within their families of origin. Gay and lesbian youth are apt to become runaways, frequently ejected from their families of origin, to engage in abuse of drugs and/or alcohol, experience academic problems, and drop out of school (Coleman & Remafedi, 1989; Hetrick & Martin, 1987; Hunter & Schaecher, 1987; O'Connor, 1992).

Lesbian and gay adolescents have few role models in society. How, then, does a young person find out about what it is like to be a gay man or lesbian? Paroski (1987) found that most gay male adolescents were educated about homosexual life-styles through sexual encounters (96%), the media (91%), word of mouth (87%), and by going to places frequented by gay men (81%). Lesbian youth acquired such information through TV and the media (88%), word of mouth (81%), and associating with lesbians (50%). Health care providers played only a small role in this process (i.e., 20%) for gay male adolescents and 13% for lesbian adolescents). Between 50 and 80 percent of the participants in Paroski's (1987) study believed common myths about homosexuality: that gay men and lesbians identify with the opposite gender, dislike members of the opposite sex, and lead unhappy and unfulfilled lives. Since lesbian and gay youth have likely been exposed to TV and the media for the longest period of time before coming out, and since the images the media have presented have, for the most part, been filled with psychopathology of one sort or another (cf., Hancock, 1991; Russo, 1987), it is little wonder that the prospect of being homosexual would be met with mixed feelings.

Without parental support, mentoring, or positive role models, gay and lesbian youth also face another tremendous difficulty: a lack of peer support. Hunter and Schaecher (1987) found that one-fifth of the lesbians and one-half of the gay male adolescents had experienced harassment, threats, and/or assault in junior high school or high school because they were perceived to be homosexual. Gay and lesbian youth are well aware of the peer and societal pressure to conform to a heterosexual standard or suffer these consequences of antigay prejudice. This awareness profoundly affects the way in which the emergent gay or lesbian identity is addressed. It may be denied, closely guarded, or disclosed with considerable caution.

Accurate information about gay and lesbian identity development and the problems associated with what Slater (1988) calls "homophobic socialization" must be obtained and used by any practitioner who provides services to adolescents (Gonsiorek, 1988; Slater, 1988). Therapists are urged to explore the psychological and psychosocial problems resulting from societal stigmatization, including alienation from peers, family of origin, and the abuse of drugs and alcohol (Remafedi, 1987; Slater, 1988). Psychodynamic approaches to treatment are discussed by O'Connor (1992), Gonsiorek (1988), and Malyon (1981). Gonsiorek (1988) cautions the psychotherapist working with adolescents who are questioning their sexual orientation not to try to resolve this issue prematurely.

A group approach to psychotherapy with lesbian and gay youth has been proposed by a number of providers (e.g., Athey, 1993; Gertsel et al., 1989; Lenna, 1992; Uribe, 1991). These models all suggest combining education and group interaction in a safe environment. Education is particularly important, to counter the homophobic myths and stereotypes gay and lesbian adolescents have internalized. The group also provides a place in which the adolescent can safely interact with other gay or lesbian teenagers, develop socialization skills, and combat isolation.

Gay and Lesbian Parenting

Gay men and lesbians have always been parents. Until about 20 years ago, this fact was primarily a result of having had children in a heterosexual marriage prior to coming out. A lesbian or gay life-style had traditionally been regarded as otherwise childless by society and by gay men and lesbians themselves. Ariel and Stearns (1992) describe the 1970s as a period in which the courts were increasingly challenged by gay men and lesbians who were fighting to retain custody or visitation rights of their children from former marriages. These parents faced enormous difficulties as the courts reflected the homophobic prejudices of society (i.e., that exposure to individuals with a homosexual orientation would be detrimental to the psychological and emotional development of children). Following a decade of such cases, however, resources for these parents have been dramatically increased, and the consciousness of the courts had been raised (at least in areas where large numbers of lesbians and gay men lived; Ariel & Stearns, 1992). In the 1980s, the number of lesbian and gay families increased. There was reference to a lesbian "baby boom." Options other than heterosexual marriage, such as foster parenting, adoption, and artificial insemination, are now widely used. Parenthood is now viewed as a viable choice for gay men and lesbians.

It is important for practitioners to realize that no evidence exists supporting the notion that having a gay or lesbian parent(s) is harmful to a child (Ariel & Stearns, 1992; Patterson, 1992). In the absence of data showing that gay or lesbian parenting is detrimental to children in the areas of sexual identity, level of personal adjustment, and social relationships, Patterson (1990) notes that psychology may need to reexamine its views regarding what facilitates healthy development in children. Despite these findings, parenthood confronts the gay or lesbian couple with new challenges. Ariel and Stearns (1992) describe them in the following manner:

> Parenthood, starting with the initial stages of conception, brings gays and lesbians into heightened contact with mainstream society. Dealing with the medical system, Lamaze classes, child care, the school system, and the child's peers and their families all bring up the issue of when and how to inform others of one's uncommon family structure. For this reason, many people report that coming out issues reemerge in a deeper way when they decide to parent. (p. 97)

The authors also point to the fact that gay and lesbian relationships enjoy no legal status. Legal definition of the relationships between the partners and between the partners and the child becomes an issue in situations such as separation, medical emergencies, and death (Ariel & Stearns, 1992). Partnership agreements, authorization to consent to medical treatment for a minor, and other legal forms are used to assist the couple in clarifying their roles and responsibilities (Pies, 1988).

Gay and lesbian parents operate without societal sanction or tradition. There are no role models to balance the heterosexual images of family life. For this reason, the therapist should be sensitive to the ways in which internalized homophobia surfaces in the couple. Lesbian and gay parents may also find themselves relatively isolated from lesbian and gay communities because of their familial obligations and responsibilities. As parents, they may not be as mobile or able to socialize as friends who are not parents. To counter the absence of guidelines for parenting and the isolation that may be associated with lesbian or gay parenthood, the provider might find it useful to acquire community information and materials about gay and lesbian parenting groups.

Because of the various options available to gay men and lesbians for becoming parents, they often have to contend with situations, decisions, and negotiations heterosexuals do not have to face. For example, one common issue for lesbian couples considering parenthood is whether or not to actively involve the male donor in a relationship with the child. The biological mother may experience some anxiety over the role the man assumes in the life of her child. The mother's partner may have to contend with feelings of being left out. Many times, lesbian couples decide that the donor remain anonymous, thereby defining their roles with regard to the child more clearly. This option is available through the process of artificial insemination. Gay men clarify their boundaries for similar reasons through adoption or the use of a surrogate mother (Ariel & Stearns, 1992). Another issue for gay and lesbian parents is that the nonbiological parent has no legal rights even though he or she is actively involved in the process from the beginning (Ariel & Stearns, 1992). Attempts on the part of the nonbiological parent to legally adopt the child still depend on state laws and regulations regarding homosexuality and the rights of gay men and lesbians to adopt children.

Parental roles and responsibilities are difficult to define in the absence of legal guidelines. The role of the nonbiological parent is particularly unclear and requires careful negotiation. As a member of a couple, to what extent does this person participate in the parenting process? The possibility of the dissolution of the relationship raises even more complex issues with regard to this parent and his/her role in the child's life following the break-up (Ariel & Stearns, 1992). The mental health practitioner is in a position to help couples develop the skills necessary to negotiate these difficult situations. It is essential that the therapist remain aware of how difficult it is to confront these issues without the social support and legal structure available to heterosexual couples.

Lesbian and gay parenthood presents other unique concerns. In addition to the fact that two people of the same sex are parenting, there may also be significant differences between couple members in their desire to parent, as well as in their expectations regarding coparenting. These concerns may involve ongoing discussions of socialization guidelines as well as parental role expectations and responsibilities. Therapists can assist in a couple's parenting concerns by working with each member to communicate clearly and negotiate compromises which respect the feelings of both partners. Therapists may also need to validate the difficulties and challenges faced by the couple with regard to parenting within a homophobic and often hostile society, which does not offer lesbians and gay men support or recognition as parents. A psychotherapist can furnish such validation and help his or her clients to develop the skills to deal with these difficulties.

The psychotherapist who works with lesbians and gay men who head families should also be aware of the various configurations of these families. Information regarding the different configurations of lesbian and gay families can be found in Ariel and Stearns (1992, Bozett and Sussman (1990), Clunis and Green (1988), and Pies (1988).

Families of Origin

Perhaps one of the most difficult and painful areas to explore in psychotherapy with gay men and lesbians is their families of origin. Families supply physical and emotional sustenance, connect us with our past, and provide a context within which we learn about the world, including the attitudes and mores of our society (Berzon, 1992a). Unfortunately, families' visions do not usually include homosexuality. Brown (1988) notes:

> As members of a stigmatized minority, whose minority status may not be shared with their families of origin (unlike ethnic and cultural minorities, where family membership is the entry point for minority status), the issues that adult lesbians and gay males must confront as members of those families raise particular challenges for the clinician. (pp. 65–66)

The conflicts over the disclosure of one's gay or lesbian identity to one's family of origin often bring the individual into psychotherapy. Situations in which a family member's homosexuality is inadvertently revealed or discovered also create family (as well as personal) crises for which both the family and the gay or lesbian member are ill-prepared. In these situations, the information pertaining to the homosexuality of the individual may not have been revealed under the most positive of circumstances. Unlike instances in which homosexuality is disclosed voluntarily, here the lesbian or gay man may be confronted by a family member (or members) and find her/himself in a stressful position. It is often with good reason that gay men and lesbians anticipate trouble with disclosure to their families of origin (Berzon, 1992a; Brown, 1988; Strommen, 1990). According to Strommen (1990), the core issue is the family's notions about homosexuality (which usually reflect the antigay biases of society) and their perceptions and expectations of the homosexual family member.

Strommen (1990) identifies several sources of antigay prejudice which affect the family's response to the disclosure of homosexuality by one of its members. These include the belief that homosexuality is "unnatural," since it does not involve heterosexual reproduction of children, and that homosexual individuals are a threat to children. This latter notion persists despite considerable evidence to the contrary (e.g., Burgess et al., 1978; Kempe & Kempe, 1984).

A final set of family issues relates to religion, since prejudices against lesbians and gay men in their families of origin are prominent in most of the religious denominations in this country (Blumenfeld & Raymond, 1988). Families with strong religious convictions often support the views of their religion even against a family member. Indeed, the literature suggests that the more a family relies on religious teachings as a source of moral strength and guidance, the more negative and severe the family's response to its gay or lesbian member will be (Collins & Zimmerman, 1983; Strommen, 1990). It is not uncommon for therapists to be confronted with a gay or lesbian client (often adolescent) who has been rejected by his or her family of origin or with a family that has thrown a lesbian or gay member out. No other minority group contends with rejection from families of origin because of religious dogma (Martin & Hetrick, 1988).

Before a family member's homosexual identity is disclosed or discovered, various coping strategies are negotiated between the individual and his or her family. Brown (1988) describes several tactics: (1) distancing, emotionally and/or geographically, from the family of origin; (2) a tacit agreement between the individual and the family that no one will discuss the individual's personal life; and (3) disclosure to one parent or sibling who is supportive, with the understanding that the individual will not tell another or other family members. Brown (1988) reminds therapists that the gay man or lesbian living under these arrangements may not present them as a problem for psychotherapy. She notes that the failure to recognize them as stressful and maladaptive reflects the internalized homophobia of the lesbian or gay member. What the provider may notice is the toll taken by these "negotiated settlements" (e.g., problems with self-esteem, relationship difficulties, and disagreements over not being "out" to one's family, etc.).

According to Strommen (1990), when the homosexual family member's sexual orientation is disclosed or discovered, the revelation initiates two processes in the family of origin. First, the family struggles for a way to understand the homosexual family member. This occurs in the context of the family's values and belief system. It is important for the psychotherapist who works with a family to which a member has just "come out" to become familiar with the family's attitudes toward homosexuality, gender roles, and religion, as each of these is related to how its members will respond (cf. Basow, 1992; Blumenfeld & Raymond, 1988; Martin & Hetrick, 1988; MacDonald & Games,

1974). As the family struggles with this "revelation crisis," they also experience a sudden alienation from the homosexual family member. Previous perceptions of him or her as a sibling, spouse, or child are negated by the new identification. The individual may be experienced as a stranger in the family. Strommen (1990) describes parental reactions of guilt and failure over their child's homosexuality, while siblings tend to respond more with anger and confusion. If the disclosure is initiated by the gay or lesbian member, the family may be told in increments, with the emotionally closest members being told first. Usually this is a sibling, and the individual may adjust the manner in which the disclosure is made based on the reactions he or she receives from this most supportive family member.

Positive outcomes to the "revelation crisis" involve the family's struggle with convention. If the concern for the gay or lesbian family member triumphs, the family adapts its attitudes and beliefs to establish a new identity for the homosexual member. It is important to note that this process, in many cases, does not occur overnight. Families who confront this new information need to grieve the loss of their previous perceptions, expectations, and dreams for the homosexual member. Many of these, as we have seen, are heterosexual in nature and will likely not be realized. The family needs time and sometimes assistance in dealing with the loss. There are many instances in which a negative initial reaction tempers and transforms into this more positive adaptation resolution with time—sometimes years. Families who are more positive in their responses may still require assistance in dealing with the homosexual member "in the context of openness" (Brown, 1988). Worth mentioning here is the difficulty these families have in figuring out how to treat this relationship and its members. The homophobia that surfaces in the simple interpersonal transactions which involve family occasions (e.g., dinners, weddings, holidays, and reunions) can be more subtle, but it is nevertheless present and can be a major problem.

One typical difficulty is that the family lacks models for dealing with same-sex relationships. The partner of the gay or lesbian family member is more apt to be treated and referred to as a friend than as a dating or committed partner. In addition, friendships are socially accepted relationships between individuals of the same sex. Viewing the relationship as a friendship allows the family to avoid the dissonance, anxiety, and other emotional responses to the sexual aspect of the homosexual relationship. Partners of gay or lesbian family members are also commonly referred to and treated as "roommates." Relationships between the family and its gay or lesbian member may become strained as a result of the individual's relationship being perceived in such a manner. Thus, the therapist should be aware of the fact that important issues surface after the disclosure or revelation of homosexuality to the family and, in these cases, be prepared to evaluate the various sources of homophobic process within the family and its gay or lesbian member as well.

Literature available for therapists on the family issues of lesbians and gay men includes the very fine articles by Strommen (1990) and Brown (1988) mentioned earlier as well as books which include material on dealing with family of origin issues (e.g., Berzon, 1992b; Blumenfeld & Raymond, 1988; Bozett & Sussman, 1990). Strommen (1990) includes a discussion of issues confronting the children whose parents disclose a gay or lesbian sexual orientation. Berzon (1992a) provides concise and pragmatic information for gay or lesbian clients who are considering disclosing their sexual orientation to their families. Psychotherapists working with these clients will find it useful as well. There are also written materials produced especially for the families of lesbians and gay men by parents of lesbians and gay men (e.g., Borhek, 1983; Fairchild, 1992; Fairchild & Hayward, 1989). These works are especially powerful because they address issues from the family's point of view. Feelings of responsibility regarding the gay or lesbian family member's sexual orientation, religious concerns, homophobia, stereotypes, relationships, and children are some of the issues addressed from the family's, particularly the parents', perspective.

Not all the resources available are written. No discussion of family of origin issues with homosexuality would be complete without mentioning the organization Parents and Friends of Lesbians and Gays (known as P-FLAG). This nationwide organization runs support groups for parents and friends of lesbians and gay men which are facilitated by family members and friends who have gone through many of the struggles mentioned here. Lesbians and gay men attend P-FLAG meetings to get support for disclosing their sexual orientation to their families of origin. Therapists who are helping clients confront disclosure or revelation issues ought to remember this valuable organizational resource.

Therapist Issues

No review of psychotherapy issues with lesbian and gay clients is complete without attention being paid to the concerns of psychotherapists who provide services to these populations (Brown, 1991, 1987; Cabaj, 1988; Gonsiorek, 1989; Isay, 1991; Stein, 1988). Stein (1988) describes several important concerns for providers, including the attitudes and beliefs of the therapist toward the view that homosexuality represents psychopathology, the psychotherapist's level of familiarity with gay and lesbian issues outside the psychopathology perspective, and the personal characteristics of the provider which directly influence the conduct of psychotherapy with these clients. In addition, it is also important to distinguish concerns unique to therapists who are heterosexual from those who are lesbian or gay.

One of the most important issues to mention is the attitude toward homosexuality. If the psychotherapist holds the belief that homosexuality represents psychopathology despite the fact that research and current thinking point to the contrary, the lesbian or gay client who receives treatment from such a therapist may be at risk for increased mental health problems (Stein, 1988). The many problems associated with internalized homophobia will very likely be perpetuated in these clients by therapists who believe homosexuality indicates psychopathology. Stein (1988) states that therapeutic neutrality is impossible when treatment is provided from this perspective because it permeates the entire treatment process and mandates the need to change the sexual orientation of the client.

Another consideration mentioned by both Stein (1988) and Cabaj (1988) is the level of familiarity with other lesbian and gay concerns. Even if the provider does not believe that gay men and lesbians are sick, he or she is working against important training deficits unless training and supervised experience in working with these populations have been obtained. Unfortunately, this sort of training is rare and usually requires extra effort on the part of the trainee. To overcome this education and training deficit, Stein (1988) suggests that therapists explore "attitudes about homosexuality and specific sexual acts, awareness of the effects of stigmatization, the relationship between normal development and homosexuality, familiarity with gay lifestyles, knowledge about the patterns and stages of coming out, and the meaning of a homosexual identity" (p. 83). He further notes that, without such education and training, the therapist's ability to establish empathy is limited, as is the therapist's ability to conceptualize about a gay man's or lesbian's experience. Unlike the view of homosexuality as mental illness, knowledge deficits can be overcome.

The personal characteristics of the service provider are also important concerns in working with gay and lesbian clients. According to Stein (1988), these include a willingness to deal with the special problems associated with a group which is oppressed and stigmatized within society, a willingness to examine one's own reactions to homosexuality and people who are homosexual, the sexual orientation of the therapist, and even the sex of the therapist. It is important to note that each affects the ability to establish and maintain empathy with the client.

As it is impossible to grow up in the United States without acquiring negative stereotypes and feelings about homosexuality, it is important for the psychotherapy service provider to be willing to look at his or her feelings about homosexuality and lesbians and gay men. To deny the presence of antigay prejudice within oneself is unrealistic even for the most enlightened of psychotherapists—homosexual and heterosexual alike. Stein (1988) notes:

> The absence of any ability to acknowledge negative feelings about homosexuality on the part of the therapist may indicate in some cases an unwillingness to examine one's own internalized homophobia. When these reactions are rigidly sealed off from consciousness, the risk is that they may then be acted out unconsciously. Thus, when therapists say too readily that they have no problem with homosexuality, they may simply be unwilling or unable to examine their true reactions and may communicate a similar message to their patients. (p. 84)

Subtle collusion with a client's homophobia may occur when the client says there is no problem with being gay or lesbian and the therapist therefore does not question the client on this subject even though the behaviors or feelings the client expresses show that he or she is operating within homophobic limitations without challenging them. These subtle limitations may also be shared by the therapist. As Cabaj (1988) points out, couples or family therapy may not be considered because of a tacit acceptance of the belief that gay and lesbian relationships are not as permanent as heterosexual relationships or that family issues are less relevant to gay men and lesbians. Therapists who are not conscious of their internalized homophobia and who in fact present themselves as having no antigay prejudice whatsoever often give clients mixed messages in treatment. Cabaj (1988) cautions the gay-affirmative therapist to avoid being overly positive and accepting, as this could prevent the therapist from spotting psychopathology or important psychodynamic issues. Such therapists might also tend to become impatient with clients who seem to resist change, accept homosexuality openly, or act out heterosexually.

The sexual orientation of the therapist and its disclosure to clients are issues which continued to be debated in the literature (e.g., Isay, 1991; Stein, 1988). Stein (1988) reasons that, since there is societal pressure for a gay man or lesbian to keep sexual orientation a secret, a willingness on the part of the therapist to share his or her sexual orientation might be helpful. He argues that, a therapist's refusal to discuss his or her sexual orientation might be construed as meaning that sexual orientation is something to be kept secret. From a more analytical perspective, Isay (1991) agrees, especially with regard to lesbian or gay therapists:

I do believe, however, that the gay analyst or therapist who hides or disguises his sexual orientation by refusing to acknowledge it implies that he is heterosexual and may further damage the self-esteem of his patients by conveying his shame, self-depreciation, or fear of disclosure. (p. 203)

It must be noted that, for the most part, therapists are assumed to be heterosexual by clients unless the sexual orientation of the therapist has been disclosed (Schwartz, 1988; Stein, 1988) or if referral is made with the therapist's gay or lesbian orientation known. Stein (1988) maintains that the degree of comfort and acceptance of sexual orientation on the part of the therapist is more important than any client knowledge of the therapist's sexual orientation. It should be mentioned here that therapists who are dealing with issues of coming out themselves or who find themselves confused about their own sexual identity ought not to work with lesbian or gay clients or clients who are struggling with sexual identity (Gonsiorek, 1989).

The gender and gender-role attributions of a therapist are also important characteristics to consider when discussing psychotherapy with lesbian and gay clients. Gender roles have traditionally defined masculinity and femininity and have been directly associated with heterosexuality. If the therapist—homosexual or heterosexual—has incorporated traditional gender roles to a large degree, he or she may become uncomfortable when confronted with a person who is more androgynous. He or she may not be conscious of the ambivalence. Stein (1988) provides an example:

. . . a traditional concept of masculinity includes a defensive rejection of homosexuality. A male therapist who has internalized this concept as a component of his identity, but who also values highly personal freedom and individuality, may communicate contradictory messages to a patient. He may be frightened or repulsed by the homoerotic sexual and affectional behaviors described by a male patient, but he may at the very same time express to the patient an acceptance of these behaviors because of his conscious values. The discordance between the rejection of the homosexuality, which may be communicated nonverbally through signs of discomfort on the part of the therapist, and spoken acceptance of homosexuality may generate considerable conflict for the patient. (p. 90).

It is crucial to keep in mind that sexism and antigay prejudice are closely aligned and any discomfort, disapproval, or anxiety should be explored in consultation.

Stein (1988) and Cabaj (1988) both discuss the difficulties heterosexually oriented therapists may experience when erotic components of the client/therapist relationship surface with someone of the same sex. Although a heterosexual therapist might be prepared for transference of this sort from a client of the opposite sex, the same therapist may well feel somewhat anxious and uncomfortable when it surfaces. The same thing applies to countertransference reactions. Cabaj (1988) states that positive feelings, particularly those with an erotic component, toward a homosexual client of the same sex may frighten and confuse the therapist. The reason for an honest and thorough self-examination of one's feelings, values, and beliefs about homosexuality becomes very clear in such situations.

A special issue for gay and lesbian psychotherapists involves the provision of services in small communities and the associated boundary issues for psychotherapists. This subject is considered by Brown (1987, 1991) and Gonsiorek (1989). Brown (1987) notes that the traditional model of psychotherapy service provision assumes that the community of the psychotherapist does not overlap with those of the client. Therapists are therefore unprepared for living and working in a world in which one meets one's clients in one's private life. Yet this is precisely what lesbian and gay psychotherapists face, even in large metropolitan areas. What surfaces are immediate issues related to boundaries and their ethical management by the psychotherapist. Brown (1991) describes the following situations:

> Common examples of overlapping relationships include the therapist finding that she is on the same committee within a community organization as a client, former client, or partner of a client. Another frequent dilemma consists of having a client meet and befriend the therapist's partner before their shared connection to the therapist is known. Or, a client may meet and form a relationship with a friend of the therapist. In either case, the client will inadvertently enter the therapist's personal and social life. (p. 327)

Therapists are ethically required to protect the therapeutic relationship and its boundaries. Unfortunately, as Brown (1991) points out, ethical guidelines are insufficient in helping the lesbian or gay therapist manage these boundaries. Gay and lesbian therapists have had to struggle with responses to these situations. Since training assumes little or no contact between client and therapist, some psychotherapists have responded by isolating themselves from their communities. Brown (1987, 1991) cautions the lesbian or gay therapist against this and suggests that therapists (1) acknowledge and validate the fact that there is greater likelihood of overlapping relationships in the gay and lesbian communities, (2) try to anticipate boundary violations and discuss these with the client in therapy, (3) learn to think about the therapeutic frame in ways that take into account the greater complexities encountered in smaller communities, and (4) empower clients regarding anticipated boundary violations (i.e., discuss what would be in the best interests of the client with the client rather than deciding this unilaterally). Gonsiorek (1989) also suggests that "gay and lesbian therapists must develop systems of consultation and support to handle the particularly intense and frequent boundary decisions which they often face" (p. 119).

Suggestions for Education, Training, and Research

All available information suggests that many psychotherapists are not adequately prepared for working with gay men and lesbians (Brown, 1991; Garnets et al., 1991; Cabaj, 1988; Stein, 1988). Knowledge deficits regarding the special issues of lesbians and gay men can be remedied through education, training, and further research. Given the high utilization rate of psychotherapeutic services among these populations, it is crucial to provide better practitioner training. Sensitivity to the many ways in which antigay prejudice permeates one's experience of the world, social interactions, and intrapsychic processes must be developed in psychotherapists. Information regarding the special problems which confront gay men and lesbians must be integrated into coursework, supervision, in-service training, and continuing education in professional psychology. The desire to eliminate homosexuality or to "cure" it must be addressed in a different way. The notion that homosexuality reflects psychopathology is an outmoded and unsupported supposition (Gonsiorek, 1991). Garnets and her colleagues (1991) point out that many of the biased, inappropriate, and counterproductive practices in the treatment of lesbians and gay men are covered in existing APA ethical guidelines. They also note that other practices, which were found to be "both questionable and disturbing," are not. The authors call for expanded ethical and professional guidelines to address these biased, inadequate, and inappropriate practices.

There is yet much psychology does not know regarding the issue of minority status within minorities. Literature is beginning to be developed on this subject (e.g., Chan, 1989; Espin, 1987; Gutierrez & Dworkin, 1992; Loiacano, 1989; Morales, 1992; Sears, 1989; Gock, 1985), but this information must be more integrated into the arena of gay and lesbian psychology and psychology as a whole. Research on the significance of sexual orientation within different cultures and on the familial attitudes toward homosexuality in these cultures would provide important information needed to train child and family therapists.

Psychology knows very little about bisexuality. The issue of bisexuality involves special complexities in human relations which even those therapists trained in gay and lesbian issues sometimes find difficult to understand, let alone negotiate in their work with bisexual clients (Zinik, 1985). The literature indicates that awareness of bisexuality seems to develop later in life than that of heterosexuality or even homosexuality. What are the reasons for this? Do bisexual individuals deny or repress homosexual attractions at earlier stages of their lives? Are there differences among homosexual, heterosexual, and bisexual individuals in familial relationships and/or personality attributes? What means does a bisexual person use to articulate identity to him/herself and to others? Psychology has much to gain from an exploration of bisexuality. The more we understand about bisexuality, the more we will understand human sexuality itself, not only variations to it.

Psychologists must consider broadening the definition of family to include gay and lesbian family members—as parents, siblings, children, and partners to family members. Families need assistance in negotiating the loss of perceptions and expectations regarding the gay man or lesbian in their midst. Strommen (1990) writes that "Family members undergoing this redefinition and development of new values and roles need factual, unbiased information about homosexuality to help them gain a balanced perspective on the trauma they are experiencing" (p. 29). Education and training in family psychotherapy should include working with such situations. Those receiving education and training in working with children and adolescents must become familiar with the issues facing the children of lesbian and gay parents, at home and in school. So, too, must psychotherapists learn to assess and treat the special problems of gay and lesbian youth with sensitivity and concern. The consequences of familial homophobia for them can be severe.

Another area for further investigation is the relationship between gender and homosexuality. Exploration of one will invariably enrich understanding of the other. (For a discussion regarding this process in the psychology of women, see Mencher, 1990.) Notions about gender and sexuality are basic to human identity—to the therapist's own identity as well as the identity of a client—and profoundly affect the way in which lesbians and gay men are treated by the mental health professions in our society. The education and training of psychotherapists must include greater knowledge, awareness, and sensitivity to these issues.

To date, the only way in which homosexuality has been understood theoretically by psychology has been as psychopathology. A literature which no longer pathologizes homosexuality needs to be considered in the light of current theoretical perspectives (e.g., self-psychology, object relations, systems theories, etc.).

> Many of the ideas about the coming out process, identity development, and internalized homophobia . . . stand apart as theoretical conceptions not tied into the main body of psychological theory. This constricts the ability of these ideas to develop further and also risks underutilization by clinicians. (Gonsiorek & Rudolph, 1991, p. 169)

The next frontier, as discussed by Gonsiorek and Rudolph (1991), will most certainly involve integrating the literature on homosexuality with current theories of psychotherapy and human development outside the realm of psychopathology.

References

American Psychological Association (1992, December). Ethical principles of psychologists and code of conduct. *American Psychologist, 47*(12), 1597–1611.

Ariel, J., & Stearns, S. (1992). Challenges facing gay and lesbian families. In S. Dworkin & F. Gutierrez (Eds.), *Counseling gay men and lesbians: Journey to the end of the rainbow* (pp. 95–112). Alexandria, VA: American Association for Counseling & Development.

Athey, K. (1993). A proposed group treatment model to provide support and advocacy for gay youth. Unpublished master's thesis. California State University, Hayward, CA.

Basow, S. (1992). *Gender: Stereotypes and roles* (3rd ed.). Pacific Grove, CA: Brooks/Cole.

Bayer, R. (1987). *Homosexuality and American psychiatry: The politics of diagnosis.* Princeton, NJ: Princeton University Press.

Bell, A., & Weinberg, M. (1978). *Homosexualities: A study of diversity among men and women.* New York: Simon & Schuster.

Berrill, K. (1992). Anti-gay violence and victimization in the United States: An overview. In G. Herek & K. Berrill (Eds.), *Hate crimes: Confronting violence against lesbians and gay men* (pp. 19–45). Newbury Park, CA: Sage Publications.

Berzon, B. (1992a). Telling the family you're gay. In B. Berzon (Ed.), *Positively gay: New approaches to gay and lesbian life* (pp. 67–78). Berkeley: Celestial Arts.

Berzon, B. (Ed.) (1992b). *Positively gay: New approaches to gay and lesbian life.* Berkeley: Celestial Arts.

Blumenfeld, W., & Raymond, D. (1988). *Looking at gay and lesbian life.* Boston: Beacon Press.

Blumstein, P., & Schwartz, P. (1976). Bisexuality in women. *Archives of Sexual Behavior, 5*, 171–181.

Blumstein, P., & Schwartz, P. (1983). *American couples*. New York: Morrow.

Blumstein, P., & Schwartz, P. (1990). Intimate relationships and the creation of sexuality. In D. McWhirter, S. Saunders, & J. Reinisch (Eds.), *Homosexuality/heterosexuality: Concepts of sexual orientation* (pp. 307–320). New York: Oxford University Press.

Borhek, M. (1983). *Coming out to parents: A two-way survival guide for lesbians and gay men and their parents*. New York: The Pilgrim Press.

Bozett, F., & Sussman, M. (1990). *Homosexuality and family relations*. New York: Harrington Park Press.

Brown, L. (1987, August). Beyond thou shalt not: Developing conceptual frameworks for ethical decision-making. In J. Gonsiorek (Chair), *Ethical and boundary issues for lesbian and gay psychotherapists*. Symposium conducted at the annual meeting of the American Psychological Association, New York.

Brown, L. (1988). Lesbians, gay men, and their families: Common clinical issues. *Journal of Gay and Lesbian Psychotherapy, 1*(1), 65–77.

Brown, L. (1991, June). Ethical issues in feminist therapy: Selected topics. *Psychology of Women Quarterly, 15*(2), 323–336.

Brownfain, J. (1985). A study of the married bisexual male: Paradox and resolution. In F. Klein & T. Wolf (Eds.), *Two lives to lead: Bisexuality in men and women* (pp. 173–188). New York: Harrington Park Press.

Burch, B. (1982). Psychological merger in lesbian couples: A joint ego psychological and systems approach. *Family Therapy, 9* (3), 201–277.

Burch, B. (1986). Psychotherapy and the dynamics of merger in lesbian couples. In T. Stein & C. Cohen (Eds.), *Contemporary perspectives on psychotherapy with lesbians and gay men* (pp. 57–71). New York: Plenum Publishing.

Burch, B. (1993). *On intimate terms: The psychology of difference in lesbian relationships*. Chicago: University of Illinois Press.

Burgess, A., Groth, A., Holmstrom, L., & Sgroi, S (1978). *Sexual assault of children and adolescents*. Lexington, MA: D.C. Heath.

Cabaj, R. (1988). Homosexuality and neurosis: Considerations for psychotherapy. *Journal of homosexuality, 15*(1/2), 13–23.

Cass, V. (1979). Homosexual identity formation: A theoretical model. *Journal of Homosexuality, 4*(3), 219–235.

Chan, C. (1989, September/October). Issues of identity development among Asian–American lesbians and gay men. *Journal of Counseling and Development, 68*, 16–20.

Chodorow, N. (1978). *The reproduction of mothering: Psychoanalysis and the sociology of gender*. Berkeley: University of California Press.

Clunis, D., & Green, G. (1988). *Lesbian couples*. Seattle: Seal Press.

Coleman, E. (1981/1982). Bisexual and gay men in heterosexual marriage: Conflicts and resolutions in therapy. *Journal of Homosexuality, 7*(2/3), 93–103.

Coleman, E. (1985a). Bisexual women in marriages. In F. Klein & T. Wolf (Eds.), *Two lives to lead: Bisexuality in men and women* (pp. 87–100). New York: Harrington Park Press.

Coleman, E. (1985b). Integration of male bisexuality and marriage. In F. Klein & T. Wolf (Eds.), *Two lives to lead: Bisexuality in men and women* (pp. 189–208). New York: Harrington Park Press.

Coleman, E., & Remafedi, G. (1989). Gay, lesbian, and bisexual adolescents: A critical challenge to counselors. *Journal of Counseling and Development, 68,* 36–40.

Collins, L., & Zimmerman, N. (1983). Homosexual and bisexual issues. In J. Hansen, J. Woody., & R. Woody (Eds.), *Sexual issues in family therapy* (pp. 82–100). Rockville, MD: Aspen Publications.

Davison, G. (1976). Homosexuality: The ethical challenge. *Journal of Consulting and Clinical Psychology, 44,* 157–162.

Davison, G. (1978). Not "can" but "ought:" The treatment of homosexuality. *Journal of Consulting and Clinical Psychology, 46*(1), 170–172.

Davison, G. (1991). Constructionism and morality in therapy for homosexuality. In J. Gonsiorek & J. Weinrich (Eds.), *Homosexuality: Research implications for public policy* (pp. 137–148). Newbury Park, CA: Sage Publications.

Espin, O. (1987). Issues of identity in the psychology of Latina lesbians. In Boston Lesbian Psychologies Collective (Eds.), *Lesbian psychologies: Explorations and challenges* (pp. 35–51). Urbana: University of Illinois Press.

Fairchild, B. (1992). For parents of lesbians and gays. In B. Berzon (Ed.), *Positively gay: New approaches to gay and lesbian life* (pp. 79–90). Berkeley: Celestial Arts.

Fairchild, B., & Hayward, N. (1989). *Now that you know: What every parent should know about homosexuality.* New York: Harcourt, Brace, Jovanovich.

Falbo, T., & Peplau, L. (1980). Power strategies in intimate relationships. *Journal of Personality and Social Psychology, 38,* 618–628.

Forstein, M. (1986). Psychodynamic psychotherapy with gay male couples. In T. Stein & C. Cohen (Eds.), *Contemporary perspectives on psychotherapy with lesbians and gay men* (pp. 103–137). New York: Plenum Publishing.

Garcia, N., Kennedy, C., Pearlman, S., & Perez, J. (1987). The impact of race and culture differences: Challenges to intimacy in lesbian relationships. In Boston Lesbian Psychologies Collective (Eds.), *Lesbian psychologies: Explorations and challenges* (pp. 142–160). Urbana: University of Illinois.

Garnets, L., Hancock, K., Cochran, S., Goodchilds, J., & Peplau, A. (1991). Issues in psychotherapy with lesbians and gay men: A survey of psychologists. *American Psychologist, 46*(9), 964–972.

Garnets, L., Herek, G., & Levy, B. (1992). Violence and victimization of lesbians and gay men: Mental health consequences. In G. Herek & K. Berrill (Eds.), *Hate crimes: Confronting violence against lesbians and gay men* (pp. 207–226). Newbury Park, CA: Sage Publications.

Gertsel, C., Feraios, A., & Herdt, G. (1989). Widening circles: An ethnographic profile of a youth group. In G. Herdt (Ed.), *Gay and lesbian youth* (pp. 75–92). New York: Harrington Park Press.

Gilligan, C. (1982). *In a different voice.* Cambridge: Harvard University Press.

Glenn, A., & Russell, R. (1986, March). Heterosexual bias among counselor trainees. *Counselor Education and Supervision, 25*(3), 222–229.

Gock, T. (1985, August). Psychotherapy with Asian/Pacific gay men: Psychological issues, treatment approach and therapeutic guidelines. Paper presented at the meeting of the Asian American Psychological Association, Los Angeles, California.

Gonsiorek, J. (1989). Sexual exploitation by psychotherapists: Some observations on male victims and sexual orientation issues. In G. Schoener, J. Milgram, J. Gonsiorek, E. Luepker, & R. Conroe (Eds.), *Psychotherapist's sexual involvement with clients: Intervention and prevention* (pp. 113–119). Minneapolis, MN: Walk-In Counseling Center.

Gonsiorek, J. (1988). Mental health issues of gay and lesbian adolescents. *Journal of Adolescent Health Care, 9,* 114–122.

Gonsiorek, J. (1991). The empirical basis for the demise of the illness model of homosexuality. In J. Gonsiorek & J. Weinrich (Eds.), *Homosexuality: Research implications for public policy* (pp. 115–136). Newbury Park, CA: Sage Publications.

Gonsiorek, J., & Rudolph, J. (1991). Homosexual identity: Coming out and other developmental events. In J. Gonsiorek & J. Weinrich (Eds.), *Homosexuality: Research implications for public policy* (pp. 161–176). Newbury Park, CA: Sage Publications.

Graham, D., Rawlings, E., Halpern, H., & Hermes, J. (1984). Therapist's needs for training in counseling lesbians and gay men. *Professional Psychology: Research and Practice, 15*(4), 482–496.

Gramick, J. (1984). Developing a lesbian identity. In T. Darty & S. Potter (Eds.), *Women identified women* (pp. 31–44). Palo Alto, CA: Mayfield.

Gutierrez, F., & Dworkin, S. (1992). Gay, lesbian, and Afro-American: Managing the integration of identities. In S. Dworkin & F. Gutierrez (Eds.), *Counseling gay men and lesbians: Journey to the end of the rainbow* (pp. 141–156). Alexandria, VA: American Association for Counseling & Development.

Haldeman, D. (1991). Sexual orientation conversion therapy for gay men and lesbians: A scientific examination. In J. Gonsiorek & J. Weinrich (Eds.), *Homosexuality: Research implications for public policy* (pp. 149–160). Newbury Park, CA: Sage Publications.

Hancock, K. (1984). On fusion in lesbian relationships: Treatment and training issues. In K. Hancock (Chair), *Training issues in lesbian psychotherapy.* Symposium conducted at the meeting of the American Psychological Association, Toronto, Canada.

Hancock, K. (1991, August). Film images of lesbian mental health: Depressed, distressed, or dead. In C. Acuff (Chair), *Lesbians in film: Images in transition.* Symposium conducted at the annual meeting of the American Psychological Association, San Francisco, CA.

Hawkins, R. (1992). Therapy with the male couple. In S. Dworkin & F. Gutierrez (Eds.), *Counseling gay men and lesbians: Journey to the end of the rainbow* (pp. 81–94). Alexandria, VA: American Association for Counseling & Development.

Hetrick, E. & Martin, D. (1987). Development issues and their resolution for gay and lesbian adolescents. *Journal of Homosexuality, 14*(1/2), 25–43.

Howard, J., Blumstein, P., & Schwartz, P. (1986). Sex, power, and influence tactics in intimate relationships. *Journal of Personality and Social Psychology, 51,* 102–109.

Hunter, J., & Schaecher, R. (1987). Stresses on lesbian and gay adolescents in schools. *Social Work in Education, 9*(3), 180–190.

Isay, R. (1991). The homosexual analyst: Clinical considerations. *The Psychoanalytic Study of the Child, 46,* 199–216.

Janoff-Bulman, R., & Frieze, J. H. (Eds.) (1983). Reactions to victimization [Special issue]. *Journal of Social Issues, 39*(2).

Kempe, R., & Kempe, C. (1984). *The common secret: Sexual abuse of children and adolescents.* New York: W.H. Freeman & Co.

Klein, F., Sepekoff, B., & Wolf, T. (1990). Sexual orientation: A multi-variable dynamic process. In T. Geller (Ed.), *Bisexuality: A reader and source book* (pp. 64–81). Hadley, MA: Times Change Press.

Krestan, J., & Bepko, C. (1980). The problem of fusion in the lesbian relationship. *Family Process, 19*(3), 277–289.

Kurdek, L. (1988). Perceived social support in gays and lesbians in cohabitating relationships. *Journal of Personality and Social Psychology, 54,* 504–509.

Kurdek, L., & Schmidt, J. (1986). Relationship quality of partners in heterosexual married, heterosexual cohabiting, and gay and lesbian relationships. *Journal of Personality and Social Psychology, 51,* 711–720.

Kurdek, L., & Schmidt, J. (1987a). Partner homogamy in married, heterosexual cohabiting, gay, and lesbian couples. *Journal of Sex Research, 23,* 212–232.

Kurdek, L., & Schmidt, J. (1987b). Perceived emotional support from family and friends in members of homosexual, married, and heterosexual cohabiting couples. *Journal of Homosexuality, 14,* 57–68.

Lenna, H. (1992). The outsiders: Group work with young homosexuals. In N. Woodman (Ed.), *Lesbian and gay lifestyles: A guide for counseling and education* (pp. 67–85). New York: Irvington Publishers.

Loiacano, D. (1989, September/October). Gay identity issues among black Americans: Racism, homophobia, and the need for validation. *Journal of Counseling and Development, 68,* 21–25.

Lourea, D. (1985). Psycho-social issues related to counseling bisexuals. In F. Klein & T. Wolf (Eds.), *Two lives to lead: Bisexuality in men and women* (pp. 51–62). New York: Harrington Park Press.

MacDonald, A., & Games, R. (1974). Some characteristics of those who hold positive and negative attitudes toward homosexuals. *Journal of Homosexuality, 1,* 9–27.

Mahler, M., Pine, F., & Bergman, A. (1975). *The psychological birth of the human infant: Symbiosis and individuation.* New York: Basic Books.

Malyon, A. (1981). The homosexual adolescent: Developmental issues and social biases. *Child Welfare, 60,* 321–330.

Malyon, A. (1982). Psychotherapeutic implications of internalized homophobia in gay men. In J. Gonsiorek (Ed.), *Homosexuality and psychotherapy: A practitioner's handbook of affirmative models* (pp. 59–69). New York: Haworth Press.

Martin, A., & Hetrick, E. (1988). The stigmatization of the gay and lesbian adolescent. *Journal of Homosexuality, 15*(1/2), 163–183.

Masters, W. H., & Johnson, V. E. (1979). *Homosexuality in perspective*. Boston: Little, Brown.

McWhirter, D., & Mattison, A. (1982). Psychotherapy for gay male couples. In J. Gonsiorek (Ed.), *Homosexuality and psychotherapy*. New York: Haworth Press.

Mencher, J. (1990). Intimacy in lesbian relationships: A critical re-examination of fusion. In *Works in Progress* (No. 46). Wellesley, MA: The Stone Center, Wellesley College.

Miller, J. (1991). The development of women's sense of self. In J. Jordan, A. Kaplan, J. Miller, I. Stiver, & J. Surrey. (Eds.), *Women's growth in connection: Writings from the Stone Center* (pp. 11–26). New York: Guilford Press.

Mitchell, V. (1989). Using Kohut's psychology of self in work with lesbian couples. In E. Rothblum & E. Cole (Eds.), *Loving boldly: Issues facing lesbians* (pp. 157–166). New York: Harrington Park Press.

Morales, E. (1992). Counseling Latino gays and Latina lesbians. In S. Dworkin & F. Gutierrez (Eds.), *Counseling gay men and lesbians: Journey to the end of the rainbow* (pp. 125–139). Alexandria, VA: American Association for Counseling and Development.

National Gay & Lesbian Task Force Policy Institute (1992). *Anti-gay/lesbian violence, victimization and defamation in 1991*. Washington, DC: National Gay & Lesbian Task Force Policy Institute.

National Lesbian & Gay Health Foundation (1987). *National lesbian health care survey: Mental health implications*. (Contract No. 86MO19832201D). Washington, DC: National Institute of Mental Health.

O'Connor, M. (1992). Psychotherapy with gay and lesbian adolescents. In S. Dworkin & F. Gutierrez (Eds.), *Counseling gay men and lesbians: Journey to the end of the rainbow* (pp. 3–21). Alexandria, VA: American Association for Counseling & Development.

Paroski, P. (1987). Health care delivery and the concerns of gay and lesbian adolescents. *Journal of Adolescent Health Care, 8*, 188–192.

Patterson, C. J. (1992). Children of lesbian and gay parents. *Child Development, 63*, 1025–1042.

Peplau, L. (1981, March). What do homosexuals want? *Psychology Today*, pp. 28–38.

Pies, C. (1988). *Considering parenthood*. San Francisco: Spinsters.

Remafedi, G. (1987). Homosexual youth: A challenge to contemporary society. *Journal of the American Medical Association, 258*(2), 222–225.

Russo, V. (1987). *The celluloid closet: Homosexuality in the movies*. New York: Harper & Row.

Saghir, M. T., & Robins, E. (1973). *Male and female homosexuality: A comprehensive investigation*. Baltimore: Williams & Wilkins.

Sanders, G. (1980). Homosexualities in the Netherlands. *Alternative Lifestyles, 3*, 278–311.

Savin-Williams, R. (1990). *Gay and lesbian youth: Expressions of identity*. New York: Hemisphere Publishing.

Schmidt, J., & Kurdek, L. (1987). Personality correlates of positive identity and relationship involvement in gay men. *Journal of Homosexuality, 13*, 101–109.

Schwartz, R. (1988). When the therapist is gay: Personal and clinical reflections. *Journal of Gay and Lesbian Psychotherapy, 1*(1), 41–51.

Sears, J. (1989). The impact of gender and race on growing up lesbian and gay in the South. *National Association of Women's Studies Journal, 1*, 422–457.

Silverstein, C. (1972, October). Behavior modification and the gay community. Paper presented at the annual convention of the Association for the Advancement of Behavioral Therapy, New York City.

Silverstein, C. (1977). Homosexuality and the ethics of behavioral intervention: Paper 2. *Journal of Homosexuality, 2*, 205–211.

Silverstein, C. (1991). Psychological and medical treatments of homosexuality. In J. Gonsiorek & J. Weinrich (Eds.), *Homosexuality: Research implications for public policy* (pp. 101–114). Newbury Park, CA: Sage Publications.

Slater, B. (1988). Essential issues in working with lesbian and gay male youths. *Professional Psychology: Research and Practice, 19*(2), 226–235.

Stein, T. (1988). Theoretical considerations in psychotherapy with gay men and lesbians. *Journal of homosexuality, 15*(1/2), 75–95.

Strommen, E. (1990). Hidden branches and growing pains: Homosexuality and the family tree. In F. Bozett & M. Sussman (Eds.), *Homosexuality and family relations* (pp. 9–34). New York: Harrington Park Press.

Surrey, J. (1991). Self-in-relation: A theory of women's development. In J. Jordan, A. Kaplan, J. Miller, I. Stiver, & J. Surrey. (Eds.), *Women's growth in connection: Writings from the Stone Center* (pp. 51–66). New York: Guilford Press.

Troiden, R. (1988). *Gay and lesbian identity: A sociological analysis.* New York: General Hall.

Uribe, V., & Friends of Project 10. (1991). *Project 10 handbook: Addressing lesbian and gay issues in our schools* (3rd ed.). Los Angeles: Friends of Project 10, Inc.

Wolf, T. (1985). Marriages of bisexual men. In F. Klein & T. Wolf (Eds.), *Two lives to lead: Bisexuality in men and women* (pp. 135–148). New York: Harrington Park Press.

Zinik, G. (1985). Identity conflict or adaptive flexibility? Bisexuality reconsidered. In F. Klein & T. Wolf (Eds.), *Two lives to lead: Bisexuality in men and women* (pp. 7–19). New York: Harrington Park Press.

Index